Roberto L. Quercetani
& Gustavo Pallicca

A WORLD HISTORY OF SPRINT RACING

"The stellar events"

**100 m., 200 m. and 4x100 m. relay - Men and Women
(1850-2005)**

Lamine Diack
President, International Association of Athletics Federations
President, International Athletic Foundation

Foreword

I am very happy to welcome this latest reference book from the legendary Athletics historian and writer, Roberto Quercetani, this time focusing on the history and development of what he calls the "pure" sprints – the 100 metres and 200 metres.

I think we can all agree that sprinters – especially those who run the 100m - offer us the purest expression of human speed and for this reason, the sprints have become "blue riband" athletic events. As I write this foreword, two wonderful athletes, Asafa Powell and Justin Gatlin are vying for the title of "world's fastest man" and both share the 100m World Record of 9.77 seconds. The glamour and excitement of the sprints can be seen in the huge media interest in their rivalry, and this is something that has been repeated throughout the history of our sport, as Roberto's latest book reveals.

As for the 200m, which is not yet a specialist event in its own right but one in which 100m aces often double up, this distance is similar to the ancient Greek sprint event the "stadion" (literally length of the stadium), but it derives from a mile-based distance, the furlong, or one-eighth of a mile.

The 200m specialist must combine the basic speed of the 100m sprinter with a running technique that allows him to cope with centrifugal forces when sprinting around the bend. Times in a 200m straight race were estimated to be around 3 to 4/10ths of a second faster than races including a bend.

In the 19th century, when the modern sport of athletics was born, the sprints were originally contested on grass or earth "cinders" tracks over the British distance of 100 yards (91.44 m) before Continental influence turned it into 100 metres and technology advances meant that synthetic tracks became the norm at the end of the 1960s. As you will learn from this book, sprinters started from a standing position until 1887, when Charles H. Sherrill dug small foot holes in the dirt track and tried a crouch start, while the IAAF officially sanctioned the use of starting blocks in 1937. A year later the IAAF stipulated that no official record shall be ratified without a wind gauge reading. The maximum tailwind permitted has remained 2 metres/second and the photo-finish camera (in use at the 1932 Olympic Games) now enables very close races to be judged fairly. Today's technology permits winning margins of as little as 1 thousandth of a second to be visible on a photofinish print.

The world of the sprinter is the domain of absolute speed. When the starting gun fires, sprinters must react instantly and summon up great explosive power and then accelerate smoothly so that once they reach top speed, they can stay relaxed with the right balance between frequency and length of stride until they reach the finish line.

For all these reasons, the sprints will always remain fascinating to fans of the sport, and I am glad that, thanks to Roberto Quercetani, we now have a book that pays tribute to the great sprinters of the past.

Lamine Diack

ACKNOWLEDGEMENTS

We wish to thank the following authorities for their valuable contribution:

International Association of Athletics Federations (IAAF)
International Athletic Foundation (IAF)
Pierre Weiss
Nick Davies
"Track & Field News", Mountain View, CA
"Athletics International", Stanmore, Middx.

Hubert Hamacher, Peter Heidenstrom, Lennart Julin, Ulf Lagerström,
Gérard Leconte, Peter Lovesey, Tony O'Donoghue, Maria Luisa Quercetani, Otto Verhoeven.

Text: Roberto L. Quercetani and Gustavo Pallicca
Graphics: Diego Galbiati
Printing and binding: Zanardi Group (Padova) ITALY
Produced by: SEP Editrice Srl (Cassina de Pecchi - Milan) ITALY
Picture acknowledgements: All Sport Photographic (UK), Roberto L. Quercetani, Gustavo Pallicca

PRINTED IN ITALY - August 2006

Via Roma 74 - 20060 Cassina de Pecchi - Milan (ITALY)
info@sepeditrice.it - www.sepeditrice.com

ISBN 978-88-87110-75-3

CONTENTS

MEN:

WOMEN:

INTRODUCTION

by Roberto L. Quercetani

My peregrination along the history of running events began in 1973 when Cordner Nelson and I edited "Runners and Races: 1500 m./ mile". For my part it continued with works on the 800 m., the long distances (5000/10,000 m.) and lately the one-lap event (400 m. and 4x400 m. relay). The present book, devoted to the sprint distances (100/200 m. and 4x100 m. relay), practically completes the series as far as flat events on the track are concerned.

Since time immemorial racing short distances has been part and parcel of the competitive sport in every civilization. There is little or no doubt that at one time or another every kid has been tempted to test his speed over short distances against that of his playmates, and if his trial was particularly successful he usually chose to remain at those distances. One day in the early Seventies I happened to discuss this theme with Valeriy Borzov, possibly the greatest ever Europe-born sprinter. I wondered why as a champion he had never returned to the 400 metres, a distance he ran in a most promising 47.6 as a youth. His reply was as simple as this: "Why prolong your labours if you can compete successfully at the shorter distances?"

In terms of popularity the sprints are certainly the most talked of among athletic events. Through the years the question I have been asked most frequently after attending this or that meet was: "Who won the 100?" As a sport journalist I know that no world record is so dear to the ears of the laymen as that for the metric century.

Events such as the 100 and 200 metres lie entirely in the sphere of anaerobic (without oxygen) running. These are distances over which a properly trained athlete can go all out from start to finish. That is probably the main reason why a great sprinter can steal the show and conquer the heart of spectators, be it in the Olympics or simply at club levels.

Throughout modern history great sprinters have come from a large variety of countries, yet USA has been easily and by far the most prolific producer of sprint talent for more than a century. In recent decades the most serious challenge to their supremacy has come from the Caribbean area.

Several factors have contributed to the advance of times in the sprints, synthetic tracks being perhaps the most important one. On the other hand, the transition from hand timing to fully automatic electric timing has been influential in a seemingly opposite direction. The world record for the 100 metres was 10.0 back in 1960, in hand-time version. Almost half a century later it is down to 9.77, in automatic-time version. In actual fact, however, the difference is greater than that, since the older system was far more generous to the runners.

Greater improvements have been registered in the 200 metres, especially with Michael Johnson's fantastic 19.32 at the 1996 Olympics in Atlanta. Most probably, this was further proof that even over short distances there is still room for improved conditioning methods.

The ever-present problem of doping found its place even here. The "Ben Johnson case" at the 1988 Olympics in Seoul made of course a lot of noise and caused the IAAF to revise its anti-doping policies and introduce "random tests". This predictably made things more difficult for prospective offenders and proved particularly effective in the women's ranks. The current world records for the distaff side still date from the time when tests were conducted only in connection with major international meets.

With the transition to professional athletics the need for exact and reliable performances has certainly become stronger than ever. As an example I may just mention the 100 metre final of the 2003 World Championships. The first four were bracketed within one hundredth of a second (10.07/10.08), yet such a trifle amounted to a difference of $45.000 in terms of price money awarded by the IAAF ($60,000 for first and $15,000 for fourth).

For this new labour of mine I was lucky enough to secure the collaboration of my friend Gustavo Pallicca, a longtime international starter. Drawing from his vast experience he was able to provide a certain number of asides (all identifiable through his initials) on various technical aspects of sprint racing and their evolution throughout the years.

As per tradition, this book has a large statistical section. In my effort to secure reliable data on old marks I was splendidly seconded by such historians as Hubert Hamacher, Peter Heidenstrom, Gérard Leconte, Peter Lovesey and Tony O'Donoghue. Even so, I am sure that there is room for additions and corrections, especially as regards 19th century marks. I will be grateful for information to that effect. In the Middle Ages authors sometimes became aware of additions and corrections to their works from leaflets nailed on the front door of their homes. I don't ask for that much - I can well do with modern methods of communication.

Roberto L. Quercetani

Firenze, May 2006

NOTE:

All times are given as originally taken, i.e. with fractions of a second in halves, quarters, fifths, tenths or – in the era of automatic timing – hundredths.

FROM FAMOUS ATHLETES OF ANTIQUITY TO BERNARD WEFERS, THE GREATEST OF 19th CENTURY SPRINTERS

1

Sprint racing certainly belongs to the remotest traditions of man's athletic endeavours, even though certain historians tend to believe that long distance running was more widely practised among primitive civilizations, notably in North America, Asia and Australia. However, the most detailed references from the sphere of Antiquity are to be found in the anthologies of ancient Greece. In all Panhellenic Games the "stadion" race, entirely on a straight course, was the chief event on the programme and eventually the one that carried the highest prestige. It was 600 "pous" (feet) in length, yet the "pous" differed from place to place and so did the distance the runners had to cover. The "stadion" was 192.28 m. at Olympia, 177.55 m. at Delphi, 181.30 m. at Epidaurus and no less than 210 m. at Pergamon. In the Olympic Games, by far the most celebrated festival of Antiquity as per Pindar's recipe ("We may sing of no contest greater than Olympia"), the "stadion" was in fact the only event on the programme since what has been commonly accepted as the first edition (776 b.C.) up to and including the 13th (728 b.C.). From the time when Olympiads began to be used for dating purposes, an Olympiad was known by its number and by the winner of the "stade". The list of Olympic victors, first reconstructed by the Elean sophist Hippias, has one Koroibos of Elis as the first "stadion" champion. The most famous "stadiodromoi" was perhaps Leonidas of Rhodes, a versatile talent who won 12 Olympic crowns in just as many years (164 b.C. – 152 b.C.), including four consecutive ones in the "stadion". Just as many victories in the short race are credited to Chionis of Sparta (668 - 656 b.C.). Nothing is known about the performances achieved in those days, since the ancient Greeks had no instrument to adequately record actual times. The stadia were generally built on the slopes of a hill, from which the judges and the public could follow the events. As often as not, running tracks were on sloping ground. The runners set off together at some word of command, but it is not known precisely what this was. Anyone who started before such a signal had some punishment inflicted on him, apparently corporal. Originally the start and the finish were simply marked by lines scratched in the earth. It was only in the 5th century b.C. that permanent starting-lines were constructed – a row of stone slabs with two continuous parallel grooves, 0.18 m. apart, in which the runners put their feet. At Olympia the track was about 29 m. in width and could accommodate as many as 20 runners! (In modern tracks each lane has a minimum width of 1.22 m).

Olympic runners were apparently clad in loincloths in the oldest times. As the story goes, in 720 b.C., one of the competitors lost his loincloth during the race, yet he went on just the same and won. From that time on nudity was favoured and somewhat later it became general behaviour. The cult of the naked body was henceforth reflected in various aspects of Greek art.

Such a basic event as the "stadion" attracted the attention of famous men for centuries to come. Philostratus the Athenian (2nd/3rd century a.C.), for example, dwelt on the natural qualities a "stadiodromos" had to possess, after carefully studying figures in motion as depicted by vase-painters of Antiquity. He thus described in detail the powerful arm action of sprinters "moving their legs with their arms to achieve speed,

George Seward, a famous American sprinter in the Forties of the XIX century.

as if winged by their hands". A concept such as the classic "a star sprinter is born, not made", so current even in our time and age, appears to have been a foregone conclusion even in remote days.

Throughout the Middle Ages sprint racing was most probably extant in folk feasts held in various European countries, yet there is no reference to any specific distance being steadily practised. One has to refer to 18th century British "pedestrianism" - as professional foot-racing came to be known - to find traces of sprint races at distances such as 100 and 120 yards. Even though times could then be read only on a running watch, the most varied methods of starting a race still co-existed in a rather hybrid fashion. Of course, this happened to be the case also on the other side of the Atlantic. According to William Curtis, quoted by Archie Hahn in "How to sprint" (1925), in the early days of the sport in America, around the middle of the 19th century, the inconveniences attending the start "by mutual consent" finally led to the idea of using a pistol as the most suitable way of starting a race. Under the former method the start was sometimes delayed for a considerable time, since contenders often tried to out-fox each other by resorting to various stratagems. To avoid this danger, a clause was included in the articles of agreement which stated: "Start by mutual consent: if not off inside one hour (or some other specified time), then to start by pistol". Resort to the latter instrument turned out to be necessary in so many cases that it gradually supplanted the mutual consent system and finally became the customary way of starting sprint races. In 1880, England's newly born "Amateur Athletic Association" had the following among its original rules: "Any competitor starting before the signal to be put back at the discretion of the starter, who shall have power to disqualify him on a repetition of the offence; all questions as to starts to be at the discretion of the starter".

William Curtis, one of the foremost characters in American athletics of the 19th century, in the arena and more so as an executive, had this to say in an article on "The Infancy and Childhood of Amateur Athletic Sport in America": "During the early years of American amateur athletic sport, all the methods of management were naturally copied from the professionals. Running was limited almost entirely to matches, as there were no open competitions in which athletes could enter, and the distances were in nine cases out of ten one of the two extremes – one hundred yards or ten miles. As there were but two starters in these match races, the methods of getting away were more primitive than at present and had been cunningly devised by veteran professionals to give the expert an advantage over the novice".

Another aspect of the early days of modern sprinting concerns the large variety of tracks. As late as in the last decade of the 19th century, on both sides of the Atlantic they varied in circumference from 1 fifth-of-a-mile (321.87 m) to 1 third-of-a-mile (536.45 m). In Britain the length of a track was measured 1 foot (30.5 cms) outward from the kerb, while in USA the prevalent measurement was 18 inches (45.72 cms).

For several decades the minimum fractions adopted in timing races were the oddest possible: halves, quarters, and sometime later fifths of a second. After all, it was only in 1862 that an instrument called chronograph was patented by Adolphe Nicole of Switzerland.

To the above considerations on starting and timing one must add the ignorance of the wind factor. Consequently, the least one can say about the times of early sprinters is that they must be taken with a grain of salt. And the fastest times were preferably recorded in "professional" races, where financial terms involved made all tricks possible. By the end of the 19th century, a keen American observer such as William Pierce looked back to the early days of modern sprinting in these terms: "Professional sprinting chroniclers have always been scarce and each has had his favourites. In most cases those we have read most about have not been in reality the fastest men .... There is conflicting testimony of the few men still living who can tell of sprinting events of 40 or 50 years ago, also of the various champions in the different localities then so far apart by the lack of our modern travelling conveniences. It has at times been next to impossible to decide in justice to whom the honour of champion belonged rightfully".

Such doubts arose even in the case of the man most historians consider as the first of great modern sprinters, American George Seward (born at New Haven, Connecticut on 16 October 1817: died at Birkenhead, England, on 10 April 1883; 1.70 m. / 72 kg.). He was probably the first "dashman" to receive plaudits on both sides of the Atlantic. On his credit were such times as 9 1/4 for 100 y:, 11 1/2 for 120 y. (109.72 m) and 19 1/2 for 200 y. (182.88 m). The first of these marks occurred at Hammersmith, England, on 30 September 1844, a few days before his 27th birthday. Seward defeated W.Robinson of England by 2 yards – the money at stake being an impressive $500 a side. According to John Cumming, author of the book "Runners and Walkers, a Nineteenth Century Sports Chronicle", that marvellous performance was evoked with respect in American track circles until 1890, when the authoritative "New York Clipper", a stern judge of running feats, decided to write it off on the strength of a "late" testimony by an eye-witness, who claimed that Seward had made it on a turnpike road, downhill, from a 10 y. flying start (another source gives the last as 30 y.). As Cumming himself surmises, the fact that in the ensuing 46 years all leading runners had failed to approach Seward's mark may have influenced the "Clipper" in its judgement. Apparently, Seward's other records were allowed to remain in the books, and they were just as great, or nearly so. The 19 1/2 for 200 yards was in London on 22 March 1847, when the American defeated Charles Westhall, English champion, by 2 1/2 yards, for $250 a side. Later in the same year, namely on 3 May in London, Seward defeated Westhall again, over 120 yards in 11 1/2, for $125 a side. This American pioneer had an unusually long career, stretching over two decades. His fame on both sides of the Atlantic must have been unrivalled, if almost half a century later William Pierce, an astute historian, had this to say on Seward in a precious little book, "Square Sports" (1898): "There can be no doubt that such a man as this must have been a wonder in his day, no matter what critics nowadays may say, and no doubt, if he were in his day now he would be as he was then, in a class by himself".

Professionals continued to rule the roost by the time amateur athletics was beginning to take shape. In America there were more or less famous "pros" throughout the Fifties, Sixties and Seventies. Foremost among them were John Thomas, C.D. "Pew" Davis, J.W.Cozad and Ed Moulton, who were involved in a lot of match races. Chroniclers of such events were usually lavish in discussing the money side of the question - $250-to-$500 a side being fairly common purses – but invariably short in details about performances. In his above-mentioned book William Curtis had reservations of his own on that subject: "These professional wolves usually travelled and prowled in pairs, one going first to a town, securing some employment, exhibiting his proficiency as a runner to a select few, and finally making a match with and beating the local champion. Then the winner would explain that he knew a man in a neighbouring town who thought he could run, and whose friends would back him heavily, but who really was several yards slower than championship speed and could be beaten easily. Negotiations would be opened with the stranger and a match arranged. All the men who had won the first race wished to double their gains, while those who lost were anxious for a chance to get even, so the betting was heavy. The stranger won, of course; the town was pretty thoroughly cleaned of spare money, and the partners changed their names and moved to fresh harvest fields".

Ultimately it fell to Britain to claim the most famous "pro" sprinter of the 19th century - Henry "Harry" Hutchens (1858-1939), who made the headlines in his own country as well as in Australia. He was credited with 9 3/4 for 100 yards in 1887, 12.4 for 131 1/4 yards (120 m.) in 1879, 14 1/2 for 150 yards in 1887, 21 4/5 for 220 yards in 1885 and 30 flat for 300 yards in 1884. Sometimes he trained with the famous Lon Myers when the American came to England in 1881. The latter, whose range extended from 100 yards to 1 mile, was at his best in the 440/880, but Hutchens was no doubt his master as a sprinter. Such a conclusion could be reached after reading what Myers himself related about his experiences in said training sessions.

Myers' career and feats were described in detail in a previous book of mine, ("A World History of the One-Lap Race"). It may suffice here to add that on his visits to England he looked so impressive as to lead such an attentive observer as Montague Shearman to say that "with such a phenomenal runner the quarter-mile is only a sprint "long drawn out".

Another famous "pro" was Thomas Malone of Ireland, who was credited with a sumptuous but hardly credible 9 3/5 for the century in Melbourne on 7 February 1885.

Even in the amateur ranks there were at times abuses, mostly connected with "appearance money" paid to athletes, yet there is no doubt that the worst things happened in the domain of the "pro" sport. An example, related by British historian Peter Lovesey: "In 1887 a pedestrian match between two sprinters, Harry Gent and Harry Hutchens, failed to start because each of the rival gangs wanted to arrange for their man to lose; the angry crowd set Lillie Bridge (Grounds, in West Brompton, London) ablaze and ended its chequered history".

In English speaking countries the 100 yards (91.44 m) was the sprint distance par excellence from the very beginning. "Beat even time", i.e. 10 seconds, was the first in a long series of dreams haunting track and field adepts. The earliest commonly accepted "10 dead" by a British amateur dates from 1855, when Thomas Bury was credited with doing just that at Cambridge on 29 November. However, Don Potts once noted that "all marks made at Oxford and Cambridge prior to 1880 were made without a pistol start, that being the first year in which pistol starts were allowed at those locations". As can be gathered from the statistical section, there was a long line of more-or-less credible 10-flat performances in the decades that followed.

Still according to Don Potts, the first genuine even time record by a US amateur should be credited to René La Montagne, who did it at Mott Haven track in New York on 29 June 1878. The wind was directly behind the runners "although not very strong". (The man's name was "Americanised" in an odd form as Reine LaMontagne). The mark was recognized by the "Spirit of the Times" and "The New York Clipper" and accepted by the AAU in 1888. The first to record such a time in a major championship race was William Wilmer at the US title meet on 12 October 1878 in New York. His time later received official sanction by the AAU, yet he was reportedly aided by a "gale of a wind". Wilmer had recorded a 10-flat even in a minor meet three months earlier, still under doubtful conditions. As the story goes, "One official time-keeper, with a cheap brass horse timer, made it a half beat under 10s; another with an ordinary timing watch, 10s even; the third, with a very superior and thoroughly tested watch, 10 1/5; one unofficial timer, with an Auburndale watch making eights, 10 1/8; and another with a Tiffany ink-dotter, 10 1/8 .... The judges agreed to call it 10.0."

Well before the establishment of the Amateur Athletic Association (AAA) in 1880, England had a title meet of some sort held under the auspices of the Amateur Athletic Club (AAC), which started in 1866 as the brainchild of an exceptional man, John Graham Chambers, a multi-star of sports if ever there was one, both as an athlete and as a promoter. The first 100-yard champion was T.M.Colmore, who was credited with 10 1/2 in the 1866 meet. The list of AAC champions notably included one Louis Junker, a Russian-born sprinter who - as per Montague Shearman - had turned to athletics just to take revenge of some friends and colleagues who had "chaffed" him for his supposed clumsiness and slowness. As the story goes, "after winning a few handicaps he soon found himself at scratch, and able to win from that position - and throughout his career he was only once beaten. In 1878 he won the 100 yards at the AAC Championships in 10 1/5.

The first notable sprinter from Scotland was Milroy Cowie, a man of medium build (1.73 m./ 63 kg.) who was credited with a 10 flat in 1884, at the second title meet organized by the Scottish AAA. The following year he ran the 220 yards in 22 1/5 in London. Both of these marks were world bests. Over a period of years he played a major role at the English AAA Championships with three wins in the 100 (1983-84-85) and two in the 440 (1883-84). It was only at the 1885 meet that he found his master, losing to Lon Myers in the "quarter".

The first 10-flat in a major English meet was credited to a Ghana-born sprinter, Arthur Wharton, who did it twice, heat and final, within half an hour in the AAA Championships at London's Stamford Bridge on 3 July 1886. A year later at Lichfield he was credited with 9.9, a doubtful mark in the eyes of authorities of the time. English historian Montague Shearman described Wharton as " a coloured gentleman ... with body bent forward and running almost on the flat of his foot". The same writer also proclaimed: "At last, after years of struggling and disputing, a genuine level time performance has been achieved". Wharton was born in Accra but his father was from Grenada and his mother was the daughter of a Scottish missionary. Wharton later became a professional soccer player as a goalie for Preston North End.

The first foreigner to win the century at the English AAA Championships was an

Start of a sprint race in New York toward the end of the 19th century. Four styles, from left to right: lunge, crouch, stand-up crouch, dab.

American, Fred Westing, who turned the trick in 1888 (time 10 1/5). On his side of the Atlantic he was for years an outstanding figure at the AAU Championhips, with a victory in the 100 (1888) and no less than three in the 220 (1887, '88 and '90), his best time being a 22 1/4 around a turn in the furlong in 1890.

The crouch start ("on all fours") was probably introduced in New Zealand around 1884 by Bobby MacDonald, a Maori. Most writers, however, accept American Charles Sherrill as the earliest adept of this method in 1887, following the advice of his coach at Yale University, the famous Mike Murphy. As the latter relates, "When he (Sherrill) used it in his first race, he was laughed at, and the starter, thinking that Sherrill did not know how to start, held up the race to give him instructions. Finally, he was made to understand that Sherrill was simply using a new method!" Yet Sherrill (who later became a General and a diplomat) had to be content of joining the large group of 10-flat performers. As for Mike Murphy, the influence of his teachings on the evolution of sprinting can hardly be disputed.

By the early Nineties more or less dubi-

Standing start - John Owen (USA), the first man to officially break "even time" in the 100 yards (1890).

ous sub-10 performances even by amateurs had been reported from several countries. In the first New Zealand Championships, held at Dunedin on 13 December 1889, Jack Hempton finished 5 yards ahead of his nearest competitor in 9 $^3/_5$ but his time was disallowed. My friend Peter Heidenstrom, who has been studying the history of New Zealand athletics like no one else, had this to say on that amazing performance: "Those 9 3/5 secs. were both a watershed and a catalyst. He created something where there had been nothing, and showed the way to New Zealand athletes ever since". Hempton went on to do 9 $^4/_5$ twice in 1892, and one of these clockings, turned in at the national title meet in Christchurch, was ratified as a record by the New Zealand AAA. In the same year Hempton went to Europe to compete in the English Championships. After an extenuating sea trip he happened to strain a leg and couldn't go beyond the 100 y. heats. In his own country, Hempton had previously beaten Australia's Bob Macpherson, himself a 9 $^4/_5$ man.

The question as to who was the first legal sub-10 performer in America's amateur ranks is still subject to debate among historians. Don Potts, the keenest of students on the subject of sprinting, favours John Owen as the "surest bet" on the strength of his 9 $^4/_5$, made at the AAU Championships held in Washington, D.C. on 11 October 1890 and later accepted by the AAU as an official US record. That time was registered on 3 watches and the race was a highly competitive test as Owen won from such a reputed crack as Luther Cary, who finished some 18 inches (0.45 m.) behind. Yet Bill Mallon, a distinguished Olympic historian, tends to believe in the authenticity of an earlier 9 $^4/_5$, credited to another American, Victor Schifferstein, on 9 September 1888 at St.Louis. Says Mallon: "The meet (Annual Western AAU) was not ratified by the AAU, presumably upset at the Western AAU holding their own championship meet". In any case Owen (born on 18 August 1861) had better credentials throughout, having scored a 100/220 y. double at the Nationals in 1889.

Luther Cary (born in New York in 1868) scored a 100/220 y. double at the 1891 AAU Championships. Earlier in the season he had won the 100 at the English AAA title meet, thereby equalling the afore-mentioned feat of his countryman Fred Westing in 1888. Cary could point to a handful of fast but partly controversial times, notably including 9 $^4/_5$ and 9 $^3/_4$ in quick succession at Princeton in 1891 - neither was accepted by the AAU. In the same year he crossed the Atlantic and chalked up a 10 $^3/_4$ for 100 metres in Paris, but one source claimed that the start was given with a handkerchief. Europeans obviously practised the metric distance. The first commonly accepted sub-11 mark for the 100 metres was 10 $^4/_5$ by Cecil Lee of Great Britain at Brussels on 25 September 1892, which was equalled by Etienne de Ré of Belgium at the Belgian Championships, still in Brussels, on 4 July 1893. But neither mark was ratified . Watches on Lee gave 10 $^3/_5$, 10 $^4/_5$ and 11.0 and Belgian officials retained the slowest mark as official. As for de Ré, he became the first Belgian record holder at the distance, but only with a slower time (11.0) achieved later the same year. The list of early sub-11 performers notably included P.J.Blignaut of South Africa who in 1898 was credited with 10 $^4/_5$ in a handicap race off scratch in Paris.

The 220 yards or furlong, a most exacting test for sprinters, had a chequered history. In England it did not appear on the programme of the AAA Championships until 1902. Yet the distance had been practiced there since the Sixties of the 19th century. The first sub-23 performance was credited to Edward Colbeck – 22 $^3/_4$ in 1867. A reporter casually noted that Colbeck, better known as a quarter-miler, won comfortably "after taking a rest".

In America the furlong attained championship status much earlier. In 1877 the Intercollegiate Association of Amateur Athletes of America (ICAAAA), the foremost body governing college sport in the East, included the furlong in the programme of its title meet. Horace Lee won in 23 $^1/_2$. Later in the same year the event made is first appearance also at the national championships, then held under the auspices of the New York Athletic Club. The winner was Edward Merritt, who did 24.0 (turn). When the jurisdiction of the meet passed to the NAAAA (National Association of Amateur

Athletes of America), Lon Myers won the 220 in three consecutive years (1879-80-81) and again in 1884, after losing to Harry Brooks in 1882 and '83. The fastest of these races was that of 1882, when Brooks did 22 3/5 and beat Myers by 5 feet (1.5 m). It should be noted, however, that on that occasion Myers was penalized one yard for a false start. Yet Myers' most amazing feat in the furlong dated from June 5, 1880, when at Clifton, N.J. he clocked 21 7/8 as a scratch runner, finishing third to handicap men. Almost inevitably, somebody concluded that the watches were lazy. But Myers' chief biographer, Don Potts, was inclined to regard the time as authentic, even considering that "it was probably run on a straight path and with a strong aiding wind". As an athletic figure Myers eventually laid all doubters at rest with his first visit to England in 1881, when he won all his races but one, a heat of the 100 yards at the AAA Championships. En passant, it may be good to remember that like all his contemporaries he used an upright stance for starting.

From 1885 onwards the 220 was mostly contested on a straight course, which usually started on a line tangent to the track. The two versions co-existed in a somewhat hybrid fashion for many years afterwards.

In his famous book "How to sprint" Archie Hahn had this to say about "strategies" in running the furlong: "There are several methods of running the longer event and it will depend upon the track available. A "two-twenty" around a curve, in which each man has a handicapped individual lane, makes it necessary for a sprinter to run through the first curve at fast speed, otherwise he may come out on the straightaway and find himself yards to the rear of a competitor running in the pole position, granting that he has an outside lane. The race is too short to allow much conservation of strength, unless it is run on a straightaway track, which allows a certain amount of checking up."

Such a duplicity existed also in England, long before the distance was introduced in the championship programme. A 22-flat made on a straightaway was credited to William Page Phillips on the Stamford Bridge track in London as early as in 1878. Like other English sprinters of those days, this powerful 6-foot (1.83 m) runner used to run both 100 and 440 y. in championship races. His record as a doubler in AAA meets was quite impressive: for three years in a row (1880-81-82) he won the 100, and placed second in the 440 just as many times. At the longer distance he tried once more in 1883, only to finish second again! Still in 1883 he was reported dead while serving in the army overseas, but much to the embarrassment of the sporting daily which had given the news he wrote them from abroad saying he was alive and well. Tragically enough, however, he died of a heart failure later in the same year, aged 25.

Another Englishman, Charles Wood, ran the furlong in 21 4/5 (heat) and 21 3/5 (final) at Stamford Bridge on 22 July 1887, still on a straight course. However, such times were not ratified by the AAA. Wood was one of those runners who could make themselves justice over a wide range of distances. In English championship meets he was three times a runner-up in the 100 (1884, '86 and '87) and won the "quarter" twice (1886 and '87). Later in the same year he improved to 21 3/5 but this mark was not ratified by the AAA. The first amateur to record an official sub-22 clocking around a turn was the above-mentioned Luther Cary, who did 21 4/5 in New York on 30 May 1891 – not bad for a man who at the time of his visit to Paris later in the same year bewildered a French journalist of "Sports Athlétiques" with the following revelations: "I lead a quiet life, carefully avoiding stress situations. I'm not particular in my eating habits and I train but little: three times a week – a warm-up session followed by some 40 or 50 y. sprints at full speed, with progressive accelerations".

The first major confrontation between "kings" of the short distances from the two sides of the Atlantic took place at Manhattan Field, New York on 21 September 1895, in connection with the historic New York AC vs. London AC dual meet. Chief characters in the play were Bernard Wefers and Charles Bradley. The former, an American, was by then a rising star. Only a week before he had scored a double at the AAU Championships (10.0 and 21 4/5 on a straight course, both wind-aided). His English rival Bradley (born on 14 March 1869; died in 1940), who had been a well-known cricketer before turning to athletics, was a strong man of medium height, by then a well established star, having won the 100 yards at the English AAA Championships for four years in a row, 1892-93-94-95. One of these victories was related with a funny situation which is dealt with in an adjoining aside. Shortly before his trip to the States Bradley was credited with 9 $^{4}/_{5}$ on two occasions – on 27 July at Cardiff and on 6 August at Stoke-on-Trent. In the latter race he tied with Alf Downer, a Jamaican-Scot. These marks, equalling the world record commonly credited to John Owen of USA, were never ratified by the AAA. At any rate. on the eve of his clash with Wefers the Briton was the favourite of most "bettors". (Mind you, as often as not betting was thriving even outside the world of "pros").

NO FAVOURS, PLEASE !

British historians commonly rate Charles Bradley as their greatest 100 yards specialist of the 19th century. His "chef-d'oeuvre" consisted in winning the AAA title at that distance four years in a row (1892 through 1895). An amusing story is told about his victory in the 1893 meet, held at Northampton's County Cricket Ground. Just before the race he was warned by officials that there was no possibility of his breaking the 100 yards record and getting credit for it because the course dropped 1 $^{1}/_{2}$ feet (45.7 cm) in the running direction and there was a following wind. To which Bradley bluntly retorted that he was ready to run uphill and against the wind, if need be. They complied with his wish by changing the direction of the race and he won in a record-equalling 10 flat! Ever since then, official books on the results of the AAA Championships have always included a note - "run uphill" – against Bradley's mark on that occasion.

The New York showdown was described in vivid fashion in "Outing" magazine by the afore-mentioned William ("Father Bill") Curtis. First, the "ambiance": "The Games were held on Manhattan Field, the most convenient and spacious grounds in the vicinity of New York City. .... This cinder path was pear-shaped, a quarter-mile in circuit, unusually wide, and having one of its straight sides prolonged into a 220 y. straightaway. ...... "The attendance numbered 8,592 and would have been several thousand greater but for the big prices, the cheapest admission being $1.00. In addition to the crowd inside, the bluff which forms the western boundary of the ground was black with people, and on the 155th Street viaduct, which towers high above the roofs of the stands on the southern edge of the field, the sidewalk was thronged with spectators, who stood for four hours in the scorching sun, to get far-off glimpses of the sport. Probably 12,000 people, inside and outside, saw the games. As the 100 y. runners thundered down the path, "Bradley wins" was heard more often and more loudly than "Wefers wins". But in the race the Englishman generally lagged behind. He made a desperate attempt with 40 y. to go, but Wefers answered so effectively that he finally won by about 4 feet (1.22 m) in 9 $^{4}/_{5}$, thus equalling the world record". Later in the day Wefers won the 220 y. on a straight course in 21 $^{3}/_{5}$, another record time. His team-mate John Crum was second, 3 yards back, and Gilbert Jordan of the rival English team third, almost 3 yards further back. Before the race, the guests thought they had their best weapon in Alf Downer, a Jamaica-born Scotsman. However, an injury forced him to stop at 50 yards. Curtis added: "Downer tried to drown his disappointment in unaccustomed draughts of ice-water but eventually became so ill that a physician was hastily summoned from among the spectators".

Reverting to the NYAC vs. LAC dual meet, it should be mentioned that the Americans won all the 11 events on the programme. This obviously led them to conclude that for the first time in the history of modern athletics they were no longer second to the British. Yet such a creditable source as "Outing" magazine had this to say about the visiting Englishmen: "They competed like men and lost like gentlemen, and their behaviour must be considered a magnificent specimen of genuine British sportsmanship". However, not all reactions to the historic event were in the same vein. Some British sport writers accused the Americans "of putting professional athletes against their amateurs".

"HE HAD BEEN SEEN TALKING TO A PROFESSIONAL"

The afore-mentioned John Crum was a student from Iowa University who earlier in 1895 had come East to score a double at the IC4A Championships in New York, with times of 10.0 and 22.0. In this connection there is an amusing story, quite revealing of the atmosphere prevalent in those days. As the story goes, "His medals were held up until charges of professionalism could be heard. The charges were based upon the allegations that no Eastern athlete knew him personally, that he ran too well for an amateur, and that he had been seen talking to a professional. In his defence, it was pointed out that his father was a banker in Bedford, Iowa. The medals were finally awarded to him."

Wefers (b. 19 February 1873 died in 1925; 1.83 m / 79 kg) went on to score the 100/220 y. double in two more US Championships (1896-97). He was not an unusually fast starter, but when well under way he could generate extraordinary speed. In the century he did 9 4/5 each year, from 1895 till '97 included, and in the 220 on a straight course he chalked up a nifty 21 1/5 (1896). All of these clockings were ratified as US records by the AAU. He would occasionally try the quarter mile. His best effort at this distance was in the 1896 Nationals in New York on 12 September. That race provided the ideal rendez-vous for three different types of runner: sprinter (Wefers). quarter-miler (Thomas Burke) and half-miler (Charles Kilpatrick), each of whom happened to be the world's no.1 man at his favourite distance. Burke had to return his fastest ever time, 48 4/5, to finally emerge the winner. Wefers was second about 8 feet (2.43 m) behind, so it can be estimated that he must have done no worse than 49 1/5. Kilpatrick was a well beaten third. It is to be noted that each of the three runners had at least one more final on his menu for that day and Wefers had in fact two (100, 220) - which he won. But then this was the prevailing trend among top runners in those days.

Wefers thus dominated the US sprint scene for three years in a row (1895-96-97). American commentators saluted him as "the fastest human in the world". And William Curtis wrote: "We never before had such a sprinter as B.J.Wefers".

The man in question had his last cry at the 1899 title meet, when he placed third in the 220.

A DREAM COMES TRUE

The "amblance" characterizing the first Olympics of the modern era was vividly described by Greek writers of the time, understandably enthusiastic about the rebirth of their onetime "child". Almost one century later, historian Thanassis Tarassouleas thus re-evoked the atmosphere of the opening day: "Athens presented a unique spectacle, as if in celebration of an unprecedented festivity. From early morning the decorated streets were crowded. The sky was cloudy and overcast. The sound of music of the bands of "Zante", "Lefkas" and Lavrium was heard everywhere.... Crowd movement was such that the traffic could pass only with great difficulty. Never before had the large Stadiou street, Philellinon street, Amalias Avenue, Olgas Avenue and Kifissias Avenue been required to hold such throngs, as people moved towards the stadium. Most of the trams were decorated with the national flag and the flags of the participating nations. The small coaches stationed on Stadiou street raised their fare from 10 lepta to 15 lepta per person..... The seats within the stadium were covered with cushions.... That evening Athens was brilliantly lit. The trade-unions organized a torch-light parade. At 9.30 pm and for half an hour the Acropolis was illuminated, entrance being allowed to foreign visitors and competitors. Everybody spent the evening in enjoyment, singing and dancing and celebrating with Greek food and retsina wine".

As destiny would have it, neither Wefers nor Britain's Bradley were among the athletes who competed in the inaugural Olympics of the modern era, which were held in Athens in the spring of 1896. A body known as the International Olympic Committee had been formed, chiefly under the stimulus of Baron Pierre de Coubertin, a genial Frenchman, in 1894. This turned out to be a major step towards the coming of age of the sport at the international level.

In a world-wide perspective, the Athens "première" aroused interest in relatively few countries and passed virtually unnoticed in many others. "The New York Times" was among the most attentive observers. On the eve of the Games it had this to say: "For scholars no less than for sportsmen there is much of interest in the fact that this Spring there is to be a revival at Athens of the ancient festivals, religious in their nature at first, but later almost purely contests of strength, speed, and physical skill, which in the great days of Greece were regarded as forming almost the most important epochs in her national history. Such a revival of the Hellenic games has been discussed and urged in Europe for several years, but there were many practical difficulties in the way. These have now all been overcome and from April 5 to 15, on the exact spot where the Panathenaea is said to have been celebrated by the almost mythical Erechtheus and Theseus and where Pisistratus and his sons certainly contended, athletes from many lands will assemble to display their prowess in races and contests, less savage and dangerous, indeed, than those of old, but perhaps not the less interesting and earnest on that account". There was at least one aspect in which the new festival was somehow reminiscent of the old ones, and that concerned the stadium. Still according to the same American source, on the opening day "more than 40,000 persons were admitted to the Stadion ... These 40,000, however, were not the only ones who witnessed the games. The Stadion has no roof, and on each side of it rise hills, from which a good view can be had within the walls. These hills were fairly black with spectators, thousands of whom were too poor to pay the small price of admission to the Stadion, but who were determined to see the revival of the ancient Greek festival. The sight was a remarkable one ...."

Yet the Athens "première", as was to be expected, left something to be desired in more than one way. No matter if Greece in general and its capital in particular, on top of their classical heredities, could also point to new experience in the sport, gathered in recent decades. The athletics events were held in the Panhellenic Stadium in Athens, which had been completely restored thanks to funds donated by Georgios Averoff, a Greek philanthropist described by contemporary writers as "a great benefactor". Participation was the weakest point: no more than 67 athletes from 10 countries for all the events (12) on the programme! Relatively few of the world's best athletes of that time happened to be there. There were no national teams in the current sense of the word and athletes were mostly recruited at the club level. Great Britain, then the undisputed leader in European athletics, was represented by only four men, none of them a prominent sprinter. The US team, chiefly put together by Professor William M. Sloane of Princeton University, included only .... one reigning national champion, the afore-mentioned Thomas Burke, a Boston student. He scored an easy double, with times of 12.0 in the 100 metres (10 April) and 54 1/5 in the 400 (7 April). Such hyper-slow times were due to a poor track which had long (about 150 m) straights and hairpin bends. Composed of very soft, slow cinders, it must have been a horror to those accustomed to American and British tracks. As explained before, Burke was America's best 440 y. runner but he was by no means no.1 in the century. In Athens he was a bit faster in the semis (11 4/5). His chief rival in the decisive race was Fritz Hofmann of Germany, who in

1893 had scored a double victory at the "Championships of the Continent" in Berlin, with times of 10 1/5 in the 100 yards and 52 3/5 in the 440 yards. Hofmann, aged 25 at the time of the inaugural Olympics, well exemplified the type of multi-star so frequent in those days. He also competed in the high jump, finishing fifth. Not only that – he also appeared in gymnastics events as a member of the German teams that won the parallel and horizontal bars.

Non-winning times were not taken – as it happened in those days even in the noblest of track countries. The 200 metres event was not included in the Athens programme nor was any sprint relay.

Of the five 100-metre finalists, only the two Americans, Burke and Francis Lane, used a crouch start.

1896 Olympics, Athens – 100 metres (10 April): 1.Thomas Burke (USA) 12.0; 2. Fritz Hofmann (Ger) 2 m. back; 3. Alajos Szokólyi (Hun); 4. Francis Lane (USA); 5. Alexandros Chalkokondilis (Gre). Last three all about 4 m. behind the runner-up. Lanes: Thomas Curtis (USA) 1(did not start), Lane 2, Szokólyi 3, Chalkokondilis 4, Burke 5, Hofmann 6.

Thomas Burke (born in Boston on 15 January 1875; died in Boston on 14 February 1929; 1.83 m. / 66 kg) was not the fastest man in the world yet he must be regarded as one of the "noblest" winners of the inaugural Olympics. He continued to perform well at his favourite distance, the quarter, throughout 1896 and '97. He turned to the half-mile towards the end of his career, winning the AAU title in 1898 and the IC4A title in '99, the latter in 1:58 4/5. In the years that followed he set up a law practice in Boston and was also a journalist.

The 1899 AAU Championships saw the emergency of a new sprint star, Arthur Duffey (born on 14 June 1879; died on 25 January 1955, 1.70 m / 62 kg). He won the 100 yards in 10.0, after recording a wind-aided 9 4/5 in a heat. In 1900 he went to England and won the AAA title, still in 10.0. The Americans scored a triple in that race, with Frank Jarvis and Walter Tewksbury finishing second and third respectively. Barely half a metre covered the three men at the end of a close struggle. This trio went on to Paris, venue of the second edition of the Olympic Games.

In 1900 the French capital hosted a great World's Fair, "Exposition Universelle". The Games were administered by the organizers of the fair, who had little or no interest in sporting events, let alone knowledge about how to organize them. The IOC had contacted them out of bare necessity, mainly to alleviate its financial burden, but Baron de Coubertin and his associates had a difficult time in trying to deal with their counterparts of the fair. The Games were held throughout the summer – merely as a sideshow to the "Exposition Universelle". And it was not easy to draw the line between Olympic events proper and the sundry ones emanating from the fair. In spite of such inconveniences, the meet was definitely richer than its Athens predecessor in terms of participation: 125 athletes from 15 countries. USA with 43 men had the biggest squad, outnumbering even that of the host nation, France (30).

The track and field events were held at Croix Catelan in the Bois de Boulogne, on the grounds of the Racing Club de France. With no proper track, the events were simply run over the grass field. The circuit was 500 metres in length and partly wound its way through a grove of trees! Due to the inadequacy of the installations, attendances were at a low level – at most only 2000-to-3000 people per day would find their way to Boulogne. Two small stands only were provided for the spectators, and as often as not only one of these was fairly filled.

The programme of the sprint events was really something though: it included three events, spread over a week, in the following order – 100, 60 and 200 metres. The 100 m. final was on Saturday 14 July, the French national holiday. Duffey was the favourite of many on the strength of his victory in the English AAA race only a week before. In Paris he went through the two preliminary rounds unscathed, with no better than 11.0. His team-mate Frank Jarvis chalked up a nice 10 4/5 – alas with the contribution of a lenient starter. In round 2 another American, Tewskbury, also did 10 4/5. There was no strict rule as to number of entries per country and in the heats the Americans fielded no fewer than 10 sprinters, exactly half the number of all participants! In the four-man final the only opposition to US might could come from Stanley Rowley of Australia, who had been credited with a 9.9 100 yards in his own country the year before. At the halfway mark Duffey was clearly in the lead but a while later he pulled up lame and had to stop. The others finished close together but Jarvis finally won in 11.0 from Tewksbury and Rowley.

Maybe Duffey could have emerged the victor in the Paris race, but for his mishap. It should be noted, however, that later in the season he narrowly lost to Maxie Long's 10 flat in the 100 yards of the AAU Championships. Long had won the 400 metres in Paris and closed his 1900 account with two blazing 440 y. performances, easily the best ever: 47 4/5 on a 321.87 m. track and 47 flat on a straightaway.

Next on the programme was the 60 metres, a rarely run distance, save perhaps in indoor meets. The final was scheduled for Sunday, 15 July. Quite a few Americans were opposed to competing on Sunday – on religious grounds. They asked for a partial revision of the time schedule but the organizers turned a deaf ear. In some events, e.g. the long jump, there were in fact defecting Americans. Not so in the sprints. Alvin Kraenzlein won the 60 metres in 7 flat, nosing out Tewksbury, with Aussie Stanley Rowley again third.

The last act of this long-drawn sprint festival, the 200 metres, was on stage a full week later. Tewksbury went into the lead past the halfway point and won comfortably from Norman Pritchard of India (more on him in the adjoining aside) and Rowley.

1900 Olympics, Paris - 60 metres (15 July): 1.Alvin Kraenzlein (USA) 7.0; 2.Walter Tewksbury (USA), centimetres back; 3.Stanley Rowley (Aus), about 30 cms. further back; 4.Edmund Minahan (USA).

100 metres (14 July): 1.Frank Jarvis 11.0; 2.Walter Tewksbury (USA) 60 cms. back; 3.Stanley Rowley (Aus) 50 cms. further back. Arthur Duffey (USA) did not finish.

A semi-final of the 100 yards at the 1896 ICAAAA Championships, won by Bernard Wefers, arguably the fastest man of the XIX century. Time, 10.0.

200 metres (22 July): 1.Walter Tewksbury (USA) 22 1/5; 2.Norman Pritchard (Ind) 2.5 m. back; 3.Stanley Rowley (Aus) 50 cms. further back, 4.William Holland (USA), almost equal 3rd.

Kraenzlein, a great talent if ever there was one, won no less than 4 events in Paris: the 110 m. hurdles (15 2/5) on 14 July; long jump (7.185) and 60 metres on 15 July; 200 m. hurdles (25 2/5) on 16 July. Still a record for the most individual victories in track and field at a single Olympic celebration. Kraenzlein (born at Augsburg, Germany, on 12 December 1876; died at Wilkes Barre, PA, on 6 January 1928; 1.83 m. / 75 kg) had emigrated to USA with his parents when he was only 3. As a student at Wisconsin in 1898 he broke the world's 120 y. hurdles record with 15 1/5. The following year he bettered the world's long jump record time and again, finally with 7.43.

After his last Olympic labour (200 m. hurdles) Kraenzlein solemnly announced: "That was my last race. I am through with athletics, and shall devote myself to something more serious". He later had a distinguished career in the coaching ranks. He was appointed coach to the German team for the 1916 Olympics to be held in Berlin, only to see the project wiped out by the outbreak of World War I. He later wound up as coach to the Cuban national team.

Frank Washington Jarvis (born at California, PA, on 31 August 1878; died at Sewickley, PA, on 2 June 1933; 1.67 m. / 58 kg), a direct descendant of famed US president George Washington, had a range stretching from 100 to 440 yards (IC4A champion of 1898 in the latter event). He later became a distinguished lawyer.

John Walter Tewksbury (born at Ashley, PA, on 21 March 1878; died at Philadelphia on 24 April 1968; 1.70 m. / 60 kg) won no less than 5 medals at the Paris Olympics. To the three gathered in the sprints he added a gold in the 400 metres hurdles (15 July) and a third place (for which there was no bronze at the time) in the 200 metres hurdles (16 July). His time in the "intermediates", 57 3/5, was remarkable in view of the primitive conditions. The hurdles were in fact telephone poles laid across the track, except for the last one, a water jump. The year before he had been clocked in 21 1/5 over 220 y. at Princeton, NJ, on 22 April, equal to Bernie Wefers' record time for a straight course. In later years he practiced dentistry. He died at the age of 90.

"WHY WAIT?"

In English speaking countries "pro" athletics was in full swing for a long time, its last fireworks occurring in the second decade of the 20th century. As often as not, the best "pro" sprinters had previously figured prominently in the amateur ranks. One of these was Alfred Downer, already mentioned in connection with the NY Athletic Club vs. London Athletic Club dual meet of 1895. Like several other leading athletes of his time, Downer became a full-time "pro" after he was ousted from the British amateur family on charges of professionalism. His hyper-activity had caused Scottish AAA officials to become suspicious and early in 1894 it was proved that he "not only had received £3 for "expenses" in a meeting, but had also overtured for payments to several clubs". He denied this but judges found his evidence to be of "a very untruthful and unsatisfactory character" and went on to condemn him. Several years later, however, Downer evoked his experiences in a book entitled "Running Recollections" and lifted the lid on the hypocrisy somewhere prevalent even in his amateur days. As for his experiences as a "pro" he said: "No one who is on the job ever dreams of waiting for the report of the pistol, or whatever the signal may be, but is generally running some five yards (this is no exaggeration) when the signal is given".

As a "pro" Downer competed up to the end of the century and was credited with such times as 12 2/5 for 128.5 y. (117. 5m) in 1898, 14.9 for 150 y. (137.16 m) in 1897, 19.9 for 200 y. (182.88 m) in 1890 and 44.8 for 400 y. (365.76 m) in 1897. He was quite a character but had a troubled existence. In the words of a Scottish writer, "In his short life (he died at 39) he quaffed to its deepest from the goblet of life – and in his dregs he found much bitterness".

The best non-American in Paris was Stanley Rowley of Australia, then 23. As related above, he finished third in all sprint events. Such was his devotion to sport that he elected to go beyond the line of duty when he volunteered to help the British in the .... 5000 metre team race. He was allowed to stop after running only seven laps of the 500-metre track (hence 3500 m.), at which stage he was far behind the other runners, who had all finished. However, officials awarded him 10 points as a member of the winning crew. He thus received a gold medal, thereby reaping more than he had achieved in the sprints! Prior to that, he won Australasian sprint titles in 1897 (10.0 in the 100 y. and 22.4 in the 220 y.) and 1899 (9.9 and 22.2)

Throughout the latter years of the 19th century continental Europeans continued to lag behind their rivals from Great Britain, let alone USA. They preferably ran over metric distances but would occasionally indulge in 100 yard races just to feel "chic", i.e. in line with their English masters! As detailed in the statistical section, several sprinters were credited with 10 $^4/_5$ for 100 metres in the last decade of the century. Among them there were two Swedes: Harald Andersson-Arbin and Isaac Westergren. The latter added to his reputation in his elder years when he became a benefactor for Swedish sport in several ways. In 1920 he donated 100,000 Swedish crowns for the trip of the Swedish national team to the Antwerp Olympics.

By the end of the 19th century English and American coaches already had clear, sound concepts about the mechanics of sprinting. If read nowadays their observations seem meticulous in matters of running form but far less demanding on the subject of conditioning methods. Montague Shearman, the acknowledged doyen of British athletics historians, who had been a good short distance runner in his youth, claims that a sprinter "nascitur, non fit", no matter if much can be done by training and practice". He goes on to say: "The best practice for a sprint race is to have continued bursts of 30 y. or so with another man, who is about as good or rather better than yourself. If practicing with a man who is inferior you should give him a short start in these spins and catch him as soon as you can. Such practice both helps a man to get into his running quickly and "pulls him out", to use a trainer's expression, i.e. leads him to do a little better than his previous best ...... After half a dozen of these spins he should take a few minutes' rest and then run the full distance, or at any rate a burst of 70 or 80 y., before he goes in to have a rub down and resume his clothes. If he is training for 220, 250 or 300 yards he must, of course, accustom himself for longer trials; but in general, even for the longest of these distances, it is quite enough to run 200 yards at full speed". Most revealing of the philosophy prevailing in those days is Shearman's conclusion: "For all practice it may be laid down that a man should very rarely run a trial for more than two-thirds of the distance for which he is training".

UNSUNG HERO

Norman Pritchard can well be regarded as India's (and Asia's) pioneer in athletics. But he also qualifies for the title of "Most unsung Olympic hero". In fact the two silver medals he won at the 1900 Olympics in Paris (200 metres flat and 200 metres hurdles) received few or no plaudits at the time. In his precious book "Great Asian Athletes", Wing Commander P.K. Mahanand reveals that Dr. Otto Peltzer of Germany, a great middle distance runner in the Twenties of the 20th century and a successful coach in India after World War II, "was in fact among the first to remind us about Pritchard's unique achievement". Then he goes on to say: "There are no action photographs available of this remarkable athlete, neither details of his life. What type of person was he? How did he train, what was his motivation? All this is lost in the heap of oblivion".
Mr. Mahanand actually wonders if Pritchard was "an Englishman born in India or a zealous Anglo-Indian" and concludes that "most probably he was an Anglo-Indian, who did India proud". Over a century after his Paris deeds, little more is known about Pritchard. He studied at St.Xaviers College in Calcutta. In Mr.

Mahanand's words, "As a prominent athlete he attracted the attention of British selectors who made him an offer to represent their country in the Paris Olympics. He chose to represent India though". In the Games he competed in five events. Besides the two afore-mentioned medals, he was 5th in the 110 m. hurdles, ran the 60 m. (heats) and the 100 m. (semi-finals). Officially he was listed as a representative of the English AAA. A week before the Games he had finished second to America's Alvin Kraenzlein in the 120 y. hurdles at the AAA Championships in London. After his Olympic labours he went to Hollywood to become a successful actor in silent films.

Of course, a history of sprint racing cannot go without a mention of what happened by the same time in the "short relays". According to the "Encyclopaedia Britannica" relay racing as a sport originated in the United States in the last decade of the 19th century, on the model of the Massachusetts firemen's "bean pot" race, in which the man running the second leg took over a small flag from the first man as he arrived, before departing on his own stage, at the end of which he would hand the flag to the awaiting next runner.

In fact, modern relay racing was conceived and launched in Philadelphia by Frank B. Ellis and H. Laussat Geyelin of the University of Pennsylvania as a four-man contest, in which a baton was used as the medium in place of the more cumbersome

1896 Olympics, Athens. 100 m. final, from left to right: Hofmann 2nd, Burke 1st, Chalkokondilis 5th, Szokólyi 3rd, Lane 4th.

flag. The inventors "deliberately searched for something to make track sports draw more contestants and spectators". The one-mile relay (4x440 y.) was first experimented in competition in 1893. The first race was such a success that it was repeated the following year. After which the Pennsylvania Committee resolved to expand the idea and hold an invitation meet in 1895, with outside schools and colleges invited. That's how the Pennsylvania Relay festival at Philadelphia was born - the first in a series of relay meets scattered in various parts of USA that were to become a vital part of the American track and field scene. (Next to follow Penn's example was Drake University at Des Moines, Iowa, which instituted its Relay meet in 1910). Even in the present day and age this type of competition seems to arouse more spectator interest than most other meets held in that country. Usually there are relay events for different age classes and they usually stretch over two days And it seems reasonable to assume that the well-known competitive "fire" of American athletes may be partly, if not chiefly, due to the practice of relay racing. However, one had to wait till late in the second decade of the 20th century to see a sprint relay (4x110 y.) included in the programme of a US meet.

Relay racing at odd distances was first experimented in England by Ranlagh Harriers in September 1895, a "flying squadron race" in which the competing teams passed on a flag from one member to another.

As far as sprint relays were concerned, continental Europeans should for once be awarded the premiership. The earliest 4x100 metre record is commonly credited to a Bohemian quartet, A.C.Sparta Praha, who covered the distance in 48 $^{1}/_{5}$ in an international meet at Prague on 26 June 1897. The runners involved were Bohuslav Pohl, Ferdinand Schnepp, Karel Malecek and Jan Havel. They won comfortably from a Hungarian quartet, timed in 50 $^{3}/_{5}$. Similar relay racing was experimented by the same time in several other European countries.

To see the 4x100 m. relay included in the programme of the Olympic Games one had to wait till 1912.

The essential of technique in relay racing concerns the passing of batons. According to Ken Doherty, the utmost American student of track and field techniques, "in all relays longer than 4x220 y. the outgoing runner (the receiver) is chiefly held responsible for correct baton passing. He consequently focuses his eyes on it until it is firmly grasped in his hands. This is called the sight or visual pass. In sprint relays and chiefly in the 4x100 m., where victory often depends on maintaining maximum velocity throughout the exchange, the universally prevalent technique is "the blind pass", with both characters in the play – giver and receiver – being responsible, more or less to the same degree, for the success of the enterprise.

MEASURING TIME

The art and craft of timing sporting efforts accurately became a reality in 1844, when Adolphe Nicole, a Swiss watch-maker from Vallée de Joux devised and later patented in England a mechanism which activated the "chronograph" invented in 1821 by his French colleague Mathieu Rieussec, in a sequence of starting, stopping and then getting back to "zero". In brief something that could aptly measure the efforts of athletes in action.

Before then, notwithstanding certain improvements on Rieussec's original invention as devised by a Frenchman, Abraham-Louis Bréguet, the stopwatch had been used in the world of sport competitions merely as a running time device, inadequate for the purpose of officializing sport results.

The afore-mentioned device was first used on 28 October 1845 on the Belle Vue track in Manchester and made it possible to release what was probably the first known aptly timed performance: 22 $^{1}/_{2}$ secs. by an English "pro", George Eastham, in the 220 yards straightaway.

Many centuries earlier, nothing of the kind was of course obtainable for Koroibos, a cook from Elis (Greece), winner of the "stadion" race in the first documented edition of the ancient Olympic Games. Chroniclers of those days describe him as the fastest man in covering that distance…but how fast, we will never know!

It was only in the second half of the 19th century that the timing of athletic efforts became a consistent practice. Stop-watches became more and more adequate to the task through subsequent improvements, up to 1878 when the Swiss Longines produced the famous 19CH stop-watch (a chronograph the size of a normal pocket watch), which made it possible to time efforts in fifths-of-a-second. Such an instrument was used at Athens in 1896 in the inaugural edition of the modern Olympic Games, brought to life chiefly thanks to Baron Pierre de Coubertin.

The wide-spread use of such timing devices came into being shortly before the birth of two important governing bodies – the English AAA (Amateur Athletic Association) in 1880 and the American AAU (Amateur Athletic Union) in 1888, which were responsible for laying the foundations of the rules that would henceforth be followed in athletics.

That was the start for timing races – obviously manual times in fifths-of-a-second and generally for winners only. All other runners were classified as per finishing order, occasionally with a notation as to "how far back" they finished.

All this originated from a well-established principle, that of gratifying an athlete only as a winner, rather than by his own performance.

At Athens in 1896 the timers' squad was directed by Charles Perry, the same Englishman who had designed the track at Panathinaikon Stadium and who will later do the same for London's White City Stadium in 1908 and Stockholm's Olympiastadion in 1912.

The timing of performances continued to evolve, from partially automatic in 1912 to fully automatic in 1972, when the tenth-of-a-second – standard of the international measuring system – will gradually be fragmented, down to a thousand-of-a-second, as to allow a minute evaluation of time, as per any other physical dimension.

G. P.

2

DUFFEY'S BAD LUCK - THE "PRO" CIRCUS

Arthur Duffey, the unlucky boy of the 1900 Olympics, more than made up for his demise in the Paris Games. Between 1901 and 1903 he dominated the sprint picture on both sides of the Atlantic and earned an international reputation never before attained by an amateur sprinter. As a student at the University of Georgetown in Washington, D.C. he equalled the world's 100 y. record (9 $^{4}/_{5}$) four times in 1901 and twice more in 1902. He had what was probably his best moment at the IC4A Championships at Berkeley Oval, New York, on 31 May 1902, when he vanquished some of America's fastest men with what was probably the first authentic 9 $^{3}/_{5}$ in the history of the century. In doing so he beat an array of good sprinters, yet the nearest to him at the tape, Billy Schick, was 2 yards back. The winner's time was registered by three watches while a fourth watch showed 9 $^{2}/_{5}$. With timing to one tenth of a second Duffey would perhaps have been credited with a 9.5. On the other hand the larger fraction then in use does explain why twelve years had to elapse between the first official 9 $^{4}/_{5}$ and the first official 9 $^{3}/_{5}$.

Duffey's record in championship races was curiously more conspicuous in England than it was in his own country. At home he won the AAU 100 yards title just once, in 1899, as related in the previous chapter. He showed up at the English AAA Championships for five years in a row, always in the 100 yards – with four wins (1900-01-02-03) and a second place (1904) when he had to bow to a local hero, Jack Morton. All of these races were won in 10 seconds flat. Duffey's career as an amateur came to an abrupt end when the AAU declared him ineligible on charges of having cashed in on his laurels in more than one way. His name was removed from all record and championship lists. Since non-winning times were not usually taken in those days, IC4A books of later years carried the name of the second place finisher with no time, simply accompanied by the following notation: "Name of winner stricken from records". Duffey was a fast starter, almost "too fast" in the opinion of some observers. In his book "Athletics of Today", F.A.M.Webster refers to Duffey's experience with a North Country starter, who is said to have uttered a warning as he stood behind Duffey's curved end: "Sitha, Duffey, lad – Ah've brought shot gun for t' startin'. Ah've blank i't first barrel an't shot i't second. Tha canst guess where that'I't get shot if tha tries any flyers". After he turned "pro", Duffey was credited with such times as 5.0 (50 y.), 7 $^{2}/_{5}$ (75 y.) and 11 $^{2}/_{5}$ (120 y.).

As a keen student of sprinting, Duffey emphasized the importance of using both arms to full advantage and also "the necessity for forward action, by lifting the knees in a straight line, ... without any of the side deviation which is such a common fault with the novice sprinter". In terms of sprinting form, little has been added since then.

In the first two decades of the 20th century there was a stagnation in sprinting standards, at the top if not in depth. Such a legendary time as that attributed to Minoru Fujii of Japan – 10 $^{24}/_{100}$ for 100 metres at the Imperial University of Tokyo on 14 November 1902 – defies examination because of inadequate information about the conditions under which it was made. No matter if James E. Sullivan, then president of the American AAU, received from Japanese officials an "affidavit" on the genuineness of

1904 Olympics, St. Louis. Archie Hahn (USA), extreme left, winning the 60 m. in 7.0.

Fujii's performance, "an electrical time recorded in hundredths of a second". Fujii, a strongly built man, was also credited with a 3.90 pole vault in 1906, then superior to the best-on-record performance for that event. Neither mark was ever accepted. The commonly accepted explanation as regards the 100 metres time was "doubtful timing".

TEMPORA MUTANTUR (?)

On the subject of Duffey's disqualification from the amateur ranks there is another version which is quite different from the official one. It was divulged by Charles Paddock, the great sprinter of the Twenties (as quoted by Kenneth Greenberg in "Track & Field News", July 1951): "In reality, the reason that Duffey was professionalized and never restored to amateur standing, even though the rules say that a man may regain his amateur status after five years, was that he deeply offended the founder of the AAU, James E. Sullivan. He (Duffey) had his (running) shoes made by an old English cobbler. Sullivan was closely associated with the A.G.Spalding & Bros. (sporting goods) Company and he gave out the story that Duffey used Spalding shoes in all of his races. Duffey vigorously denied the statement and being so much under the displeasure of Sullivan and his cohorts he was never allowed to run in amateur competition again".

At that time Sullivan was also Editor of an excellent annual, "Spalding's Official Athletic Almanac". In the 1906 edition he wrote: "The Editor takes it upon himself on this occasion to act aside from all governing bodies and expunges the name of A.F.Duffey". There can be little doubt that Mr. Sullivan had a strong impact on the athletic world of those days. In the book "Irish Athletic Record 1906" one could see a page fully devoted to A.G.Spalding & Bros., London Branch, advertising among other things "a shoe worn by J.W.Morton, English 100 y. champion".

In America wide publicity was given to some performances credited to a "pro" by the name of R.P.Williams, who between 1904 and 1906 collected four 9 1/5 marks in the century, and even one 9 flat, reportedly recorded by three timers at Winthrop, MA., in 1906. Williams was also credited with 47 2/5 in the quarter-mile on a course with four turns, hence over two laps. If there was a trick of some sort, in his case as well as in Fujii's, we obviously cannot say, but those exploits certainly sound "fishy".

At the same time there were of course amateur sprinters of proven ability. Outstanding among them was Archibald ("Archie") Hahn (born at Dodgeville, WI. on 14 September 1880; died at Charlottesville, VA., on 21 January 1955; 1.67 m./ 64 kg.), who on account of his tiny figure was nicknamed "the Michigan Midget". As a student at Michigan U. he first hit the headlines with a 100/220y double at the 1903 AAU Championships at Milwaukee, alas with unimpressive marks (10 1/5 and 23 1/5) – but on a track "noted to be in terrible condition". He rose in stature, so to say, when he scored a triple at the 1904 Olympics.

The third edition of the quadrennial Games was at first awarded to Chicago, but after some rather intensive struggling the honour & burden befell St. Louis, MO., which was then busy organizing a World's Fair. First scheduled for 1903, the fair was delayed until 1904. Once again, the Games were in fact a sideshow to a much bigger event, and "The New York Times" actually referred to it as "The World's Fair Olympic Games". The sporting events spread – just as in Paris – over a period of several months (!) Olympic events were interspersed in a rather confused fashion with all sorts of handicap events and other oddities. The biggest handicap, however, was the all-too-modest quota of foreign countries – only 9 for a total of 38 athletes. Exempli gratia: on the grounds of travelling expense, no British team was sent to St.Louis! In sharp contrast with this, the host nation was represented by 103 men! Neutral observers were understandably eager to describe the Games as a US Inter-Club Championship! Foremost absentee from the British ranks was Jack Morton (born on 13 February 1879; died on 5 September 1950), who as related above had broken Arthur Duffey's winning streak at the English AAA Championships. Throughout the same year, the Englishman beat Duffey time and again in several British meets. No doubt Morton would have been a prime threat to the Americans if he had shown up at the St.Louis Olympics. Between 1904 and 1907 he collected four straight victories at the AAA Championships and on the very last occasion he again won from a leading American, Nathan Cartmell. His best 100 yards time was 9.8 at Montreal on 4 September 1905. He was a most consistent performer, no matter if he apparently liked to depict himself as a chain smoker and a heavy drinker.

At the Olympic gathering in St.Louis the real plus was unquestionably a good cinder track. Especially built for the Games, it was 1/3 of a mile (536.45 m.) in length and had one long straightaway. Just as in Paris four years earlier, there were three sprint races on the programme, in the following chronological order: 60, 200, 100 metres. With Morton and Duffey not in the game, Hahn obviously had a relatively easy task at the St.Louis Games. For the first – and, so far, only – time in Olympic history, the sprint finals were an all-American affair as foreign competitors, very few in number, were all eliminated in the qualifying rounds. In the 60 metres a very fast start helped Hahn to build up a strong lead early, and he won comfortably in 7.0. He went on to win the 200 metres (straight course) hands down in 21 3/5 after the three other finalists were all penalized 1 yard for false starts. (More on the subject in an adjoining aside). His third and last victory, in the century (11.0), was fairly easy too: well as usual, he held off Nate Cartmell's final dash without major trouble.

1904 Olympics, St.Louis - 60 metres (29 August): 1.Archie Hahn (USA) 7.0; 2.William Hogenson (USA) 1 m. back; 3.Fay Moulton (USA) equal 2nd; 4.Clyde Blair (USA) equal 3rd; 5.Meyer Prinstein (USA), 6.Frank Castleman (USA).

100 metres (3 September): 1.Archie Hahn (USA) 11.0; 2.Nate Cartmell (USA) 1 1/2 m. back; 3.William Hogenson (USA) 1 m. f.b.; 4.Fay Moulton (USA) 1 1/2 m.

f.b.; 5.Fred Heckwolf (USA); 6.Lawson Robertson (USA).

200 metres - straight course (31 August): 1.Archie Hahn (USA) 21 $^{3}/_{5}$; 2.Nate Cartmell (USA) 3 m. back; 3.William Hogenson (USA); 4.Fay Moulton (USA).

DISCOUNT ON PENALTIES

False starts have always been a major problem for athletics legislators. In the early days of modern amateurism there was a rule, valid both in Britain and USA although with different specifications, which penalized anyone accused of a false start. Usually the penalty consisted in putting the "culprit" 1 or 2 yards back when the gun was fired again. During the 1904 Olympics in St.Louis there were rather amusing episodes in the sprint races, according to Olympic historian Bill Mallon. In a heat of the 60 metres Béla de Mezö of Hungary false started once. He was to be penalized 2 yards according to the rule then in force, but the starter decided not to penalize him - on the grounds that "as a foreigner he had difficulties in understanding instructions". In the 200 metres final three Americans – Nate Cartmell, William Hogenson and Fay Moulton – were to be penalized 2 yards for the same reason. Yet they obtained a "50% discount" and were put back only 1 yard, claiming that "there was not room to put them back any more".

With Arthur Duffey's 9 $^{3}/_{5}$ expunged from record lists, the first official 9 $^{3}/_{5}$ over 100 yards was achieved by another American, Daniel Kelly. This happened in the Pacific Northwest AAU meet at Spokane on 23 June 1906 and the performance caused quite a stir in US track circles, mostly because of the fact that Kelly (born on 1 September 1883; died on 9 April 1920), an Oregon University student, was little known on a national scale as he happened to be far removed from the East, then the fulcrum of US athletic might. To tell the truth, Kelly had a national reputation of some sort as in 1905 he had placed second .... in the long jump (6.88 m.) at the AAU Championships held in his own backyard at Portland, Ore. There was a curious circumstance surrounding his 9.6. A paper from Portland, "Oregonian", told the story: "The afternoon was warm and during the meet the steel tape, which had been used to measure the course, lay unrolled in the sun. After Kelly had won in that course, it was found to be 5 inches (12.7 cms.) short of the required 100 yards .... Then it was realized that the unrolled steel tape expanded under the heat of the sun and after it had cooled off another measurement showed the course to be slightly over 100 yards. Proper affidavits were forwarded to the AAU and the performance became the world's and American record".

Kelly was no doubt a good athlete. In the very same meet of his 9 $^{3}/_{5}$ century he also equalled Wefers' American record for 220 yards straight with 21 $^{1}/_{5}$. And a few weeks before he had done 7.37 in the long jump, the world's longest leap for that year. In fact, it was in the long jump that he showed at his best in big meets: AAU champion in 1907, second in the 1908 Olympics.

Earlier in 1906 there had been an unusual event: the "interim" Olympics in Athens. Mind you, the Greeks have always regarded that festival as a full-fledged Olympic celebration. After the two sloppy editions of 1900 in Paris and 1904 in St.Louis, in which Baron de Coubertin's "child" had survived merely as a side-show to World's Fairs, the Greeks came up with the idea of regularly holding an official version of their own in Athens in the middle year between Olympic celebrations. The IOC and the Baron himself consented as far as the 1906 event was concerned but later made it a point that Olympic celebrations should occur every fourth year as per old .... Greek tradition. Consequently the 1906 affair has since been branded as "unofficial" in IOC history books. Apart from such "technicalities", the Games of 1906 in Athens turned out to be the best ever seen up to that moment - first and foremost, in terms of international participation. As far as track and field was concerned, there were 21 countries for a total of 254 athletes. The events were run off between 25 April and 1 May, virtually before the opening of the track season in most Northern Hemisphere countries. For the first time, most countries appeared with a national team, i.e. with uniforms of their own. Theatre of the events was once again the Panhellenic Stadium with its difficult curves and loose cinders – just as in the "première" of the modern Games in 1896. And the sprint department again consisted of just one event, the 100 metres. Jack Morton of Great Britain was the most notable absentee. The best non-American candidates were Nigel Barker of Australia and Knut Lindberg of Sweden. Both made the final, along with four US sprinters. There were several false starts in the early rounds as the runners had difficulties in understanding instructions, given in Greek. In the decisive race, after a fair start, Archie Hahn went into an early lead, as per his custom, and won rather comfortably from his countryman Fay Moulton. The winner's time, 11 1/5, was rather unimpressive by top international standards yet much faster than those returned on the same track in the 1896 Games. Barker took third and Lindberg, a slow starter, was sixth and last.

1906 "Interim" Olympics, Athens - 100 metres (27 April): 1.Archie Hahn (USA) 11 1/5; 2.Fay Moulton (USA) 1 m. back; 3.Nigel Barker (Aus) 30 cms. f.b.; 4.William Eaton (USA) 1.5 m. f.b.; 5.Lawson Robertson (USA); 6.Knut Lindberg (Swe). Moulton and Eaton won their semi-finals in 11 1/5. Lanes: Hahn 1, Eaton 2, Moulton 3, Lindberg 4, Robertson 5, Barker 6.

Versatility was the rule for many outstanding athletes of those days. Lindberg also placed second in the javelin and sixth in the pentathlon. Later in the same year, this 24-year-old Swede made the headlines with a fast 10 3/5 in the 100 metres in a meet at Göteborg on 26 August. This was the fastest time recorded until then over the metric century. Amazingly enough, the three watches read 10 1/5, 10 2/5 and 10 3/5. Swedish rules of the time provided for the slowest watch to be taken as official and the 10 3/5 version was consequently ratified as a national record. The IAAF, which was yet to come at that time, later ruled that in all races the middle time would have to be accepted as official, in which case Lindberg's feat would have been ratified as 10 2/5. There is a PS though: according to Ulf Lagerström, a keen Swedish student of athletics history, the Göteborg race was started with a flag rather with the firing of a pistol. Lindberg, who was also a good soccer player, had his best competitive days in 1907, when he had mixed fortunes with England's Jack Morton in Swedish meets and once ran 150 metres in 16.0, then the fastest time on record at this seldom run distance.

Archie Hahn thus reaped a lot of international honours in his career, no matter if partly aided by the fact that the 1904 and 1906 Olympic festivals were deserted by some of the best sprinters of those days. He was at any rate one of the most useful athletes of his generation. A keen student of technique, he later became a track coach, first at Princeton and then at the Virginia University. What's even more perhaps, in 1925 he edited a golden booklet, "How to sprint", which may still be regarded as a classic. He usually indulges in many fine details about running form, much less perhaps on what we now call conditioning methods. In fact, he writes: "A six-day training week is a drawback from the oldtime professional system. Of recent years there has been a decided tendency toward underwork, and during the competitive season a three or four-day week is sufficient when finished up by hard Saturday competition".

More or less mysterious marks continued to crop up now and then. In 1907 one such was reported from Helsinki. In an international meet held there on 1 September a Scot then living in Finland, George Easton, was credited with a nifty 10.4 for the metric distance. In his wake, Uuno Railo of Finland was timed in 10.6. To tell the truth, Railo had been credited with 10.6 also four days earlier at Tampere, but for some reason the Finnish Athletics Federation did not ratify these marks. Railo only got official credit for a 10.8 made at the national championships earlier in the season. As for Easton, he went on for some time but he never approached his wondrous but hardly believable 10.4.

In early July 1908 two notable overseas sprinters starred at the English AAA Championships, held in London's brand-new

White City Stadium, which only a few weeks later was to be the theatre of the 4th Olympic Games (as previously noted, the 1906 "interim" edition in Athens was ignored for all official purposes).

The two men in question were Robert Kerr of Canada and Reggie Walker of South Africa, the latter barely 19 at the time. In the English title meet, which at the time ranked as the most important rendez-vous of international talents, Kerr scored a double with 10.0 (100 y.) and 22 2/5 (220 y.). Walker was runner-up in the shorter race, ahead of Britain's pride, Jack Morton. That was an alarm-clock which turned out to be the fore-runner of greater things to come.

In previous years no official US team had been selected for the Games, but in 1908 sectional meets were used as Tryouts for the Olympic team selection – a fore-runner of the nation-wide Olympic Tryouts which were to follow in the Twenties. As it usually happened in those days, the strongest cohort of US Olympic candidates for the 100 metres emerged from the Eastern tryouts, in which Lawson Robertson, James Rector and Nate Cartmell finished 1-2-3 in that order, all in 11 flat. Rector was set back 1 yard after making a false start. In the same meet, Cartmell won the 200 metres in 21 4/5. It should be added that earlier in the season Rector, apparently the nervous type of sprinter, had been credited with a sensational 9 2/5 in the 100 yards, albeit with the aid of a strong wind.

For once, however, the US cohort proved not strong enough for the Olympic tests. Time-wise the preliminary rounds of the 100 and 200 metres were perversely interspersed, making things difficult for prospective doublers, with the finals on consecutive days. At the shorter distance the fastest qualifiers were Rector and Walker, with 10 4/5. Only four men were admitted to the final: the above two, plus Robert Kerr and Cartmell. The youngest of them all, 19-year-old Walker, was the early leader, while Kerr got off badly. At the mid-way point Rector just passed Walker, the others being close. Then Walker spurted magnificently, got level with Rector and finally shot ahead to win by the better part of a metre. Rector just nipped Kerr for second. Cartmell was a well-beaten fourth.

In the 200 Kerr ran the fastest heat with 22 1/5, then went on to win the final in slower time, 22 3/5. He was the best starter and in the closing stage he narrowly repulsed a strong attack by Robert Cloughen of USA to win by no more than 20 centimetres. The American was barely 19 at the time.

1908 Olympics, London - 100 metres (22 July): 1.Reginald Walker (SA) 10 4/5; 2.James Rector (USA) 10.9e; 3.Robert Kerr (Can) 11.0e; 4.Nate Cartmell (USA) 11 1/5e. Lanes: Walker 1, Rector 2, Cartmell 3, Kerr 4.

200 metres (23 July): 1.Robert Kerr (Can) 22 3/5; 2.Robert Cloughen (USA) 22 3/5e: 3.Nate Cartmell (USA) 22.7e; 4.George Hawkins (UK) 22.9e.

Reginald "Reggie" Walker (born at Durban on 16 March 1889; died in 1914; 1,70 m, / 61 kg,) was the most precocious talent in Olympic sprint history. At home he had made the headlines in 1907, when only 18, winning the South African 100 yards title in 10 flat. The following year, before coming to Europe, he lowered the South African record to 9 4/5, but lost to E.J.Duffey at the national title meet. The South African federation just selected Duffy for the Olympics and it was only at the unanimous request of a group of friends and acquaintances from Nepal, who accompanied their pleas with fund raising, that Walker was finally sent to London. His subsequent success in the Games made him famous – to the point that a "Reginald Walker Day" was proclaimed in his home town. He went through hectic days amid celebrations.

Walker confirmed his international status in 1909, notably with a victory in the 100 yards (10.0) at the English AAA meet, beating Nathan Cartmell of USA and Kerr of Canada. The following year the South African ace had mixed fortunes in his duels with Fred Ramsdell of USA, who notably nipped him in the AAA championship race (10 1/5). Well realizing that running was after all the best thing he could do, by the end of that year Walker decided to take maximum advantage by turning "pro". He did so in spite of the fact that a South African millionaire made him a very generous offer in hopes

Coach Sam Mussabini and one of his most famous protégés, South African Reginald Walker.

that he would remain in the amateur ranks up to the 1912 Olympics. Walker's outstanding performances in the "pro" circus are summarized in an adjoining aside.

Robert Kerr (born in Ireland on 9 June 1882; died on 12 May 1963; 1.71 m. / 66 kg.) was just a child when his family crossed the Atlantic and settled down in Canada. He went to work while still in his teens and, as he recalled many years later "I just made the best of it, training after work – and that was the age of the twelve-hour day". He was 20 by the time he achieved prominence with a stunning triple (100, 440, 880 y.) at the Hamilton Coronation Games in 1902. Two years later he was rated good enough to represent the (unofficial) Canadian team at the St.Louis Olympics. As the story goes, his $75 expense money came out of his own savings. He made the trip in a day coach and slept on the floor at a St.Louis friend's house. He didn't go beyond the prelims though. In the next few years Kerr made further progress. In 1907 he ran the century in 9 4/5 and later scored a 100/220 y. double at the Canadian Championships in Toronto. 1908 was of course the year of his comethrough, with the fine performances we have already mentioned. The following year, on straight courses, he was twice credited with 21 2/5. He continued to compete until 1912, but chose not to enter the Stockholm Olympics, feeling that at 30 he was past his prime. His contemporaries described him as "a man of strong character and of sound sense". He displayed these qualities also in his later life as an army officer and finally as a driving force behind the inaugural British Empire Games, held at Hamilton in 1930.

US sprinters thus experienced a momentary eclipse in 1908, but in the years that followed they amply re-affirmed their world leadership. By then talents came from practically every section of the vast country. Texas, "the Lone Star State", practically entered the game with Gwinn Henry, the offspring of a farmers' family who raised cattle and horses. As a boy he loved various sports but found it difficult to convince his father that to pursue his dream he would have to stay away from their ranch now and then. Yet he proved very fast in running in the fields and ultimately won his father's assent. In 1909, aged 22, he excelled in intercollegiate competition, notably with 9.6 in the 100 yards, not ratified though. He soon became a well-known figure even in Eastern circles and in 1910 he went to New York to compete for the Irish-American AC under Lawson Robertson, a former sprinter and now a famous coach. At AAU meets Gwinn won the 220 yards in 1910 (22.6) and the 100 in 1911 (10.0). Perhaps his most noteworthy mark was at the odd distance of 125 yards (114.3 m.) – 12.2 in New York in 1911. This powerfully built sprinter (1.80 m. / 71 kg.) ultimately failed to live up to expectations though.

Germany's first sterling sprinter was Richard Rau (born in Berlin on 26 August 1889; died at Vyasma, USSR, on 6 November 1945; 1.78 m. 7 67 kg.). Between 1909 and 1920 he won thirteen national titles, including one over 110 metres hurdles. He began in 1908 and in the following year he ran the 100 metres in 10 4/5. Clockwise he was at his best in 1911, by which time he had two worthy rivals in his own country, Emil Ketterer and Erwin Kern. In a spring meet Rau was timed in 10 3/5, thus equalling Lindberg's world's best. In close succession but in different races, first Ketterer then Rau were timed in 10.5 (timing in tenths of a second was an optional in those days).

Britain had by then a first-class sprinter in William Reuben Applegarth, a medium-size runner who was at his best in the furlong (born in Scotland on 11 May 1890, died in New York on 5 December 1958). Described as "a diminutive runner who ran with machine-like precision". In 1910, at the age of 20, he first came to prominence by finishing third in the 100 yards at the AAA Championship behind Fred Ramsdell (USA), 10 1/5, and Reggie Walker. Still in the English title meet, in 1912, Applegarth made the grade with a first in the 220 (22.0) and a second in the 100, won by George Patching of South Africa (9 4/5).

On the eve of the Stockholm Olympics (1912) America's best appeared to be Howard Drew (born at Lexington, Virginia on 28 June 1890; died on 20 February

1956; 1.72 m. / 72 kg.), who may be regarded as the first black sprinter of world calibre of the 20th century. He was once remembered by Charles Paddock, the great American sprinter of the Twenties, as "the smoothest piece of running machinery the world had ever seen". He was still in high school at Springfield, MA, when he showed up at the Eastern Olympic Trials at Cambridge in 1912. The pre-race favourite was Ralph Craig, a tall man with plenty of staying power who had twice equalled the world's best on a straight course, 21 1/5 – on 28 May 1910 in Philadelphia and on 27 May 1911 at Cambridge, MA, both in the ICAAAA Championships. But in the Eastern Olympic Trials, Drew upset Craig first in a 100 metre semi-final, then in the final – 10 4/5 to 10.9est.

The Stockholm Olympics marked a decided step forward in the evolution of track and field at the international level. In fact they witnessed the birth of the IAAF (International Amateur Athletic Federation), chiefly if not entirely the brain child of two Swedes, J.Sigfrid Edström and Leopold Englund. For official purposes the constitution of the new body was ratified at Berlin a year later and Edström was elected president. There were 26 nations on the original membership list.

The athletics events of the 1912 Games were held in a brand new stadium. The cinder track was 385 metres in length. Technical innovations notably included timing in tenths of a second. For the first time in Olympic history, most if not all non-winning times were officially recorded. And for the first time the sprint parade included a 4x100 metres relay. The two individual events were run off without improper interspersions, a rule which would henceforth be applied to all future editions. Only strange thing, if viewed through present-day lenses, the 4x100 metres relay was placed in between the two individual races.

Ralph Craig (USA) winning the 100 m. at the 1912 Olympics in Stockholm.

In the 16th heat of the 100 metres Donald Lippincott of USA was clocked in 10.6, a performance which was to be ratified by the IAAF as the first official world record for this distance. In the semi-finals, with winners only advancing to the decisive race, there were such notable "victims" as Richard Rau and William Applegarth. The only non-American who managed to qualify for the final was Patching of South Africa. Howard Drew, the favourite of many, strained a tendon in winning his "semi" in 10.7 and had to stay away from the final. This was a bad loss for the US cohort which nonetheless managed to dominate the picture in the decisive race. The final was countersigned by seven (!) false starts, three of which reportedly by Ralph Craig. No penalties were contemplated though. At the right start Patching soon forged ahead and had a half-metre lead at 40 metres. Then Craig began to close, caught the South African at 60 metres and was a fraction ahead at 75 metres. Craig pulled away in the closing stage and finally won by about 60 cms. in 10.8. His countrymen Alvah Meyer and Lippincott followed in that order, relegating Patching to fourth.

The heats of the 200 metres followed three days later. Here again Lippincott was the fastest qualifier, wining his "semi" in 21.8. The two top-rated Europeans, Applegarth and Rau, fared better than in the 100 and eventually made the final as did Americans Craig, Lippincott, Charles Reidpath (who was to annex the 400 metres two days later) and Donnell Young. Coming out of the turn Applegarth had a slight lead, but Craig and Lippincott soon came abreast of him and led in that order at the half-way mark. They subsequently increased their lead, with Craig a safe winner at the end, after brilliantly holding off Lipppincott's last attack. Applegarth edged Rau for third.

The 4x100 metre relay was virtually a European invention. The Americans would include a 4x110 yards (402.34 m.) event in the programme of their relay carnivals only after World War 1. On the eve of the Stockholm Games the best-on-record performance for the metric sprint relay belonged to a German Club, SC Charlottenburg, with a time of 43.5, made in Berlin on 9 May 1912 by a quartet consisting of Otto Röhr, August Sandvoss, Willy Schöltz and Richard Rau. Not surprisingly, this mark was beaten time and again in the qualifying rounds of the Olympics. Even so, the Americans had the best sprinters and hardly anyone thought that they could be beaten in the Olympic "première". As it was, they managed to beat themselves, so to say. It happened in a semi-final: a US team consisting of J.Ira Courtney, Frank Belote, Clement Wilson and Carl Cooke won in 42.2, a new world's best, but was disqualified for passing out of the zone. In another "semi" Germany provided the best qualifying time, 42.3, and thus loomed as a favourite for the decisive race. Here they too were disqualified and victory went to Great Britain.

1912 Olympics, Stockholm - 100 metres (7 July): 1.Ralph Craig (USA) 10.8; 2.Alvah Meyer (USA) 10.9; 3.Donald Lippincott (USA) 10.9: 4.George Patching (SA) 11.0; 5.Frank Belote (USA); Howard Drew (USA) did not start. Lanes: Drew 1, Meyer 2, Craig 3, Patching 4, Lippincott 5, Belote 6.

200 metres (11 July): 1.Ralph Craig (USA) 21.7; 2.Donald Lippincott (USA) 21.8; 3.Willie Applegarth (UK) 22.0; 4.Richard Rau (Ger) 22.2; 5.Charles Reidpath (USA) 22.3; 6.Donnell Young (USA) 22.3. Lanes: Applegarth 1, Reidpath 2, Young 3, Craig 4, Rau 5, Lippincott 6.

4x100 metres (9 July): 1. UK (D.Jacobs, H.MacIntosh, V.d'Arcy, W. Applegarth) 42.4; 2.Swe (I.Möller, C.Luther, T. Persson, K.Lindberg) 42.6; Ger (O.Röhr, M.Herrmann, E.Kern, R.Rau), disqualified.

Ralph Craig (born on 21 June 1889 at Detroit, MI; died on 21 July 1972 at Lake George, NY; 1.83 m. / 77 kg.) thus reached his peak at the right moment, reportedly as a result of unusually intensive training. Curiously enough, he failed to add other important titles – e.g. AAU or English AAA – to his relatively short career record. But a long while later he was unique in at least one more detail, as related in the adjoining aside.

RARE COMEBACKS

Ralph Craig, the double Olympic sprint champion of 1912, was in the sporting news again 36 years later. He had taken up yachting and in 1948 he was a member of the US team at the London Olympics. By then a 59-year-old senior, he was given the honour of carrying the US flag at the opening ceremony. Contrary to widely spread reports, however, he was on the yachting team as an alternate and did not compete. Athletes who have appeared in the Olympics in two different sports are obviously a rarity. Notable in this respect is the case of Willie Davenport of USA, who represented his country in four Olympics, winning gold in the 110 metres hurdles in 1968 and bronze in 1976. In 1980 he competed in the Olympic Winter Games at Lake Placid, NY, as a member of the US team in the 4-man bobsled.

Donald Lippincott was probably at his best in 1913, when he tied the world's best for 220 yards straightaway, 21 1/5, in winning the ICAAAA title on the Harvard track at Cambridge, MA. on 31 May. He could hold his own even in the quarter-mile and in 1915 he was a member of the Univ. of Pennsylvania team that lowered the world record for the 4x440 yards relay to 3:18.0. On that occasion he ran the penultimate leg in 49 1/5 before handing over to Ted Meredith, then the no.1 man at the distance, who ran the anchor leg in 47 4/5.

The unlucky Drew fought back bravely. Later in 1912 he won the AAU 100 y. title (10.0) from Alvah Meyer, the Olympic runner-up. Although born in the East, he had his best days while attending the University of Southern California in Los Angeles, whose athletes, known under their battle name, "Trojans", were to remain a dominant factor in US intercollegiate track for many years. In 1913 Drew won both sprints at the AAU meet, with lacklustre performances that's true. But on another occasion he was credited with 9 3/5 in the century, a time which was not ratified as a record. 1914 was his best season, clock-wise at least. Operating in sunny California, he began with a record-tying 21 1/5 for the 220 y. straightaway at Claremont on 28 February, then equalled the 100 y. record (9 3/5) at Berkeley on 28 March. There was no wind rule at the time and all decisions on this were left to officials, who apparently considered the wind not strong enough to nullify the record. Both these marks were thus ratified by the AAU and later by the newly-born IAAF as well. Drew continued to run intermittently till the Olympic Tryouts of 1920, in which he reached the semi-finals in both 100 and 200 metres. He was described as a dusky youth of medium build and powerful legs. Many years later Charles Paddock, his true successor, wrote: "If he (Drew) had faced real competition during his best college years he would undoubtedly have shattered both sprint records".

The world record for the 220 yards straightaway, 21 1/5, was equalled once more towards the end of 1914, when George Parker, a massive runner (1.86 m. / 78 kg.), did just that at Fresno on 2 October.

Willie Applegarth of Britain continued to perform at high levels and won both sprints at the AAA Championships in 1913 and again in 1914. In the latter meet (London, 4 July) he was credited with a swift 21 1/5 over 220 yards, until then the fastest time ever recorded on a course with one turn. The latter was in fact no more than 70 yards (64 m.) but photos of the Stamford Bridge ground suggest that the turn was sharper than those now in vogue. Second to Applegarth, 4 1/2 y. behind, was his Olympic relay colleague Victor d'Arcy. For the sake of completeness it must be said that Australian "pro" Jack Donaldson had been credited with a slightly slower time, 21 1/4, at Glasgow on 26 July 1913. Applegarth himself turned "pro" near the end of 1914 and among his "scalps" in that new world was Donaldson, known in "pro" circles as the "Blue Streak" of Australia.

Another prominent European whose career was cut short by World War I was Richard Rau of Germany. He managed to do 21.6 for 200 metres on a straight course, his best ever, in 1914. After the war he attempted a comeback and did 10.7 (1920) and 10.6w (1921) in the century when well in his thirties. As destiny would have it, many years later another World War put an end to his life while he, by then a major in the Luftwaffe, was in a Russian POW camp.

FIREWORKS OF THE "PRO" CIRCUS

The revival of the Olympic Games under the banner of the International Olympic Committee sanctioned the demise of professionalism, so clearly in fact that some optimistic observers came to regard it as definitive. (But the "monster" was to rise again many years later with the "Trojan Horse" method, i.e. from within amateurism itself).
However, "pro" races continued to thrive here and there, at least for some time. Between 1908 and 1914 a "pro" circus chiefly involving sprinters was a major attraction in Australia, South Africa and even in Great Britain, the acknowledged motherland of amateurism. Among the stars of those match races were Reggie Walker, Willliam Applegarth and two Aussies, Jack Donaldson and Arthur Postle. Applegarth beat Donaldson in two widely heralded matches at Manchester, with 9.9 (100 y.) in November 1914. and 22 $^{1}/_{4}$ in April 1915. But the performances that really astounded experts were returned Down Under. Here is a summary:

Arthur Postle – 50 y. 5 $^{1}/_{5}$ (1908), 60 y. 6.0 (1906); 70 y. 7 $^{1}/_{16}$ (1910); 80 y. 7 $^{3}/_{4}$ (1908); 100 y. 9 $^{1}/_{2}$ (1906); 150 y. 14 $^{1}/_{5}$ (1912); 200 y. 19.0 (1912).
Jack Donaldson – 65 y. 6 $^{1}/_{2}$ (1910); 80 y. 7 $^{15}/_{16}$ (1909); 100 y. 9 3/8 (1910); 120 y. 11 $^{1}/_{4}$ (1909); 130 y. 12.0 (1911); 150 y. 14.0 (1911); 220 y. 21 $^{1}/_{4}$ (1913); 300 y. 29 $^{61}/_{64}$ (1913).
Reggie Walker – 50 y. 5 $^{1}/_{5}$ (1912); 90 y: 8 $^{4}/_{5}$ (1912); 100 y. 9 2/5 (1912); 110 y. 10 $^{2}/_{5}$ (1911); 120 y. 11 $^{2}/_{5}$ (1908); 130 y. 12 $^{2}/_{5}$ (1909).

Some of these performances were to remain superior to the official amateur records for a long time. For example, Donaldson's 9 $^{3}/_{8}$ for 100 yards, made in beating Postle at Johannesburg in 1910, was officially bettered by an amateur only in 1948 (Mel Patton, USA, 9.3). Of course, the South African city is located 1753 metres above sea level and, as we know, a rarefied atmosphere can be beneficial in events lying in the anaerobic sphere. Then it should be added that the rules prevailing in the "pro" ranks were definitely more flexible than those in force in amateur athletics. For example, the track on which Postle recorded his 9 $^{1}/_{2}$ for 100 yards at Kalgoorlie on 28 December 1906 dropped 3 ft. (0.91 m.) in the running direction.

Now and then, incredibly good times continued to crop up. In 1913 a 20-year-old American high school boy, Albert Robinson, was credited with 9 $^{3}/_{5}$ and 20 $^{4}/_{5}$ (straight course) for the English distances. True, he had finished second in the 220 at the AAU meet the year before, but apart from that he was to remain a flash in the pan. The aforementioned Emil Ketterer of Germany was said to have done 10.1 for 100 metres at Prague on 9 June 1912, according to press reports. A revolutionary mark, for those days. Many years later, German statisticians discovered that Ketterer's real mark on that occasion was 10 $^{1}/_{5}$ for .... 100 yards. Apart from misprints, it should be noted that starting and timing methods differed considerably from one country to another, sometimes even within the same country; and the wind factor was often ignored. As for German sprint times it should be said that as often as not they were partly the result of "fast guns". Comparison with the slower ones usually made in Britain by the same men seems to substantiate such a hypothesis.

The advent of Charles Paddock (born at Gainesville, Texas, on 11 August 1900; died at Sitka, AK, on 21 July 1943; 1.72 m. / 72 kg.) coincided with the end of World War I. In 1919, while still a junior, he made his international debut at the Inter-Allied Games, held in the new Stade Pershing in Paris: he won both metric sprints in 10 $^{4}/_{5}$ and 21 $^{3}/_{5}$. That was only the beginning: for the better part of a decade Paddock was the outstanding star of the American sprint scene, and a widely discussed one. He lived in sunny California throughout his career. In 1920, after posting a promising 9 4/5 in the 100 yards, he came East to compete in the AAU Championships, held at Cambridge, MA. For the first time this meet served as an Olympic Tryout, hence as a door-opener for the Antwerp Olympics. In the 100 yards he had to bow to Loren Murchison (10.0) and Jackson Scholz, but in the 220, his 6th race in just over 24 hours, he won easily in 21 2/5 from Morris Kirksey and Murchison. Notwithstanding such mixed fortunes Paddock was by then a famous star, were it only for his habit of taking a leap of about 4 metres in going into the tape, a technique which was widely discussed by experts and laymen. Regardless of whether he really gained something by such a stratagem, it has been sensibly suggested that he certainly caught the eye of the judges on the finish line.

Great Britain had by then a new star in the person of Harry Edward, a tall sprinter from British Guiana. He had in fact emerged just before the outbreak of World War I when as a 19-year-old boy he ran a brilliant 200 metres in Berlin, barely losing to Richard Rau. He quickly scaled the heights after the war, notably with an impressive double at the 1920 AAA Championships - 10.0 and 21 3/5 for the English distances.

The war had caused the cancellation of the 1916 Olympics, which were originally scheduled to be held in Berlin. When the tale was resumed, the IOC chose Antwerp as venue of the 1920 edition. Pierre de Coubertin and his colleagues deemed it advisable not to extend invitations to Germany, Austria, Hungary, Bulgaria and Turkey, which countries had incidentally emerged as losers from the conflict. As the Baron himself pointed out in his "Mémoires Olympiques" many years later, it would have been particularly risky to allow a German team to appear before a prevalently Belgian crowd, so shortly after the end of the war in

1912 Olympics, Stockholm. The first team to be crowned Olympic champion in the 4x100 m. relay represented Great Britain. From left to right: Willie Applegarth, Vic D'Arcy, David Jacobs and Henry Macintosh.

1920 Olympics, Antwerp. 100 m. final. Charles Paddock goes home the winner in 10.8, using his famous jump style. Morris Kirksey (USA), extreme right, is 2nd, and Harry Edward (UK), extreme left, is 3rd.

which Belgium had been invaded by German troops. On the other hand he well realized than an open proclamation of ostracism would be tantamount to establishing what he termed as "un précédent dangereux". The decision not to invite Germany and her allies was at best a crooked compromise, which may well go down in history as the first example of an Olympic boycott.

Antwerp had a newly-laid 389.80 metre track which was not fast. Unstable weather conditions did not help either. Even so, in the qualifying rounds of the 100 metres, 10.8s clockings were recorded by four Americans, Paddock, Scholz, Kirksey, Murchison, plus one Englishman, Edward. In the final the clerk of the course cautioned Paddock not to put his hands over the mark just as the men were about to start. Murchison, accustomed to the methods of American starters in similar instances, expected an order to "stand up" and proceeded to arise just as the others were off. Naturally, he was never in the race and finished a distant sixth and last. At the half-way mark Scholz led Edward by 60 cms., with Kirksey and Paddock close. All four came fast, Paddock using his characteristic "jump" finish to beat Kirksey by 30 cms. At first, Scholz was placed fifth behind Ali Khan of France. Later, however, the judges placed Scholz 4th. And some observers at the finish were inclined to believe that he had actually finished 3rd.

Three days elapsed between the final of the 100 and the first preliminary round of the 200. Britain's Edward had the fastest time (22.0) among qualifiers. He suffered a muscle injury in the next round yet managed to qualify for the final. In the decisive race Paddock was off in front and led entering the straight, with Woodring close. As they neared the tape Paddock gathered for his customary "jump" but Woodring shot past him to take the race. Edward, starting poorly, surprisingly held off Murchison for 3rd. The winner's time was 22.0. Edward, his thigh strapped up to offset hamstring trouble, thus collected another bronze.

The third and final act of the Antwerp sprint saga, the 4x100 metres relay, saw the US men win rather easily from France and Sweden, while Britain finished no better than fourth. The winners' time was a new world record – 42 1/5.

1920 Olympics, Antwerp - 100 metres (16 August): 1.Charles Paddock (USA) 10.8; 2.Morris Kirksey (USA) 10.8; 3.Harry Edward (GB) 11.0; 4.Jackson Scholz (USA) 11.0; 5.Emile Ali Khan (Fra) 11.1; 6.Loren Murchison (USA). Lanes: Kirksey 1, Murchison 2, Paddock 3, Ali Khan 4, Scholz 5, Edward 6.

200 metres (20 August): 1.Allen Woodring (USA) 22.0; 2.Charles Paddock (USA) 22.1; 3.Harry Edward (UK) 22.2; 4.Loren Murchison (USA); 5.George Davidson (New Zealand); 6.Jack Oosterlaak (SA). Lanes: Davidson 1, Oosterlaak 2, Woodring 3, Paddock 4, Edward 5, Murchison 6.

4x100 metres relay (22 August): 1.USA (C.Paddock, J.Scholz, L.Murchison, M.Kirksey) 42.2 (world record); 2.Fra (E.Ali Khan, R.Lorain, R.Tirard, R. Mourlon) 42.6; 3.Swe (A.Holmström, W.Petersson, S.Malm, N.Sandström) 42.9; 4.UK; 5.Den; 6.Lux.

Allen Woodring (born at Bethlehem, PA, on 15 February 1898) was the real upset of the 1920 Games. He had finished no better than fifth in the 220 yards at the AAU Championships and was certainly not expected to outfox Paddock in the Games. While at Syracuse University, however, he was in the news again in 1921, when he won the 220 at the ICAAAA meet in 21 $^2/_5$ and more so perhaps in 1923, when he won the 440 at the same meet in 48.2.

Jackson Scholz (born at Buchanan, MI, on 15 March 1897; died on 26 October 1986; 1.72 m. / 61 kg.) was in the initial stage of a wondrous international career. After the Games he had another glorious day at Stockholm on 16 September, when he tied Lippincott's world record for the 100 metres, 10.6, leaving Nils Engdahl 5 metres back. The latter, a good Swedish all-around sprinter, had won a bronze medal in the 400 metres at the Antwerp Olympics. Such an overwhelming victory margin in a world record race over 100 metres is indeed a rarity. Scholtz was truly impressive on that occasion. As a Swedish reporter put it, "One could hardly believe one's eyes".

Scholz was to become the first sprinter to make Olympic finals in three editions of the Olympic Games. Strangely enough, he had fewer successes in national title meets. After placing fourth in the 100 yards in the 1917 AAU meet and second in 1920, he had to wait till 1925 to annex his one and only crown at the Nationals – in the furlong.

By 1920 the map of athletics had extended to other areas of the world. Strangely enough, the first continent to have championships of its own was South America, which had been lagging behind rather considerably in the sport. The inaugural meet was held at Montevideo, Uruguay in 1919. Sprint times on that occasion were all but sensational. Henry Bowles of Uruguay won the 100 metres in 11 $^4/_5$ and Isabelino Gradin, also of Uruguay, took the 200 in 23 $^1/_5$. The second edition, held the following year at Santiago de Chile, produced much better results: Marcelo Uranga of Chile won the 100 in 10 $^4/_5$ and Gradin took the 200 again in 22 $^2/_5$. The last two marks are usually listed as the first official South American records.

In other continents the best up to 1920 had invariably occurred in English speaking countries like South Africa, Canada and Australia. The deeds of Olympic champions Reggie Walker and Robert Kerr have been recounted already. In Australasia the fastest 100 yards times dated from long ago: 9 $^4/_5$ by W.T.Macpherson (1891) of Australia and Jack Hempton (1892) of New Zealand. Best in the 220 was Nigel Barker of Australia, 21 $^4/_5$ in 1905. In the greater part of Africa and Asia the sport was still in the dormant stage.

As related above, British and German sprinters had been the cream of Europe, along with Sweden's aces Lindberg (10.6 for 100 metres in 1906) and Engdahl (21.9 for 200 metres in 1920). In addition there were several other countries which could claim a national record of 10 $^4/_5$ for the metric century, such as Belgium (P.Brochart, 1919), Austria (F.Weinzinger, 1906), Hungary (I. Jankovich, 1914), Holland (J.Grijseels, 1915) and Finland (U. Railo, 1907). Officially at least, no one in either France or Italy was in that class, but it should be noted that particularly in France there had been sub-11 marks by the acre which for one reason or another did not hold water in the eyes of federation officials.

PEGS AND ROPES

The main problem confronting the constructors of tracks in the early days, apart from the ground structure and the shape of curves, was that of providing for the homestretch of flat and hurdle races a set of pegs and ropes likely to define corridors, later called lanes. By such a provision all runners were obliged to keep a definite course of motion without making inroads on other runners' territory.

The term "lane" defined a well-confined space apt to facilitate motion, without impediments of sort, and far from the precarious vagaries of road courses along avenues lined with trees or grass tracks on which even sprint races once used to be contested.

The legendary "stadion" race, the first competition included in the inaugural edition of the ancient Olympics in 776 b.C., was run on an inadequately dug track, rectangular in shape (roughly 215 m x 32 m.), located on the hills of mount Cronion, where Olympia once stood, in the Elis area. As far as we know there were no marks to avoid interferences among runners.

At a much later date, images regarding the inauguration in April 1877 of the Stamford Bridge track in London, one of the theatres of early deeds in the history of modern athletics, show an aptly levelled stretch but still with no marks on the ground likely to assure a controlled and protected running direction.

However, the first general book on amateur athletics, H.M.Wilkinson's "Modern Athletics" (1868) states: "For sprint races the course to be kept by each competitor shall be divided by pegs and ropes about two feet (0.60 m.) above the ground and at least four feet (1.21 m.) apart". Later referred to as stakes and strings, these were widely used in Britain and even in USA. One of those who contributed to such an innovation at the international level was an Englishman, Charles Perry, who laid down the project for the track at the Panathinaikon stadium in Athens, theatre of the inaugural Olympics of the modern era (1896). On that occasion the lanes for the 100-metre race were designed through strings stretched among six rows of stakes. No such provision was made for the 110 metre hurdles as it was then felt that the very necessity of clearing hurdles facing the running direction would prevent anyone from interfering with others. Cords and pickets were used also in the Olympics of 1900 (Paris), 1904 (St.Louis), 1908 (London) as well as in the Interim Games of 1906 (Athens). Such a system was abolished at Stockholm in 1912. The afore-mentioned Charles Perry, designer of the Olympiastadion track, had the boundaries of each of the six lanes marked in white plaster. In harmony with the innovating spirit that characterized that edition of the Games, the use of stakes and strings was thus abandoned. Notwithstanding such positive results, however, conservatives thought it advisable to go back to the old method, which was therefore in use at the 1920 (Antwerp) and 1924 Olympics (Paris), only to be discontinued for good from 1928 onwards.

G. P.

1920 Olympics, Antwerp. 4x100 m. final, last change. Loren Murchison (USA), extreme left, hands over to Morris Kirksey, who will go home first in 42.2, a new world record. France (lane 3) will take 2nd, and Sweden (lane 5) 3rd.

3

THE INCOMPARABLE J.C.OWENS

As a "merchant of speed" Charles Paddock had his greatest year in 1921. Curiously enough, all of his 18 races that year were in sunny California. By then he was attending the University of Southern California in Los Angeles, whose athletes were known in sport jargon as "Trojans". His first rendezvous with records was on 26 March in Berkeley, during the dual meet between USC and the University of California. First he ran the 100 yards in 9 $^{3}/_{5}$, thus equalling the world record jointly held by his predecessors Kelly and Drew. Then he sped the 220 on a straight course in 20 $^{4}/_{5}$ – the first sub-21 mark in the history of the furlong. According to a newspaper report, "No sooner had the gun gone up for the start than the wind sprang up, blowing decidedly in the face of the runners". Under such circumstances nobody gave Paddock a chance to break the record, yet this is what he did, partly with the benefit of some competition offered by Robert Hutchison, who finished only 1 $^{1}/_{2}$ y. behind and was timed in 21 $^{1}/_{5}$. (Timing to one fifth of a second probably explains the difference). Only 3 days later Paddock did 9.6 again, this time at Palo Alto. He was pitted against Morris Kirksey of Stanford, who ultimately lost by only 1 foot. Throughout his career Kirksey was Paddock's nemesis in countless instances but never managed to beat the "jumper".

Paddock then decided to go metric and on 23 April at Redlands he did 10 $^{2}/_{5}$ for the century and 33 $^{1}/_{5}$ for the seldom run 300 metres – two more world records. The timers' crew was very efficient and in the longer race they caught Paddock in 21 $^{1}/_{5}$ at 200 metres and 21 $^{2}/_{5}$ at 220 yards. What was perhaps the greatest feat of the series came at Pasadena on 18 June, when Paddock was caught in 10 $^{1}/_{5}$ for 110 yards (100.58 m.) This has been dubbed as doubtful by some historians, due to the fact that Paddock was credited with 9 $^{3}/_{5}$ for 100 yards while enroute. A time differential of only $^{3}/_{5}$ths of a second for a distance of 9.14 m. may appear superhuman, but here again the timing, "confined" to one fifth of a second, can explain things to a large extent. Be that as it may, the AAU did not have the 110 yards in their record list and so Paddock's 10 $^{1}/_{5}$ was confined to the column of "noteworthy performances".

In the AAU Championships, held at Pasadena, CA, on 4 July, Paddock climaxed his perfect season with a fine double, with times of 9.6 and 21.8 for the English distances. He suffered his only defeat of the year in a heat of the furlong. His overall record that year was undoubtedly the most impressive ever seen in the domain of sprinting. He could point to five 9 $^{3}/_{5}$ clockings in the 100 yards, three of which made AAU and IAAF books.

Allen Woodring, who had upset Paddock in the Olympic 200 metres the year before, only competed in Eastern meets during 1921. He got credit for a record tying 9 $^{3}/_{5}$ in the 100 yards during a triangular college meet at Syracuse on 7 May. This was virtually a solo run as the runner-up finished 6 yards behind. There were four watches on Woodring, two of which showed 9 $^{2}/_{5}$ and two 9 $^{3}/_{5}$. The slower time was accepted as official.

The New York Athletic Club accounted for a new world record of 42 $^{2}/_{5}$ for the 4x110 yards relay in the AAU Championships at Pasadena. The man in the lead-off leg was Bernard Wefers Jr., a son of the great runner who had outshone every one else in the domain of sprinting in the last decade of the 19th century.

1921 did not offer much in terms of international competition. The AAA Championships in London was an all-British affair, with Harry Edward, the double bronze medallist of the Antwerp Olympics, winning the 100 yards (10 1/5) and the 220 (22 1/5). Runner-up in both races was Harold Abrahams, a law student from Cambridge who was to make history three years later.

THE "DISCOVERY" OF ALTITUDE

Retrospectively, the most intriguing mark of 1922 must be credited to Cyril Coaffee of Canada – a record-equalling 9 3/5 for the 100 yards, made at Calgary on 12 August. I do say "retrospectively" for one very simple reason: Calgary is located 1048 metres above sea level and this was the first occasion on which a world record had been set at high altitude (save for Jack Donaldson's 9 3/8 over the same distance in a "pro" race at Johannesburg in 1910). It would not be until the 1955 Pan American Games at Mexico City that track observers really began to understand that the rarefied atmosphere of a mountain venue could be advantageous to athletes engaged in a short-lived effort, i.e. in an event lying in the so-called anaerobic sphere. At the time it was made, Coaffee's record was tentatively attributed to doubtful timing and/or wind assistance. In the early twenties no one apparently recognized that the altitude could be a factor – let alone an advantageous one.

My friend Bob Phillips, editor of "Track Stats", the precious quarterly publication of the National Union of Track Statisticians (NUTS), was in Canada in 2004 and thought it advisable to make a pilgrimage to Calgary in an effort to throw further light on that performance. Local papers related that it was a miserably cold day and that a light wind was blowing from the West. Six men got off the marks to a perfect start and for the first 15 yards ran in a bunch. In the second half of the race Coaffee leaped forward and finished in whirlwind style. There are conflicting reports as to his winning margin. The ATFS credits the runner-up, 30-year-old Laurie Armstrong, with an estimated 9.9. Later in the same day, Coaffee won the 220 yards in 21 4/5. From the very beginning Coaffee had made a strong visual impression, as he was handicapped by a disabled arm and ran with a leaning style, with his legs "spitting out behind", according to a local observer. After his record performance he became a member of the Illinois Athletic Club and competed in a lot of US meets. Best he could do was placing fourth in the 100 yards and third in the 220 at the 1924 AAU Championships, well behind the winner, Charles Paddock, who equalled his own world records with 9 3/5 and 20 4/5.

In his two Olympic experiences, Antwerp '20 and Paris '24, Coaffee never went beyond the sprint semi-finals. Even so, between 1921 and 1928 he amassed a strong array of 9 4/5 performances for the 100 yards, which would amply justify his peak day of 1922. Especially if the altitude factor is taken into consideration.

Paddock continued to add to his collection of fast times for several more years. He was probably the first American world class athlete who discovered the pleasure of competing in various parts of the world. In 1922 he produced yet another 9 3/5 for the century at Honolulu. The following year he was again in Paris and ran 100 metres in 10 2/5. Both marks equalled the respective world records but were never ratified, thereby joining the destiny of that large number of marks which for one reason or another never made the official books. For several years Paddock's fiercest rivals were Loren Murchison and Jackson Scholz, both medium size and very consistent. Among the three of them they won no less than 10 AAU sprint titles at the standard distances: Paddock 5. Murchison 4 and Scholz 1. But the last one, as related above, had the longest life span at the international level.

By the same time Germany's shares as a sprint power continued to rise. Rau's rightful successor was Hubert Houben (born at Goch on 24 February 1898; died at Krefeld on 9 November 1956; 1.69 m./ 67 kg.). He reached international class in 1922 with times of 10.5 and 21.9 for the metric distances. By 1924 he was one of the fastest men in the world. Early in the season he ran the 100 metres in 10.5 on no less than 4 occasions in home meets. Then he hit the headlines in an international meet at Copenhagen: on 22 June he did 11.0 (heat) and 10.5 (final) in the 100 metres, and on the 24th he chalked up a surprising 9.5 in the 100 yards and closed his day's work with 22.8 (heat) and 21.7 (final) in 200 metres. Of course it was his 9.5 that made the news: it was made in a handicap race and no less than 8 watches registered that time, one tenth below the official world record – at a time when most if not all sprint races were obviously timed to the nearest fifth of a second. Much to Houben's disgrace, however, Germany had not been invited to the Paris Olympics and thus lost the Games for the second time in a row (her Allies in WW1 had since been "reinstated").

The US Olympic Tryouts were held at Cambridge, MA, on 13 and 14 June. On this occasion there was a more flexible approach: a certain number of leading athletes did not make the top-4 but were nonetheless selected for the Games because of their consistency in previous competition. Among those who benefited were sprinters Alfred LeConey and Loren Murchison, 5th and 7th respectively in the 100 metres at the Tryouts. Chester Bowman won the race in 10.6, barely ahead of Paddock and Scholz. This last confirmed his brilliant form winning the 200 comfortably in 21.0. Here Paddock had to slow down because of an injury and finished no better than sixth. Here it was his turn to benefit from the above-mentioned proviso and he was selected just the same.

Great Britain rose to the occasion at the right time with a strong duo – Harold Abrahams and Eric Liddell. The former (born in Bedford on 15 December 1899; died at Enfield on 14 January 1978; 1.83 m. / 75 kg.) lost little or no time in showing promise and in 1919 he beat Willie Applegarth, his boyhood hero, in a handicap race over 100 yards: given a start of 2 yards, Abrahams won by six in 10.0. In 1920 he recorded "evens" at the English distance, then went to the Antwerp Olympics. After winning his 100 metres heat in 11.0 he was eliminated in the second round. As a law student at Cambridge he reached national prominence in 1921 by placing second to Harry Edward in both sprints at the AAA Championships. He was also an excellent long jumper and in 1923 he actually won his first AAA title in that event with 7.23 – a mark which earned him a tie for 6th in the World List of that year. He was by then under the tutelage of Sam Mussabini, who had previously coached Applegarth and Edward. Normally he used to train two or three times a week, which was just about average in those days. He worked most diligently on technical details, particularly to improve his arm action. In 1924 he had an excellent pre-Olympic season: on 7 June at Woolwich he ran 100 yards in a nifty 9.6 and won the long jump with 7.38.

Harold Abrahams (GB) no.419, winning the 100 metres at the 1924 Olympics in Paris. Time, 10.6. Others from left to right are: A. Porritt (N.Z.), 3rd; C. Bowman (USA), 4th; L. Murchison (USA) 6th; J. Scholz (USA) 2nd; C. Paddock (USA) 5th.

CHARLES PADDOCK AND A BIT OF "DOLCE VITA"

Charles Paddock went to Paris for the 1924 Olympics as the "World's Fastest Human" and a clear favourite for the sprint titles. In the 100 metres he could point to a world record (10.4 in 1921) and an Olympic victory (1920), not forgetting his world mark for the 100 yards (9.6), a time he achieved on several occasions. His credentials for the 200 metres were also great, clock-wise at least, plus his second place in the 1920 Olympics.

Yet the great California comet went down to unsuspected defeats in Paris: barely fifth in the 100 metres, won by Harold Abrahams of Britain; and second in the 200 behind his countryman Jackson Scholz; finally, an injury kept him away from the sprint relay. Coaches and reporters found it hard to explain such reversals as the man had been until then the dominant figure of the early Twenties.

Somebody thought that a plausible explanation could be found on the strength of recent gossips. Charles Paddock was a longtime friend of Douglas Fairbanks Jr., an outstanding Hollywood star in successful films. The American actor had made the trans-Atlantic trip on the steam ship "America" with the US Olympic team and during the Games he was in Paris with his second wife, actress Mary Pickford (Gladys Smith) to promote his latest film, "The Thief of Bagdad". In 1919 Mary Pickford had been one of the founders of the United Artists production company, along with David W. Griffith and Charlie Chaplin. Mary made the trip to Paris with her husband to contact Maurice Chevalier, the famed French "chansonnier", and possibly engage him for a forthcoming musical, meant to be an early example of sound films. Fairbanks once witnessed a Paddock training session at Colombes. By then in rather low spirits after his far from flamboyant races in the early rounds of the 100 metres, Paddock reportedly told his friend: "Doug, I'm too old". Then he told Fairbanks about a bet he had with the Prince of Wales, – invite the whole British team to dinner if Harold Abrahams beat him in the Olympic final. To which Fairbanks reacted thus: "You need relaxation. Why don't you come down to Paris with me and enjoy yourself? Stay away from track for a while and tomorrow you'll be your real self again". The four of them – Douglas, Mary, Maurice and Charles – had dinner at the exclusive Carillon restaurant, with plenty of champagne. Then they made the small hours at "la Revue Nègre", a club featuring a famous black singer/dancer hailing from St.Louis, Josephine Baker, who then worked with the Claude Hopkins Band, a highly successful jazz band that had in its ranks a famous clarinettist, Sidney Bechet.

In the early hours of the following day Paddock returned to Colombes, where he shared an apartment with his friend and rival Loren Murchison, while the US team was housed in the Rocquencourt castle, once the residence of prince Murat.

The following day Paddock was soundly beaten by Harold Abrahams in a semi-final of the 100 metres. Maybe he then began to have second thoughts about the bet he had made with the Prince of Wales!

G.P.

The latter was ratified as an English record, but the sprint mark was discounted on account of an aiding wind. He went on to win both events at the AAA Championships, the 100 with 9.9. His fiercest rival in Britain was Eric Liddell (born in Tientsin, China, on 16 January 1902; died in a Japanese Internment camp at Weihsien on 21 February 1945; 1.75 m. / 70 kg.) whose range as a sprinter went from 100 to 440 yards. The son of a missionary, he set foot on British soil at the age of 5. As a boarder at Eltham College he did very well both as a student and as a budding athletic genius. Yet it was only in 1921, while attending Edinburgh University as a pure science student, that he began to make a strong impact as an athlete, winning his first Scottish titles in the sprints. In 1922 he set Scottish records of 10.0 and 21.8 (straight course). His real breakthrough at the international level was in 1923, when he won British titles with 9.7 and 21.6, the former a new national record which was to stand for 35 years! In view of the 1924 Olympics he was forced to make a choice in accordance with his strong Sabbatarian views as an evangelical Christian: when he learnt that the first round of the 100 metres would be on a Sunday, he decided to bypass that event to concentrate on 200 and 400 metres. At the AAA Championships he confined himself to the quarter, which he won easily in 49.6 from David Johnson of Canada and Bill Stevenson of USA, who had won the event at the 1921 AAU Championships in 48.6.

The 1924 Olympics were actually held at Colombes, a suburb north-west of Paris. The installation, built by Racing Club de France shortly before WW1, had a 500-metre cinder track which proved pretty fast. The 100 metres came first and Harold Abrahams soon displayed his excellent condition. He had the fastest time, 10.6, both in the 2nd and the 3rd round, equalling the Olympic record. In the decisive race he was pitted against four Americans – Paddock, Scholz, Bowman, Murchison - and Arthur Porritt of New Zealand. The starter, Dr. E.Moir of Britain, dispatched the finalists to a magnificent start on the first attempt. At 25 metres they were all together, but at the half-way mark Abrahams was clear of Scholz and Bowman. The Englishman held his lead and won from Scholz by about 60 centimetres. Porritt finished with an astounding burst to nip Bowman for third, while Paddock and Murchison closed up the rear in that order. Abrahams' time once again was 10.6 – or 10.52 to be exact. He had reached his peak at the right time, to an extent very seldom registered in such cases. He thus became the first European to win the blue riband event of the Games. Abrahams paid tribute to his trainer Sam Mussabini. "Under his guidance I improved that decisive one per cent, which made all the difference between supreme success and obscurity" he said. In the 200 metres the Englishman clocked 22.0 in a quarter-final for a personal best but in the decisive race he looked rather weary and trailed home last. The Americans were obviously seeking a revenge and finally got it. Their toughest opponent here was Eric Liddell, yet he had to be content with third. After a gigantic battle Jackson Scholz won from Paddock by about half a metre in 21.6, equalling the Olympic record.

In the 4x100 metres relay the world record (42 1/5 for USA at the Antwerp Olympics) was beaten time and again: 42.0 by Britain and Holland, then 41.2 by USA in the heats; 41.0 in the semi-finals, and finally equalled by USA in the final with 41 flat, the line-up being Frank Hussey, Louis Clarke, Loren Murchison and Alfred LeConey. Yet Britain, with Abrahams in the lead-off leg, was a strong contender and finally lost by no more than 1 1/2 metres.

1924 Olympics, Paris (Colombes) - 100 metres (7 July): 1.Harold Abrahams (UK) 10.6, 2.Jackson Scholz (USA) 10.8. 3.Arthur Porritt (NZ) 10.9, 4.Chester Bowman (USA) 10.9, 5.Charles Paddock (USA) 10.9, 6.Loren Murchison (USA) 11.0. Lanes: Paddock 1, Scholz 2, Murchison 3, Abrahams 4, Bowman 5, Porritt 6.

200 metres (9 July): 1.Jackson Scholz (USA) 21.6, 2.Charles Paddock (USA) 21.7, 3.Eric Liddell (UK) 21.9, 4.George Hill (USA) 22.0, 5.Bayes Norton (USA) 22.0, 6.Harold Abrahams (UK) 22.3. Lanes: Norton 1, Abrahams 2, Hill 3, Scholz 4, Liddell 5, Paddock 6.

4x100 metres relay (13 July): 1.USA (F.Hussey, L.Clarke, L.Murchison, A.LeConey) 41.0; 2.UK (H.Abrahams, W.Rangeley, L.Royle, W.Nichol) 41.2, 3.Hol (J.Boot, H.Broos, J.de Vries, M.van den Berge) 41.8, 4.Hun 42.0, 5.France 42.2; Swz (42.0) disqualified. Lanes: USA 1, Hun 2, Swz 3, UK 4, Hol 5, Fra 6.

1928 Olympics, Amsterdam. 200 m. final. Percy Williams (Canada) completes his sprint double, winning in 21.8 from Walter Rangeley (UK), lane 3 and Helmut Körnig (Germany), lane 4.

UNKNOWN FOOLS SPRINT STARS

by Otto Verhoeven

Hubert Houben savoured the first success of his career, on a modest scale that's true, in an inter-service meet at Warsaw in 1917. On his return from WWI most of his thoughts were obviously centered on shaping up as a tradesman. However, in 1920 he witnessed a national meet in Krefeld and when it was over he challenged the sprint stars to a "match race", boasting that he could vie with them in pure blazing speed. After an impressive getaway he fooled them all and thereby secured himself a place on the national scene.
In his first appearance at the national championships Houben reached the semi-finals. But in 1921 he managed to win both sprints at the title meet in Hamburg, a double he repeated in 1922 and 1923. Such a triple is so far unequalled in the history of Germany's national championships. In 1924 he stayed away from the 200 metres but won the 100 quite comfortably. He went on with an impressive number of victories and repeatedly ran the distance in 10.5, best-on-record time by a European. He seemed to be up there with the best in the world too but, as explained elsewhere in the text, Germany was barred from the 1924 Olympics. In Colombes the 100 metres went to Harold Abrahams of Great Britain, who upset the favourite Americans.
On 6 August 1924, however, a "meet of sprint giants" was staged in Berlin. This marked the first appearance of American athletes in Germany since the end of World War I. Houben traded wins with Charles Paddock and Loren Murchison, beating them in the 100 metres (10.8) and losing to them in the 200, won by Paddock in 21.4. By then the two Yanks had formed between them a sort of "Sprint Co. Inc." and travelled around the world. After that post-Olympic event, the talk in Germany was all about "unser Houben" (our Houben). He quickly became a symbol of Germany's resurgence to high class athletics.
After seeing his Olympic dream shattered in 1924, Houben managed to secure a place on the national team for the Amsterdam Olympics four years later. Before the Games the Germans set a new world record of 40.8 for the 4x100 metre relay. But in Holland Houben and Helmut Körnig failed to connect properly in the last exchange and Germany had to be content with second behind USA (41.2 to 41.0).

NB: Otto Verhoeven is a member in good standing of the "Association of Track and Field Statisticians" and one of the leading wheels of the DGLD (Deutsche Gesellschaft für Leichtathletik-Dokumentation). He is one of the acutest students of German t&f history.

Abrahams could have added to his record as a sprinter and long jumper if he had not been stopped by a serious leg injury while jumping in May 1925. He thus decided to leave the arena. Always a wise man, he later supplied the following reflection: "I wonder if, in a sense, that was not another piece of good-bad luck. How many people find it almost impossible to retire at the right time."

The New Zealander who won bronze in the Olympic century, Arthur Porritt, was a 23-year-old medical student from Wanganui. He had caught the eye of keen observers the year before, in what historian Peter Heidenstrom defines as "the most famous race ever run in New Zealand – the 100 yards championship at Athletic Park, Wellington". Running in a star-studded field, he finished a fairly close third behind Morris Kirksey of USA (9 4/5) and Edwin "Slip" Carr of Australia. In 1924 Porritt came to Europe and as an Achilles club man he placed third in the furlong at the English AAA championship, before going to the Olympics. The following year he ran the 100 yards in 9.8 twice. He too could have added to his excellent record – except that he was one of those young men, fairly frequent in those days, for whom sport was still only fun. He thus chose to concentrate on his surgical studies. He eventually reached the top of that profession and in sport hierarchy as well, when he was elected to the International Olympic Committee. He later became New Zealand's first native-born Governor General.

A MAN OF MANY PARTS

Very few people, if any, are likely to have contributed to the world of track and field in so many ways as did Harold Abrahams. As an athlete, he was Europe's first sprinter to win an Olympic 100 metres title. Later on, as a member of the Fourth Estate, he was for many years one of Britain's best known athletics writers and radio commentators, as well as author of several books on the sport. As a track legislator, he was for a long time a leading wheel in the IAAF Technical Committee and his lucid reasoning, partly the result of his training as a lawyer, was often reflected in the rule book. As an administrator he played an important role in the English AAA for years, finally becoming its President in 1976. As a timekeeper he was absolutely tops. Last but not least, in the years between the two World Wars he was one of those rare track writers who showed a penchant for the statistical facet of the game.

I first got in touch with him in 1948, when he used the inaugural "Olympic Handbook", edited by Don Potts and myself, for the seeding of Olympic events at Wembley. When eleven of us statistical "nuts" founded the ATFS at Brussels in 1950, Norris McWhirter (a would-be co-author of the famous "Guinness Book of Records") and I thought of him as Honorary President of the newly formed body. Over the years he always showed a keen interest in the affairs of the ATFS, attending most, if not all, our Conventions. I was lucky enough to meet Harold many times in various corners of the globe. Apart from his unquenchable love for athletics, he was a man of many talents. He could talk perceptively on such sundry subjects as Roman monuments and the world of lyrics. He did not live long enough to see the beautiful film "Chariots of Fire", which featured him and Eric Liddell in their glorious days at the 1924 Olympics. I wish I knew how he would have reacted to such a romanticized tribute.

Eddie Tolan (USA), nearest camera, winning the 100 metres by a hair's breadth from Ralph Metcalfe (USA) at the 1932 Olympics in Los Angeles. Both were given the same time, 10.3. Others from left to right are: T. Yoshioka (Japan), 6th; D. Joubert (S.A.) 5th; G. Simpson (USA) 4th; A. Jonath (Germany) 3rd.

The man who had to stay away from the Olympics, Hubert Houben of Germany, got a chance to lock horns with several illustrious Olympians in the latter part of the season. In an international meet at Berlin on 6 August, he had mixed fortunes with the Americans: he won the 100 metres in 10.8 from Murchison and Paddock, then had to be content with third in the 200, behind Paddock (21.4) and Murchison. Later in the same month, still in Berlin, he beat Edwin Carr of Australia and Arthur Porritt of New Zealand in the 100 with a wind-aided 10.6. If present in the Paris Olympics, Houben could have vied for one or more medals.

Back home, the Americans appeared to be still full of running. At Allentown, PA, Alfred LeConey beat Paddock in a wind-aided 100 yards, their times being 9.4 and 9.5 respectively. The AAU Championships were at West Orange, NJ, on 6 Sep and Paddock won the 100 yards in 9.6, thus equalling the world record. Loren Murchison was second (9.7e), LeConey third and Cyril Coaffee of Canada fourth. In that meet Paddock equalled yet another world record, winning the 220 (straight course) in 20.8. Here he outclassed Murchison (21.4e) and Coaffee.

A P.S. to the Olympic tale seems in order: two days after finishing third in the 200 metres, Eric Liddell won the 400 in 47.6. This time was officially ratified as a world record, apparently in disregard of a faster time credited to "Ted" Meredith of USA over a .... longer distance (440 yards) in 1916. The IAAF erased Liddell's marks from its books in 1926. Apart from this, Liddell was unquestionably the greatest all-around sprinter (100-to-400 m.) of the early Twenties. As such he crowned his competitive days in Europe with a triple (10.0w in the 100 yards, 22.2 in he 220 and 49.2 in the 440) at the 1925 Scottish Championships. Then he went back to China as a missionary. Over there he ran a few races now and then, but his main energies were obviously devoted to his missionary work. Many years after his death (1945), one of the chief characters in the award-winning film "Chariots of Fire" was named after him. To this end the script-writer of the film was assisted by John Keddie, the inspired historian of Scottish athletics. In Keddie's own words, "Liddell made a great impact on his generation, not merely on account of his athletic triumphs but principally because of his stand for righteous principles".

The man who first managed to break Paddock's monopoly in the record department was a slim Nebraskan, Roland Locke. Usually at his best in the furlong, he had his peak year in 1926, at the age of 23, when he did 20.5, then 20.7 twice in the 220 yards, always at Lincoln, NE. In his fastest race, on 1 May (his time was of course ratified as 20.6) he ran the first 96 yards (87.78 m.) around a turn and the remaining 124 y. (113.38 m.) on the straight – which mathematician Don Potts computed as "a quarter turn". Locke went through that season without a loss but he did not compete in the AAU Championships. In other years he produced good times now and then, yet he never finished higher than 3rd in the 100 and 2nd in the 220 in AAU meets, both in 1927.

Paddock offered his last flash as a record-breaker with yet another 9.6 in the century at the Memorial Coliseum in Los Angeles on 15 May 1926. That was probably his fastest ever though, as three watches showed 9.5 and a fourth 9.6. As usual, the official time had to be ratified in fifths-of-a-second. He won by the proverbial whisker from Charles Borah, who is rightfully credited by statisticians with 9.5. Maxwell Stiles, a famous West Coast chronicler, wrote in the "Los Angeles Examiner": "There was the wildest confusion as Borah leading by more than 2 feet (60.96 cm.) with two yards to go, was caught by Paddock's savage finish (his famous leap). They broke the tape together and Borah (a student at Southern California) was raised on the shoulders of a Trojan serpentine and carried off the field as the conqueror of the mighty Paddock. So certain was the writer that Borah had won by inches that he went straight to Paddock and began to offer sympathy for the latter's defeat.

Paddock, thinking he had won, glared back in surprise. When the official announcer named Paddock as the winner a mighty roar of protest swept the vast enclosure with cries of "robber! robber!" Don Potts had two pictures of the finish and in his opinion there was no doubt that Paddock won. Borah, not yet 20 at that time, eventually won the AAU title (9.8) later in the season – in the absence of Paddock. For the rest of his career Borah, (1.77 m. / 68 kg.) had his share of glory in national meets, with two victories in the 220 at the AAU Championships (1927 and '28), but failed to make an adequate impact in international competition.

England's time-honoured AAA Championships were throughout the Twenties and Thirties the most "international" meet in the world, next to the Olympics of course. In the 1925 edition Loren Murchison of USA won both sprints (9.9 and 21.6). Runner-up in the shorter distance was André Théard of Haiti, one of the earliest sprinters to come out of Central America, which was to develop into one of the world's greatest speed reservoirs. In the years that followed Germany's rising power was well in evidence in the AAA Championships, with victories by Richard Corts in 1926 (10.0 in the 100 y.), Helmut Körnig (10.1) and Hubert Houben (21.8 in the 220 y.) in 1927 and Friedrich Wichmann in 1928 (21.7).

Helmut Körnig (born on 12 September 1905 at Glogau; 1.76 m. / 66 kg.) rose to national class in 1925 and hit the international headlines the following year with a scintillating 10.3 for the 100 metres during the German Championships in Leipzig on 8 August. He was hard pressed as Kurt Dreibholz and Werner Wege finished next in that order, both in 10.4. Hubert Houben was fourth in 10.5. The winner's time was accepted as a German record as 10 2/5, as per rule then in force. However, when the mark was submitted to the IAAF for approval as a world record, it was finally rejected on a double account: 7 cms. sloping ground, aiding wind 3-to-4 m/s. In the same year Körnig also did 10.4 on two occasions. His best in the 200 metres was 21.5, in the above-mentioned German title meet. Yet the longer distance was to become his forte in the Olympic year 1928.

BARRIENTOS, "EL PRIMERO RELÁMPAGO CARIBE"

The Central American and Caribbean area has long been described by sport writers as "tierra de relámpagos" (land of lightnings). Throughout the last sixty years of the 20th century Jamaica, Cuba, Trinidad and other islands from that area have produced sprinters and quarter-milers galore. Chronologically, the first dashman to be given such a label was José Eduardo ("Pepe") Barrientos of Cuba (1905-1945). In home meets he was credited with a long array of fast times, especially in the metric century, but for one reason or another he failed to do himself justice in international meets.

While still a junior at the University of La Habana he exhibited good talent in the dashes and the long jump. 1926 was the year of his breakthrough. He became Cuba's first sub-11 secs. man in the 100 metres with a time of 10 $^4/_5$. Later in the same year he was to make his international debut at the inaugural Central American Games at Mexico City but at the very last moment he had to undergo an operation for appendicitis and that put paid to his chances. In 1927 he did 10 $^2/_5$ for a new Cuban record. On 8 May of that year, still at La Habana, he improved to 10 $^1/_5$, but this mark never made the Cuban record list, let alone that of the IAAF. The historical lists of the ATFS carry it as wind assisted. Curiously enough, on that very day Barrientos also ran the 200 metres in 21 $^3/_5$ and this was ratified as a Cuban record. In 1928 the Cuban ace produced another 10 $^1/_5$ which befell exactly the same destiny as the former one, and later another 10 $^2/_5$ which was apparently OK. His next venture was at the Amsterdam Olympics, where he failed to respond to the classic "Hic Rhodos, hic salta": after winning his heat in 11.0, he was eliminated in the quarter-finals. Cuban sport writer Enrique Montesinos attributes such failures to the fact that « Pepe » was one of those athletes who loved to spread themselves thin in too many sports. He also loved baseball, rugby football and rowing, and in this last he had a remarkable success. He eventually became an aviator and found his death in an air crash. He was immortalized after WW2 when the Cuban Athletics Federation decided to name their foremost track meet after him.

A rare example of sprinter/long jumper of the highest class was William DeHart Hubbard, a US Negro from Michigan University. At the 1925 NCAA Championships he scored a rare double, with 9 4/5 in the century and 7.89 m. in the horizontal jump, the latter being a new world record. The following year he tied the world mark for the 100 yards, 9 3/5 at Cincinnati on 5 June. A man of medium build endowed with a great stamina, Hubbard was unquestionably the outstanding long jumper of the pre-Owens era. In this event he conquered Olympic gold in 1924 and won the AAU title for six years in a row (1922 through 1927).

Shortly before the Amsterdam Olympics (1928), a new star sprinter emerged – Frank Wykoff (born at Des Moines, IA, on 29 October 1909; 1.75 m. / 66 kg.). He made the headlines as a schoolboy in the spring of that year, when he beat the declining Paddock and other good sprinters with eye-catching metric times – 10 3/5 and 20 4/5. At the US Olympic Tryouts, held at Cambridge, MA, early in July, he scored a sweeping victory in the 100 metres, equalling his personal best, 10 3/5. Paddock was better in the 200, although he lost to 22-year-old Charles Borah (21 2/5), then his team-mate in the Los Angeles AC. Although the Olympic race had been run over a course starting on a curve since 1908, the US Tryout race continued to be on a straight course.

Germany was back in the Olympics after missing two editions. Prior to the Games its national relay team showed excellent form, notably with three 40.8 clockings in the 4x100 m. event, 0.2 secs. under the official world record set by a US national team at the 1924 Olympics. For some reason unknown to this writer, none of these marks was ratified by the IAAF, which however approved a record-equalling 41.0 credited to a club team, Eintracht Frankfurt, at Halle on 10 June. Individually the best German prospect appeared to be Helmut Körnig, but Richard Corts, Ernst Geerling and Friedrich Wichmann also looked promising. Veteran Houben seemed to be over the hill though.

Britain seemed to have a mighty weapon in Jack London, who like Harry Edward hailed from British Guyana. According to British historians, London broke all the rules of good sprinting technique. Some of his deficiencies disappeared when he began to be counselled by Albert Hill, the man who had scored a great 800/1500 metre double at the 1920 Olympics.

But on the days that mattered most all the above-mentioned sprinters had to bow to a Canadian marvel – Percy Williams (born in Vancouver on 19 May 1908; died in Vancouver on 29 November 1982: 1.78 m. / 58 kg.). He emerged pratically from nowhere to run the metric 100 in 10 3/5 at the Canadian Trials. Even so, European papers identified him as an outsider - at best. The Amsterdam track was 400 metres in length, which would henceforth be the standard size for the Games. Yet the surface was not particularly fast. Williams first caught the eye of keen observers in the second round of the 100 metres, when he equalled the Olympic record, 10 3/5. The same clocking was credited to several others in the penultimate round. In the final there were two false starts, first by Wilfred Legg of South Africa, then by America's boy wonder Wykoff. The third time the runners were away together. Williams soon took the lead. He stayed in front all the way and won by about 60 cms. from the powerful London, who nosed out Körnig by about 30 cms. Wykoff, not yet 19 at the time, had to be content with fourth. The winner's time was no better than 10 4/5. Even after that, few observers if any gave Williams a real chance for the 200 metres. To the best of our knowledge, he had never beaten 22 secs. before the Games. He did so in the second round at Amsterdam with 21 4/5, but losing to Körnig, who equalled the Olympic record with 21 3/5. Among the victims of the qualifying rounds was Paddock, by then 28. In the decisive race Körnig entered the straight in front, with Jackson Scholz close. With 50 metres to go Williams and Walter Rangeley of Britain went past the German champion. In the closing metres the young Canadian pulled away from the Briton to win by about 60 cms.The judges could not separate Körnig and Scholz and bracketed them for third place. Later they decided on a run-off but the American declined and third was given to Körnig. A photo of the finish clearly shows that Körnig deserved third anyway. The winner's time was 21 $^{4}/_{5}$. The "dead" track had apparently taken a lot out of the runners. For the first time in Olympic history America's sprinters thus failed to win medals in the individual sprint events. Some put the blame for their poor form on the long trans-Atlantic trip by sea ... Be that as it may, they did recover in time to win the 4x100 m. relay in 41.0, ahead of the crack German quartet (41.2). The two teams were practically even when the last leg got under way, but here Henry Russell gained about 1 $^{1}/_{2}$ metres on his German counterpart, Helmut Körnig. Britain was a well beaten third.

1928 Olympics, Amsterdam – 100 metres (30 July): 1.Percy Williams (Can) 10.8; 2.Jack London (UK) 10.9; 3.Georg Lammers (Ger) 10.9; 4.Frank Wykoff (USA) 11.0; 5.Wilfred Legg (SA) 11.0; 6.Robert McAllister (USA) 11.0. Lanes: Legg 1, Lammers 2, Williams 3, London 4, McAllister 5, Wykoff 6.

200 metres (1 August): 1.Percy Williams (Can) 21.8; 2.Walter Rangeley (UK) 21.9; 3.Helmut Körnig (Ger) 21.9; 4.Jackson Scholz (USA) 21.9; 5.John Fitzpatrick (Can) 22.1; 6.Jakob Schüller (Ger) 22.2. Lanes: Schüller 1, Williams 2, Rangeley 3, Körnig 4, Scholz 5, Fitzpatrick 6.

4x100 metres relay (5 August): 1.USA (F.Wykoff, J.Quinn, C.Borah, H. Russell (USA) 41.0; 2.Ger (G.Lammers, R.Corts, H.Houben, H.Körnig) 41.2; 3.UK (C.Gill, E.Smouha, W.Rangeley, J.London) 41.8; 4.Fra 42.0; 5.Swz 42.6. Can, disqualified. Lanes: USA 1, UK 2, Can 3, Ger 4, Swz 5, Fra 6.

"IT ACTUALLY MADE ME TIRED TO WATCH HIM"

Percy Williams' double victory at the 1928 Olympics still stands as one of the most unexpected feats in the history of the sprints. Better said, it was a major upset – but only in the eyes of European observers. In his own country, Canada, there were people who believed in him, one in particular being his coach Bob Granger.

"If ever there was an unlikely and unwilling hero in Canadian sports history, it was surely Percy Williams", wrote a Canadian historian. As a child he had a long bout of rheumatic fever, which apparently left him with a damaged heart – so doctors said. Even so, as an 18-year-old youngster he caught the eye of a coach, Bob Granger. On their first vis-à-vis, however, the latter had the impression that Percy "violated every known principle in the running game. He ran with his arms glued to his sides. It actually made me tired to watch him". Under Granger's guidance, Percy improved gradually on his training and running techniques. Yet some of Granger's methods may sound strange nowadays. For example, he believed in conserving the boy's energy in the vicinity of major tests. As the story goes, just before the final of the 200 metres at the Amsterdam Olympics, when all his rivals were engaged in warming-up exercises, Percy was lying in his dressing room buried under a pile of blankets. It is also known that on cold days, before a race the coach would rub his pupil's body with cocoanut butter and dress him in three track suits and sweaters to prevent loss of valuable body heat.

As related in the text, Williams hit the headlines again in 1930, clock-wise at least, but his career practically came to an end two years later. After a long spell in business, he fell seriously ill and late in 1982, aged 74, he committed suicide.

In the period between Amsterdam (1928) and Los Angeles (1932) the dominant figures of the sprints were Wykoff, George Simpson and Eddie Tolan in USA, Williams in Canada, Körnig and Lammers in Germany and Daniel Joubert in South Africa. One by one all of Paddock's world records were removed from the books, while standards went up in practically every corner of the globe.

1929 was long to remain one of the greatest non-Olympic years in history, with fast times galore, only a few of which happened to be ratified though. One who was able to shine on both sides of the Atlantic was an American, Thomas Edward "Eddie" Tolan (born at Denver on 29 September 1908; died at Detroit on 31 January 1967; 1.70 m. / 65 Kgs.), a relatively short but compact Negro who used to run with spectacles taped to his temples. He was the first to be officially credited with an official 9.5 in the 100 yards. This was in the Big Ten Championships at Evanston, Illinois, on 25 May 1929 with an aiding wind of 1.9 m/s. Tolan won by about a foot (30.48 cms.) from his arch rival, pale-faced George Simpson (born at Columbus, Ohio, on 21 September 1908; died at Columbus, Ohio on 2 December 1961; 1,80 m. / 75 kg.). In the same meet, the latter evened the count, beating Tolan in the 220 yards straightaway with a classy 20.6 which never made the book of records. Simpson, tall and slender, had a very long stride and a uniform running action, while Tolan, a natural talent refined in years of assiduous coaching, exhibited a fast leg work. Later in the same year Tolan came to Europe, where he twice equalled Paddock's world record for the 100 metres with two officially accepted 10.4's, (Stockholm, 8 August and Copenhagen, 25 August). His toughest rival in Germany was Georg Lammers, the Olympic bronze medallist, with whom he had mixed fortunes. Between the two of them they chalked up no less than twelve 10.4's during the season but for some reason only two, both by the American, received official IAAF sanction.

The year 1929 was especially memorable for the introduction of a new device in

1932 Olympics, Los Angeles. Eddie Tolan achieving a sprint double with his victory in the 200 metres, well ahead of George Simpson, Ralph Metcalfe and Arthur Jonath. (See text for story behind the story re: Metcalfe).

major competitions: starting-blocks. These turned out to be an obvious advantage if compared to man-made starting-holes. The invention was conceived by two keen students of athletics, George Bresnahan and William Tuttle in 1927. From experiments conducted on a large scale they came to the conclusion that the normal gain derived by a sprinter in a 100 y. race could be valued at an average of 34 thousandths of a second, i.e. about 30 cm. in actual running distance. Equally if not more important was the psychological advantage of having a firm foothold for a fast getaway. In the very same year 1929 this new device apparently paid dividends in the NCAA Championship 100 y. race at Chicago on 8 June when Simpson was clocked in 9.4 in a windless race, winning from Claude Bracey and Tolan, who had estimated times of 9.5 and 9.6 respectively. Of course, the new device had not been accepted yet by either the AAU or the IAAF. Simpson found partial consolation in .... 1944, when the AAU finally ratified his time as an American record.

Frank Wykoff gradually made amends for his poor show in the 1928 Olympics. He had his greatest year in 1930. On 10 May at Patterson Field in Los Angeles he became history's first official 9.4 man for the 100 y. – using normal starting-holes. A month later he duplicated his record time in the NCAA Championships at Chicago, clearly beating Simpson, Emmett Toppino and Tolan, who finished in that order. Wykoff did not like the furlong, even though he was once timed in 20.5 over a 218 y. (199.33 m.) straight course in 1931.

Double Olympic champion Percy Williams confirmed his class on several occasions. In 1929 he once beat Tolan by inches in a 9.6 100 y. race. The following year, in a 100 metres race at Vancouver, 1 July, he had to be content with third behind Tolan and Simpson in a 100-metre race. The shortest of the three, Tolan, won in 10.2, reportedly on a wind-free day. Simpson evened the count with Tolan in the 220 yards, with both timed in 20.6. This was started on a slight curve, with all the rest on a straight course. These marks never made the IAAF books though. Later in the season, Williams did get recognition for a 10.3 he ran at Toronto on 9 August. The Canadian wound up his seasonal record with a victory over 100 y. in the inaugural edition of the British Commonwealth Games, held at Hamilton, Ontario. The winner's time was no faster than 9.9, but it must be added that Williams suffered a thigh-muscle strain with 30 y. (27.43 m.) to go and was in real trouble throughout the last stretch of land. After that he gradually lost form and was ostensibly past his peak by the time of the Los Angeles Olympics in 1932.

Daniel Joubert is still regarded as one of the greatest sprinters ever to come out of South Africa. In the Inter-varsity Championships at Grahamstown (altitude 530 m.) on 16 May 1931 he amazed Springbok experts with two sterling 100 y. performances: a wind-assisted 9.3 (heat) and a legal 9.4 (final), plus a 21.3 for 220 y. around a turn and a 15.2 in the 120 y. hurdles. Strangely enough, his 9.4 for the century was submitted to the IAAF only in 1946 and was ratified just 2 years before the occurrence of the first official 9.3 ! Later in the year Joubert locked horns with one of America's best, Emmett Toppino. Such encounters received enormous publicity in South Africa. Toppino emerged the winner on both occasions.

The 1931 season also saw a record-breaking effort in the 4x110 yards relay. It occurred in the West Coast Relays at Fresno on 9 May when a So.California team composed of Roy Delby, Milton Maurer, Maurice Guyer and Frank Wykoff was clocked in 40.8.

In Europe most if not all the fastest times continued to be returned by Germans. During a "tournée" in the Far East in 1929, Eugen Eldracher ran a wind-assisted 10.3 for the 100 m. at Keijo (Seoul). In view of the 1932 Olympics attention was primarily focussed on a rising star, Arthur Jonath (born at Bentrop on 9 September 1909; 1.79 m. / 73 kgs.), a most consistent performer who on 5 June 1932 at Bochum became the first European to clock an official 10.3 for the metric century. Oddly enough, this mark was ratified as a German and European record but not as an IAAF record.

Early in 1932 the US scene was dominated by a rising star, Ralph Metcalfe (born at Atlanta, Georgia, on 29 May 1910; died in Chicago on 10 October 1978; 1.80 m. / 83 kg.). He first attained national prominence as a high school boy in 1928, when he ran the 100 y. in 9.8 and had a wind-aided 21.1 in the furlong (straight course). Three years later, while a freshman at Marquette University, he was fifth in the 100 y. and second to Tolan in the 220 y. at the AAU Championships in Lincoln, Nebraska. In May 1932 he started in high gear with a wind-aided 20.4 for 220 y. straightaway. At the NCAA Championhips, held at Chicago on 11 June, he scored a great double with 10.2 in the 100 m. and 20.5 in the 220 y. straight. While enroute, he was clocked in 9.5 (100 y.) and 20.3 (200 m.). Like numerous other records made in NCAA competition, Metcalfe's marks were ratified by the collegiate body, but for some mysterious reason he never gained AAU (nor, for that matter, IAAF) approval. At the US Final Tryouts in Palo Alto, Metcalfe beat Tolan in both 100 (10.6) and 200 metres (21.5). George Simpson qualified for the Games with two third places, very precious indeed as in the meantime the maximum number of Olympic entries in each event had been cut to three per country. Frank Wykoff, recovering from an early-season injury, was a close fourth in he 100, which barely sufficed to earn him a place on the 4x100 m. relay team. A new timing device called the "Kirby Photo-electric Camera" (from the name of its inventor, Gustavus T. Kirby) was in use in that meet. It gave times in one-hundredths of a second and was used as a verification of official results, given in the usual one-tenth version. At Palo Alto its verdicts for the century were as follows: Metcalfe 10.64, Tolan 10.71, Simpson 10.76 and Wykoff 10.79.

CARLTON, A MYSTICAL AFTERMATH

One of the most peculiar episodes in the history of sprinting concerns Aussie star James Andrew Carlton (born at Lismore, NSW on 10 February 1908). He first revealed his talent by running the English distances in 10.0 and 21.8 as a junior in 1927. The following year he was good enough to reach the quarter-finals at the Amsterdam Olympics in both 100 and 200 metres. By 1930 he was capable of 9.6 and 21.3 (the latter around a turn) in the English distances. His next (and last) clash with a top-class international sprinter occurred in New Zealand in 1931, when he beat the famous George Simpson of USA on two occasions. Before the year was out, Carlton was credited with a wind-aided 9.4 in the 100 y. and 21.0 (around a turn) in the 220 y.

What happened at the Sydney Cricket Ground on 18 January 1932 is still a matter of controversy among Australian oldtimers. The 220 y. was run around a full turn of the oval track. Carlton, in lane 2, soon pulled away from the rest and won with 8 yards (7.31 m.) to spare on Ewan Davidson, a sprinter of national class. Timers caught Carlton in a surprising 20.6, easily and by far the fastest time ever recorded on a full-turn course. No wind gauge was available, and so referee Laurie Drake used a piece of wool to test the "feelings" of the air – and finally decided to rule the time wind-assisted. In doing so, he sparked an Australia-wide furore, since many eye-witnesses disputed his verdict. The argument subsided somewhat five days later, when it was announced that Carlton "had run his last race". On that very day the fastest man from Down Under entered a training centre for Sacred Heart Missionaries, a Catholic seminary. He was ordained as Father Carlton in 1939 and for a long while he remained out of the public eye, only to re-emerge in 1945, when he left the priesthood to marry. This great sprinter - in the words of an Aussie commentator, "almost too fast for his own good" – thus remained a virtual unknown in the eyes of the outside world. He died in 1951 at the age of 43. In the opinion of former Australian sprint star "Slip" Carr, "he set standards of achievement and conduct that came as close as possible to the ideal".

In the Olympic arena, the magnificent Memorial Coliseum in Los Angeles, Metcalfe appeared to be slightly past his peak for the season, while Tolan was visibly gathering momentum. In the second round of the 100 metres Tolan set a new Olympic record of 10.4. The final brought together three Americans – Tolan, Metcalfe, Simpson – a South African, Joubert, a German, Jonath, and a Japanese, Takayoshi Yoshioka, i.e. a cast from four continents. The 23-year-old Yoshioka, barely 1.65 m. in height, used to run with a handkerchief round his head. He lived up to his reputation as a very fast starter: off in front, he led for almost half the distance. Then Tolan pulled ahead and with 30 metres to go he had 30 cms. on Metcalfe. The latter pulled even at 80 metres and the two struggled mightily till the end. The two Americans hit the tape virtually even. Finally it was announced that Tolan was the winner. Movies later showed the margin of victory to be only an inch (2.54 cms). Curiously enough, watches on Tolan showed 10.3, 10.3 and 10.4, whereas Metcalfe got 10.3 on all three! Not even the Kirby camera could separate them, as it showed 10.38 for both. The wind was negligible, + 0.4 m/s. Even so, only Tolan got credit from the IAAF for equalling the world record! Jonath ran a steady race and finished third, just ahead of Simpson. Tolan confirmed his superb condition in the 200 metres final two days later and won easily in 21.2 (electric time, 21.12), while Simpson and Metcalfe shunted Jonath to fourth place. Later on, news filtered through to the effect that Metcalfe, who was timed in 21.5, had been given a handicap of about a metre because of a hideous error in the measurement of his lane. To his credit it must be said that he refused to ask for a rerun, since he did not wish to jeopardize Uncle Sam's clean sweep.

The 4x100 metre relay closed the Los Angeles epic in fine style. The US leadership dispensed Tolan and Metcalfe from further work and lined up with an all-white team with Robert Kiesel, Toppino, Dyer and Wykoff. They sped to a new world record, 40.6, in the first round and improved to a spectacular 40.0 in the final. According to a European reporter, the announcement of such a time was followed by "a thunderstorm, the like of which had never been heard before". Two teams from Europe, Germany and Italy, finished second and third in that order. The latter in particular, well trained in baton exchanging, did very well in relation to the speed aggregate of its members.

1932 Olympics, Los Angeles – 100 metres (1 August) w start +0.2 m/s crosswind; at 50 m. – 1.4 m/s crosswind; finish: +0.4 m/s: 1.Eddie Tolan (USA) 10.3 (electric camera, 10.38); 2.Ralph Metcalfe (USA) 10.3 (10.38), 3.Arthur Jonath (Ger) 10.4 (10.50), 4.George Simpson (USA) 10.5 (10.53), 5.Daniel Joubert (SA) 10.6 (10.60); 6.Takayoshi Yoshioka (Jap) 10.7 (10.79). Lanes: Yoshioka 2, Joubert 3, Metcalfe 4, Simpson 5, Jonath 6, Tolan 7.

200 metres (3 August): 1.Eddie Tolan (USA) 21.2 (electric camera, 21.12); 2.George Simpson (USA) 21.4; 3.Ralph Metcalfe (USA) 21.5, 4.Arthur Jonath (Ger) 21.6; 5.Carlos Bianchi Luti (Arg) 21.7, 6.William Walters (SA) 21.9. Lanes: Tolan 2, Metcalfe 3, Simpson 4, Bianchi Luti 5, Walters 6, Jonath 7.

4x100 metres relay (7 August): 1.USA (R.Kiesel, E.Toppino, H.Dyer, F.Wykoff) 40.0 (electric camera, 40.10); 2.Ger (H.Körnig, F.Hendrix, E.Borchmeyer, A.Jonath) 40.9; 3.Ita (G.Castelli, G.Salviati, R.Maregatti, E.Toetti) 41.2; 4.Can 41.3; 5.Jap 41.3; 6.UK 41.4. Lanes: USA 1, Ita 2, Can 3, Ger 4, Jap 5, UK 6.

Tolan chose to call it a day after his glorious Olympic season. As for his great rival Metcalfe, his best days still lay ahead. He closed his 1932 season with a sizzling 19.8 for 220 yards (straight course, save for a slight curve initially) in a handicap race at Toronto on 3 September, an effort which was apparently nullified by several circumstances, such as doubtful timing and start given by waving a handkerchief.

In 1933-34 Metcalfe proved to be the World's Fastest Human in no uncertain way. During that period he experienced only one possible "scare", namely in the 100 m. of the 1934 AAU meet when he had to come from behind to barely nip one Jesse Owens at the tape – time for both 10.4. In both 1933 and '34 Metcalfe came to Europe and made men like Christiaan Berger of Holland, Erich Borchmeyer and Arthur Jonath of Germany look like "pikers", or just about. In 1934 he visited Japan and treated Takayoshi Yoshioka in a like manner. Clockwise Metcalfe had one of his greatest days on 17 June 1933 in the NCAA Championships in Chicago, when he ran the English distances in 9.4 and 20.4 – once again his times were ratified as records by the NCAA but not by the AAU. During his "tournées" abroad in 1933-34 he ran the 100 m. in 10.3 on five occasions and at Budapest on 12 August 1933 he sped over a 200 m. course with a quarter turn in 20.6 (handicap race), which time was accepted as a world record. In 1934 he covered the same distance on a straight course in 20.2 twice, first in Tokyo, then at Dairen, with a wind at his back on both occasions.

Metcalfe is recalled as one of the fastest finishers in the annals of sprinting. He was rather slow in rounding into top gear, apparently due to his far from perfect form in the early stages. But once he got into his real 8 ft. 6 in. (2.59 m.) stride he was well-nigh invincible. He was still in his prime when two other Greats appeared on the American scene. Both came from the "Deep South". One was Eulace Peacock (born at Dothan, Alabama, on 27 August 1914; 1.82 m. / 82 kg.), a heavily muscled sprinter who in 1934-35 competed with great success even in European meets, recording two legitimate 10.3 marks for the metric century, and losing only two races. The other rising star was Jesse Owens (born at Oakville, Alabama, on 12 September 1913; died at Tucson, Arizona, on 31 March 1980; 1.78 m. / 71 kg.). There is a story behind this name: thirteenth and last in a long line of children generated by Henry and Emma Owens, the boy was actually christened James Cleveland, but his name was so-to-say remoulded the day he entered Bolton Elementary School. When his teacher asked him his name, the boy reportedly replied: J.C.Owens, in a thick Southern drawl. The teacher understood him to say Jesse and asked if that was correct. "J.C. ma'am", he timidly mumbled. Once more she misunderstood and again asked him if he had said: Jesse. Eager to please, the boy gave up: "Yes, ma'am, Jesse Owens". That is how Jesse for ever replaced James Cleveland in the eyes of the world.

As an athlete, Owens was less impressive than Metcalfe or Peacock in sheer muscular power but he was built on well-proportioned, statuesque lines and had the agility and strength of a panther. He reached athletic greatness in the Middle West, after his peasant family left the "Deep South" to settle down in Cleveland. In 1932, while a student at the East Technical High School, he ran the 100 metres in 10.3 with an assisting wind. Subsequent pre-Olympic tests proved that he was not yet ripe for championship races. In his own admission: "I tightened up under the pressure of competition against older, more mature athletes". Then maybe his interest in those days lay elsewhere. In July he married his long-time girl friend Ruth Solomon. Both were minors at the time and had to elope to Erie, Pennsylvania (a state with rather lax marriage requirements) in order to be declared husband and wife by a Justice of the Peace. Early in August, Jesse and Ruth had their first child, a girl. Father celebrated with two wins and a second place in a post-Olympic meet held in Cleveland, notably running 100 y. around a turn in 9.6!

In 1933, his last year at East Technical High School, Owens had his real breakthrough. In the Interscholastic Championships at Chicago, on 17 June, he ran the sprints in 9.4 and 20.7 and long jumped 7.56. His time for the century was unmatched as an American Interscholastic record until 1954! Years later, he was asked about the difference, if any, between his 9.4 in High School competition and his 9.4's of later years in college. He replied: "About 6 yards (5.48 m.)". This was probably underestimating his ability as a youth, yet the anecdote serves to convey the useful idea that times of seemingly equal face value, especially if made in different grades of competition, can often differ strongly in intrinsic value.

In 1934, while a freshman at Ohio State University, Owens had a limited athletic activity, yet he closed the season on a high note by finishing second to Metcalfe in the

AAU 100 m., time for both 10.4. Owens really began to make history in 1935. Incidentally, it was chiefly thanks to his High School coach Frank Riley (who helped him "on and off the track" for years) that Jesse made it to Ohio State. Once there, he came under the tutelage of Larry Snyder, one of America's best known coaches, after a notable career as an athlete (52.4 in the 400 m. hurdles in 1924, second best in the world that year). The results of Snyder's refining work became apparent in the spring of 1935. Competing in three or four events virtually every weekend, Jesse chalked up times of 9.5 and 9.4 in the 100 y. as well as 20.9 and 20.7 in the furlong. And also did 22.9 in the 220 y. hurdles and 7.97 in the long jump! His Day of Days fell on 25 May at Ferry Field, Ann Arbor, Michigan, in the Western Conference ("Big Ten") Championships. A few days earlier, while indulging in the innocent game of touch football with some of his team-mates, Owens sustained a back injury. On the eve of the big two-day meet he and his coach were uncertain whether he could be able to contribute an all-out effort for the benefit of his Ohio State team ("The Buckeyes"). In this connection, however, the story related in an adjoining aside may be of interest to readers. However, on the first day, 24 May, Owens went through the prelims without a hitch, with such marks as 9.7 (100 y.), 21.4 (220 y.), 7.65 (long jump) and 24.9 (220 y. hurdles). Still, doubts lingered on. The next day Jesse and his coach agreed that he would try the first event, the 100 y. final, and then see .... What happened that afternoon at Ann Arbor belongs to the greatest tales in track history. Here it is, in chronological order (note revised timetable vis-à-vis information contained in some of my previous books):

Under a new IAAF rule, his furlong marks (made on a straight course) were also acceptable as world records for the shorter metric distance, so he actually bettered five world records and equalled another in his most glorious HOUR. Jesse was so busy during that fateful hour that he found the time for just one attempt in the long jump – and he broke the world record by 15 cms., with a mark that was to resist all assaults for 25 years! Especially in the sprints he was up against good competition: Robert Grieve was second in the 100 y. in 9.5, and Andrew Dooley trailed him in the 220 y. in 20.7. On that occasion Owens started from holes since he did not have the benefit of starting-blocks. Ken Doherty, a former decathlon star and later one of America's most famous track scholars, was among the lucky spectators (about 10,000) at Ferry Field and actually acted as meet director. In his book "Modern Track and Field" he gives enlightening details on timing conditions: "Large dialed tenth-second watches were used, with hands that move in tiny segments and therefore stop between as well as on the tenth-second markers. The hands of all three official watches (in the 100 y. final) were actually closer to 9.3 than to 9.4, but of course the slower time had to be recorded officially. Further, the starter for the race was W.J.Monilaw, who was insistent in his starting that the "set" should be held at least two seconds so that the chances of a "flyer" would be minimized. There was no international rule on wind at that time, yet Owens' efforts were measured also along that line – and all happen to be within the maximum wind assistance (+2.0 m/s) allowed under present rules.

15.15 hrs	100 y.	9.4	wind +1.55 m/s	(eq.WR)
15.25 hrs	long jump	8.13 (26-8 1/4)	wind +1.49 m/s	(WR)
15.45 hrs	220 y.	20.3	wind +0.83 m/s	(WR)
16.00 hrs	220 y.hurdles	22.6	wind +0.46 m/s	(WR)

"ARGUABLY THE INJURY WORKED TO HIS ADVANTAGE"

Seventy years have elapsed since Jesse Owens's heyday, yet it would be difficult even today to find any other "name" more universally known in the sport of track and field. Many have dwelt on his sterling performances but very few have endeavoured to delve into Owens the man. In the latter respect no one seems to have gone deeper than William J. Baker, a professor of history at the University of Maine and author of the excellent book "Jesse Owens, an American Life". He departed from widely spread beliefs in some cases, e.g. as regards Jesse's back injury on the eve of his Day of Days. "Some of Jesse's team-mates think "the bad back story" has been overdone to romanticize his struggle against the odds. Arguably the injury worked to his advantage. As only an athlete knows, an injury forces him to concentrate, to reach within himself for strength, making opponents and spectators irrelevant. That was Owens's experience at Ann Arbor. Years later he confided to an interviewer that once he warmed up and got into position for his first sprint, he "ran the entire day without a pain anywhere".

In June Owens continued to sweep the board in college meets and won the esteem of West Coast fans with four wins at the NCAA Championships in Berkeley. Such a hard schedule probably caused him to lose part of his springtime sparkle, and defeat finally came to him – in the biggest test of the season, the AAU Championships. On 4 July, Independence Day, 15,000 spectators gathered at the University of Nebraska Memorial Stadium in Lincoln to see what was probably the greatest trio of sprinters ever assembled in a 100 m. race: Jesse Owens, Ralph Metcalfe, a three-time winner of the title (1932-33-34), and Eulace Peacock, a redoubtable challenger. The latter, a powerful sprinter (1.82 m. / 81 kg.), showed what he could do by beating Owens in a sizzling 10.2 heat. This record time was made with an assisting wind of 2.22 m/s. In the final, the three Negroes had only one white challenger who seemed to have the ghost of a chance - George Anderson, who a few weeks earlier in California had run what could be described as the fastest 9.5 in the history of the 100 y. Incredible as it may sound, no less than seven timers out of eight caught Anderson in ....9.2, and only one in 9.5. Although this one admitted that his visual attention had been diverted by the flash of a photographer, the 9.5 version was accepted as official! In the Lincoln final, Anderson managed to stay the course in the early goings, after which he had to give way to his great rivals. Peacock pulled away near the halfway point. Once again, Metcalfe came up with his devastating finish, passed Owens but fell 2 ft. (60.96 cm.) short of Peacock at the tape. The winner's time was again 10.2 but a following wind of 3.47 m/s nullified it for record purposes. Metcalfe and Owens finished second and third in that order with estimated times of 10.3 ad 10.4 respectively, while Anderson was fourth. In the same meet, Peacock also beat Owens in the long jump, while Metcalfe easily won the 200 m. (21.0w) from Anderson and Foy Draper, who tied for second (21.3w). Peacock defeated Owens in two more races before the end of the season and closed his 1935 outdoor account having won three out of five sprint finals with the Ohio State flash.

In the years between Los Angeles and Berlin the leading European sprinters were Christiaan Berger of Holland, Erich Borchmeyer of Germany, Paul Hänni of Switzerland and József Sir of Hungary. Berger had his best season in 1934, when he beat Eulace Peacock in the 100 m. at Amsterdam (10.5 to 10.6), equalled Jonath's continental record (10.3) and finally won both sprints at the inaugural European Championships in Turin (10.6 and 21.5). Borchmeyer, the heavy type of sprinter, ran 10.3 on several occasions (but never got IAAF recognition) and was second to Berger in the 100 m. at Turin. Hänni traded wins with Peacock at Basel in 1935 with times of 10.4 and 21.2. Sir scored a double in the seventh World Student Games at Budapest in 1935. The English AAA Championships lost part of their international splendour with the advent of the European Championships, yet it should be recorded that in the period 1933-36 Berger, Osendarp and Sir won title races there. In 1934 London's White City Stadium acted as host to the second edition of the British Commonwealth Games and Arthur Sweeney of England scored a double (10.0 and 21.9), obviously over the English distances.

In 1936 Owens made no mistakes. Although not visibly faster than the year before, he appeared to have gained in staying power. Still alternating his sprint labours with hurdling and long jumping chores, he went through that exacting season virtually unscathed. He tried the furlong around a turn and by the end of May he was down to 21.1. He also had a 20.5 for the 220 y. straightaway , a wind-aided 9.3 and a legal 9.4 for the 100 y. On the first day (19 June) of the NCAA Championships in Chicago he clocked 11.2 over a course which on re-measurement was found to be 10 m. in excess of the supposed 100 metres! The following day, under perfect conditions (aiding wind, 1.2 m/s) he won the final in 10.2, after being officially timed in 9.4 at the 100 y. mark. In doing so, he whipped a fine field: 2.Foy Draper 10.3, 3.Sam Stoller 10.3, 4.Adrian Talley 10.4, 5.Harvey Wallender 10.4, 6.George Boone 10.4, 7.Donald Dunn 10.5, 8.Perrin Walker 10.5, 9.Morris Pollock 10.6. However, upon rer-measurement the course was found to be 99.985 m.! (In 1938, after considering all the factors involved, the IAAF decided to ratify Owens's mark as a world record).

At the AAU Championships, held in early July at Princeton, N.J., Owens won the 100 m. in 10.4 and left the way free for Metcalfe in the 200 m. (21.2 over a straight course). A week later, in the US Final Tryouts in New York, Owens won the 100 m. on the first day, again in 10.4, with Metcalfe second and Frank Wykoff third in a brilliant comeback. Eulace Peacock, still nursing an early-season injury, had been eliminated in the first round. He was admittedly the rival Owens feared most, and we'll never know what he could have done in Berlin, if healthy and present. Obviously, Peacock did not have the staying power of his great rival.

The next day of the New York meet Owens won the 200 m. around a turn in 21.0 from Mack Robinson and Robert Packard, while the usually dependable Metcalfe ran one of the poorest races of his career and finished fourth.

Owens' legendary "Week of Weeks" at the Berlin Olympics is best related by a chronological list of his achievements:

- 2 August:	11.29 a.m.,	100 m. heat,	1st in 10.3 (+1.7 m/s);
	3.04 p.m.,	100 m. quarter-final,	1st in 10.2 (+ 2.3 m/s).
- 3 August:	3.30 p.m.,	100 m. semi-final,	1st in 10.4 (+2.7 m/s);
	5.00 p.m.,	100 m. final,	1st in 10.3 (+2.7 m/s).
- 4 August:	10.30 a.m.,	long jump, qualifying round: achieved the qualifying distance, 7.15, on his third and last try;	
	10.45 a.m.,	200 m. heat,	1st in 21.1 (adverse wind);
	3.44 p.m.,	200 m. quarter-final,	1st in 21.1 (aiding wind);
	4.30 p.m.,	long jump final,	1st with 8.06 (aiding wind).
- 5 August:	3.05 p.m.,	200 m. semi-final,	1st in 21.3 (aiding wind);
	6.00 p.m.,	200 m. final,	1st in 20.7 (allowable wind assistance):
- 8 August:	3.00 p.m.,	4x100 m. relay, heat,	1st, time 40.0 (eq.WR), first leg.
- 9 August:	3.15 p.m.,	4x100 m. relay, final,	1st, time 39.8 (WR), first leg.

In all the above-mentioned events Owens invariably emerged as the undisputed winner. He collected four gold medals without ever being seriously challenged, save perhaps in the long jump. In the 100 m. final Metcalfe had a poor getaway and a strong finish, and wound up second ahead of 20-year-old Martinus Osendarp of Holland, who nosed out veteran Wykoff in the battle for bronze. In the 200 m. final, which was run in a drizzle, Owens appeared to be trying hard near the end, yet he won easily from Mack Robinson and Osendarp.

In the sprint relay Americans were once again in a class by themselves. They equalled the world record (40.0) in a heat. In the decisive test Owens gained a lead of more than 5 metres on the first leg and that was virtually the end of the race. His team-mates gradually increased the lead and USA finally won in 39.8, a new world record. The battle for the other medals was close and a well-tuned Italian team without stellar performers finished ahead of Germany. In actual fact, Holland was third but met disqualification as anchor leg man Osendarp dropped the baton 25 metres from home.

1936 Olympics, Berlin - 100 metres (3 August) w +2.7 m/s: 1.Jesse Owens (USA) 10.3w; 2.Ralph Metcalfe (USA) 10.4w; 3.Martinus Osendarp (Hol) 10.5w; 4.Frank Wykoff (USA) 10.6w; 5.Erich Borchmeyer (Ger) 10.7w; 6.Lennart Strandberg (Swe) 10.9w. Lanes: Owens 2, Strandberg 3, Borchmeyer 4, Osendarp 5, Wykoff 6, Metcalfe 7.

200 metres (5 August) w under 2.0 m/s: 1.Jesse Owens (USA) 20.7; 2.Mack Robinson (USA) 21.1; 3.Martinus Osendarp (Hol) 21.3; 4.Paul Hänni (Swz) 21.6; 5.Lee Orr (Can) 21.6; 6.Wijnand van Beveren (Hol) 21.9. Lanes: Osendarp 2, van Beveren 3, Owens 4, Robinson 5, Hänni 6, Orr 7.

4x100 metres relay (9 August): 1.USA (J.Owens, R.Metcalfe, F.Draper,

Jesse Owens winning the 200 metres at the 1936 Olympics in Berlin. Time 20.7. Right behind him is Mack Robinson (USA), 21.1, who passed away early in 2000. Only other visible finalist is L.Orr (Canada), 5th.

F.Wykoff) 39.8 (WR); 2.Ita (O.Mariani, G.Caldana, E.Ragni, T.Gonnelli) 41.1; 3.Ger (W.Leichum, E.Borchmeyer, E.Gillmeister, G.Hornberger) 41.2; 4.Arg 42.2; 5.Canada 42.7; Hol, (third in 41.2) disq. Lanes: Arg 2, Ger 3, Hol 4, USA 5, Ita 6, Can 7.

It should be added that Mack Robinson, who finished second in the 200 m., was also a good long jumper (7.76 / 25-5 1/2 in 1937). In the course of time, however, he was to be chiefly remembered as "the elder brother of Jackie Robinson", the first black American to play major league baseball in modern times. By the way, Jackie too was an excellent long jumper: in 1938, aged 19, he topped the World Year List in that event with 7.78 / 25-6 1/2.

Quite understandably, Owens did not take the post-Olympic meets too seriously. On 10 August at Cologne he was second to Ralph Metcalfe in a 100 m. race, the story of which can in no way detract from Jesse's fame. With only 20 m. to go, Owens was leading Metcalfe by almost 2 m., then he suddenly decided to ease up ... in order to give way to his rival and friend Ralph, who went on to win in 10.3. On hearing the winner's time, Owens (second in 10.4) probably realized that he had thrown away the chance of his lifetime. But then that was not the only day on which he appeared to have no undue affection for records. Until recently there were old-timers who thought that he could have done better in this or that event if he had shown a greater singleness of purpose. But that is of course idle speculation.

Owens was attracted toward professional activities soon after the Berlin Olympics. His last appearance as an amateur was at the White City Stadium, London, on 15 August, when he ran the third leg in a 4x100 yards relay which was won by USA over a Commonwealth foursome in 37.4. Metcalfe closed his career by the same time, after his second European campaign. He had the rare distinction of twice placing second in an Olympic 100 m. final. Even more remarkable perhaps was his record in AAU meets: between 1932 and 1936 he won eight titles (three in the 100 m. and five in the 200 m.). Peacock never regained his 1935 form yet he continued for many more years and chiefly distinguished himself as a fine all-rounder in pentathlon competitions.

1936 was an important year in the annals of sprinting for another reason too: at their Convention in Berlin the IAAF introduced a new rule which read like this: "For all records up to 220 y. and for the long jump and hop, step and jump, information as to wind conditions must be available. If the component of the wind measured in the direction of the racing behind the competitor exceeds 2.0 m. (6 feet 6 3/4 in.) per second the record will not be accepted". The period for which the wind component would be measured was 10 secs. for the 100 m. and 20 secs. for the 200 m. and 220 y. If the longer distance was run on a curve, the component would be measured for a period of 10 secs., commencing as the runners entered the straight.

The problem of "ruling the winds" had bothered the minds of track legislators for years. The 1936 dictum came as the consequence of a proposal advanced by the "Deutscher Leichtathletik Verband". In fact, the Germans had proposed a maximum allowance of only 1 m/s, which the majority of the (conservative?) IAAF delegates regarded as punitive. Hence the final agreement on the 2 m/s limit. It must be said that several years had to go by before the majority of national federations affiliated to the IAAF took the habit of complying with the new rule.

THE OTHER SIDE OF THE MEDAL

Incredible as it may sound, Jesse Owens, the most widely acclaimed athlete of the XX century, hung up his spikes a few weeks before turning 23. After his triumphs in Berlin and a parade in his honour in Cleveland, he soon discovered the ephemeral side of his glory. In the Thirties no champion could expect to derive more than medals and records from his athletic talent. Having by then a family to support, he decided to leave Ohio State University to concentrate on earning a decent living. He was soon attracted by "pro" shows of various kinds, like running against a horse. Later on, as a businessman, he had his share of ups and downs. His chief biographer William J. Baker describes him as "a man of heart, who eventually became a polished speaker and promoter, even though he never managed to write fluently". In his old age, Owens was employed by the American Olympic Committee as a popular PR man, ever ready to voice age-old American beliefs such as: "In America, anyone can still become somebody .... It happened to me, a kid who had come from the worst poverty to be thrown wildly to the top of the tallest mountain, and somehow had landed on his feet".

Martinus Osendarp of Holland (born at Delft on 21 May 1916; died at Heerlen on 20 June 2002; 1.76 m. / 80 kg.) was Europe's Fastest Human for several years. He would suffer an occasional defeat now and then, e.g. to Lennart Strandberg of Sweden over 100 m. in a post-Olympic meet at Malmö in 1936 (10.6 to 10.3), but on the whole he was a most dependable performer. In 1938 he scored a double at the European Championships in Paris (10.5 and 21.2). Possibly the only man who could have challenged him if he had been present in Paris was Cyril Holmes of Britain, who earlier in the year had scored a similar double over the English distances (9.7 and 21.2) at the British Empire and Commonwealth Games in Sydney. A solid sprinter with no weak points, Osendarp never did better than 10.4 or 21.1 officially (although he once did 10.3 with a following wind), but his ability as a competitor was unquestionable. Other fine sprinters of the late Thirties were Orazio Mariani of Italy, Jakob Scheuring and Karl Neckermann of Germany.

Even after the departure of Owens and Metcalfe, good sprinters continued to be a dime a dozen on the American market. At the 1939 AAU Championships in Lincoln, Nebraska, a classy 100 m. field was assembled. After a furious battle, Clyde Jeffrey emerged the winner in a wind-aided 10.2. Among the place-winners were Ben Johnson, a man with a Blitz start who in 1938 in an indoor meet ran 60 yards (54.86 m.) in 6 seconds flat, a time the AAU refused to ratify; and tall, long striding Perrin Walker, a poor starter with an excellent pick-up. Both competed with great success even in Europe. Jeffrey equalled Owens's 100 y. record (9.4) in 1940, but like other champions of those days he was deprived of his Olympic chance by World War II.

Central America was about ready to join the battle for sprint honours. An advance signal came from the Central American Championships held at Panama City early in 1938. The fireworks came from Jennings Blackett of Panama and Jacinto Ortiz of Cuba, who won their respective semi-finals of the 100 m. in 10.3. The next day Blackett beat Ortiz in the final, the time for both being a wind-aided 10.4.

ABOUT THE START

Reliable historical sources attribute the invention of the start "on all fours" to Mike Murphy (1861-1913), an American coach of Irish extraction, very well known in his time and age for promoting some revolutionary innovations, partly the result of his medical studies.

Other sources claim that the "crouching start" was first experimented in 1884 in Scotland by Bobby MacDonald, an athlete of Maori extraction residing in the United Kingdom.

In his book "Athletic Training" (published in 1890 by Charles Scribner & Sons of New York) Murphy claimed to have invented and experimented that revolutionary start in 1887 with his pupil Charles Sherrill, then 21 and a student at Yale University.

Prior to then starting methods used by sprinters and middle distance men could be classified under three varieties: lunge start, dab start and stand-up crouch start. All three called for a standing start of sorts. The only difference concerned the position of the arms. For example, in the lunge start the runner kept his arms wide open, one pointing down and the other pointing up and kept behind. That was after the discontinuation of the start "by mutual consent", richly dealt with by Archie Hahn in his famous book "How to sprint" (1925), mainly in the chapter "Early Days of Athletics in the United States".

Prior to Mike Murphy's invention, the most widely used starting method, both in USA and in Europe, was the "dab start", in which the stand-up style was mitigated somewhat by bending the upper body.

The third variety, the stand-up crouch start, was generally similar to the dab-start, except in the position of the arms, pointing down. This method was very popular among "pros".

On 18 May 1888 at Cedarhurst, Long Island (NY) Charles Sherrill used the form devised by his coach in the 100 yards race of the Rockaway Hunt Club Games. Two months after that the "Athletic Journal" published a short article summarizing the new starting form used by Sherrill and related that the starter, one Mr. Turner, was quite upset as he thought the athlete did not know how to start and went to extreme lengths in trying to instruct him ....

The news concerning the new starting method soon reached Europe. On this continent it was first experimented by Tom Nicholas of Monmouth A.C., back from a sojourn in the States. For various reasons, however, he was unable to use it in official competition. The first to divulge it on this side of the Atlantic was Ernest Pelling of the London AC, who used it to good advantage in winning the 100 yards at the 1889 AAA Championships.

Continental Europeans first saw the crouching start at the 1896 Athens Olympics, thanks to Burke, Lane and Curtis, three Americans who competed in the 100 metres.

G.P.

AN AMERICAN SKY (WITH SCATTERED EUROPEAN CLOUDS)

World War II with its implications far and wide caused the cancellation of two editions of the Olympic Games, 1940 and 1944. The former (12th of the series) had been originally assigned to Tokyo, but the decision had to be revised at the time of the Japanese invasion of Northern China. In 1938 Helsinki was awarded the Games but here again war had the last word as Finland was invaded by USSR troops. The 13th edition (1944) was scheduled to take place in London, but Britain's involvement in WW2 made it necessary to delay it till 1948. According to a well established IOC habit, however, the London Games of 1948 went down in history as the 14th edition.

Among the many crack sprinters who suffered most because of this sad state of affairs was Harold Davis, the "California Comet", who ruled the roost in America during the early Forties. Davis (born at Salinas, California, on 5 February 1921; 1.78 m. / 72 kg.) was one of those tremendously gifted athletes who can do marvellous things virtually from the beginning. In 1938, as a 17-year-old High School boy, he ran the English distances in 9.7 and 21.0 (straight course). He began to give the full measure of his greatness in 1940. Don Potts, a keen student of sprinting history, thus recalled the unusual circumstances of Davis's breakthrough at Los Angeles on 17 May 1940: "They had lined up a crack field in the 100 y. dash, including Mozel Ellerbe of Tuskegee, twice NCAA champion. It was Ellerbe who won the race (9.7), but the man who finished fourth attracted much attention. He stumbled at the start, fell on all fours, recovered and then made up 4 to 7 m. on some of the nation's crack sprinters in the last 65 m. The runner was young Harold Davis from Salinas Junior College". Even apart from falls, Davis never rose above the average in starting ability. But he went on to impress observers more and more with his amazing finishing kick. In the four years of his reign as the king of American sprinters (1940-43), he never lost a race in the furlong and was beaten on only one important occasion in the century, namely by Norwood "Barney" Ewell in the 1941 AAU 100 m. at Philadelphia. And Davis probably ran one of his greatest races on that very occasion: an atrocious start caused him to lag 3 m. behind Ewell at the half-way mark, but a fantastic rush in the closing stage brought him within centimetres of his great rival at the tape. If I add that both were timed in 10.3, it seems reasonable to assume that Davis must have come very close to the maximum of known human potential in the second half of that incredible race. "Bud" Winter, who was Davis's coach at Salinas, has committed to history some interesting splits for Davis's fastest races. On 6 June 1941 at Compton, when he equalled Owens's world record for the 100 m. (10.2), Davis covered the first half in 5.7 and the second half in 4.5. In his two 20.2 straightaway races, aided on both occasions by a wind over the limit, Davis ran halves of 10.3 and 9.9, namely at Fresno on 17 May 1941 (220 y.) and in New York on 20 June 1943 (200 m.). Between 1940 and 1943, Davis won seven AAU titles – three in the 100 m., four in the 200 m. He also equalled the world's 100 y. record, 9.4. and in the same year, 1942, he achieved his best legitimate time for the furlong, 20.4. Had the Olympics taken place in 1940 and 1944, only one man could have made things a bit difficult for him, the above-mentioned Ewell, one of the most durable sprinters the world has ever seen. Ewell (born at Harrisburg, PA., on 25 February 1918; died at Lancaster, PA., on 4 April 1996; 1.80 m. / 71 kg.) figured among the fastest sprinters in America, and for that matter in the world, from 1937 to 1948, apart from a spell during WW2 when he was in the Services. In 1941 he traded wins with Davis at the AAU Championships, winning the 100 by the proverbial whisker, as related above, and finishing second to the "California Comet", 20.5 to 20.4, in the 200 m. straightaway. He won six AAU titles, the first in 1939, the last in 1948, and he was AAU Junior champion in 1936, at the age of 18. And just like other great sprinters of the past he was also a leading long jumper: 7.68 indoors in 1942.

In early post-war years two excellent sprinters emerged in North America, Melvin Patton of USA and Lloyd LaBeach of Panama. The former (born in Los Angeles on 16 November 1924; 1.85 m./ 72 kg.), a dashman with a silken stride, came to the fore in 1942 with times of 9.9 and 21.4 for the English distances. The following year he improved to 9.8 and 21.2. Then the war put a brisk halt to his promising career, and it was only in 1946 that he resumed his athletic activity, as a freshman at the University of Southern California. In 1947 he equalled the world's 100 y. record, 9.4, twice and ran the furlong in 20.4 (straight course) three times. For some curious reason he never appeared in AAU meets.

By then, Patton's fiercest rival was Lloyd LaBeach (born at Panama City on 28 June 1922; died in New York on 19 February 1999; 1.85 m. / 73 kg,). Both of his parents were born in Jamaica. Lloyd's father was a passionate cricketer and apparently used to get his sons up early in the morning to run a few miles. And if there was ever an athletic family, that was Señor LaBeach's. All of his six sons were active sprinters at one time or another, with Lloyd being by far the best of them. He was educated first in Jamaica, then in USA but in international competition, from 1946 onwards, he chose to represent his native country. He began to make the headlines in 1943, when he was credited with such times as 9.5 (100 y.), 10.2w and

Start and finish of the 100 metres final at the 1948 Olympics in London. The winner is hurdler Harrison Dillard (USA), extreme left, time 10.3. Others from left are: A. McCorquodale (GB), 4th; E. McDonald Bailey (GB) 6th; L. LaBeach (Panama), 3rd; N. Ewell (USA) 2nd; and M. Patton (USA), 5th.

10.4 (100 m.) and 21.2 (200 m.). One of his main rivals at that time was Leroy "Coco" Brown of Jamaica, an early phenomenon whose career ended prematurely because of WW2. LaBeach entered major international competition in 1946, while a student at Wisconsin Uiversity. He collected a string of second places – in both sprints at the NCAA meet and in the 200 m. at the AAU meet, where he lost to Barney Ewell. He closed his busy year placing 4th in the 100 m. and 2nd in the 200 at the Central American and Caribbean Games, held at Barranquilla, Colombia. Winner of both races was Rafael Fortún of Cuba (10.4 and 21.6).

Being basically a self-taught and self-advised athlete, LaBeach amassed a superb series of fast times throughout his career but he was not always at his best on big occasions. The first major clash between him and Mel Patton occurred at Los Angeles in 1947 and resulted in a tie, with the Californian first in the 100 m. (10.5) and LaBeach winning the 220 y. (20.8). The most memorable chapter of their feud unfolded at Fresno on 15 May 1948. In the 100 y., after several false starts, Patton was off fast and appeared to have a decisive lead on LaBeach. Even though Patton's pick-up was considered nonpareil, LaBeach managed to close the gap almost entirely and finished only a foot (30 cm.) back at the end. The winner was rewarded with a new world record, 9.3, while LaBeach was given 9.4. As one keen observer pointed out, chance had a large part in awarding the first official 9.3 to Patton and not, say, to Simpson or Owens. In fact, the three official watches on Patton read 9.3, 9.3, 9.4, while two alternates showed 9.3 and 9.4. Both Simpson at Chicago in 1929 and Owens at Ann Arbor in 1935 were timed alternatively in 9.3 or 9.4, except that the majority of timers designated as official before the races were on the 9.4 side. In the days of manual timing it took three watches to make the verdict official, yet records were not infrequently determined by one timepiece – operated, like all others, by the fallible human element – going this way or that way. Later in the same afternoon at Fresno, LaBeach ran the 100 m. in 10.2, with Patton not in the race. On 4 June at Compton, the Panamanian ace posted another 10.2 and ran the 220 y. straightaway in 20.3 (time at 200 m., 20.2). Although the wind on these occasions was within the permissible limit, for some obscure reason the Compton marks were never ratified by the IAAF.

AGE RIDDLE

According to most historians and statisticians, Lloyd LaBeach's date of birth was 28 June 1923, apparently confirmed in obituaries published in foreign papers at the time of his death (1999). Just a year before that sad occurrence, Ulf Lagerström, one of the keenest students of Central American track and field, had offered a different version in his excellent book "The Kingston Flyers". Here is what he wrote on the subject: "His brother Sam guarantees that Lloyd's birth certificate states 28 June 1922. The reason for the former date being used by Lloyd may have been his strong desire to participate in class-I and junior events in Jamaica despite being overage".
On another note it may be worth recording that shortly before Lloyd's death the Panamanian Government decided to inaugurate a Lloyd LaBeach Street in Panama City. Jamaica too has been lavish in honouring her onetime athletic Greats in similar ways.

A few weeks before the London Olympics, Patton and LaBeach reigned supreme in the thoughts of (amateur) prognosticators, who at best gave an outsider's chance to veteran Barney Ewell. But to make things difficult for both athletes and tipsters there came a trouble-maker: hurdler Harrison Dillard of USA. Holder of the world's record for the 120 y. hurdles (13.6 early in 1948) Dillard could point to a personal best of 10.3 in the 100 m. flat, made in Stockholm in 1947. It so happened that at the US Final Tryouts at Evanston Dillard unexpectedly met disgrace in his favourite event: after hitting several hurdles rather badly, he came to a halt at the eighth hurdle. But he had been wise enough to secure a berth on the team by placing third in the 100 m. flat the day before, merely three hundredths of a second ahead of the fourth man! Here is the result of that race (9 July) – official times first and in parentheses the versions given by an electronic device, the Bulova Phototimer, which was activated by the sound of the gun, not by its actual firing as it happens with nowadays fully automatic timing. 1.Norwood "Barney" Ewell 10.2 (10.33); 2.Mel Patton 10.3 (10.45); 3.Harrison Dillard 10.4 (10.50); 4.Ed Conwell 10.4 (10.53); 5.Donald Campbell 10.5 (10.58); Bill Mathis did not finish. Ewell thus became a co-holder of the world record at the age of 30. And Dillard, the great hurdler, just sneaked into he team, centimetres ahead of Conwell, a wizard of the start if ever there was one.

After the race Patton's coach, the honourable and venerable Dean Cromwell, reportedly stated that his protégé had run "like a plow-horse". Such a shrewd judgement apparently had the power to revitalize Patton. On the following day he evened the count with Ewell in the 200 m. Both were officially timed in 20.7, but Patton actually won by 2 ft. (60 cm.). Cliff Bourland, a world class quarter-miler in 1941, was third in 21.0 and thus became one of the rare pre-war stars who managed to "survive" till the 1948 London Olympics.

On the eve of the London rendez-vous the European armour appeared to be weaker than usual. With Osendarp serving a prison term for collaborating with the Germans during the war and Strandberg well past his peak, none of the sprinters from the old continent loomed as a threat to America's representatives. Two year earlier, at the European Championships in Oslo, Jack Archer of Britain had won the 100 m. in 10.6. Yet he was not the fastest man in the British Isles, because that title rightly belonged to Emmanuel McDonald Bailey, a copybook stylist hailing from the Caribbean area (born at Williamsville, Trinidad, on 8 December 1920; 1.80 m. / 65 kg.). "Mac" was for many years a dominant figure in British athletics circles and in the words of Mel Watman, "if any sprinter personified poetry in motion, it was McDonald Bailey". He emerged as a sprint talent in his native Trinidad (9.8 and 21.2), but soon moved to England, where he spent the better part of his career. Between 1946 and 1953 he collected no less than 14 AAA titles. Just a few days before the London Olympics a home-made British sprinter, Alistair McCorquodale, came to the fore in meteoric fashion and began to talk on even terms with the great "Mac".

The Wembley track (specially laid for the Olympics, it was in fact dismantled as soon as the Games were over!) turned out to be the fastest surface in the history of British athletics. On 31 July, 84,000 spectators saw the final of the 100 m. Patton, in the inside lane, practically lost the race at the start, as did "Mac" – and they never looked like their real selves. Dillard, who had gone through the prelims with times of 10.4, 10.4 and 10.5, was in the outside lane and held a narrow but decisive lead from gun to tape. At the other end of the track, Ewell looked dangerous as he closed the gap gradually. The 30-year-old veteran actually thought he had won as he went through the tape. Having waited for that supreme moment many years, he indulged in an impromptu dance to celebrate. The official verdict, awarding the victory to Dillard, thus came as a bitter pill for the durable Ewell. LaBeach, though not as good as in his best days, was third, just ahead of McCorquodale, a squat-shouldered rugby player, while Patton and Bailey closed up the rear in that order. The official times for the first three were 10.3, 10.4 and 10.6, but it was apparent that they bore no relation to the actual intervals. According to an electric timer, only 11 hundredths of a second covered the first four, which means that McCorquodale, fourth, should have been credited with 10.4. Non-wining times given below were in fact construed on the differentials shown by the electric timing device.

Patton was burnt by a strong desire to make amends for his poor show in the century. On 3 August he went to the starting line of the 200 m. final fully determined to prove his greatness to the big international audience. Ewell, by then in the twilight of his career, was moved by an even more stringent necessity; for him it was obviously a case of now or never. Ewell was off faster than Patton, but the latter had an early pick-up, collared his rival in the final part of the turn and shot into the lead on entering the homestretch. Ewell fought back with dogged determination, but Patton held on gamely and won by half a metre. Both were timed in 21.1, while LaBeach was again third (21.2).

The Americans once and again had things under control in the sprint relay, but for the first time they failed to break or even tie the listed world record. In actual fact, their quartet – Ewell, Lorenzo Wright, Dillard, Patton - was at first disqualified due to an allegedly faulty changeover between Ewell and Wright, but after a careful study of the official film, the jury reinstated the US team. Far behind were Britain and Italy, second and third respectively. The latter thus won a medal in this event for the third successive time.

1948 Olympics, London - 100 metres (31 July) w + 1.7 m/s: 1.Harrison Dillard (USA) 10.3; 2.Barney Ewell (USA) 10.4; 3.Lloyd LaBeach (Pan) 10.4; 4.Alistair McCorquodale (UK) 10.4; 5.Mel Patton (USA) 10.5; 6.Emmnauel McDonald Bailey (UK) 10.6. Lanes: Patton 1, Ewell 2 LaBeach 3, McCorquodale 4, McDonald Bailey 5, Dillard 6.

200 metres (3 August) w - ?: 1.Mel Patton (USA) 21.1; 2.Barney Ewell (USA) 21.1; 3.Lloyd LaBeach (Pan) 21.2; 4.Herb McKenley (Jam) 21.2; 5.Cliff Bourland (USA) 21.3, 6.Leslie Laing (Jam) 21.6. Lanes: McKenley 1, Patton 2, LaBeach 3, Ewell 4, Bourland 5, Laing 6.

4x100 metre relay (7 August): 1.USA (B.Ewell, L.Wright, H.Dillard, M.Patton) 40.6; 2.GB (J.Archer, J.Gregory, A.McCorquodale, Ken Jones) 41.3; 3.Ita (M.Tito, E.Perucconi, C.Monti, A.Siddi) 41.5; 4.Hun 41.6; 5.Can 41.9; 6.Hol 41.9. Lanes: Hun 1, Hol 2, USA 3, UK 4, Ita 5, Can 6.

William Harrison Dillard (born at Cleveland on 8 July 1923; 1.78 m. / 70 kg.) was reportedly won to the cause of track as a teenager in 1936, the day he witnessed in his hometown a parade in honour of Jesse Owens, coming home from his glorious Berlin campaign. As the story goes, right then and there the boy decided to emulate the feats of the "Ebony Antelope". "Bones", as he was called on account of his skinny physique, first made the headlines in 1942,

Patton, no.71, took revenge in the 200 metres (1948 Olympics), winning from veteran "Barney" Ewell, no.70. Time for both, 21.1. Others from left: C. Bourland (USA) 5th; L. LaBeach (Panama) 3rd; H. McKenley (Jamaica) 4th. Not visible, in lane 6, L. Laing (Jamaica) 6th.

33

with worthy marks in the entire variety of hurdling events – highs, lows and intermediates. WW2 put a halt to his progress, but right after the end of the conflict he did his best in service meets held in Italy and Germany. I happened to see P.f.c. Dillard in action several times when he was serving with the 5th US Army. He was primarily an outstanding hurdler, even though his height appeared to be a bit inadequate in relation to the 1.06 m. barriers. In 1945 he did 14.6 in the highs but also ran the century on the flat route in 10.6. Back home, he improved rapidly. He is often remembered as the guy who in time of need turned to the 100 metres flat to find consolation for failing to make the US Olympic team in his favourite event. Putting it that way is not strictly correct though: as related above, he qualified for the Games in the sprint event before meeting disgrace in the hurdles. After winning gold in the century in 1948 he patiently waited another four years and finally won Olympic gold in the hurdles as well. Consequently, it seems proper to remember him as the only athlete who ever managed to score the 100m/110mH double, in different editions of the Games, that's true.

After his victory in the Olympic 200 m. final, Mel Patton had the incentive he needed for another season of full action on the cinder path. His greatest moments in the struggle against time came on 7 May 1949 at Westwood, Los Angeles, in a dual meet between UCLA and their cross-town rivals, USC, Mel's university. Running as only a great champion does in his most inspired moments, he offered an uninhibited, smooth display of sprinting ability. He began with a splendid 9.1 in the 100 y, alas assisted by a wind of 2.90 m/s., then continued with a legal 20.2 in the 220 y. straightaway. In the latter race the wind in his favour was 1.50 m/s. In the century the three official watches gave 9.1, 9.1 and 9.0. Had the wind staid within the permissible limit, he would have probably earned a legal 9.2. In the furlong two watches gave 20.2 and one showed 20.1. Patton won both races by a "block". He was second to none of his contemporaries in pure blazing speed, but he tended to be rather nervous on occasions. Moreover, his habit of bypassing the AAU Championships probably cost him a few points in the eyes of experts, more perhaps than his rare defeats (two in the 100 m. and one in the furlong) in the three-year period 1947-48-49.

In his last major race, the 220 y. final of the 1949 NCAA Championships, Patton (20.4) was extended by a newcomer, Andy Stanfield, who finished a close second (20.5). The latter, a statuesque runner (born in Washington, D.C. on 29 December 1927; died in Livingston, NJ., on 15 June 1985; 1,85 m. / 77 kg.) went on to score a double at the AAU Championships (10.3 and 20.4w) and thus established himself as the new king of American sprinters. In later years, recurrent muscle injuries prevented him from showing a consistency equal to his class. On 26 May 1951 at Philadelphia he ran the 220 yards around a full turn in 20.6. By then the IAAF had finally decided to distinguish between marks made on a straight course and those made around a turn. Stanfield's mark thus became the first official record for the latter category. In USA the straightaway event was discontinued only in the late Sixties.

Lloyd LaBeach had his best year as a record-breaker and globe-trotter in 1950. In European meets he twice clocked 20.7 for the 200 m. around a turn, beating among others Herb McKenley of Jamaica and Emmanuel McDonald Bailey of Trinidad. Then, on 7 October at Guayaquil, Ecuador, LaBeach was credited with a sensational 10.1 for the metric century. There was no wind gauge though and this obviously prevented ratification by the IAAF. The time of the runner-up, Andres Fernandes Salvador, 10.3, was accepted as Ecuadorian record though. However, the timing was regarded as doubtful by some observers.

By the same time, Bailey continued to rule the roost on British tracks. As often as not, however, he had to go abroad to post his fastest times. On 25 August 1951 at Belgrade he ran the 100 m. in 10.2, thus equalling the official world record. His mark was also ratified as a European record, since the Trinidad speedster had been a resident of Great Britain for more than the required five years. In 1950, he was not admitted to the European Championships, and the continental titles, contested by a relatively mediocre lot, had gone to Etienne Bally of France in the 100 m. (10.6) and to Brian Shenton of Britain

Final of the 100 m. at the 1956 CISM Games in Berlin. Willie Williams (nearest camera) beating Ira Murchison, 10.1 to 10.2. Both had done 10.1 in the qualifying rounds on previous days, thus breaking Jesse Owens' twenty-year old world record of 10.2.

in the 200 m. (21.5). Holland seemed to have exhausted her onetime vein, and Germany was not yet ready to return to her tradition.

Early in 1952 the leading American candidates for Olympic honours were Stanfield, agile and consistent Art Bragg and powerful Jim Golliday. This last (born at Sacramento, California, on 23 April 1931; 1.76 m. / 76 kg.) looked like the class of the nation when he downed a crack field at the NCAA Championships, running the 100 m. against a stiff wind in 10.4. But a muscular ailment prematurely put paid to his Olympic chances. In his absence. Bragg won the 100 m. at the Final Olympic Trials (as they began to be called) in 10.5, the other qualifiers being Lindy Remigino and Dean Smith. It should be added that Smith actually tied for third with Jim Gathers but Olympic coaches decided to give preference to Smith .... after they saw Gathers secure a berth for himself in the 200 m. The longer race was easily won by Stanfield, who went home in 20.6, with Thane Baker and Gathers following in that order, both in 20.9. Lindy John Remigino (born in New York on 3 June 1931; 1.73 m. / 67 kg.) was in fact the least known of the Olympic qualifiers. Then a junior at Manhattan College, he had sharpened his competitive spirit in relay meets as well as in indoor races.

At Helsinki, Bragg too fell the victim of muscular trouble. After many years, the throne of American sprinters seemed likely to be overturned. McKenley, who was at his best in the one-lap race, chose to try the 100 m., supposedly to warm up for the 400 m. Maybe the field for the final was not in a class with those of the last three editions, yet it was such as to offer a close, fascinating race. Remigino was in the lead at the half-way point, but McKenley was coming on like a whirlwind. With a driving finish he caught Remigino at the tape and shot ahead of him just after crossing the finish line. This circumstance probably led some onlookers to believe that McKenley had won. The finish was the closest possible and the photo finish had to be supplemented by a set-square, through which it was possible to determine that Remigino's right shoulder was fractionally ahead of McKenley's torso at the tape. "Mac" was a close third, with Smith centimetres further back. The first four were all credited with 10.4. A photo-timer used as unofficial "supplementary evidence" gave a more exact and far less generous set of times for the first four: 10.79, 10.80, 10.83 and 10.84.

Andy Stanfield had no problems in the 200 m. He was clearly the class of the field and had the fastest time, 20.9, in the preliminary rounds. In the final "Mac" Bailey got a good start but Stanfield was already in the lead as they entered the straight, with Thane Baker pretty close. Stanfield, smooth and steady, won comfortably from Baker, while Jim Gathers had no trouble in securing third place. Once again, Bailey lost part of his zip in the moments that mattered most and finished no better than fourth. Stanfield equalled Owens's Olympic record (20.7).

Dillard, who had previously won the 110 m. hurdles, got a chance to add to his collection of medals as a member of the sprint relay team. In the final the Americans met unsuspected resistance from a well-drilled USSR team. The Soviets actually led over the first two legs, mainly because of their good passes. Remigino cut their lead considerably in the third leg, and Stanfield was off almost even with Vladimir Sukharyev. The Olympic 200 m. champion had no trouble in securing a safe margin and finally won comfortably. Hungary passed Britain on the last leg to take third.

1952 Olympics, Helsinki - 100 metres (21 July): Lindy Remigino (USA) 10.4 (el. time 10.79) ; 2.Herb McKenley (Jam) 10.4 (10.80); 3.Emmanuel McD.Bailey (UK) 10.4 (10.83); 4.Dean Smith (USA) 10.4 (10.84); 5.Vladimir Sukharyev (SU) 10.5 (10.88); 6.John Treloar (Aus) 10.5 (10.91). Lanes: Sukharyev 1, McKenley 2, Remigino 3, Smith 4, McDonald Bailey 5, Treloar 6.

200 metres (23 July) w +1.0: 1.Andy Stanfield (USA) 20.7 (20.81); 2.Thane Baker (USA) 20.8 (20.97); 3.Jim Gathers (USA) 20.8 (21.08); 4.Emmanuel McDonald Bailey (UK) 21.0 (21.14); 5.Leslie Laing (Jam) 21.2 (21.45); 6.Gerardo Bönnhoff (Arg) 21.3 (21.59). Lanes: Bourland 1, Stanfield 2, McD.Bailey 3, Laing 4, Gathers 5, Baker 6.

4x100 metres relay (27 July): 1.USA (D.Smith, H.Dillard, L.Remigino, A.Stanfield) 40.1 (40.26); 2.SU (B.Tokaryev, L.Kalyayev, L.Sanadze, V.Sukharyev) 40.3

(40.58); 3.Hun (L.Zarándi, G.Varásdi, G.Csányi, B.Goldoványi) 40.5 (40.83); 4.UK 40.6 (40.85); 5.Fra 40.9 (41.10); 6.CSR 41.2 (41.41). Lanes: UK 1, USA 2, SU 3, Hungary 4, CSR 5, Fra 6.

THE LUCK OF THE GAME

In discussing sport results, fans sometimes fail to fully appreciate how infinitesimal can be the difference that separates victory from defeat. The luck of the game, that is. On occasion even such an important laurel as an Olympic title may come as the result of a long series of close decisions, or "lucky" cards. Typical in this respect is the case of Lindy Remigino, winner of the 100 m. at the Helsinki Olympics. In the States he was regarded merely as a good sprinter – one of many – with a fierce competitive spirit. In the spring of 1952 there were at least three Americans who clearly excelled him as 100 m. aces: Jim Golliday, the strongest of them all, was sidelined with a muscle injury on the eve of the Olympic Trials; Andy Stanfield, another injury-prone sprinter, decided to put all his eggs in one basket, the 200 m. Art Bragg, winner of the 100 m. at the Trials in 10.5, was stopped by an injury in one of the Olympic semi-finals. Remigino, a 21-year-old medium-size sprinter of Italian (Piedmontese) extraction, went through the ordeal of the selection process almost unnoticed: fifth in the NCAA meet in 10.8; eliminated in the semi-finals at the AAU meet; second in the all-important test of the Olympic Trials in 10.6 – the same time credited to three others who finished close behind him. At Helsinki he won Olympic gold in 10.4, actually with one-hundredth of a second to spare vis-à-vis runner-up Herb McKenley. However, it must be conceded that Remigino was at his best at the right time. After all, even luck needs assistance (from man) in order to be effective. The story has a P.S. A few days after the Games, Remigino ran the 100 m. in 10.2, aided by a wind of 2.08 m/s, barely above the permissible limit.

The surprise winner of the century at Helsinki, Lindy Remigino, had a meteoric career, in the sense that he practically disappeared from the scene just as quickly as he had appeared on it. He placed sixth in the 100 m. at the 1953 AAU Championships, then failed to make the final in the same event in 1954. In later years he became a successful high school coach.

In the four-year period between Helsinki and Melbourne the select group of leading "speed merchants" also included three non-Americans: Mike Agostini of Trinidad, Hector Hogan of Australia, and Heinz Fütterer of Germany. Agostini, the offspring of a sports-minded family of Portuguese descent, was a most precocious talent. At 18 he ran the English distances in 9.4 and 21.1 (turn). An excellent starter, despite – or perhaps because of – his not so good hearing, he played a prominent role for many years. A first-rate globe-trotter with an amusing personality, at the end of his career he could match anybody's knowledge about athletes, starters and tracks from practically every corner of the world.

Hogan, known as the "Queensland Hurricane", was an Aussie of medium build who got off the marks like a bullet and used a very long stride while in high gear. Clockwise, he had his greatest day on 13 March 1954 at Sydney, when he tied Mel Patton's 100 y. world record (9.3). Later in the day he also ran the 100 m. in 10.2. The latter mark, however, could not be submitted to the IAAF since it was made in a "mixed" handicap with three men pitted against three women, the males running 100 m. and the distaff side only 100 y. (Best of the latter group was Marlene Mathews, who did 10.5). Later in the season, however, Hogan was soundly beaten in both sprints at the British Empire Games in Vancouver. Winner of the 100 y. was Agostini (9.6). Hogan also excelled as a long jumper (7.65).

The first European native who proved a consistent world-class sprinter in post-war years was Heinz Fütterer (born at Illingen-am-Rhein on 14 October 1931; 1.64 m. / 72 kg.), a former soccer player, on the small side but very compact. He first gave the measure of his ability at the international level in 1953, when he had no less than six tussles with Art Bragg of USA, ending always on the losing side, as often as not by scanty margins. In 1954 he won a double (10.5 and 20.9) at the European Championships in Bern, then went to Japan and brought a perfect season to a climax with two 10.2 clockings in the 100 m. and 20.8 in the 200 m. (full turn). His second 10.2 (Yokohama, 31 October) was accepted as a world record by the IAAF. Still strong in 1955, when he did 20.6 for the 200 m. at Cologne on a course with a light turn, Fütterer began to fade in the Olympic year 1956.

Meanwhile, Bragg, Golliday and Stanfield continued to dominate the picture in the States. On 14 May 1955 at Evanston, Illinois, the powerful Golliday equalled the world's 100 y. record (9.3). With three official watches showing 9.2, 9.3 and 9.3 and two alternates showing 9.2 and 9.4, his final time was a "fast" 9.3, if not a slow 9.2. The wind in his favour was 1.5 m/s. American experts, notably including Don Potts, wondered what Golliday might have achieved if his muscles had not failed him now and then. At his best he looked very much like the perfect sprinter.

Still in 1955 a new star appeared on the American firmament: Bobby Joe Morrow (born at Harlingen, Texas, on 15 October 1935; 1.85 m. / 75 kg.). He proved well-nigh invincible in interscholastic competition, with best times of 9.6 and 21.1 for the English distances in 1954. It may be regarded as typical of the vagaries of hand timing that he was credited with some of the fastest times of his career before his actual breakthrough on the national scene. It happened on 3 and 4 June 1955 at Abilene: on the first day he ran the English distances in 9.4 and 20.6 (around a turn) in the prelims; on the following day he won the finals in 9.1 and 20.9. All these times, save for the 9.4 mark in the century, were made with an aiding wind well beyond the permissible limit. Even so, his 9.1 (wind +3.12 m/s) equalled Patton's fastest wind-aided mark. True, over the years the winds of Texas had yielded quite a number of fast times, but here was a man who wanted to prove that the Lone Star

Bobby Morrow (USA) winning the 200 metres at the Melbourne Olympics (1956) from A. Stanfield (USA), no.88. Others from left: J.T. da Conceição (Brazil) 6th; T. Baker (USA) 3rd; B. Tokaryev (USSR) 5th and M. Agostini (Trinidad) 4th. Winner's time, 20.6.

State had sprinters who could beat the world under any circumstance. He began to prove this later in the same year at the AAU Championships in Boulder, Colorado (altitude, 1655 m.), where he won the 100 y. in 9.5, beating among others Rod Richard, who earlier in the year had scored a "metric" double at the Pan-American Games in Mexico City (10.3 and 20.7), beating Mike Agostini among others.

The year 1956 was to be one of the most eventful in the annals of sprinting. Agostini started the fireworks in March, when he sped over a new, lightning-fast track at Bakersfield, California to clock 20.1 for the 220 y. straightaway. But later in the season a well-built thoroughbred from Duke University did even better. The man in question was David William Sime (born at Paterson, NJ, on 25 July 1936; 1.88 m. / 81 kg.). Hardly known prior to 1956 (the year before his best in the century was 9.6), Sime got started in the Olympic season on 21 January at Washington, D.C. with a 9.5 century, leaving Andy Stanfield 2 m. behind. This was a new American indoor record for the 100 y., a distance seldom run in undercover meets as very few indoor arenas have a straight course of that length. Then, in outdoor meets, read-headed Dave really let himself go. Between 26 March and 9 June, counting legal marks only, he did 9.3 twice and 9.4 six times for the 100 y.; and 20.0, 20.1, 20.2, 20.3 (twice) and 20.4 for the 220 y. straightaway ! Most of these were in "cold" races in the warm Southern climate, but he probably had his greatest day at Sanger, California, on 9 June, when he beat Agostini twice, 9.3 to 9.4, in the 100 y. and 20.0 to 20.4 in the 220 y. In the latter race Sime had an ordinary start and Agostini managed to hold him back till 120 y. The wind in his favour was a legal 1.35 m/s.

With the US Olympic Trials only three weeks away, nobody would have dared to predict the exclusion of the new speedball from the Melbourne-bound team. Yet the "Blue Devil of Duke" met defeat and disaster in the meets that mattered most. At the NCAA Championships in Berkeley he was pitted against Bobby Morrow, whom he had beaten at the Drake Relays in April (9.4 to 9.5), not without the benefit of a dubious start. At Berkeley, however, the reliable Morrow won the 100 m. in 10.4 from Sime, Agostini (both 10.6) and Leamon King (10.7), who finished in that order. King had been credited with a record-equalling 9.3 for the 100 y. at Fresno a few weeks earlier. A bitter surprise awaited Sime in the 200 m. around a turn. Until then he had never run the curve in competition and whether or not this had anything to do with what followed, he did in fact pull a muscle just as he was going round the turn. Morrow won in 20.6.

That was the end of Sime's Olympic dream. True, the Melbourne Games were more than four months away, but under the rigid American system the tickets for the trip Down Under were to be assigned at Final Trials two weeks later. In the absence of his great rival, Morrow was again a double winner, with 10.3 and 20.6. The other Olympic berths went to Ira Murchison and Thane Baker (both 10.4) in the 100 m., to Baker (20.7) and Stanfield (20.9) in the 200 m. The last two thus qualified for their second trip to the Olympics. Even after the demise of the unlucky Sime, further circumstances occurred which showed up the negative side of the AAU selective system. Early in August, Berlin's "Olympiastadion" was the theatre of the CISM (Conseil International du Sport Militaire) Championships. Among the entries in the 100 m. were two Americans, stocky Willie Williams and little Ira Murchison. The former had failed at the Trials, not without the complicity of a pulled muscle. In the Berlin heats (3 August) he created quite a stir, running the metric century in 10.1, with an aiding wind of 0.7 m/s. The next day, in a semi-final, Murchison (who stood only 1.62 m. but weighed 65 kg.) returned the same time, with a plus wind of 1.0 m/s. Quite understandably, the outcome of the final was awaited with great curiosity in metric-minded Europe. The two characters in the play had dreams of a 10-flat performance ... But on 5 August the famous track was washed by the rains, which let up just an hour before the race. Murchison, an explosive starter, held a minor lead in the initial stage, but Williams had a good pick-up and finally won by about 30 cm. The winner's time was again 10.1, while Murchison was given 10.2. The wind in their favour was no more than 0.55 m/s.

Yet for some unexplained reason only the first two of the three 10.1's were ratified by the IAAF. Williams was by no means an unknown. He had won the NCAA 100 y. title twice (1953-54). He was to be heard from again in 1957, when he had wind-aided times of 9.3 and 20.3 for the English distances.

One month before the Melbourne Olympics, the new 100 m. record, 10,1, was equalled by another American, Leamon King, a smooth-striding dashman who could sometimes produce a terrific lift in the final stages. But just like Williams, he had failed at the Trials ... Morrow had a virus infection in the fall months, yet he managed to recover in time for the big test. In all his appearances at the Melbourne Cricket Ground he proved as great a sprinter as any ever seen in Olympic history. He went through the 100 m. motions without a loss, with times of 10.4 (heat), 10.3 (quarter-final), 10.3 (semi-final) and 10.5 (final). In all these races except the first he ran against the wind. In the ultimate test he battled a cold, adverse wind of 5 m/s and won by a good metre from his compatriot Thane Baker, who was also timed in 10.5. Hector Hogan of Australia finally confirmed his 9.3 (100 y.) potential and finished a very close third in 10.6, ahead of Murchison, Manfred Germar of Germany and Agostini. An automatic but unofficial timing device caught the first three in 10.62, 10.77 and 10.77. In the 200 m. Morrow ran with a bandaged thigh and ostensibly saved his energies for the last round, in which he produced the third legitimate 20.6 of his career and won from defending champion Stanfield (20.7), while Baker easily held off Agostini for third. Baker, endowed with a great competitive heart and a supreme ability in negotiating the curve, brought his tally of Olympic medals to three (two silver, one bronze). He had to wait for the relay to hit gold at last.

Once again, the Russians were the toughest rivals for USA in the 4x100 m. relay. Although clearly inferior to their American counterparts in speed aggregate, they showed such a good technique in passing the baton that the outcome looked uncertain till the last leg. After some worse-than-average changes on their part, the Americans only had a narrow lead by the time Morrow took off for the last battle against Vladimir Sukharyev. The double Olympic champion confirmed his superior vein and won easily. The winners' time was 39.5, three tenths under the previous world record, set up by Owens & Co. twenty years earlier in the Berlin Olympics. The clever Russians were rewarded with a new European record of 39.8. Germany was a distant third.

1956 Olympics, Melbourne - 100 metres (24 November) w -2.0 m/s: 1.Bobby Morrow (USA) 10.5 (autom. 10.62); 2.Thane Baker (USA) 10.5 (10.77); 3.Hector Hogan (Aus) 10.6 (10.77); 4.Ira Murchison (USA) 10.6 (10.79); 5.Manfred Germar (Ger) 10.7 (10.86); 6.Mike Agostini (Tri) 10.7 (10.88). Lanes: Murchison 3, Agostini 4, Baker 5, Morrow 6, Germar 7, Hogan 8.

200 metres (27 November) w under 2.0 m/s: 1.Bobby Morrow (USA) 20.6 (autom. 20.75); 2.Andy Stanfield (USA) 20.7 (20.97); 3.Thane Baker (USA) 20.9 (21.05); 4.Mike Agostini (Tri) 21.1 (21.35); 5.Boris Tokaryev (SU) 21.2 (21.42); 6.José Telles da Conçeicão (Bra) 21.3 (21.56). Lanes: Agostini 1, Tokaryev 2, Morrow 3, Stanfield 4, Telles da Conçeicão 5, Baker 6.

4x100 metres relay (1 December): 1.USA (I.Murchison, L.King, T.Baker, B.Morrow) 39.5 (autom. 39.60); 2.SU (B.Tokaryev, V.Sukharyev, L.Bartenyev, Y.Konovalov) 39.8 (39.93); 3.Ger (L.Knörzer, L.Pohl, H.Fütterer, M.Germar) 40.3 (40.34); 4.Ita 40.3 (40.43); 5.UK 40.6 (40.74); 6.Pol 40.6 (40.75). Lanes: Ger 1, UK 2, Ita 3, SU 4, Pol 5, USA 6.

The rising star of Europe was Manfred Germar (born at Cologne on 10 March 1935; 1.82 m. / 72 kg.), who in 1957-58 rose to heights previously unknown to Europe-born sprinters. His class was especially clear in the 200 m., at which distance he remained undefeated from 1956 till July 1960. His best times for the metric distances were 10.2, 20.6 (full turn) and 20.4 (slight turn). Unfortunately for him, the Melbourne Games found him not yet ripe, and the Rome Games four years later came when he was visibly past his peak. At the 1958 European Championships in Stockholm he won the 200 m. in 21,0 but suffered a bitter and partly unexpected defeat in the century. Making his first major international appearance in that race was a new phenom, Armin Hary (born at Quierschied, Saarland, on 22 March 1937; 1.82 m. / 71 kg.), a German citizen since 1957, when Saar became the tenth "Land" (state) of the German Federal Republic. Already a 10.4 man the year before, Hary made the grade at the 1958 German Championships, when he finished a close second to Germar in the 100 m., the time for both being 10.2. In the continental title meet at Stockholm the powerful Hary, known as an explosive starter, took what in the opinion of most onlookers was a blatant flyer and was never headed. Germar and a new British star, Peter Radford, chased him all the way and both had a strong finish, yet failed to catch Hary, who won in 10.3, with Germar and Radford next in that order, both in 10.4. Of course, there were people who said that Hary was second to none in terms of reaction time to the gun, yet such an acute observer as Sweden's Lennart Julin has aptly called the Stockholm act "The mother of all false starts".

The debate was still raging when, on the evening of 6 September, the news was flashed to the athletic world that a 21-year-old German had run the metric century in the startling time of 10 seconds flat, the wind in his favour being a negligible 0.2 m/s. This happened in the afternoon of that day at Friedrichshafen, a town on Lake Constance. And the man in question was Armin Hary. However, that high-sounding time was made in an unsanctioned race, which was run at the request of Hary and other sprinters, after the European champion had done 10.3 in the official event. Apart from technicalities, it was found that the track was sloping gently in the running direction. In a book he wrote years later, Hary himself curiously gave the following version: "As I was later informed ...all lanes had a gradient of less than 10 cms. other than the one in which I ran". Be that as it may, the time was made in an unsanctioned race, and consequently it could not be submitted to approval.

Germany's growing ascendance was confirmed in 1958 by a significant effort in the 4x100 m. relay. A quartet consisting of Manfred Steinbach, Lauer, Fütterer and Germar equalled the world record, 39.5, on 29 August at Cologne. The last two were

Armin Hary (Germany) at the tape of history's first official "10 flat" for the metric century (Zurich 1960). Heinz Müller (Switzerland) was second (10.3) and Jürgen Schüttler (Germany), extreme right, third (10.4). This was Hary's second 10.0 of the day, but the first one was annulled because of a faulty start.

1960 Olympics, Rome. Armin Hary (nearest camera) edging Dave Sime at the tape of the 100 metres. Both were timed in 10.2. Peter Radford of Britain was third (10.3).

thus seconded by a classy long jumper, Steinbach, and a would-be world record holder in the high hurdles, Lauer.

Germar and Hary found a worthy opponent in Peter Radford (born at Walsall on 20 September 1939; 1.80 m. / 61 kg.), whose emergence as an athlete looked very much like a fairy tale. At the age of 5 he contracted a serious kidney disease and for a long time he was confined to a wheelchair. The very necessity to combat such an adversity probably led him to practice sport: he began running at 12 and attained international class while still a junior. In 1958 he was fourth in the 100 y. at the British Commonwealth Games and, as previously related, third in the 100 m. at the European Championships. He invariably exhibited a great finishing power and before the year was out he was credited with 10.3 and 20.8 at the metric distances, a few days before his 19th birthday. In 1959 he was down to 9.4 in the 100 y. He had his best year in 1960: on 28 May at Wolverhampton, running on one of Britain's fastest tracks, he did 9.4 (heat) and 9.3 (final) in the 100 y., and 20.5 in the 220 y. around a turn. In all these races he was aided by a slight wind, which crept over the allowable limit only during the 9.3 century. His furlong time was ratified as a world record by the IAAF. Such a mark occurred in what was virtually a solo race as the runner-up did no better than 22.4 – a rare example in the annals of sprinting.

France had by then two sprinters of international calibre in Jocelyn Delecour (10.3 and 20.9 in 1958) and Abdoulaye Seye from Senegal, who in the pre-Olympic weeks of 1960 posted such times as 10.2 and 20.7, plus a remarkable 45.9 in the 400 m.

Italy, another country with relatively modest traditions in sprinting, joined the debate shortly before the Games with Livio Berruti (born in Torino on 19 May 1939; 1.80 m. / 66 kg.), a natural talent with the silken stride of a gazelle. He equalled the Italian 100 m. record, 10.4, at 18 years of age. In 1959 he was good enough to beat Hary in the 100 m. and Seye in the 200 m. during a hexagonal match at Duisburg. Later in the same year in Sweden he took some lessons from Ray Norton of USA but ran the 200 m. around a turn in 20.8 the only time he managed to beat his American rival.

In the States Bobby Morrow continued to reign supreme for two more years (1957-58), but in 1959 muscular ailments began to slow him down. Yet many international experts agree, even today, that his competitive record between 1955 and 1958 suffices to stamp him as one of best competitors ever seen in the annals of sprinting. In that four-year period he won all the major titles for which he vied, with only one exception – the AAU 220 y. in 1955, the year of his debut in big-time competition. Counting legitimate times only, he ran the 100 y. in 9.3 once (Austin, 14 June 1957) and in 9.4 sixteen times; the 100 m. in 10.2 seven times, the 200 m. around a turn in 20.6 three times, and the 220 y. straightaway in 20.4.

Morrow's arch rival, Dave Sime, potentially second to none of the great sprinters in pure blazing speed, had an uneven record. Yet he managed to make a good comeback in 1960. On the eve of the Rome Olympics, however, the no.1 American sprinter was Ray Norton (born on 22 September 1937 at Tulsa, Oklahoma; 1.88 m. / 91 kg.), a tall, powerful man who between 1958 and 1960 compiled a fine set of marks: 9.3 in the 100 y. three times, 10.1 in the 100 m., 20.6 in the 220 y. around a turn and 20.1 on a straight course (with 19.9 for 200 m. enroute). Other strong candidates were Charles Tidwell and Stone Johnson. The former was credited with a nifty 20.2 for 220 y. around a turn at Abilene on 16 April 1960, on a course which turned out to be 1.57 m. short. He also ran the 100 m. in 10.1, but an injury stopped him on the threshold of the Olympic Trials, which were held at Palo Alto, California. In this crucial meet Norton won the 100 m. from Frank Budd, Sime and Paul Winter, as all four were credited with 10.4. Sime actually tied for third with Winter, but later in the summer he posted a fast 10.1 and thus earned the coveted berth. Norton also won the 200 m. in a record-tying 20.5 from Stone Johnson (20.8) and Les Carney (20.9), who shut out the great Bobby Morrow (21.1). It should be added that Johnson too had a legal 20.5 in the prelims. In both these record-tying efforts the wind was nil.

Yet the most sensational of all pre-

Olympic marks were returned in Switzerland and Canada. On 21 June 1960, running on the magic Letzigrund track in Zurich, Armin Hary was credited with 10.0 for the 100 m. not once but twice! The duplicate was necessary though, as only the later mark was done under acceptable conditions. In the first race Hary took a flyer – à la Hary, as some malign commentators hastened to add. The starter had a pistol for recall in his left hand but somehow failed to use it. He later admitted his mistake and the race was annulled. Hary, who had won from Abdoulaye Seye (10.3), protested at first, then he calmed down and went back to his marks, fully determined "to show 'em". There was a new starter for the re-run, incidentally the same man who had sent another German, Martin Lauer, off to a happy 13.2 record journey over 110 m. hurdles on the same track in 1959. Only two contestants from the former race lined up alongside Hary at the start: Jürgen Schüttler of Germany and Heinz Müller of Switzerland. This time Hary was off correctly. With his characteristic early pick-up he soon put daylight between himself and the opposition, then continued to run hard till the end. He was rewarded with another "even time" clocking, his third since 1958, but for official purposes the first in the history of the metric century. Müller (10.3) and Schüttler (10.4) respectively equalled and bettered their previous bests. The three official

1960 Olympics, Rome: Livio Berruti (Italy) becomes the first European sprinter to win the 200 m. crown, equalling the world record, 20.5. Les Carney (USA), nearest camera, is second, and Abdoulaye Seye (Fra), centre, is third.

watches on Hary showed 10.0, 10.0 and 10.1. The favourable wind was 0.9 m/s and the Longines electric timer showed 10.25 (In the preceding race the reading was 10.16).

History's second official "10 flat" came a few weeks later, on 15 July at Saskatoon, Canada, and was achieved by a Canadian, Harry Jerome (born at Prince Albert, Saskatchewan on 30 September 1940; 1.80 m. / 77 kg.). He had previously shown his class in several US meets, yet his record, made in the Canadian Olympic Trials, caused quite a stir. Conditions were checked and found correct: a legal aiding wind of 1.8 m/s. and a distance which turned out to be 5 cm. long. Jerome's comment was as simple as this: "I got a good start, and I felt like running".

The Rome Olympics came at the right time to solve the riddle: "Who was the World's Fastest Human anno 1960?" When the chips were down, Hary was the name. His early acceleration impressed experienced American observers as truly phenomenal. Furthermore, he displayed a combination of arrogance and coolness such as only few sprint "demons" can command. In the second quarter-final Hary lowered the Olympic record to 10.2 in winning from Sime, 10.3 (adverse wind 0.32 m/s). A photo-timer caught them in 10.32 and 10.37 respectively. In the first of the semi-finals Harry Jerome was eliminated – he was in front when he pulled a muscle and had to give up at 50 metres. In the final the two men regarded by many as the top contenders were curiously placed a maximum distance apart – Sime in lane 1 and Hary in lane 6. At the first start both men appeared to jump, but the gun was not fired. At the next attempt Hary broke and the vigilant starter, Primo Pedrazzini, did not let him go away with it and the recall gun was fired. (There was a rumour that Signor Pedrazzini had spent a sleepless night, anticipating the heavy task awaiting him in connection with Hary's "Blitz Start"). At the next attempt Hary was off well and correctly. The interval between "pronti" (set) and the gun was a normal 1.9 secs. The German built up a sizable lead in the early part of the race. Even the great Sime appeared to be hopelessly out of it at the half-way mark. But in the closing stage the "Blue Devil of Duke" came back like a whirlwind and made up valuable ground on Hary. At the tape, however, the German was still ahead by a narrow but visible margin. Officially both were timed in 10.2, but an automatic timer gave 10.32 for Hary and 10.35 for Sime. Peter Radford had an unimpressive getaway and a grand finish, which gave him a close third, just ahead of Enrique Figuerola of Cuba and Frank Budd of USA, as all three were timed in 10.3. (The automatic timer was more discerning: 10.42, 10.44 and 10.46). Ray Norton, far from his best form, was a disappointing sixth. Sime, who had never won a major title at home, certainly closed his career on a high note. Hary did not run the 200 m., a distance he had often by-passed in German meets too, even though he had marks of 20.5 (slight turn) and 20.9 (full turn). Livio Berruti, Italy's hope, had chosen to concentrate on the 200 m. He came to the Olympic rendez-vous in the form of his lifetime, with a fresh personal best of 20.7 (plus an earlier 10.2 m. in the 100 m.) and plenty of self-confidence. He had lost once, to Peter Radford in the England vs. Italy match at London's White City (10.6 to 10.4), but the century was clearly not his forte.

In the early rounds of the 200 m. (2 September) Berruti looked sharp, with 21.0 (heat) and 20.7 (quarter-final). The following day, on a windless afternoon, he offered a superlative display of his ability as a curve-runner. In his semi-final the 21-year-old Italian, wearing his customary sun glasses, was pitted against Norton, Johnson and Radford, i.e. the three men who held the official world record at 20.5 (the Briton had done it over the longer 220 y. course). That could hardly be regarded as a piece of good seeding. Berruti was thus confronted with the task of beating at least one of the three record holders in order to make the final. He ran an inspired race and beat them all! He came off the turn with a decisive lead and went home in 20.5, equalling the world record. Norton was second (20.7) ahead of Johnson (20.8). Radford put on a game effort but could do no better than fourth (20.9) and was eliminated. The other "semi" was not so hectic: Seye won in 20.8 from Marian Foik of Poland (21.0) and Les Carney (21.1), who was believed to be America's third string. The final was to follow less than 3 hours later and in the intervening time Berruti, who had created quite a bedlam with his superb effort in the "semi", thought it advisable to keep quiet and have a rest ... watching his rivals in their warm-up work. The line-up from the inside was as follows: Foik, Seye, Johnson, Berruti, Norton and Carney. There was one jump, with both Johnson and Berruti getting away but neither was charged. At the next start, Berruti blazed the turn to lead into the straight. Norton also ran around the turn hard and was second with 80 m. to go. At that stage, however, he had nothing left. Johnson ran poorly from the beginning and was never in the hunt. It was later learnt that he ran with a temperature. Carney unexpectedly proved the best of the Americans and closed slightly on Berruti in the final part of the race. Seye probably ran too easily on the turn, but later made up ground and finished a brilliant third ahead of the fast closing Foik. Closing up the rear were Johnson and Norton, well below their pre-meet credentials. The winner duplicated his record time, 20.5, while Carney was timed in 20.6. It should be noted that the electric timer used as a reserve caught Berruti in 20.62 (as opposed to 20.65 in the semi-final).

Among those who failed to reach the 200 m. final was Edward Jefferys of South Africa, who in March at Pretoria (altitude, 1333 m.) had run 220 y. on a straight course in 20.2 (200 m. time, 20.1). The Rome events certainly raised the stock of European sprinters as no previous Olympics had ever done. Hary had emulated Harold Abrahams in the century, and Berruti was the first European to strike gold in the 200 m. The Americans, although deprived of a man like Charles Tidwell, were nonetheless clever in defeat as they had placed three men in each of the two finals.

In the first round of the 4x100 m. relay a crack German quartet tied the world record, 39.5 (autom. timer 39.61) and clearly indicated it was out to challenge the traditional supremacy of USA. The latter, despite indifferent passing, won its heat in 39.7. The Germans took the first semi-final in 39.7 and the American did likewise in the second, also in 39.7. In the decisive race the first pass between Frank Budd and Ray Norton was clearly out of the zone, yet the latter continued to run and actually took the lead – only

Two sprint kings from different generations get together during the 1960 Olympics in Rome: Armin Hary and Jesse Owens.

to lose ground with another bad pass. Dave Sime started two metres behind Martin Lauer and finally overhauled him to hit the tape nearly a metre in front, time 39.4. But all was in vain as USA was disqualified. The Germans were therefore the official winners, equalling their world record time (39.5) of the heats. The automatic device better reflected the actual time differential between the first two finishers: USA 39.59, Germany 39.66. The USSR, with only fair sprinters but excellent passing, collected its third consecutive silver medal.

1960 Olympics, Rome - 100 metres (1 September) w under 2.0 m/s: 1.Armin Hary (Ger) 10.2 (autom. 10.32); 2.Dave Sime (USA) 10.2 (10.35); 3.Peter Radford (UK) 10.3 (10.42); 4.Enrique Figuerola (Cub) 10.3 (10.44); 5.Frank Budd (USA) 10.3 (10.46); 6.Ray Norton (USA) 10.4 (10.50). Lanes: Sime 1, Norton 2, Budd 3, Figuerola 4, Radford 5, Hary 6.

200 metres (3 September) w under 2.0 m/s: 1.Livio Berruti (Ita) 20.5 (autom. 20.62); 2.Les Carney (USA) 20.6 (20.69); 3.Abdoulaye Seye (Fra) 20.7 (20.83); 4.Marian Foik (Pol) 20.8 (20.90); 5.Stone Johnson (USA) 20.8 (20.93); 6.Ray Norton (USA) 20.8 (21.09). Lanes: Foik 2, Seye 3, Johnson 4, Berruti 5, Norton 6, Carney 7.

4x100 metres relay (8 September): 1.Ger (B.Cullmann, A.Hary, W.Mahlendorf, M.Lauer) 39.5 (autom. 39.66); 2.SU (G.Kosanov, L. Bartenyev, Y. Konovalov, E.Ozolin) 40.1 (40.24); 3.UK (P.Radford, D.Jones, D.Segal, N. Whitehead) 40.2 (40.32); 4.Ita 40.2 (40.33); 5.Ven 40.7 (40.83). Disqualified: USA (Frank Budd, Ray Norton, Stone Johnson, Dave Sime) (39.4 / 39.59). Lanes: USA (disq.)2, Ven 3, Ita 4, SU 5, Ger 6, UK 7.

Just about the only notable race of post-Olympic meets was in the Italy vs. France match at Milan, with Abdoulaye Seye scoring a narrow win over Berruti in the 200 m. (slight curve). Time for both, 20.7. The Senegal-born Frenchman was just as good, if not better, in the one-lap event (45.7 earlier in the season).

"DON'T LET THE BOY DO THAT!"

100 and 200 metres obviously belong to one and the same family, were it only for the fact that both are entirely in the sphere of anaerobic running. Even so, the two distances imply partly different problems and consequently quite a few sprinters show a marked penchant for one or the other. Chef-de-file of those who preferred the longer distance is, of course, Michael Johnson, who committed to history what many of us consider the "record of records" – 19.32 for the 200 – but seemingly neglected the 100, to the point of (almost) never trying it in high-class competition.

Livio Berruti of Italy also showed a marked preference for the 200 throughout his career, though not to the same extent as Johnson. A fluid curve runner, in 1960 Berruti became the first European to win the 200 in the Olympics, and did so after equalling the world record twice (semi and final) in the same afternoon.

Berruti first entered Italy's coaching scheme in 1956, aged 17. The Italian Athletics Federation (FIDAL) has in its archives a letter which was then sent to the head of the national coaching department by Michele Berruti, Livio's father. He had heard and even read that his offspring was being led towards training for the 200 metres, in addition to the 100, "the only event for which I have given my assent and for which he joined your group". "If what I heard is true - wrote Sig. Berruti Sr. - please note that I strongly object to such a design and will never allow him to practise an event (the 200) which I consider as too exacting for his physique and his age and consequently harmful to this health".

Notwithstanding his vehement opposition, coaches did not retreat, nor did Livio himself. To the benefit of all concerned, including I dare say even Livio's loving father.

THE ADVENT OF ELECTRIC TIMING

The 1912 Games in Stockholm marked a notable advance in more than one way. True Olympic spirit, revived four years earlier in London, was further enhanced for the benefit of both competitors and officials, thanks to the great Swedish tradition and to the efforts of untiring organizers.

Timing in athletics events was manual, to the tenth of a second; in sprint events only the winner's time in each race was made official. However, subsidiary evidence was supplied by a semi-automatic apparatus conceived by a Swede, R.Carlstedt, who called for a connection with a still camera, placed high up alongside the finish line. This was in a rudimentary way the fore-runner of nowadays photo-finish. Semi-automatic times taken in the Stockholm Games were not divulged.

In the editions of 1920, 1924 and 1928 timing devices were essentially similar, save for a return to fifths-of-a-second. At the 1932 Olympics in Los Angeles, the timing was entrusted for the first time to a private enterprise: Omega Company, which supplied 30 stopwatches, all tested and approved as per IAAF prescriptions. The timers' crew was headed by Ottó Misángyi of Hungary. In addition to manual watches, timers also used another instrument apt to time finishes electrically in hundredths-of-a-second.

Such a device was called Kirby Two-Eyed Camera and was named after its inventor, Gustavus T. Kirby, a real expert in all matters concerned with athletics. He had officiated as a judge at the 1904 Olympics in St.Louis, then president of the American Olympic Committee and member of the IAAF Technical Commmission. The instrument he devised was made by Western Electric Co. of New York and was also known as Kodak-Bell Lab's Camera after the name of the company that produced it under the trademark ERPI (Electrical Research Products Inc.), belonging to the Bell group.

The IAAF had discussed the timing problem at its Berlin Convention on 20 and 21 May 1930. The German Athletics Federation proposed its Löbner electric timing, used at the Amsterdam Olympics (1928). They hoped it would be in force also at Los Angeles and suggested that the Rules and Records Commission approve as world records only electrical times taken with such an instrument. The IAAF accepted the proposal only in part and decided that the last paragraph of Rule 10 be replaced with the following one: "One of the three abovementioned stopwatches (minimum required for the ratification of a world record) can be replaced by an electric timer supplied by the organizers, provided that such an instrument has been accepted by the federation of the country acting as host".

Mr. Kirby asked that in the rule book the word "mechanic" (referring to the stopwatch) be replaced with "electrical". This was consented when the Congress ratified the proposal on 21 May 1930. That's how the word "electrical", referred to timing, officially entered the IAAF rule book.

At the 1932 Olympics in Los Angeles the Kirby Two-Eyed Camera was used only as a finish judge. Its use proved precious to throw light into close finishes, notably including that of the men's 100-metre final in which Eddie Tolan just prevailed over Ralph Metcalfe.

G.P.

SPEED DEMONS GALORE. BOB HAYES, THE BRIGHTEST STAR

This period was characterized by important technical innovations and also by a partial shift in the balance of powers, race-wise at least. First of all, the adoption at the international level of automatic electrical timing in hundredths of a second. According to IAAF rules, this was to be assured with "equipment which is started automatically by the starter's gun and which records the finish time automatically". As previously related, something of the kind had been experimented in major Games as early as in 1932 (Los Angeles Olympics), but only as an aid to official manual timing, mainly to verify and possibly correct place differentials. Starting with the 1968 Olympics in Mexico City, automatic timing became official, thus replacing the traditional hand timing. In inverted roles, the latter was to be used merely as a back-up in case of malfunction of the electrical apparatus. At the Mexico Olympics the IAAF allowed a 0.05 sec. bonus to compensate for the reaction time, and marks thus obtained were rounded off to the tenth. The era of automatic timing without adjustments began with the Munich Olympics (1972).

It is commonly accepted that hand times are faster than automatic ones. This is probably due to the fact that timers, stationed alongside the finish line, tend to anticipate a runner's finish, rather than allow for the same delay as is caused by reaction to the flash of the starter's gun, obviously fired 100 or more metres away from the timers' stand. Experiments made during the Munich Olympics revealed an average plus of 0.24 sec. in the case of a 100 m. race timed automatically. Under this assumption, a "manual" 10.3 should be regarded as the theoretical equivalent of 10.54 with auto timing. However, it would be dangerous to take this as a fully reliable guideline, since hand timing practices varied from one country to another, sometimes even within the same country. In some cases, timers were so trained that their verdicts equated rather consistently with automatic times; in other areas the difference could be as great as three tenths of a second. In any case, the introduction of automatic timing resulted in clearly more reliable verdicts, especially in the sprint races where the relative magnitude of error under hand timing was relatively greater.

The second relevant factor concerned tracks. Towards the end of the Sixties, conventional cinder tracks were gradually replaced by surfaces in synthetic materials. These so-called "all-weather tracks" (initially known under their first trade name of "Tartan") soon proved more consistent and faster than the old cinder ones. The advantages derived from this innovation were certainly great, although obviously difficult to evaluate in actual fractions of time.

The third factor regarded the growing impact of negro sprinters, who during this period gradually outshone their white colleagues. Of course there had been a black victor in the Olympics as early as in 1932 (Eddie Tolan), but in the second half of the Sixties the trend became more and more evident, so much in fact that the eight finalists of the 100 m. at the Mexico Olympics (1968) were all black! This change was particularly evident in USA. Since Bobby Morrow's 100 / 200 m. double at Melbourne (1956) and Dave Sime's second place in the 100 m. in Rome (1960) no white sprinter from USA has ever won a medal in an Olympic sprint final! As an eyewitness to the 1976 and 1980 US Olympic Trials in Eugene, Oregon, I noticed that non-black sprinters were reduced to a negligible minority even in terms of quantity, and no one of them would usually advance beyond the semi-finals. If one considers that whites account for 75 % of the US population and blacks for only 12 %, it seems reasonable to assume that most Caucasians attending colleges and universities have chosen to stay away from the sprints, obviously scared by the prowess of their black brothers. In the period under consideration the best specimens of the white race in this department came from Europe: after Hary and Berruti, the greatest menace to black supremacy was provided by the likes of Borzov, Mennea and Wells.

FURTHER ON ELECTRIC TIMING

The 1964 Olympics, held in Tokyo, were featured among other things by an event destined to be identified as an important milestone in the history of athletics – a further step towards the final demise of hand timing. For the first time, the IAAF decided to accept as official all automatic times registered by Seko. However, the international organ intended to move gradually in this direction and thus requested that such verdicts be released in tenths of a second, after calculating a bonus of 0.05, as a supposed compensation of the timer's reaction time to the gun, and rounding off to the traditional tenth (by defect from 0.00 through 0.04 and by excess from 0.05 through 0.09). Times were released as official only after such adjustments. The new IAAF policy, initially applicable only to marks made in the Olympics, remained in force till May 1st, 1971.

The time of the 100 metre final at the 1964 Olympics in Tokyo, won by Robert Hayes of USA, was officialized as 10.0. This resulted from an adjustment by defect of the original 10.06. With the deduction of the 0.05 bonus this was the equivalent of a fast 9.9, maybe 9.8. (At first the photo-finish was read as 10.05, which on the basis of the afore-mentioned conversions wouldn't change things a bit).

Sometime later, when somebody deemed it advisable to do full justice to the great American sprinter, Japanese officials revealed the actual hand times taken for Hayes in that race: two 9.9's and one 9.8 ! It was therefore by plain injustice that he had been officially credited with the slower version.

Several commentators wrote that Hayes had been faster than anyone else up to that time. In fact one had to wait till 1984 to see a faster time in an Olympic final held at or near sea level (9.99 by Carl Lewis in Los Angeles). In the intervening time, however, synthetic tracks had entered the game. In its convention of 25 August 1970 in Stockholm the IAAF Technical Commission had partly amended its rule, and the new form was to be introduced on May 1st, 1971 and be therefore in use at the 1972 Olympics. Rule 119, paragraph 6, now reads thus: "Fully automatic electrical timekeeping equipment shall be used in the Olympic Games, World Championships and, wherever possible, in all Area and group Championships. Whenever fully automatic electrical timekeeping equipment is used at any meeting, the time recorded shall be the official time".

It was further decided that in all running events up to and including the 10,000 metres, photo-finish times would be read in hundredths of a second and registered as such. Manual timing would still be used but only as a reserve in case of malfunctioning of the automatic device.

Effective January 1st 1977 the Records Commission would take into consideration fully automatic times only in races up to and including the 400 metres. For all longer distances, up to and including the 10,000 metres, the same timing system was to become effective as of January 1st, 1981. After such a date, therefore, only results registered with fully automatic timing would be ratified as official.

In its Rome Convention of 1974, held in connection with the European Championships, the IAAF decided that the first list of world records registered with fully automatic timing would be officialized on January 1st, 1975 and have, wherever possible, a retroactive effect.

The first world record for the 100 metres in the new era (fully automatic timing) was 9.95, by Jim Hines of USA at the 1968 Olympics in Mexico City.

G.P.

As it was, it fell to black Americans to stage a counter-attack after the bitter defeats suffered by Uncle Sam in the 1960 Olympics. First to lead the "vengeance parade" was Francis "Frank" Budd (born at Long Branch, NJ, on 20 July 1939; 1.78 m. / 76 kg.). A year after finishing fifth in the 100 m. in Rome, this compact sprinter sped to a new world record of 9.2 for the 100 y. It happened in the AAU Championships in New York on 24 June 1961 (an automatic Bulova timer caught him in 9.36). This broke a long sequence of 9.3 clockings, beginning with Mel Patton's first (1948) and lately including no less than four by Dennis Johnson of Jamaica, between March and May 1961. The same post-Olympic year was also featured by a new world record in the 4x100 m. relay, made in the USSR vs. USA dual in Moscow, third edition of what was then the most widely advertised meet of the international track menu. The guests - Hayes Jones, Frank Budd, Charles Frazier and Paul Drayton - won in 39.1. Even more surprising perhaps was the time of the host team, 39.4, since Edvin Ozolin, Nikolay Politiko, Yuriy Konovalov and Leonid Bartenyev were good but not exceptional sprinters. A year later, at the European Championships in Belgrade, the Russians inexplicably flopped, failing to make the final. Germany, with Germar in the anchor leg, nipped Poland for the title (both 39.5).

A new IAAF rule introduced in 1960 made the full lap (i.e. two turns) course mandatory for any record set in the sprint relay. Shortly before the Tokyo Olympics (1964), however, this disadvantage was counter-balanced by a liberalization in another sense: "Members of a team other than the first runner may commence running not more than 10 m. outside the take-over zone" (obviously with the exchange still occurring inside said zone). The advantages of this innovation first became apparent in the France vs. Italy dual at Annecy in 1964, when both teams broke the European record, with the French winning by one tenth in 39.2.

Harry Jerome, eager to avenge his unlucky show in the crucial part of 1960, had in the meantime won more confidence with a couple of 9.2 clockings for the 100 y. in 1962, then equal to Budd's world record.

Olympic 100 m. final in Tokyo (1964), the first with eight sprinters in the game. From left to right: M. Pender (USA), tied for 6th; T. Robinson (Bah) 8th; W. Maniak (Pol) 4th; H.Jerome (Can) 3rd; G. Kone (Ivory Coast) tied for 6th; E.Figuerola (Cuba) 2nd; H.Schumann (Ger) 5th; and Bob Hayes (USA) 1st in 10.0, equalling the world record.

And in 1964 he won the NCAA title in the metric century, clocking 10.1 in both semi and final. In the meantime, two exceptional talents had come to the fore: Bob Hayes and Henry Carr, great physical specimens although quite different from each other. Robert Lee "Bob" Hayes (born on 20 December 1942 at Jacksonville, Florida; died on 18 September 2002 at Jacksonville; 1.82 m. / 86 kg.) was essentially a power runner, endowed with a tremendous pick-up which made him almost unbeatable in the century. He ran the furlong on relatively rare occasions yet proved capable of challenging the world's best even at that distance. In 1961 he emerged practically from nowhere to chalk up times of 9.3 and 20.1 (straight course) for the English distances. In the next three years he was unquestionably the world's fastest 100 y. / 100 m. man. Between 1963 and 1964 he was caught in 9.1 for the 100 y. on four occasions, but for some reason only one of these clockings was ratified as a world record by the IAAF, namely his 9.1 in winning the AAU title on a rubberized asphalt track at St.Louis on 21 June 1963, aided by a legal wind of 0.85 m/s. Undefeated in the century in 1963-64, he went to the Tokyo Olympics as an odds-on favourite.

In addition to Jerome, the opposition notably included Enrique Figuerola of Cuba (born on 25 July 1938 at Santiago de Cuba; 1.67 m. 67 kg.), the stocky little fellow who had placed fourth in the 100 m. at the Rome Olympics. In 1963 he won the 100 m. at the Pan-American Games in São Paulo (10.46), beating Ira Murchison of USA among others. He rounded into top form during a European tour in the summer of 1964, with a new personal best of 10.1 for 100 m. at Tartu and a victory in the English AAA meet over 100 y. (9.4). Another interesting prospect was Horacio Esteves of Venezuela, an Olympic semi-finalist in 1960 at the age of nineteen. In 1964, shortly before the Tokyo Olympics, he made the headlines by running history's third official 10-flat for 100 m. on 15 August at Caracas (922 m. above sea level). At the last moment, an ill-timed injury kept him away from the Tokyo rendez-vous.

When the chips were down, nobody was able to make an impression on the formidable Hayes. On the Tokyo track – which was to remain the last "conventional" surface used in the Olympics – he lost no time in laying his cards on the table. In his semi-final of the 100 m. he sped to a blistering 9.9, aided by a wind of 5.3 m/s. (The actual automatic time was 9.91). In the final, later in the same day (15 October), he and Figuerola were off well, then Hayes "exploded" and soon gained a full one-metre lead, which he increased to about 2 m. at the end of the race. One commentator described his margin of victory as "almost insulting to an Olympic final field". His official time was announced as a record equalling 10.0. In fact, his actual time was an automatic 10.06, which made his effort clearly superior in intrinsic value to all previous 10-flat marks returned with hand timing. Figuerola just nipped Jerome for second as both were officially credited with 10.2 (auto times, 10.25 and 10.27 respectively). The aiding wind was an allowable 1.03 m/s. For the first time in Olympic history, the number of 100 m. finalists was up to eight, a norm that has been followed ever since.

In Tokyo the two greatest US sprinters, Bob Hayes and Henry Carr, took different paths. The former concentrated on the century, whereas the latter only appeared at his favourite distance, the 200 m. Carr (born on 27 November 1942 in Momtgomery, Alabama; 1.90 m. / 84 kg.) was a powerful yet smooth runner. Like Jesse Owens, he came from the "Deep South" and, like Owens, he emerged as a speed demon while living in the Middle West, namely at Detroit, capital of the automobile. Consequently and almost inevitably he was defined "the fastest Car(r) ever to come out of Detroit". At nineteen he ran the English distances in 9.5, 20.6 (straight track) and 47.8. By then, however, Americans had abandoned their traditional 220 y. straightaway in favour of the Olympic (one turn) course. After his High School days in the Middle West, Carr moved to a college in Arizona. In 1963, at Tempe, he ran the 220 y. round a turn in a record shattering 20.3 and on 4 April 1964, still at Tempe, he improved to 20.2, aided by a wind of 0.5 m/s. On the eve of the Tokyo Games the only man who looked capable of giving him something to think about was Paul Drayton. In fact, the latter had done more than just that at the final US Olympic Trials in Los Angeles one month before the Games. On that occasion Carr had the only gloomy day of his 1964 season, finishing no better than fourth in 20.8 (200 m.), while Drayton won in 20.4 from Dick Stebbins (20.5) and Bob Hayes (20.7). According to one report, in the closing stage "Hayes was gazing over at Carr in disbelief at his poor form". As the Games drew nearer, the selectors felt that Carr was in reasonable shape. And Hayes indirectly helped them by choosing to stay away from the 200.

In the Tokyo final of the 200 m. (17 October) Carr was not to be denied. Running in the favourable lane 7, against a wind of 0.78 m/s in the stretch, he disposed of his rivals as he pleased to win in 20.3 (actual auto time, 20.36) from Drayton, 20.5, and Edwin Roberts of Trinidad, 20.6 (or 20.58 and 20.63 respectively). Jerome was fourth in 20.7 (20.79) and defending champion Livio Berruti of Italy was fifth in 20.8 (20.83). The last named had ostensibly "taken ten" after his 1960 victory in Rome, yet his Tokyo race in the unfavourable lane 1 amounted to one of his best efforts ever.

Clock-wise at least, Herny Carr outshone the great Herb McKenley as a "complete" sprinter. In addition to 9.3 (100 y.), 10.2 (100 m.) and 20.2 (220 y.) in the "pure" sprints, he had a significant 45.4 in the 400 m.

In Tokyo the customary US victory in the sprint relay hung in the balance till the last exchange. Anchor leg man Bob Hayes, the "World's Fastest Human", had instructed his team-mates before the race in simple terms: "Just give it to me close". But Paul Drayton, Gerry Ashworth and Dick Stebbins were far from flawless in their "stick-work" (US track jargon for baton passing) and by the time Hayes received the baton the team was only fourth, about 3 m. behind France, the leader. But within a few seconds the large crowd was treated to a rare spectacle of explosive speed: the phenomenal Hayes not only closed the 3-metre gap but finally won by a similar margin, giving his team the gold medal and a new world record: 39.0 (auto time 39.06). Poland (39.3), France (39.3) and Jamaica (39.4) came next in that order. A time of 8.6 has been often quoted for Hayes' anchor leg.

1964 Olympics, Tokyo - 100 metres (15 October) w + 1.03 m/s: 1. Bob Hayes (USA) 10.0 (autom. 10.06); 2. Enrique Figuerola (Cub) 10.2 (10.25); 3.Harry Jerome (Can) 10.2 (10.27); 4.Wieslaw Maniak (Pol) 10.4(10.42); 5.Heinz Schumann (Ger) 10.4 (10.46); 6. (tie) Gaoussou Kone (IC) 10.4 (10.47) and Mel Pender (USA) 10.4 (10.47); 8.Thomas Robinson (Bah) 10.5 (10.57). Lanes: Hayes 1, Schumann 2, Figuerola 3, Kone 4, Jerome 5, Maniak 6, Robinson 7, Pender 8.

200 metres (17 October) - 0.78 m/s: 1.Henry Carr (USA) 20.3 (autom. 20.36); 2.Paul Drayton (USA) 20.5 (20.58); 3.Edwin Roberts (Tri) 20.6 (20.63); 4.Harry Jerome (Can) 20.7 (20.79); 5.Livio Berruti (Ita) 20.8 (20.83) 6.Marian Foik (Pol) 20.8 (20.83); 7.Dick Stebbins (USA) 20.8 (20.89); 8.Sergio Ottolina (Ita) 20.9 (20.94). Lanes: Berruti 1, Ottolina 2, Jerome 3, Foik 4, Drayton 5, Stebbins 6, Carr 7, Roberts 8.

4x100 metre relay (21 October): 1.USA (P.Drayton, G.Ashworth, D.Stebbins, B.Hayes) 39.0 (autom. 39.06); 2.Pol (A. Zielinski, W.Maniak, M.Foik, M.Dudziak) 39.3 (39.36); 3.Fra (P.Genevay, B.Laidebeur, C. Piquemal, J.Delecour) 39.3 (39.36); 4.Jam 39.4 (39.49), 5.SU 39.4 (39.50), 6.Ven 39.5 (39.53); 7.Ita 39.5 (39.54), 8. UK 39.6 (39.69). Lanes: UK 1, Fra 2, Ita 3, Jam 4, Ven 5, Pol 6, USA 7, SU 8.

The Tokyo relay was Hayes' final race. He turned to pro football right after that and eventually became one of the great players of that game. Unfortunately, in later years he ran into trouble with the law for possession and trafficking in illegal drugs and had to serve a two-year jail term. He died just before turning 60.

Henry Carr also chose to call it quits after the 1964 Olympics. He too went on to a good but not exceptional career in pro football. A devout Christian, he later worked as a lay preacher. Many of us still wonder what he could have done as a full-time one-lap runner. In Tokyo he ran a 44.5 anchor leg to lead USA to a new 4x400 m. world record of 3:00.7.

"STILL THE FASTEST EVER?"

Such was the title of an article which appeared in the American magazine "Track & Field News" at the time of Bob Hayes' death late in 2002. The question was posed to four experts. What follows is a synthesis of their answers.

Cordner Nelson (with his brother Bert one of the founding editors of T&FN). "I firmly believe Bob Hayes had the most natural speed of any sprinter in the entire history of track. Today's sprinters run faster, but on artificial surfaces much faster than anything Hayes knew. Today's sprinters are pros who train year-round, while he spent only about three months on the track". Jim Dunaway (Eastern Editor of T&FN): "I think of Bob Hayes as some kind of sprinting genius. He had none of the benefits of today's scientific knowledge about diet, running technique, shoes and so forth. And he won the big races not by inches, but by yards. I don't think I've yet seen anyone capable of beating him over 100 m. at his best".

R.L. Quercetani (European Editor of T&FN) "I just cannot remember a sprinter who outshone his contemporaries as insultingly as Hayes in his banner years. Nonpareil in the century, he ran the furlong but sparingly, yet he was 2-1 vis-à-vis Henry Carr, then WR holder at that distance. Most probably the strongest 100 m. man ever seen in the long era of conventional tracks, but I am still not prepared to give him the nod vis-à-vis Carl Lewis, since champions can rightly be valued only for what they did under the conditions existing in their time and age."

Howard Schmertz (director of the famous "Millrose Games"). "I saw him run 60 y. at our 1964 indoor Games. He was 2 y. back after a sluggish start and was still a yard behind Sam Perry, "New York's Fastest Human", with 20 y. to go. But Hayes, driving with his head down, caught his rival in the final stride and averted a stunning defeat with a powerful desperate lunge. Any sprinter who could win against a quality field in this fashion must be the World's Fastest Human. And none of the great sprinters I have seen since have changed my opinion".

In the late Sixties, good "merchants of speed" could be found in several parts of the world. Enrique Figuerola had revived a Cuban tradition born in the Twenties with José Barrientos. In 1966 he won the Central American and Caribbean title in 10.2 and the following year he posted a record-equalling 10.0 at Budapest. Even Asia had some notable sprinters, like Hideo Iijima of Japan (10.1 in 1964) and Chen Chia-chuan of China, who in 1965 at Chungking (Chongqing in the Pinyin phonetic alphabet) was credited with 10.0 in the 100 m., a mark the IAAF could not take into consideration, since the Chinese People's Republic was not a member of the international body at that time.

Harry Jerome probably had his luckiest season in 1966. First he tied Hayes' world record for the 100 y., 9.1, at the Canadian Championship, with negligible wind assistance (0,5 m/s). Then he won the same event at the Commonwealth Games with 9.41 (automatic timing). In Europe, France had by the same time a promising sprinter hailing from Guadeloupe, Roger Bambuck, who in 1966 won the 200 m. at the European Championships in Budapest, thereby becoming the first black athlete to win a European sprint title. In the late Eighties, Bambuck was to become Minister of Sports and Recreation in the French Government.

Halfway between the Tokyo and the Mexico Olympics, two exceptional talents emerged in USA: Jim Hines and Tommie Smith. The former (born on 10 September 1946 at Dumas, Arkansas; 1.83 m. / 81 kg.) was a 9.4 performer at eighteen. He was coached at Texas Southern by former Olympic sprint champion Bobby Morrow. Although hampered for some time by a false start problem, he eventually developed into a top-class sprinter. In 1967 he "exploded" with record equalling performances in both 100 y. (9.1 at Houston) and 100 m. (10.0 at Modesto). In the latter race he was extended by Willie Turner, also timed in 10.0. Shortly afterwards, another up-and-coming star, Charles Greene (born on 21 March 1945; 1.73 m. / 69 kg.) took some advantage of the rarefied atmosphere of Provo, Utah (1387 m.) to clock 9.1 for the 100 y. An automatic timer caught him in 9.21, which

1968 Olympics, Mexico City. 100 m. final. Midway in the race, the field is tightly bunched. At the tape, Jim Hines (lane 3) is clearly ahead of Lennox Miller (lane 4), Charlie Greene (lane 1), Pablo Montes (lane 2), who finished next in that order. The winner's time was 9.95, the first official sub-10 secs. as per automatic timing.

Tommie "Jet" Smith (USA), one of the All Time "Greats" in the 200 m.

was to remain the fastest auto-time ever registered for the time-honoured English distance. In 1976 all imperial distances except the mile would be dropped from the official list of world records.

Tommie Smith (born at Acworth, Texas, on 5 June 1944; 1.90 m. / 84 kg.) is still regarded as one of the most talented sprinters in the annals of track. In terms of sustained speed he was arguably the greatest of all. At 20 he was capable of 21.0 (200 m.) and 46.5 (440 y.). Like Carr, he would have discovered new worlds in the one-lap event, but in his adult years he generally stayed away from that distance – with one serious, highly significant exception, a head-to-head confrontation with Lee Evans at San Jose in 1967. The race, over a quarter-mile, was won by Smith in 44.8, a new world record, with Evans second in 45.3. (Within a year, Evans was to become the master of that event and bring the metric world record down to 43.8). Smith was in any case instrumental in raising 200 m. running to a new dimension. In this respect he began to astound experts in 1966, while a student at San Jose State under Bud Winter, a dedicated and ebullient coach. On 7 May of that year, on his home track at San Jose, "Tommie Jet", as he was called, was credited with an incredible 19.5 for 220 y. straightaway – an average speed of 37.139 km. per hour. A truly superlative effort, even if favoured by a wind of 1.9 m/s in the stretch and sanctioned by somewhat controversial readings: the watches showed 19.4, 19.5 and 19.6 at 200 m., 19.5, 19.5 and 19.6 at 220 y. Later in the season, on 11 June at Sacramento, Smith ran the same distance round a turn in 20.0 (wind nil), virtually the first sub-20 secs. effort if converted to its 200 m. equivalent.

The 1968 Olympics were to be held at Mexico City, located some 2250 m. above sea level. This very fact created great expectations. The advantages of a rarefied atmosphere in the sprints were again in evidence the year before, when a US college team ran a 4x110 y. relay in 38.6, which according to the Association of Track & Field Statisticians (ATFS) is rated the equivalent of 38.4 for the Olympic/metric event. It happened at Provo, Utah (altitude, 1387 m.) on 17 June 1967 and the team was that of Southern California – Earl McCullough, Fred Kuller, O.J.Simpson and Jamaica's Lennox Miller. The time was better than the official world record for the 4x100 m. relay, 39.0 by USA at the 1964 Tokyo Olympics. An interesting entry was of course "O.J.", a 9.4 100 y. man who was to become one of the greatest running backs in American football. Still in 1967, a French foursome made of Marc Berger, Jocelyn Delecour, Claude Piquemal and Roger Bambuck represented Europe in the first dual meet with America at Montreal and did an excellent job, winning in 39.1. The America's team, actually an all-US quartet, finished in 39.3 but was disqualified for passing out of their zone.

1968 was a memorable year in the domain of sprinting. The highlights were provided by the AAU Championships and the Mexico Olympics. In the former, held on 20 June at Sacramento on a conventional yet very fast track, Jim Hines got the ball rolling with a sensational 9.8 in the first heat of the 100 m., aided by an illegal wind of 2.8 m/s. In the first "semi" the wind was down to 0.8 m/s and Hines chalked up history's first sub-10 secs. performance under legal conditions. His 9.9 was supported by an impressive auto time, 10.03. Ronnie Ray Smith finished about a metre behind Hines yet received the same manual 9.9 – and a more truthful auto time, 10.14. In the other "semi" Charles Greene also won in 9.9, with an aiding wind of 0.9 m/s (auto time, 10.10), with Lennox Miller of Jamaica and Roger Bambuck of France next, both in 10.0. The latter thus equalled the European record. The final offered a close fight between Greene and Hines, with the former winning by a scant margin and both credited with a wind-aided 10.0. Next came Lennox Miller of Jamaica, Roger Bambuck of France and Ronnie Ray Smith in that order, all in 10.1. Really a mind blowing day for sprint enthusiasts!

In the 200 m. the pre-Olympic fireworks were provided by the US Olympic Trials, held at Echo Summit (altitude, 2250 m.) on 12 September. That mountain site assured US technicians that conditions would be similar to those that were to be expected at Mexico City. An imposing figure by the name of John Carlos (born on 5 June 1945 in New York; 1.93 m. / 85 kg.) had his Day of Days on that occasion. Well known since the year before, when he had run the English distances in 9.4 and 20.3, Carlos won the Trials race over 200 m. in 19.7 (auto time, 19.92), handing the great Tommie Smith (20.0/20.18) one of his rare defeats. The assisting wind (1.9 m/s) was within the allowable limit, yet Carlos' mark could not be submitted to the IAAF since he (and Smith) had used multi-spike "brush" shoes. The rules state that each shoe may have six spikes up front and two in the heel at the maximum. Smith ran in lane 1, while Carlos was in lane 4.

POSTHUMOUS TRIBUTE

In October 2005, i.e. thirty-seven years after their Mexico City demonstration, Tommie Smith and John Carlos saw their stance memorialized at their alma mater as San Jose State University unveiled a statue of their gesture against racial discrimination. They were honoured in the presence of, among others, Lee Evans, the 1968 Olympic champion in the 400 metres, and Australian Peter Norman, who finished second in the Mexico City 200 m., behind Smith and ahead of Carlos. The 20-foot (6.09 m.) statue, the work of a sculptor known as Rigo 23, was commissioned by San Jose State's student association, who paid most of the $300,000 cost of the big monument. Quite predictably, the event aroused mixed comments in USA. In our opinion, the most appropriate was that of prof. Ethel Pitts Walker, who said: "This sculpture honours them (i.e. Smith and Carlos) but is also for future generations. No student should pass it by without asking: 'What can I do to make this world a better place?'

In Mexico City the same rarefied atmosphere and the Tartan track caused an even greater "explosion" in the sprints, which notoriously lie in the sphere of anaerobic (without oxygen) running. The 100 m. prelims produced a host of fast times. In the final (14 October) eight men lined up at the start and for the first time in Olympic annals all of them were black. Little Mel Pender of USA was fastest off the blocks, but Hines soon began his long, hard drive and built up a lead. From then on he was never headed. Greene was expected to be his toughest rival, but in the closing stage he sensed a pull in his hamstring, eased up a little before resuming high speed, alas too late. He had to give way to Lennox Miller for second place. Aided by a rather negligible wind (0.3 m/s), Hines was credited with 9.95 – history's first sub-10' secs. mark with automatic timing. He won comfortably from Miller (10.04), Greene (10.07), Pablo Montes of Cuba (10.14) and Bambuck (10.15). The Frenchman had done better (10.11) in a semi-final.

The 200 m. crown was awarded on 16 October. Tommie Smith was limping badly after his "semi", but two hours later he showed up for the final, "wrapped up from the waist to the lower edge of his running shorts". In the heat of competition, however, he never seemed to be bothered. He was in lane 3, with his most feared rival, Carlos, just ahead of him in lane 4. The latter was out to duplicate his Echo Summit trick and got off like a bullet. At the half-way mark he led Smith by a metre, but when "Tommie Jet" got into high gear it was really no contest. He drew away with supreme ease with 60 m. to go. About 15 m. before the finish, Smith threw both arms up in a victory gesture. that probably cost him some precious fractions of time, yet he managed to finish in a record-breaking 19.8 (auto time, 19.83; aiding wind 0.9 m/s). Meanwhile Carlos, probably suffering the effects of his hyper-fast getaway, lost second place to a relatively little known Australian, Peter Norman, who had a pre-Games best of 20.5. Both were officially credited with 20.0, their auto times being 20.06 and 20.10 respectively. Next came Edwin Roberts of Trinidad and Bambuck. Before the final, Smith and Carlos badly wanted to mount the victory dais also for another reason. Like Lee Evans and a few other black Americans, they had adhered to the project of Prof. Harry Edwards, a sociologist who advocated using the Olympic "limelight" (to be seen by millions of TV viewers around the world) to demonstrate in favour of his "Olympic Project for Human Rights", more exactly to highlight black Americans' struggle for civil rights. Smith and Carlos thus appeared on the dais wearing black gloves, black socks and no shoes (symbols of black poverty) and saluted with clenched fists. Such a show, widely discussed in USA and elsewhere, created a split in the US team, to some extent even among black athletes. The majority seemed to disapprove the idea of using the Olympic arena for what was after all a political demonstration. The US Olympic Committee decided to expel Smith and Carlos from the Games Village.

The 4x100 m. relay was no exception to the rule: here too there was an avalanche of fast times. Jamaica got the ball rolling with two record-breaking performances, 38.6 in a heat and 38.3 in a "semi" (auto times, 38.65 and 38.39). Their line-up in both races was Erroll Stewart, Michael Fray, Clinton Forbes and Lennox Miller. In the final, however, they failed to improve and USA was again on top as Charles Greene, Melvin Pender, Ronnie Ray Smith and Jim Hines chalked up a new world record – 38.2 (auto time 38.24). No surprise, after all: these men were all credited with 10-flat or better in the individual event! In actual fact, however, it wasn't so easy: once again, some passes were far from good and after the last exchange USA was only third after Cuba and the GDR (German Democratic Republic). But just as in Tokyo four years earlier, the anchor leg man, in this case Jim Hines, played in favour of the team with the highest speed aggregate. Cuba, anchored by the ever reliable Figuerola, was a fairly close second (38.3 / 30.40), ahead of France and Jamaica.

1968 Mexico City Olympics - 100 metres (14 October) w +0.3 m/s: 1.Jim Hines (USA) 9.9 (autom. 9.95); 2.Lennox Miller (Jam) 10.0 (10.04); 3.Carles Greene (USA) 10.0 (10.07); 4.Pablo Montes (Cub) 10.1 (10.14); 5.Roger Bambuck (Fra) 10.1 (10.15); 6.Mel Pender (USA) 10.1 (10.17); 7.Harry Jerome (Can) 10.1 (10.20); 8.Jean-Louis Ravelomanantsoa (Mad) 10.2 (10.28). Lanes: Greene 1, Montes 2, Hines 3, Miller 4, Bambuck 5, Pender 6, Jerome 7, Ravelomanantsoa 8.

200 metres (16 October) w +0.9 m/s: 1.Tommie Smith (USA) 19.8 (autom. 19.83); 2.Peter Norman (Aus) 20.0 (20.06); 3.John Carlos (USA) 20.0 (20.10); 4.Edwin Roberts (Tri) 20.3 (20.34); 5.Roger Bambuck (Fra) 20.5 (20.51); 6.Larry Questad (USA) 20.6 (20.62); 7.Michael Fray (Jam) 20.6 (20.63); 8.Jochen Eigenherr (FRG) 20.6 (20.66). Lanes: Fray 1, Bambuck 2, Smith 3, Carlos 4, Questad 5, Norman 6, Eigenherr 7, Roberts 8.

4x100 metre relay (20 October): 1.USA (C.Greene, M.Pender, R.R.Smith, J.Hines) 38.2 (autom. 38.24), 2.Cub (H.Ramirez, J.Morales, P.Montes, E.Figuerola) 38.3 (38.40); 3.Fra (G.Fenouil, J.Delecour, C.Piquemal, R.Bambuck) 38.4 (38.42); 4.Jam 38.4 (38.47); 5.GDR 38.6 (38.66); 6.FRG 38.7 (38.76); 7.Ita 39.2 (39.22); 8.Pol 39.2 (39.22). Lanes: Cub 1, USA 2, Pol 3, GDR 4, Jam 5, Ita 6, FRG 7, Fra 8.

After the revolutionary results of Echo Summit and Mexico City, many observers came to the conclusion that the problem of record marks made at high altitude certainly deserved consideration. Some people felt that it would be advisable to separate such "inflated" marks from those made at or near sea level – as it was done in other sports. Jean Creuzé, a French student of statistics and aerodynamics, calculated that the effect of rarefied atmosphere at Mexico City was such as to equate, over a 100 m. course, that of an assisting wind of 1.2 m/s. Considering that in the Olympic final Hines was aided by a negligible breeze of 0.3 m/s, then his 9.95 would remain legal even in the theoretical "double account" of altitude and wind (1.2 + 0.3 = 1.5). But in other cases, including for instance some of the superlative triple jumps made at Mexico City with the aid of a 2.0 m/s wind, the total advantage would excel the allowable limit. The problem of setting a borderline in terms of altitude is of course a very difficult one, which may partly explain why the IAAF has not pronounced judgement on this matter. The Association of Track & Field Statisticians (ATFS) has tentatively set 1000 m. as the borderline to distinguish between altitude and non-altitude marks in the following events: 100, 200, 400 m. flat, 110 and 400 m. hurdles, long jump, triple jump, 4x100 and 4x400 m. relays – which could roughly be described as the domain of "short-lived" (mostly anaerobic) efforts. In its World Lists, the ATFS denotes marks made at altitudes over 1000 m. with an "A", but does not keep them separate from other marks.

To wind up the tale of the Mexico Olympics, I may add that the continued banning of South Africa from the Games (due to its "Apartheid" policies) resulted in the non-participation of Paul Nash, a 21-year-old sprinter who in 1968 had done 10.0 and 20.1 over the metric distances at the famous Zurich "Weltklasse" meet – in the space of 50 minutes.

Towards the end of 1968, the European Junior Games, held at Leipzig, revealed a bright new prospect from USSR, Valeriy Borzov, who scored an impressive double with 10.4 and 21.0. A few weeks later, just before turning nineteen, he ran the century in 10.2. This man (born on 20 October 1949 at Sambor, Ukraine; 1.82 m. / 82 kg.) was to become one of the greatest sprinters of the Seventies and probably the greatest Europe-born one. A compact runner, if ever there was one, he had no weak points. A very fast starter, cool and poised in every phase of the race, he ran like a well-oiled machine from start to finish. He added to his natural gifts through years of hard and systematic work, mostly under the tutelage of Valentin Petrovskiy, a physiologist. In 1969 Borzov won the European 100 m. title in Athens (10.4) and in subsequent years he began to take the measure of the top Americans, beating them twice - in the USSR vs USA dual meet at Leningrad in 1970 he won the 100 m. in 10.4 from Ben Vaughan and Ivory Crockett (10.5 both) and at Berkeley in 1971 he did it again, in the USA-USSR-World All Stars 1971, winning in 10.5 from Jim Green (USA), 10.5, and Lennox Miller (Jamaica), 10.6. The latter race was against a wind of 3.4 m/s. True, Jim Hines and Tommie Smith had by then retired and their successors were not in the same class. As for John Carlos, however, he had two more seasons of excellent running before sinking into oblivion. On 10 May 1969 at Fresno he equalled the world's 100 y. record, 9.1, with a truly negligible wind of 0.05 m/s. Exactly seven days before, at San Jose, he had turned in a 9 flat, leaving the likes of Ronnie Ray Smith, Bill Gaines and Charles Greene (all timed in 9.3) well behind: on that occasion, however, Aeolus went out of his way, producing an aiding gale of 7.0 m/s. Carlos came to a halt in the 1970 AAU meet, when he pulled up lame in the 100 y. and jogged across the finish. He signed a pro football contract soon after and missed, among other things, the dual meet with USSR.

Borzov went on to score a fine double at the 1971 European Championships in Helsinki, with times of 10.27 and 20.30. The sprint relay in this meet turned out to be a comedy of errors. West Germany failed to finish after fouling up the second exchange, East Germany and France were disqualified for changing outside the zone. USSR, sans Borzov, fell below expectations. Czechoslovakia won in 39.3.

In the meantime two "gems" had appeared elsewhere in the world, both destined to fear no foes in terms of durability. They were Don Quarrie of Jamaica and Pietro Mennea of Italy. The former (born on 25 February 1951 at Kingston; 1.73 m. / 70 kg.) qualified for the Mexico Olympics while still a teen-ager, but an injury stopped him on the eve of the Games. In later years he improved rapidly and in 1970 he was able to score a significant double (10.24w and 20.56) at the British Commonwealth Games in Edinburgh. He reached the top on 3 August 1971 at the Pan American Games in Cali, Colombia (altitude, 1046 m.), when he came dangerously close to Tommie Smith's world record for the 200 m. with a sparkling 19.86, aided by a legal wind of 0.9 m/s. A relatively short man, the Jamaican showed an amazingly fast leg work. As a competitor, he made the grade in US collegiate ranks and soon proved a hard nut to crack for anybody.

Pietro Mennea (born on 28 June 1952 at Barletta; 1.79 m. / 68 kg.) also emerged as a teen-ager, finishing fifth in the 200 m. at the 1970 European Junior Championships. He worked hard for many years with coach Carlo Vittori, a former Italian sprint champion (10.6 in 1952 and 21.6 in '53). Mennea was very selective in choosing his commitments throughout the season and knew how to concentrate on major Games. This may have been not the last reason for his longevi-

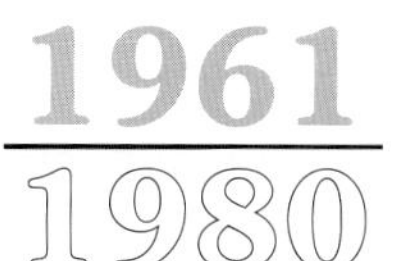

Valeriy Borzov (USSR) taking the baton in a relay race. The only European sprinter to score the 100/200 m. double in the Olympics (Munich, 1972).

Don Quarrie (Jamaica), a durable and highly competitive sprinter.

ty as a top-class sprinter – he competed in five editions of the Olympics, 1972 through 1988! Just like his predecessor Livio Berruti, he showed a preference for the 200 m., and in 1971 he placed sixth in this event at the European Championships in Helsinki with a new personal best of 20.88 (Borzov won in 20.30, as previously related). In June 1972 he and Borzov met at Milan over 100 m. and the Ukrainian won by a scant margin as both equalled the European record, "manual" version (10.0). The next day, with Borzov not in the race, Mennea took the 200 m. in 20.2, equalling the European record set by Borzov himself at Moscow in 1971.

A man who looked capable of playing a prominent role in the Munich Olympics was Jean-Louis Ravelomanantsoa of Madagascar. After finishing eighth in the century at the Mexico Olympics, he made steady progress and in 1971 he compiled a fine set of 100 m. performances, including a 10.0 at Helsinki, enough to earn second place in the "Track & Field News" World Ranking for that year, behind Borzov. Unfortunately, he happened to be hampered by physical problems at Munich and could not go beyond the 100 m. "semis".

As per tradition, the US pre Olympic season culminated with the Trials held for the first time at Eugene, Oregon, which by offering enthusiastic crowds soon turned out to be a choice location for such a meet, to the point of winning in later years the bold but not unjust label of America's "Track Capital". In fact, Eugene was to be the venue of the Olympic Trials on several more occasions. The 100 metres offered plenty of exciting moments. Aiding winds inflated performances in the prelims, with 9.9 marks by Robert Taylor in a quarter-final and no less than five 9.9's in the first semi-final, as Rey Robinson, Norbert Payton, Warren Edmonson, Eddie Hart and Willie Deckard finished in that order, all in 9.9. By the time of the final, near 8 p.m. on 1 July, the aiding wind was down to a legal 0.9 m/s. Hart emerged the winner in the closing stage, beating Robinson by about 6 inches (15.24 cms.). Both were timed in 9.9, thus equalling the world record, and Taylor earned the vital third place in 10.0. There was no automatic timer, only a hand-started Data Timer which gave 9.88 for Hart and 9.90 for Robinson.

A MISSED RENDEZ-VOUS

What happened to Eddie Hart and Rey Robinson at the 1972 Olympics in Munich certainly has right of place in the chapter of track's strangest memorabilia. On the eve of the Games these young US sprinters ranked among the favourites for the 100 m. crown. As related in the main text, they had equalled the world record (9.9) at the US Olympic Trials. In the Munich "Olympiastadion" they easily won their heats in the morning of 31 August, thus qualifying for the quarter-finals, which in their opinion (and that of US team coach Stan Wright) were to take place at 6 p.m. the same day – rather than 4 p.m. as indicated in the official timetable. (As it later transpired, Wright had been using a 15-month old schedule issued by the US Olympic Committee).
According to "Track & Field News", things went like this. Around 4 p.m., Hart and Robinson were in the ABC building just outside the Olympic Village, in the company of third US qualifier Robert Taylor. Fully relaxed, they were viewing on a TV set some races being run off at "Olympiastadion". "Hey, what's that? A re-run of the heats this morning?" asked one. "No, that's live", said another, "It's happening right now. That's our race!" Before one could say (Jack) Robinson, they were rushed to the stadium, half a mile away, in an ABC car. But by the time they arrived there, both Robinson's and Hart's races had been run, and only Taylor, scheduled for a later "quarter", was "still alive". The lucky escaper warmed up in a hurry, then lined up at the start, with Borzov and others. With his adrenalin obviously running high, he finished right behind Borzov (10.07) in 10.16, his best auto time ever! Coach Stan Wright admitted it was entirely his fault if two co-holders of the world record missed the rendez-vous of their life. From the looks of things, Hart could have been a hard nut to crack for everybody, possibly including Borzov, but in my opinion the Ukrainian would have won anyhow. As for Robinson, 20, he appeared to be limping after winning his heat in the morning.

In Munich's "Olympiastadion" Valeriy Borzov left no doubts as to the identity of the World's Fastest Human anno 1972. In the 100 m. he was partly favoured by a strange incident (the Hart-Robinson case, dealt with in an adjoining aside). Yet the Ukrainian looked perfect in all his appearances. After lowering the European "automatic" record to 10.07 in the prelims, he won the final in fine style from Robert Taylor of USA, 10.14 to 10.24. Excellent times in virtually windless (-0.30 m/s) conditions. (In pre-meet predictions made by "experts", Taylor was generally considered America's second string, next to Hart). Lennox Miller, the powerful Jamaican, again won a medal, ahead of little Aleksandr Kornelyuk of USSR, a very fast starter. Incidentally, in Munich there was a machine known as "Startkontrolle" which verified the reaction time (to the starter's gun) of every sprinter. In the various rounds of the 100 m. the lowest differential, 0.12 sec., was credited to Borzov and Kornelyuk.

In the 200 m. final, three days later, Borzov's superiority was, if possible, even more apparent. After a perfect journey, he threw his arms in the air before crossing the line – in 20.00, a new European record and the fastest "auto" time ever at or near sea level (Munich: 520 m.) and in windless conditions. Larry Black of USA ran an excellent race in lane 1 to take second place in 20.19, ahead of Pietro Mennea and another American, Larry Burton.

By the time the sprint relay came up, the Americans were obviously thirsty for revenge. The incredible Hart-Robinson case in the 100 m. had obviously caused quite a stir, and US coach Stan Wright in particular, chosen by the media as the main "culprit", was in search of relief. He got it when Black, Taylor, Gerald Tinker and Hart ran a near perfect race and went home the winners in 38.2, equalling the world record set by another US team at Mexico City in 1968. In actual fact, the auto-time, 38.19, was better than the 38.24 credited to the 1968 team. USSR had Borzov as anchor leg man. He started 0.3sec. behind his US counter-part, Hart, and found the margin unsurmountable. The Ukrainian was apparently happy just to hold second, ahead of West Germany.

1972 Olympics, Munich - 100 metres (1 September) w –0.3 m/s: 1.Valeriy Borzov (SU) 10.14; 2.Robert Taylor (USA) 10.24; 3.Lennox Miller (Jam) 10.33; 4.Aleksandr Kornelyuk (SU) 10.36; 5.Michael Fray (Jam) 10.40; 6.Jobst Hirscht (FRG) 10.40: 7.Zenon Nowosz (Pol) 10.46. Did not finish: Hasely Crawford (Trinidad). Lanes: Nowosz 1, Borzov 2, Crawford 3, Taylor 4, Miller 5, Kornelyuk 6, Hirscht 7, Fray 8.

200 metres (4 September) w 0.0 m/s: 1.Valeriy Borzov (SU) 20.00; 2.Larry Black (USA) 20.19; 3.Pietro Mennea (Ita) 20.30; 4.Larry Burton (USA) 20.37; 5.Chuck Smith 20.55; 6.Siegfried Schenke (GDR) 20.56; 7.Martin Jellinghaus (FRG) 20.65; 8.Hans-Joachim Zenk (GDR) 21.05. Lanes: Black 1, Mennea 2, Smith 3, Jellinghaus 4, Borzov 5, Burton 6, Zenk 7, Schenke 8.

4x100 metre relay (10 September): 1.USA (L.Black, R.Taylor, G.Tinker, E.Hart) 38.19; 2.SU (A.Kornelyuk, V.Lovyetskiy, J.Silovs, V.Borzov) 38.50; 3.FRG (J.Hirscht, K.-H.Klotz, G.Wucherer, K.Ehl) 38.79; 4.Cze 38.82; 5.GDR 38.90; 6.Pol 39.03, 7.Fra 39.14. 8.Ita 39.14. Lanes: USA 1, Ita 2, Fra 3, SU 4, Pol 5, GDR 6, FRG 7, CSR 8.

Borzov never fully regained the splendid condition he had exhibited in Munich. In subsequent years he mostly concentrated on the century. At the 1974 European Championships in Rome he won from Mennea, 10.27 to 10.34. A very fast starter, Borzov won no less than seven European indoor titles at 50/60 m. between 1970 and 1977. He stayed away from that meet in 1973 for the purpose of making a visit to US boards – and over there he suffered defeats in both the AAU Championships and the USA vs USSR indoor match.

Borzov apparently had a moderate affection for the 200 m. and never again tried the 400 m., a distance he had run in 47.6 at the age of twenty. I once asked him why and his reply, in a joking tone, was as simple as this: "Why add to your labours when you can beat everybody at the shortest distance?"

In the Munich Olympics, Don Quarrie was stopped by a pulled muscle in the next-to-last round of the 200 m. Really too bad for an athlete who had lost his first Olympic chance for a similar reason in 1968, when only 17. But he was stubborn enough to overcome – he would have a third and a fourth Olympic chance. Throughout his long career he won the 100/200 double in two editions of the British Commonwealth Games (1970 and '74) and the 100 again in 1978. During the Seventies he also annexed seven AAU titles. His most serious rival in those years was Steve Williams (born on 13 November 1953; 1.92 m. / 79 kg.), a magnificent US sprinter who amassed a lot of classy marks and won many important races but simply had no luck in Olympic years: in 1972 and again in 1976 he was stopped by injuries on the threshold of the Games. Then his physical prowess was not always accompanied by an adequate singleness of purpose. On 12 May 1973 at Fresno he equalled the world's 100 y. record (9.1) with the aid of a maximum allowable wind (2.0 m/s), winning from Quarrie (9.3); and on 21 June 1974 at Westwood he matched the 100 m. mark (9.9). In 1975-76 he amassed three more 9.9's and was once timed in 9.8, in a heat of the 1975 AAU Championships at Eugene, but on that occasion hand timing was only used unofficially and the "auto" time for him was no better than 10.19. Still at Eugene, on 7 June 1975, he was narrowly edged by Quarrie in a thrilling 220 y. race, with both credited with a record-shattering 19.9.

The early Seventies also featured a number of meteoric figures. At least three of these seem to deserve mention:

1) Ivory Crockett, a lithe American, was AAU 100 y. champion twice, and on 11 May 1974 at Knoxville, Tennessee he ran history's first official 9.0 for the 100 y. (wind nil) and got official credit for it.

2) Dr. Delano Meriwether, a haematologist who at the age of 28 took time out off his medical duties to win the 1971 AAU 100 y. title in 9.0, aided by an illegal wind of 3.0 m/s. He won by a whisker from little known Jim Green, also timed in 9.0. The men who came next were such well-known sprinters as Quarrie and Charles Greene (9.1 both). And Eddie Hart was 8th and last in 9.2! As the

Pietro Mennea (Italy) setting a new world's 200 m. record (19.72) at the Universiade in Mexico City, 1979.

story goes, Meriwether became a track addict the day he saw Valeriy Borzov win the 100 m. in the USA-USSR match in 1970. He told his wife he could do better, and what sounded like a wild dream turned out to be quasi-reality a year later. The doctor kept at it for another two years, with declining success. At the 1972 US Olympic Trials he was eliminated in the prelims.

3) Houston McTear, an explosive starter who in 1975, aged eighteen, equalled Crockett's 100 y. mark (9.0) in a High School meet. The following year he qualified for the US Olympic team but at the crucial moment he was stopped by an injury. In 1977 he fared well in several European meets, notably with a 10.13 for the 100 m. at Cologne.

In 1975 (apart from Quarrie's and Williams' feats, previously related) one of the highlights was offered by the Zurich "Weltklasse" meet, which had by then risen to the no.1 rank among European Invitationals. In the 100 m. Steve Riddick of USA beat his rival and friend Steve Williams, 10.05 to 10.08, while Borzov was third (10.16) – exceptional times, in view of an adverse wind of 1.2 m/s. In the same year, Borzov barely held off Pietro Mennea in the 100 m. of the European Cup at Nice (both 10.40), then lost to the Italian for the first time in the 200 m., 20.61 to 20.42. These two had ruled the roost at the European Championships in Rome the year before, with Borzov winning the 100 m. as related above, and the Italian taking the 200 m. title comfortably (20.60).

New stars came to the fore on the eve of the 1976 Olympics in Montreal. At the US Olympic Trials in Eugene, 19-year-old Harvey Glance won the 100 m. in 10.11; in the 200 m. Millard Hampton won from an 18-year-old lad, Dwayne Evans, 20.10 to 20.22. In the meantime, the Caribbean area was capable of fielding two gems in the persons of Don Quarrie of Jamaica and Hasely Crawford of Trinidad. The latter had made the Olympic 100 m. final in 1972, pulling up lame after a few strides. In later years this solid but somewhat unpredictable sprinter fared well on both sides of the Atlantic.

At the Montreal Olympics, athletes competed in a huge stadium, which looked like a giant concrete mushroom. Its massive curving walls arched out to produce a wondrous roof which kept all snug and dry. Only an oval hole at the top kept the whole thing from being an indoor facility, which would have made possible record marks unacceptable under IAAF rules ("The record must be made out of doors"). Few Games, if any, were ever exempt from the wind factor as those held in Montreal.

In the sprints, Central America simply K.O.'d both USA and Europe. During the 100 m. final (24 July) the wind was virtually nil (-0.1 m/s). At the start, Harvey Glance was out in front, with Borzov close behind. Quarrie began to move up at the half-way mark and went into the lead in the next 20 metres. But in the closing stage Crawford came up to nip Quarrie at the finish by the proverbial whisker (10.06 to 10.07). Borzov passed the fading Glance to get the bronze in 10.14, curiously the same time that had earned him gold four years earlier. With Glance no better than fourth (10.19), USA failed to win a medal – for the first time since 1928. Reaction times to the starter's gun were officially released for the first time. In the final Quarrie (0.122) was the quickest of them all, followed by Borzov (0.125) and Crawford (0.129). All others varied from 0.141 to 0.167 – and remained off the podium!

In the 200 m., two days later, Quarrie's tenacity was finally rewarded. He ran a consistent race throughout. Millard Hampton of USA turned out to be his most serious challenger, but Quarrie repulsed all his attacks and finally won safely, if not comfortably (20.22 to 20.29). Young Dwayne Evans hung on for third despite a strong stretch run by Mennea, who had the inside lane. Crawford, obviously happy for his great success in the century, met his old foe again in the decisive race of the 200 m. After about 50 m. a spasm in a hamstring muscle forced him to leap high in the air and then stop running. Then he gallantly walked till the finish line.

The 4x100 m. relay was remarkable in at least one way: for the first time since 1952 the winning team failed to break or tie the world record! It was clear that only the Americans could beat the Americans. For once, however, their passes were generally, if not always, good, and they won by a safe margin from GDR and USSR, in that order. Times, 38.33, 38.66, 38.78.

BORZOV COMPROMISES WITH CROUCHING TECHNIQUE

The crouching start was first used on May 18, 1888 at Cedarhurst, Long Island, New York, by Charles Sherrill, then US 100 yards champion (1887) and a pupil of coach Mike Murphy. That new technique, successfully introduced in the international arena at the 1896 Olympics in Athens, was then used for over 85 years and nobody ever thought of changing it. Until March 9, 1974, when during the European Indoor Championships at Göteborg the Olympic 100 metre champion of 1972, Valeriy Filipovich Borzov, created a sensation by using only three pushaways instead of four in the 60 metre dash. He did so by placing only his right hand on the ground and keeping the other one high on his back. He did so in both semi-final and final. In the latter he won comfortably in 6.58. At the starter's gun. Borzov projected his left arm forward, much as a boxer in delivering a blow to his rival, probably adding new impetus to his powerful getaway.

Later in the same year (2/8 September), Rome's Stadio Olimpico acted as host to the European Championships. This writer was officiating in the starters' team. As such I had carefully studied most of the sprinters who were expected to play a prominent role. The variation introduced by Borzov, on the advice of Valentin Petrovskiy, a physiologist/coach who was his adviser, had been widely described in several athletics publications. I read that in Borzov's opinion his start "on threes" originated as a counter-measure to an injury in his left wrist, suffered in a meet at Minsk. However, some people found this hard to believe as the wrist in question had no visible sign of a possible injury. Personally I was worried more than somewhat. The possibility that at the signal "pronti" (set) we could see an arm straying from the general line-up was disturbing. This impression was confirmed by experiments made with athletes living in my hometown. Shortly before the Europeans I discussed the matter with Pietro Mennea, who told me that he was unable to see what advantages, if any, could be derived by his great rival in using that technique. And he simply concluded: "Let's wait and see". I came to the same conclusion: we only had to wait till the afternoon of September 2, when the first round of the 100 metres would get under way. Borzov happened to be at in heat 1, with among others Chauvelot of France and Nowosz of Poland. As expected, Borzov resorted to his "unusual" technique and in connection with the "pronti" (set) we saw his left arm rise well above the line of his rivals's backs and rest as prescribed by the rule. We were prepared for this, so we had no difficulties. Borzov won his heat easily in 10.49. Surprisingly though, he returned to the classic start "on all fours" the next day in both semi-final and final. In the latter he won in 10.27, with Mennea second in 10.34.

Only in March 1977 at San Sebastian, shortly after winning his sixth European indoor title in the 60-metre dash, Borzov revealed in an interview with Gianni Merlo of "La Gazzetta dello Sport" that his start "on threes" had been nothing more than an occasional experiment. Which obviously failed to provide any real advantage and was later abandoned.

G.P.

Valeriy Borzov, centre, and his "compromise" with the crouching technique at the 1974 European Championships in Rome.

1976 Olympics, Montreal - 100 metres (24 July) w: -0.01 m/s: 1.Hasely Crawford (Tri) 10.06; 2.Don Quarrie (Jam) 10.07*; 3.Valeriy Borzov (SU) 10.14; 4.Harvey Glance (USA) 10.19; 5.Guy Abrahams (Pan) 10.25; 6.Johnny Jones (USA) 10.27; 7.Klaus-Dieter Kurrat (GDR) 10.31; 8.Petar Petrov (Bul) 10.35. Lanes: Crawford 1, Petrov 2, Borzov 3, Quarrie 4, Glance 5, Jones 6, Kurrat 7, Abrahams 8.

*Quarrie's official time was 10.08, but Bob Sparks, the newly elected President of the ATFS, corrected it to 10.07 after a close examination of the film.

200 metres (26 July) w +0.72 m/s: 1.Donald Quarrie (Jam) 20.22; 2.Millard Hampton (USA) 20.29; 3.Dwayne Evans (USA) 20.43; 4.Pietro Mennea (Ita) 20.54; 5.Rui da Silva (Bra) 20.84; 6.Bogdan Grzejszczak (Pol) 20.91; 7.Colin Bradford (Jam) 21.17; 8.Hasely Crawford (Tri) 79.6 (injured). Lanes: Mennea 1, Quarrie 2, Bradford 3, Hampton 4, Crawford 5, Grzejszczak 6, Evans 7, da Silva 8.

4x100 metre relay (31 July): 1.USA (H.Glance, J.Jones, M.Hampton, S.Riddick) 38.33; 2.GDR (M.Kokot, J.Pfeifer, K.-D. Kurrat, A.Thieme) 38.66; 3.SU (A.Aksinin, N.Kolyesnikov, J.Silovs, V.Borzov) 38.78; 4.Pol 38.83; 5.Cub 39.01; 6.Ita 39.08; 7.Fra 39.16; 8.Can 39.47. Lanes: GDR 1. USA 2, Pol 3, Cub 4, Ita 5, Can 6, SU 7, Fra 8.

Hasely Joaquim Crawford (born on 16 August 1950 in San Fernando, Trinidad; 1.90 m. / 78 kg.) first reached international class at the age of twenty, when he placed third in the 100 m. at the Commonwealth Games in Edinburgh, close behind Quarrie an Lennox Miller. After his mishap in the 1972 Olympic final he had to labour quite a bit to resurge again. At the end of 1975 he could point to personal bests of 9.35 (100 y.) and 10.18 (100 m.).

In 1977 the unlucky Steve Williams won what was virtually the only major international honour of his career when he beat Eugen Ray of the GDR, 10.13 to 10.15, in the 100 m. of the inaugural World Cup at Düsseldorf. Silvio Leonard of Cuba (10.19) was third, well ahead of Pietro Mennea, who later made amends by finishing a very close second to Clancy Edwards of USA in the 200 m. (both 20.17). The main event of the year regarded the 4x100 m. relay though. In the World Cup at Düsseldorf, a US team consisting of Bill Collins, Steve Riddick, Cliff Wiley and Steve Williams broke the world record with 38.03, "passing about as well as any American national team has ever done", as one commentator put it. A GDR team was a distant second in 38.57.

1978 saw the emergence of a not-so-green Scotsman, Allan Wells (born on 3 May 1952 at Edinburgh; 1.83 m. / 77 kg.). It is in fact rather unusual for a sprinter to reach world class at 26. Until then Wells had done no better than 10.55 and 21.10 (as well as 7.32 in the long jump). So it was only in 1978, after working harder than ever under the guidance of Wilson Young, a former "pro" sprinter, that Wells finally made the grade at the international level. After setting a British 100 m. record of 10.15 in his native city, he went to Edmonton, Canada, to compete in the British Commonwealth Games. In that important test he held his own against Don Quarrie, barely losing to him in the 100 m., 10.07 to 10.03 (wind-assisted) but winning the 200 m. in 20.12 ("windy" again), after Quarrie was stopped by an injury in the prelims.

In 1978 Mennea enjoyed the first of three nearly perfect seasons. Unlike his countryman Livio Berruti, who relied mostly if not exclusively on his great natural talent, Mennea was a hard worker. His best work that year in terms of both quality and quantity was at the European Championships in Prague. He won the 100 m. in 10.27 (after a 10.19 in the prelims, a new Italian record), beating the likes of Eugen Ray, Wells and Borzov, who was by then plagued by tendon troubles; then he won the 200 m. hands down in 20.16. In the space of six days, counting individual and relay events (prelims and finals) he made ten appearances, and in his last effort he ran a leg of the 4x400 m. relay in 44.4. His potential for the one-lap event had become apparent in 1977, when he did 45.87 outdoors, and was confirmed early in 1978, when he won the European indoor title. But like many top-class sprinters Mennea disliked the "longest dash" and subsequently forgot about it.

Other outstanding sprinters of 1978 were Silvio Leonard of Cuba (10.08 and 20.06) and Clancy Edwards of USA (10.07 and 20.03). Also worthy of note was Eddie Hart's attempted comeback. Six years after experiencing a frustrating disappointment in the Munich Olympics, he ran the metric century in 10.07 at high altitude but failed to make an impact in major competitions.

Clock-wise at least, Mennea reached his peak in 1979. His main target for the season was the "Universiade" (World Student Games) to be held at Mexico City in September. His not-so-secret aim was to break Tommie Smith's famous 200 m. world record (19.83), made on the same track eleven years earlier. While preparing for that event with his usual singleness of purpose, he rounded into form gradually. In August he had mixed fortunes in the European Cup at Turin, barely winning the 100 m. in 10.15 from Marian Woronin of Poland (10.16) and Allan Wells (10.19) and losing to the Scotsman in the 200 m., 20.31 to 20.29 (wind-assisted). Mennea went to Mexico early and thus had plenty of time to acclimatize to the rarefied atmosphere. The benefits soon became apparent when in tune-up races held on consecutive days (3 and 4 September) he first returned a "manual" 19.8 for the 200 m., then 10.01 for the century with an aiding wind of 0.9 m/s, thereby beating Borzov's European record (10.07). In the "Universiade" proper he chose to concentrate on his favourite distance, the 200 m., and on three consecutive days (10-11-12 September) he produced the following series: 19.96 (heat), 20.04 (semi-final) and 19.72 (final) for a new world record. In the decisive race he was in his beloved lane 4, which in Italian meets had been his for years, almost by divine right. Aided by a 1.8 m/s wind down the stretch, he ran a beautiful race, winning as he pleased from Leszek Dunecki of Poland, who came home in 20.24, a personal record. It was a race under favourable conditions throughout: all eight finalists but one chalked up new personal bests. The lonely exception was Otis Melvin of USA, who had improved on his PB in a semi-final! The average gain per man vis-à-vis previous bests at or near sea level was an eye-catching 0.38 secs. Having done better than "Tommie Jet" Smith under similar conditions, Mennea could at any rate claim a record of substance. He and Wells had stayed away from the World Cup, held at Montreal a few weeks earlier. Under the strictly "aseptic" conditions evidenced by the 1976 Olympics, a heavily muscled American, James Sanford, won the 100 m. from Silvio Leonard, 10.17 to 10.26, while the Cuban took the 200 m. in 20.34.

In the two-year period 1978-79 there were no major deeds in the sprint relay department. Poland won at the 1978 European Championships in Prague in 38.58. In the second World Cup, held at Montreal in 1979, a US team lost to the Americas (two Brazilians and two Cubans) 38.77 to 38.70. Later in the same year an Italian team anchored by Pietro Mennea, then at his very best, did 38.42 in the "Universiade" at Mexico City, equalling the European record set by France on the same track during the 1968 Olympics.

The Olympic Games of 1980 in Moscow suffered heavily as a result of the new inroads of world politics into sport. USA and other non-Communist countries decided to boycott the Moscow event. The protest, led by US President Jimmy Carter, was over the invasion of Afghanistan by Soviet troops in 1979. A sad affair, four years after the African boycott of the Montreal Games. In some Western countries, notably including Britain and Italy, national Olympic Committees refused to follow the line taken by their Governments and sent their teams to Moscow anyhow – they would compete under the colours of the International Olympic Committee .... Outstanding among the absentees were USA, the German Federal Republic, Japan and Kenya. Quite understandably, the absence of the US sprinters altered the picture in the sprint, although it should be noted that 1980 did not look like a vintage year for Uncle Sam's dashmen. At their Olympic Trials in Eugene, run off as a symbolic gesture, 19-year-old Stanley Floyd won the 100 m. from Harvey Glance, 10.26 to 10.27. Fourth in this race was another youngster, 19-year old Carl Lewis, bound to be heard from again and again in subsequent years. Had USA taken part in the Moscow Games, he would have run the 4x100 m. relay. James Butler topped the 200 m. field in 20.49. Potentially at least, the best American sprinter of 1980 may have been James Sanford, who ran the century in 10.02, then a low-altitude world record – reportedly after "stumbling about 15 y. (13.7 m.) out of the blocks"; and he also ran the 200 m. in 20.26. Unfortunately, he was bogged down by injuries when the important races came around. Stanley Floyd was the most consistent of the Americans throughout the year and might have been dangerous in the century, if he had been able to compete in Moscow.

Valeriy Borzov, by then 31, tried to qualify for his third Olympic venture, but recurrent ankle problems (he had been operated on not long ago) prevented him from taking part. In the Games, Allan Wells showed he was ready by running a quarter-final of the 100 m. in 10.11, his best ever. In a semi-final, Quarrie and Mennea had their gloomiest day and failed to survive. In the decisive race Wells had to give all he had to narrowly edge consistent Silvio Leonard, with both running 10.25. Petar Petrov of Bulgaria was third in 10.39. To everybody's surprise, Mennea and Quarrie were back in good form by the time the 200 m. final came around. The Italian was in lane 8, with Wells right behind in 7, Quarrie in 4 and Leonard in the pole lane. Wells went out fast, too fast perhaps, and led by nearly 2 m. at the half-way point. Then Mennea began to close the gap, collared his rival in the last stretch of land and beat him, 20.19 to 20.21. Quarrie was a solid third (20.29), just ahead of Leonard (20.30). The three medal winners averaged just over 28 years in age. Contrary to his custom, Mennea had trained rather inconsistently before going to Moscow, probably as a result of contradictory reports

Allan Wells (UK), nearest camera, winning the 100 m. title at the 1980 Olympics in Moscow. Others visible in the picture, from left to right, are Panzo (Fra) 8th, Lara (Cuba) 5th, Woronin (Pol) 7th, Petrov (Bul) 3rd and Leonard (Cuba) 2nd.

about the participation of Italy in the Moscow Games.

In the absence of the Americans, the Russian relay team, with Vladimir Muravyov, Nikolay Sidorov, Aleksandr Aksinin and Andrey Prokofyev was expected to have a relatively easy job in the 4x100 m. relay. But Poland made it difficult for them, although finally losing, 38.33 to 38.26. France was third (38.53). It should be noted that a few days earlier the Russian anchor man, Prokofyev, had placed fourth in the 110 m. hurdles in 13.49.

1980 Olympics, Moscow - 100 metres (25 July) w +1.11 m/s: 1.Allan Wells (UK) 10.25; 2.Silvio Leonard (Cub) 10.25; 3.Petar Petrov (Bul) 10.39; 4. Aleksandr Aksinin (SU) 10.42: 5.Osvaldo Lara (Cub) 10.43; 6.Vladimir Muravyov (SU) 10.44; 7.Marian Woronin (Pol) 10.46; 8.Herman Panzo (Fra) 10.49. Lanes: Leonard 1, Aksinin 2, Muravyov 3, Woronin 4, Petrov 5, Panzo 6, Lara 7, Wells 8.

200 metres: (28 July) w +0.88 m/s: 1.Pietro Mennea (Ita) 20.19; 2.Allan Wells (UK) 20.21; 3.Donald Quarrie (Jam) 20.29; 4.Silvio Leonard (Cub) 20.30; 5.Bernhard Hoff (GDR) 20.50; 6.Leszek Dunecki (Pol) 20.68; 7.Marian Woronin (Pol) 20.81; 8.Osvaldo Lara (Cub) 21.19. Lanes: Leonard 1, Woronin 2, Hoff 3, Quarrie 4, Dunecki 5, Lara 6, Wells 7, Mennea 8.

4x100 metre relay (1 August): 1. SU (V.Muravyov, N.Sidorov, A.Aksinin, A.Prokofyev) 38.26; 2.Pol (K.Zwolinski, Z.Licznerski, L.Dunecki, M.Woronin) 38.33; 3.Fra (A.Richard, Pascal Barré, Patrick Barré, H.Panzo) 38.53: 4. UK 38.62; 5.GDR 38,73; 6.Bul 38.99; 7.Nig 39.12; 8.Bra 39.54. Lanes: Pol 1, Fra 2, Bul 3, Bra 4, UK 5, SU 6, Nig 7, GDR 8.

Mennea reached his best-ever form in post-Olympic meets: between 5 August and 27 September he competed in eight 200 m. races all over the world (Italy, Belgium, Japan and China), winning them all and averaging a phenomenal 20.07. His fastest time, 19.96, was achieved in his native town of Barletta. As for Allan Wells, having won a gold and a silver in the Olympics, he certainly deserved a place of honour among Europe's best ever. Only Borzov, among continentals, had done better in the history of the Games. In post-Olympic meets, however, Wells showed a slightly declining form and lost 1-to-2 in direct clashes with young Stanley Floyd of USA in the 100 m.

TRACKS AND CIRCLES - FROM CINDERS TO TARTAN

The track used at the inaugural Olympics of the modern era was, in the opinion of chroniclers of the time, absolutely dreadful. Made of a soft, loose kind of cinders, it could not stand the challenge of rain, which came down during the games and made it virtually unusable.

Charles Perry, the Englishman who designed the track, had taken inspiration from the primitive form of the ancient Olympia stadium, built by Herod Atticus in 180 b.C., and characterized by very tight curves (with a radius of no more than 15 m.) and long straightaways, about 150 m., all of which obviously had a negative effect on performances made in the running events.

Even the grass track of Racing Club de France, used for the Paris Olympics in 1900, was far from perfect. Far more consistent was the track designed by Charles Perry for the 1912 Games at the "Olympiastadion" in Stockholm. The track, 385 metres in length, had three layers of scoriae. The first of these, 18 cms., was made of minute fragments of bricks derived from demolitions, interspersed with pieces of granite. The second layer, 12 cms., was made of stones of medium size, and supported the third layer (15 cms.), which consisted of a mixture of carbon scoriae, 50% of which came from leftovers of fossil material used for locomotives, and the remaining 50% from leftovers used in electric workshops and from sand used for constructions.

Better materials were used in subsequent years and the 1924 Paris Olympics were run off on a 500-metre track (400 m. runners thus had to negotiate only one turn), with the bottom covered by a layer of clay in reddish colour, very compact and elastic. The track, ratified by Pierre Larousse, an engineer, received plenty of plaudits from runners, who did not hesitate in proclaiming it the fastest in the world!

In due time came the advent of synthetic tracks, made with materials used as supports for tennis courts. Red materials became the vogue in the Olympics and all major sports events throughout the world, before giving way to Tartan, a polyurethan resin produced by the American "Minnesota" company in the mid-Sixties and known under the "3M" trademark. Such a product had proven most useful and many American and Canadian universities used it for new tracks and surfaces in their stadiums.

Given the steadiness and comfort (reduced maintenance) offered by the new product, the organizing Committee of the Mexico Olympics (1968) proposed to the IAAF the use of such materials for the Games. Such a plan was discussed at the IAAF Congress of 1966 in Budapest. The international body posed a veto, claiming that such synthetic materials were by then used only in North America. Its adoption, so claimed the IAAF, would be discriminating for all those countries where Tartan was unknown as they would not have the opportunity of becoming familiar with it. Mexican officials, headed by Prof. César Moreno Bravo, now a member of the IAAF Council and in 1968 head officer for athletics in the Olympics, stood fast by their project and finally succeeded in getting the assent of the IAAF for the use of the new materials. However, the international body requested an experimentation of the new product. The Mexicans thus presented two venues, with different installations: one with track and circles in traditional materials and the other – the magnificent "Estadio Olimpico de la Ciudad Universitaria". Technical IAAF delegates Adriaan Paulen and Donald Pain were invited to witness preliminary ventures in both venues, to become acquainted with the reaction of the athletes. Those who were not familiar with Tartan soon accepted it enthusiastically. The new product thus found its way in the history of athletics. The "3M" was produced in three different colours – grey, green and blue. However, IAAF technical delegates opted for a red colour as per tradition until then prevailing in all previous Games. The Minnesota Company had never used that colour before yet had no difficulties in complying with such a wish!

G.P.

CARL LEWIS SUPERSTAR MJ AND HIS RECORD OF RECORDS - 19.32

The last twenty years of the 20th century were characterized by a steady growth of the international athletics calendar. First and foremost was the appearance of a World Championship meet entirely dependent on the IAAF. Several other sports already had "Worlds" of their own, while the IAAF had long adhered to the concept that such a championship meet was embodied in the Olympic Games, in which track and field had long been acclaimed as the no.1 sport. In fact Rule 10, paragraph 2 of the IAAF book read: "The Olympic Games shall be regarded as World Championships in track and field athletics". In the course of time, however, the growth of the sport at all levels and the strongly felt necessity of having such a global meet more frequently than every fourth year inevitably led to the introduction of an autonomous IAAF World Championship. The first edition was held at Helsinki in 1983 (7-14 August), Initially such a meet was scheduled for pre-Olympic years only, but from 1991 onwards a biennial frequency was adopted, with the meet held in every odd year. As a result, only one year out of four is now without a global (Worlds or Olympics) championship.

Invitational meets at the international level also grew in number. Beginning with 1985, the most important ones were made part of the Grand Prix IAAF/Mobil, after the name of the sponsoring company that made it possible for the IAAF to award prizes to the most successful athletes. In 1998 the leading Grand Prix meets joined to form the IAAF Golden League, which offered a jackpot of 1 million US dollars to be divided among leading men and women. Primo Nebiolo, who was elected President of the IAAF in 1981, thought that such a reform would reinforce the concept of prize money, while attempting to discontinue the trend of over-inflated appearance fees, a phenomenon that had been growing "under the table" during the Seventies.

Two sprinters were head and shoulders above the rest during the Eighties: Carl Lewis of USA and Ben Johnson of Canada. The former was great, versatile and most durable as a top-notch performer in the 100, 200 m. (and long jump); the latter was simply phenomenal as a single event (100 m.) man but eventually saw his athletics stature tarnished by the doping evil, as explained in an adjoining aside.

Frederick Carlton "Carl" Lewis (born at Birmingham, Alabama, on 1 July 1961; 1.88 m. / 79 kg.) collected a record number of noble medals between 1983 and 1996 – eight golds, one silver and one bronze in the World Championships; nine golds and one silver in the Olympic Games. In 1984, at Los Angeles, he equalled Jesse Owens' legendary feat from the 1936 Olympics, winning four gold medals – in exactly the same events as the "Ebony Antelope": 100, 200 m., long jump and 4x100 m. relay. A unique series, especially if one considers that in order to qualify for those meets he had to pass every time through the "Caudine Forks" of the US Olympic Trials (or the US Championships), a test which as often as not was just as hard as the "global" championships themselves. In my opinion, such honours amply suffice to stamp Lewis as one of the greatest athletes of all time – if not the greatest. Clockwise, the man who was dubbed "Figlio del vento" (Son of the Wind) by Italian sportswriter Franco Arturi, can point to the following series of marks:

- **100 m.** Fifteen legitimate marks between 9.86 (a world record in 1991)and 9.99. Twelve marks between 9.78 and 9.99 with the aid of winds exceeding 2 m/s.
- **200 m.** Ten legitimate marks between 19.75 and 19.99.
- **4x100 m. relay.** Twelve marks between 37.40 (a world record in 1992) and 37.99, always as anchor man.
- **Long jump.** Nine legitimate marks between 8.87 and 8.70. Eight marks between 8.91 and 8.70 with the aid of winds exceeding 2 m/s.

Tall and statuesque, Lewis was not considered a great starter, yet he held at one time the world's indoor record for the 60 y. (6.02 at Dallas in 1983). His pickup midway in the race was undoubtedly his "atout maître". Always a reliable competitor on big occasions, he diligently followed the advice given him by coach Tom Tellez. Comparing him as an athlete with Jesse Owens – who incidentally came from Alabama, just like Lewis – is well nigh impossible, since so many things have changed in athletics during the half century that separated them. Each won four Olympic gold medals in exactly the same events. But the similarity ends here: on his return from the Berlin Olympics Owens found that medals and records could not be converted into money – that is, along the amateur path of his time. Having a family to support he was forced to leave school and athletics as well, in search of financially more rewarding paths. Lewis, on the contrary, happened to evolve at a time when it was finally possible for a top-class athlete to be a self-avowed professional. After his four golds of 1984 in Los Angeles he was thus able to continue as a top-class athlete for another 12 years. Outside the track Lewis was advised by an intelligent manager, Joe Douglas, and thus appeared to be ever conscious of the image he was likely to offer, even to the point of occasionally losing something in terms of spontaneity.

Lewis was a precocious talent. He started at age 7, "not very seriously, of course". Sprinting was his first concern but, curiously enough, he first made the headlines as a long jumper, with 24-10 (7.57 m.) and a wind-aided 25-9 (7.85) at age 17, by which time he could also point to a promising 10.5 for the metric century. In 1979, while in High School at Willingboro, New Jersey, the 18-year-old Carl was quoted as saying: "This may sound funny, but my goal is to be the best of all time".

Doubts that the lad might be overestimating his potential were soon dispelled. A few weeks later he placed third in the long jump at the Pan-American Games at San Juan, Puerto Rico with 8.13 - exactly the distance of Jesse Owens' world record on his Day of Days at Ann Arbor in 1935! The 18-year-old Carl achieved that mark on his 6th and last try. As a sprinter he first reached national class in 1980, with a 100-200 m. double in the US Junior Championships – times 10.21 and 20.66. As previously related, he was fourth in the century at the US Olympic Trials in Eugene, good enough to earn a place on the sprint relay team. But USA had previously decided to boycott the Moscow Olympics and he had to stay away from the Games. Carl did visit Europe though and finished second to Stanley Floyd in the 100 m. (10.23 to 10.20) in Rome.

Lewis continued to progress throughout the next two years, yet he suffered an unexpected rout in the 1981 World Cup, held in Rome. In the 100 m. he was laid low by a re-injury midway in the race and wound up ninth and last. By then, however, his best for that distance was a sound 10.00 - apart from a windy 9.99. He reiterated his 10-flat in 1982, when he also began to reveal his potential as a 200 m. man with 20.27.

Benjamin Sinclair "Ben" Johnson (born at Falmouth, Jamaica, on 30 December 1961; 1.80 m. / 75 kg.) left his native country at 15, when his mother, Gloria, following a split in the family, emigrated to Canada with her six children. Ben, affected by balbuties, had a troubled youth but found partial solace in practicing various sports, notably including athletics, in which he caught the eye of coach Charles Francis. Although not so precocious as his American rival, Ben managed to run the century in 10.25 shortly before turning twenty. His first clash with Carl Lewis was at Sudbury late in 1980. The Canadian lost badly in a 100 m. event – 10.88 for sixth, while Lewis won in 10.43. Save for a 50 y. race indoors in 1982, in

Ben Johnson, a Jamaican-born Canadian, with a build more akin to a boxer than a sprinter. He made the news, good and bad, in the late Eighties.

which he narrowly beat Lewis, the Canadian was to retain his underdog status vis-à-vis his American rival till August 1985. During such a period the score was 9-to-1 in Lewis' favour. Johnson faced his first major international task at the 1982 Commonwealth Games in Brisbane, Australia, where he placed second to Allan Wells in the 100 m., 10.05 to 10.02 (aiding wind, 5.9 m/s). In the 200 m. the Scotsman had to be content with a tie for first with Mike McFarlane of England (time for both, 20.43). It should be added that Johnson did not like this distance. He seldom tried it, with a best of 20.41 in 1985 (plus a wind-aided 20.37 in '82).

The big event of 1983 was the inaugural edition of the World Championships. The venue chosen for such a historic "première" was Helsinki, capital of Finland, one of the noblest track countries. Next to Lewis, the most redoubtable pre-meet prospect was another American, Calvin Smith (born on 8 January 1961 at Bolton, Mississippi; 1.78 m. / 64 kg.), the type of sprinter who throve off hard racing. Very much in evidence since 1982, when he was credited with 10.05 and 20.31 (plus wind-aided 9.91 and 20.20). He rose to stardom on 3 July 1983 when he cracked Jim Hines' world's 100 m. record with 9.93, aided by a legal wind of 1.38 m/s.This mark also had the benefit of a rarefied atmosphere, since it was made at Air Force Academy (Colorado), 2195 m. above sea level. Smith won by a sound margin, as runner-up Bernard Jackson was timed in 10.19. But then Lewis too looked very sharp in pre-Worlds meets. At Modesto in May he had his first sub-10 in the century – 9.97. In the US Championships at Indianapolis on 19 June he came dangerously close to Pietro Mennea's 200 m. world record with a magnificent 19.75. Apart from the fact that this was made at sea level, Lewis thrust both arms into the air before crossing the finish line. This surely cost him vital fractions, but eye-witness Bert Nelson, one of the founding editors of "Track & Field News", noted that Lewis seemed to be far less concerned about the lost record opportunity than were the record-hungry fans. Another great long jumper, Larry Myricks, was second (20.03) and Calvin Smith third (20.13).

Lewis was content with three events in the Helsinki rendez-vous – 100, 4x100 m. and long jump. He came out of it with three gold medals, exhibiting a superiority seldom if ever seen in meets of this calibre. His victory in the century was outrageously easy. In fact the only trouble he had to face was .... a bee which molested him just before the start of the final. He slapped at it with his left hand, then walked away from the blocks. No false start was called. At the right getaway he lagged well behind Calvin Smith, but in the closing stage he came up so strongly that his rival was simply swollen. Lewis won by a wide margin – 10.07 to 10.21. Emmit King made it a clean sweep for USA, just ahead of Allan Wells. Ben Johnson only made it up to the "semis". So did Frank Emmelmann of the GDR, who had won the European title the year before.

With Lewis not in the game, the 200 metres was a very easy job for Calvin Smith, who won hands down in 20.14 from his countryman Elliott Quow (20.41). The only non-US medallist in the sprints was Pietro Mennea, who was third just ahead of Allan Wells. The world record holder, by then 31, was far from his 1979-80 form, yet he also contributed to Italy's silver medal in the sprint relay with a fine anchor leg, well behind USA, of course. King, Willie Gault, Smith and Lewis chalked up history's first sub-38 secs. mark with a nifty 37.86. Incidentally, this was Carl's first world record. And for the first time, eight teams bettered 39 secs. in the same race. It should be added that for once the relay came midway in the week, after the 100 m. and before the 200 m.

1983 World Championships, Helsinki – 100 metres (8 August) w –0.3 m/s: 1.Carl Lewis (USA) 10.07; 2.Calvin Smith (USA) 10.21; 3.Emmit King (USA) 10.24; 4.Allan Wells (UK) 10.27; 5.Juan Nuñez (Dom.Rep.) 10.29; 6.Christian Haas (FRG) 10.32; 7.Paul Narracott (Aus) 10.33; 8.Desai Williams (Can) 10.36. Lanes: Wells 1, King 2, Lewis 3, Haas 4, Williams 5, Narracott 6, Nuñez 7, Smith 8.

200 metres (14 August) w +1.1 m/s: 1.Calvin Smith (USA) 20.14; 2.Elliott Quow (USA) 20.41; 3.Pietro Mennea (Ita) 20.51; 4.Allan Wells (UK) 20.52; 5.Frank

Emmelmann (GDR) 20.55; 6.Innocent Egbunike (Nig) 20.63; 7.Carlo Simionato (Ita) 20.69; 8.João da Silva (Bra) 20.80. Lanes: Simionato 1, Egbunike 2, Smith 3, Wells 4, Mennea 5, Quow 6, Emmelmann 7, da Silva 8.

4x100 metre relay (10 August): 1. USA (E.King, W.Gault, C.Smith, C.Lewis) 37.86; 2.Ita (S.Tilli, C.Simionato, P.Pavoni, P.Mennea) 38.37; 3.SU (A.Prokofyev, N.Smirnov, V.Muravyov, V.Bryzgin) 38.41; 4.GDR 38.51; 5.FRG 38.56; 6.Pol 38.72; 7.Jam 38.75; 8.Fra 38.98. Lanes: SU 1, Jam 2, USA 3, FRG 4, Ita 5, Pol 6, GDR 7, Fra 8.

The most notable event of post-Worlds weeks was a 200 m. race at the Zurich "Weltklasse", which saw Lewis suffer a crushing defeat at the hands of Calvin Smith, who lowered his best to 19.99, while Lewis, probably past his peak for the season, both physically and mentally, did no better than 20.21. In the final of the European Cup in London, Wells beat Mennea over the same distance, 20.72 to 20.74.

For the first time in athletics annals, track fans were offered global meets in consecutive years, 1983 and 1984. But while the Worlds had been exempt from the evils of politically inspired boycotts, the Los Angeles Olympics suffered from the prolonged effects of the so-called "Cold War". This time it was USSR's turn to stay away from the Games, officially because "they would feel insecure" in the Los Angeles area, but most probably because they wanted to "repay" USA for their boycott of the 1980 Olympics in Moscow. The GDR and other countries of the Communist bloc sided with USSR, all except Romania, which courageously chose to have its own team present in LA. In terms of sprint potential, however, none of the absentees could have vied for medals in Los Angeles.

Fifty-two years after the 1932 Olympics, the Los Angeles Memorial Coliseum became the first stadium to host two editions of the Games. And this time Carl Lewis decided to play at four, not three, tables. As far as the finals were concerned, his events came in the following sequence: 100, long jump, 200, 4x100. Prior to that, he had a rehearsal of the three individual events at the US Olympic Trials, which were held some 7 weeks before at the same Los Angeles venue. Carl went through the motions with easy wins and the following marks: 100 m., 10.06 (Sam Graddy 2nd, 10.21), 200 m., 19.86 (Kirk Baptiste 2nd, 20.05), LJ 8.71 (Larry Myricks 2nd 8.25).

Lewis went on to make his dream come true: win four Olympic gold medals, just as Jesse Owens had done at Berlin in 1936, incidentally at the same age, 23. The timetable of his exploits read like this:

- 3 August,	10.05	a.m.,	100 m. heat,	1st 10.32.
- 3 August,	0.40	p.m.,	100 m. quarter-final,	1st 10.04.
- 4 August,	4.35	p.m.,	100 m. semi-final,	1st 10.14.
- 4 August,	7.10	p.m.,	100 m., final,	1st 9.99.
- 5 August,	4.10	p.m.,	long jump, qual. round,	8.30w.
- 6 August,	10.00	a.m.,	200 m., heat,	1st 21.02.
- 6 August,	12.00	a.m.,	200 m. quarter-final,	1st 20.48.
- 6 August,	5.40	p.m.,	long jump, final,	1st 8.54.
- 8 August,	4.00	p.m.,	200 m. semi-final,	1st 20.27.
- 8 August,	6.30	p.m.,	200 m. final,	1st 19.80.
- 10 August,	12.00	a.m.,	4x100 m. heat, USA	1st 38.89.
- 11 August,	10.30	a.m.,	4x100 m. semi-final, USA	1st 38.44.
- 11 August,	4.50	p.m.,	4x100 m. final. USA	1st 37.83 (WR).

Carl Lewis (USA) winning the 100 m. at the 1991 World Championships in Tokyo. His team-mates Leroy Burrell (lane 3) and Dennis Mitchell (lane 6) were second and third respectively. Winner's time, 9.86, a new world record.

The climax of it all probably coincided with the long jump final: Carl opened with a stupendous 8.54 and went on with a foul, after which he decided to call it a day (he finally won with 30 cms. to spare!). While approaching the victory podium, Lewis was booed by the most unknowledgeable section of the crowd. To which Carl, forever the gentleman, reacted with the following words: "I was shocked at first. But after I thought about it, I realized they were booing because they wanted to see more of Carl Lewis. I guess that's flattering".

Even in the sprint department, Lewis was obviously in a class by himself. He won the 100 m. crown in 9.99, with 0.20 sec. to spare vis-à-vis Sam Graddy, who relegated Ben Johnson (10.22) to third. In the 200 m. Carl was vastly ahead of his countryman Kirk Baptiste, 19.80 to 19.96. Pietro Mennea, in his fourth Olympiad, had to be content with seventh. Same as in Helsinki the year before, the Americans were at their best in the 4x100 m. relay, lowering the world record to 37.83. To this they came with the following contributions: Sam Graddy 10.29, Ron Brown 9.19, Calvin Smith 9.41 and Carl Lewis 8.94.

1984 Olympics, Los Angeles - 100 metres (4 August) w +0.2 m/s: 1.Carl Lewis (USA) 9.99; 2.Sam Graddy (USA) 10.19; 3.Ben Johnson (Can) 10.22; 4.Ron Brown (USA) 10.26; 5.Mike McFarlane (UK) 10.27; 6.Raymond Stewart (Jam) 10.29; 7.Donovan Reid (UK) 10.33; 8.Tony Sharpe (Can) 10.35. Lanes: Brown 1, McFarlane 2, Sharpe 3, Johnson 4, Graddy 5, Reid 6, Lewis 7, Stewart 8.

200 metres (8 August) w - 0.9 m/s: 1.Carl Lewis (USA) 19.80; 2.Kirk Baptiste (USA) 19.96, 3.Thomas Jefferson (USA) 20.26; 4.João da Silva (Bra) 20.30; 5.Ralf Lübke (FRG) 20.51; 6.Jean-Jacques Boussemart (Fra) 20.55; 7.Pietro Mennea (Ita) 20.55; 8.Ade Mafe (UK) 20.85. Lanes: Mafe 1, Boussemart 2, Baptiste 3, Jefferson 4, Mennea 5, Lübke 6, Lewis 7, da Silva 8.

4x100 metre relay (11 August): 1.USA (S.Graddy, R.Brown, C.Smith, C.Lewis) 37.83; 2.Jam (A.Lawrence, G.Meghoo, D.Quarrie, R.Stewart) 38.62; 3.Can (B.Johnson, T.Sharpe, D.Williams, S.Hinds) 38.70, 4.Ita 38.87; 5.FRG 38.99; 6.Fra 39.10; 7.UK 39.13; 8.Bra 39.40. Lanes: Jam 1, FRG 2, Ita 3, UK 4, USA 5, Can 6, Fra 7, Bra 8.

Nothing sensational happened in post-Olympic meets held in Europe. Carl Lewis chalked up his third 9.99 of the year in the 100 m. at the "Weltklasse" in Zurich. Cubans Osvaldo Lara and Leandro Peñalver, probably the most notable absentees at Los Angeles, failed to make any impression on top US sprinters.

Ben Johnson made an important step forward in 1985. In the World Cup at Canberra late that year he won the century in 10.00 from Chidi Imoh of Nigeria, 10.11, Frank Emmelmann of the GDR and Kirk Baptiste, (both 10.17). In outdoor meets held in 1985, Johnson and Lewis met three times and "King" Carl beat his growing rival 2-to-1. Consistent Kirk Baptiste, then 22 , was US champion in both 100 (10.11) and 200 m. (20.11).

It was in 1986 that "Big Ben" really began to turn the tables on Lewis. The Canadian met his rival three times in the century and always won. In fact none of those races was close. Johnson had the fastest time of the year, 9.95, in a meeting designed to offset at least in part the negative effects of Olympic boycotts - the Goodwill Games, held in Moscow. Chidi Imoh of Nigeria was second (10.04) and Lewis third (10.06). In the same meet, Floyd Heard of USA won the 200 m. in 20.12, the fastest time of the year.

The Johnson vs. Lewis saga reached a fever pitch in 1987. The meet of the year was scheduled for Rome – the second edition of the World Championships. To add spice to the eagerly awaited confrontation, the two rivals offered a preview in a century at Sevilla late in May. Johnson won by the proverbial whisker, 10.06 to 10.07. The American gave further signs of his return to top form a few days later in Madrid, when he ran the 200 m. in 19.92. In Rome he exhibited a brilliant form in the prelims, with such times as 10.05 (heat) and 10.03 (semi-final). Johnson apparently took it easy, if that is correct in the case of 10.14 (quarter-final) and 10.15 (semi-final) times. The showdown at 6.40 in the afternoon was anticipated ahead of all other confrontations by the large crowds. The Canadian was the favourite, although one could notice that press-box sympathies still lay with Lewis. The draw added further heat to the debate, putting them side by side – Johnson in 5 and Lewis in 6. Johnson clearly outshone his rival in reaction time at the start – 0.109 vs. 0.196. He led by a clear margin at the halfway mark (5.53 vs. 5.64). Lewis' famous finishing speed made little or no difference on that occasion. He regained only a trifle (0.01) in the second half of the race, and the final verdict was a clear-cut decision: Johnson 9.83, Lewis 9.93. Even allowing for the fact that Lewis lost 0.087 vis-à-vis Johnson on reaction time alone. The Canuck thus obliterated Calvin Smith's world record by 0.10 sec. and Lewis tied it. Through his record performance Johnson really brought the crowd to its feet. To the point of obscuring another event that followed only 12 minutes later – Stefka Kostadinova's world mark (2.09) in the women's high jump. (At the time of writing, 19 years later, Stefka's feat is still unsurpassed ...). Third in this historic race was Ray Stewart of Jamaica (10.08).

By comparison, the 200 m. was demoted to the rank of a quasi-ordinary event. Yet it offered a fascinating finish, with the first three wrapped up in the space of 0.02 sec. With Lewis not in it, Calvin Smith was considered a clear favourite, yet he had to fight hard all the way. He was only sixth at the half-way mark (10.63), well behind leader Vladimir Krilov of USSR (10.49). But the ever consistent Calvin came back strongly and finally won in 20.16, barely ahead of Gilles Quénehervé of France and John Regis of Britain (20.16 and 20.18). Smith was not able to run a faster turn because of a groin injury picked up in the semi-final. Given this condition, he was happy to get lane 8 though.

In the relay the US quartet once again compensated for their mediocre baton passing with their vastly superior speed. At the last exchange Vladimir Krilov started with a lead of about 2 metres vis-à-vis Carl Lewis. The latter easily turned the tables on his rival though. With a superlative 8.86 leg he was even faster than in the Olympic race at Los Angeles in 1984, and USA thus beat USSR - 37.90 to 38.02, the latter being a new European record.

There was unfortunately a belated PS to Johnson's 100 m. heroics in Rome. His 9.83 for the century was initially ratified by the IAAF, but after his 9.79 in the 1988 Olympics in Seoul and his subsequent disqualification for a doping offence, he was stripped of his former (Rome) record as well. In September 1989 the IAAF decided that the gold medal and record from Rome should go to Carl Lewis. Consequently, Raymond Stewart of Jamaica was raised to second and Linford Christie of Great Britain to third.

BEN'S START WAS O.K.

The 100 metre final of the 1987 World Championships in Rome – won by Ben Johnson in 9.83 – was characterized by a circumstance which apparently eluded the attention of the Fourth Estate.

On that occasion I happened to be there as a counter-starter or recaller (shortly afterwards I would act as starter in the women's 100 metre final). The timing system was that of Seiko, a Japanese company that also supplied the control apparatus for false starts. Contrary to what was the rule of the time, the allowed minimum of a runner's reaction time was fixed at 0.120 secs., against the 0.100 then in use. Seiko justified such a change on strictly technical reasons. Here is the detailed story of what happened at 18.40 hrs on that Sunday, the 30th of August.

Ben Johnson's reaction time was truly exceptional: 0.109 sec. For some unknown reason, the figure first released to the press was 0.129 sec., yet the documentary evidence still in my possession unequivocally confirms the former figure. Johnson's reaction time was 0.087 sec. faster than that of his chief rival Carl Lewis (0.196 sec.).

At this stage somebody could ask: if the minimum reaction time was then set at 0.120

sec., wasn't Johnson's start "illegal" ? Such a hypothesis was not taken into consideration as the Canadian's start appeared to be visually correct in the opinion of both the starter and the recaller.

By 1987 the rule book included some innovations introduced at the IAAF Convention of 1986 in Stuttgart. A propos starting blocks, rule 162 paragraph 9-V stated: "Starting blocks may be fitted with approved false start detection apparatus to assist starters". Such a rule remained in force throughout the 1988 Olympics in Seoul and the 1991 World Championships in Tokyo. In actual fact the sentence "to assist starters" reaffirmed the basic conception that the starter remained the ultimate judge. He was offered a helping hand by the start control apparatus, yet it was up to him to avail himself of a headphone signalling, with a high pitched ring in his ears, that a runner had reacted in excess of the allowed minimum time. Somebody may wonder why I'm using such a dubitative form. We knew from experiments made as well as from statements of the English operators of Seiko material that the control instruments reacted not only to actual false starts but also to the contraction of muscles, to the hardening of a limb or even to any imperceptible movement of the feet after the "set" command. Hence it was entirely up to the starter and/or recaller to decide, regardless of acoustic signals, whether a start was visually correct and runners were actually still (motionless) as required by the rule. Starters at the 1987 World Championships in Rome behaved accordingly. In the 100 metre final the start was correct in the opinion of both the starter and the two recallers. And the latter were located where they could have a different view of the field vis-à-vis that of the starter. Add that starter Gianfranco Cipelli, the only one to use a headphone, confirmed that he did not hear any signal likely to advise him otherwise.

At the IAAF Convention of 1993 in Stuttgart, for the purpose of removing all possible doubts, rule 162 was enriched with a new paragraph, 10, which made it compulsory to connect the blocks with the instrument signalling false starts. And for the starter to use a headphone connected with such an instrument, in order to perceive a signal any time a runner reacted to the gun in less than 100 thousandths of a second. By introducing such an innovation the technical commission of the IAAF virtually made the starter subordinate to the machine. In my opinion, however, this will not be the solution of all problems, as evidenced by some embarrassing cases which occurred at the 1995 World Championships in Göteborg.

Getting back to the Rome 100 metre final, the correctness of Ben Johnson's start was further confirmed by a text, "Time Analysis of the Sprints at the 2nd WC, Rome 1987", edited by Moravec, Ruzicka, Dostal, Susanka, Kojecs and Nosek, researchers of the department of computerized bio-mechanics at the Charles University in Prague. This was contained in the "Scientific Report on the 2nd World Championships in Athletics, Rome 1987", published in London, 1988, by the IAF (International Athletic Foundation). On the basis of registrations made by a high velocity TV-camera, which supplied 196 images per second, it was possible to analyse all starts and reaction times and compare them with those furnished by the starting blocks. Here are the figures concerning Johnson and Lewis. The former reacted after 0.109 sec. as per starting blocks, whereas the rapid TV camera showed 0.143, hence well within the limits of the rule. For Lewis the response of the TV-camera was slightly "heavier" than that of starting blocks: 0.199 sec. to 0.196. All this leads me to conclude that suspicions on Ben Johnson's start were to be attributed exclusively to his peculiar starting motion, quite different from that of his rivals.

G.P.

1987 World Championships, Rome - 100 metres (30 August) w +1.0 m/s: 1. Carl Lewis (USA) 9.93; 2.Raymond Stewart (Jam) 10.08; 3.Linford Christie (UK) 10.14; 4.Attila Kovács (Hun) 10.20; 5.Viktor Bryzgin (SU) 10.25; 6.Lee McRae (USA) 10.34; 7.Pierfrancesco Pavoni (Ita) 16.23 (injured). Ben Johnson (Can) 1st in 9.83, but retroactively disqualified. Lanes: Brizgin 1, Pavoni 2, Stewart 3,

Kovács 4, Johnson 5, Lewis 6, McRae 7, Christie 8.

200 metres (3 September) w -0.4 m/s: 1.Calvin Smith (USA) 20.16; 2.Gilles Quéneherve (Fra) 20.16; 3.John Regis (UK) 20.18; 4.Robson da Silva (Bra) 20.22; 5.Vladimir Krilov (SU) 20.23; 6.Floyd Heard (USA) 20.25; 7.Pierfrancesco Pavoni (Ita) 20.45; 8.Atlee Mahorn (Can) 20.78. Lanes: Mahorn 1, Regis 2, Heard 3, da Silva 4, Krilov 5, Quéneherve 6, Pavoni 7, Smith 8.

4x100 metre relay (6 September): 1.USA (L.McRae, L.McNeill, H.Glance, C.Lewis) 37.90; 2.SU (A.Yevgenyev, V.Bryzgin, V.Muravyov, V.Krilov) 38.02; 3.Jam (J.Mair, A.Smith, C.Wright, R.Stewart) 38.41; 4.FRG 38.73; 5.Hun 39.04; 6.Ita 39.62; 7.Chi 39.93; Can, 4th in 38.47, retroactively disqualified because of Ben Johnson's drug offence. Lanes: Chi 1, Ita 2, SU 3, Can 4, USA 5, Jam 6, FRG 7, Hun 8.

Johnson's record in 1987 was indeed phenomenal: from January through September he ran twenty-one 100 m. races (counting finals only) and never lost! He ducked under 10 seconds five times, counting a wind-assisted 9.7, manual time. Lewis was no.1 in the 200 metres, even if he did not compete in this event in Rome. Before and after that meet he beat Smith every time they met.

1988 offered even greater exploits and the two main characters in the play were once more Ben and Carl. The apex was reached at the Seoul Olympics, when the Canadian iterated his victory of the year before in Rome with an even faster time, only to meet disgrace only a few hours later when it was announced that he had turned positive in a doping test.

Prior to the Seoul rendez-vous the Big Two locked horns only once, in the Zurich "Weltklasse" meet. Lewis won in a hair-raising finish. Calvin Smith was also in the race and actually relegated Johnson to third. Times: 9.93, 9.97 and 10.00. The wind was a favourable but legal +1.1 m/s. In fairness to Johnson, somebody said that he still felt the effects of a hamstring injury he suffered in an indoor meet.

The US Olympic Trials, held at Indianapolis, were as usual an ebullient affair. Lewis ran both 100 and 200 m. At the shorter distance an aiding wind of 5.2 m/s., well over the limit, brought seven of the eight finalists to duck under 10 seconds, with Lewis an impressive winner in 9.78, followed by Dennis Mitchell (9.86) and Calvin Smith (9,87). The 200 m. came as the last exertion of the week for Lewis, i.e. after he had won both 100 m. and long jump. For once he was beaten at his forte, i.e. the closing stage: with 20 m. to go he was baffled by Joe DeLoach, his team-mate at Santa Monica Track Club, 20.01 to 19.96. The latter had previously placed no higher than fifth in the century. This powerful sprinter (born on 5 June 1967 at Bay City, Texas; 1.84 m. / 75 kg.) had emerged four years earlier, taking both sprints at the Pan-American Junior Championships. He continued to progress gradually, showing a marked preference for the 200 m. Even so, his overall record was uneven and what he did at Indianapolis therefore surprised many people. After his breakthrough he said: "This was the most pressure I ever felt in my life; it's a big relief to get this over with". Yet that was only the first of the two mountains Americans had to climb: the other one was at Seoul two months later.

At Seoul the 100 m. tale unfolded very much as it had done in Rome a year before, i.e. with Lewis sprightly in the prelims (9.99 quarter-final and 9.97 semi-final) and Johnson unassailable in the final. This time the Canadian was only a little bit faster than Lewis in reacting to the gun: 0.132 vs 0.136. It was in the first half of the race that Johnson gained a decisive lead vis-à-vis his American rival – 5.52 to 5.65. Lewis' legendary pickup in the closing stage was for once ineffective. In fact he did not gain in the second half of the race. Johnson thus won by a decisive margin, 9.79 to 9.92, truly a K.O. verdict. The Canadian exhibited shorter but quicker steps - 47 to Lewis' 44 for the entire race. In fact, the truly close duel was between Lewis and Linford Christie for second place, and Carl finally had the edge by 0.05. The Englishman wound up with 9.97, a new European record.

The bomb, probably the noisiest ever in Olympic annals, exploded three days later, when the IOC disqualified Johnson after his urine samples tested positive for stanozolol, an anabolic steroid. As an inevitable consequence, Johnson was inflicted an automatic 2-year ban by the IAAF. He lost his gold medal and the world record as well. More on this in the adjoining aside. Carl Lewis became the first 100 m. man to create an official world record while finishing second.

Lewis won a gold medal in the long jump before facing his third assignment, the 200 m. final. However, to make sure against such a tough rival as Larry Myricks, he had to take all six tries, not just two as in Los Angeles four years earlier. How much all this took out of Lewis was hard to say, even for coach Tom Tellez, who acted as mentor to both Carl and Joe DeLoach. Be that as it may, in the 200 m. final the latter ran the race of his life and won. It was a fascinating spectacle: for once Lewis, in lane 3, led his rival, in lane 6, at the halfway point – 10.31 to 10.35. Then DeLoach truly surpassed himself, achieving what very few mortals, if any, had ever been able to achieve: run faster than Lewis – 9.40 to 9.48 - in the second half of the race. DeLoach won by a narrow margin, 19.75 to 19.79, equalling Lewis's American record, which was also a low altitude world record. Not the least part of DeLoach's satisfaction may have come from the words of his team-mate and friend Carl: "I feel very good for Joe. I'm very proud of him. We have worked together a lot, but he has done it all himself".

A PS to the 200 m. tale should be reserved to Pietro Mennea. By then 36, the Italian entered the Games for the fifth time. In the latter part of his long career he had announced his retirement twice, only to come back again and again. In Seoul he barely passed the first round with 21.10 – then wisely decided to laugh at himself and call it a day. He had made the final of that event on all his previous tries, a unique achievement in the annals of sprinting.

In the relay the favourite Americans met disgrace in the very first round. Competing with a team mostly made of alternates, they went out of the exchange zone in the last pass and were disqualified. This opened the door to the USSR, whose team was made as usual of well-tuned relay men. They won from Great Britain, whose anchor leg man was Linford Christie. In the poisoned atmosphere prevailing after the Johnson affair, Christie had first been named as testing positive for a banned substance, but was later cleared. He celebrated by moving from fifth to second in the anchor leg.

THORNY QUESTION

The widely publicized " Johnson affair" caused the IAAF to revise its doping rules, making them stricter and far-reaching. Doping controls were intensified and in 1989 they were extended to random out-of-competition tests conducted in training camps. Johnson's belated confession was probably instrumental in the addition of the following paragraph (Rule 55/6): "An admission may be made either orally or in a verifiable manner or in writing. For the purpose of these rules, a statement is not to be regarded as an admission where it was made more than six years after the facts to which it relates. Ben Johnson was deprived not only of the world record he set at Seoul, where he proved positive to a forbidden substance, but also of the one he set the year before in Rome, where in the admission of competent officials he had proven negative to a test conducted after the race. As a result, this retroactivity seems at best debatable. It amounts to an indirect admission, on the part of the IAAF, that control techniques used at the 1987 World Championships were far from faultless. Such a suspicion could easily be extended to other medal winners in that meet or, for that matter, any previous championship meet. If methods used at the time were inadequate, I see little or no utility in trying to "correct the past" on the strength of lone admissions or confessions. It is more important to concentrate on enforcing the law at the present time as uniformly as possible.

1988 Olympics, Seoul - 100 metres (24 September) w +1.1 m/s: 1.Carl Lewis (USA) 9.92; 2.Linford Christie

(UK) 9.97; 3.Calvin Smith (USA) 9.99; 4.Dennis Mitchell (USA) 10.04; 5.Robson da Silva (Bra) 10.11; 6.Desai Williams (Can) 10.11; 7.Raymond Stewart (Jam) 12.26 (injured). Ben Johnson (Can), first in 9.79, was later disqualified for a doping offence. Lanes: R.da Silva 1 Stewart 2, Lewis 3, Christie 4, Smith 5, Johnson 6, Williams 7, Mitchell 8.

200 metres (28 September) w +1.7 m/s: 1.Joe DeLoach (USA) 19.75; 2.Carl Lewis (USA) 19.79; 3.Robson da Silva (Bra) 20.04; 4.Linford Christie (UK) 20.09; 5.Atlee Mahorn (Can) 20.39; 6.Gilles Quénehervé (Fra) 20.40; 7.Michael Rosswess (UK) 20.51; 8.Bruno Marie-Rose (Fra) 20.58. Lanes: Quénehervé 1, Mahorn 2, Lewis 3, R.da Silva 4, Christie 5, DeLoach 6, Marie-Rose 7, Rosswess 8.

4x100 metre relay (1 October): 1.SU (V.Bryzgin, V.Krilov, V.Muravyov, V.Savin) 38.19; 2.UK (E.Bunney, J.Regis, M.McFarlane, L. Christie) 38.28; 3.Fra (B.Marie-Rose, D.Sangouma, G. Quénehervé, M.Morinière) 38.40; 4.Jam 38.47; 5.Ita 38.54; 6.FRG 38.55; 7.Can 38.93; 8.Hun 39.19. Lanes: Can 1, FRG 2, UK 3, SU 4, Ita 5, Fra 6, Jam 7, Hun 8.

Late in 1988 the Canadian Government decided to start an investigation on doping abuses in Canadian sports. The "Dubin Inquiry", as it was called after Charles Dubin, the judge presiding over it, inevitably involved Johnson and his clan. Prior to the athlete's testimony, his physician Dr. Mario ("Jamie") Astaphan and his coach Charles Francis, as well as some athletes, made clear admissions which were subsequently confirmed by Johnson himself. He said he had been using steroids, testosterone and human growth hormone since 1981, following the advice of his mentors. After his tearful confession he said: "I did wrong, but I was confused at the time". He then urged young athletes to stay away from it. In the fall of 1988 the IAAF suspended Johnson for two years. Nobody can say to what extent he derived benefits from his long use of drugs. In 1991, being again eligible, he tried to make a comeback but turned out to be only a shadow of his previous self. In a widely publicized rematch with Carl Lewis at Villeneuve-d'Ascq, France, the Canadian finished a disappointing 7th in the 100 m. with 10.46 as Lewis (10.20) was second to Dennis Mitchell (10.09). That was the first meeting between Carl and Ben since Seoul '88 and possibly the richest in the history of the sport (they would split $500,000), but results looked ridiculous vis-à-vis the ballyhoo made in advance about the affair. The Johnson story was to end on an even sadder note. In 1992 he managed to do 10.16 in the 100 m. but in the Barcelona Olympics he did not go beyond the semi-finals. And early in 1993 he again tested positive, this time to testosterone, and the IAAF banned him for life. He made repeated attempts to be reinstated – to no avail.

Robson Caetano da Silva of Brazil (born on 4 September 1964 at Rio de Janeiro; 1.87 m. / 74 kg.) could by then be acclaimed as the best sprinter ever seen in South America. In the Seoul Olympics he was fifth in the 100 m. and third in the 200 m. He gained further credentials in 1989, when he posted the world's fastest time for the 200 m., 19.96, and won at the World Cup in Barcelona with 20.00, well ahead of Floyd Heard (USA), 20.36. A strongly built man, he was no. 1 for the longer distance in the "Track & Field News" World Ranking. In what was a rather pale season for US sprinters, no.1 in he 100 m. was Daniel Sangouma of France. He split (1-1) in direct confrontations with Carl Lewis and had a tougher schedule throughout the year.

However, the truly rising stars were by then Linford Christie of Britain and Leroy Burrell of USA. They finished first and second in that order (10.10 and 10.15 respectively) in the 100 m. of the World Cup. The Briton (born on 2 April 1960 at St.Andrews, Jamaica; 1.89 m. / 77 kg.) was really what is commonly described as a late comer. By the end of 1985, aged 25, his best for the century was 10.33. Then he decided to give it a truly serious try, spurred on by his coach, Ron Roddan. And he began to live up to his great potential. In 1986 he won the European 100 m. title (10.15) and had a seasonal best of 10.04. In 1988, as previously related, he was second to Lewis at the World Championships in Rome with 9.97, the first sub-10 by a European. In 1990 Britons

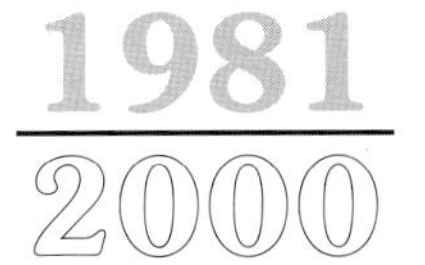

Carl Lewis during a visit to Palazzo Vecchio, Florence, in the late Nineties, revering a statue of "The Labours of Hercules" group.

CANADA
1192
NAMIBIA
1962

swept the board at the European Championships in Split, Croatia, with Christie winning the 100 m. in a wind-aided 10.00 from Sangouma (10.04) and John Regis, also of Britain, taking the 200 m. in 20.11. This meet also offered a superlative mark: a French foursome made a successful inroad in the favourite alley of US sprinters by conquering the world record for the 4x100 m. relay with 37.79. The runners and their splits were as follows: Max Morinière 10.58, Daniel Sangouma 8.90, Jean-Charles Trouabal 9.21, Bruno Marie-Rose 9.10. They were duly extended by a good British team, who wound up second in 37.98.

Leroy Burrell (born on 21 February 1967 at Philadelphia; 1.80 m. / 82 kg.) grew to world class in the shadow of Carl Lewis, mainly as his team-mate at the by then famous Santa Monica Track Club. And like Carl he could do well in the long jump too. In 1989 he won the US national title in the century with a superlative 9.94, best in the world for the year. In the high altitude of Provo, Utah, he did 8.37 in the long jump. The following year he had a superlative season, with times of 9.94, best in the world that year, in the 100 m. and 20.14 in the 200 m. At the shorter distance he was 2-1 against Lewis. On two other occasions they happened to be in the same meet but chose to run in different sections. He gained further in consistency during 1990, with no less than five sub-10 clockings, his legitimate best being a world leading 9.96. At the longer distance, however, he and the rest of the US élite were outshone by a phenomenal newcomer, who was to be the dominant force on the 200/400 m. axis for a long time to come.

The man in question was Michael Johnson (born on 13 September 1967 at Dallas; 1.83 m. / 77 kg.). In 1988 he could point to such marks as 20.07 (200 m.) and 45.23 (400 m.). Injury-prone in his early years, he had his first full season in top-class competition in 1990, when he was so impressive at both his favourite distances that "Track & Field News" voted him Athlete of the Year, on a world-wide basis that is. And the same magazine also ranked him no.1 in both 200 and 400 m. – the first-ever double of the kind in the history of the ranking (started in 1948).

From the very beginning Johnson was an anomalous sprinter, in the sense that he usually stayed away from the century. At this distance he showed up on very few occasions - he had a wind-aided 10.19 in 1988 and reached his career best, 10.08, in 1994. In the same year he ran his only US Championship race at this distance, pulling up lame at the half-way mark and walking in eighth and last. In other words, he never had the feeling as a century man. To compensate for this, he did marvellous things in the 200 m. and in the course of time he broke the world record and ..... put it out of sight. In 1990, his first super-season, he ducked under 20 secs. on four occasions, his best being 19.85, and ran the one lap in 44.21. His seasonal record also included a mind-boggling mark which could never make the books: true, accurate splits are tough to come by in the 4x200 metre relay, but his coach at Baylor University, Clyde Hart, caught him in 18.5 on the last leg of a 4x200 m. event at the Texas Relays (Austin, 6 April). "That's the time I got", said Hart, "but I'm not sure I believe it – but then, he made up at least 10 m. .....". The new trends then prevailing in the sport allowed the new champ to receive as much as $60,000 for one race in Europe. By the end of 1990 he also earned a marketing degree from Baylor. All this notwithstanding, he was described by a team-mate as "a regular guy who was not affected by the limelight". His upright running style with relatively little knee lift and quick, short strides made a considerable impact on track observers.

In 1991 Johnson went on with a flawless record, always on the 200/400 m. axis. In the 100 m. two men, Leroy Burrell and Carl Lewis, battled for supremacy and their duel was so hot that both broke the world record – in different races. The first round was in the US Championship race, held on 14 June at Downing Stadium on Randall's Island, New York. Lewis had been charged with a false start, and the subsequent getaway was disastrous for him. Burrell led throughout and repulsed his rival's attacks to win in world record time, 9.90 (aided, that's true, by a wind of 1.9 m/s, pretty close to the limit). Lewis was second in 9.94 - veteran observers said they couldn't recall ever having seen anyone

Donovan Bailey, left, and Frank Fredericks at the end of a heavy tussle in the 100 m. of the 1996 Olympics in Atlanta. The Canadian lowered the world record to 9.84 and Fredericks was runner-up in 9.89.

finish that well as he did. Dennis Mitchell was third in 10.00. At the longer distance, with Lewis not in the race, Burrell had to surrender to Michael Johnson, 20.42 to 20.31.

Burrell beat Lewis two more times in 100 m. races held in Europe. Carl thus entered the World Championship arena in Tokyo with an alarming record (0-3) vis-à-vis his team-mate. But he had one bolt in reserve and he shot it on the most important occasion. The 100 m. final on 25 August was aptly described as the greatest of all time – 6 athletes beating 10 secs. and the first two under the listed world mark! As generally expected, Burrell was faster than Lewis in reacting to the gun, 0.120 vs. 0.140, but three others too were faster: Dennis Mitchell 0.090 (more on this later on), Raymond Stewart 0.114 and Linford Christie 0.126. Stewart, Burrell and Mitchell were the early leaders, running abreast till the halfway mark which saw the Jamaican (5.54) just ahead of the other two (5.55). Lewis was barely sixth (5.61) at that stage. Then he put on his legendary finish, yet it was only with 10 m. to go that he gained a scant advantage on Burrell (9.00 to 9.01). Carl gained a little bit more before reaching the finish in 9.86, a new world record. The wind in the runners' favour was a legal 1.2 m/s. Burrell (9.88) was also under the previous limit and Mitchell was a close third (9.91). It was over this last that a controversy arose, right after the race. Mitchell's reaction time (0.090) actually beat the false start limit set for automatic recall (0.100). This was not picked up as the starter Hideo Iijima, (in his younger days Japanese record holder for the century – 10.1, hand time, in 1964) was inadvertently not wearing the headphones which would have made him aware of that with a high-pitched ring in his ears. It should be added that according to the IAAF rule the starter is not strictly obliged to do so, being "the sole judge of any fact connected with the start of the race". Linford Christie was fourth in 9.92, a new European record, and Frank Fredericks fifth in 9.95, a new African record.

As the tale goes, before the race an eyewitness who was sitting near the finish line predicted a winning time of ...9.86. His name? Ben Johnson of Canada.

Another Johnson, Michael by first name, had things going his way in the 200 m. With Lewis and Burrell not in the race, he won the world title hands down in 20.01. Not bad, considering that a strong wind (3.4 m/s) was blowing against the runners in the stretch. Frank Fredericks of Namibia was second in 20.34.

The Americans were obviously eager to regain the world relay record they had lost to France in 1990. So eager in fact that before the Tokyo rendez-vous they took early revenge, not once but twice. At Monaco, on 3 August, a Santa Monica Track Club team with Mike Marsh, Burrell, Floyd Heard and Lewis equalled the world record (37.79), while the French made a mistake at the first exchange and did not finish. Only four days later, at the "Weltklasse" meet in Zurich, a US national team with Marsh, Burrell, Mitchell and Lewis, did even better – 37.67 – while France had to be content with 38.39. The Tokyo affair followed the same line. Using "somewhat conservative passing", Andre Cason, Burrell, Mitchell and Lewis went home as easy winners, beating their brave French rivals, so much inferior in speed aggregate, 37.50 to 37.87. The French ran with the same team that had made history at Split the year before. The world record was thus bettered once again.

It wouldn't be proper to dismiss the 1991 Worlds without mentioning the Mike Powell vs. Carl Lewis clash in the long jump – in this writer's opinion the most memorable duel in the annals of track & field. Powell, who was only a fair quantity as a sprinter (10.45 in the 100 m. and 21.21 in the 200 m.) had only one superlative jump, but that was the longest in history, 8.95 – a distance still unmatched at the time of writing, fifteen years later. Lewis reacted with the best series ever, four jumps over 8.80, namely 8.83w, 8.91w, 8.87 and 8.84, but had to be content in winding up as "the greatest loser in history".

1991 World Championships, Tokyo – 100 metres (25 August) w +1.2 m/s: 1.Carl Lewis (USA) 9.86, 2.Leroy Burrell (USA) 9.88; 3.Dennis Mitchell (USA) 9.91; 4.Linford Christie (UK) 9.92; 5.Frank Fredericks (Nam) 9.95;

6.Raymond Stewart (Jam) 9.96; 7.Robson da Silva (Bra) 10.12; 8.Bruny Surin (Can) 10.14. Lanes: Surin 1, Stewart 2, Burrell 3, Christie 4, Lewis 5, Mitchell 6, Fredericks 7, da Silva 8.

200 metres (27 August) w - 3.4 m/s: 1.Michael Johnson (USA) 20.01; 2.Frank Fredericks (Nam) 20.34; 3.Atlee Mahorn (Can) 20.49; 4.Robson da Silva (Bra) 20.49; 5.Olapade Adeniken (Nig) 20.51; 6.Jean-Charles Trouabal (Fra) 20.58; 7.Nikolay Antonov (Bul) 20.59; 8.Aleksandr Goryemykin (SU) 20.78. Lanes: da Silva 1, Adeniken 2, Johnson 3, Fredericks 4, Mahorn 5, Antonov 6, Trouabal 7, Goryemykin 8.

4x100 metre relay (1 September): 1.USA (A.Cason, D.Mitchell, L.Burrell, C.Lewis) 37.50; 2.Fra (M.Morinière, J.C. Trouabal, D.Sangouma, B.Marie-Rose) 37.87; 3.UK (T.Jarrett, D.Braithwaite, J.Regis, L.Christie) 38.09; 4.Nig 38.43; 5.Ita 38.52; 6. Jam 38.67; 7. SU 38.68; 8.Can 39.51. Lanes: Can 1, SU 2, Nig 3, USA 4, Fra 5, UK 6, Ita 7, Jam 8.

Linford Christie was reportedly on the verge of calling it quits after the great 100 m. final of the 1991 World Championships. His time in that race, 9.92, was his fastest ever, yet it only earned him a fourth place. At 31 his disappointment was quite understandable. In the weeks that followed, however, the mighty warrior had second thoughts and began to think seriously about trying once more – at the 1992 Olympics in Barcelona. As things turned out, his was a winning bet and at 32 he became the oldest Olympic 100 m. champion ever.

True, the most famous Americans did not have a particularly happy season. Lewis had problems stemming from a viral infection at the time of the US Olympic Trials, held at New Orleans in late June and placed only fifth in the 100 m. and fourth in the 200 m. Michael Johnson won the longer race in a classy 19.79 from Mike Marsh (19.86) but later caught a virus infection and could not go beyond the 200 m. semi-finals in the Olympics. As for Leroy Burrell, he did have ups and downs. Of course, the inexhaustible US reservoir had something in reserve: Dennis Mitchell, first in the 100m. at the Trials (10.09), had his best ever season, and Marsh was even more brilliant at the longer distance.

In the Barcelona Olympics, Christie hit top form at the right time. In the penultimate round of the 100 m. Burrell looked well-nigh unbeatable as he won from the Briton, 9.97 to 10.00 – incredible times, in the face of a 1.3 m/s wind. But in the final, after two false starts, the American was rather slow in reacting to the gun, after which he was never in the hunt. Christie, off reasonably well, lagged behind Bruny Surin of Canada in the first half, but went into the lead with 40 m. to go and won comfortably in 9.96. Consistent Frank Fredericks of Namibia took second ahead of Dennis Mitchell (10.02 to 10.04), while Burrell wound up a disappointing fifth.

Yet old man Christie described his long-sought gold as almost anti-climactic: "Chasing it is the best part", he was quoted as saying. "You think there's going to be this elated joy, because you're looking for it, but it doesn't happen". It was certainly enjoyable winning though!"

The 200 m. offered a rather unusual happening: the fastest time, easily and by far, stemmed from a semi-final, thanks to Mike Marsh. With a headwind of 0.2 m/s the American went home in 19.73, missing Pietro Mennea's world record by a mere 0.01. The visual impression of expert onlookers was that he had eased off at the end, which may have cost him a world record. The next day in the final the American could not do it again. Running against a wind of greater force (1.0 m/s) he had to be content with 20.01. Yet he won rather comfortably from Fredericks (20.13).

The Americans were at their best in the 4x100 m. relay. A formidable quartet made of Marsh, Burrell, Mitchell and Lewis showed plenty of speed and fairly good passes, finally lowering the world record to 37.40. All except Mitchell came from the Santa Monica Track Club. Some watches caught Lewis in 8.8. A Nigerian team, partly trained in USA, took second in 37.98, a new African record.

1992 Olympics, Barcelona - 100 metres (1 August) w +0.5 m/s: 1.Linford Christie (UK) 9.96; 2.Frank Fredericks (Nam) 10.02; 3.Dennis Mitchell

(USA) 10.04; 4.Bruny Surin (Can) 10.09; 5.Leroy Burrell (USA) 10.10; 6.Olapade Adeniken (Nig) 10.12; 7.Raymond Stewart (Jam) 10.22; 8.Davidson Ezinwa (Nig) 10.26. Lanes: Surin 1, Stewart 2, Fredericks 3, Mitchell 4, Christie 5, Burrell 6, Ezinwa 7, Adeniken 8.

200 metres (6 August) w -1.0 m/s: 1.Michael Marsh (USA) 20.01; 2.Frank Fredericks (Nam) 20.13; 3.Michael Bates (USA) 20.38; 4.Robson da Silva (Bra) 20.45; 5.Olapade Adeniken (Nig) 20.50; 6.John Regis (UK) 20.55; 7.Oluyemi Kayode (Nig) 20.67; 8.Marcus Adam (UK) 20.80. Lanes: Bates 1, Adeniken 2, Regis 3. Marsh 4, Fredericks 5, da Silva 6, Kayode 7, Adam 8.

4x100 metre relay (8 August): 1.USA (M.Marsh, L.Burrell, D.Mitchell, C.Lewis) 37.40; 2.Nig (O.Kayode, C.Imoh, O.Adeniken, D.Ezinwa) 37.98; 3.Cub (A.Simon Gómez, J.Lamela, J.Isasi, J.Aguilera) 38.00; 4.UK 38.08, 5.CIS (former SU) 38.17; 6.Jap 38.77; 7.Aut 39.30; 8.I.C. 39.31. Lanes: Aut 1, IC 2, Cub 3, USA 4, Nig 5, UK 6, Jap 7, CIS 8.

Michael Marsh (born on 4 August 1967 in Los Angeles; 1.78 m. / 68 kg.) had reached national class as a sprinter while in college at UCLA, with times of 10.07 (1989) and 20.35 (1988). He grew in stature when he joined the Lewis clan at Santa Monica Track Club. His first gold medal came at the

1992 Olympics in Barcelona. Linford Christie (UK), 32, becoming the oldest 100 m. champion ever. Following him, in order, were Fredericks (lane 3), Mitchell (lane 4), Surin (lane1), and Burrell (lane 6).

1991 Worlds, when he ran in the heats of the US sprint relay.

Frank Fredericks (born on 2 October 1967 at Windhoek, South Africa; 1.80 m. / 70 kg.) became able to compete internationally when Namibia gained independence in 1990 and IAAF affiliation in 1991. By then he had resolved that track would take precedence over soccer as his favourite sport. Frank was the type of young man who could do equal justice to both study and sport. The right opportunity came when he was sent to USA by a uranium company to study computer science at Brigham Young University in Colorado. In 1991 he won both sprint titles at the NCAA Championships, the first non-US sprinter to score such a double. As previously reported, he won silver in the 200 m. at the 1991 Worlds. The two medals of the same colour he won at Barcelona a year later were the first ever by a Namibian citizen in the Olympics.

The World Championships had by then become a biennial affair and 1993 saw another edition – in Stuttgart, a German city that could point to an excellent tradition as the venue of major international meets. At 33 Linford Christie had another superlative season as a century man and Fredericks finally became the leader of the 200 m. fraternity. The US Championships, acting as Trials for the Stuttgart rendez-vous, were held at Eugene, America's track capital (in Western eyes at least). Andre Cason, at 5-7 (1.70 m.) one of the shortest men in élite sprinting, won the 100 m. with a wind-aided 9.85 from Mitchell (also 9.85) and Lewis (9.90), while Burrell was no better than fifth. In the 200 m. Marsh beat Lewis, 19.97 to 20.07, again with the benefit of a fairly strong wind. Michael Johnson was content to qualify for the Worlds in the one-lap event.

In Stuttgart, however, Christie lived up to the reputation he had earned at Barcelona a year before and ran the century faster than ever. He sped to 9.87 – a new British and European record. Given the conditions (a negligible aiding wind of 0.3 m/s), this may have been one of the fastest ever. Americans thus learnt that they could miss the world crown two years in a row, no matter if Cason (9.92) and Mitchell (9.99) ran just about as fast as could be expected. Lewis, no longer in his prime but still great enough, finished fourth.

In the 200 m. Frank Fredericks abandoned his label as "man of silver" by finally hitting gold with a superb 19.85, a new personal and African record. John Regis of Britain ran the race of his life (19.94) to take second. Lewis (19.99) was third and best of the Americans here, ahead of Marsh. Carl's bronze was cheerfully described as "his first amulet of that colour".

US sprinters partly avenged their defeats in the individual events with a victory in the 4x100 m. relay. John Drummond, Cason, Mitchell and Burrell curiously did better in a semi-final than in the decisive race. In the former they equalled the world record (37.40) set at Barcelona the year before by another US team, in the latter they won in 37.48, while Great Britain was a magnificent second in 37.77, just ahead of Canada, 37.83, national records both. Thirteen years later, that 37.40 is still unsurpassed.

1993 World Championships, Stuttgart - 100 metres (15 August) w +0.3 m/s: 1.Linford Christie (UK) 9.87; 2.Andre Cason (USA) 9.92; 3.Dennis Mitchell (USA) 9.99; 4.Carl Lewis (USA) 10.02; 5.Bruny Surin (Can) 10.02; 6.Frank Fredericks (Nam) 10.03; 7.Daniel Effiong (Nig) 10.04; 8.Raymond Stewart (Jam)10.18. Lanes: Fredericks 1, Surin 2, Lewis 3, Christie 4, Effiong 5, Cason 6, Mitchell 7, Stewart 8.

200 metres (20 August) w +0.3 m/s: 1.Frank Fredericks (Nam 19.85; 2.John Regis (UK) 19.94; 3.Carl Lewis (USA) 19.99; 4.Michael Marsh (USA) 20.18; 5.Dean Capobianco (Aus) 20.18; 6.Jean-Charles Trouabal (Fra) 20.20; 7.Emmanuel Tuffour (Gha) 20.49; 8.Damien Marsh (Aus) 20.56. Lanes: D.Marsh 1, Tuffour 2, Capobianco 3, M.Marsh 4, Fredericks 5, Regis 6, Lewis 7, Trouabal 8.

4x100 metre relay (22 August): 1.USA (J.Drummond, A.Cason, D. Mitchell, L.Burrell) 37.48; 2.UK (C.Jackson, T.Jarrett, J.Regis, L.Christie) 37.77; 3.Can (R.Esmie, G.Gilbert, B.Surin, A.Mahorn) 37.83; 4.Cub 38.39; 5.Aus 38.69; 6.Ger 38.78; 7.I.C. 38.82; 8.Swe 39.22. Lanes: Ger 1, IC 2, USA 3, UK 4, Can 5, Aus 6, Swe 7, Cub 8.

Michael Johnson chose to compete in the one-lap event at Stuttgart and again outclassed his rivals. He did run the 200 m. too on occasions, but here he did not have a particularly lucky season. In his clashes with world champion Fredericks he lost 1-to-3.

There was no "global" championship meet in 1994, yet Johnson did well enough to earn the no.1 spot in both 200 and 400 m. in "Track & Field News" World Ranking. His record vis-à-vis Fredericks at the shorter distance was a non-committal 2-to-2 though. Linford Christie continued to perform at his favourite distance, the century. First he successfully defended his Commonwealth and European titles - the former at Victoria, Canada, with 10.14, and the latter in Athens with a sprightly 9.91. And he closed his seasonal account with a victory (10.21) in the World Cup in London. Amazingly steady form for a 34-year-old lad. He lost by a scant margin to Dennis Mitchell (10.13 to 10.12) in the final of the Grand Prix, this being perhaps the deciding factor in the eyes of the "Track & Field News" set, who chose Mitchell over Christie as no.1 of the year for that event. Leroy Burrell, hampered by injuries now and then, had a checkered season - the last of an exciting but uneven career. He did close on a high note though: on 6 July at Lausanne he broke Lewis's world record by 0.01 with a sparkling 9.85. The wind in his favour was a legal but useful 1.2 m/s. Davidson Ezinwa (Nigeria) was second and Mitchell third, both in 9.99.

Canada had by then discovered Ben Johnson's "vindicator" in the person of Donovan Bailey (born on 16 December 1967 at Manchester, Jamaica; 1.83 m. / 82 kg.). Like "Big Ben", he came from Jamaica, the cradle of so many "speed demons". He emigrated to Canada in 1981. He was a late comer, almost 24 by the time he first broke 11 secs. for the century (10.42 in 1991). Maybe he would have joined the ever abundant "lost sheep" variety if Dan Pfaff, a dedicated coach, had not succeeded in convincing him that "he had all the tools to become the world's fastest man". Donovan was henceforth quick in gathering momentum and reached world class in 1994 with 10.03. His first banner year was 1995, when he engaged a long-drawn battle with Linford Christie. The Briton finally emerged the winner, 5-to-4, in head-to-head decisions, but the Canadian had a clear edge in the meet that mattered most - the World Championships, held at Göteborg, Sweden. The final of the 100 m. (6 August) should be remembered in the annals of sprinting as Canada's Day. Bailey and Bruny Surin, both running for the Maple Leaf, finished one-two in the century. Bailey had a poor start but was quick to recover. From midway on he appeared to be fully in charge and finally won in 9.97. Surin barely held off Ato Boldon of Trinidad in the battle for second (both 10.03). Off the podium were the likes of Fredericks, Marsh and Christie, who came next in that order. Oddly enough, the aging Briton probably had his best-ever reaction time (0.110), but then his wrapped right leg began to give him trouble and he faded rather badly at the halfway mark.

Michael Johnson had by then resolved that he was ready to play at both his favourite tables, 200 and 400 m. He had an excellent rehearsal at the US Championships in Sacramento with times of 43.66 and 19.83w, after going through six races, counting prelims and finals, all this in the space of five days. But the task awaiting him in Göteborg was even more appalling: eight rounds altogether between 5 and 11 August, with the 400 m. coming first. He won his first challenge in 43.39, second fastest time in the history of the event – next to Butch Reynolds's 43.29 in 1988. And he did so leaving the runner-up more than one second behind! The task awaiting him in the 200 m., with world champion Fredericks as his main rival, was more difficult, yet he handled it masterfully. Less than 3 hours after an impressive 20.01 "semi", Johnson was wise enough not to overuse his sprinting potential in the early stages of the final. He came on strongly in the second half, finally beating Fredericks to win by a large margin – 19.79 to 20.12. No one had ever managed a 200/400 m. double in a "global" (Olympic or World) competition. And the inimitable Michael had seemingly done so with astounding ease. In reality, his post-race comment was: "I'm exhausted. This was a tough, tough job". On second thought, however, he added a flamboyant: "I hope to do it again next year".

In the sprint relay, the Canadians saw their chances grow considerably when their US rivals failed to connect on the second pass in the first round and went out of the zone. And again when Great Britain "sans Christie" and France were eliminated in the "semis". In the decisive race the only serious challenge came from a surprisingly good Australian team, yet with Surin and Bailey in the two final legs Canada went home a clear winner in 38.31. The Aussies won silver in 38.50.

1995 World Championships, Göteborg - 100 metres (6 August) w +1.0 m/s: 1.Donovan Bailey (Can) 9.97; 2.Bruny Surin (Can) 10.03; 3.Ato Boldon (Tri) 10.03; 4.Frank Fredericks (Nam) 10.07; 5.Michael Marsh (USA) 10.10; 6.Linford Christie (UK) 10.12; 7.Olapade Adeniken (Nig); 8.Raymond Stewart (Jam) 10.29. Lanes: Christie 1, Fredericks 2, Surin 3, Boldon 4, Bailey 5, Marsh 6. Stewart 7, Adeniken 8.

200 metres (11 August) w +0.5 m/s: 1.Michael Johnson (USA) 19.79; 2.Frank Fredericks (Nam) 20.12; 3.Jeff Williams (USA) 20.18; 4.Robson da Silva (Bra) 20.21; 5.Claudinei da Silva (Bra) 20.40; 6.Geir Moen (Nor) 20.51; 7.John Regis (UK) 20.67; 8.Iván Garcia (Cub) 20.77. Lanes: Regis 1, Garcia 2, Fredericks 3, Johnson 4, R.da Silva 5, Williams 6, C.da Silva 7, Moen 8.

4x100 metre relay (13 August): 1,Can (R.Esmie, G.Gilbert, B.Surin, D.Bailey) 38.31; 2.Aus (P. Henderson, T.Jackson, S.Brimacombe, D.Marsh) 38.50; 3.Ita (G.Puggioni, E.Madonia, A.Cipolloni, S.Floris) 39.07; 4.Jam 39.10; 5.Jap 39.33; 6.Bra 39.35; 7.Ukr 39.39; Swe, disq. for passing out of zone. Lanes: Bra 1, Swe 2, Ita 3, Can 4, Aus 5, Jam 6, Ukr 7, Jap 8.

In 1996 Donovan Bailey confirmed his leadership in the 100 m. with a brilliant victory at the Atlanta Olympics. To be sure, his seasonal record left something to be desired as he lost to Frank Fredericks, 2-to-3, in direct clashes and in sequence of marks as well. What the Canadian did at Atlanta was simply superlative though: he won gold in world record time, 9.84, a rare combination in competitions of such a calibre. That sufficed to earn him the no.1 position even in "Track & Field News" World Ranking. Just as in Sweden the year before, there was no US sprinter on the podium, a bad pill to swallow for the home crowd. The hard Atlanta track yielded a high number of fast times. Ato Boldon and Fredericks won their quarter-finals in 9.95 and 9.93 respectively. And they were very much in evidence in the "semis" too, the Namibian winning the first from Bailey, 9.94 to 10.00, and Boldon the second in 9.93, with Mitchell next (10.00), The stage was set for a superlative final. Such was the tension that there were three false starts. And Linford Christie, at 36 the oldest finalist, fell into the trap twice and was disqualified. The British veteran looked incredulous and lingered in and around the track until a referee told him he was no longer welcome in the area. In reality, his reaction time turned out to be an illegal 0.086. At the fourth report of the starting gun all seven sprinters were understandably hesitant and Fredericks had the fastest reaction time with no better than 0.143. Bailey was the slowest of them all (0.174), yet he progressively grew in stature as the race went on. From mid-race on he was not to be denied. Fredericks and Boldon offered a stubborn resistance but finally had to surrender, finishing second and third in that order. Bailey won in 9.84, shaving 0.01 off Leroy Burrell's world record. His actual time in hundredths was 9.835. The wind in his favour was a legal 0.7 m/s. Dennis Mitchell as the best US man had to be content with fourth.

Michael Johnson wanted to duplicate in the Games his marvellous 200/400 m. double of the year before at the Göteborg Worlds. He had his rehearsal at the US Olympic Trials, aptly held on the same Atlanta track in the second half of June. After winning the one-lap race comfortably from world record holder Butch Reynolds, 43.44 to 43.91, he scaled new heights on 23 June, finally breaking Pietro Mennea's world record for the 200 m. with a blistering

19.66. Running in lane 5, he covered the first half in 10.26 and the second in 9.40. Here again there was no opposition worthy of the name, as the second finisher, Jeff Williams, came home in 20.03. just ahead of Michael Marsh, 20.04. All this with an aiding wind of 1.7 m/s down the stretch. The two events came in the same order in the Games and Johnson was once again in a class by himself. In the 400 m. he went through four races on just as many consecutive days with the following series: 45.80, 44.62, 44.59 and 43.49. He won the decisive race with almost one second to spare vis-à-vis Roger Black of Britain, second (44.41). After a day of rest, he took care of his 200 m. pensum with four races in the space of two days: 20.55, 20.37, 20.27 and ..... 19.32. This last (1 August) was obviously his chef-d'oeuvre. At the time of writing, ten years later, many track observers still consider his 19.32 as the greatest exploit ever seen in the domain of sprinting. In actual fact, it reflects a speed of 37.267 km. per hour – the highest ever attained by man in a race from a standing start. Tommie Smith's 19.5 for 220 yards (201.16 m.) in 1966, with the double advantage of a straight course and hand timing, expressed a speed of 37.139 km. per hour. Johnson won by a quasi-insulting margin from Fredericks (19.68) and Boldon (19.80), who also bettered their personal records. In the prelims Johnson had wisely administered his reserves and in the final test he "exploded" with 100 m. splits of 10.12 and 9.20. The relative figures for his main rivals were: Fredericks 10.14+9.54 and Boldon 10.18+9.62. Just before the finish MJ – as he was now called in track circles – felt a twinge in his lower right hamstring. In crossing the line he glanced to his left at the clock, frozen at a historic reading. A while later he strapped an ice bag to his aching hamstring and ran a lap of honour to the chorus of "You're unbelievable". His 200-400 m. double was the first ever in Olympic history, but of course it came a year after his similar prodigy at the Worlds in Göteborg.

In the sprint relay the Canadians were eager to confirm their Göteborg victory in a head-to-head confrontation with their US rivals. This time the latter made the final all right, but here they didn't do so well in the game of passing the baton and the Canadians, intrinsically inferior in speed aggregate, won by a large margin – 37.69 (new national record) to 38.05. Brazil, easily and by far the no.1 power in South American sprinting, took third in 38.41, another national record.

After three silver medals in "global" meets, Frank Fredericks (centre) became the first Namibian athlete to strike gold with his strong finish in the 200 m. of the 1993 Worlds in Stuttgart. Others, from left to right, are Carl Lewis, (3rd), John Regis (2nd), Mike Marsh (4th) and Dean Capobianco (5th).

1996 Olympics, Atlanta - 100 metres (27 July) w +0.7 m/s: 1.Donovan Bailey (Can) 9.84; 2.Frank Fredericks (Nam) 9.89; 3.Ato Boldon (Tri) 9.90; 4.Dennis Mitchell (USA) 9.99; 5.Michael Marsh (USA) 10.00; 6.Davidson Ezinwa (Nig) 10.14; 7. Michael Green (Jam) 10.16. Linford Christie (UK) disqualified.

Lanes: Marsh 1, Christie 2, Boldon 3, Mitchell 4, Fredericks 5, Bailey 6, Ezinwa 7, Green 8.

200 metres (1 August) w +0.4 m/s: 1.Michael Johnson (USA) 19.32; 2.Frank Fredericks (Nam) 19.68; 3.Ato Boldon (Tri) 19.80; 4.Obadele Thompson (Bar) 20.14; 5.Jeff Williams (USA) 20.17; 6.Iván Garcia (Cub) 20.21; 7.Patrick Stevens (Bel) 20.27; 8.Michael Marsh (USA) 20.48. Lanes: Marsh 1, Williams 2, Johnson 3, Garcia 4, Fredericks 5, Boldon 6, Stevens 7, Thompson 8.

4x100 metre relay (3 August): 1.Can (R.Esmie, G.Gilbert, B.Surin, D.Bailey) 37.69; 2.USA (J.Drummond, T.Harden, M.Marsh, D.Mitchell) 38.05; 3.Bra (Arnaldo Silva, R.C. da Silva, E.Ribeiro, Andre da Silva) 38.41; 4.Ukr 38.55; 5.Swe 38.67; 6.Cub 39.39; Fra, disq., and Gha, did not start. Lanes: (vacant) 1, Swe 2, Bra 3, USA 4, Cub 5, Can 6, Ukr 7, Fra 8.

The man who finished fourth in the historic 200 m. final, Obadele Thompson of Barbados, could claim nothing less than the fastest 100 m. time ever. It happened on 13 April at El Paso, Texas (altitude, 1130 m), and the lad, barely 20, was timed in 9.69. There was a strong following wind, alas unmeasured as the anemometer had broken down just before the race. Eyewitnesses estimated that the wind was in the 4-to-5 m/s range at the time of Thompson's effort. He won comfortably from Andrew Tynes (10.01). Thompson, who had done 10.08 in 1994 (high altitude again), aged 18, was to be heard from again in subsequent years.

Americans were eager to regain the sceptre in the 100 m., after suffering crushing defeats at the hands of Christie and Bailey in the period from 1992 to 1996 included. In 1997 they found the man for the purpose in Maurice Greene (born on 23 July 1974 in Kansas City; 1.76 m. / 75 kg.), a gifted sprinter who improved from 10.43 at 19 to 10.08 at 22. In September 1996 he moved from his native Kansas to California to train under coach John Smith, former holder of the world record for the quarter mile (44.5 in 1971). The benefits of such a move were to become crystal clear in 1997, the year of the World Championships in Athens.

NOBLE ART

The career of Carl Lewis epitomizes the noble art of sport at its best. In him power and style combined to form a truly unique figure. In terms of quality and quantity of exploits, no contemporary athlete can match his record: 20 medals in global championships (10 in the Olympics, 10 in the Worlds), broken down as follows: 17 gold, 2 silver and 1 bronze. Such a harvest was put together over a period of thirteen years, 1983 through 1996, in the range of four events: 100 m., 200 m., 4x100 m. relay and long jump.
Lewis had his share of world records too, yet he never went after them the way other top athletes did, i.e. looking for specially favourable conditions. For the greater part of his career he was after two world records - Pietro Mennea's 19.72 (200 m.) and Bob Beamon's 8.90 (long jump) – both made at Mexico City, hence with the benefit of high altitude, notoriously advantageous in events lying in the anaerobic sphere. Lewis sought hot competition rather than records, but was obviously happy when the latter came as the logical consequence of the former, as it happened in the 100 m. of the 1991 World Championships or in relay races. As a rule, his best marks occurred in the competitions that mattered most. The long jump was apparently his favourite event and clearly his main job in the latter part of his career. The four Olympic gold medals he collected in this event (1984 through '96) stand out as his greatest competitive achievement.

Prior to the big rendez-vous, however, there was an odd event that really made the headlines, a self-avowed professional match race between Donovan Bailey and Michael Johnson at Toronto on 1 June. A multinational company had conceived the idea of matching the reigning Olympic champions for 100 and 200 m. just to find out who was the "World's Fastest Human". They guaranteed $ 500,000 to each, plus another 1 million dollars to the winner! The race, held indoors, was at the odd but "neutral" distance of 150 m. The Canadian soon built up a lead, 5.74 to 5.83 at 50 m., 10.24 to 10.63 at 100 m. Johnson, normally a great curve runner, was beaten at his own game for once. But he was visibly limping due to a damaged quadriceps and had to call it quits. Bailey went on unopposed and finished in 14.99. Outdoors the fastest time on record for that seldom run distance was 14.97 by Linford Christie at Sheffield in 1994, beating Donovan Bailey among others. Back in 1983 at Cassino, Pietro Mennea had a hand-timed 14.8. Seen in retrospect, the Toronto affair, featured by an inadequate organisation and a concert of blabbering mouths before and after, was not an enlightening show for athletics. Johnson recovered just in time for the summer season, during which he chose to concentrate on the 400 m. Having conquered the world's 200 m. record to the point of putting it out of sight, his target now was the one-lap record, which had hitherto eluded him.

Greene offered a preview of his new form at the US Championships, which normally acted as the key to the Worlds. The meet, held at Indianapolis, was featured by a

Leroy Burrell (USA), no. 239, celebrating his world record time of 9.85 in the 100 m. of the Lausanne meet in 1994.

turnover, with new men taking over from established quantities. Greene won a virtually windless (+0.2 m/s) century in a pompous 9.90. That was just about what he needed to stay ahead of Tim Montgomery (9.92). Marsh was third (10.03), beating out John Drummond and Leroy Burrell, among others. Drummond came back two days later to win the 200 m. (20.23).

The stage was set for great things in the meet of the year as Bailey and Fredericks also had promising pre-Games marks in the century, 9.91 and 9.94 respectively. The Athens track proved very fast. In the prelims Ato Boldon of Trinidad had a superlative 9.87, but in the decisive race he was afflicted with cramps and had to be content with fifth. Here Greene was irresistible. He dominated the race practically from start to finish and won in 9.86, with 50 m. splits of 5.55 and 4.31. Next came Bailey (9.91), Montgomery (9.94) and Fredericks (9.95).

Boldon did not give up though. He sought and found revenge in the 200 m., winning from Fredericks, 20.04w to 20.23w. Claudinei da Silva of Brazil was a close third (20.26w). The absence of Michael Johnson was surely felt in US ranks: Drummond, as the best American, was only seventh. (MJ won the one-lap race with a normal, for him, 44.12).

In the sprint relay Americans met their quasi-traditional troubles early. In their heat they were disqualified for passing out of zone. The usually well-drilled Canadians emerged the winners (37.86) only in the last leg, thanks to Donovan Bailey. Nigeria nosed out Great Britain for second.

The ever reliable Fredericks could look back to a remarkable season – ten sub-10 clockings in the 100 m. and four sub-20 in the 200 m. He split with Greene in the century (2-2) and beat Boldon (3-1) in the 200 m. He found partial relief for his defeats at Athens when he saw himself on top of the "Track & Field News"World Ranking in both 100 and 200 m.

1997 World Championships, Athens – 100 metres (3 August) w + 0.2 m/s: 1.Maurice Greene (USA) 9,86; 2.Donovan Bailey (Can) 9.91; 3.Tim Montgomery (USA) 9.94; 4.Frank Fredericks (Nam) 9.95; 5.Ato Boldon (Tri) 10.02; 6.Davidson Ezinwa (Nig) 10.10; 7.Bruny Surin (Can) 10.12; 8.Michael Marsh (USA) 10.29. Lanes: Surin 1, Fredericks 2, Greene 3, Bailey 4, Ezinwa 5, Boldon 6, Montgomery 7, Marsh 8.

200 metres (8 August): w + 2.3: 1.Ato Boldon (Tri) 20.04w; 2.Frank Fredericks (Nam) 20.23w; 3.Claudinei da Silva (Bra) 20.26w; 4.Iván Garcia (Cub) 20.31w; 5.Yiorgos Panayiotopoulos (Gre) 20.32w; 6.Obadele Thompson (Bar) 20.37w; 7.Jon Drummond (USA) 20.44w; 8.Patrick Stevens (Bel) 20.44w. Lanes: Drummond 1, Thompson 2, Boldon 3, Fredericks 4, C.da Silva 5, Garcia 6, Panayiotopoulos 7, Stevens 8.

4x100 metre relay (10 August): 1.Can (R.Esmie, G.Gilbert, B.Surin, D.Bailey) 37.86; 2.Nig (O.Ezinwa, O.Adeniken, F.Obikwelu, D.Ezinwa) 38.07; 3.UK (D.Braithwaite, D.Campbell, D.Walker, J.Golding) 38.14; 4.Cub 38.15; 5.Gha 38.26; 6.Bra 38.48; 7.Spa 38.72. Fra disq. Fra 1, Bra 2, Nig 3, Gha 4, UK 5, Cub 6, Spa 7, Can 8.

There were no global titles at stake in 1998, yet Greene in the 100 m. and Boldon in the 200 m. amply lived up to their form of the year before. At the shorter distance the former had a very impressive series of marks and beat Boldon 6-3 in direct clashes. The Trinidad man ran the 200 m. in only four meets, without losses. Boldon (born on 30 December 1973 at Port-of-Spain; 1.76 m. / 75 kg.) was one more in the long queue of talented sprinters from the Caribbean area who had made the grade after emigrating to USA. He had soccer as his first love, but after moving from New York to California he became a full-time athlete. In addition to honours I have already alluded to, he claimed the best-ever one-day sprint double: 9.90 and 19.77 at Stuttgart on 13 July 1997. His first name, Ato Jabari, apparently comes from the Yoruba language of Nigeria and translates as "Brilliant Leader".

In the domain of sprinting the most important title of 1998 was awarded at the Commonwealth Games, held in a brand-new, costly stadium at Kuala Lumpur,

Malaysia. This was in the 100 m. and Boldon beat his arch rival Frank Fredericks, 9.88 to 9.96. Neither competed in the 200 m., won by Julian Golding of England in 20.18. Even after the retirement of Linford Christie, Great Britain well retained the role of no.1 sprint power in Europe. At the continental championships, held in Budapest, Darren Campbell won the 100 m. in 10.04 and Doug Walker the 200 m. in 20.53. Britain took no less than five of the six medals at stake in these events.

The closing act of 1998 was the European Cup, held at Johannesburg. High altitude probably helped Obadele Thompson of Barbados to chalk up a resplendent 9.87 in the century. Fredericks won the 200 m. as he pleased (19.97).

Maurice Greene reached the peak of his form in 1999, at the age of 25. He combined major wins with a resplendent record time. The latter came early in the season, on the same site where he had won the world title in 1997 – Athens. In practically windless conditions (+0.1 m/s) he ran the 100 m. in 9.79, with his arch rival Boldon second in 9.86. By official standards Greene's time was a new world record by 0.05, yet followers of the sport no doubt remembered that eleven years ago in Seoul another man had been credited with exactly the same time before sinking into official oblivion following a disqualification .... Later in the same afternoon Boldon turned the tables on his rival and friend, still over-elated, in the 200 m. – 19.86 to 20.03. Boldon was subsequently sidelined with an injury, which made it impossible for him to appear at the World Championships in Sevilla. Greene was mentally prepared to run both distances in Spain, yet at the US title meet he cut his work short by skipping the 100 m., availing himself of the new IAAF rule which provided a "wild card" admittance to defending champions. He secured a berth for the 200 m. by winning the title race in 19.93w, well extended by Rohsan Griffin (19.98w).

Sevilla provided a marvellous atmosphere for sprinting and Greene surpassed himself by winning three golds in the space of a week. He had his toughest job in the century vs-à-vis Canada's Bruny Surin, who at 32 turned out to be faster than ever. The latter was a bit faster in reaction time (0.127 to 0.132). Greene stumbled slightly but remained cool, moving up gradually as the race went on. He finally won in a splendid 9.80, still with a negligible wind (+0.2 m/s). Surin, who was contesting his fifth World Championship final, did better than ever with 9.84. Dwain Chambers won bronze for Britain with a new personal best (9.97), shunting Obadele Thompson of Barbados to fourth. Veteran Frank Fredericks was stopped by an injury in a semi-final. He tried again in the 200 m., gallantly made the final but could not run it.

Greene went on relentlessly and in his eighth race of the meet he won the 200 m. title in 19.90, clearly ahead of Brazil's Claudinei da Silva (20.00). Their respective 100 m. splits were: 10.25+9.65 and 10.32+9.68. Greene thus became the first sprinter to win both dashes in the same edition of the Worlds. Francis Obikwelu of Nigeria shunted the unlucky Thompson to another fourth place.

The men who ran the 4x100 m. relay for USA - Drummond, Montgomery, Brian Lewis and Greene – had been involved in mishaps in the recent past. This time, however, the major casualty was defending champion Canada, who was disqualified in the heats for passing out of zone. In the final the Americans had to fight all the way to beat a sharp GB team – 37.59 to 37.73, the latter being a new European record. Nigeria, third in 37.91, later lost the bronze medal when Daniel Effiong was charged with a doping offence. Brazil (38.05, a new South American mark) thus moved from fourth to third.

1999 World Championships, Sevilla – 100 metres (22 August) w +0.2 m/s: 1.Maurice Greene (USA) 9.80; 2.Bruny Surin (Can) 9.84; 3.Dwain Chambers (UK) 9.97; 4.Olapade Thompson (Bar) 10.00; 5.Tim Harden (USA) 10.02; 6.Tim Montgomery (USA) 10.04; 7.Jason Gardener (UK) 10.07; 8.Kenneth Streete-Thompson (Cayman Islands) 10.24. Lanes: Thompson 1, Streete-Thompson 2, Harden 3, Chambers 4, Greene 5, Surin 6, Gardener 7, Montgomery 8.

200 metres (27 August) w +1.2

Maurice Greene (USA) can point to such 100 m. times as 9.79, 9.80 and 9.82, all in virtually windless conditions – in intrinsic value probably the fastest times ever.

Michael Johnson (USA) owns the most incredible record in the history of sprinting: 19.32 for the 200 m.

m/s: 1.Maurice Greene (USA) 19.90; 2. Claudinei da Silva (Bra) 20.00; 3.Francis Obikwelu (Nig) 20.11; 4.Obadele Thompson (Bar) 20.23; 5.Marcin Urbas (Pol) 20.30; 6. Kevin Little (USA) 20.37; 7.Julian Golding (UK) 20.48. Frank Fredericks (Nam) did not start. Lanes: Golding 1, vacant in Fredericks'absence 2, Greene 3, Obikwelu 4, Urbas 5, C. da Silva 6,Thompson 7, Little 8.

4x100 metre relay (29 August): 1.USA (J.Drummond, T.Montgomery, B.Lewis, M.Greene) 37.59; 2.UK (J.Gardener, D.Campbell, M.Devonish, D.Chambers) 37.73; 3.Bra (R.de Oliveira, Claudinei da Silva, E.Ribeiro, André da Silva) 38.05; 4.Cub 38.63; 5.Pol 38.70; 6.SA 38.74; 7.Hun 38.83; Nig (I.Asonze, F.Obikwelu, D. Effiong, D.Aliu) third in 37.91, later disqualified for doping offence. Lanes: Pol 1, Cub 2, UK 3, Bra 4, USA 5, Niga 6, SA 7, Hun 8.

Michael Johnson had chosen the 400 m. as his favourite alley for 1999, obviously in search of the world record that had eluded him for so long. The reward he so badly deserved finally came his way at the Sevilla Worlds. He succeeded Butch Reynolds (43.29 in 1988) with a sparkling 43.18, achieved with 200 m. splits of 21.22 and 21.96. And he did so in a virtual "solo", his nearest rival ending 1.11 sec. back. Scoring tables value his 19.32 for the 200 m. as a much better mark – under the current IAAF table it is worth 1335 points, 42 more than his 400 m. mark. Out of his own experience "MJ" himself offers the following explanation: the one-lap adventure is simply a more difficult one.

ABOUT LANES

The assignment of lanes in short running events has always been a delicate matter. Consequently, IAAF legislators have been most attentive in this respect, more so in fact as years went by and the sport continued to evolve.

Of course, short races run in lanes can differ greatly from the longer ones where such a problem does not exist.

As often as not it has been taken for granted that lanes located in the middle of the track are generally the most favourable ones. If this is true in sprint races started from a single starting line, as in the 100 metres, it is even more so in those started in intercalated lanes as in the 200 metres, where runners placed in the outer lanes can have the benefit of easier turns.

Since the earliest days of modern athletics the problem of lane assignment has been chiefly left to casual decisions. Initially there was in fact no section of officials particularly committed to such a task. The judge acting as a starter sorted out lanes using leaflets numbered from 1 to 6, taking them out of his cap or from a purse. The most diligent starters used a small sack in which they placed small pieces of wood marked with the numbers concerned. Runners themselves were asked to draw the numbers.

By 1939 it became necessary to entrust such a task to a specific official, who drew lanes for both individual and relay races. Once on the track, athletes went to their marks as per instructions received from said official. The starter merely had to verify that every runner was on the lane assigned to him. Number 1 was placed in the inner lane, number 2 in lane two, and so on. In races with a single starting line, however, runners were placed in lanes according to their best times in the prelims, with the owner of the fastest time in lane 1, and others placed in accordance from lane 2 onwards. For no reason whatsoever, e.g. if someone scratches at the last moment, can the lane assignment be changed. Not even the starter has the right to do so.

In 1954 a new rule came into force: in the most important meets (Olympics, area championships and the like) the lane draw could be made the day before a given race. Athletes were informed as to place and time in which the operation would take place, so that they could witness he operation or have someone represent them during the operation.

At the 1991 IAAF Convention in Tokyo important innovations were introduced in respect to lane assignment. Casualness was abandoned and athletes were henceforth judged on the basis of their previous marks. It was decided that in races from 100 to 800 metres included and for the 4x100 and 4x400 metre relays, when one or more preliminary rounds were on the programme, lanes would be drawn as follows: In the first round the lane order would be drawn by lot; for the following rounds there would be two draws: one for the four highest ranked athletes or teams to determine placings in lanes 3, 4, 5 and 6; the other for the four lowest ranked athletes or teams to determine placings in lanes 1,2, 7 and 8.

Such a change implied that the whole matter would henceforth be transferred to the chief meet director.

G.P.

Even after the retirement of Linford Christie in 1997, Europe had its share of good sprinters, mostly stemming from the same country, Britain. But no one of them seemed able to top the world as Linford had so splendidly done. However, Greece had a surprise in store for the last year of the 20th century. The man in question was Konstadinos Kedéris (born on 11 June 1973 at Mitilini, island of Lesbos; 1.80 m. / 78 kg.), who just like "MJ" had shown a marked preference for the 200/400 m. axis from the beginning of his career. At the 1991 European Junior Championships, held in his native country at Thessaloniki, he was fourth in the 400 m. in 47.03. In the 200 m. he progressed slowly but gradually, from 21.63 in 1991 to 20.50 in 1999. In the one-lap race he could point to a good 45.60 (1998). At the dawn of 2000, an Olympic year, his mind was definitely on the shorter race though. His early season results were good but by no means eye-catching. He went to Sydney with no better credential than a 20.25 (aided by a wind of 1.9 m/s), followed by a third place in the European Cup, in a race won by Charles Malcolm of Britain in 20.48. Prognosticators ignored him completely on the eve of the Games ...

The US Olympic Trials, held at Sacramento, evidenced Maurice Greene's steady form (1st in he 100 m., time 10.01) and the brightness of John Capel, who won a terrific 200 m. after a furious battle with Floyd Heard, 19.85 to 19.88. Elsewhere, no one was sprightlier than Ato Boldon, who authored yet another precious one-day double at Lausanne – 9.95 and 19.97. As for MJ, he had his eyes on the 400 m.

The Olympics returned to Australia almost half a century after the Melbourne event. As of today (anno 2006) these are the only editions held in the Southern hemisphere. Sydney provided a splendid setting and unprecedented crowds, with attendances ranging between 85,806 and 97,432 for the morning sessions and between 99,428 and 112,524 for the evening sessions.

Maurice Greene confined his business to the century and won his third global title at this distance in the space of three years (1997-2000). Irresistible from start to finish, he sped home in 9.87, splendid time in a windless race (- 0.3 m/s). Boldon was second (9.99) ahead of Obadele Thompson (10.04), who finally reached the podium.

Kedéris reportedly felt very confident before his test in the 200 m. "I knew I had a chance ... I said Konstan The Greek would win. I feared nobody". On known evidence few onlookers, if any, were prepared to share his view. But in Sydney he improved on his personal best not once but twice with 20.14 in a quarter and 20.09 in the final. One of the pre-race favourites, John Capel of USA, had a tragic getaway in the decisive race. He was left at the start as he moved early and then rocked back onto his blocks as the gun went – for a resulting reaction time of 0.348, far worse than Kedéris (0.163) and Boldon (0.174). The American never managed to remedy and wound up a poor eighth. Kedéris was only fourth as they entered the straight, but his quick recovery brought him into the lead with 50 metres to go. He won from another European, Darren Campbell of

Britain, while Boldon was a disappointing third. Kedéris was in all probability the most surprising of Olympic victors in the sprint department. At any rate he was the first Greek man to win an Olympic running title since … 1896.

US sprinters fared better in the 4x100 m. relay. Their team – Drummond, Bernard Williams, Brian Lewis, Greene – was as usual nonpareil in terms of speed aggregate, yet they had to labour more than somewhat to emerge the winners against a well-drilled Brazilian foursome that lowered the South American record to 37.90. The winners appeared to be extravagantly exuberant in their victory celebrations, to such a degree as to induce criticism even from some US pressmen.

2000 Olympics, Sydney – 100 metres (23 September) w -0.3 m/s: 1.Maurice Greene (USA) 9.87; 2.Ato Boldon (Tri) 9.99; 3.Obadele Thompson (Bar) 10.04; 4.Dwain Chambers (UK) 10.08; 5.Jon Drummond (USA) 10.09; 6.Darren Campbell (UK) 10.13; 7.Kim Collins (St.Kitts & Nevis) 10.17; Abdul Aziz Zakari (Gha) did not finish (injured). Lanes: Campbell 1, Zakari 2, Chambers 3, Thompson 4, Greene 5, Drummond 6, Collins 7, Boldon 8.

200 metres (28 September) w -0.6 m/s: 1.Konstadinos Kedéris (Gre) 20.09; 2.Darren Campbell (UK) 20.14; 3.Ato Boldon (Tri) 20.20; 4.Obadele Thompson (Bar) 20.20; 5.Christian Malcolm (UK) 20.23; 6.Claudinei da Silva (Bra) 20.28; 7.Coby Miller (USA) 20.35; 8.John Capel (USA) 20.49. Lanes: C.da Silva 1, Miller 2, Malcolm 3, Capel 4, Kedéris 5, Campbell 6, Thompson 7, Boldon 8.

4x100 metre relay (30 September): 1.USA (J.Drummond, B.Williams, B.Lewis, M.Greene) 37.61; 2.Bra (V.de Lima, E.Ribeiro, André da Silva, Claudinei da Silva) 37.90; 3.Cub (J.Cesar, L.Pérez Rionda, I.Garcia, F.Mayola) 38.04; 4.Jam 38.20; 5.Fra 38.49; 6.Jap 38.66; 7.Ita 38.67; 8.Pol 38.96. Lanes: Pol 1, Jap 2, Cub 3, Bra 4, USA 5, Jam 6, Fra 7, Ita 8.

Kim Collins, the man who put St. Kitts & Nevis on the map of athletics through his victory in the century at the 2003 Worlds.

MARBLE STONES, HOLES AND STARTING BLOCKS

The necessity of having a firm support from which to "fly" at the starting signal has been felt since time immemorial. Among the famous remains found in the ruins of the ancient stadium at Olympia are two stones located on the narrow sides of the onetime track. Lengthwise they show holes from which the runners competing in the "stadion" race apparently took off.

Only after the advent of cinders first, and tartan later, runners began to use starting holes, usually made with mason's spatules and deep enough for the athlete to set his feet in them. The hole used for the foot from which the main impulse had to derive was slightly larger than the other one. A detailed description of starting holes is contained in Archie Hahn's famous book "How to sprint" (1925). As often as not there were practical difficulties in supplying a sufficient number of instruments for all runners, so that the operation was likely to cause long delays. Add that the friability of materials tracks were made of (usually slags from fossils used in locomotives and live sand for building purposes) was such as to make for a precarious stability at the starting moment. Until in 1927 two Americans, George T. Bresnahan, coach and PE instructor, and William W. Tuttle, a physiology professor, both from Iowa University, conceived a new instrument which replaced the traditional holes, providing for a greater stability on the ground and a more effective impulse at the start. The project, submitted by Bresnahan, was patented on 5 February 1929 under the denomination "foot support". In their experiments, the two inventors found that the advantage given by starting blocks vis-à-vis the old starting holes in a 100 yard race amounted to 34 thousandths of a second.

However, some time went by before starting blocks were used in official competition. Some athletes using them saw their performances disallowed by IAAF censors. That is what happened to George Simpson for his 9.4 of 1929 in the 100 yards, which would have been a world record. Same for an equal time credited to Hubert Meier in 1930. The subject of starting blocks was first taken into serious consideration by the IAAF in its 10th Convention, held in Berlin in the spring of 1930. Szilard Stankovits of Hungary, after studying the problem, concluded that the use of such instruments should not be allowed in international competitions and that no record made with their support should be ratified.

Such a status prevailed for many more years. With the IAAF Technical Commission entrenched in their disbelief, starting blocks were not in use at the Los Angeles (1932) and Berlin (1936) Olympics, even though renowned experts and many athletes were in favour of using them. As late as in 1939, said Technical Commission aired the following view on the subject: starting blocks or foot supports may be used not as a material aid to athletes but to preserve tracks from wear and tear problems and speed up the competition schedule.

One will have to wait till the 1948 Olympics in London to finally see such instruments in use. As a matter of fact they revolutionized starting techniques and marked another step forward in the evolution of sprint racing.

G.P.

7

THE BATTLE GOES ON: GREENE, GATLIN AND POWELL

Maurice Greene was the world's no.1 century man even in the first year of the new millennium. His leadership over a period of four years (1998-2001) certainly established him among the event's all time greats. If we exclude an early season race which was marred by a starter's blunder in allowing a runner to get away before the trigger was pulled, Greene had a faultless season record, with nine sub-10 clockings. What's more, he won at the World Championships in Edmonton under far from perfect physical conditions. Running with a bad knee, he led from start to finish. About 15 metres from home he was hit by two pulls, quadriceps and hamstring, yet he managed to hold on and won his third global title at the distance. A superlative effort, countersigned by a great time – 9.82 in virtually windless conditions (-0.2 m/s). Tim Montgomery was a close second in 9.85 and Bernard Williams made it a clean sweep for USA, relegating Ato Boldon to fourth. "Mo" Greene, usually famous for his grimaces, showed that he could suffer and still emerge the winner. He well epitomized the dictum "frangar non flectar".

Konstadinos Kedéris of Greece lived up to his heroics of the year before and again beat the cream of the world in the 200 m. He appeared only in a handful of meets. After a 20.10 in early season and a victory in the European Cup, he reached the top at the Worlds: after a new personal and national record (20.03) in the "semis", he won the final in 20.04, well ahead of his nearest pursuers – actually a flock of six sprinters wrapped up in the range 20.20-20.25. Chris Williams of Jamaica won silver in 20.20, barely ahead of Shawn Crawford (USA) and Kim Collins (St.Kitts) who could not be separated and tied for third in 20.20. The winner had 100 m. splits of 10.3 and 9.7. Seemingly unable to hold his form over a long period of time, Kedéris suffered his only defeat in the "Weltklasse" meet in Zurich at the hands of Bernard Williams of USA (20.19) and Malcolm of Britain. Earlier in the season, Kedéris had lowered his 100 m. best to 10.15.

In the sprint relay the US quartet won in 37.96, the slowest winning time by Americans in a global meet since 1976. That well sufficed to stay comfortably ahead of a surprisingly good South African team, who shunted Trinidad to third. In fact, the would-be winners had met real trouble in the heats. Their lead-off man Jon Drummond, afflicted by muscle problems, ran outside his lane for a short while. The team went on to qualify but was initially disqualified, only to be later reinstated on the sound consideration that by straying into the lane outside his Drummond had gained no advantage and impeded nobody. Other prospective finalists – Britain, Cuba, Germany – were not so fortunate: still in the prelims, they had problems in exchanging the baton and did not make the final.

2001 World Championships, Edmonton (Alberta) - 100 metres (5 August) w -0/2 m/s: 1.Maurice Greene (USA) 9.82; 2.Tim Montgomery (USA) 9.85; 3.Bernard Williams (USA) 9.94; 4.Ato Boldon (Tri) 9.98; 5.Dwain Chambers (UK) 9.99; 6.Kim Collins (St.Kitts) 10.07; 7.Christian Malcolm (UK) 10.11; 8.Abdul Aziz Zakari (Gha) 10.24. Lanes: Zakari 1, Malcolm 2, Montgomery 3, Greene 4, Boldon 5, Williams 6, Collins 7, Chambers 8.

2003 World Championships in Paris-St.Denis. One of the closest finishes in the annals of the metric century, with merely one hundredth of a second between first and fourth. From left to right: Emedolu (Nig) 8th, D.Campbell (UK), 3rd, Montgomery (USA) 5th, Chambers (UK) 4th, Brown (Trin) 2nd, Williams (USA) 6th, Aliu (Nig) 7th and winner Kim Collins (St.Kitts & Nevis), timed in 10.07.

200 metres (9 August) w +0.1 m/s: 1.Konstadinos Kedéris (Gre) 20.04; 2.Chris Williams (Jam) 20.20; 3.(tie) Shawn Crawford (USA) and Kim Collins (St. Kitts) 20.20; 5.Christian Malcolm (UK) 20.22; 6.Stéphan Buckland (Mau) 20.24; 7.Kevin Little (USA) 20.25; 8.Marlon Devonish (UK) 20.38. Lanes: Collins 1, Crawford 2, C.Williams 3, Kedéris 4, Malcolm 5, Little 6, Buckland 7, Devonish 8.

4x100 metre relay (12 August): 1.USA (M.Grimes, B.Williams, D. Mitchell, T.Montgomery) 37.96; 2. SA (M.Nagel, C.Du Plessis, L.Newton, M.Quinn) 38.47; 3.Tri (M.Burns, A.Boldon, J. Harper, D.Brown) 38.58; 4.Aus 38.83; 5.Jap 38.96; 6.IC 39.18; 7.Pol 39.71; Bra, did not finish. Lanes: Pol 1, IC 2, Jap 3, USA 4, Tri 5, Bra 6, Aus 7, SA 8.

Tim Montgomery (born on 28 January 1975 at Gaffney, South Carolina; 1.78 m. / 73 kg.) had his first rendez-vous with fame in 1994, when he won the 100 m. at the Junior Colleges Championships in 9.96. The wind gauge showed a legal + 1.7 m/s, but it was improperly placed on the outside of the track, instead of the inside as mandated by the rules. Then the course turned out to be short by the proverbial whisker - 99.96 m. Consequently the mark could not be accepted as a World Junior record. As previously related, Montgomery had his breakthrough in 1997, joining the sub-10 élite and finishing third at the World Championships.

In 2002, with no global championship meet on the programme, the most relevant fact was Montgomery's new world record for the 100 m., especially significant as it occurred in the Grand Prix final, the conclusive test of the IAAF Invitational series. With 9.78 he shaved 0.01 off Greene's three-year old mark, thanks to a perfect combination of favourable factors. First, he was off with a reaction time (0.104) that could hardly have been better; then, he had an aiding wind of 2.0 m/s, exactly the maximum allowable. He forged much of his winning margin in the first few steps. Dwain Chambers of Britain was runner-up (9.87), Jon Drummond third (9.97) and Kim Collins (St.Kitts) fourth (9.98). The happy winner took home a cheque of $250,000 – broken down as follows: $100,000 for the overall Grand Prix title, $50,000 for the individual event win and $100,000 as world record bonus. For

once he outshone his girl friend Marion Jones, the "World's Fastest Human", who on the same occasion clinched the overall GP title for the women's section and won a total of $150.000.

A careful examination of facts leads one to reflect that even in these days of non-stop scientific advance, the title of "World's Fastest Human" can sometimes be attributed in a tricky way. For sure, Maurice Greene can point to not one but three marks all intrinsically better than Montgomery's record: 9.79 (w +0-1 m/s) and 9.80 (w +0.2 m/s) both in 1999, and 9.82 (w –0.2 m/s) in 2001.

Greene himself had an uneven seasonal record in 2002 and was no better than third in "Track & Field News" World Ranking for the century, behind Montgomery and Chambers. As for the 200 m., Kedéris had a minimal involvement – only 3 finals, bringing his total to just 12 finals in the last three years. Yet he lowered his personal record to 19.85 in winning the European title from Francis Obikwelu, a former Nigerian who had become a Portuguese citizen late in 2001. Frank Fredericks, by then 35, had a richer seasonal record and earned the no. 1 spot in the "T&FN" Ranking. This marked his 11th ranking ever and made him the most durable 200 m. runner, just ahead of Pietro Mennea, who also figured in the ranking for over a decade.

Great sprinters may come from practically any corner of the globe. This well-known thesis was reinforced in 2003, when Kim Collins of Saint Kitts and Nevis crowned years of constant progress with a victory in the 100 m. at the World Championships in Paris. To be sure, said insular group lies in a somewhat secluded corner of Central America, the richest reservoir of sprint talent outside USA. Collins (born on 5 April 1976; 1.75 m. / 64 kg.) had a rather long apprenticeship. His international career began in 1995, when he won silver in the 100 m. at the Pan-American Junior Championships in Santiago de Chile. The following year he was at the Atlanta Olympics but failed to survive the second round of the century, In 1997 he began studies in sociology at Texas Christian University, where he had access to better opportunities for training. Yet he went through two uneventful appearances at the Worlds (1997 and '99) before his breakthrough at the 2000 Olympics in Sydney, where he was 7th in the 100 m. final (10.17) and made the "semis" in the 200 m. The following year he won his first important medal, in the Worlds at Edmonton – third in the 200 m., as previously related in my account of said meet. At the dawn of 2003 he could point to personal bests of 9.98 (2002) and 20.20 (2001).

In 2003 the no. 1 American sprinter was John Capel (born on 27 October 1978 at Brooksville, Florida; 1.80 m. / 83 kg.). From the very beginning he had "deux amours", football and track. Given the duplicity of his commitments, his results in the latter sport were startling, to say the least. By 1999 he could point to such times as 10.03 and 19.87. In the 2000 Olympics he ran the fastest time in the "semis" (20.10) but was left at the start in the final. In 2003 he earned a berth on the US team for the Worlds in the 200 m.

It should be mentioned that an important novelty was in force since the beginning of 2003. During the 2001 IAAF Congress in Edmonton a new rule on starting was introduced (on a close vote: 81 to 74) to the effect that only one false start per race would henceforth be allowed and that any athlete subsequently false starting would be disqualified immediately. It was also agreed that this rule would not be introduced until 1 January 2003 to allow for a significant period of adaptation by competitors.

The meet of the year was held in the spacious "Stade de France" at Saint-Denis, a suburb of Paris. There were notable victims in the early rounds. Jon Drummond and Asafa Powell (Jamaica) were disqualified for false starting (their reaction times were 0.052 and 0.086 respectively). The American remonstrated at length, stirred up the crowd and lay down on the track, hereby causing a long delay. He was ultimately disqualified "for behaviour likely to bring the sport into disrepute". Maurice Greene had to say goodbye in the "semis", due to an injured left leg. The final was a beautiful race to watch, with the first four wrapped up in the space of 0.01 and world record holder Tim Montgomery no better than fourth. Collins, the smallest man in the field, was dressed in black. Running in lane 1, he took a clear lead by the 50 m. mark, then repulsed strong attacks and finally won by a scant margin in 10.07. Darrel Brown (Trinidad), Darren Campbell and Dwain Chambers (both of GB) finished next in that order, all in 10.08. A further disappointment was in store for Chambers: he was disqualified in retrospect when it was found that he had committed a doping violation on 1 August.

Said Collins, the happy winner: "I was thought to be the dark horse of the race, so I decided to wear a black outfit".

In the longer sprint the surprise item was the last-minute withdrawal of Konstadinos Kedéris – reportedly due to a hamstring injury. The final saw another exciting finish, in which Capel emerged the winner by a narrow margin from his team-mate Darvis Patton, 20.30 to 20.31. Shingo Suetsugu of Japan was third in 20.38.

The Paris Worlds offered exciting sprint races throughout, and that included the 4x100 m. relay. USA had a good but not exceptional foursome, which did very well in the face of strong British rivals and won the day, 38.06 to 38.08. What was even worse for the British, their silver turned to nothing when an earlier positive doping test on Chambers was confirmed. With Britain's disqualification, Brazil moved from third to second, adding to its rich recent tradition.

2003 World Championships, Paris-Saint Denis – 100 metres (25 August) w 0.0 m/s: 1.Kim Collins (Saint Kitts & Nevis) 10.07; 2.Darrel Brown (Tri) 10.08; 3.Darren Campbell (UK) 10.08; 4.Tim Montgomery (USA) 10.11; 5. Bernard Williams (USA) 10.13; 6.Deji Aliu (Nig) 10.21; 7.Uchenna Emedolu (Nig) 10.22. Dwain Chambers (UK), 4th in 10.08, was later disqualified for a doping violation committed on 1 August. Lanes: Collins 1, Aliu 2, Williams 3, Brown 4, Chambers 5, Montgomery 6, Campbell 7, Emedolu 8.

200 metres (29 August) w +0.1 m/s: 1.John Capel (USA) 20.30; 2.Darvis Patton (USA) 20.31; 3.Shingo Suetsugu (Jap) 20.38; 4.Darren Campbell (UK) 20.39; 5.Stéphan Buckland (Mau) 20.41; 6.Joshua J. Johnson (USA) 20.47; 7.Frank Fredericks (Nam) 20.47; 8.Uchenna Emedolu (Nig) 20.62. Lanes: J.Johnson 1, Campbell 2, Buckland 3, Patton 4, Suetsugu 5, Capel 6, Fredericks 7, Emedolu 8.

4x100 metre relay (31 August): 1.USA (J.Capel, B.Williams, D.Patton, J. J. Johnson) 38.06; 2.Bra (V.de Lima, E.Ribeiro, André da Silva, C. de Souza) 38.26; 3.Hol (T.Beck, T.Douglas, P.van Balkom, C.Douglas) 38.87; 4.Nig 38.89; 5. Pol 38.96; 6. Jap 39.05. Jam did not finish; UK, 2nd in 38.08, was later disqualified due to Chambers' doping offence. Lanes: Jap 1, Pol 2, Jam 3, Bra 4, UK 5, USA 6, Hol 7, Nig 8.

It should be noted that a relay time of 37.77 had been credited to a US foursome (Drummond, .Williams, Patton, Greene) in the ISTAF meet at Berlin on 10 August. At the time of writing, early in 2006, this is the fastest time registered so far in the new millennium.

Notwithstanding his hairline victory in the Worlds, Kim Collins had to be content with the third spot in "Track & Field News" World Ranking for the 100 m., behind Capel and Bernard Williams, who had a more consistent seasonal record. In a clearer decision, Capel was first also in the 200 m.

2004 was yet another year of partly conflicting results. Jamaica's Asafa Powell (born on 11 November 1982 at St.Catherine; 1.90 m. / 88 kg.) made the grade in no unmistakable terms. As a junior he had done no better than 10.50 (2001), but in subsequent years he progressed gradually – 10.12 in 2002 and 10.02 in 2003. As previously reported, in the 2003 Worlds he was ousted for a false start in the quarters. In 2004 he amassed nine sub-10 sec. marks, with a peak of 9.87 in Brussels. He had his most glorious day in the final of the Golden League series at Monaco, where he won over both distances (9.98 and 20.06). Unfortunately, Athens added one more to his list of unlucky days in meets that mattered most.

The US Olympic Trials, again at

2001
2005

Sacramento, saw Maurice Greene in the vein of his best days. He won a great 100 m. in 9.91, barely ahead of newcomer Justin Gatlin (9.92) and Shawn Crawford (9.93). Coby Miller, fourth (9.99), gained the unenviable distinction of running the first legal sub-10 while failing to qualify for the Games. Greene did not contest the 200 m., which saw Crawford and Gatlin on top, in that order (19.99 and 20.01).

Over a century after their "première", the Olympic Games finally returned to Athens. In actual fact, the Greek capital had nurtured hopes of securing the centennial edition (1996) but was out-sprinted at the right moment by Atlanta. After waiting another eight years, Athens lived up to the task in a most dignified way. USA practically swept honours, wining 5 of the 6 medals at stake. In the 100 m. the recent tradition of very close finishes was honoured in a splendid way: the first three were bracketed in the space of 0.02 sec. and Gatlin came through the winner with a strong finish in 9.85, barely ahead of Francis Obikwelu (9.86) and Maurice Greene (9.87). The runner-up, a Nigerian at birth, ran in the colours of his new homeland, Portugal, and broke Linford Christie's European record by 0.01. Powell, fifth, suffered what was to remain his only defeat of 2004!

Shawn Crawford won the 200 m. by what could be described as a "street", at least under the standards of the new millennium. He lowered his personal record to 19.79, leaving runner-up Bernard Williams 0.22 behind. Gatlin was third, well ahead of 37-year-old Frank Fredericks.

The sprint relay saw a rather unusual event, that of US sprinters beaten in a head-to-head confrontation and not by ... disqualifications. Great Britain emerged the victor in a thrilling finish, 38.07 to 38.08. The British foursome consisted of Jason Gardener, Darren Campbell, Marlon Devonish and Mark Lewis-Francis. The "Union Jack" had last won this event in 1912, the first year it was contested at the Olympics. Nigeria was third (38.23) – sans Obikwelu, of course. There is a PS though: in one of the heats USA had finished well ahead of Britain, 38.02 to 38.53. Winning the wrong race, that is.

Shawn Crawford (born on 14 January 1978 at Van Wyck, South Carolina; 1,81 m. / 83 kg.) could point to a rather long career, featured by a gradual, steady progress. He went from 10.62 and 21.57 in 1996, aged 18, through 10.16 and 20.09 in 2000, up to 9.94 and 19.85 in 2002. He is said to call himself "The Cheetah Man", after racing against a zebra and a cheetah in a TV show.

Francis Obiorah Obikwelu (born on 22 November 1978 in Nigeria; 1.95 m. / 74 kg.) emigrated to Portugal in 1994, but as related above he did not obtain the Portuguese citizenship until the fall of 2001. Prior to that he represented his native country in the Olympics twice and in the Worlds also twice, winning bronze once in the latter (200 m. in 1999). In 2004 he became yet another European record holder hailing from a different continent.

2004 Olympics, Athens - 100 metres (22 August) w +0.6 m/s: 1.Justin Gatlin (USA) 9.85; 2.Francis Obikwelu (Por) 9.86; 3.Maurice Greene

Justin Gatlin (USA), lane 5, topping a crack field with astounding ease at the 2005 World Championships in Helsinki. He won by 0.17 from Michael Frater (Jam), lane 4. Early in 2006 Gatlin equalled the world's 100 m. record, 9.77.

(USA) 9.87; 4.Shawn Crawford (USA) 9.89; 5.Asafa Powell (Jam) 9.94; 6.Kim Collins (Saint Kitts & Nevis) 10.00; 7.Obadele Thompson (Bar) 10.10; Abdul Aziz Zakari (Gha) did not finish. Lanes: Collins 1, Zakari 2, Gatlin 3, Crawford 4, Obikwelu 5, Powell 6, Greene 7, Thompson 8.

200 metres (26 August) w +1.2 m/s: 1.Shawn Crawford (USA) 19.79; 2. Bernard Williams (USA) 20.01; 3.Justin Gatlin (USA) 20.03; 4.Frank Fredericks (Nam) 20.14; 5.Francis Obikwelu (Por) 20.14; 6.Stéphane Buckland (Mau) 20.24; 7.Tobias Unger (Ger) 20.64; Asafa Powell (Jam) did not start. Lanes: Unger 1, Powell 2, Williams 3, Crawford 4, Gatlin 5, Obikwelu 6, Buckland 7, Fredericks 8.

4x100 metre relay (28 August): 1.UK (J.Gardener, D.Campbell, M.Devonish, M.Lewis-Francis) 38.07; 2. USA (S.Crawford, J.Gatlin, C.Miller, M.Greene) 38.08; 3.Nig (O.Fasuba, U.Emedolu, A.Egbele, D.Aliu) 38.23; 4.Jap 38.49; 5.Pol 38.54; 6.Aus 38.56; 7.Tri 38.60; 8.Bra 38.67. Lanes: Aus 1, Bra 2, UK 3, Nig 4, USA 5, Pol 6, Jap 7, Tri 8.

2005 amply confirmed the stature of Justin Gatlin, who scored a magnificent double at the Worlds. And also the great potential of Asafa Powell, who lowered the world's 100 m. record to 9.77 but again missed connections with the meet of the year. Gatlin (born on 10 February 1982 at Brooklyn, NY; 1.85 m. / 79 kg.) emerged as a sprinter-hurdler in 2002. On 12 May of that year he starred in the Southeastern Conference Championships at Starkville, Mississippi, when in the space of 105 minutes he went through the following labours:

1) second leg for his team, the University of Tennessee in the 4x100 m. relay (won by UT in 38.66);

2) 2nd to Ron Bramlett in the 110 m. hurdles, as both ran 13.41;

3) 1st in the 100 m. in 10.11 (he had done 10.07 in a heat the day before);

4) 1st in the 200 m. in 19.86, a new collegiate record.

Eye-witnesses were so impressed that somebody ventured to compare Justin's stunning efforts to those of the legendary Jesse Owens on his Day of Days at Ann Arbor in 1935. Gatlin simply replied: "I feel tremendously honoured to be thought of in the same category as him. And I also know that my best years are ahead of me".

However, there was a PS. which is

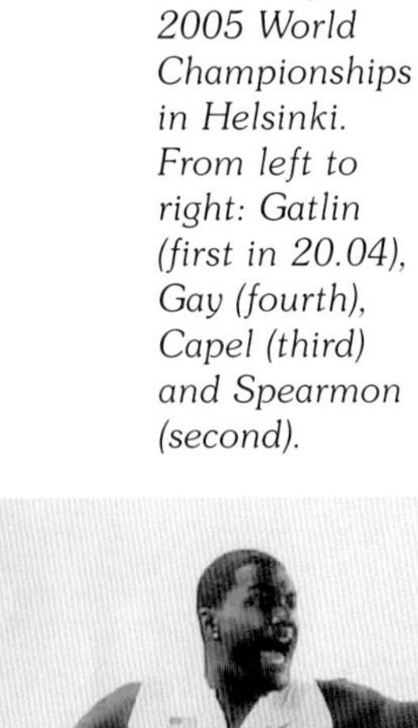

Americans scoring an unprecedented 1-2-3-4 in the 200 m. of the 2005 World Championships in Helsinki. From left to right: Gatlin (first in 20.04), Gay (fourth), Capel (third) and Spearmon (second).

worth a mention. A few days later, the US Anti-Doping Agency (USADA) announced a decision confirming that "Gatlin had "inadvertently committed a doping violation" at last year's US Junior Championships. He tested positive for amphetamine – a substance which carries a 2-year ban – in a prescription medication he has taken for a decade. Gatlin stopped taking the medication several days before the meet, but it had not fully cleared his system and trace amounts in his urine resulted in the positive test. The final decision went like this: "Mr. Gatlin's inadvertent violation of (IAAF) rules was at most a technical or paper-work violation". At most, he should have raised his medical condition for a review before the meet, instead of after it. The IAAF inflicted a 2-year suspension from international events, retroactive to last July (2001), but eventually reinstated Gatlin in July 2002. In the meantime he had been going on in US competition. Having practically abandoned the high hurdles to concentrate on the sprints, he improved to 9.97 and 20.04 in 2003, doing very well at the Athens Olympics the following year.

In 2005 Gatlin and Asafa Powell met only once, in a torrid 100 m. at Eugene on 4 June. Aided by a strong wind (+3.4 m/s) both finished in 9.84 and Gatlin got the verdict. Exactly ten days later the Jamaican was in Athens. Running on what was considered one of the world's fastest tracks, he sped to 9.77, thus shaving 0.01 sec. off Tim Montgomery's world record.

The wind in his favour was a considerable but legal 1.60 m/s. His reaction time was "normal", at best: 0.150. Aziz Zakari of Ghana as a distant second did 9.99. Earlier in the day, Powell had run a 9.98 heat.

Gatlin went through the US Championships at Carson, California, without any hitch. He won over both distances, with 10.08 and 20.04. In the century he won from Leonard Scott and Crawford, in the 200 m. from Tyson Gay and Crawford. Once again, the phalanx seemed to be ready for the big event of the year, the Worlds.

Powell ran into trouble shortly before that event, on 22 July in London. Here he and Gatlin were expected to meet again. The Jamaican won his heat in 10.02 and Gatlin his in 10.01, neither man trying unduly hard. In the final Powell pulled up after a few strides with a groin injury. Gatlin went on to win in 9.89. Apparently, the Jamaican had first sensed the trouble several weeks before, even on the day of his clash with Gatlin at Eugene. The story had a sad end: the new world record holder - incidentally a sports medicine student at the Kingston University of Technology – had to stay away from the Worlds.

Helsinki hosted the Worlds for the second time, twenty-two years after the inaugural edition. Weather conditions were not the best that could be hoped for, yet Gatlin was in great form and won over both distances in a most impressive way. He took the 100 m. as he pleased in 9.88, leaving runner-up Michael Frater of Jamaica 0.17 behind. The latter barely held out Kim Collins, as both finished in 10.05. In the 200 m. the US phalanx really made history, filling the first four places. Of course they availed themselves of the recent IAAF rule that from 2001 allowed defending champions to qualify as automatic entrants. John Capel, the 2003 champion, was thus enabled to join the three Trials qualifiers. Here Gatlin was no sure-fire favourite, yet he won rather comfortably in 20.04, from Wallace Spearmon (20.20), Capel (20.31) and Tyson Gay (20.34). The best non-American was Stéphane Buckland of Mauritius (20.41). Before the maximum of three-per-event was introduced in 1932, such a 1-2-3-4 sweep by one country had last occurred in the Games of 1920 , when the Finns turned the trick in the javelin throw. In the 200 m. it had happened at the 1904 Olympics in St.Louis, when nearly all the competitors were American anyway.

In the relay USA was to run with Scott, Greene, Gay and Gatlin, a quartet likely to endanger the world record of 37.40. As it was, a bad pass put them off the race in the prelims. France and Trinidad battled it out for first in the final, with the former finally winning by a close margin (38.08 to 38.10). The French had as lead-off man the newly crowned world champion of the 110 m. hurdles, Ladji Doucouré.

FROM ATHLETES TO STARTERS

We know but little about Spiridon Avrantis, the gentleman with a bowler hat who officiated as starter in the inaugural edition of the modern Olympics in 1896. But we know that Papadiamantopoulos, starter of the marathon in those Games, was the commanding colonel of a regiment that had among its soldiers one Spiridon Louis, who turned out to be the winner of that marathon.

Among officers who acted as starters in subsequent editions of the Games we find several former athletes, especially sprinters. That was the case of Charles L. Lockton, an Englishman, who acted as starter at the 1908 Games in London. In his youth he had been a rugby international as well as English long jump champion and a 10.2 sprinter in the 100 yards.

The Games of 1924 in Paris saw in action among starters Charles Poulenard of France, who twelve years earlier in Stockholm had run with his national team in the 4x400 metre relay, finishing second behind USA. After World War I he became a well-known coach. Among his pupils we may mention Jules Ladoumègue, a famous miler, and Séraphin Martin, another middle distance man of world class.

Jacobus Hoogveld of Holland, a good sprinter at the 1908 Olympics in London, acted as starter in the Amsterdam Games twenty years later. An even greater fame as an athlete had Robert Kerr of Canada, who was one of the judges at Los Angeles in 1932 along with Theodore Leslie Wright of New Zealand and Franz Miller, a German sport journalist for the "Münchener Neueste Nachrichten". Kerr had competed in the 1904 Olympics in St.Louis without success, only to make amends four years later in London. He went to the latter as a holder of the "Harvey Memorial Cup", having won a sprint double at the 1908 AAA Championships. In the Olympic arena he won gold in the 200 metres and bronze in the 100.

Two of the starters and one of the assistants officiating at the 1948 Olympics in London had been excellent athletes. Fred Hulford had distinguished himself first as a swimmer and then as a football player. Before turning to athletics and winning the AAA 4 mile title in 1906. At the Stockholm Olympics (1912) he reached the semi-finals of the 800 metres and ran the1500 too (eliminated in the first round).

Assistant George Nicol had been a semi-finalist in the 400 metres at the 1908 Olympics. He later competed in the Stockholm Games (1912), winning a bronze medal in the 4x400 metre relay. In 1913 he won the AAA quarter-mile title and ran with the Polytechnic Harriers teams that won the 4x440 yard relay in the title meet in 1913, 1914 and 1915.

Heikki Mäkinen of Finland, starter of the 100 metres at the 1952 Olympics in Helsinki, had been national triple jump champion in 1930, 1931 and 1932, with a personal bes of 14.90.

The starters' trio officiating at the Rome Olympics (1960) notably included Ruggero Maregatti, who as a sprinter had represented Italy in three editions of the Olympics – 1924 (as a reserve), 1928 and 1932. On the last occasion he ran with the Italian team that earned a bronze medal in the 4x100 metre relay. One of the assistants at the Rome Olympics (1960) was Vasco Lucci, who had been a leading sprinter in Italian ranks for a long time, winning the national 4x100 metre title with "Giglio Rosso" of Florence in 1930.

Franz "Bubi" Buthe-Pieper of Germany had been one of Europe's fastest men for several years long before acting as Chief Judge at the Munich Olympics in 1972. Almost two decades later, in connection with the 1991 World Championships in Tokyo. a famous name appeared in the officers' cadre, that of Hideo Iijima, who acted as starter of the 100-metre final. Formerly a world class sprinter, he had represented Japan at the 1964 Olympics in Tokyo, making it to the semi-finals in both the 100 and the sprint relay. And four years later he competed in the Mexico Games with similar results, doing 10.2 in the prelims, one tenth shy of his own Japanese record. Right now the tradition of sprinters joining the starters' ranks seems to be well-nigh extinct.

G.P.

2005 World Championships, Helsinki - 100 metres (7 August) w +0.4 m/s: 1.Justin Gatlin (USA) 9.88; 2.Michael Frater (Jam) 10.05; 3.Kim Collins (St.Kitts & Nevis) 10.05; 4.Francis Obikwelu (Por) 10.07; 5.Dwight Thomas (Jam) 10.09; 6.Leonard Scott (USA) 10.13; 7.Marc Burns (Tri) 10.14; 8.Abdul Aziz Zakari (Gha) 10.20. Lanes: Burns 1, Collins 2, Scott 3, Frater 4, Gatlin 5, Zakari 6, Thomas 7, Obikwelu 8.

200 metres (11 August) w -0.5 m/s): 1.Justin Gatlin (USA) 20.04; 2.Wallace Spearmon (USA) 20.20; 3.John Capel (USA) 20.31; 4.Tyson Gay (USA) 20.34; 5.Stéphane Buckland (Mau) 20.41; 6.Patrick Johnson (Aus) 20.58; 7.Tobias Unger (Ger) 20.81; 8.Usain Bolt (Jam) 26.27 (injured). Lanes: Bolt 1, Unger 2, Spearmon 3, Capel 4, Gay 5, Gatlin 6, Buckland 7, P.Johnson 8.

4x100 metre relay (13 August): 1.Fra (L.Doucouré, R.Pognon, E.de Lépine, L.Dovy) 38.08; 2.Tri (K.Pierre, M.Burns, J.Harper, D. Brown) 38.10; 3.UK (J.Gardener, M.Devonish, C.Malcolm, M.Lewis-Francis) 38.27: 4.Jam 38.28; 5.Aus 38.32; 6.Netherlands Antilles 38.45; 7.Ger 38.48, 8.Jap 38.77. Lanes: Jap 1, Aus 2, Tri 3, Fra 4, UK 5, Jam 6, NA 7, Ger 8.

FALSE START CONROL APPARATUS

For many years two problems, obviously connected with man's fallibility, have had negative effects on the results of short races: lack of consistency in timing and disrespect of starting rules.

The timing problem was solved with the introduction of steadily improved instruments, while adequate instruments for the detection of false starts became available only in the Sixties of the century just past.

The attention of technicians working in the field of timing devices concentrated more and more on athletes' reaction time to the gun and more exactly on the lapse of time in leaving the starting blocks after the firing of the starter's gun.

Starting blocks devised in 1927 by two Americans, George Bresnahan and William Tuttle, were gradually improved through the experiments conducted by Dr. Henry Franklin in 1947 and by Friedrich Assmus and Otto Ambruster in 1969. This led to the setting of 100 thousandths of a second as the minimum reaction time – say the borderline of honesty, below which any getaway was to be considered as irregular and therefore subject to penalties.

Officially an apparatus for the detection of false starts was first used by Junghans during the 1972 Olympics in Munich. A team from the University of Giessen conducted experiments on a large scale (1037, of which 652 were on men athletes and 385 on women athletes). The fastest reaction times were those of two USSR sprinters, Borzov and Kornelyuk: both 0.12 secs.

Later on even Swiss Timing (a trademark originating from the fusion of Longines and Omega, of which even Swatch was to become part) and Seko (supplier of the electric timing apparatus for the 1964 Olympics in Tokyo) carefully studied the problem of false starts and means to control them.

Swiss Timing was first to offer an adequate apparatus in this respect, namely in connection with the 1974 European Championships in Rome. This writer had the privilege of being among the earliest users of the system in Italy.

At the time of the 1976 Olympics in Montreal a control apparatus was introduced as an "aid to the starter": a headphone which conveyed to him adequate signals in the case of false starts. However, the starter remained the ultimate judge in all doubtful cases.

The IAAF Congress of 1993 in Stuttgart, judging on the strength of what had happened in the 100 metre final at the 1991 World Championships in Tokyo (a reaction time of 0.090 by Dennis Mitchell of USA, not detected by Hideo Iijima, starter of the race), further restricted the starter's decision area, obliging him to put a halt to the proceedings any time the control apparatus signalled a false start.

Asafa Powell (Jamaica), co-holder of the world record (9.77) for the metric century.

Instruments used to this effect have become more and more precise. Nowadays those used by Seiko and Omega are supplied with an electronic pistol (not with traditional bullets, but emanating a similar sound) which gives a recall signal anytime one or more athletes react to the gun in less than 100 thousandths of a second.

IAAF rules have evolved likewise on the strength of experience made on the fields of competition. However, such innovations have confirmed that human judgment remains necessary to support any control apparatus. The situations that are likely to arise are so many and so different as to imply the help of human rationale.

G.P.

No matter how important the technical innovations introduced throughout the 20th century – from starting blocks to synthetic tracks - I have a strong suspicion that nowadays top-class sprinters are generally if not always "a bit faster" than their predecessors. Training methods have improved time and again and their intensity has increased considerably. For example, a sprinter like Pietro Mennea of Italy, adimittedly no phenom in terms of physical qualities, achieved world record heights in the 200 metres (19.72 in 1979) mostly thanks to the intensity of his methodical daily work. His coach Carlo Vittori once said: "Mennea should get credit for demystifying the sprints. Even the most gifted of sprinters should comprehend that natural talent isn't enough, and that work is always the ultimate key." Sometime later, a man with superior physical qualities like Michael Johnson crowned years of very intense work on the 200/400 metres axis with a 19.32 for the 200, a mark which appears to be practically out of sight for present-day stars.

But no matter how short the sprint distances, there will always be room for further improvement.

P.S.: Throughout the text - for both men and women - I have purposely omitted to mention sprint marks made indoors, since conditions in the so-called undercover meets differ greatly from those prevailing outdoors in several aspects. Generally speaking, due to lack of space the "century" (100 yards or 100 metres) has never figured on the programme of major indoor meets. That also applies, to a lesser extent that's true, to the 200 metres and the 220 yards.

The main sprint distance in U.S. indoor meets was for many years the 60 yard dash, while on the European continent such a role belonged to the 60 metres. In the inaugural edition of the World Indoor Championships, held at Indianapolis in 1987, the IAAF decided to have both 60 and 200 metres on the programme, even though the longer distance had to be contested over a full lap, hence with two turns, standard indoor tracks being 200 metres in perimeter. With banked board tracks being generally the rule in indoor arenas, the advantage of the outer lanes came into play. For example, two of the last three world indoor records for the 200 metres were set in lane 6 of the fast Liévin track, dubbed by David Powell of the London "Times" as the "choice of champions". Obviously, organizers were eager to assign that upper lane to the fastest man in the field. In 1996 the great Frank Fredericks used that to good advantage to clock 19.92, the first sub-20 in indoor annals. The IAAF, alerted by the opinion of several observers, finally decided that from 2006 this event would be removed from the programme of the World Indoor Championships because "it was clear that top performances depended solely on the lane draw".

Even considering the differences in distances and nature of tracks, we feel that indoor sprints would deserve a tale of their own. Were it only to give full credit to explosive starters such as Bob Hayes, Valeriy Borzov and Maurice Greene, who made history in the 60 yards and/or 60 metres. Greene holds the present world record for the metric distance with 6.39 (2001). Irina Privalova has to her credit the fastest time for the distaff side, 6.92 (1995).

LATEST NEWS 2006

Early in 2006 Justin Gatlin and Asafa Powell engaged in a fascinating ding-dong battle for the world's 100 metre record. Within three months the listed mark (9.77 by Powell in 2005) was equalled - not once but three times. (This is being written on 23 August and forthcoming meets may add to the story). Gatlin got the ball rolling at Doha, Qatar, on 12 May. Aided by a 1.7 m/s wind, the American won comfortably from Olusoji Fasuba of Nigeria, who set a new African record of 9.85. Oddly enough, Gatlin's time was first announced and divulged all over the world as 9.76. A few days later the IAAF announced that the time, actually 9.766, had been erroneously adjusted by defect and not by excess, as prescribed by the rules. It was therefore corrected to 9.77.

The following month, on 11 June at Gateshead, Powell also did 9.77, aided by a 1.5 m/s wind. He won by a street from Michael Frater of Jamaica (10.06). The Jamaican did it again in Zurich on 18 August, winning from Tyson Gay (9.84). On this occasion the aiding wind was 1.0 m/s. Just out of curiosity some statisticians took (unofficial) thousandths of a second into consideration. The ranking would then read as follows: Powell 9.762 (Zurich 2006), Powell 9.763 (Gateshead, 2006), Gatlin 9.766 (Doha, 2006) and Powell 9.768 (Athens, 2005). Wind conditions in the four races: a favourable breeze ranging from 1.0 m/s to 1.7 m/s. Still a considerable help, at least in the opinion of two experts who have studied the problem in depth - Jesús Dapena, an exercise physiologist, and Nicholas Linthorne, a mathematician. They studied the influence of wind and altitude in sprint marks made on a straight course and devised charts offering the "corrected" value of times. Their adjusted versions may not be 100% "truthful", because other factors – e.g. the size of athletes – can also affect the situation. Still, their "corrected" lists are no doubt truer, in intrinsic value, than the traditional ones based on official results. Their All Time List is currently topped by Maurice Greene, who in his heydays had marks of 9.79, 9.80 and 9.82, all under practically windless conditions (as detailed in the preceding text). They "translate" into recalculated marks all in the range 9.80-9.81. As for the four 9.77's by the Powell-Gatlin duo, the best of them (Powell at Gateshead and Zurich this year) convert to no better than 9.84.

By the end of July an explosive news-item hit the headlines: Gatlin announced that he had tested positive for testosterone at the Kansas Relays on 22 April, three weeks before his 9.77 at Doha. He agreed to attend a hearing before the US Anti-Doping Agency. Considering what happened to him in 2001 (as related earlier in the text), he could well suffer a life ban. Up to now he and Powell have met 9 times over 100 metres and the American leads 6 to 3.

In mere face value, the fastest century of the early season was credited to 22-year-old Churandy Martina of the Dutch Antilles – 9.76 at El Paso on 13 May. Wind (+6.1 m/s) and altitude (1126 m.) richly contributed to such a product. This is worth no better than 10.00 under Mr. Dapena's corrected version.

In the 200 metres Xavier Carter of USA made the headlines with a surprisingly fast 19.63 at Lawrence on 11 July (wind +0.4 m/s). He was duly extended by Tyson Gay, 19.70. These are the fastest clockings of the post-Johnson era and rank their authors second and fourth respectively in the All Time List. Carter, who will turn 21 in December, had delivered a clear fore-warning the month before at Sacramento, 10 June, when he ran the century in 10.09 and the 400 metres in 44.53 – in the space of 32 minutes!

"Konstas" Kedéris of Greece, winner of the 200 metres at the 2000 Olympics and the 2001 Worlds, had been involved in a long-drawn "querelle" with his own Federation for failing to show up at three doping tests in 2004, which caused him to stay away from the Athens Olympics of that year. Provisionally suspended by the IAAF, the Greek sprinter finally came to an agreement with the Court of Arbitration for Sport in June 2006, after admitting his violation of the anti-doping rules. He'll be able to re-enter international competition at the end of 2006, aged 33.

WOMEN
FROM THE VASSAR PIONEERS TO HELEN STEPHENS, THE "MISSOURI TORNADO"

8

Sport historians are generally inclined to believe that women's athletics originated a long time ago, though perhaps in forms rather different from those prevailing nowadays. For example, it is a known fact that in ancient Egypt women engaged in gymnastics and acrobatics since the early days of the Middle Kingdom, about 2000 b.C.

In ancient Greece married women were not allowed to attend the celebrated men's games, under pain of punishment that extended to the death penalty. This veto did not apply to unmarried girls though. Yet, contrary to a widespread "lieu commun", Greek women had athletic competitions of their own, held at Olympia every four years, entirely separate from the men's games. The festival was in honour of Hera, wife of Zeus, and was called Heraia, a series of races for girls. The competitors were divided into three age

Finish of a sprint race at Vassar College.

groups – children, adolescents, and young women – and competed over a distance of 500 feet (160.22 m.) or 5/6th of the "stadion". They ran with their hair unbound, and wearing a short "chiton" which left their right shoulder uncovered to the breast. The prize for the winner consisted of a crown of olive, a portion of the cow that was sacrificed to Hera, and the right to have a portrait of themselves. There were women's races even in other parts of ancient Greece, e.g. at Sparta and Cyrene, but those at Olympia were the most celebrated. Above all this there was of course the myth of Atalanta, the swift-footed huntress who was often taken as a symbol of females engaged in sports activities.

In those days, however, even illustrious men had mental reservations about the participation of women in sports. Unfortunately, this prejudice subsisted even in the early days of modern athletics. It was vaguely explained with the "differences" between the sexes, but in reality it stemmed from the subordinate role traditionally reserved to women in the social life of most if not all civilizations, a role which made it difficult for them to engage in sport as independent individuals. There are, however, Teutonic legends which occasionally refer to women's sports.

Modern historians refer to two handicap races over 100 yards and 440 yards in a meeting held in Dublin in 1891 as "the first of known timed track performances". According to Eric L. Cowe, the foremost historian of women's athletics for the early days, the sprint race was won by Miss A. Foulds, who did 13.0 off 2 1/2 y. (2.28 m.) and finished inches ahead of 15-year-old Eva Francisco (scratch). These girls were British born and members of circus families. Private secondary schools established in Britain in the mid 19th century are recognized as the cradle of modern women's athletics.

In fact, the earliest 100 yards record was probably made in USA, one year before the afore-mentioned Dublin meet. It was a "modest" 17.0 credited to an American, Mamie Hubbard, at New York on 11 August 1890. What is generally considered as the earliest organized women's meet of modern times took place in USA, namely at Vassar College on 9 November 1895, when in the words of a local chronicler a group of "nimble, supple and vivacious girls" engaged in running and jumping events, under unfavourable weather conditions. Vassar College, a private school for women founded in 1861 by Matthew Vassar, was located at Poughkeepsie in the state of New York. We are told that the young women wore no hats. Marks were recorded under the careful supervision of women officials and the programme consisted of five events, plus a basketball competition. Almost needless to say, there was a 100 yards race, which was aptly won by Miss Elizabeth Forbes Vassar, a niece of the college's founder, in 16.0. Times made in the heats were faster: 15 1/4 by Annie Wilkinson and 15 1/2 by Vassar herself. There was also a furlong race, won by Helen Haight in 36 1/4, regarded by historians as a best-on-record mark for the 220 yards.

SECURITY FIRST

The inaugural Vassar "Field Day" of 1895 was what we would now describe as an exclusive affair. Said a paper of the time: "Every effort was made to have the programme carried through without publicity. The oval field is admirably adapted to secure the girls from undesired spectators, being surrounded by a thick evergreen hedge, about 12 ft. (3.65 m.) high. Orders were given to exclude reporters and also all masculine visitors". The girls wore divided skirts and white sweaters, loose enough to disguise every curve of the body, but which did not hide the broad, well-developed shoulders of the athletes. Black stockings and rubber-soled canvas shoes without heels completed the costumes. The young women wore no hats. They scorned mackintoshes and umbrellas, although by 11 a.m. the rain settled into a downpour".

P.S.: In connection with "undesired spectators", that 12. ft. hedge was just the thing. At that time the best-on-record mark for the men's pole vault was 11 ft. 9 in. (3.58 m.) .... (by Richard Dickinson of Britain in 1891, using the so-called "climbing technique").

The Vassar meet became an annual feature and yielded gradually better results. And surely it did not pass unnoticed, if it is true, as reported, that in connection with the second edition (1896) "college boys had a peep at the Field Day" fun " ... In 1900 the 220 yards record was brought down to 32 2/5 by Ruth Wells of USA. By the same time the 100 yards mark was relatively better: 12.0 by Mabel Guinness and F. Nolan, both of Britain, in "a magnificent dead-heat" at Dublin in 1898.

By the turn of the century several English speaking countries such as UK, USA, Ireland, Australia, New Zealand and South Africa held women's meets regularly. Even prior to that there had been a widespread walking activity involving college women.

Unfortunately, the revivers of the modern Olympics did not have progressive views on the subject of women participating in sports events, baron Pierre de Coubertin himself being no exception. Yet, by a curious twist of circumstances the real boost for the advent of the distaff-side in the international arena came from France, more exactly from a fervent "suffragette" named Alice Milliat, who in 1917 founded the "Fédération Féminine Sportive de France". Two years later, her request to have women's events included in the Olympic programme was refused by the IOC. The tenacious French pioneer and her associates from several other countries went ahead by themselves and decided to organize the first multi-national women's meet. This was held in the Principauté de Monaco from 24 to 31 March 1921 and was essentially an Anglo-French festival, with eleven events on the programme. Mary Lines of England (born on 3 December 1893; 1.65 m. / 62 kg.), although virtually a novice, had the lion's share. She won the 60 m. in 8 $^{1}/_{5}$, the 250 m. in 36 $^{3}/_{5}$, the long jump at 4.70 and anchored two victorious British relay teams. Just for good measure, she also placed second in the 800m. !

Later in 1921, Madame Milliat and her associates founded the "Fédération Sportive Féminine Internationale" (FSFI). Six countries were represented: France, UK, Czechoslovakia, Italy, Spain and USA. Madame Milliat was elected President of the newly born organization, which held the inaugural Women's World Games at Stade Pershing, just outside Paris, on 20 August 1922. The whole programme, 11 events (partly with preliminary rounds), was completed in one day. The meet was witnessed by

1928 Olympics, Amsterdam. Betty Robinson (USA), centre, becomes the first woman to be crowned Olympic champion in the 100 m. She is flanked by Fanny Rosenfeld (Canada), left, and Erna Steinberg (Germany), right, second and fourth respectively. Not in the picture is Ethel Smith (Canada), lane 1, who finished third.

about 20,000 spectators! There were three sprint races, all of which produced new world records. Marie Mejzliková II Czechoslovakia) won the 60 metres in a record 7.6 from Mary Lines, while Nora Callebout (UK) took the 100 yards in 12.0. At the latter distance Mejzliková II did 11.4 in a heat for a new world record, but had to be content with second in the decisive race. Finally, a British foursome won the 4x110 y. relay in 51.8, getting credit for a 51.4 at 4x100 m. while enroute, another world record.

1922 World Games, Paris - 60 metres (20 August): 1.Marie Mejzliková II (Cze) 7.6; 2.Mary Lines (UK) 7.7e; 3.Nora Callebout (UK) 7.8e; 4. Lucie Prost (Fra) 7.9e.

100 yards (20 August): 1.Nora Callebout (UK) 12.0; 2.Marie Mejzlková II (Cze); 3.Mary Lines (UK); 4.Lucie Prost (Fra).

4x110 yard relay (20 August): 1.UK (M.Lines, N.Callebout, D.Leach, G.Porter) 51.8 (timed in 51.4 for 4x100 m.); 2.Fra (L.Prost, L.Robin, Y.de Wynne, Noeppel); 3.Cze (Marie Mejzliková I, Marie Mejzliková II, B. Sramková, M. Jirasková); 4.USA.

Oddly enough, Mary Lines was credited with a 100 m. time of 12.8, from a set start on the first leg of the relay. This was ratified as a world record by the FSFI, but of course it would be unacceptable by modern standards.

Marie Mejzliková II (née Majerová on 13 December 1903) and Nora Callebout (born on 29 April 1895, died on 26 January 1995; 1.67 m. / 60 kg.) thus made history as the first women to be crowned world champions in the sprints. Neither of them, however, had such a wide range as Mary Lines. The English woman spread herself thin by competing in four events and in addition to a third in the 100 yards she won three firsts: 300 metres (44.8), long jump (5.06) and, as related above, sprint relay.

The untiring efforts of the FSFI certainly contributed to the coming of age of women's athletics at the international level. At the outset this pioneer body was practically ignored by the IAAF, but the latter had reasons to reconsider as time went on. Mrs. Milliat's organization managed to hold three more editions of the World Games: Göteborg (1926), Prague (1930) and London (1934), by which time the number of countries involved was up to nineteen.

The Göteborg meet of 1926 was a three-day affair and yielded much better results. Once again, the programme showed a curious mixture of English and metric events, maybe as a happy compromise between English and continental (read, FSFI) traditions. There were no less than four sprint events. The outstanding sprinter was Marguerite Radideau of France (born on 5 March 1907), who won the 60 metres (7.8) and the 100 yards (11.8), was third in the 250 metres and second with the French team in the relay. The outstanding figure of the Games was, however, a tiny Japanese girl, Kinue Hitomi (born on 1 January 1907 at Okayama; 1.57 m./ 45 kg.) who showed a fantastic range with wins in the long jump – both running and standing versions – and placings in the 60 m. (5th), the 100 y. (3rd), the 250 m. (6th) and the discus (2nd) ! Not surprisingly, this 19-year-old girl was voted the outstanding athlete of the Games.

1926 World Games, Göteborg - 60 metres (29 August): 1.Marguerite Radideau (Fra) 7.8; 2.Florence Haynes (UK) 7.8; 3.Rose Thompson (UK) 7.8; 4.Zdenka Smolová (Cze) 8.0; 5.Kinue Hitomi (Jap) 8.0; 6.Ludmila Sychrová (Cze) 8.0; 7.Janka Grabicka (Pol) 8.2.

100 yards (27 August): 1.Marguerite Radideau (Fra) 11.8; 2.Rose Thompson (UK) 11.8; 3.Kinue Hitomi (Jap) 12.0; 4.Florence Haynes (UK) 12.0; 5.Ludmila Sychrová (Cze) 12.0; 6.Yolande Plancke (Fra) 12.8; 7.Signe Johansson (Swe) 12.8.

250 metres (27 August): 1.Eileen Edwards (UK) 33.4; 2.Vera Palmer (UK) 34.6; 3.Marguerite Radideau (Fra) 35.4; 4.Yolande Plancke (Fra) 35.8; 5.Julija Khmizovska-Volfa (Lat) 36.4; 6.Kinue Hitomi (Jap) 37.0.

4x100 metre relay (29 August): 1.UK (D.Scoular, F.Haynes, E. Edwards, R.Thompson) 49.8; 2.Fra (L.Bellon, G.Laloz, Y.Plancke, M.Radideau) 51.2; 3.Cze (M.Vidlaková, S.Kucerová, L.Sychrová, Z.Smolová) 52.8; 4.Sweden 53.0.

DEAR OLD WORSTED

Sometime in the early days of the 20th century track addicts conceived the idea of using a worsted or woolen yarn to be stretched across the track between the two posts for the purpose of assisting the referee and judges in placing the competitors. Mind you, this was not meant to infringe the basic rule that competitors were to be placed exclusively "in the order in which any part of their bodies, i.e. torso, including neck, as distinguished from the head, arms, legs, hands or feet - reach the nearer edge of the finish line drawn on the ground".

However, what to officials and timers was meant merely as an additional help, soon became the guiding factor to spectators in general. Most fans and even journalists began to rave about "victories snatched at the last possible moment" or about athletes "breaking the tape after a furious battle".

From a photo of Archie Hahn at the end of the 100 metre final in the intermediate Olympics of 1906 in Athens we can gather that the worsted had not entered the picture yet. But it was there all right when Reginald Walker of South Africa won the same event at the 1908 Olympics in London. The same for his successors, for many years afterwards. The presence of a white yarn was of great visual help in the very close finish involving Eddie Tolan and Ralph Metcalfe at the 1932 Olympics in Los Angeles. Little Eddie's breast appeared to be slightly ahead of Ralph's, no matter if a Kirby camera caught both in the same electric time – 10.38.

Even athletes sometime happened to ignore that the worsted or yarn was by no means the official "judge". Journalists seconded such a belief and their imagination often ran wild. Anecdotes abound. In 1936 Italy won its first Olympic gold medal in the women's ranks thanks to Ondina Valla, who emerged the winner in the 80 metre hurdles from a closely bunched field (the first four in the space of 7 hundredths of a second). Somebody suggested that it was Ondina's breast to reach the tape first, to which she retorted: "That's not true: I've never had too much of it, so I had no advantage of the sort..."

With the advent of photo-electric cells the dear old worsted went into a sad retreat. For some time many athletes regretted that, missing what to many of them had been a useful reference point. Not to mention the nice sensation they experienced when breaking it as winners.

G.P.

In that very same year, 1926, the IOC finally took notice of the serious purposes that animated Madame Milliat and her associates and voted (12 to 5) to include women's events in the Olympics. The occasion for this historic event were the Games of 1928 in Amsterdam. The women's programme was very thin, consisting of only five events. Included in that number were the 100 metres and the 4x100 m. relay. It must be said that this debut was saluted with mixed feelings by the press in general. There were malicious remarks too, e.g. by a Swedish paper which carried a picture showing a woman athlete in training. The accompanying caption was: "Eva tränar för A'dam" (Eve training for A'dam, an obvious contraction of Amsterdam).

The first Olympic champion in the 100 metres was Elizabeth "Babe" Robinson of USA (born on 23 August 1911 at Riverdale, IL; 1.67 m. / 58 kg.). In her first track season she amazed experts by coming through in the race that mattered most. Two of the six finalists, Myrtle Cook of Canada and Leni Schmidt of Germany, were disqualified for false starts. Robinson won rather comfortably in 12.2. Canadians took partial revenge in the sprint relay, with Cook holding off Robinson in the anchor leg. The winners broke the world record with 48.4.

1928 Olympics, Amsterdam – 100 metres (31 July): 1.Elizabeth Robinson (USA) 12.2; 2.Fanny Rosenfeld (Can) 12.3e; 3.Ethel Smith (Can) 12.3e; 4.Erna Steinberg (Ger) 12.4e. Myrtle Cook (Can) and Leni Schmidt (Ger) disq. for false starts. Lanes: Smith 1, Schmidt 2, Cook 3, Steinberg 4, Robinson 5, Rosenfeld 6.

4x100 metre relay (5 August): 1.Can (E.Smith, F.Rosenfeld, F.Bell, M.Cook) 48.4; 2.USA (M.Washburn, J.Cross, L.McNeil, B.Robinson) 48.8e; 3.Ger (R.Kellner, L.Schmidt, A.Holdmann, L.Junker) 49.0e 4.Fra 49.6e; 5.Hol 49.8e; 6.Ita 53.6e. Lanes: Can 1, USA 2, Ita 3, Fra 4, Hol 5, Ger 6.

VENI, VIDI, VICI

One of the best "rags-to-riches" stories in women athletics is connected with the name of Elizabeth "Babe" Robinson of USA, the first woman to be crowned Olympic champion in a sprint race. Amazingly enough, the Amsterdam affair was only the fourth meet of her career, according to Louise Mead Tricard, the leading historian of US women's athletics. Of course, Babe's love for the sport was evident since her school days – "anytime anyone was having races I was in them". Yet her official debut in the sport only came in an indoor meet in March 1928. She wound up second to Helen Filkey, then a US record holder. In her second meet, outdoors, she simply ran the .... fastest time ever recorded for the metric century – 12.0 at Chicago on 2 June. At the Olympic Trials "Babe" finished second to Elta Cartwright. Then came the Amsterdam Olympic test. In the 100 metres (three rounds), she won the decisive race in 12.2. Then she ran the anchor leg in the sprint relay, earning second place and silver for USA. Not bad for a newcomer, not yet 17!

"Babe" performed at the highest level for another two and a half years, notably with US records in the 100 yards (11.2 in 1929) and in the 220 (25.1 in 1931). Then she suffered facial lacerations, a crushed arm and a broken leg in an airplane accident. All this seemed to put pay to her career. She did miss the 1932 Los Angeles Olympics, yet by 1936 she staged a miraculous comeback, contributing to America's gold in the 4x100 metre relay at the Berlin Olympics. A truly amazing career, no doubt.

Even after the acceptance of women's athletics in the Olympic family, the FSFI deemed it advisable to organize two more editions of its World Games. In 1930 it was the turn of Prague, the capital of Czechoslovakia, again on a 3-day basis (6,7,8 September) and again with four sprint races. The meet marked the advent on the international stage of the redoubtable Pole, Stanislawa Walasiewicz (born on 3 April 1911 at Wierzchownia; died on 4 December 1980 at Cleveland, OH; 1.62 m. / 54 kg.), who was truly unparalleled in athletic longevity. Erich Kamper, a well-known Austrian track writer and historian, recently discovered that at birth she was actually named Stefania, although the athletics world always knew her as Stanislawa. Her parents emigrated to the USA when she was two. Although she took the name Stella Walsh, she always represented her native country in international competition. Her masculine appearance gave rise to perplexity in some quarters. As destiny would have it, suspicions were confirmed in 1980, when she was shot dead while accidentally involved in a robbery just outside a grocery store in Cleveland. An autopsy revealed a situation certainly not compatible with participation in women's sports. Cases of physical ambiguity could make the identification of sex difficult in the early decades of the 20th century, when medical knowledge was far from today's sophisticated levels. Consequently, it is pretty hard for a track observer to adequately value Walasiewicz's results in the light of women's athletics.

For a long period of time Stella was prominent in both USA and Europe in a wide variety of events – sprints, long jump and pentathlon. Her ultimate best times for the short distances were 11.6 for the 100 metres (Berlin, 1 August 1937) and 23.6 for the 200 (Warsaw, 4 August 1935), both ratified as world records by the IAAF. On the latter occasion she succeeded so-to-say on second try: in the first race she did 22.2 on a course which upon re-measurement turned out to be a sizable 12 m. short. In a re-run, half an hour later, she did 23.6 on a course of 200.17 m. In 1939 she had an unratified 6.12 in the long jump.

Walasiewicz was the dominant figure at the 1930 World Games in Prague, winning all three sprint events.

WOMEN ON THE RISE

Women's events became part of the Olympic programme only in 1928. Since then they have never ceased to gain ground and nowadays they practically equal the men's quota even in number. Apart from rare exceptions (e.g. weight of throwing implements and height of hurdles), the rule book is substantially the same for both sexes.

Even starting blocks are the same and no difference is foreseen in the evaluation of reaction times, even though we know that women's impulses on the blocks are less powerful than those of men.

World records for men and women are no longer miles apart as they once used to be. As recently as in 1992 "Nature" magazine went so far as to predict that women would soon excel men even in terms of records. This conclusion was arrived at on the basis of a conception that seems to be arguable at best: in recent years women's records were bettered more often and more rapidly than those of the other sex. According to consequent calculations, in the marathon women were expected to excel men by 1998. As everybody knows this did not happen, no matter if the best-on-record time for a woman – Paula Radcliffe's 2 hrs 15:25 in 2003 – is to be considered an excellent performance even by men's standards. Apart from such a case, the difference between men's and women's records has remained virtually unchanged in recent years. Right now it is difficult to hypothesize substantial changes for the near future. I think that the "Nature" analysts, instead of limiting themselves to the study of statistical data, should have paid more attention to the fact that the mechanisms producing energy are less developed in women, same as muscular power in general. Furthermore, women are different in body fats and skeleton structure. At this stage it seems well nigh impossible to foresee even vaguely a date when sexes will perform on a similar basis in athletics. There are at any rate physiological prerequisites which may lead, at least in some sports, to a further reduction of performance levels between the two sexes.

G.P.

1930 World Games, Prague - 60 metres (7 September): 1.S.Walasiewicz (Pol) 7.7; 2.Lisa Gelius (Ger) 7.8; 3.Kinue Hitomi (Jap) 7.8; 4.Ivy Walker (UK) 8.0; 5.Marguerite Radideau (Fra) 8.1; 6.Rosa Kellner (Ger) 8.2.

100 metres (8 September): 1.S.Walasiewicz (Pol) 12.5; 2.Tollien Schuurman (Hol) 12.6; 3.Lisa Gelius (Ger) 12.6; 4.Eileen Hiscock (UK) 12.7; 5.Daisy Ridgley (UK) 12.8; 6.Kitty ter Horst (Hol) 13.0.

200 metres (8 September): 1.S.Walasiewicz (Pol) 25.7; 2.Tollien Schuurman (Hol) 25.8; 3.Nellie Halstead (UK) 26.0; 4.Detta Lorenz (Ger) 26.6. (Kinue Hitomi of Japan and Marie Dollinger of Germany, both scratched due to competing in other events later in the day).

4x100 metre relay (8 September): 1.Ger (R.Kellner, A.Karrer, L.Holzer, L.Gelius) 49.9; 2.UK (E.Scott, I.K.Walker, E.Hiscock, D.Ridgley) 50.5; 3.Pol (A.Hulanicka, F.Freiwald, S.Walasiewicz, F.Schabinska) 50.8; 4.Jap 52.0; 5.Fra 53.0; 6.Aut 53.8.

In the meantime the IAAF continued to be far from generous in opening new frontiers for the distaff side. In the 1932 Olympics in Los Angeles the number of women events was increased but minimally – from 5 to 6 - vis-à-vis the première of four years earlier in Amsterdam. Again, only two sprint events. Stella Walasiewicz had to fight hard in order to emerge the winner against a petite sprinter from Montreal, 22-year-old Hilda Strike. The latter was only 5 ft. 4 ins. (1.62 m.) and weighed about 105 pounds (47 kg.), yet it was only in the final stretch of land that she was passed by the Pole. Both were timed in 11.9, equalling the world record set earlier in the year by Tollien Schuurman of Holland.

The sprint relay offered a close fight

between USA and Canada, with the former finally prevailing by a scant margin in new world record time, 46.9.

1932 Olympics, Los Angeles - 100 metres (4 August): 1.S.Walasiewicz (Pol) 11,9; 2.Hilda Strike (Can) 11.9; 3. Wilhelmina von Bremen (USA) 12.0; 4.Marie Dollinger (Ger) 12.2; 5.Eileen Hiscock (UK) 12.3; 6. Elizabeth Wilde (USA) 12.5. Lanes: von Bremen 1, Wilde 2, Strike 3, Dollinger 4, Walasiewicz 5, Hiscock 6.

4x100 metre relay (7 August): 1.USA (M.Carew, E.Furtsch, A.Rogers, W.von Bremen) 46.9; 2.Can (Mildred Frizzell, L.Palmer, Mary Frizzell, H.Strike) 47.0; 3.UK (E.Hiscock, G.Porter, V.Webb, N.Halstead) 47.6; 4.Hol 48.0e: 5.Jap 48.9e; 6.Ger 50.0e. Lanes: Jap 1, Hol 2, Can 3, USA 4, UK 5, Ger 6.

The fourth and last edition of the World Games organized by the FSFI was held in 1934 at London's White City Stadium, a dignified venue for such a farewell occasion. Walasiewicz did win the 60 metres, but in the longer races she chanced upon a worthy rival, who beat her in both 100 and 200 metres: Käthe Krauss of Germany (born on 29 November 1906 in Dresden; 1.76 m. / 72 kg.), a powerful sprinter who also helped Germany in winning gold in the 4x100 metre relay. By that time Germany was shaping up as the world's no.1 power in women's athletics, more in the field events than in the running department though.

1934 World Games, London - 60 metres (11 August): 1.S.Walasiewicz (Pol) 7.6; 2.Gretel Kuhlmann (Ger) 1 y. back: 3.Ethel Johnson (UK) in. f.b.; 4.Barbara Burke (SA); 5.Elsie Maguire (UK); Tollie Schuurman (Hol) scratched.

100 metres (11 August): 1.Käthe Krauss (Ger) 11.9; 2.S.Walasiewicz (Pol) 12.0e; 3.Eileen Hiscock (UK) 12.1e.; 4.Marie Dollinger (Ger); 5.Audrey Dearnley (Can); 6.Barbara Burke (SA).

200 metres (11 August): 1.Käthe Krauss (Ger) 24.9; 2.S.Walasiewicz (Pol) 25.0e; 3.Eileen Hiscock (UK) 25.2e; 4.Lilian

Relay final at the 1936 Olympics in Berlin turns into drama for leading German team as Marie Dollinger (left) and Ilse Dörffeldt lose baton in the last change. Picture on the opposite page shows the entire field: Helen Stephens (lane 3) will anchor the US team to victory in 46.9; picture here shows the "drama" in detail. In a "re-match" at Wuppertal a few days later, the Germans won over the Americans after a hot duel (46.6 to 46.7).

The incomparable Fanny Blankers-Koen (Holland), as a runaway winner in the 200 metres at the London Olympics (1948).

Palmer (Can); 5.Aileen Meagher (Can); 6.Marie Dollinger (Ger).

4x100 metre relay (11 August): 1.Ger (S.Grieme, K.Krauss, M.Dollinger, I.Dörffeldt) 48.6; 2.Hol (C.Aalten, I.Martin, J.Dalmolen, A.Doorgeest) 50.0; 3.Aut (E.Spanader, G.Gottlieb, V.Kohlbach, J.Vancura-Wendler) 51.2; 4.Jap; 5.Fra; UK did not finish. Lanes: UK 1, Ger 2, Aut 3, Hol 4, Jap 5, Fra 6.

The glorious FSFI merged with the IAAF in the mid-Thirties. And so did world records, which at the end of 1935 were as follows: 100 yards – 11.0 Barbara Burke (SA) at Pretoria (1935); 100 metres – 11.6 Helen Stephens (USA) at Kansas City (1935); 200 metres – 23.6 Stanislawa Walasiewicz (Poland) at Warsaw (1935).

On the eve of the 1936 Olympics a new star seemed to dominate the sprint picture, Helen Stephens of USA (born on 3 February 1918 at Fulton, Missouri; died on 17 January 1994 at St.Louis, Missouri; 1.82 m. / 70 kg.). In only three years of track activity she ran over 100 races and was never beaten. With her impressive physique, well above the women's average of those days, she dwarfed her rivals. In her first race, at the age of 17, she equalled the world indoor best for 50 metres (6.6) and beat none other than Stella Walsh. Later in the same year, 1935, she had fast times galore, including some world records, most of which remained unratified. She ran the 100 yards in 10.8 (twice) and 10.9 (three times), the 100 metres in 11.6 (twice), 11.8 (once) and 11.9 (twice) and the 220 yards (straight course) in

Betty Cuthbert (Australia), right, nipping Heather Armitage (UK) at the end of the 4x100 m. relay in the 1956 Olympics in Melbourne. The official times were 44.5 (world record) and 44.7, but a more reliable electric timer caught them in 44.65 and 44.70 respectively.

Wilma Rudolph (USA), who won three gold medals at the 1960 Olympics in Rome.

23.9. Clock-wise her best day was at Toronto on 2 September: 10.4 (heat) and 10.6 (final) in the 100 yards and 23.2 in the 220 (straight course). These were branded as mere "exhibitions" though.

On the eve of Olympic year 1936 Stephens obviously looked as the dominating figure. Even Walasiewicz, seven years her senior, seemed helpless in her regard. In pre-Olympic meets Helen was her usual speedy self, notably with a wind-assisted 11.3 in the metric century at St.Louis. When she went on board ship to the Olympics she had to train on the deck under far from ideal conditions and developed a case of shin splints. Be that as it may, she performed at her best in Berlin. In the Games there were, as usual, only two sprint events, the 100 and the 4x100 relay. Helped by winds in the 2-to-4 m/s range, the 18-year-old American chalked up times of 11.4 (heat) and 11.5 (semi-final and final). In the decisive race she left Walasiewicz (11.7) well behind. Käthe Krauss of Germany was a well beaten third.

Helen was out for a second gold as anchor-leg runner in the relay. Here the US team was confronted by a well-oiled German team – Emmy Albus, Käthe Krauss, Marie Dollinger and Ilse Dörffeldt – who were credited with a new world record, 46.4, in one of the heats, while the Americans won theirs in 47.1. In the final the next day the Germans were clearly in the lead up to the last pass, in which Dollinger and Dörffeldt failed to connect properly and had to call it quits, much to the despair of the large German crowd. Stephens coasted to an easy win in 46.9, well ahead of Great Britain.

A few days later, at Wuppertal, there was a re-match and the Germans emerged the winners over the Americans after a hard fight– 46.6 to 46.7. In this meet Helen had the closest call of her glorious season, emerging the winner over Walasiewicz in the 200 metres by a scant margin, 24.1 to 24.2.

Her seasonal record was again great, with two apparently valid 11.5 marks in the 100 metres.

1936 Olympics, Berlin - 100 metres (4 August) w: +3.5 m/s: 1.Helen Stephens (USA) 11.5; 2.S.Walasiewicz (Pol) 11.7; 3. Käthe Krauss (Ger) 11.9; 4. Marie Dollinger (Ger) 12.0; 5.Annette Rogers (USA) 12.2; 6.Emmy Albus (Ger) 12.3. Lanes: Dollinger 1, Rogers 2, Albus 3, Stephens 4, Krauss 5, Walasiewicz 6.

4x100 metre relay (9 August): 1.USA (H.Bland, A.Rogers, B.Robinson, H.Stephens) 46.9; 2.UK (E.Hiscock, V.Olney, A.Brown, B.Burke) 47.6; 3.Can (D.Brookshaw, M.Dolson, H.Cameron, A.Meagher) 47.8; 4.Ita 48.7; 5.Hol 48.8. Ger, did not finish. Lanes: UK 1, Ita 2, USA 3, Ger 4, Can 5, Hol 6.

In 1937 Stephens ran in exhibitions as a "pro", notably with a 10.5 for the 100 yards. That was the end of a short yet phenomenal career. She remained in close touch with the sport in several ways and in the early Eighties, at 60-plus, she starred in the Senior Olympics.

1938 saw the inaugural edition of the European Women's Championships, held in Vienna. Stanislawa Walasiewicz, by then 27, scored an impressive double, with 11.9 in the 100 metres and 23.8 in the 200. Käthe Krauss was second in both races (12.0 and 24.4), always ahead of a Dutch girl, Fanny Koen (12.0 and 24.9). Then 20, the latter happened to be on the rise at what turned out to be the wrong time, i.e. just before the outbreak of World War II. But she managed to survive and eventually reached immortality in post-war years, as will be related in the next chapter.

STARTERS AND GUNS

At the inaugural Olympics of 1896 in Athens races were started by firing a pistol. The task was entrusted to Spiridon Avrantis, committed to posterity thanks to Albert Meyer of Germany, the official photographer of the Games.

The use of a pistol as a starting signal had been introduced a few years before, exactly when and where we don't know for sure.

Surely the use of an instrument likely to emit a strong clear sound was connected with provisions made in the early days of the sport, presumably when the first athletics federations came to life, the English AAA in 1880 and the American AAU in 1888. We know that prior to that other signals had been used, like the trill of a trumpet or the sound of a drum – as an alternative to pristine methods (handkerchiefs or flags).

Historians tell us that in the ancient Olympics, prior to the competitions proper, there were other events involving trumpeters and heralds to select the ones who were to act as starters. A famous trumpeter, who might arguably be considered as history's first starter, was Herodoros of Megara who acted as such from 328 B.C. to 292 B.C.

In trying to locate the first use of a gun for starting races one can receive valuable help from the writings of William B. Curtis, the foremost figure in American athletics of the early days, then known affectionately as "Father Bill". Curtis (1837-1900) was an excellent athlete in his youth: national champion in hammer throwing for three years (1876, 1878 and 1880) and in weight lifting once (1878). Later on he was among the founders of the New York A.C. and the AAU. He left valuable writings, e.g. a book on "The infancy and childhood of amateur athletics sport in America" (1899), which was published only after his death, when he was caught in the middle of a tempest while on a climbing adventure on Mount Washington in the company of a close friend, Allan Ormsbee.

William Curtis is also indicated as the first athlete to use spiked shoes in running. That was in connection with an indoor meet held at New York's Empire Skating Rink in 1868. He also claims that the use of a gun in starting races was made necessary to do away with the long delays caused by the so-called "mutual consent" starts. The latter procedure was well illustrated by Curtis in 1899, but his notes appeared in the "New Athletic Journal" only a few years after his death. Further information on the start by mutual consent was later supplied by Archie Hahn in his book "How to sprint". In the early days of modern track, most races were a two-men affair. A maximum of four runners could sometimes occur. The men were placed 15 to 20 strides from the starting line, on which the starting judge was located. Runners came forward gradually, joining hands, a contact which was broken as they came alongside the starter, this moment being tantamount to a starting signal. However, such a mutual consent was hard to achieve as some runners tried by various ways and means to "steal" the race. The maximum time allowed for the start to materialize was set at .....one hour. Even so, difficulties survived – and that was the reason why a pistol shot was ultimately chosen as the starting signal in cases of long delays. Owing to the persistent mal-conduct of runners, the new method ultimately emerged as the final answer to the problem.

G.P.

9

THE FIRST QUEEN COMES FROM HOLLAND

Francina "Fanny" Blankers née Koen (born on 26 April 1918 in Amsterdam, died on 25 January 2004 in Amsterdam; 1.75 m. / 63 kg.) was the first "queen" of modern athletics in a truly international perspective. Through her smashing victories, her many records and, last by not least, her unassuming behaviour, she put women's athletics in a new dimension. A most versatile talent, she emerged as a teen-ager in 1935 with a 2:29.0 in the 800 m., her first national record. At the Berlin Olympics in 1936 young Fanny tied for sixth in the high jump at 1.55 and contributed to Holland's fifth place in the sprint relay. She set her first world record at Amsterdam in 1938: 11.0 in the 100 y., a record tying effort. In the same year, as previously related, she also wound up third in both sprints at the inaugural European Championships. In 1940 she married her coach Jan Blankers, a former triple jumper of international calibre (14.69 in winning the 1933 AAA tile in London). The following year, Jan Jr. was born. Mammy stayed away from track only the minimum necessary and in 1942, still in Amsterdam, she tied Claudia Testoni's world record for the 80 m. hurdles (11.3). In 1943 she conquered two more global marks, with 1.71 in the high jump at Amsterdam and 6.25 in the long jump at Leiden. In 1944 she lowered the world's 100 y. record to 10.8. WW2 had obviously deprived her, and many others, of two editions of the Olympic Games (1940 and '44), yet she managed to stay at it and reaped plenty of honours in the post-war years. In 1946, shortly after the birth of her second child - a daughter named Fanny – she was bold enough to compete in four events at the European Championships in Oslo, and good enough to win two gold medals, in the 80 m. hurdles and in the sprint relay.

This magnificent athlete earned worldwide fame at the 1948 Olympics in London. Before the Games she broke the world's 100 m. record with 11.5, on a windless day (The same clocking had been credited to her in rather dubious conditions five years earlier, still on home soil, in a "mixed race, finishing behind two men). In London the Dutch sprinter won four gold medals: 100 m. (11.9) and 200 m. (24.4), 80 m. hurdles (11.2) and the 4x100 m. relay (47.5) – all this at the age of 30. In the sprints she was head and shoulders above her rivals and in the 200 m. – a distance included in the Olympic programme for the first time – she left the runner-up, Audrey Williamson of Britain, a haunting 7 tenths behind (actually 0.80 as per electric timer used as a back-up). In the 200 metre final, Audrey Patterson of USA was given third just ahead of Shirley Strickland of Australia, both with a time of 25.2. Years later, however, Bob Sparks, then president of the ATFS, gained access to a photo finish print and found that it was actually Strickland who finished third, one hundredth of a second ahead of her American rival.

In the sprint relay Fanny was only fourth as she took the baton for the anchor leg, but she stormed through and eventually moved to first, thus securing her fourth gold medal. The winners' time was 47.5, essentially worse than a world record 47.4 made by the same Dutch quartet in a pre-Games meet at Ryswyk over the longer 4x110 yards route.

1948 Olympics, London - 100 metres (2 August) w = adverse: 1.Fanny Blankers-Koen (Hol) 11.9; 2.Dorothy Manley (UK) 12.2; 3.Shirley Strickland (Aus) 12.2; 4.Viola Myers (Can) 12.3; 5.Patricia Jones (Can) 12.4; 6.Cynthia Thompson (Jam) 12.6. Lanes: Myers 1,

Marlies Göhr (East Germany) as anchor leg runner in the victorious 4x100 m. relay team at the 1985 World Cup. Time, 41.37, still standing as a world record.

Thompson 2, Blankers-Koen 3, Strickland 4, Jones 5, Manley 6.

200 metres (6 August) w 0.0 m/s: 1.Fanny Blankers-Koen (Hol) 24.4; 2.Audrey Williamson (UK) 25.1; 3.Shirley Strickland (Aus) 25.2; 4.Audrey Patterson (USA) 25.2; 5.Margaret Walker (UK) 25.4; 6.Daphne Robb (Can) 25.5. NB: Patterson officially given as third, ahead of Strickland (see story above). Lanes: Robb 1, Blankers-Koen 2, Strickland 3, Walker 4, Williamson 5, Patterson 6.

4x100 metre relay (7 August): 1.Hol (X.Stad-de-Jong, J.Witziers-Timmer, G.van der Kade/Koudijs, F.Blankers-Koen) 47.5; 2.Aus (S.Strickland, J.Maston, B.McKinnon, J.King) 47.6; 3.Can (V.Myers, N.Mackay, D.Foster, P.Jones) 47.8; 4.UK 48.0; 5.Den 48.2; 6.Aut 49.2. Lanes: Aus 1, Can 2, UK 3, Aut 4, Hol 5, Den 6.

"ALL I DID WAS WIN SOME FOOT RACES"

After her glorious days at the 1948 Olympics in London, Holland's Fanny Blankers-Koen was widely hailed by the media as a female version of Jesse Owens (who had also won 4 Olympic gold medals, twelve years earlier). Upon her return to Amsterdam she was treated to a big parade. She sat with her husband Jan (by then a well-known sports journalist) in an open "landau" drawn by four white horses. Amidst a hailstorm of applause by her admiring countrymen, she seemed mildly bemused. Years later she recalled: "I could not understand why everyone was so excited. All I did was win some foot races".
John Hendershott, in his fascinating book "Track's Greatest Women", reveals another funny story about the Dutch wonder in those memorable days. On her way home from London, she was concerned about customs. I had bought a raincoat and some towels in London, so I was concerned about customs, but all the officer wrote that I had to declare was: "Some gold medals".
Anyone who happens to reflect on this nowadays is bound to conclude that quite a few things have changed in the world of track in the intervening time.

Between 1938 and 1951 Blankers-Koen collected world records galore. In addition to those already mentioned, she had the following: 24.2 in the 220 y. (Brescia, 1950), 11.0 in the 80 m. hurdles (Amsterdam, 1948) and 4692 points in the pentathlon (Amsterdam, 1951). Her furlong record at Brescia was practically made in a solo race as she left her nearest rival over 4 seconds behind! Surely a rare achievement in the annals of sprinting. In three editions of the European Championships (1938, '46 and '50) she won eight medals, including five golds. She was in the Olympic arena even in Helsinki (1952), at the age of 34, but in those days she happened to be suffering from boils and thus failed to do herself justice. Even so, she did not retire until 1955. Some time later, in her hometown of Amsterdam, a statue was erected to immortalize her achievements. She was believed to be the first woman athlete ever to receive such an honour.

Australia had some superlative sprinters in the early Fifties. Shirley Strickland de la Hunty competed in three editions of the Olympics (1948, '52 and '56) and collected no less than 7 medals and her tally could have been 8 but for the afore-mentioned misjudgement in the London 200 metres. Very good as a sprinter, she was even better in the 80 metre hurdles, with two firsts (1952 and '56) and a third (1948) at the quadrennial Games. Her dedication bordered on fanaticism, yet one of her rivals described her as one of those "natural-born athletes who need only some coaching and training to be successful".

Marjorie Jackson (born on 13 September 1931 at Coffs Harbour, New South Wales; 1.72 m. / 66 kg.), known Down Under as "The Lithgow Flash", had her first superlative season in 1950, when she won both sprints at the Commonwealth Games in Auckland with times of 10.8 and 24.3 for the English distances, finishing well ahead of Strickland (11.0 and 24.5). She was barely 18 and a half at the time. In the same year she collected three world records, with 10.8 and 10.7 in the 100 yards and 24.3 in the 220. In 1952 she was truly superlative. She lowered the 100 y. record to 10.4 before going to Helsinki for the Olympic Games, in which she outclassed her rivals in both sprints, chalking up four world record marks: 11.5 twice (semi and final) in the 100 metres, 23.6 (heat) and 23.4 (semi) in the 200. She won the final of the longer distance in 23.7. Her victory margin in the decisive races was outrageous: 0.3 in the 100 and 0.5 in the 200. In the relay she helped her team to a new world record of 46.1 in the preliminary round but in the final the highly favoured Aussie team met an unexpected defeat due to a fumbled last pass between Winsome Cripps and Jackson. Commentator Norris McWhirter put it this way: "The shapely Cripps knee knocked the baton from Marjorie's grasp and despite one of the fastest pieces of retrieving ever seen the Lithgow girl could not hope to catch her rivals". Australia finished a disappointing fifth. As for gold, USA and Germany fought it out between themselves till the end, finishing in that order, both in 45.9, a new world mark.

1952 Olympics, Helsinki - 100 metres (22 July) w = + 1.7 m/s: 1. Marjorie Jackson (Aus) 11.5 (electric time 11.67); 2.Daphne Robb-Hasenjager (SA) 11.8 (e 12.05); 3.Shirley Strickland de la Hunty (Aus) 11.9 (e 12.12); 4.Winsome Cripps (Aus) 11.9 (e 12.16); 5.Maria Sander (FRG) 12.0 (e12.27); 6.Mae Faggs (USA) 12.1 (e12.27). Lanes: Faggs 1, Hasenjager 2, Sander 3, Strickland 4, Jackson 5, Cripps 6.

200 metres (26 July) w. legal: 1.Marjorie Jackson (Aus) 23.7 (e 23.89); 2.Bertha Brouwer (Hol) 24.2 (e 24.25); 3.Nadyezhda Khnykina (SU) 24.2 (e 24.37); 4.Winsome Cripps (Aus) 24.2 (e 24.40); 5.Helga Klein (FRG) 24.6 (e 24.72); 6.Daphne Robb-Hasenjager (SA) 24.6 (e 24.72). Lanes: Jackson 1, Brouwer 2, Hasenjager 3, Cripps 4, Khnykina 5, Klein 6.

4x100 metre relay (27 July): 1.USA (M.Faggs, P.Jones, J.Moreau, C.Hardy) 45.9 (e 46.14); 2.FRG (U.Knab, M.Sander, H.Klein, M.Petersen) 45.9 (e 46.18); 3.UK (S.Cheeseman, J.Foulds, J.Desforges, H.Armitage) 46.2 (e 46.41); 4.SU 46.3 (e 46.42), 5.Aus 46.6 (e 46.86); 6.Hol 47.8. Lanes: Aus 1, SU 2, USA 3, FRG 4, UK 5, Hol 6.

Jackson crowned her 1952 season with one more world record: 11.4 in the 100 metres, competing as a guest in the Japanese Championships at Gifu on 4 October.

USSR was by then the no.1 power in women athletics, with good runners in the sprints too. In 1953 Vyera Kalashnikova, Zinaida Safronova, Nadyezhda Khnykina/Dvalishvili and Irina Turova lowered the world record for the 4x100 m. relay to 45.6. In 1955 Shirley Strickland offered one more flash, wresting the world's 100 m. record from her compatriot Mary Jackson with a time of 11.3. This happened in Warsaw in a meet called World Youth Games. Shirley, by then 30, was still very young at heart.

Australia's most amazing athlete was yet to come though. She bore the name of Elizabeth "Betty" Cuthbert (born on 20 April 1938 at Merrylands, Sydney; 1.69 m./ 57 kg.). The first of twin girls, Betty was spotted as a great talent when she was only 13. In 1954 she ran the 100 yards in 10.9 (and 10.8w). Two years later, at the Melbourne Olympics – the first ever held in the Southern hemisphere – she drove the large home crowd crazy with a series of amazing performances. Prior to the Games she had offered a great glimpse of what was to come with a new world record of 23.2 for the 220 yards, a distance on which she seemed to do better than in the century. In the Games, however, anything she touched invariably turned into gold. In the 100 metres she did 11.4 in a heat for a new Olympic record, then won the final as she pleased in 11.5. In the 200 her superiority was even greater: after a 23.5 in round 1, she won the decisive race in 23.4. In both finals she won from Christa Stubnick of Germany and another Aussie, Marlene Mathews, who finished in that order. For the first time since the end of WW2, Germany was in the Games with a unified team (FRG + GDR, i.e. West and East).

This time the Australian girls did no mistakes in the relay and Cuthbert anchored the team to victory in 44.5, a new world record. A surprisingly good British team took second in 44.7, a new European record.

1956 Olympics, Melbourne - 100 metres (26 November) w = -2.3 m/s: 1.Betty Cuthbert (Aus) 11.5 (e 11.82); 2.Christa Stubnick (Ger) 11.7 (e 11.92); 3.Marlene Mathews (Aus) 11.7 (e 11.94); 4.Isabelle Daniels (USA) 11.8 (e 11.98); 5.Giuseppina Leone (Ita) 11.9 (e 12.07); 6.Heather Armitage (UK) 12.0 (e 12.10). Lanes: Stubnick 1, Armitage 2, Mathews 3, Cuthbert 4, Leone 5, Daniels 6.

200 metres (30 November) w - legal: 1.Betty Cuthbert (Aus) 23.4 (e 23.55); 2.Christa Stubnick (Ger) 23.7 (e 23.89); 3.Marlene Mathews (Aus) 23.8 (e 24.10); 4.Norma Croker (Aus) 24.0 (e 24.22); 5.June Foulds-Paul (UK) 24.3 (e 24.30), 6.Gisela Köhler (Ger) 24.3 (e 24.68). Lanes: Mathews 1. Foulds-Paul 2, Köhler 3, Croker 4, Cuthbert 5, Stubnick 6.

4x100 metre relay (1 December): 1.Aus (S.Strickland de la Hunty, N. Croker, F.Mellor, B.Cuthbert) 44.5 (e 44.65); 2.UK (A.Pashley, J.Scrivens, J.Foulds-Paul, H.Armitage) 44.7 (e 44.70); 3.USA (M.Faggs, Margaret Matthews, W.Rudolph, I.Daniels) 44.9 (e 45.04); 4.SU 45.6 (e 45.81); 5.Ita 45.7 (e 45.90); 6.Ger 47.2 (e 47.29). Lanes: USA 1, Ger 2, Aus 3, UK 4, SU 5, Ita 6.

After her fabulous Olympiad Betty inevitably became the toast of the athletic world. However, the 18-year-old Australian marvel was not prepared for all the publicity that suddenly surrounded her. As she later wrote in her autobiography "Golden Girl" (1966), "my life wasn't my own anymore". Be that as it may, in the two following sea-

Evelyn Ashford (USA) winning the 100 m. at the 1984 Olympics in Los Angeles.

Florence Griffith (USA) in her most glorious week (1988 Olympics), here winning the 100 m.

sons she was outshone by her compatriot Marlene Mathews-Willard, who scored a 100/220 y. double at the 1958 Commonwealth Games in Cardiff (10.70 and 23.65), in which races Betty had to be content with fourth and second respectively. Later in the same season, however, she suddenly rose to a new dimension in a different event, winning a 400-metre race at Göteborg in 54.4, which turned out to be the world's fastest time for that year. In 1959 she twice bettered the quarter-mile world record with 55.6 and 54.3, but before the end of that season she was dislodged by Maria Itkina of USSR, who in a race at Krasnodar was clocked in 53.4 (400 m.) and 53.7 (440 y.).

Cuthbert returned to the sprints in view of the 1960 Olympics in Rome, where a bad leg put paid to her chances in a quarter-final of the 100 metres. In the meantime a new star had entered the scene, American Wilma Rudolph (born on 23 June 1940 at Clarksville, Tennessee; died on 12 November 1994 at Nashville, Tennessee; 1.81 m. / 60 kg.), a sprinter who combined speed and grace to an extraordinary degree.

Yet her early steps in life had been far from lucky: the 20th of 22 children born in the family of a poor handyman, Wilma contracted paralysis in her left leg as an infant and was unable to walk normally until she was ten. She first tried sprinting two years later as a member of the Tennessee State Track Club under coach Ed Temple. At the time that club offered the best collegiate programme in US women athletics. In 1956 Wilma had her first taste of the Olympics at the tender age of 16. Eliminated in the prelims of the 200 metres, she won a bronze medal in the 4x100 m. relay. She rose further in athletic stature in the years that followed, although she missed the 1958 season after the birth of her first child, a daughter. In 1960 she was in a class by herself, in America and in the world. She won a double at the AAU meet at Corpus Christi, Texas, with times of 11.5 and 22.9 for the metric distances. The latter made her the first woman to duck under 23 secs.

Her Rome adventure started on a bad note. The day before the first round of the 100 metres she stepped in a hole on a practice field and twisted an ankle. Medical examination revealed that it was only a bad sprain though. In the races that counted she put on a superb show: 11.5 in both heat and quarters, 11.3 (semi) and 11.0w (final). Her semi-final time equalled the world record set by Vera Krepkina of USSR two years earlier. In the decisive race, however, she was helped by a wind over the limit, 2.8 m/s. She won by an overwhelming margin (0.25 as per electric timer) over Dorothy Hyman of Britain, while Giuseppina Leone of Italy was a close third.

Even in the 200 metres Rudolph was overwhelmingly superior. She went through the four rounds with times of 23.7, 23.2, 23.7 and 24.0. In the final she had to fight with an adverse wind, yet she beat her nearest rival, Jutta Heine of Germany, by an outrageous 0.45. The American crowned her splendid adventure by anchoring the US relay team to victory in 44.5. In a heat the American team did 44.4 for a new world record.

1960 Olympics, Rome - 100 metres (2 September) w = +2.8 m/s: 1.Wilma Rudolph (USA) 11.0 (e 11.18); 2.Dorothy Hyman (UK) 11.3 (e 11.43); 3.Giuseppina Leone (Ita) 11.3 (e 11.48); 4. Mariya Itkina (SU) 11.4 (e 11.54); 5. Catherine Capdevielle (Fra) 11.5 (e 11.64); 6.Jennifer Smart (UK) 11.6 (e 11.72). Lanes: Capdevielle 1, Hyman 2, Rudolph 3, Itkina, 4, Smart 5, Leone 6.

200 metres (5 September) w = adverse: 1.Wilma Rudolph (USA) 24.0 (e 24.13); 2.Jutta Heine (Ger) 24.4 (e 24.58); 3.Dorothy Hyman (UK) 24.7 (e 24.82); 4. Maria Itkina (SU) 24.7 (e 24.85); 5. Barbara Janiszewska (Pol) 24.8 (e 24.96); 6. Giuseppina Leone (Ita) 24.9 (e 25.01). Lanes: Rudolph 1, Leone 2, Itkina 3, Hyman 4, Heine 5, Janiszewska 6.

4x100 metre relay (8 September): 1.USA (M.Hudson, Lucinda Williams, P.Jones, W.Rudolph) 44.5 (e 44.72); 2.Ger (M.Langbein, A.Biechl, B.Hendrix, J.Heine) 44.8 (e 45.00); 3.Pol (T.Wieczorek, B. Janiszewska, C. Yesionowska, H. Richter) 45.0 (e 45.19); 4.SU 45.2 (e 45.39); 5.Ita 45.6 (e 45.80); UK did not finish. Lanes: UK 1, SU 2, USA 3, Ger 4, Ita 5, Pol 6.

Rudolph had two more brilliant seasons. In 1961 she starred in the dual meet with the Soviet Union in Moscow, matching her own world record (11.3) in the 100 metres and finishing off the job of Willye White, Ernestine Pollards and Vivian Brown in the 4x100 m. relay with a new world record of 44.3. Only three days later, in Stuttgart, she ran the century in 11.3 (wind +0.7 m/s.) for another global mark. She left the arena in 1962 at twenty-two, even earlier than Jesse Owens. She was a cool competitor and in fact she was called "The great frozen face". Wilma's likeness stands in Madame Tussaud's Wax Museum in London.

Not so famous perhaps but still a two-time winner of the 100 metres in the Olympics – an exploit until then unmatched by either men or women – was another black American, Wyomia Tyus (born on 29 August 1945 at Griffin, Georgia; 1.70 m. / 61 kg.). Just like Rudolph, she blossomed as a pupil of coach Ed Temple at Tennessee State and had the benefit of developing alongside another talent, Edith McGuire. The two "Tigerbelles", as the girls of that club were known, rose to world class in 1963, while still teenagers. Just prior to the 1964 Olympics, McGuire was slightly ahead of her club-mate and even coach Temple reportedly said that she was the girl most likely to fill Wilma Rudolph's shoes. A similar concept prevailed in Europe too. The German weekly "Leichtathletik" had McGuire 1st and Tyus only 6th in its Olympic prediction for the 100 metres.

But the Games in Tokyo told another story. Tyus competed only in the century but proved the class of the field from the very beginning, with times of 11.3 (heat) and 11.2 (quarters). The latter, favoured by a negligible wind of +0.22, tied Wilma Rudolph's world record. She went on with 11.3 (semi) and 11.4 (final). In the latter race she surged ahead around 30 metres and was never really threatened. She won clearly from McGuire (11.6), even though the electric timer saw only 0.13 between the two "Tigerbelles". Third went to Ewa Klobukowska of Poland, who in 1967 was barred from international athletics because of her failure to pass a sex test.

McGuire emerged the winner from a magnificent 200 metre final in 23.0, barely ahead of Irena Kirszenstein of Poland and Marylin Black of Australia. Poland, with Klobukowska in the anchor leg, won the sprint relay in 43.6, a new world record, well ahead of USA (43.9). Poland's mark was later deleted because of the participation of Klobukowska, and USA thus saw its 43.9 retroactively listed as a world record.

Perhaps the most sensational event of the Tokyo Olympics was offered by an Aussie girl who had swept the sprint board in Melbourne eight years earlier, Betty Cuthbert. By the early Sixties she had found a new "residence" in the one-lap event. After bettering the 440 y. world record twice with 53.5 and 53.3, both in 1963, she won the Olympic crown over the metric distance in Tokyo with a great 52.0, one tenth shy of the world record set by Shin Keum-Dan of North Korea in 1962. After which she retired – on the happiest note one could possibly imagine.

1964 Olympic Games, Tokyo - 100 metres (16 October), w = -1.2 m/s: 1.Wyomia Tyus (USA) 11.4 (e 11.49); 2.Edith McGuire (USA) 11.6 (e 11.62); 3. Ewa Klobukowska (Pol) 11.6 (e 11.64); 4.Marylin White (USA) 11.6 (e 11.67); 5. Miguelina Cobián (Cub) 11.7 (e 11.72); 6. Marilyn Black (Aus) 11.7 (e 11.73); 7.Halina Górecka (Pol) 11.8 (e 11.83); 8.Dorothy Hyman (UK) 11.9 (e 11.90). Lanes: Klobukowska 1, Hyman 2, Górecka 3, Cobián 4, Black 5, Tyus 6, McGuire 7, White 8.

200 metres (19 October): 1.Edith McGuire (USA) 23.0 (e23.05); 2.Irena Kirszenstein (Pol) 23.1 (e 23.13); 3.Marilyn Black (Aus) 23.1 (e 23.18); 4.Una Morris (Jam) 23.5 (e 23.58); 5.Lyudmila Samotyosova (SU) 23.5 (e 23.59); 6. Barbara Janiszewska-Sobotta (Pol) 23.9 (e 23.97); 7.Janet Simpson (UK) 23.9 (e 23.98); 8.Daphne Arden (UK) 24.0 (e 24.01). Lanes: Morris 1, Samotyosova 2, McGuire 3, Kirszenstein 4. Simpson 5, Janiszewska 6, Arden 7, Black 8.

4x100 metre relay (21 October): 1.Pol (T.Wieczorek-Ciepla, I.Kirszenstein, H.Richter-Górecka, E.Klobukowska) 43.6 (e 43.69); 2.USA (W.White, W.Tyus, M. White,

Merlene Ottey (Jamaica), the most durable of female sprint stars.

Irena Szewinska (Poland), a female version of Jesse Owens as a leading sprinter & long jumper.

E.McGuire) 43.9 (e 43.92); 3.UK (J.Simpson, M.Rand, D.Arden, D.Hyman) 44.0 (e 44.09); 4.SU 44.4 (e 44.44); 5.Ger 44.7; 6Aus 45.0; 7.Hun 45.2; 8.Fra 46.1. Lanes: Aus 1, UK 2, Ger 3, Pol 4, USA 5, Hun 6, SU 7, Fra 8.

1965 was a prolific year in the record book. The 200 m. silver medallist from Tokyo, Irena Kirszenstein, was very much in evidence. Born to Polish parents in Leningrad on 24 May 1946, she was quite young when her family moved back to their native country. Her mother was once quoted as saying: "As I remember, Irena never walked to school – she always ran". At 17 she caught the eye of coach Andrzej Prokowski, who was impressed by her mental attitude and her athletic talent. She had an ideal build (1.76 m. / 63 kg.) too and for several years she did excellent things in the sprints and long jump. At the Tokyo Olympics, when only 18 years old, she won no less than three medals: gold in the sprint relay and silver in the 200 metres (as related above) plus another silver in the long jump with 6.60 behind Mary Rand of Britain, who chose the occasion to raise the world record to 6.76.

In 1965 the Polish star set new world records for the metric distances: 11.1 in the 100 and 22.7 in the 200. In the former race, in Prague, she actually finished a very close second to Ewa Klobukowska, also credited with 11.1. As mentioned before, Klobukowska was disqualified from women's competition in 1967 and another three years later she saw all her records deleted.

Kirszenstein won three golds (200, long jump and 4x100 m. relay) at the 1966 European Championships. The following year she married Janusz Szewinski, a devoted athlete himself (53.4 in the 400 m. hurdles) and by then her chief adviser.

Tyus also had an excellent season in 1965, with world records on both sides of the Atlantic: 10.3 in the 100 yards at Kingston and a record tying 11.1 for the metric century in the match with the Soviet Union at Kiev, both times winning from Edith McGuire (10.6 and 11.4) by a comfortable margin. By 1967 she had a serious rival in Barbara Ferrell, who won the AAU 100 m. title in 11.1, equalling the world record and beating Tyus among others. Ferrell was in the forefront also in 1968, but Tyus once again rose at the right time to steal the show in the Mexico Olympic arena. The double effect of high altitude and new synthetic tracks contributed to make 1968 in general and the Mexico Games in particular a memorable passage in the history of women's sprinting. Tyus got the ball rolling with a record equalling 11.1 for 100 metres in a warm-up meet in the Mexican capital in April. The same clocking was credited to Lyudmila Samotyosova of the Soviet Union in August. As generally expected, the Mexico Olympics yielded fast times galore. In the very first round of the 100 metres all three US entries – Tyus, Ferrell and Margaret Bailes - were credited with 11.2. In the quarter-finals, Ferrell and Irena Szewinska eqalled the world record with 11.1, while Tyus chalked up an 11 flat with an ading wind of 2.7 m/s, hence over the limit. After a quieter set of times in the semis, the final provided a full explosion. Tyus successfully defended her 1964 title and went home in a new record time – 11.0. Right behind her three athletes did 11.1 and one of them consequently failed to reach the podium.

Szewinska looked as the strongest finisher in the 100, yet she had to be content with third. She put her superior staying power to full advantage in the 200 metres, which she won in 22.5, two tenths under her own world record. There was a benevolent wind of just 2.0 m/s down the homestretch.

USA won the sprint relay hands down. Here again there was a new world mark, an impressive 42.8.

1968 Olympics, Mexico City - 100 metres (15 October) w = + 1.2 m/s: 1.Wyomia Tyus (USA) 11.0 (e 11.08); 2.Barbara Ferrell (USA) 11.1 (e 11.15); Irena Kirszenstein-Szewinska (Pol) 11.1 (e 11.19); 4.Raelene Boyle (Aus) 11.1 (e 11.20); 5.Margaret Bailes (USA) 11.3 (e 11.37); 6.Diane Burge (Aus) 11.4 (e 11.44); 7.Chi Cheng (Taipei) 11.5 (e 11.53); 8. Miguelina Cobián (Cub) 11.6 (e 11.61). Lanes: Chi Cheng 1, Boyle 2, Tyus 3, Bailes 4, Ferrell 5, Cobián 6, Szewinska 7, Burge 8.

200 metres (16 October) w = + 2.0 m/s: 1.Irena Kirszenstein-Szewinska (Pol) 22.5 (e 22.58); 2.Raelene Boyle (Aus) 22.7 (e 22.74); 3.Jennifer Lamy (Aus) 22.8 (e 22.88); 4.Barbara Ferrell (USA) 22.9 (e 22.93); 5.Nicole Montandon (Fra) 23.0 (e 23.08); 6.Wyomia Tyus (USA) 23.0 (e 23.08); 7.Margaret Bailes (USA) 23.1 (e 23.18); 8.Jutta Stöck (FRG) 23.2 (e 23.25). Lanes: Ferrell 1, Bailes 2, Tyus 3, Montandon 4, Lamy 5, Boyle 6, Szewinska 7, Stöck 8.

4x100 metre relay (20 October): 1.USA (B.Ferrell, M.Bailes, M.Netter, W.Tyus) 42.8 (e 42.88); 2.Cub (M.Elejarde, F.Romay, V.Quesada, M.Cobián) 43.3 (43.36); 3.SU (L.Zharkova, G.Bukharina, V.Popkova, L.Samotyosova) 43.4 (e 43.41), 4.Hol 43.4 (e 43.44); 5.Aus 43.4 (e 43.50); 6.FRG 43.6 (e 43.70); 7.UK 43.7 (e 43.78), 8.Fra 44.2 (e 44.30). Lanes: Fra 1, FRG 2, Hol 3, USA 4, UK 5, Cu 6, SU 7, Aus 8.

Tyus thus offered the rare example of a 100 m. sprinter capable of reaching the top of her condition at the right time in two editions of the Games. She did not like the 200 just as much, yet she was able to run her best ever (23.0) in finishing sixth in the 1968 Olympic final. As for her winning time in the 100 , it was the first record mark to go down in the IAAF book in its automatic version, 11.08.

Chi Cheng, the girl who finished seventh in the 100 m. final, later turned out to be the greatest talent ever to come out of Asia since the distant days of Japan's Kinue Hitomi. A Chinese from Taipei (Taiwan), she spent the greater part of her career in USA, where she was coached by Vince Reel. Like her Japanese predecessor she was a great all-rounder, her range extending from the sprints to the high hurdles, and the long jump. She was at her best in 1970, aged 26, when she went undefeated through 83 competitions and set world records of 10.0 (100 y.), 11.0 (100 m.) and 22.4 (200 m.). Unfortunately, a vicious hip injury cut short her career. In 1981 she was elected to the Taiwan senate. She also headed the Taiwan Athletics Federation.

GERMAN DYNASTY, ASHFORD, THEN HURRICANE "FLO-JO"

Ever since the end of WW2, Germany was split in two "countries", West (FRG) and East (GDR). Such an unnatural situation obviously had bearing on sport. As it happened before and after in many authoritarian states, the political leaders of the GDR used sport as a major vehicle to gain a high profile in the eyes of the world. Superb results were achieved in the domain of women athletics. In the early Seventies the dominant figure in the sprint department was Renate Stecher née Meissner (born on 12 May 1950 at Süptitz near Torgau; 1,70 m. / 69 m.), a solidly built woman who at the 1972 Olympics in Munich was branded as a female version of Valeriy Borzov of USSR. This was an easy reflection as both scored sprint doubles in those days. Clock-wise, the German had first made the grade in 1970, equalling the world's 100 m. record, 11.0, a time she duplicated in '71 and early in '72. In the Munich Olympics her strongest rival was Raelene Boyle of Australia, a precocious runner who had finished second in the 200 metres at the Mexico Olympics at the tender age of 17.

In the Munich 100 m. final the muscular Stecher had things going her way from start to finish. After an even start she pulled steadily away and won from Boyle by over a metre. Her time, 11.07, was a new world record in the automatic version – a splendid achievement with a slightly adverse wind (-0.20 m/s). Boyle offered a sterner resistance in the 200 but still had to be content with a close second to the German – 22.45 to 22.40. Irena Szewinska was third, partly making amends for her disappointing show in the 100, where she was eliminated in the semis.

In the 4x100 m. relay Stecher was expected to lead the GDR to victory but in the anchor leg she found a very hard nut to crack in Heidemarie Rosendahl of the FRG, the "coqueluche" of the Munich crowd who had previously won the long jump and finished second in the pentahlon. The latter was a stride ahead when she took the baton. Amidst a monumental crescendo of cheering she surpassed herself and flashed over the finish line more than a metre in front. The time, 42.81, was a new world record.

1972 Olympics, Munich - 100 metres (2 September) w = - 0.20 m/s: 1.Renate Stecher (GDR) 11.07; 2.Raelene Boyle (Aus) 11.23; 3.Silvia Chivás (Cub) 11.24; 4.Iris Davis (USA) 11.32; 5. Annegret Richter (FRG) 11.38; 6.Alice Annum (Gha) 11.41; 7.Barbara Ferrell (USA) 11.45; 8.Eva Glesková (Cze) 12.48. Lanes: Boyle 1, Richter 2, Stecher 3, Davis 4,Ferrell 5, Chivás 6, Glesková 7, Annum 8.

200 metres (7 September) w = + 1.1 m/s: 1.Renate Stecher (GDR) 22.40; 2. Raelene Boyle (Aus) 22.45; 3.Irena Kirszenstein-Szewinska (Pol) 22.74; 4.Ellen Stropahl (GDR) 22.75; 5.Christina Heinich (GDR) 22.89; 6.Annegret Kroniger (FRG) 22.89; 7.Alice Annum (Gha) 22.99; 8. Rosie Allwood (Jam) 23.11. Lanes: Kroniger 1, Allwood 2, Stropahl 3, Boyle 4, Szewinska 5, Stecher 6, Heinich 7, Annum 8.

4x100 metre relay (10 September): 1.FRG (C.Krause, I.Mickler, A.Richter, H.Rosendahl) 42.81; 2.GDR (E.Kaufer, C.Heinich, B.Struppert, R.Stecher) 42.95; 3.Cub (M.Elejarde, C.Valdes, F.Romay, S.Chivás) 43.36; 4. USA 43.39; 5.SU 43.59; 6.Aus 43.61; 7. UK 43.71; 8.Pol 44.20. Lanes: UK 1, GDR 2, Pol 3, FRG 4, Aus 5, SU 6, Cub 7, USA 8.

Stecher continued to rule over the sprint sorority in 1973. In the GDR Championships of that year in Dresden she set new world records of 10.8 and 22.1, both of which made the IAAF book as the last records as per manual timing, no matter if there was also an "automatic" version on them (11.07 and 22.38). In the following year, however, Stecher was outshone by Irena Szewinska. At the European Championships in Rome the Polish star beat her German rival in both sprints – 11.13 to 11.23 in the 100 and 22.51 to 22.68 in the 200. On another occasion Szewinska set what turned out to be the first "electronic" world record – 22.21 (22 flat in the "manual" version).

By 1976 Szewinska had chosen the 400 metres as her new weapon. Using her staying power to full advantage, she opened new horizons to one-lap runners and won the Olympic crown in Montreal with a new world record, 49.29 (later corrected to 49.28 by Bob Sparks, president of the ATFS, on re-reading the photo finish). That performance was one of the greatest ever in the history of women's athletics as Irena left her nearest rival well over a second behind. The shorter sprints were dominated by the Germans, who won all six medals at stake. And the Western sector was for once equal to its Eastern counterpart as each of the two secured three medals. Annegret Richter née Irrgang of the FRG (born on 13 October 1950; 1.68 m / 52 kg.) was not counted among the top favourites in pre-Montreal predictions for the 100 metres, but she rose to new heights at the right time with 11.05 (quarter) and a record breaking 11.01 (semi). She was a shade slower in the decisive race (11.08) yet she pulled away in the second half of the race and won from defending champion Stecher, 11.08 to 11.13. In the 200 the feud was even closer but Richter finally had to give way to Bärbel Eckert (GDR). The latter (born on 21 March 1955 in Leipzig; 1.74 m. / 62 kg.) was an even greater surprise. After winning 200 flat and 100 hurdles at the 1973 European Junior Championships, Eckert had been relatively quiet, so to say, partly because of an early season injury in 1975. Her best before the Montreal Games was 22.91. In the Olympic arena she improved on that three times in a row: 22.85 (quarter), 22.71 (semi) and 22.37 (final). The last one sufficed to give her a narrow lead vis-à-vis Richter. The two leaned together in the very last stretch of land and only the "electronic eye" saw the East German ahead by 0.02. Defending champion Stecher was third. Australia's glorious veteran Raelene Boyle had been disqualified for false starts in the penultimate round, after placing fourth in the 100.

The GDR girls just beat their FRG rivals in the 4x100 metre relay (42.55 to 42.59), mostly thanks to Bärbel Eckert's superb effort in the anchor leg. The world record had been lowered to 42.50 in a pre-Olympic meet by a GDR quartet .... sans Eckert.

1976 Olympics, Montreal - 100 metres (25 July) w = -0.2 m/s: 1.Annegret Richter (FRG) 11.08; 2.Renate Stecher (GDR) 11.13; 3.Inge Helten (FRG) 11.17; 4.Raelene Boyle (Aus) 11.23; 5.Evelyn Ashford (USA) 11.24; 6.Chandra Cheeseborough (USA) 11.31; 7.Andrea Lynch (UK) 11.32; 8.Marlies Oelsner (GDR) 11.34. Lanes: Helten 1, Cheeseborough 2, Lynch 3, Stecher 4, Ashford 5, Oelsner 6, Richter 7, Boyle 8.

200 metres (28 July) w = nil: 1.Bärbel Eckert (GDR) 22.37; 2.Annegret Richter (FRG) 22.39; 3.Renate Stecher (GDR) 22.47; 4.Carla Bodendorf (GDR) 22.64: 5.Inge Helten (FRG) 22.68; 6.Tatyana Prorochenko (SU) 23.03; 7.Denise Robertson (Aus) 23.05; 8.Chantal Rega (Fra) 23.09. Lanes: Prorochenko 1, Eckert 2, Robertson 3, Bodendorf 4, Richter 5, Rega 6, Helten 7, Stecher 8.

4x100 metre relay (31 July): 1. GDR (M.Oelsner, R.Stecher, C.Bodendorf, B.Eckert) 42.55; 2.FRG (E.Possekel, I.Helten, A.Richter, A.Kroniger) 42.59; 3. SU (T.Prorochenko, L.Zharkova-Maslakova, N.Besfamilnaya, V.Anisimova) 43.09; 4. Can 43.17; 5.Aus 43.18; 6.Jam 43.24; 7. USA 43.35; 8.UK 43.79. Lanes: FRG 1, USA 2, UK 3, Aus 4, Jam 5, Can 6, SU 7, GDR 8.

Among those who just failed to reach the limelight at Montreal was a 19-year-old East German who was destined to make history:

Marita Koch (born on 18 February 1957 at Wismar; 1.71 m. / 63 kg.). Unlike Cuthbert and Szewinska who had turned from the sprints to the one-lap event only in the latter part of their careers, Koch operated on such a large front throughout her entire athletic venture. At the age of 15 she was credited with 12.2, 25.5 and 60.3. She was an undisputed leader in her age group and could beat quite a few boys too ... By 1976 she was down to 22.0 and 50.19. In the Montreal Olympics she ran the 400, but after doing 51.87 in the quarters she had to call it quits in the semis because of the flare-up of an old leg injury. She came back in great style and in 1978 she set new world records in both 200 (22.06) and 400 (48.94), the latter in winning the European title in Prague. The following year she became the first sprinter to crack the 22 secs. barrier with a sparkling 21.71 during an international match at Karl-Marx-Stadt.

Those were the golden years of the GDR. As we have since learnt, e.g. from Brigitte Berendonk's well-documented book "Doping" (1992), over there nothing was left untried to enhance performances. Anabolic steroids were in large use – as in many other parts of the world, that's true, except that the "state vice", as we like to call the practice of authoritarian states, was harder to detect than the "private vice" existing in (more-or-less) democratic countries, were it only for the different role of the media.

First to break 11 seconds in the century under the harsher rule of automatic timing was Marlies Oelsner (later Göhr, born on 21 March 1958 at Gera; 1.65 m. / 54 kg.) who was credited with 10.88 at Dresden on 1 July 1977, aided by a wind of just 2.0 m/s. A relatively small sprinter endowed with a truly explosive "fire", she amassed plenty of

Marita Koch (East Germany) was at one time holder of world records for both 200 and 400 metres. She still owns the mark for the longer distance (47.60).

honours in Europe, including three continental titles (1978, '82 and '86) in the 100 metres but in the Olympics she had a harsher lot, even though she took relay gold twice.

As explained in the men's section, the 1980 Olympics in Moscow suffered greatly as a result of the vicious "boycotting game" of political inspiration. As far as the women's sprints were concerned, however, most of the best runners came from Eastern Europe, so the Moscow cast was truly representative of the best potential. USA and FRG, the big absentees, did not seem to have particularly strong candidates that year. Evelyn Ashford, after shining in 1979 with times of 10.97 and 21.83, was forced to rest by an injured leg for most of the 1980 season. Her best days were yet to come.

Generally speaking, the Russians surpassed themselves in the Moscow Olympic arena. Lyudmila Kondratyeva (born on 11 April 1958; 1.68 m. / 58 kg.) was such an example. In the 100 metre final, although reportedly hampered by a pain in her right hamstring, she nosed out the top favourite, Marlies Oelsner-Göhr, 11.06 to 11.07. Bärbel Eckert-Wöckel of the GDR successfully defended her 200-metre title against another Russian who surpassed herself, Natalya Bochina. The world record holder at this distance, Marita Koch, chose to concentrate on the 400, which she won as she pleased. The GDR girls very nearly outclassed their Russian rivals in the sprint relay and lowered the world record to 41.60.

1980 Olympics, Moscow - 100 metres (26 July) w: +1.0 m/s: 1.Lyudmila Kondratyeva (SU) 11.06; 2.Marlies Oelsner-Göhr (GDR) 11.07; 3.Ingrid Brestrich-Auerswald (GDR) 11.14; 4.Linda Haglund (Swe) 11.16; 5.Romy Müller (GDR) 11.16; 6.Kathy Smallwood (UK) 11.28; 7.Chantal Rega (Fra) 11.32; 8.Heather Hunte (UK) 11.34. Lanes: Haglund 1, Rega 2, Hunte 3, Auerswald 4, Kondratyeva 5, Smallwood 6, Müller 7, Göhr 8.

200 metres (30 July) w = +1.5 m/s: 1.Bärbel Eckert-Wöckel (GDR) 22.03; 2.Natalya Bochina (SU) 22.19; 3.Merlene Ottey (Jam) 22.20; 4.Romy Müller (GDR) 22.47; 5.Kathy Smallwood (UK) 22.61; 6.Beverley Goddard (UK) 22.72; 7.Denise Robertson-Boyd (Aus) 22,76; 8.Sonia Lannaman (UK) 22.80. Lanes: Eckert-Wöckel 1, Lannaman 2, Ottey 3, Boyd 4, Goddard 5, Bochina 6, Smallwood 7, Müller 8.

4x100 metre relay (1 August): 1.GDR (R.Müller, B.Wöckel, I.Auerswald, M.Göhr) 41.60; 2.SU (V.Komisova, L.Zharkova-Maslakova, V.Anisimova, N.Bochina) 42.10; 3.UK (H.Hunte, K.Smallwood, B.Goddard, S.Lannaman) 42.43; 4.Bul 42.67; 5.Fra 42.84; 6.Jam 43.19; 7.Pol 43.59; Swe did not finish. Lanes: SU 1, Pol 2, Jam 3, Bul 4, Swe 5, Fra 6, UK 7, GDR 8.

Evelyn Ashford (born on 15 April 1957 at Shreveport, Louisiana; 1.65 m. / 52 kg.) was for several years the only serious threat to East German supremacy. With her tiny build and her competitive ability she evoked the paraphrase: "Dynamite comes in small boxes". She was precocious too for she managed to place fifth in the 100 metres in her first Olympic adventure, Montreal '76. As previously related, her breakthrough to the highest world class was in 1979. The following year was an unlucky one: besides being unable, as an American, to compete in the Moscow Olympics, she was bogged down with an injury. In the early Eighties she was better than ever. In 1983 another global goal was provided by the first-ever World Championships, scheduled for Helsinki in August. That was a year of mixed fortunes though. Her chief rival Marlies Göhr was at her very best and she started on a high note. In a very close duel with Marita Koch in Berlin she lowered the world record to 10.81, just edging Marita, 10.83. In a dual meet with USA Göhr beat Ashford, 11.39 to 11.53. But a few days later Evelyn took advantage of the rarefied atmosphere of the US Air Academy in Colorado (2195 m. above sea level) to lower the world record to 10.79. Yet she met bad luck in the final and most important test of the year, Helsinki. In the decisive race Göhr was the early leader. Shortly before the half-way point Evelyn made a strong move to catch her, but a few moments later she hopped into the air, hobbled a few steps on her injured right leg and then fell. That was the end of her dream and she pounded the track with her right fist, in frustration. Göhr won from her compatriot Marita Koch, 10.97 to 11.02. The latter won the 200 from Merlene Ottey of Jamaica. In between the two individual races, the GDR had won the relay hands down. A few days earlier, in a pre-Worlds test in Berlin, the same foursome – Gladisch, Koch, Auerswald, Göhr – had lowered the world record to 41.53.

1983 World Championships, Helsinki - 100 metres (8 August) w = -0.5 m/s: 1.Marlies Göhr (GDR) 10.97; 2.Marita Koch (GDR) 11.02; 3.Diane Williams (USA) 11.06; 4.Merlene Ottey (Jam) 11.19; 5.Angela Bailey (Can) 11.20; 6.Helinä Marjamaa (Fin) 11.24; 7.Angella Taylor (Can) 11.30; Evelyn Ashford (USA) did not finish. Lanes: Marjamaa 1, Ashford 2, Taylor 3, Koch 4, Ottey 5, Williams 6, Bailey 7, Göhr 8.

200 metres (14 August) w = +1.5 m/s: 1.Marita Koch (GDR) 22.13; 2.Merlene Ottey (Jam) 22.19; 3.Kathy Cook (UK) 22.37; 4.Florence Griffith (USA) 22.46; 5.Grace Jackson (Jam) 22.63; 6.Anelia Nuneva (Bul) 22.68; 7.Angela Bailey (Can) 22.93; 8.Ewa Kasprzyk (Pol) 23.03. Lanes: Griffith 1, Bailey 2, Cook 3, Kasprzyk 4, Nuneva 5, Koch 6, Ottey 7, Jackson 8.

4x100 metre relay (10 August): 1.GDR (S.Gladisch, M.Koch, I.Auerswald, M.Göhr) 41.76; 2.UK (J.Baptiste, K.Cook, B.Callender, S.Thomas) 42.71; 3.Jam (L.Hodges, J.Pusey, J.Cuthbert, M.Ottey) 42.73; 4.Bul 42.93; 5.Can 43.05; 6.SU 43.22; 7.Fra 43.40; 8.Cze 43.78. Lanes: Fra 1, Jam 2, GDR 3, SU 4, Cze 5, Bul 6, Can 7, UK 8.

As far as the vicious "boycotting game" was concerned, the 1984 Olympics in Los Angeles could be described as the return match of Moscow 1980. In other words, USSR and its allies stayed away from the feast. Sprint events obviously suffered greatly as the likes of Göhr and Koch were on the absentees' list. The Americans had a relatively easy task in Los Angeles and won most of the medals at stake, yielding only two bronzes to Jamaica's Merlene Ottey. In the century Ashford had no troubles. She won in 10.97, not bad with an adverse wind of 1.2 m/s. The real surprise was Valerie Brisco-Hooks (born on 6 July 1960 at Greenwood, Mississippi; 1.69 m. / 59 kg.) who ran the race of her life and won the 200 m. crown in 21.81 (halves in 11.20 ad 10.61), moving to third on the All Time List. This completed an unusual double as she had won the 400 in 48.83 three days before. She came practically from nowhere: on the eve of the Olympic year her personal records were no better than 23.10 and 52.08. So, when her name appeared as "Brisco-Hoo" on the scoreboard of the Los Angeles Coliseum, reportedly for lack of space, there were wits who pronounced it "Brisco-Who".

The easiest US victory was in the sprint relay (41.65), in which Canada, the nearest opponent, was left more than a second behind.

1984 Olympics, Los Angeles - 100 metres (5 August) w -1.2 m/s: 1.Evelyn Ashford (USA) 10.97; 2.Alice Brown (USA) 11.13; 3.Merlene Ottey (Jam) 11.16; 4.Jeanette Bolden (USA) 11.25; 5.Grace Jackson (Jam) 11.39; 6.Angela Bailey (Can) 11.40; 7.Heather Hunte-Oakes (UK) 11.43; 8.Angella Taylor (Can) 11.62. Lanes: Bolden 1, Taylor 2, Hunte-Oakes 3, Ashford 4, Bailey 5, Ottey 6, Brown 7, Jackson 8.

200 metres (9 August) w -0.1 m/s: 1.Valerie Brisco-Hooks (USA) 21.81; 2.Florence Griffith (USA) 22.04; 3.Merlene Ottey (Jam) 22.09; 4.Kathy Smallwood-Cook (UK) 22.10; 5.Grace Jackson (Jam) 22.20; 6.Randy Givens (USA) 22.36; 7.Rose-Aimée Bacoul (Fra) 22.78; 8.Liliane Gaschet (Fra) 22.86. Lanes: Gaschet 1, Ottey 2, Cook 3, Griffith 4, Givens 5, Bacoul 6, Brisco 7, Jackson 8.

4x100 metre relay (11 August): 1.USA (A.Brown, J.Bolden, C. Cheeseborough, E.Ashford) 41.65; Can (A.Bailey, M.Payne, A.Taylor, F.Gareau) 42.77; 3.UK (S.Jacobs, K.Smallwood-Cook, B.Callender, H.Hunte-Oakes) 43.11; 4.France 43.15; 5.FRG 43.57; 6.Bah 44.18; 7.Trinidad 44.23; 8. Jam 53.54. Lanes: UK 1, Jam 2, Bah 3, Tri 4, USA 5, Canada 6, FRG 7, France 8.

After the mutilated Games, track fans were eager to see all the world's best in real head-to-head competition. The organizers of Europe's most famous invitational meet, Weltklasse in Zurich, served them well on 22 August, matching the Los Angeles heroines against their rivals from the Eastern Bloc. In the domaine of sprinting the challenge ended in a draw, 1-1. The century was one of those races no real track fan can ever forget. Marlies Göhr was her usual explosive self in the early stage, but Ashford pulled even with some 40 metres to go and then ahead. She won in 10.76, a new world record. An aiding wind of 1.7 m/s no doubt played its part. Göhr, second in 10.84, missed her best ever by 0.03. A capacity crowd of 29,000 went wild as Ashford ran her victory lap, after which Göhr and her teammate Ingrid Auerswald each grabbed one of Evelyn's hands and hoisted them aloft. That was sport at its best.

In the 200 metres Olympic champ Brisco-Hooks had absolutely no chance against Marita Koch. The German won in 21.87 ahead of her compatriot Wöckel (22.10) as Brisco was only fourth (22.26). At the end of the year "Track & Field News" gave undefeated Ashford a rightful edge vis-à-vis Göhr in the 100 but also put things right – in its way, that's true - in the 200, with Koch, Wöckel and Göhr, in that order, all ahead of Brisco. Koch had equalled her own world record (21.71) in a pre-Olympic meet.

Göhr and Koch dominated the picture in 1985, while Ashford had to step aside, after giving birth to a daughter. The big event of that year was the World Cup in Canberra, where a GDR quartet consisting of Gladisch, Rieger, Auerswald and Göhr chalked up a great 41.37 in the 4x100 metre relay for a new world record. It was virtually a solo race, with USSR a distant second in 42.54. A fast lead-off leg by Silke Gladisch was enough to give the Germans a sound lead and nobody expected that her team-mates would spread themselves thin, especially as Marita Koch had been replaced with young Sabine Rieger. That is what they did though – and the record is still unsurpassed at the time of writing, almost twenty-one years later. As for Koch, she saved her ammunitions for an all-out attack on the world's 400 metre record. And the result was an incredible 47.60 - another global mark that is still unchallenged!

Evelyn Ashford had one more good season in 1986, when a new star, Heike Drechsler of the GDR, hit the headlines with a couple of record-equalling 21.71's in the 200. 1987 was the year of the second World Championships, held at Rome's Stadio Olimpico. The above-mentioned Silke Gladisch (later Möller, born on 20 June 1964 at Stralsund; 1.68 m. / 59 kg.), who had long been regarded as the successor to Göhr, finally came into her own and scored a double in the meet of the year. She first won the 100 in 10.90, well ahead of sprinter/long jumper Heike Drechsler, also of the GDR, and Merlene Ottey. In the 200 she just ran the race of her life with a classy 21.74, easily repulsing the late rush of her American rival Florence Griffith. In the sprint relay USA upset a disappointing GDR foursome to win in 41.58. Göhr was for once not at her best. She had previously failed to make the final in the century.

1987 World Championships, Rome - 100 metres (30 August) w - 0.5 m/s: 1.Silke Gladisch (GDR) 10.90; 2.Heike Drechsler (GDR) 11.00; 3.Merlene Ottey (Jam) 11.04; 4.Diane Williams (USA) 11.07; 5.Angella Issajenko (née Taylor) (Can) 11.09; 6.Anelia Nuneva (Bul) 11.09; 7.Angela Bailey (Can) 11.18; 8.Pam Marshall (USA) 11.19. Lanes: Marshall 1, Williams 2, Issajenko 3, Drechsler 4, Ottey 5, Gladisch 6, Nuneva 7, Bailey 8.

200 metres (3 September) w +1.2 m/s: 1.Silke Gladisch (GDR) 21.74; 2.Florence Griffith (USA) 21.96; 3.Merlene Ottey (Jam) 22.06; 4.Pam Marshall (USA) 22.18; 5.Gwen Torrence (USA) 22.40; 6.Mary Onyali (Nig) 22.52; 7.Ewa Kasprzyk (Pol) 22.52; 8.Nadezhda Georgieva (Bul) 22.55. Lanes: Marshall 1, Kasprzyk 2, Gladisch 3, Ottey 4, Griffith 5, Onyali 6, Georgieva 7, Torrence 8.

4x100 metre relay (6 September): 1.USA (A.Brown, Diane Williams, F.Griffith, P.Marshall) 41.58; 2.GDR (S.Gladisch, C.Oschkenat, K. Behrendt, M.Göhr) 41.95; 3.SU (I.Slyusar, N.Pomoshchnikova, N.German, O.

Antonova) 42.33; 4.Bul 42.71: 5.FRG 43.20; 6.Can 43.26; 7.Cub 43.66; 8.Fra 43.75. Lanes: Cub 1, Bul 2, Can 3, SU 4, USA 5, GDR 6, FRG 7, Fra 8.

All the above feats were outshone in 1988 by an American who had been prominent for several years and who now rose to a new dimension, Florence Griffith (born on 21 December 1959 at Los Angekles; died on 21 September 1998 at Mission Viejo, CA; 1.70 m. / 59 kg.). "Flo-Jo", as she was called, did 11.51 and 22.55 in 1980, before turning 21. Her progress in subsequent years was gradual and steady: in 1984 she improved to 10.99 and 22.04 and won a silver medal in the 200 m. at the Los Angeles Olympics. In the next three years she improved but little (10.96 and 21.96), yet she won silver again at the Rome Worlds in 1987. Even so, until then her fame curiously rested more on her highly styled beauty and eccentricity, e.g. in sporting 10 cms. fingernails and flashy bodysuits than on her valuable athletic skill.

During the winter 1987/88 she worked harder than ever, mostly under the guidance of her husband and coach Al Joyner, the 1984 Olympic triple jump champion. In 1988 she made a great leap forward, rather unusual in a sprinter approaching her thirties. Clock-wise she improved by the equivalent of 5-to-6 metres over both sprint distances! She made history in two important meets, the US Olympic Trials at Indianapolis and the Olympic Games in Seoul. Times and wind readings aptly tell the tale (she won all these races):

1988 US Olympic Trials

100 m.	10.60w	(+3.2)	Heat	16 Jul
	10.49*	(0.0)	Q-F	16 Jul
	10.70	(+1.6)	S-F	17 Jul
	10.61	(+1.2)	Final	17 Jul
200 m.	21.96	(+0.6)	Heat	22 Jul
	21.77	(-0.1)	Q-F	22 Jul
	21.90w	(+2.4)	S-F	23 Jul
	21.85	(+1.3)	Final	23 Jul

1988 Olympic Games

100 m.	10.88	(+1.0)	Heat	24 Sep
	10.62	(+1.0)	Q-F	24 Sep
	10.70w	(+2.6)	S-F	25 Sep
	10.54w	(+3.0)	Final	25 Sep
200 m.	22.51	(+0.7)	Heat	28 Sep
	21.76	(+0.7)	Q-F	28 Sep
	21.56*	(+1.7)	S-F	29 Sep
	21.34*	(+1.3)	Final	29 Sep

*World Record.

That fabulous 10.49 in a quarter-final at the Trials created quite a stir, representing an improvement of 0.27 sec. vis-à-vis Evelyn Ashford's world record. Several eye-witnesses questioned the wind reading (officially "nil"), noting that in the men's triple jump, going on virtually alongside at the same time and in the same running direction, there were only 3 legal readings out of 46, notably including a 4.3m/s on the board just as the 10.49 race began. However, wind gauge operators and the company they worked for firmly confirmed the correctness of the verdict, and Griffith's time made the IAAF book.

Apart from that incredible mark, Griffith could point to clearly legal clockings as

10.61 and 10.62, plus a windy 10.54. They still represented a remarkable progress vis-à-vis Ashford's previous record (10.76). Then what "Flo-Jo" did at Seoul, especially in the 200 metres, largely suffices to confirm that she had reached a new dimension. East German coach Horst-Dieter Hille, certainly not a partisan source, studied the Seoul races carefully and came to the conclusion that "Flo-Jo" had the speed of an excellent male sprinter in all but the first 10 m. and the last 10 m. She won by unusually wide margins: 0.29 on Ashford in the 100 m. and 0.38 on Grace Jackson of Jamaica in the 200 m. And every time she had a radiant smile on her face well before coming home the winner! Of course, some observers wondered how a sprinter pretty close to the age of thirty could improve by as much as 0.47 (100 m.) and 0.62 (200 m.) in one year. "Strength work and repeated videotape study of the starts of the fastest humans of all" – that was the reply given by "Flo-Jo" and her new coach Bob Kersee. Some commentators, obviously influenced by the Ben Johnson case which unfolded at the same time, were inclined to suspect that drugs may have entered the picture even in Griffith's case. But no light had gone up when she was subjected to tests, in the States and in Seoul. Under such conditions, the dictum "honni soit qui mal y pense" seems to be in order. Be that as it may, the Doubting Thomases seemingly gained new vigour when "Flo-Jo" announced her retirement from track shortly after the Seoul Games. Genuine track fans simply regretted that she would no longer have a chance to give the 400 m. a truly serious try. (Griffith, the 1983 NCAA champion at that distance, had been quoted as saying: "I especially like the 400 m. because it is the most challenging event").

As destiny would have it, the life of the fastest woman of modern times was to pass away almost as rapidly as her most memorable races. On a September day of 1998 the track world was struck by the news that Dolorez Florence Griffith had died in her sleep while at home in Mission Viejo, California, three months before turning 39. An autopsy revealed that her death was due to "suffocation following an epileptic seizure". She had a congenital brain abnormality known as "cavernous angioma". Dr. Richard Fukumoto, chief of forensic medicine at the Orange County Coroner's Office, incidentally remarked that said "abnormality never has been associated with steroids or any other drugs".

Getting back to the Seoul Olympics, it should be mentioned that Griffith, besides winning both sprints by outrageous margins, also starred in the relays, contributing to US gold in the 4x100 m. and to silver in the 4x400 m. There was only 30 minutes between the two finals and "Flo-Joe" was timed in 48.1 in the anchor leg of the longer race. She was outshone by a fresher Russian rival, Olga Bryzgina, who was clocked in 47.9 (A few days earlier, Bryzgina had won the individual event in 48.65). The end result of this great duel was a new world record for USSR, 3:15.18, and a new US record for Griffith & Co., 3:15.51.

1988 Olympics, Seoul - 100 metres (25 September) w + 3.0: 1.Florence Griffith-Joyner (USA) 10.54; 2.Evelyn Ashford (USA) 10.83; 3.Heike Drechsler (GDR) 10.85; 4.Grace Jackson (Jam) 10.97; 5.Gwen Torrence (USA) 10.97; 6.Natalya Pomoshchnikova (SU) 11.00; 7.Juliet Cuthbert (Jam) 11.26; 8. Anelia Nuneva (Bul) 11.49. Lanes: Torrence 1, Pomoshchnikova 2, Griffith 3, Nuneva 4, Drechsler 5, Ashford 6, Cuthbert 7, Jackson 8.

200 metres (29 September) w + 1.3 m/s: 1.Florence Griffith-Joyner (USA) 21.34; 2.Grace Jackson (Jam) 21.72; 3. Heike Drechsler (GDR) 21.95; 4.Merlene Ottey (Jam) 21.99; 5.Silke Gladisch-Möller (GDR) 22.09; 6.Gwen Torrence (USA) 22.17; 7.Maya Azarashvili (SU) 22.33; 8. Galina Malchugina (SU) 22.42. Lanes: Drechsler 1, Azarashvili 2, Ottey 3, Gladisch-Möller 4, Griffith 5, Jackson 6, Malchugina 7, Torrence 8.

4x100 metre relay (1 October): 1.USA (A.Brown, S.Echols, F.Griffith, E.Ashford) 41.98; 2.GDR (S.Gladisch-Möller, K.Behrendt, I.Auerswald-Lange, M.Göhr) 42.09; 3.SU (L.Kondratyeva, G.Malchugina, M.Zhirova, N. Pomoshchnikova) 42.75; 4.FRG 42.76; 5.Bul 43.02; 6.Pol 43.93; 7.Fra 44.02; 8. Jam did not start. Lanes: Fra 1, (Jam 2),

FRG 3, SU 4, GDR 5, USA 6, Bul 7, Pol 8.

Throughout the Nineties no female sprinter came reasonably close to the records set by the flamboyant "Flo-Jo". Ashford went on for several years but she was clearly past her peak. The most consistent of them all appeared to be Jamaica's Merlene Ottey (born on 10 May 1960 at Cold Spring; 1.73 m. / 59 kg.), who was to outshine all her predecessors in at least one respect, longevity at high levels. As related above, she had already won a fair number of "lesser" medals in global competitions. In 1989-90 she rose to the no.1 rank in both sprints, her bests in the latter year being 10.78 and 21.66.

The third edition of the World Championships was held at Tokyo in 1991. Ottey had a peerless record in pre-Tokyo weeks, but on the occasion that mattered most she could not get rid of her "lesser medals" role. Victory over both distances went to a German nine years her junior, Katrin Krabbe (born on 22 November 1969 at Neubrandenburg; 1.82 m. / 64 kg.). 1991 was incidentally the first year that saw Germany appear with a combined West-East team in global competitions, following the unification of the country. Krabbe, a sleek and blond beauty, had grown to athletic stardom in the GDR ranks and in 1990 she scored the 100/200 double at the European Championships. In Tokyo she upset the likes of Gwen Torrence (USA) and Ottey and won over both distances. Her times, 10.99 and 22.09, were excellent in view of strong adverse winds.

Merlene Ottey's long-delayed rendezvous with gold finally materialized when she anchored the Jamaican team to victory in the sprint relay (41.94). USA met disqualification in the prelims due to poor baton passing. In the final Germany was partly penalized by its inadequacies in the same department.

1991 World Championships, Tokyo - 100 metres (27 August) w -3.0 m/s: 1.Katrin Krabbe (Ger) 10.99; 2.Gwen Torrence (USA) 11.03; 3.Merlene Ottey (Jam) 11.06; 4.Irina Privalova (SU) 11.16; 5.Evelyn Ashford (USA) 11.30; 6.Juliet Cuthbert (Jam) 11.33; 7.Mary Onyali (Nig) 11.39; 8.Carlette Guidry (USA) 11.52. Lanes: Ashford 1, Guidry 2, Krabbe 3, Ottey 4, Torrence 5, Privalova 6, Onyali 7, Cuthbert 8.

200 metres (30 August) w -2.4 m/s: 1.Katrin Krabbe (Ger) 22.09; 2.Gwen Torrence (USA) 22.16; 3.Merlene Ottey (Jam) 22.21; 4.Irina Privalova (SU) 22.28; 5.Galina Malchugina (SU) 22.66; 6.Dannette Young (USA) 22.87; 7.Pauline Davis (Bah) 22.90; 8.Yelena Vinogradova (SU) 23.10. Lanes: Malchugina 1, Davis 2, Krabbe 3, Torrence 4, Ottey 5, Young 6, Privalova 7, Vinogradova 8.

4x100 metre relay (1 September): 1. Jam (D.Duhaney, J.Cuthbert, B.McDonald, M.Ottey) 41.94; 2. SU (N.Kovtun, G. Malchugina, Y.Vinogradova, I.Privalova) 42.20; 3.Ger (G.Breuer, K.Krabbe S.Richter, H.Drechsler) 42.33; 4.Nig 42.77; 5.Fra 43.34; 6.Cub 43.75; 7.Ita 43.76; 8.Aus 43.79. Lanes: Aus 1, Fra 2, Ger 3, Nig 4, Jam 5, SU 6, Ita 7, Cub 8.

There was no truly dominant figure in 1992. Especially in the century the top runners took turns in beating one another. The most coveted title was awarded at the Barcelona Olympics and an American sprinter-hurdler upset them all, winning the 100 metres in 10.82. She was Gail Devers (born on 19 November 1966 at Seattle; 1.60 m. / 52 Kg.), a fast sprinter/hurdler, almost a female version of Harrison Dillard (memories of 1948). A serious thyroid disorder caused her to miss competition in 1989/90 and she was close to having a foot amputated, yet she managed to stage a great comeback in 1991, when she finished second in the 100 m. hurdles at the Worlds in Tokyo. The following year she was favoured to win this event in the Olympics but tripped over the last hurdle when well clear of the field. However, this happened five days after she had surprised a lot of people by winning "the wrong race", i.e. the 100 metres flat! It was one of the closest finishes ever seen, as no more than 0.06 covered the first five. Devers won in 10.82 from Juliet Cuthbert, who was only 0.01 behind. Merlene Ottey, her usually unlucky self, had to be content with fifth.

The Olympic 200 metre crown went to another American, Gwen Torrence (born on 12 June 1965 at Atlanta; 1.70 m. / 57 kg.), who five days earlier had finished a disappointing fourth in that hectic century. She was quite upset after that race and reportedly said: "Two of the three medallists are not clean. I'm sick and tired of it". An obvious reference to performance enhancing drugs, which had been the talk of the town for years. Be that as it may, Torrence did herself justice by winning the 200 in 21.81, with Cuthbert again second and Ottey third. After which Torrence used a milder tone in a public statement: "My personal opinions have perhaps come across too strongly. I am sorry that any of my opinions expressed here have brought harm to anyone, especially great athletes and my team-mates in particular".

USA made it three in the relay, despite some (usual?) trouble with passes.

Second went to CIS, a combined team assembling athletes from the dismantled USSR. This was a momentary solution: in later years each of the republics from the former Soviet empire would compete with a team of its own.

1992 Olympics, Barcelona - 100 metres (1 August) w –1.0 m/s: 1.Gail Devers (USA) 10.82; 2.Juliet Cuthbert (Jam) 10.83; 3.Irina Privalova (CIS) 10.84; 4.Gwen Torrence (USA) 10.86; 5.Merlene Ottey (Jam) 10.88; 6.Anelia Nuneva (Bul) 11.10; 7.Mary Onyali (Nig) 11.15; 8.Liliana Allen (Cub) 11.19. Lanes: Allen 1, Devers 2, Cuthbert 3, Ottey 4, Torrence 5, Privalova 6, Nuneva 7, Onyali 8.

200 metres (6 August) w –0.6 m/s: 1.Gwen Torrence (USA) 21.81; 2.Juliet Cuthbert (Jam) 22.02; 3.Merlene Ottey (Jam) 22.09; 4.Irina Privalova (CIS) 22.19; 5.Carlette Guidry (USA) 22.30; 6.Grace Jackson (Jam) 22.58; 7.Michelle Finn (USA) 22.61; 8.Galina Malchugina (CIS) 22.63. Lanes: Malchugina 1, Finn 2, Privalova 3, Cuthbert 4, Ottey 5, Torrence 6, Guidry 7, Jackson 8.

4x100 metre relay (8 August): 1.USA (E.Ashford, E.Jones, C.Guidry, G.Torrence) 42.11; 2.CIS (Russia) (O.Bogoslovskaya, G.Malchugina, M. Trandenkova, I.Privalova) 42.16; 3.Nig (B.Utondu, F.Idehen, C.Opara-Thompson, M.Onyali) 42.81; 4.Fra 42.85; 5.Ger 43.12; 6.Aus 43.77; Cuba and Jamaica did not finish. Lanes: Aus 1, Fra 2, USA 3, Nig 4, Jam 5, CIS 6, Ger 7, Cub 8.

Merlene Ottey's long quest for gold in an individual event came to a happy end in 1993. Until then the fleet-footed Jamaican had collected a record number of "lesser medals" in global competitions – one silver and 8 bronze! And only in 1991 she had tasted victory in the 4x100 metre relay.

The turning point was provided by the 1993 World Championships in Stuttgart. But she succeeded only on second try as the 100 saw her once more on the losing side – by the most infinitesimal of margins, 1 thousandth of a second! At the end of a grand duel explosive Gail Devers nosed her out, 10.811 to 10.812. Officially they were credited with the same time, 10.82. The American led for the greater part of the race, 4.09 to 4.13 at 30 m., 6.95 to 6.98 at 60 m. The Jamaican had a slight lead at 80 m. – 8.87 to 8.88, but Devers again surged ahead in the very last stretch of land. The crowd sensed the drama of the Jamaican and rewarded her with a two-minute standing ovation at the victory ceremony. Three days later Ottey was confronted with a similar headache in the 200 metres, but at the crucial moment she repulsed Gwen Torrence's last minute attack and won by a scanty margin – 21.98 to 22.00. "I finally got it", exclaimed the happy Jamaican, "after 13 years of waiting I have the gold".

In the last leg of the 4x100 m. relay Gail Devers was involved in another tight photo-finish, but this time she just lost the verdict to Irina Privalova of Russia. Both teams were credited with 41.49. Jamaica was a distant third, but Ottey as anchor leg runner won her third medal in a few days – as did Devers, who in the meantime had won her favourite event, the high hurdles.

1993 World Championships, Stuttgart - 100 metres (16 August) w – 0.3 m/s: 1.Gail Devers (USA) 10.82, 2.Merlene Ottey (Jam) 10.82; 3.Gwen Torrence (USA) 10.89; 4.Irina Privalova (Rus) 10.96; 5.Mary Onyali (Nig) 11.05; 6. Natalya Voronova (Rus) 11.20; 7.Nicole Mitchell (Jam) 11.20; 8.Liliana Allen (Cu) 11.23: Lanes: Allen 1, Mitchell 2, Torrence

3, Privalova 4, Devers 5, Ottey 6, Onyali 7, Voronova 8.

200 metres (19 August) w 0.0 m/s: 1.Merlene Ottey (Jam) 21.98; 2. Gwen Torrence (USA) 22.00; 3.Irina Privalova (Rus) 22.13; 4.Marie-José Pérec (Fra) 22.20; 5.Mary Onyali (Nig) 22.32; 6. Natalya Voronova (Rus) 22.50; 7.Galina Malchugina (Rus) 22.50; 8.Dannette Young (USA) 23.04. Lanes: Young 1, Onyali 2, Privalova 3, Ottey 4, Malchugina 5, Torrence 6, Pérec 7, Voronova 8.

4x100 metre relay (22 August): 1.Rus (O.Bogoslovskaya, G.Malchugina, N. Voronova, I.Privalova) 41.49; 2.USA (M.Finn, G.Torrence, W.Vereen, G.Devers) 41.49; 3.Jam (M.Freeman, J.Campbell, N.Mitchell, M.Ottey) 41.94; 4.Fra 42.67; 5. Ger 42.79; 6.Cub 42.89; 7.Fin 43.37; 8. UK 43.86. Lanes: Fra 1, UK 2, USA 3, Rus 4, Jam 5, Ger 6, Fin 7, Cub 8.

Gritty Gwen Torrence was the no.1 sprinter in the two seasons that followed. In 1995 she went so far as to score a double at the World Championships in Göteborg, or so she thought - until she was disqualified in the 200 metres for stepping on the line at least three times around the turn. She had been clocked in 21.77, a stunning time into a 2.2 m/s. wind, with Ottey and Russia's Privalova next in that order, almost four metres behind. Prior to that the American had won the 100 metres in 10.85, still ahead of Ottey and Privalova, second and third respectively. The Russian had a reaction time of 0.233, very slow, especially if compared to Torrence's 0.135.

Following the judges' decision after the longer race, Ottey was moved to first and thus won her second gold in an individual event at the age of 35. Torrence was back in stride for the sprint relay, in which she outshone her great rival Merlene in the anchor leg and thus gave USA yet another gold.

1995 World Championships, Göteborg - 100 metres (6 August) w +0.9 m/s: 1.Gwen Torrence (USA) 10.85; 2.Merlene Ottey (Jam) 10.94; 3.Irina Privalova (Rus) 10.96; 4.Carlette Guidry (USA) 11.07; 5.Zhanna Pintusevich (Ukr) 11.07; 6.Melanie Paschke (Ger) 11.10; 7.Mary Onyali (Nig) 11.15; 8.Juliet Cuthbert (Jam) 11.44. Lanes: Onyali 1, Pintusevich 2, Ottey 3, Guidry 4, Torrence 5, Paschke 6, Privalova 7, Cuthbert 8.

200 metres (10 August) w - 2.2 m/s: 1.Merlene Ottey (Jam) 22.12; 2.Irina Privalova (Rus) 22.12; 3.Galina Malchugina (Rus) 22.37; 4.Melanie Paschke (Ger) 22.60; 5.Silke Knoll (Ger) 22.66; 6.Mary Onyali (Nig) 22.71; 7.Marina Trandenkova (Rus) 22.84. Gwen Torrence (USA), 1st in 21.77, was disqualified: Lanes: Trandenkova 1, Knoll 2, Malchugina 3, Ottey 4, Privalova 5, Torrence 6, Paschke 7, Onyali 8.

4x100 metre relay (13 August): 1.USA (C.Mondie-Milner, C.Guidry, C.Gaines, G.Torrence) 42.12; 2.Jam (D. Duhaney, J.Cuthbert, B.McDonald, M.Ottey) 42.25; 3.Ger (M.Paschke, S.Lichtenhagen, S.Knoll, G.Becker) 43.01; 4.Bah 43.14; 5.Fra 43.35; 6.Fin 44.46; 7.Col 44.61. Rus did not finish. Lanes: Fin 1, Bah 2, Fra 3, Rus 4, USA 5, Jam 6, Ger 7, Col 8.

Torrence gained a clair first over both distances in the 1995 World Ranking of "Track & Field News". This was a true reflection of her superiority throughout the season. In the 200 metres she ducked under 22 secs. five times, before and after her Olympic "faux pas".

The cast of leading characters was very much the same also in 1996, year of the Atlanta Olympics, save for one important addition, Marie-José Pérec of France (born on 9 May 1968 at Basse-Terre, Guadeloupe; 1.80 m./ 60 kg.). She already had a high reputation as a 400 m. runner, having won this event in the 1992 Olympics and in the 1991 and '95 Worlds. In the last of these meets she also finished fourth in the 200 m. A most gifted but somewhat lazy athlete, she began to come close to her great potential as a sprinter when she transferred to USA and joined the powerful squad directed by John Smith, a former holder of the world's quarter-mile record. She once said of her American coach: "He puts the bar very far – a variation of the bar very high". Hard work paid dividends in 1996, when she scored a great 400/200 m. double at the Atlanta Olympics. That's the chronological order in which it evolved: after winning the one-lap event in 48.25 (third best ever) on 29 July, she came back three days later to beat Merlene Ottey for the 200 m. title, 22.12 to 22.24. Her great staying power was evidenced by her halves – 11.38 + 10.74, as opposed to Ottey's 11.28 + 10.96.

Earlier in the week Ottey had lost the 100 m. to Gail Devers in yet another close decision as both were timed in 10.94. A close examination of the photo finish revealed that Devers won by a mere 55/1000 sec. !

USA also won the sprint relay in 41.95 as Bahamas nosed out Jamaica for second, despite a great 9.83 by Ottey in the anchor leg.

1996 Olympics, Atlanta - 100 metres (27 July) w – 0.7 m/s: 1.Gail Devers (USA) 10.94; 2.Merlene Ottey (Jam) 10.94; 3.Gwen Torrence (USA) 10.96; 4. Chandra Sturrup (Bah) 11.00; 5.Marina Trandenkova (Rus) 11.06; 6.Natalya Voronova (Rus) 11.10; 7.Mary Onyali (Nig) 11.13; 8.Zhanna Pintusevich (Ukr) 11.14. Lanes: Voronova 1, Trandenkova 2, Devers 3, Ottey 4, Onyali 5, Torrence 6, Pintusevich 7, Sturrup 8.

200 metres (1 August) w + 0.3 m/s: 1.Marie-José Pérec (Fra) 22.12; 2.Merlene Ottey (Jam) 22.24; 3.Mary Onyali (Nig) 22.38; 4.Inger Miller (USA) 22.41; 5.Galina Malchugina (Rus) 22.45; 6.Chandra Sturrup (Bah) 22.54; 7.Juliet Cuthbert (Jam) 22.60; 8.Carlette Guidry (USA) 22.61. Lanes: Cuthbert 1, Guidry 2, Pérec 3, Onyali 4, Ottey 5, Malchugina 6, Miller 7, Sturrup 8.

4x100 metre relay (3 August): 1.USA (C.Gaines, G.Devers, I.Miller, G.Torrence) 41.95; 2.Bah (E.Clarke, C.Sturrup, S.Fynes, P.Davis) 42.14; 3.Jam (M.Freeman, J.Cuthbert, N.Mitchell, M.Ottey) 42.24; 4. Rus 42.27; 5.Nig 42.56; 6.Fra 42.76; 7.Aus 43.70; 8.UK 43.93. Lanes: UK 1, Bah 2, Fra 3, Rus 4, USA 5, Jam 6, Nig 7, Aus 8.

Until then all the fast runners in circulation had remained well behind „Flo-Jo"'s fabulous records. To reduce the gap at least to some extent there came a tremendously gifted athlete, Marion Jones of USA (born on 12 October 1975 at Los Angeles; 1.78 m. / 68 kg.). She had dual nationality as her mother was born in Belize, but she opted for USA. She began to show tremendous promise at a very early age. In the summer of 1991, just before turning 16, she astounded experts by placing 4th in the 200 metres (time, 22.76) at the national championships, narrowly missing selection for the World Championships in Tokyo. A year later she came close to making the US Olympic team at the national Trials, finishing 5th in the 100 and 4th in the 200. Her best times that year (1992) were 11.14 and 22.58. Then she turned her attention to … basketball, in which she progressed to the point of winning the NCAA title, playing point guard on the North Carolina team. In 1995 she suffered fractures of the left foot twice, after which she decided to forget about contact sports and returned to athletics. It took her a while to regain top form, but in 1997 she joined world class with such times as 10.76 and 21.76, plus 6.93 in the long jump. At the World Championships of that year in Athens she won the 100 in 10.83, nosing out the redoubtable Zhanna Pintusevich (10.85), but was only 10th in the long jump, in which her technique still left much to be desired. Merlene Ottey was not at her best, having lost training through illness. After placing no better than 7th in the 100, she looked better in the 200, but finally faded to third. Even so she became the oldest ever women's medallist at 37. Victory went to Ukrainian Zhanna Pintusevich (née Tarnopolskaya on 6 July 1972 at Nezhin near Chernigov; 1.64 m. / 62 kg.), a small but explosive talent who had progressed gradually and steadily. She won in 22.32, after a hard fight with Susanthika Jayasinghe of Sri Lanka. A well-balanced US team won the sprint relay by a comfortable margin.

1997 World Championships, Athens - 100 metres (3 August) w + 0.4 m/s: 1. Marion Jones (USA) 10.83; 2.Zhanna Pintusevich (Ukr) 10.85; 3.Sevatheda Fynes (Bah) 11.03; 4.Christine Arron (Fra) 11.05; 5.Inger Miller (USA) 11.18; 6.Melanine Paschke (Ger) 11.19; 7. Merlene Ottey (Jam) 11.29; 8.Chryste Gaines (USA) 11.32. Lanes: Fynes 1, Paschke 2, Jones 3, Arron 4, Pintusevich 5, Ottey 6, Miller 7, Gaines 8.

Marie-José Pérec (France) won a great 200/400 m. double at the 1996 Olympics in Atlanta.

200 metres (8 August) w - 0.7 m/s: 1.Zhanna Pintusevich (Ukr) 22.32; 2. Susanthika Jayasinghe (Srl) 22.39; 3. Merlene Ottey (Jam) 22.40; 4.Yekaterina Leshchova (Rus) 22.50; 5.Inger Miller (USA) 22.52; 6.Marina Trandenkova (Rus) 22.65; 7.Melinda Gainsford-Taylor (Aus) 22.73; 8. Sylvianne Félix (Fra) 22.81. Lanes: Trandenkova 1, Gainsford-Taylor 2, Ottey 3, Jayasinghe 4, Pintusevich 5, Miller 6, Leshchova 7, Félix 8.

4x100 metre relay (9 August): 1.USA (C.Gaines, M.Jones, I.Miller, G.Devers) 41.47; 2.Jam (B.McDonald, M.Frazer, J.Cuthbert, B.Grant) 42.10; 3.Fra (P.Girard, C.Arron, D.Combé, S.Félix) 42.21; 4.Ger 42.44; 5.Rus 42.50; 6.Bah 42.77; 7.Nig 43.27; 8.Chi 43.32. Lanes: Nig 1, Chi 2, Fra 3, Jam 4, USA 5, Bah 6, Rus 7, Ger 8.

In 1997 Marion Jones was unquestionably no.1 in the 200 metres too, no matter if she did not run that distance at the Worlds. The following year she topped the world again in both 100 and 200 and eventually moved to no.2 in the All Time Lists of such events. This

Marion Jones (USA), the greatest sprinter of the post Griffith era.

happened at Johannesburg and altitude most probably gave her a helping hand. First she did 21.62 in the 200 (11 September), then 10.65 in the 100 (12 September). Even though all this happened in no smaller meet than the World Cup, Marion won by wide margins - 0.32 in the 100 and 0.63 in the 200. And she had plenty of good marks at or near sea level too: eight in the range 10.71/10.79 in the 100 and 21.80 in the 200. The only defeat she suffered throughout her long season came in the long jump, at the hands of Germany's Heike Drechsler.

In 1999 Jones decided to raise the bar, aiming for a quadruple (100-200-LJ-4x100) in the World Championships, scheduled for late August in Sevilla. She won the century in a brilliant 10.70, practically with no wind, but had to be content with third in the long jump. Then came the 200: halfway down the stretch in her semi she broke down and did not finish, after which she had to go home. Apparently her problem was cramping and spasms in her back. Even so, gold medals on her family account were two, because J.C.Hunter, her husband since October 1998, won the men's shot put.

The 200 m. crown went to another American, Inger Miller (born on 12 June 1972 at Los Angeles; 1.63 m. / 55 kg.), the daughter of Lennox Miller, who had been one of the world's fastest men in his younger days, winning two Olympic medals in the 100 metres – silver in 1968 and bronze in '72.

Inger rose to new heights at Sevilla. In the 100 she improved on her personal best three times and in the final she wound up second in 10.79. In the longer distance she ran her best race ever and won by an overwhelming margin in 21.77.

In the sprint relay the US quartet was still the favourite of many, even without Jones, but fell below expectations, finishing only fourth. Bahamas, with a US trained quartet, stole the show with a good 41.92.

An event cast a shadow over the Sevilla celebration. Veteran Merlene Ottey withdrew after a positive test for nandrolone on 5 July 1999 in Lucerne. However, a year later the IAAF Arbitration Panel decided that there were "not the grounds to maintain her suspension from competition and accordingly the suspension ended with immediate effect."

1999 World Championships, Sevilla - 100 metres (22 August) w - 0.1 m/s: 1.Marion Jones (USA) 10.70; 2.Inger Miller (USA) 10.79; 3.Ekaterini Thanou (Gre) 10.84; 4:Zhanna Pintusevich (Ukr) 10.95; 5.Gail Devers (USA) 10.95; 6. Christine Arron (Fra) 10.97; 7.Chandra Sturrup (Bah) 11.06; 8.Mercy Nku (Nig) 11.16. Lanes: Pintusevich 1, Arron 2, Miller 3, Thanou 4, Jones 5, Devers 6, Sturrup 7, Nku 8.

200 metres (27 August) w + 0.6: 1.Inger Miller (USA) 21.77; 2.Beverly McDonald (Jam) 22.22; 3T.Merlene Frazer (Jam) and Andrea Philipp (Ger) 22.26; 5: Debbie Ferguson (Bah) 22.28; 6.Fatima Yusuf (Nig) 22.42; 7.Lauren Hewitt (Aus) 22.53; 8.Juliet Campbell (Jam) 22.64. Lanes: Hewitt 1, Campbell 2, Miller 3, Ferguson 4, Frazer 5, Philipp 6, Yusuf 7, McDonald 8.

4x100 metre relay (29 August): 1.Bah (S.Fynes, C.Sturrup, P.Davis, D.Ferguson) 41.92; 2.Fra (P.Girard, M.Hurtis, K.Benth, C.Arron) 42.06; 3.Jam (A.Bailey, M.Frazer, B.McDonald, P.Dowdie) 42.15; 4.USA 42.30; 5.Ger 42.63; 6.Can 43.39; 7.Pol 43.51; 8.UK 43.52. Lanes: UK 1, Ger 2, Bah 3, USA 4, Fra 5, Jam 6, Pol 7, Can 8.

"AN ACT OF GOD"

Marion Jones went to the 1999 World Championships in Sevilla with the declared aim of winning four gold medals. As related above, defeat in the long jump and then injury in a 200 m. semi shattered her dreams. "Track & Field News" made the following remarks: "Perhaps it was the cumulative and dehydrating effect of gearing up again and again on 100° (F)-degree Sevilla days for rounds and finals in three events. Or maybe it was the hard track or her awkward landing in the long jump. Maybe it was simply what the insurance companies call "An act of God". Or maybe, I dare say , her dream of winning four golds was simply put off till the 2000 Olympics in Sydney".

The Olympic season of 2000 proved, beyond any reasonable doubt, that Marion Jones was a diehard indeed. As soon as she regained full fitness she began to rave about a dream even greater than the one she had fostered the year before – why not aim for five, instead of four, medals? Both sprints, both relays (4x100 and 4x400) and long jump. After all, for most athletes the Olympics still had a greater appeal than the World Championships. At the US Trials in Sacramento she looked like her best self, winning both sprints by comfortable margins (10.88, against a 1.0 m/s wind, and 21.94) plus the long jump (7.02).

In the unique atmosphere of Sydney's Oympic arena, with attendances over 100,000 in every evening session, Marion Jones did win five medals – three golds and two bronze. As usual, she looked well-nigh unbeatable in the individual sprints, winning the 100 m. in 10.75 and the 200 m. in 21.84, with huge margins vis-à-vis her nearest rival, 0.37 and 0.43 respectively. As expected, she had a tougher job in the long jump and finally had to be content with third (6.92). At least three of her four fouls looked like a potential winning jump. The American completed her marathon stint in fine style, contributing to the US bronze in the 4x100 m. relay and to a gold in the 4x400. In the latter her third leg time of 49.40 was the fastest of the race. Of course, she had tried the one-lap event but rarely (best of 49.59 earlier in 2000). Just as in the case of her great predecessor "Flo-Jo", we will never know what she could have done at this distance. At any rate her total of 5 Olympic medals was the highest ever amassed by a woman at one Games. Add that she achieved all that in spite of off-track complications connected with her husband, shot-putter C.J.Hunter, who was found positive in a drug test in July and had to stay away from the Games. Talking about her Sydney adventure in retrospect, Marion summed it up with a brief but wonderful "this was a good experience".

The Bahamas quartet who had won the sprint relay at the 1999 Worlds – Savatheda Fynes, Chandra Sturrup, Pauline Davis-Thompson and Debbie Ferguson – turned the trick again in Sydney, ahead of Jamaica and USA. Davis-Thompson, 34, was in her fifth Olympics. She had previously won silver in the 200 m. The Jamaican team had the incomparable Merlene Ottey as anchor leg runner. At 40 she became the oldest women's medallist in Olympic history.

2000 Olympics, Sydney - 100 metres (23 September) w –0.4 m/s: 1.Marion Jones (USA) 10.75; 2.Ekaterini Thanou (Gre) 11.12; 3.Tanya Lawrence (Jam) 11.18; 4.Merlene Ottey (Jam) 11.19; 5.Zhanna Pintusevich (Ukr) 11.20; 6.Chandra Sturrup (Bah) 11.21; 7.Sevatheda Fynes (Bah) 11.22; 8.Debbie Ferguson (Bah) 11.29. Lanes: Lawrence 1, Ferguson 2, Ottey 3, Thanou 4, Jones 5, Sturrup 6, Pintusevich 7, Fynes 8.

200 metres (28 September) w +0.7 m/s: 1.Marion Jones (USA) 21.84; 2.Pauline Davis-Thompson (Bah) 22.27; 3.Susanthika Jayasinghe (Sri) 22.28, 4.Beverly McDonald (Bah) 22.35, 5.Debbie Ferguson (Bah) 22.37; 6.Melinda Gainsford-Taylor (Aus) 22.42; 7.Cathy Freeman (Aus) 22.53; 8.Zhanna Pintusevich (Ukr) 22.66. Lanes: McDonald 1, Freeman 2, Davis-Thompson 3, Jones 4, Ferguson 5, Jayasinghe 6, Gainsford-Taylor 7, Pintusevich 8.

4x100 metre relay (30 September): 1.Bah (S.Fynes, C.Sturrup, P.Davis-Thompson, D.Ferguson) 41.95; 2.Jam (T.Lawrence, V.Campbell, B.McDonald, M.Ottey) 42.12; 3.USA (C.Gaines, T.Edwards, N.Perry, M.Jones) 42.20; 4.Fra 42.42; 5.Rus 43.02; 6.Ger 43.11; 7.Nig 44.05; 8.Chi 44.87. Lanes: Ger 1, Chi 2, Jam 3, Fra 4, Bah 5, USA 6, Nig 7, Rus 8.

Jones was clearly the dominant figure in the last decade of the century, yet she too had been unable to come close to "Flo-Jo"s fantastic times of 1988. A noteworthy European record for 100 metres had been set by Christine Arron, a French girl born in Guadeloupe: 10.73 at the continental title meet of 1998 in Budapest. This mark was favoured by an aiding wind of 2.0 m/s, the maximum allowable, and this may be one of the reasons why Arron has so far failed to come close to it again.

WAITING FOR M.LLE GODOT ?

The first five years of the 21st century were characterized by a persistent standstill in women's sprinting. For example, there was not a single sub-22 secs. mark in the 200 metres throughout this period, and only one sub-10.80 in the 100. Marion Jones figured in the top ranks for another two years (2001-02) but failed to improve on her personal bests. On the eve of the 2001 World Championships in Edmonton, Canada, she could look back to a great win streak over 100 metres - 42 finals, from February 1998 till August 2001, if we overlook a false start disqualification in 1999. This chain was broken at the end of the 100 m. final, when Zhanna Pintusevich-Block, now representing Ukraine, beat her by a scant margin, 10.82 to 10.85. In fact, most of Zhanna's winning margin was gained at the start thanks to her faster reaction time (0.123 vs. 0.146). The American later won the 200 in 22.39 from Debbie Ferguson of Bahamas and finally contributed to the US victory in the sprint relay. However, the latter title was lost .... three years later, when Kelli White, the US lead-off runner, was disqualified for doping violations going back to 2000. This obviously penalized the entire US team and victory went to Germany.

2001 World Championships, Edmonton – 100 metres (6 August) w –0.3 m/s: 1.Zhanna Pintusevich-Block (Ukr) 10.82; 2.Marion Jones (USA) 10.85; 3.Ekaterini Thanou (Gre) 10.91; 4.Chandra Sturrup (Bah) 11.02; 5.Chryste Gaines (USA) 11.06; 6.Debbie Ferguson (Bah) 11.13; 7.Mercy Nku (Nig) 11.17. Kelli White (USA), 7th in 11.15, was posthumously disqualified for doping offence. Lanes: Gaines 1, Nku 2, Jones 3, Pintusevich-Block 4, Thanou 5, Sturrup 6, White 7, Ferguson 8.

200 metres (10 August) w-0.8 m/s: 1.Marion Jones (USA) 22.39; 2.Debbie Ferguson (Bah) 22.52; 3.LaTasha Jenkins (USA) 22.85; 4.Cydonie Mothersill (Cay) 22.88; 5.Juliet Campbell (Jam) 22.99; 6. Alenka Bikar (Slo) 23.00; 7. Myriam Mani (Cmr) 23.15. Kelli White (USA), 3rd in 22.56, was posthumously disqualified for doping offence. Lanes: Mothersill 1, Campbell 2, White 3, Ferguson 4, Jones 5, Mani 6, Jenkins 7, Bikar 8.

4x100 metre relay (11 August): 1.Ger (M.Paschke, Gabi Rockmeier, Birgit Rockmeier, M.Wagner) 42.32; 2.Fra (S.Félix, F.Bangué, M.Hurtis, O.Sidibé) 42.39; 3.Jam (J.Campbell, M.Frazer, B.McDonald, A.Walker) 42.40; 4.Nig 42.52; 5.UK 42.60; 6.Gre 43.25; 7.Rus 43.58. USA (White, Gaines, Miller, M.Jones), 1st in 41.71, was posthumously disqualified due to Kelli White's doping violations. Lanes: Rus 1, UK 2, Fra 3, Ger 4, Nig 5, USA 6, Jam 7, Gre 8.

Grand Prix meets dominated the picture in 2002, a season with no global championship on the programme. Marion Jones had a peerless record and for the sixth straight year she was no.1 in the World Rankings of "Track & Field News" over both distances. She went through fourteen finals in the 100 and three in the 200 without a loss. In the century she beat her old rival Pintusevich-Block 3-0. After her separation from husband C.J.Hunter in 2001, Jones found a new partner in Tim Montgomery, officially labelled as the fastest man in the world following his 9.78 in the century (2002). They had a son in 2003 and Marion consequently had to bypass the World Championships in Paris-St.Denis, "clou" of that year in athletics. Her successor as no.1 in the sprints was her compatriot Kelli White (born on 1 April 1977 at Oakland, California; 1.63 m. 52 kg.), who won the 100 in 10.85 and the 200 in 22.05. However, she lost these titles a year later as a result of the long-drawn investigation to which we have already hinted. She had tested positive to a stimulant, modafinil, and all her results from December 2000 onwards were consequently annulled. Following this "retarded burst" the 2003 world titles reverted to the runner-up, Torri Edwards of USA in the 100 (10.93), and Anastasiya Kapachinskaya of Russia in the 200 (22.38).

The prospect of disqualification had been hanging over Kelli White and hours before the relay final the US leadership decided not to use her in that race. This measure was not enough to secure victory though, because in the anchor leg Torri Edwards was caught and then passed by Christine Arron of France – to the immense delight of the Paris crowd, that is obvious. It may be interesting to note that a few days earlier, in the individual 100 m. race, Arron had finished no higher than fifth, 0.13 behind winner Edwards. The real opposite of what was to happen when the two clashed again in the relay. Sometimes it may well happen that a runner surpasses himself or herself if "driven" by a large friendly crowd. Let's remember a classic: Rosendahl vs. Stecher in the relay of the 1972 Olympics in Munich.

Unfortunately there is another PS to the chapter of "sad stories". Both Kapachinskaya and Edwards committed doping violations in early 2004, and each began serving bans of two years.

Zhanna Pintusevich-Block (Ukraine) rejoycing over her victory (over Marion Jones) in the 100 m. of the 2001 World Championships in Edmonton.

2003 World Championships, Paris-St.Denis - 100 metres (24 August) w +0.9 m/s: 1.Torri Edwards (USA) 10.93; 2.Zhanna Pintusevich- Block (Ukr) 10.99; 3.Chandra Sturrup (Bah) 11.02; 4.Ekaterini Thanou (Gre) 11.03, 5.Christine Arron (Fra) 11.06; 6.Aleen Bailey (Jam) 11.07; 7.Gail Devers (USA) 11.11. Kelli White (USA), 1st in 10.85, was posthumously disqualified for doping offence, as related above. Lanes: Edwards 1, Pintusevich-Block 2, Arron 3, Thanou 4, White 5, Sturrup 6, Devers 7, Bailey 8.

200 metres (28 August) w -0.3 m/s: 1.Anastasiya Kapachinskaya (Rus) 22.38; 2.Torri Edwards (USA) 22.47; 3.Muriel Hurtis (Fra) 22.59; 4.Zhanna Pintusevich-Block (Ukr) 22.92; 5.Beverly McDonald (Jam) 22.95; 6.Natalya Safronnikova (Blr) 22.98; 7.Anzhela Kravchenko (Ukr) 23.00. K.White (USA), 1st in 22.05, later disqualified, as related above. Lanes: Safronnikova 1, Edwards 2, Pintusevich-Block 3, Hurtis 4, Kapachinskaya 5, White 6, Kravchenko 7, McDonald 8.

4x100 metre relay (30 August): 1.Fra (P.Girard, M.Hurtis, S.Félix, C.Arron) 41.78; 2.USA (Angela Williams, C.Gaines, I.Miller, T.Edwards) 41.83; 3.Rus (O.Fyodorova, Y.Tabakova, M.Kislova, L.Kruglova) 42.66; 4.Ukr 43.07; 5.Ger

Blind pass exemplified: Me'Lisa Barber takes the baton from Muna Lee midway in the 4x100 m. relay final of the 2005 World Championships in Helsinki. The American team wound up first in 41.78.

Christine Arron (France), holder of the European 100 m. record (10.73).

43.27; 6.Bel 43.45; 7.Belarus 43.47; Jam did not finish. Lanes: Bel 1, Belarus 2, USA 3, Rus 4, Ukr 5, Fra 6, Jam 7, Ger 8.

In 2004 Marion Jones made a comeback of sorts, concentrating on the long jump. She won with a fine 7.11 at the US Trials but had to be content with 6.85w and fifth in the Athens Olympic final. It wasn't a great year for sprinters and the season's fastest time in the 100 metres – 10.77 by Ivet Lalova of Bulgaria - was regarded as rather doubtful by observers. In the Olympics Lalova, the 20-year-old offspring of two good sprinters, had to be content with fourth in the 100 and fifth in the 200. Winner of the title at the shorter distance was Yuliya Nesterenko of Belarus (née Bartsevich on 12 October 1980; 1.80 m. / 81 kg.), a powerful sprinter who was at her best at the right time, with 10.92 in a semi and 10.93 in the final. She won from Lauryn Williams (USA), while Christine Arron, the favourite of prognosticators, failed to make the final. Veronica Campbell of Jamaica (born on 15 May 1982 at Trelawny, 1.63 m./ 61 kg.) crowned a peerless season over 200 metres with a clear victory in 22.05, a personal best. In 2000, aged 18, she had won both sprints at the World Junior Championships. She also anchored the Jamaican team to victory in the 4x100 m. relay. The time, 41.73, was a new Jamaican and Commonwealth record. The Americans used Marion Jones, who had just finished long jumping, but were deficient in baton passing and failed to finish.

2004 Olympics, Athens - 100 metres (21 August) w -0.1 m/s: 1.Yuliya Nesterenko (Belarus) 10.93; 2.Lauryn Williams (USA) 10.96; 3.Veronica Campbell (Jam) 10.97; 4.Ivet Lalova (Bul) 11.00; 5.Aleen Bailey (Jam) 11.05; 6.Sherone Simpson (Jam) 11.07; 7.Debbie Ferguson (Bah) 11.16; 8.LaTasha Colander (USA) 11.18. Lanes: Lalova 1, Bailey 2, Campbell 3, Williams 4, Simpson 5, Nesterenko 6, Colander 7, Ferguson 8.

200 metres (25 August) w +0.8 m/s: 1.Veronica Campbell (Jam) 22.05; 2.Allyson Felix (USA) 22.18; 3.Debbie Ferguson (Bah) 22.30; 4.Aleen Bailey (Jam) 22.42; 5.Ivet Lalova (Bul) 22.57; 6.Kim Gevaert (Bel) 22.84; 7.(tie) Muna Lee (USA) and Abi Oyepitan (UK) 22.87. Lanes: Gevaert 1, Lalova 2, Felix 3, Campbell 4, Oyepitan 5, Bailey 6, Lee 7, Ferguson 8.

4x100 metre relay (27 August): 1.Jam (T.Lawrence, S.Simpson, A.Bailey, V.Campbell) 41.73; 2.Rus (O.Fyodorova, Y.Tabakova, I.Khabarova, L.Kruglova) 42.27; 3.Fra (V.Mang, M.Hurtis, S.Félix, C.Arron) 42.54; 4.Bah 42.69; 5.Belarus 42.94; 6.Bel 43.11; 7.Nige 43.42; USA did not finish. Lanes: Belarus 1, Fra 2, Bah 3, Jam 4, USA 5, Rus 6, Bel 7, Nig 8.

2005 offered yet another example of mixed fortunes for the top contenders. The tenth edition of the World Championships was held at Helsinki, as had been the case for the inaugural affair of 1983. This time the event was marred by unfavourable weather

Yuliya Nesterenko née Bartsevich (Belarus), the latest Olympic 100 m. champion (2004).

conditions, with a fair amount of cold and rain especially on the middle days. The 100 metre title went, rather surprisingly, to Lauryn Williams of USA (born on 11 September 1983 at Pittsburgh, PA; 1.59 m./ 50 Kg.), who nosed out Veronica Campbell – 10.93 to 10.95. That was a real upset as the Jamaican suffered what was to remain her one and only defeat of the year at the distance. Off the title she had won at the 2004 Worlds, Campbell seemed to have a better chance in the 200 metres, but she failed to make the podium. Here too victory went to an American, Allyson Felix (born on 18 November 1985 in Los Angeles; 1.68 m. / 57 kg.), a student at the University of So. California. Three months before turning 20 she won the world title by a comfortable margin in 22.16, ahead of her compatriot Rachelle Boone-Smith. Christine Arron of France, more consistent than in previous years, finished third over both distances. USA completed their hat trick by taking revenge over Jamaica in the sprint relay, 41.78 to 41.99.

2005 World Championships, Helsinki – 100 metres (8 August) w +1.3 m/s: 1.Lauryn Williams (USA) 10.93; 2.Veronica Campbell (Jam) 10.95; 3.Christine Arron (Fra) 10.98; 4.Chandra Sturrup (Bah) 11.09; 5.Me'Lisa Barber (USA) 11.09; 6.Sherone Simpson (Jam) 11.09; 7.Muna Lee (USA) 11.09; 8.Yuliya Nesterenko (Belarus) 11.13. Lanes: Simpson 1, Barber 2, Sturrup 3, Campbell 4, Arron 5, Williams 6, Nesterenko 7, Lee 8.

200 metres (12 August) w + 0.2 m/s: 1.Allyson Felix (USA) 22.16; 2.Rachelle Boone-Smith (USA) 22.31; 3.Christine Arron (Fra) 22.31; 4.Veronica Campbell (Jam) 22.38; 5.LaTasha Colander (USA) 22.66; 6.Yuliya Gushchina (Rus) 22.75; 7.Kim Gevaert (Bel) 22.86; 8.Cydonie Mothersill (Cay) 23.00. Lanes: Mothersill 1, Colander 2, Gevaert 3, Boone-Smith 4, Arron 5, Felix 6, Campbell 7, Gushchina 8.

4x100 metre relay (13 August): 1.USA (A.Daigle, M.Lee, M.Barber, Lauryn Williams) 41.78; 2.Jam (D.Browning, S.Simpson, A.Bailey, V.Campbell) 41.99; 3. Belarus (Y.Nesterenko, N.Sologub, Y.Nevmerzhitskaya, O.Dragun) 42.56; 4. Fra 42.85, 5.Bra 42.99; 6.Col 43.07; 7. Nig 43.25; 8.Pol 43.49. Lanes: Col 1, Pol 2, Fra 3, Jam 4, Belarus 5, Rus 6, Bra 7, Nig 8.

The early years of the new century have amply confirmed the standstill existing in women's sprinting. The world records set by Florence Griffith-Joyner in 1988 (10.49 and 21.34) look like a most distant cry. One of the reasons for such an impoverishment may be found in the present and more severe policy of the IAAF in enforcing its anti-doping campaign. It was only in 1989 that the international body began to conduct out-of-competition doping controls (random tests). Until then the athletes were subjected to doping controls only in connection with major international meets such as the Olympics/Worlds or continental championships. There can be little or no doubt that before that date quite a few athletes were able to circumvent anti-doping rules by discontinuing the "treatment" shortly before such major dates, i.e. once or twice a year.

As related before, there were rather strong reasons to doubt the wind reading officially released in connection with "Flo-Jo"s 100 m. record, that incredible 10.49 she was credited with at the 1988 US Olympic Trials. Her next best marks under surely correct conditions were 10.61 and 10.62. Second best in the All-Time List is Marion Jones with 10.65 (1998), alas with the advantage of high altitude. Jones' best at or near sea level is 10.70.

Griffith's superiority remains even more appalling in the 200 metres. Her 21.34 in winning the 1988 Olympic title in Seoul is largely superior to anything her successors have been able to do. Next bests are Marion Jones with 21.62 (high altitude) in 1998 and Merlene Ottey with 21.64 (1991) at sea level.

To be sure, anti-doping violations occur even under today's harsher rules. As previously related, the most recent lists of offenders include such top-class sprinters as Kelli White and Torri Edwards of USA and Anastasiya Kapachinskaya of Russia. We can only hope that infractions may become more and more difficult to perpetrate.

Judging from the present look of things,

Allyson Felix (USA) won the world's 200 m. title at Helsinki in 2005, just before turning 20.

one is almost tempted to say that identifying the possibility of new record-holders in women's sprinting for the near future is just like waiting for (M.lle) Godot, to paraphrase the sense implicit in the title of one of Samuel Beckett's plays. But, of course, one can never know .....

THE EMPRESS OF SPRINTLAND

Merlene Ottey has no peers in terms of longevity in the high spheres of sprinting. Throughout a quarter of a century she has been at or near the top of the world in this domain, where durability is undoubtedly harder to achieve than in most other sections of the sport. She can boast an unrivalled number of medals in major competitions: 8 in the Olympic Games (4 silver, 4 bronze) and 14 in the World Championships (3 gold, 4 silver and 7 bronze). The grand total, 22 medals, puts her two notches ahead of Carl Lewis, the most prolific collector of "global" medals in the men's department.
Jamaican-born Ottey, a magnificent specimen of "beauty in motion", achieved her bests at a rather advanced age: 10.74 in the 100 metres in 1996, aged 36, and 21.64 in the 200 in 1991, aged 31. These marks rank her as no.4 and no.3 respectively in the All-Time Lists of such events. She has never figured in the select group of world record holders, save for some indoor events of lesser significance (50, 60, 200 m.). And she won her first gold in an individual event at 33 years of age – in the 200 metres of the 1993 World Championships. Her debut in global meets dated from 1980, when she was third in the 200 metres at the Moscow Olympics.
Ottey had previously missed gold by very scant margins, at the latest three days before her breakthrough, when she was nipped by Gail Devers of USA in the 100 metre final by one thousandth of a second - 10.812 to 10.811 !
The fleet-footed Ottey spent part of her career in Italy and since 2000 she lives in Liubljana, Slovenia, a country she represented in her seventh Olympic adventure in 2004, when an injury forced her to withdraw in the semis of the 200. (A few weeks earlier she ran the 100 in 11.09, not bad for a 44-year-old woman!)
Of course, Ottey is destined to remain the pride and joy of her native land, Jamaica, which has been lavish in honouring her. Between 1979 and 1997 she was named Jamaican Sportswoman of the Year 15 times. And she was appointed a roving ambassador for Jamaica in 1993. Last but not least, early in 2006 a 2.4 m. bronze statue of Merlene - the work of sculptor Basil Watson - was unveiled in front of the National Arena in Kingston.

LATEST NEWS 2006

The main newsitem of the early season was the return to action of Marion Jones, now almost 31. In the Paris meeting of 8 July she turned in a good 10.92 for the century on a practically windless day, winning from up-and-coming Sherone Simpson of Jamaica, 10.98. The latter, a tiny girl (1.60 m. / 50 kg.) of 22, managed to turn the tables on her American rival on two later occasions though – 10.87 to 10.91 (Rome, 14 July) and 11.00 to 11.05 (London, 28 July). The Jamaican had previously run the 200 metres in 22.00.

However, early in August a sad chapter was added to Jones' glorious but often troubled life story. It was announced that she was found positive for EPO. The ultimate judgment is eagerly awaited. Of course, it could practically put an end to her career.

Prior to that, another chapter of the ever ebullient doping department had come to a conclusion. Ekaterini Thanou of Greece, involved in the same case of her countryman Kedéris for failing to appear at doping tests in 2004, finally admitted her violation before the Court of Arbitration for Sport and will be able to resume international competition at the end of 2006.

STATISTICS
MEN

ABBREVIATIONS

A	=	made at an altitude over 1000 metres
e	=	estimated non-winning time (generally derived from a study of the finish picture as per conservative evaluation)
E	=	automatic electric time
h	=	heat
hcp	=	made in a handicap race from scratch
qf	=	quarter-final
s	=	semi-final
T	=	tie (ex-aequo)
*	=	220 y. time less 0.1 (in 200 m. list) 4x110 y. time less 0.2 (in 4x100 m. list)

NB. Only 1 mark per country is given in the 4x100 m. relay lists.

WORLD YEAR LISTS 1860 - 1900

1860

100 yards

John Watkins	UK		10.0	1)	Oxford	14 Mar
Henry Pepys	UK	40	10.0	1)	Oxford	15 Mar
Charles Turnbull	UK	43	10.0	1)	Cheltenham	21 Apr
T. R. Monro	UK		10.0	1)	Cheltenham	21 Apr
Edward Boyle	UK		10.0	1)	Oxford	11 May
George Goodricke	UK		10.0	1)	Rugby	02 Oct
Charles Edmondes	UK	38	10.0	1)	Sherborne	25 Oct

Note (from Peter Lovesey): marks at Cheltenham, Rugby and Sherborne were in school sports, probably timed to the nearest second.

Doubtful:

James Stewart	Ire		10.0	1)	Dublin	09 Jun

1861

100 yards

James Mason	UK	40	10.0	1)	Cambridge	01 Jun
Arthur Poole	UK	40	10.0	1)	Oxford	28 Nov

Doubtful conditions:

Edward Estridge	UK	40	9.0	1)	Tonbridge	16 Apr

(made in school sports – see note above)

1862

100 yards

R. B. Fenwick	UK		10.0	1)	London	26 Apr
Arthur Powell	UK	44	10.0	1)	Bradfield	21 Oct
Frederick Evans	UK	42	10.0	1)	Oxford	12 Nov
William Heap	UK	43	10.0	1)	Oxford	22 Nov

Doubtful conditions:

Thomas Poole	UK	43	9.25	1)	Uppingham	May

Note - Bradfield and Uppingham were school sports – see note above.

1863

100 yards

T.W. Master	UK		10.0	1)	Oxford	16 Feb
F. D. Barker	UK		10.0	1)	Durham	05 Mar
F. A. Hyett	UK		10.0	1)	Tonbridge	21 Mar
A. Mitchell Inness	UK		10.0	)	London	30 May
W. J. MacKintosh	UK		10.0	)	London	17 Jun
Buckmaster	UK		10.0	1)	Rugby	29 Sep
George Morrell	UK	45	10.0	1)	Oxford	24 Nov
William Kettlewell	UK	45	10.0	1)	Oxford	26 Nov
Alban Harrison	UK	43	10.0	1)	Cambridge	08 Dec

Note – Buckmaster in school sports, see note above.

Doubtful timing:

Benjamin Derbyshire	UK	45	9.5	1)	Oxford	12 Nov

1864

100 yards

Edward Estridge	UK	43	10.0	1)	Oxford	03 Feb
Edmund Pigott	UK	43	10.0	)	Cambridge	24 Feb
J. King	UK		10.0	1)	Durham	10 Mar
Charles McArthur	UK		10.0	)	Bristol	07 Apr
Tomkinson	UK		10.0	)	Liverpool	26 Apr
Robert Reid	UK		10.0	1)	Cheltenham	06 May
H. Hunter	UK		10.0	)	Stubbington	14 May
H. Hawthorne	UK		10.0	)	London	04 Jun
Julius Elliott	UK	42	10.0	)	Brighton	22 Jun
William Mitchell	UK	38	10.0	1)h	Liverpool	09 Jul
John Trevor	UK		10.0	1)	Liverpool	09 Jul
William Burton	UK		10.0	)	Sandhurst	16 Sep
Joseph Green	UK		10.0	1T)	Rugby	14 Oct
Roland Poole	UK		10.0	1T)	Rugby	14 Oct
A. Randolph	UK		10.0	1)	Reading	29 Oct
John Gilmore	Aus		10.0	1)	Oxford	10 Nov
Richard Webster	UK	42	10.0	1)	Cambridge	12 Nov
Marcus Martin	UK	42	10.0	1)	Cambridge	07 Dec

Note – The Cheltenham and Rugby marks were in high school sports. See above.

Doubtful:

F.F.Groom	Aus		9.5	1)h	Melbourne	Sep
G.Tait	Aus		10.0	1)h	Melbourne	Sep

1865

100 yards

Robert Vidal	UK	43	10.0	1)	Oxford	10 Mar
John Boyle	UK	45	10.0	1)	Marlborough	17 Mar
Henry Jollye	UK	41	10.0	1)	Oxford	18 Mar
Sydney Richards	UK		10.0	)	Cheltenham	28 Apr
Arthur Atkins	UK		10.0	)	Cheltenham	29 Apr
Theodore Calliphonas	UK		10.0	)	Felstead	Apr
C.R.G. Beresford	UK		10.0	1)	Fareham	10 Jun
Henry Harrison	Aus	36	10.0	)	Melbourne	08 Jul
F. H. Field	UK		10.0	1)	Cirencester	15 Nov
Jack Harris	Aus		10.0	)	Melbourne	18 Nov
William Armstrong	UK	49	10.0	1)	Sherborne	

Doubtful:

John Sandilands	UK	47	9.5	1)	Uppingham	Apr

Note – The marks at Marlborough, Cheltenham, Felstead, Fareham, Sherborne and Uppingham were in school sports. See above.

1866

100 yards

Hector Gurdon-Rebow	UK	46	10.0	1)	Colchester	10 Jan
John Prothero	UK	43	10.0	1)	Oxford	13 Feb
Cecil B. Hornby	UK	43	10.0	1)	Tonbridge	15 Mar
James Fairlie	UK	48	10.0	1)	Glenalmond	28 Apr
J. Thompson	UK		10.0	1)	Horsley	24 Aug
Benjamin Connolly	UK	45	10.0	1)	Oxford	07 Nov
Jack Harris	Aus		10.0	1)	Melbourne	11 Nov

Note – B.Connolly "under 10 secs with the wind" (Bell's Life).
The Glenalmond mark was in school sports - see above.

200 metres (half-to-full turn)

William Collett	UK	43	22.9*	1)	London	24 Nov
C. G. Emery	UK		23.15*	1)	London	19 May

1867

100 yards

Jack Harris	Aus		10.0	1)	Melbourne	22 Apr
John Baines	UK	47	10.0	1)	Cheltenham	03 May
William Tennent	UK	45	10.0	1)	Buersil	15 Jun

Doubtful:

Neale	UK		9.0	1)	Aldershot	24 Sep
Archer	UK		10.0	1)	Aldershot	24 Sep

"Pros":

C. D. Davis	USA		9.75	1)	Bloomington,IL	25 May
George Adams	USA	36	10.0	1)	Newark, OH	

100 metres

William MacLaren	UK		11.0°	1)	Haslingden	27 Jul

° = 110y. (100.58m.) time

200 metres (half-to-full turn)

Edward Colbeck (*22 3/4 220 y.)	UK	47	22.65*	1)	London	31 May
William Collett (4 yds back)	UK	43	23.15*e	2)	London	31 May
C. G. Emery (*23 1/4 220 y.)	UK		23.15*	1)	Liverpool	29 Jun

1868

100 yards

Charles Absolom	UK	46	10.0	1T)	Cambridge	19 Mar
Charles Corfe	UK	47	10.0	1T)	Cambridge	19 Mar
John Tennent	UK	46	10.0	1)	London	03 Apr
T. Clerk	UK		10.0	1)	Wimbledon	30 May
William Tennent	UK	45	10.0 w	1)h	London	19 Jun
Arthur Gwatkin	UK	50	10.0	1)	Cambridge	14 Nov

Doubtful:

T. Sturgeon	UK		10.0	1)	Tamalpore	03 Jan
Lewis Evans	UK	51	10.0	1)	Canterbury	28 Apr
T. Clerk	UK		10.0	1)	Wimbledon	30 May
P. Callaghan	UK		10.0	1T)	Sandhurst	25 Sep
R. Lonsada	UK		10.0	1T)	Sandhurst	25 Sep

200 metres

Charles Bauchope	UK	43	22.9*	1)	London	10 Oct

Doubtful:

William Gair	UK	46	21.9*	1)	Edinburgh	18 Jun
H. D. Parry	UK		22.2*e	2)	Edinburgh	18 Jun

"Pro":

John Rothwell	UK	42	23.4*	1)	Manchester	14 Nov

1869

100 yards

Charles Greenwood	UK		10.0	1)	Durham	27 Feb
John Duckworth	UK	c45	10.0	1)	Ormskirk	15 May

Downhill:

W. Hackingley	UK		10.0	1)h	Aldershot	08 Jul
Ferdinand Tidmarsh	UK		10.0	1)	Aldershot	08 Jul

200 metres (half-to-full turn)

Walter Eaton	UK	48	23.3*	1)	London	15 May
Frederick Hartung	UK	c46	23.4*e	3)hcp	South Norwood	12 Jun

Doubtful:

J. Godfrey	UK		22.4*	1)	Milton Chapel	26 Jul

1870

100 yards

William Dawson	UK	50	10.0	1)	Cambridge	11 Mar
Alfred Baker	UK	c47	10.0	1)	London	02 Apr
John Tobin	Ire		10.0	1)	Cork	07 Apr
John Wilson	UK	48	10.0	1)	London	07 Apr
Thomas Jones	UK	c49	10.0	1)	Birmingham	23 Jul
Charles Pickering	UK	c48	10.0	1)	Knutsford	30 Jul

"Pros":

Frank Hewitt	UK	45	9.75	1)	Melbourne	07 Mar
Jack Harris	Aus		9.75	2)	Melbourne	07 Mar

Downhill and wind assisted:

George Mole	UK	42	9.75w	1)	Liverpool	25 Jun

100 metres

William Dawson	UK	50	11.3°	1)	Cambridge	09 Nov

° = actual time 11 1/3 for 110 y. (100.58 m.)

200 metres (half-to-full turn)

Thomas Hooman	UK	51	23.1*	1)	Walthamstow	01 Oct
T. Lee	UK		23.15*	1)	Hughton	11 Jul
W. Page	UK		23.2*e	2)	Walthamstow	01 Oct
John Clegg	UK	50	23.25*e	2)hcp	Macclesfield	18 Jun

1871

100 yards

John Clegg	UK	50	10.0	1)	Ormskirk	20 May
William Collett	UK	43	10.0	1)	Dublin	07 Jun

Doubtful:

Charles Monnington	UK		10.0	1)	Cirencester	24 Oct

100 metres

F. Salmon	UK		10.7e°	1)	Cambridge	04 Nov

° = actual time 11.0 for 102.9 m.

200 metres (half-to-full turn)

R. Matthews	UK		22.3*e	1)	Horney	13 May

* = actual time 22.2 for 199.8 m.

Doubtful:

John de Haviland	UK	52	22.9*	1)	Oxford	11 Nov

1872

100 yards

Brownlow Martin	Ire		10.0	1)	Dublin	25 May
William Dawson	UK	50	10.0	1)	Sheffield	13 May
A.G. Burn	UK		10.0	1)	Ilminster	01 Jun

200 metres (half-to-full turn)

G. R. Johnstone	UK		23.3*	1)	London	25 May
R. Mathews	UK		23.5*	1)	London	20 Jul

1873

100 yards

George Urmson	UK	c51	10.0	1)	London	31 Mar
Marceline Chabrile	Ire	c51	10.0	1)	Cork	23 Apr

Downhill:

John Clegg	UK	50	9.8	1)	Leicester	26 Jun

100 metres

H. W. Armstrong	UK		11.1e°	1)	London	09 Aug

° = actual time 11.4 for 103 m.

200 metres (half-to-full turn)

John Reay	UK	53	22.7*	1)	London	17 May
G. R. Johnstone	UK		22.9*e	2)	London	17 May

1874

100 yards

Clement Woodland	UK	51	10.2	1)	Cambridge	14 May
Charles Barrett	UK	c51	10.2	1)	Oxford	18 Mar
Edward Nash	UK	c53	10.2	1T)	Oxford	18 Mar
William Gordon	UK	c53	10.2	1T)	Oxford	18 Mar
Jenner Davies	UK	51	10.2	1T)	London	27 Mar
Michael Glazebrook	UK	53	10.2	1T)	London	27 Mar
George Templer	UK	51	10.2	1T)	London	27 Mar
A. H. Pearson	UK		10.2	1)	London	30 Mar
Walter Blaxter	UK	54	10.2	1)	Nottingham	23 May
John McLean	Ire	51	10.2	1)	Dublin	10 Jun
Douglas Ogilby	Ire	53	10.2	1)	Dublin	11 Jun

100 metres

A. G. Tindall	UK		11.3e°	1)	London	18 Jul

° = actual time 11.5 for 102 m.

200 metres (half-to-full turn)

George Blaxter	UK	56	23.4*	1)	Hyde	25 Jul
George Gower	UK	49	23.6*e	3)	London	02 May
Thomas Wraith	UK	c55	23.65*	1)	Gateshead	15 Aug

1875

100 yards

Edward Evans	UK	54	10.2	1)	Oxford	06 Mar
Clement Woodland	UK	51	10.2	1)	London	19 Mar
James Heron	Ire		10.2	1)	Belfast	01 May
John Potter	UK		10.2	1)	Belfast	12 Jun
George Kenny	Ire	55	10.2	1)	Dublin	22 Jun
Frederick Elborough	UK	52	10.25	1)	Sheffield	05 Jul
Walter Blaxter	UK	54	10.25	1)	Widnes	10 Jul

Started by word of mouth – wind assisted:

Douglas Ogilby	Ire	53	10.2w	1)	Dublin	22 May

100 metres

H. McDougall	UK		11.0e°	1)	Wakefield	18 Sep

° = actual time 11.25 for 102.4 m.

200 metres (half-to-full turn)

Douglas Ogilby	Ire	53	23.1*	1)h hcp	Dublin	08 Jun
Frederick Elborough	UK	52	23.15*	1)	London	13 Mar
George Blaxter	UK	56	23.2*e	2)	Sale	26 Jun
A. G. Tindall	UK		23.2*e	2)	Northampton	02 Aug

1876

100 yards

Douglas Ogilby	Ire	53	10.0	1)hcp	Belfast	06 May
Brownlow Martin	Ire		10.0	1)	Dublin	25 May
Montague Shearman	UK	57	10.2	1)	London	07 Apr
A. C. Hunt	USA		10.2	1)	Princeton	24 Jun

Doubtful:

Fred Saportas	USA		10.2	)		

100 metres

F. Goodfellow	Aus		11.0e°	1T)	Newark	05 Jun
G. H. Blaxter	UK		11.0e°	1T)	Newark	05 Jun

° = actual time 11.0 for 110 y. (100.58 m)

200 metres (half-to-full turn)

Frederick Elborough	UK	52	22.5*	1)	London	07 Oct
Charles Lockton	UK	56	22.7*e	2)hcp	Northampton	07 Aug
Alfred Powles	UK	53	23.1*	1)	Dublin	05 Jun
P. Cronhelm	Ire		23.1*	1)	Dublin	26 Aug

1877

100 yards

Horace Lee	USA	59	10.0	1)	Philadelphia	05 May
W. McCord	Ire		10.0	1)h hcp	Belfast	09 Jun
Béla Lipthay	Hun		10.0	1)	Budapest	May

100 metres

E. P. White	UK		11.3e°	1)	Pinner Hill	25 Jul

° = actual time 11.6 for 103.3 m.

200 metres (half-to-full turn)

William Barter	Ire		22.7*e	2)hcp	Dublin	16 Jun
Fred Saportas	USA		22.9*	)	Mott Haven, NY	01 Sep
Horace Lee	USA	59	23.4*	1)	Mott Haven, NY	16 Jul

Doubtful:

Edward Merritt	USA		22.9*			

220 yards (straight course)

Horace Crossley	UK	55	22.7e	2)hcp	London	07 Jul
Charles Lockton	UK	56	23.2	1)	London	27 Oct

1878

100 yards

Horace Lee	USA	59	10.0	1)	Philadelphia	25 May
William Phillips	UK	58	10.0	)	London	25 May
René LaMontagne	USA	56	10.0	1)	Mott Haven, NY	29 Jun
William Wilmer	USA		10.0	1)	New York	06 Jul

Unconfirmed:

Louis Junker	Rus	54	10.0	1)	Woodbridge	22 Apr

100 metres

A. C. Smith	UK		11.25e°	1)	Watton	04 Sep

° = Made over 110 y. (100.58 m.)

200 metres (half-to-full turn)

William Wilmer	USA		22.8*	1)	New York	12 Oct

Doubtful:

Herbert Sturt	UK		22.2*	-)h hcp	Catford Bridge	22 Jun

220 yards (straight course)

William Phillips	UK	58	22.0	1)hcp	London	25 May
John Shearman	UK	56	22.8e	2T)hcp	London	30 Mar
Montague Shearman	UK	57	22.8e	2T)hcp	London	30 Mar

1879

100 yards

Charles Gilbert	UK	55	10.0	1)	Langport	28 Aug
René LaMontagne	USA	56	10.0 +	1)	Mott Haven, NY	20 Sep

+ actually ran 101y (92.35 m.) as he was penalized (1y) for a false start.

Reported as wind-assisted and probably downhill:

Allan	UK	10.0	1)	Birmingham		09 Jun

200 metres (half-to-full turn)

Lon Myers	USA	58	22.65°	1)	Mott Haven, NY	20 Sep

° actually 22 3/4 for 220y.

220 yards (straight course)

Lennard Stokes	UK	56	22.8	1)	London	02 Jul
H. M. Massey	UK		22.9e	2)	London	02 Jul

1880

100 yards

Edward Lucas	UK	60	10.0	1)	Cambridge	09 Mar
Lon Myers	USA	58	10.0	1)hcp	New York	18 Sep
Francis Lucas	UK	62	10.0w	1)	Cambridge	16 Nov

Downhill:

Evert Wendell	USA		10.0	)		

Doubtful:

William Phillips	UK	58	10.0	1)	Woodbridge	31 Mar

100 metres

T. H. Holt	UK		10.9e°	1)	South Norwood	12 Jun

° = actual time 11.2 for 103.3 m.

200 metres (half-to-full turn)

J. H. Stewart	Ire		22.8*e	3)hcp	Dublin	03 Apr
Thomas Clulee	UK	57	22.9*	1)hcp	Northampton	02 Aug
Robert Haley	USA		22.9*	1)	San Francisco	11 Sep
Lon Myers	USA	58	23.1°	-)	Plainfield, NJ	15 Sep

° actual time 23 1/8 for 220y.

220 yards (straight course)

Lon Myers	USA	58	21.8°w	3)hcp	Clifton, NJ	5 Jun

° actual time 21 7/8.

1881

100 yards

W. W. Beveridge	UK		10.0	1)	Glasgow	21 May
Evert Wendell	USA	60	10.0	1)	Cambridge, MA	24 May
Arthur Waldron	USA	61	10.0	1)	New York	11 Jun
C. G. Wilson	USA		10.0	1)	Princeton	18 Jun
E. H. Jones	USA		10.0	1)	Placerville	08 Sep

100 metres

J. Ferguson	UK		10.8e°	1)	Ramsbotham	28 May

° = actual time 11.2 for 103.8 m.

200 metres (half-to-full turn)

Lon Myers	USA	58	22.4°	2)hcp	New York	15 Sep
Henry Brooks	USA	64	23.1"	1)		
Evert Wendell	USA		23.1*	1)	New York	28 May

° Myers ran on an oversize track, with a curve about 60y (54.86 m.) in length.
" Actually 23 1/8 for 220y.

1882

100 yards

Robert Haley	USA		9.8	1)	San Francisco	23 Sep
John White	USA		10.0	1)	(in Canada)	
G. M. Worden	USA		10.0	1)	Mott Haven	29 May
M. W. Ford	USA		10.0	1)	New York	03 Jun
C. G. Words	USA		10.0	1)	Beccles	06 Jul

Doubtful:

G. M. Rowland	SA		9.6	1)	Port Elizabeth	
Tom Malone	Ire	57	9.8	1)	Limerick	15 Jun

"Pros":

N. K. Kettleman	USA		9.75	1)	Bloomington	04 Jul
J. Fitzer	USA		9.75	1)	Salamanca	08 Nov

100 metres

Doubtful:

Galland	Fra	54	11.2	1)	Paris	

200 metres (half-to-full turn)

Henry Brooks	USA	64	22.5*	1)	New York	10 Jun

also: 22 5/8 for 220 y. 1) New York 27 May

Lon Myers	USA	58	22.7*e	2)	New York	10 Jun

Note – Myers was penalized (1 yd) for a false start.

Doubtful:

Galland	Fra	54	22.25	1)	Paris	

1883

100 yards

B. W. McIntosh	USA		10.0	1)	Lafayette	23 May
D. H. Madara	USA		10.0	1)	Minneapolis	09 Jun
A. C. Waldron	USA		10.0	1)	New York	25 Jun
W. C. Lubbock	USA		10.0	1)	Oakland, CA	17 Nov

Downhill:

Frank Ritchie	UK	64	9.8	1)	Birmingham	17 Sep
James Cowie	UK	59	10.0	1)	Birmingham	09 Jun
W. R. Thompson	Can		10.0	1)	Montreal	06 Oct

"Pros":

M. K. Kittleman	USA		9.3/4	1)hcp	Portland, OR	21 Oct
Tom Malone	Ire	57	9.8	1)	Melbourne	Jan
J. T. Crossley	USA		10.0	1)	Richmond	25 May

200 metres (half-to-full turn)

James Cowie	UK	59	22.2*e	4)hcp	London	22 Sep
(2 yds behind 21.9*)						
Henry Brooks	USA	64	22.7*	1)	Mott Haven, NY	02 Jun
Lon Myers	USA	58	22.8*e	2)	Mott Haven,NY	02 Jun

1884

100 yards

L. Roberts	USA		9.8	1)	Macon	16 Apr

Doubtful:

G. W. Rolland	SA		9.9	1)	Durban	04 Oct

"Pros":

H. M. Johnson	USA		9 3/8	1)	San Francisco	Jul
F. Rogers	USA		9 3/8	1)	Trenton	08 Sep
N. K. Kettleman	USA		9.3/4	1)	San Francisco	05 Feb
J. T. Crossley	USA		9.3/4	1)	San Francisco	27 Nov
Tom Malone	Ire	57	9.8	1)	Sydney	Oct

100 metres

Kenyon	UK		11.2e°	1)	Widnes	21 Jun
Henry Potter	USA		11.2#	1)	New York	11 Jun
Thomas Potter	USA		11.25#	1)	New York	25 May

° = actual time 11.4 for 102.4 m.
= made over 110 y. (100.58 m.)

"Not legal":

Arpad Tollinusz	Hun		11.0	)		03 Aug

"Pro":

Tom Malone	Ire	57	10.8e°	1)	Rochester	04 Jun

° = actual time 10.8 for 110 y (100.58 m.)

200 metres (half-to-full turn)

Wendell Baker	USA	64	22.3*	1)	New York	24 May

220 yards (straight course)

Wendell Baker	USA	64	22.4	1)	New York	24 May

Henry Brooks	USA	64	22.5	1)	New Haven	22 May

"Pro":

Tom Malone	Ire	57	21.6	)	Stawell	Nov

1885

100 yards

James Cowie	UK	59	9.8w	1)	Widnes	13 Jun
(Cowie			10.0	1)	Belham	16 Jul
H. M. Raborg	USA		10.0	1)	Jersey City	30 May
G. E. Painter	USA		10.0	1)	Brushton	27 Jun
A. C. Davies	USA		10.0	1)	Woodford	11 Jul
F. J. McQuiggan	USA		10.0	1)	Gloucester	04 Aug
James Scott	Can	c61	10.0	1)	Toronto	01 Sep

Downhill:

Frank Ritchie	UK	64	9.8	1)	Birmingham	12 Sep

"Pros":

Tom Malone	Ire	57	9.6	1)	Melbourne	07 Feb
J. Quirk	USA		9.3/4	1)		23 Jun
H. M. Johnson	USA		9.8	1)	Miamisburg, OH	13 Jul

100 metres

Marshall	USA		11.0e°	1)	Strathroy	Dec

° = 110 y. (100.58 m.) time.

200 metres (half-to-full turn)

James Cowie	UK	59	22.1*	1)hcp	Catford Bridge	25 Jul

"Pro":

Harry Hutchens	UK	58	21.7*	1)	London	11 May

1886

100 yards

Thomas English	USA		10.0	)	Jersey City	12 Jun
William Evans	USA		10.0	1)		19 Jun
F. Walker	USA		10.0	1)	New Haven	20 Oct
Wendell Baker	USA	64	10.0	1)	Boston	01 Jul
Arthur Wharton	UK	65	10.0	1)h	London	03 Jul

Downhill:

Frank Ritchie	UK	64	10.0	1)	Birmingham	17 Jul

"Pros" - doubtful:

E. Boardley	USA		9.75	1)	Philadelphia	30 Oct
Harry Johnson	USA		9.8	)	Cleveland	31 Jul

100 metres

Wendell Baker	USA	64	11.2°	1)	Cambridge, MA	23 May

° = 110 y. (100.58 m.) time

Flag start:

Charles Wood	UK	61	11.2	1)	Paris	01 Nov

"Pro":

F. N. Bonine	USA		11.0e°	1)	New York	29 May

° = 110 y. (100.58 m.) time

200 metres (half-to-full turn)

Charles Wood	UK	61	22.1*	1)	Catford Bridge	24 Jul

220 yards (straight course)

Wendell Baker	USA	64	22.0	1)	Boston	14 Jun
Charles Wood	UK	61	22.2	1)	London	25 Sep

1887

100 yards

Thomas English	USA		9.8	1)	Jersey City	30 May
N. Sheldon	USA		10.0	1)	Racine	26 May
J. A. Murphy	USA		10.0	1)	San Louis	30 Jul
L. D. Goodshall	USA		10.0	1)	Lafayette	28 Jun
Arthur Wharton	UK	65	10.1	1)	Stourbridge	02 Jul

"Pros":

H. M. Johnson	USA		9.5	1)	Springfield	17 Sep
F. Stone	USA		9.5	1)	Helena	09 Oct
Harry Hutchens	UK	58	9.3/4	1T)	Melbourne	29 Jan
W. Clarke	Aus		9.3/4	1T)	Melbourne	29 Jan
H. Ghent	Can		9.3/4	1)	Ottawa	25 Oct

100 metres

Unverified:

Charles Wood	UK	61	10.8	1)	Paris	

200 metres (half-to-full turn)

J. T. Priestley	UK		22.4*	2)hcp	Bradford	23 Jul
Alfred Vigne	Ire		22.7*°	1)	Dublin	30 May
Daniel Bulger	Ire	65	23.3*°	1T)	Dublin	30 May
T. Blair	UK		23.5*	)	Glasgow	26 May

° = In the final of the Irish Ch., Vigne and Bulger dead-heated in 23.4y (23.3*). There was then a run-off and Vigne won easily in 22.8y (22.7*)

220 yards (straight course)

Charles Wood	UK	61	21.8	1)	London	25 Jun
Ernest Pelling	UK	66	22.2e	2)	London	25 Jun

Word of mouth start:

Charles Wood	UK	61	21.6	1)hcp	London	22 Jul

1888

100 yards

Victor Schifferstein	USA	63	9.8	1)	St.Louis	09 Sep

(ratified by the NAAA, not by the AAU – Bill Mallon studied several sources, says this can be considered "the first legal sub-10").

Fred Westing	USA	66	10.0	1)	New Haven	30 Apr
J. S. King	USA		10.0	1)	Princeton	10 May
Walter Dohm	USA	69	10.0	1)	Princeton	20 Oct
C. A. Brand	USA		10.0	1)	Annapolis	Dec

"Pros":

Harry Bethune	Can		9.8	1)	Sioux Falls	28 Aug
H. M. Johnson	USA		9.8	1)	San Louis	16 Oct

200 metres (half-to-full turn)

Fred Westing	USA	66	22.5*	1)	Dublin	09 Jul

220 yards (Straight course)

Fred Westing	USA	66	22.2	1)	Detroit	19 Sep

"Pro":

Harry Bethune	Can		22.2	1)	Oakland, CA	22 Feb

1889

100 yards

Jack Hempton	NZ	63	9.6w	1)	Dunedin	14 Dec
John Owen	USA	61	9.8w	1)	Detroit	03 Aug
J. P. Haughn	USA		10.0	1)	Hot Springs	22 Apr
Fred Westing	USA	66	10.0	1)h	New Haven	30 Apr
CHarles Sherrill	USA	67	10.0	1)	Staten Island	18 May
Luther Cary	USA	68	10.0	1)	Detroit	15 Jun
Peter Vredenburgh	USA	69	10.0	1)	Princeton, NJ	01 Nov
H. F. Greenwood	NZ		10.0w	1)h	Dunedin	14 Dec

"Pros":

J. Kettleman	USA		9.75	1)	Wichita	26 Jan
J. W. Flynn	UK		9.75	1)	New Haven	04 May

100 metres

Charles Sherrill	USA	67	11.2	1)	New York	15 Jun

Actually 110 y. (100.58 m.)

200 metres (half-to-full turn)

Ernest Pelling	UK		22.2°	1)	Catford Bridge	27 Jul

° Exact distance 199.9 m.

1890

100 yards

John Owen	USA	61	9.8	1)	Washington, DC	11 Oct
Luther Cary (1 ft. back)	USA	68	9.9e	2)	Washington, DC	11 Oct
Fred Westing (18 in. f.b.)	USA	66	9.9e	3)	Washington, DC	11 Oct
Charles Sherrill	USA	67	10.0	1)	Cambridge, MA	03 May
C. H. Vincent	SA		10.0	1)	(Natal Ch)	

"Pros":

D. F. Lonergan	USA		9.4	1)	Providence	23 Nov
L. L. Galvin	USA		9.6e	2)	Providence	23 Nov

100 metres

Emile de Ré	Bel		11.0	1)	Bruxelles (Belg.Ch)	
Luther Cary	USA	68	11.2*	1)	New York	07 Jun

* = 110 y. (100.58 m.) time.

Flag start:

Ricardo de Zevallos	Spa		11.2	1)	Paris	08 May

200 metres (half-to-full turn)

Luther Cary	USA	68	21.9*	1)	Princeton, NJ	18 Oct
Fred Westing	USA	66	22.15°	1)	Washington, DC	11 Oct
Thomas Lee	USA		22.3*	1)	New York	Jun
John Owen	USA	61	22.3*	1)	Montreal	27 Sep

° = 220 y. time (22 1/4) less 0.1

1891

100 yards

Luther Cary	USA	68	9.3/4	1)	Princeton, NJ	06 Jun
William Macpherson	Aus		9.8	1)	Auckland	07 Feb
G. R. Swain	USA		9.8	1)	Princeton	09 May

"Pros":

E. S. Skinner	USA		9.3/4	1)	Spokane	06 Jan
J. Gibson	USA		9.8 e	2)	Spokane	06 Jan

100 metres

Emile de Ré	Bel		11.0	1)	Bruxelles (Belg.Ch)	
A. Margis	Fra		11.0	1)r1	Paris	21 May
Charles Bernard	Fra		11.0	1)r4	Paris	21 May
J. Hébert	Fra		11.0	1)	Valéry-en-Caux	30 Aug
Bellon	Fra		11.0	1)	Neuilly-sur-Seine	27 Sep

Flag start:

Luther Cary	USA	68	10.3/4	1)	Paris	04 Jul

200 metres (half-to-full turn)

Mortimer Remington	USA	c68	21.9*	1)	New Ross	04 Jul
Harry Jewett	USA	69	22.1*	1)	New York	17 Oct
Luther Cary	USA	68	22.3*	1)	Huddersfield	Jun
William McPherson	Aus		22.3*	1)		
Harry Carr	Can		22.5*	1)	Montreal	27 Jul

220 yards (straight course)

Luther Cary	USA	68	21.8	1)	New York	31 May
Harry Jewett	USA	69	22.0	1)	Detroit	05 Jul
Mortimer Remington	USA		22.0	1)	New York	19 Sep
James Lee	USA		22.2	2)	New York	31 May
Peter Vredenburgh	USA	69	22.2	3)	New York	31 May

Note – Lee and Vredenburgh actually timed as non-winners.

1892

100 yards

Jack Hempton	NZ	63	9.8	1)	Christchurch	06 Feb
(had a previous 9.8 – Napier 15 Jan – which was not ratified)						
Charles Bradley	UK	69	9.8	1)	London	11 Jul
Harry Jewett	USA	69	9.8w	1T)	Cleveland	13 Aug
John Owen	USA	61	9.8w	1T)	Cleveland	13 Aug
C. W. Jones	SA		9.8	1)	Kimberley	03 Oct

100 metres

Cecil Lee	UK		10.8	1)	Bruxelles	25 Sep
Harald Andersson Arbin	Swe	67	11.0	1)	Göteborg	18 Sep

Flag start:

André Tournois	Fra		10.9	1)	Paris	22 May
A. Margis	Fra		11.0	2)	Paris	22 May

Doubtful:

Doisy	Aus		11.0	1)	Lille	07 Jul

200 metres (half-to-full turn)

Harry Jewett (°)	USA	69	21.5*	1)	Montreal	24 Sep
Edward Allen	USA		22.0*e	2)	Montreal	24 Sep
A. Leithend	Can		22.0*e	3)	Montreal	24 Sep
Norman Macleod	UK	70	22.9*	1)	Glasgow	02 Jul
D. F. Horgan	Ire		23.1*	1)	Dublin	10 Sep

(°) Electrically timed in 21.95 and approved as such by the AAU.

220 yards (straight course)

Harry Jewett	USA	69	21.8w	1)h	New York	01 Oct
William Swayne	USA		22.0	1)	New York	28 May
Luther Cary	USA	68	22.2	)h	New York	01 Oct
Carey Spence	USA		22.2	)h	New York	01 Oct

1893

100 yards

Charles Stage	USA		9.8w?	1)	Cleveland	02 Sep
William Macpherson	Aus		9.9	)	Melbourne	09 Nov
A. E. D'Arcy	NZ		10.0	1)h	Masterton	23 Feb
Charles Bradley	UK	70	10.0	1)	Huddersfield	17 Jun
(also: 10.0 1) Northampton 1 Jul- run uphill!)						
J. M. Hendricks	USA		10.0	1)	Saragota	04 Jul
John Crum	USA		10.0	)		
Arthur Wharton	UK		10.0	)		

Doubtful:

J. S. Barnes	USA		9.6	1)	St.Paul	16 Sep

"Pros":

T. C. Morris	USA		9.8	1)h1	Goshen, IN	15 Jul
Sten Farrell	USA		9.8	1)h2	Goshen, IN	15 Jul
Jack Marsh	Aus	74	9.9	1)h	Sydney	Jul
Jim Collins	USA		9.9e	2)	Goshen, IN	15 Jul

100 metres

Emile de Ré	Bel		10.8	)	Bruxelles	04 Jul
Jean-Guy Gauthier	Fra	75	11.0	)	Paris	04 May

Doubtful:

Delmas	Fra		11.0	)	Constantine	23 Feb?

200 metres (half-to-full turn)

Charles Stage	USA		22.1*	1)h	Chicago	16 Sep
Charles Bradley	UK	70	22.4*?	)		
John Crum	USA		22.5*	)		
D. R. McCulloch	UK		22.5*	1T)	London	03 Jun
J. Black	UK		22.5*	1T)	London	03 Jun
W. T. Macpherson	Aus		22.5*	1)	Melbourne	11 Nov

220 yards (straight course)

Charles Stage	USA		21.6	1)	St.Louis	23 Sep
S. M. Merrill	USA		22.2	1)	Cambridge, MA	29 Apr

1894

100 yards

Charles Bradley	UK	70	9.9w	1)	Manningham	26 May
Jack Hempton	NZ	63	10.0	1)	Wellington	07 Mar
F. H. Bigelow	USA		10.0	1)		
Piet Blignaut	SA		10.0	)		
W. T. Macpherson	Aus		10.0	)		
Frank Stephenson	UK		10.0	1)	Highgate	09 Apr
Ernest Ramsdell	USA	72	10.0	1)	New York	26 May
W. T. Davis	USA		10.0	1)	??	26 May
J. W. Scoggins	USA		10.0	)	Champaign,IL	07 Jun
A. R. Lester	UK		10.0	)		Jul
Thomas Lee	USA		10.0	1)	Montreal	29 Sep
F. Petersen	Den		10.0?	)		

"Pros":

Jack Marsh	Aus	74	9.8	1)hcp	Melbourne	09 Jun
A. S. Henderson	USA		9.8	1)	Denver	19 Aug
H. Appleman	USA		9.9	)		
W. H. Copple	USA		9.9	)		
T. C. Morris	USA		9.9	)		
W. A. Pulley	USA		10.0	)		

100 metres

Charles Bradley	UK	70	10.7e	)	Glasgow	11 Aug
Jean-Guy Gautier	Fra	75	11.0	)	Paris	20 May
Armin Villányi (Weisz)	Hun		11.0	)	Budapest	17 Jun
F. Swaby	UK		11.0	)	Mexbro	12 Jul

Doubtful:

de Joanis	Fra		11.0	1)	Paris	10 May

200 metres (half-to-full turn)

Thomas Lee	USA		21.7*	1)	Montreal	29 Sep

"Pro":

Harry Hutchens	UK 58		21.7*	1)	Paisley	06 Jan

220 yards (straight course)

Ernest Ramsdell	USA	72	22.0	1)	New York	26 May
S. M. Merrill	USA		22.2	1)	New Haven	12 May
J. B. Smull	USA		22.2	)h	New York	26 May
A. Pond	USA		22.3e	2)	New York	26 May
F. H. Bigelow	USA		22.4	)	Worchester	
E. R. Bering	USA		22.4	1)		

1895

100 yards

Charles Bradley	UK	70	9.8w	1)	Cardiff	27 Jul
H. Sharpe	USA		9.8	1)	Cincinnati	29 May
John Crum	USA		9.8	1)	Chicago	15 Jun
H. Sturza	Hun		9.8	1)	Steinamanger	20 Jun
S. M. Alford	USA		9.8	1)	Lexington	29 Aug
Bernard Wefers	USA	73	9.8	1)	New York	21 Sep

One watch only:

Alfred Downer	UK	73	9.8	1T)r2	Stoke-on-Trent	06 Aug
Charles Bradley	UK	70	9.8	1T)r2	Stoke-on-Trent	06 Aug

"Pros":

Edward Donovan	USA		9.6	1)	Brockton, MA	02 Sep
T. C. Morris	USA		9.75e	2)	Brockton, MA	02 Sep

(downhill? w?)

100 metres

L. Atcherley	UK		10.8	1)h	Frankfurt/M	13 Apr
Jean-Guy Gautier	Fra	75	10.8	1)hcp	Asnières	19 May
Harry Beatton	UK		10.8	1)	Rotterdam	28 Aug

(or 22 Aug?)

200 metres (half-to-full turn)

John Crum	USA		21.7*	1)	Chicago	30 Aug
Alfred Downer	UK	73	22.15°	1)	Glasgow	20 Jul
James Maybury	USA	75	22.2*e	2)	Chicago	30 Aug

° = 22 1/4 for 220 y.

220 yards (straight course)

Bernard Wefers	USA	73	21.6	1)	New York	21 Sep
John Crum	USA		21.9e	2)	New York	21 Sep
Gilbert Jordan	UK		22.1e	3)	New York	21 Sep
Ralph Derr	USA		22.2	)		
Charles Stage	USA		22.2e w	3)	New York	14 Sep
Thomas Lee	USA		22.2e w	4)	New York	14 Sep
Armin Villányi (Weisz)	Hun		22.2	1)	Budapest	23 Jun

1896

100 yards

D. Smith	USA		9.8		1)	Danville	18 Apr
Bernard Wefers	USA	73	9.8		1)	New York	30 May
E. A. Robinson	NZ		10.0		1)	Christchurch	04 Jan
W. Meikle	SA		10.0		1)	Kimberley	
C. A. Sulzer	USA		10.0		1)		
Henderson	USA		10.0		1)	Annapolis	02 May
Arthur Holder	NZ	70	10.0		1)	Napier	09 May
J. H. Rush	USA		10.0		1)	Iowa City	23 May
Ralph Derr	USA		10.0		1)	Princeton	23 May
Alfred Downer	UK	73	10.0		1)	Barrow-in-Furness	28 May
James Maybury	USA	75	10.0		1)	Chicago	10 Jun
Charles Bradley	UK	70	10.0		1)	Crewe	13 Jun
J. J. Keane	USA		10.0		1)	Newark	09 Aug
F. K. Schnepp	Boh		10.0		1)	Praha	13 Sep
J. M. O'Mara	USA		10.0		1)	New York	27 Sep
T. C. Morris	USA		10.0	A	1)	Denver	03 Oct
Scott	USA		10.0	A	)	Denver	03 Oct

"Pro":

E. F. Donovan	USA		9.6		1)		

100 metres

Harald Andersson-Arbin	Swe	67	10.8	1)	Helsingborg	09 Aug
E. M. Baker	UK		11.0	)	(in Germany)	
Leleu	Fra		11.0	1)	Rouen	07 May
(downhill ?)						
A. Garnier	Fra		11.0	1)	Paris	04 Jun
Joseph Roffo	Fra		11.0	1)	Paris	04 Jun
Ferd Pedersen	Den		11.0	)	København	08 Sep
F. K. Snep (Schnepp)	Boh		11.0	)	Klatovy	04 Oct

200 metres (half-to-full turn)

James Maybury	USA	75	21.7*	1)	Madison, WI	09 May
Bernard Wefers	USA	73	21.7*	2)hcp	New York	13 Jun
Alfred Downer	UK	73	22.0*e	)hcp	Lancaster	25 May

220 yards (straight course)

Bernard Wefers	USA	73	21.2	1)	New York	30 May
H. C. Woodyatt	UK		21.9e	)	London	04 Jun

1897

100 yards

J. Brunton	USA		9.8	1)	Syracuse	08 Apr
Heywood	USA		9.8	1)		08 May
James Maybury	USA	75	9.8	1)	Madison	08 May
(also 9.8 1) Chicago 5 Jun- more authentic?)						
John Rush	USA	75	9.8	1)	Des Moines	28 May
Bernard Wefers	USA	73	9.8	1)	New York	28 Aug

100 metres

Kurt Doerry	Ger	74	11.0	1)	Berlin	27 Jun
Bruno Diebold	Ger		11.0	1)hcp	Berlin	15 Aug
Alfred Svensson	Swe	76	11.0	1)	Göteborg	05 Sep
L. T'Serstevens	Bel		11.0	)		09 Sep

Doubtful:

Chales Bradley	UK	70	10.8	)		
A. Faverd	Fra		11.0	)	Paris	18 Apr
Falour	Fra		11.0	)	Sceaux	20 May
H. Geiger	Fra		11.0	)	Vincennes	25 Jun

200 metres (half-to-full turn)

James Maybury	USA	75	21.3*	1)	Chicago	05 Jun
H. M. Price	USA		22.1*	)	New York	05 Jun
Philip Blignaut	SA		22.3*	1)	Grahamstown	08 May
(or 22.1* ?)						
Stanley Rowley	Aus	76	22.3*	1)	Sydney	02 Oct

220 yards (straight course)

A. S. Henderson	USA		21.2	1)	Annapolis	08 May
Bernard Wefers	USA	73	21.4	1)	New York	28 Aug
John Rush	USA	75	21.8	1)	Des Moines	28 May
James Maybury	USA	75	21.8e	2)	New York	28 Aug
(11 ft. – 3.35 m. - beh. Wefers' 21.4)						
Alvin Kraenzlein	USA	76	21.8	)		

4x100 metre relay

AC Sparta Praha	Boh		48.2	1)	Praha	26 Jun
(B.Pohl, F.Schnepp, K.Malecek, J.Havel)						

1898

100 yards

Charles Burroughs	USA		9.8	1)	Chicago	04 Jun ?
John Rush	USA	75	9.8	1)	Chicago	18 Jun
James Maybury	USA	75	9.9e	2)	Chicago	18 Jun
Maxwell Long	USA	78	9.9e	3)	Chicago	18 Jun

Doubtful:

W. G. Knapp	USA		9.8	1)	Princeton, NJ	22 Apr

Downhill:

Charles Thomas	UK	75	9.9	1)	Abergavenny	03 Aug

100 metres

Bieth	Fra		10.8	)	Toulouse	25 May
Philip Blignaut	SA		10.8	1)hcp	Paris	10 Jul
Isaac Westergren	Swe	75	10.8	)	Gävle	11 Sep

200 metres (half-to-full turn)

Charles Burroughs	USA		21.9*		1)	Chicago	04 Jun
Maxwell Long	USA	78	21.9*		1)	Montreal	24 Sep
Frank Jarvis	USA	78	22.1*		)		
Alfred Downer	UK	73	22.1*		1)	Glasgow	
F. L. Stephen	Can		22.1*		)	Charlottestown	10 Sep
John Tewksbury	USA	76	22.1*	?	2)e	Montreal	24 Sep

220 yards (straight course)

John Tewksbury	USA	76	21.6	1)	New York	28 May
Alvin Kraenzlein	USA	76	21.8 ?	1)		
John Rush	USA	75	21.9e	2)	New York	28 May
Maxwell Long	USA	78	22.0	1)	Princeton	21 May
Bernard Wefers	USA	73	22.0	1)	New Orleans	15 May
Connelly	USA		22.0	1)	Brooklyn, NY	05 Sep

1899

100 yards

John Rush	USA	75	9.8	)		
John Tewksbury	USA	76	9.8	)	Elmira	May
Frank Jarvis	USA	78	9.8	1)	Elmira	30 May
Arthur Duffey	USA	79	9.8w	1)h	Newton, MA	26 Aug
Stanley Rowley	Aus	76	9.9	1)	Brisbane	11 Nov

Doubtful conditions:

Ernö Schubert	Hun	c81	9.8	1)	Praha	02 Jul

100 metres

Isaac Westergren	Swe	75	10.8w	1)	Gävle	10 Sep

Doubtful:

Massip	Fra		10.6	)	Agen	

200 metres (half-to-full turn)

Stanley Rowley	Aus	76	22.1*	1)	Brisbane	11 Nov
Maxwell Long	USA	78	22.3*	1)	Newton, MA	26 Aug
Frank Stephens	Can		22.4*e	2)	Newton, MA	26 Aug
Z. Speidl	Hun		22.4w	1)	Budapest	17 Sep
Charles Burroughs	USA		22.5*	1)	Chicagop	03 Jun
William Welsh	UK	79	22.5*	1)	Edinburgh	
John Morrow	Can		22.5*	1)	Montreal	13 Oct

220 yards (straight course)

John Tewksbury	USA	76	21.2	1)	Princeton, NJ	22 Apr
D. Boardman	USA		21.6	1)	New Haven	22 Apr
F. B. Fox	USA		21.6	1)	Milwaukee	20 May
Frank Stephens	Can		22.0	1)	Halifax	17 Aug

1900

100 yards

John Tewksbury	USA	76	9.8	)		
Alfred Hind	UK	78	9.8w?	1)	Cambridge	12 Mar
Arthur Duffey	USA	79	9.8	1)	Philadelphia	28 Apr

100 metres

John Tewksbury	USA	78	10.8	1)	Philadelphia	12 Jun
Frank Jarvis	USA	78	10.8	1)h3	Paris	14 Jul
Angely	Fra		11.0	1)	Marseille	13 May
Marmonnier	Fra		11.0	1)	Grenoble	10 Jun
Henriquez	Fra		11.0	1)	Grenoble	21 Jun
Leblanc	Fra		11.0	1)	Grenoble	21 Jun
Arthur Duffey	USA	79	11.0	1)s1	Paris	14 Jul
Stanley Rowley	Aus	76	11.0	1)°	Paris	14 Jul
(° repêchage)						
Carl Levi	Ger		11.0	1)	Stöckach	02 Sep
H. Hellmich	Hun		11.0	)	Wien	02 Sep
Erich Ludwig	Ger		11.0	1)	Frankfurt/M	09 Sep
Max Wartenberg	Ger		11.0	1)h hcp	Hamburg	22 Sep

Downhill:

Geo Malfait	Fra	78	10.9	1)	Roubaix	19 Aug

On road:

Carl Ljung	Swe		10.8	)	Stockholm	23 Sep

200 metres (half-to-full turn)

M. F. Canyon	USA		21.9*	1T)	Chicago	12 May
Henry Slack	USA	77	21.9*	1T)	Chicago	12 May
Maxwell Long	USA	78	21.9*	1)	Whitehaven	17 Aug
R. W. Albertson	USA		22.1*	1)	Milwaukee	14 Sep
John Tewksbury	USA	76	22.2	1)	Paris	22 Jul
A. Cadogan	USA		22.3*	1)	Chicago	02 Jun

220 yards (straight course)

William Schick	USA	81	21.6	1)	Cambridge, MA	09 Jun
P. L. Van Nuis	USA		21.8	1)	Princeton	21 Apr

Fay Moulton	USA	78	22.2e	2)	Princeton	21 Apr
H. L. Taylor	USA		22.2	1)	Syracuse, NY	05 May
Ira Richards	USA		22.2	1)h	Cambridge, MA	12 May
D. Boardman	USA		22.2	1)	Cambridge, MA	12 May
C. D. Young	USA		22.2	)	Ithaca	12 May
H. H. Cloudman	USA		22.2	)	Worcester	19 May
S. M Sears	USA		22.2	)	Ithaca	02 Nov

Doubtful:

M. J. Cregan	USA		21.5	1)	New York	30 May

ALL TIME WORLD LIST OF BEST AMATEUR PERFOMERS AS AT THE END OF 1900

100 yards

Jack Hempton	NZ	63	9.6w	1)	Dunedin	14 Dec 89
Luther Cary	USA	68	9.3/4	1)	Princeton, NJ	06 Jun 91
Robert Haley	USA		9.8	1)	San Francisco	23 Sep 82
L. Roberts	USA		9.8	1)	Macon	16 Apr 84
James Cowie	UK	59	9.8w	1)	Widnes	13 Jun 85
Thomas English	USA		9.8	1)	Jersey City	30 May 87
Victor Schifferstein	USA	63	9.8	1)	St. Louis	09 Sep 88
John Owen	USA	61	9.8	1)	Washington,D.C.	11 Oct 90
William Macpherson	Aus		9.8	1)	Auckland	07 Feb 91
G. R. Swain	USA		9.8	1)	Princeton, NJ	09 May 91
(J. Hempton			9.8	1)	Christchurch	06 Feb 92
Charles Bradley	UK	69	9.8	1)	London	11 Jul 92
Harry Jewett	USA	69	9.8w	1T)	Cleveland	13 Aug 92
C. W. Jones	SA		9.8	1)	Kimberley	03 Oct 92
Charles Stage	USA		9.8w ?	1)	Cleveland	02 Sep 93
H. Sharpe	USA		9.8	1)	Cincinnati	29 May 95
John Crum	USA		9.8	1)	Chicago	15 Jun 95
H. Sturza	Hun		9.8	1)	Steinamanger	20 Jun 95
S. M. Alford	USA		9.8	1)	Lexington	29 Aug 95
Bernard Wefers	USA	73	9.8	1)	New York	21 Sep 95
D. Smith	USA		9.8	1)	Canville	18 Apr 96
J. Brunton	USA		9.8	1)	Syracuse	08 Apr 97
Heywood	USA		9.8	1)		08 May 97
James Maybury	USA	75	9.8	1)	Madison	08 May 97
John Rush	USA	75	9.8	1)	Des Moines	28 May 97
Charles Burroughs	USA		9.8	1)	Chicago	04? Jun 98
John Tewksbury	USA	76	9.8	)	Elmira	May 99
Frank Jarvis	USA	78	9.8	1)	Elmira	30 May 99
Alfred Hind	UK	78	9.8w?	1)	Cambridge	12 Mar 00
Arthur Duffey	USA	79	9.8	1)	Philadelphia	28 Apr 00

100 metres

F. Salmon	UK		10.7e	1)	Cambridge	04 Nov 71
Charles Bradley	UK	70	10.7e	)	Glasgow	11 Aug 94
J. Ferguson	UK		10.8e	1)	Ramsbotham	28 May 81
Cecil Lee	USA		10.8	1)	Bruxelles	25 Sep 92
Emile de Ré	Bel		10.8	)	Bruxelles	04 Jul 93
L. Atcherley	UK		10.8	1)h	Frankfurt/M	13 Apr 95
Jean-Guy Gautier	Fra	75	10.8	1)	Asnières	19 May 95
Harry Beatton	UK		10.8	1)	Rotterdam	28 Aug 95
Harald Andersson-Arbin	Swe	67	10.8	1)	Helsingborg	09 Aug 96
Bieth	Fra		10.8	)	Toulouse	25 May 98
Philip Blignaut	SA		10.8	1)hcp	Paris	10 Jul 98
Isaac Westergren	Swe	75	10.8	)	Gävle	11 Sep 98
John Tewksbury	USA	78	10.8	1)	Philadelphia	12 Jun 00
Frank Jarvis	USA	78	10.8	1)h3	Paris	14 Jul 00

200 metres (half-to-full turn)

James Maybury	USA		21.3*	1)	Chicago	05 Jun 97
Harry Jewett	USA	69	21.5*	1)	Montreal	24 Sep 92
Thomas Lee	USA		21.7*	1)	Montreal	29 Sep 94
John Crum	USA		21.7*	1)	Chicago	30 Aug 95
Bernard Wefers	USA	73	21.7*	2)hcp	New York	13 Jun 96
Luther Cary	USA	68	21.9*	1)	Princeton, NJ	18 Oct 90
Mortimer Remington	USA	c68	21.9*	1)	New Ross	04 Jul 91
Charles Burroughs	USA		21.9*	1)	Chicago	04 Jun 98
Maxwell Long	USA	78	21.9*	1)	Montreal	24 Sep98
M. F. Canyon	USA		21.9*	1T)	Chicago	12 May 00
Henry Slack	USA	77	21.9*	1T9	Chicago	12 May 00

220 yards (straight course)

Bernard Wefers	USA	73	21.2	1)	New York	30 May 96
A. S. Henderson	USA		21.2	1)	Annapolis	08 May 97
John Tewksbury	USA	76	21.2	1)	Princeton, NJ	22 Apr 99
Charles Stage	USA		21.6	1)	St. Louis	23 Sep 93
D. Boardman	USA		21.6	1)	New Haven	22 Apr 99
F. B. Fox	USA		21.6	1)	Milwaukee	20 May 99
William Schick	USA	81	21.6	1)	Cambridge, MA	09 Jun 00

4x100 metre relay

AC Sparta Praha	Boh		48.2	1)	Praha	26 Jun 97
(B.Pohl, F.Schnepp, K.Malecek, J.Havel)						

1901

100 yards

Alfred Hind	UK	78	9.8w	1)	Cambridge	14 Mar
Lee Deming	USA		9.8	1)	St.Louis	18 May
Frank Stephens	Can		9.8	1)	Halifax	19 May
Arthur Duffey	USA	79	9.8	1)	New York	24 May
Frank Sears	USA		9.8	1)	Buffalo, NY	15 Jun
G. E. Ross	USA		9.8	1)		04 Jul
Archie Hahn	USA	80	9.8w	1)		
Pat Webster	NZ		9.9	1)	Wanganui	22 Jan

"Pros":

Lachie McLachlan	NZ		9.6	1)	Wanganui	22 Jan
F. H. Somers	NZ		9.9e	2)	Napier	23 Feb

100 metres

Otto Lindemann	Ger	81	11.0	1)	Berlin	14 Jul
Max Wartenberg	Ger		11.0	1)	Hamburg	22 Sep
Fritz Götze	Ger		11.0	1)	Frankfurt/M	29 Sep

Downhill:

Jimmy Carré	Fra		10.8	1)	Rouen	09 Jun
E. Fabre	Fra		10.8e	2)	Rouen	09 Jun
Basil Wood	UK		11.0	1)h	Rouen	09 Jun
Coulon	Fra		11.0e	2)h	Rouen	09 Jun

Doubtful conditions:

Gomond	Fra		10.4	1)	Alençon	09 Jun
Chachignon	Fra		11.0	)	Paris	19 May
Emil Bär	Ger		11.0	1)	Leipzig	Sep

200 metres (half-to-full turn)

Clifford Bell	USA		21.9*	1)	Madison	17 May
Edward Merrill	USA		22.5*	1)	Chicago	01 Jun
H. Henderson	Aus		22.6*	1)	Melbourne	11 Nov
T. Heaney	USA		22.7*	1)	Madison	
J. McLean	UK		22.7*	1)	London	27 Jul
George Moir	USA		22.7*	1)h	Auckland	21 Dec

"Pro":

Lachie McLachlan	NZ		21.9*	1)	Pachiatua	23 Jan

220 yards (straight course)

N. H. Hargrave	USA		21.4	1)	New Haven, CT	03 May
Frank Sears	USA		21.6	1)	New York	24 May
William Schick	USA	81	21.6	1)	Cambridge, MA	05 Jun
L. V. Bell	USA		21.8	1)	Champaign, IL	25 May
A. Cadogan	USA		22.0	1)	Eugene	06 May
C. Dupee	USA		22.0	1)	Cambridge, MA	11 May
H. H. Cloudman	USA		22.0	1)	New York	24 May

4x100 metre relay

Tampere SLU	Fin		47.4	1)	Helsinki	

(Rydman, Alenius, Groublom, Volanen)

1902

100 yards

Arthur Duffey	USA	79	9.6	1)	New York	31 May
William Schick	USA	81	9.8	1)	Cambridge, MA	24 May
Herbert Hunter	Aus		9.8	1)	Melbourne	10 Nov
Nigel Barker	Aus	84	9.9	1)	Sydney	
Fay Moulton	USA	76	9.9e	2)	Cambridge, MA	31 May
John Westney	USA	80	9.9e	3)	New York	31 May

Doubtful conditions:

Arthur Duffey	USA	79	9.5	)hcp	Wolverhampton	28 Jun

100 metres

Ernest Kuhn	Swz	79	11.0	1)	Bordeaux	08 Jun
Eugène Choisel	Fra	81	11.0	1)	Le Mans	15 Jun
Grass	Ger		11.0	1)hcp	Berlin	20 Jul
Max Wartenberg	Ger		11.0	1)	Hannover	03 Aug
Fritz Carlsson	Swe	78	11.0	1)	Stockholm	17 Aug
Carl Moldestad	Nor		11.0	1)	Bergen	24 Aug
Harald Åsbrink	Swe		11.0	1)	Gävle	28 Sep

Doubtful electric time:

Minoru Fujii	Jap		10.24	-)	Tokyo	14 Nov

200 metres (half-to-full turn)

Patrick Walsh	USA		21.5*	1)	Montreal	21 Sep
James Craig	Can		21.6*e	2)	Montreal	21 Sep
Frederick Moloney	USA		21.9*	1)	Chicago	17 May
Clyde Blair	USA		21.9*	1)	Chicago	07 Jun

"Pro":

Lachie McLachlan	NZ		21.3*	1)	Napier	19 Feb

220 yards (straight course)

John Haigh	USA		21.6	1)s1	New York	30 May
Milton Lightner	USA		21.6	1)	New York	31 May
George Poage	USA	80	21.8	1)	Champaign, IL	16 May
William Schick	USA	81	22.0	1)	Cambridge, MA	24 May
Victor Rice	USA		22.0	1)	Terre Haute	07 Jun

4x100 metre relay

IFK Gävle	Swe		46.0	1)	Gävle	28 Sep

(Westergren, Lidén, Åsbrink, Arnell)

1903

100 yards

Fay Moulton	USA	76	9.8	1)	New Haven, CT	09 Mar
Clyde Blair	USA		9.8	1)	Chicago	30 May
Frank Sears	USA		9.8	1)		
Arthur Duffey	USA	79	9.8	1)	Birmingham	11 Jul
William Schick	USA	81	9.9e	3)	New York	30 May

Note – Name of winner in New York, 30 May (Arthur Duffey) stricken from records, as explained in the text.

100 metres

Ernest Kuhn	Swz	79	10.8	1T)	Gradignan	14 Jun
André Passat	Fra		10.8	1T)	Gradignan	14 Jun

Doubtful:

Harald Grönfelfdt	Den		10.8	1)	Aarhus	05 Jul

Downhill:

Geo Malfait	Fra	78	10.8	1)	Roubaix	19 Jul
Eric Frick	Swe		10.8	1)	Jönköping	09 Aug

Short track (99.79 m.):

Reinhold Herting	Ger	78	10.8	1)hcp	Berlin	23 Aug

200 metres (half-to-full turn)

Archie Hahn	USA	80	21.5*	1)	Chicago	30 May
William Hogenson	USA	84	22.1*	1)	Chicago	06 Jun
Nathan Cartmell	USA	83	22.3*	1)	Nashville, TN	02 May
L. B. Webster	NZ		22.5*	1)	Dunedin	07 Mar
Walter Eckersall	USA		22.5*	1)h	Chicago	06 Jun
Reginald Wadsley	UK		22.5*	1)		

"Pros":

Beauchamp Day	Ire	82	22.1*	1)	Rochdale	16 Sep
Reginald Wadsley	UK		22.2*e	2)	Rochdale	16 Sep

220 yards (straight course)

Fay Moulton	USA	76	21.6	1)	Princeton	09 May
Frank Sears	USA		21.6	1)	Ithaca, NY	16 May
Milton Lightner	USA		21.6	1)h	New York	30 May
Frank Castleman	USA	77	21.6	1)	New York	30 May
H. K. Tootle	USA		22.0	1)	Baltimore	07 May
Archie Hahn	USA	80	22.0	1)	Ann Arbor	09 May
William Schick	USA	81	22.0	1)	Cambridge, MA	16 May
Walter Eckersall	USA		22.0	1)	Champaign	16 May

4x100 metre relay

TV München 1879 (W.Keyl, O.Reissner, J.Buchheit, J.Keyl)	Ger		47.4	1)	Frankfurt/M	23 Aug
Allmänna IK, Sthlm (Carlsson-Carling, Lindquist, Ljung, Insulander)	Swe		48.6	1)	Stockholm	Aug

1904

100 yards

John Churchill	UK	81	9.8w	1)	Cambridge	09 Mar
W. J. Torrey	USA		9.8	1)	New Haven	30 Apr
Archie Hahn	USA	80	9.8	1)	Ann Arbor	14 May
G. L. Swasey	USA		9.8	1)	Hanover	14 May
William Eaton	USA	82	9.8	1)	Boston	04 Jul
William Schick	USA	81	9.8	1)	London	23 Jul
John Morton	UK	79	9.8	1)	London	17 Sep

"Pro":

Ettore Capucci	Ita		9.8	1)	Glasgow	15 Feb

100 metres

John Morton	UK	79	10.9e	)	London	24 Sep
Ferdinand Asimus	Ger	80	11.0	1)	Stuttgart	07 Aug
Willy Kohlmey	Ger	81	11.0	1)h3 hcp	Stettin	14 Aug
Archie Hahn	USA	80	11.0	1)	St. Louis	03 Sep

Unconfirmed:

Willy Kohlmey	Ger	81	10.8	)	Berlin	

Doubtful timing:

Max Schreiber	Ger		10.8	1)	Halle	18 Sep

200 metres (half-to-full turn)

Victor Rice	USA		22.1*	1)	Chicago	21 May
Nigel Barker	Aus	84	22.3*	1)h	Melbourne	01 Feb
C. H. Jones	SA		22.3* A	1)	Johannesburg	Apr
John McEniry	Ire		22.3*	1)	Cork	28 May
William Murray	Ire	85	22.3*	1)hcp	Glasgow	13 Aug
Patrick Walsh	USA		22.3*	1)	Montreal	24 Sep

"Pro":

Ettore Capucci	Ita		22.3*	1)	Berwick	30 Apr

220 yard (Straight course)

Nathaniel Cartmell	USA	83	21.4	1)	Ithaca, NY	14 May
William Schick	USA	81	21.4	1)	Philadelphia	28 May
Archie Hahn	USA	80	21.6	1)	Ann Arbor	14 May
Charles Long	USA	82	21.8	1)	New Haven	07 May
L. Leventritt	USA		21.8	1)	Princeton	14 May
William Hogenson	USA	85	21.8	1)	Chicago	28 May
H. E. Martın	USA		21.8	1)	St. Louis	11 Jun
Fay Moulton	USA	76	21.8	1)	St. Louis	30 Jul

4x100 metre relay

University Team (Alenius, Volanen, Jääskeläinen, Hällström)		Fin	46.6	)		

1905

100 yards

William Schick	USA	81	9.8	1)	New Haven	20 May
Harry Hillman	USA	81	9.8	1)	Albany	04 Jul
Charles Parsons	USA		9.8	1)	Portland, OR	05 Aug
Eldridge Eatman	Can		9.8	1)	Moncton	02 Sep
John Morton	UK	79	9.8	1)	Montreal	04 Sep
George Queyrouze	USA		9.8	1)	Birmingham, AL	28 Oct

100 metres

Vincent Duncker	Ger/SA	84	10.8	1)h	Berlin	06 Aug
Fritz Carlsson	Swe	78	10.9	1)	Stockholm	09 Sep
Hermann Lindqvist	Swe	86	10.9	1)	Stockholm	10 Sep

Downhill:

G. Bürger	Ger		10.9	)	Kempten	25 Jul

200 metres (half-to-full turn)

Nigel Barker	Aus	84	21.7*	1)	Sydney	22 Apr
William Hogenson	USA	85	21.9*	1)	Chicago	03 Jun
Harvey Blair	USA		22.1*	1)	Chicago	10 Jun
Archie Hanh	USA	80	22.1*	1)	Portland, OR	05 Aug

Charles Parsons	USA		22.2*e	2)	Portland, OR	05 Aug
Clyde Blair	USA		22.2*e	3)	Portland, OR	05 Aug

Doubtful:

John Morton	UK	79	22.1*	1)	Darlington	

"Pro":

T. F. Keane	USA		21.7*	1)	Glasgow	04 Feb

220 yards (straight course)

William Schick	USA	81	21.4	1)	New Haven	20 May
Forrest Smithson	USA	81	21.4	1)	Salem	10 Jun
Harry Hyman	USA		21.8	1)	Philadelphia	12 May
William Hogenson	USA	85	21.8	1)	Ann Arbor	20 May
L. E. Waller	USA		21.8	1)	Champaign, IL	20 May

4x100 metre relay

Turun SLU	Fin		46.3	)		
(Simola, Heikkilä, Tefke, Tiiri)						

1906

100 yards

Dan Kelly	USA	83	9.6	1)	Spokane, WA	23 Jun
Lee Carey	USA		9.8	1)	Annapolis	12 May
John Morton	UK	79	9.8	1)	Crewe	23 Jun
Robert Kerr	Can	82	9.8	1)	Toronto	02 Jul
Joseph White	Can	87?	9.8	1)	Toronto	01 Sep

"Pro" - downhill:

Arthur Postle	Aus		9.5	)	Kalgoorlie	28 Dec

100 metres

Knut Lindberg	Swe	82	10.6	1)	Göteborg	26 Aug
Emile Lesieur	Fra	85	10.8	1)	Saint-Cloud	06 May
Vincent Duncker	Ger/SA	84	10.8	1)	Mittweida	27 May
Leonard Tremeer	UK	74	10.8	1)	Bruxelles	21 Jul
Paul Schröder	Ger	82	10.8	1)	Mönchen-Gladbach	26 Aug
Heinrich Berger	Ger		10.8	1)h	Köln	02 Sep
Ivar Neuman	Swe		10.8	1)	Sundsvall	23 Sep

200 metres (half-to-full turn)

Lee Carey	USA		21.9*	1)	Annapolis	12 May
Harvey Blair	USA		22.1*	1)	Chicago	30 Jun
Lawson Robertson	USA	83	22.3*	1)h	New York	08 Sep
Ralph Young	USA		22.3*	1)	New York	08 Sep
Robert Kerr	Can	82	22.3*	1)	Montreal	22 Sep

220 yards (straight course)

Dan Kelly	USA	83	21.2	1)	Spokane, WA	23 Jun
(„slightly curved track")						
J. D. Whitham	USA		21.8	1)	Philadelphia	05 May
Lawrence Dodge	USA		21.8	1)	Cambridge, MA	19 May
Robert Branham	USA		21.8	1)		
Robert Kerr	Can	82	22.0	1)	Toronto	02 Jul

4x100 metre relay

AIK Stockholm	Swe		45.4	1)	Stockholm	16 Sep
(Ljung, Frick, Carlsson -later Carling-, Ljung)						

1907

100 yards

Charles Parsons	USA		9.8	1)	Los Angeles	30 Mar
William May	USA	78	9.8	1)	Chicago	01 Jun
Nathaniel Cartmell	USA	83	9.8	1)	Norfolk, VA	22 Jun
Robert Kerr	Can	82	9.8	1)	Toronto	20 Jul
Harold Huff	USA	81	9.8	1)	Chicago	31 Aug

"Pro":

Walter Knox	Can	78	9.6	1)	San Francisco	25 Jul

100 metres

Heinrich Rheder	Ger	87	10.8	1)	Hamburg	30 Jun
Arno Neumann	Ger	85	10.8	1)	Dresden	Jul
Uuno Railo	Fin	87	10.8	1)	Tampere	04 Aug
Knut Stenborg	Swe	90	10.8w	1)	Göteborg	13 Oct

Flying start:

K. Dopheide	Ger		10.6	1)	Bielefeld	04 Aug
H. Kobold	Ger		10.8	1)s	Barmen	01 Sep

Doubtful:

George Easton	UK		10.4	1)	Helsinki	01 Sep
Uuno Railo	Fin	87	10.6	1)	Tampere	28 Aug

200 metres (half-to-full turn)

Nathaniel Cartmell	USA	83	21.5*	1)	Norfolk, VA	22 Jun
Frank Hamilton	USA	84	21.7*	1)	Chicago	31 Aug
Harold Huff	USA	81	21.9*	1)	Chicago	01 Jun
Dan Kelly	USA	83	21.9*e	2)	Norfolk, VA	22 Jun
Frederick Ramsdell	USA		21.9*e	3)	Norfolk, VA	22 Jun
Patrick Roche	Ire	86	22.1*	1)	Cork	09 Jun
W. J. Keating	USA		22.1*	1)	Norfolk, VA	06 Sep

220 yards (straight course)

Dan Kelly	USA	83	21.6	1)	Eugene	15 May
Jay Whitham	USA		21.8	1)	Philadelphia	05 May
Nathaniel Cartmell	USA	83	21.8	1)	Cambridge, MA	01 Jun

4x100 metre relay

Combined Team	Swe/UK	44.6	1)	Stockholm	08 Sep
(Stenborg/Swe, Möller/Swe, Lindberg/Swe, Morton/UK)					
AIK Stockholm	Swe	45.0	1)	Stockholm	04 Aug
(Ljung, Frick, Almqvist, Carlsson – later Carling -)					

1908

100 yards

James Rector	USA	84	9.4w	1)	Charlottesville	09 May
Les Morgan	Aus		9.8	1)	Melbourne	25 Apr
Ernest Nelson	USA		9.8	1)	Cambridge, MA	02 May
R. K. Mason	USA		9.8	1)	Atlanta	23 May
William May	USA	78	9.8	1)	Chicago	06 Jun
Reginald Walker	SA	89	9.8	1)	Glasgow	Jul
H. J. Fay	Aus		9.8	1)	Brisbane	25 Jul
Robert Kerr	Can	82	9.8	1)	Halifax	03 Sep
William Martin	USA		9.8	)		

Downhill:

Reginald Walker	SA	89	9.4	1)	Abergavenny	04 Aug

100 metres

Willy Spreng	Ger	84	10.8	1)	Langen	05 Jul
Reginald Walker	SA	89	10.8	1)s1	London	21 Jul
James Rector	USA	84	10.8	1)h	Philadelphia	06 Jun
Harold Huff	USA	81	10.8	1)	Pittsburgh	20 Jun
Jean Konings	Bel		10.8	1)	Bruxelles	15 Aug
Knut Lindberg	Swe	82	10.8w	1)	Göteborg	30 Aug

Doubtful:

Willy Trautmann	Ger		10.6	1)	Mannheim	02 Aug
Fr. Schäfer	Ger		10.8	)		
Kurt Lattas	Ger		10.8	2)	Mannheim	02 Aug

200 metres (half-to-full turn)

Robert Kerr	Can	82	21.3*	1)	Toronto	26 Sep
Reuben Povey	SA	89	21.9*	1)	Port Elizabeth	09 Nov
Harold Huff	USA	81	22.1*	1)	Chicago	06 Jun
William Hamilton	USA	84	22.1*	1)	Chicago	12 Sep
Lon Siebert	Can		22.2*e	2)	Halifax	29 Aug

"Pro":

Beauchamp Day	Ire	82	21.65*	1)	Oldham	14 Nov

21 3/4 over 220 y. (201.16 m.)

220 yards (straight course)

Nathaniel Cartmell	USA	83	21.9°	1)	Philadelphia	06 Jun
Huston	USA		22.0	1)	Pullman	16 May
William Hamilton	USA	84	22.1°	1)	Colombes	01 Aug

° = 200 m. time plus 0.1

4x100 metre relay

Berlin Team	Ger		44.0	1)	Frankfurt/M	30 Aug

(Kohlmey, Rau, Falk, Hoffmann) with standing baton changes

1909

100 yards

Jack Nelson	USA		9.7e		)hcp	Pullman	29 May
(actually 9.6 over 99.5 y. = 90.9 m)							
Reginald Walker	SA	89	9.8	A	1)	Johannesburg	07Apr
Lee Carey	USA		9.8		1)	Annapolis	08 May
Robert Kerr	Can	82	9.8		1)	Toronto	11 Sep

100 metres

Reginald Walker	SA	89	10.7	A	1)	Pretoria	01 Jan
Frederick Ramsdell	USA		10.8°		1)	New York	31 May
A. Nieschlag	Ger		10.8		1)	Hannover	25 Jul
Knut Lindberg	Swe	82	10.8		1)	Göteborg	12 Sep
Richard Rau	Ger	89	10.8 w		1)	Duisburg	08 Aug
Fritz Weinzinger	Aut	90	10.8		1)	Wien	03 Oct

° = 110 y. (100.58 m.) time

Unconfirmed:

Willy Kohlmey	Ger	81	10.8	1)	Praha	04 Jul

200 metres (half-to-full turn)

Lee Carey	USA		21.5*	1)	Annapolis	08 May
Ron Opie	NZ	90	21.9*	1)s	Christchurch	03 Apr
Nathaniel Cartmell	USA	83	21.9*	1)	London	03 Jul
Robert Kerr	SA	82	21.9*	1)	London	18 Jul
William Hamilton	USA	84	21.9*	1)	Chicago	06 Aug
Reuben Povey	SA	89	21.9*	)		
Leroy Dorland	USA	89	22.1*	1)	Montreal	15 Sep

220 yards (straight course)

Robert Kerr	Can	82	21.4	1)	Ottawa	21 Apr
Reginald Foster	USA		21.4	1)	New Haven	15 May
Warring Dawbarn	USA		21.6	1)	Princeton	08 May
William May	USA		21.6	1)	San Francisco	21 Aug

Note – Kerr did 21.4 again at Toronto on 11 Sep. Only the latter was ratified.

4x100 metre relay

Wiener AC	Aut	44.2	1)	Wien	04 Jul

(Brünner, Tekusch, Schönecker, Weinzinger)

1910

100 yards

Marion Roberts	USA		9.6w		1)	Amherst	07 May
Clement Wilson	USA	91	9.6		1)	Cedar Rapids	11 Jun
Billy Woodger	NZ		9.8ew		2T)hcp	Wellington	19 Feb
Waldo Throop	USA		9.8		1)	Claremont	19 Mar
Stanley Hill	USA		9.8		1)	Madison, WI	14 May
F. T. Haddock	USA		9.8		1)	Lawrence	14 May
Byrd	USA		9.8		1)	Clemson	14 May
Robert Kerr	Can	82	9.8		1)	Ottawa	23 May
Frank Lukeman	Can		9.8		1)	Toronto	04 Jun
John Nelson	USA	85	9.8		1)		
Huston	USA		9.8				
P. Redmond	Aus		9.8		1)h	Sydney	03 Dec

Doubtful:

George Patching	SA	86	9.5				

"Pros":

Jack Donaldson	Aus	86	9.375	A	1)	Johannesburg	12 Feb
Arthur Postle	Aus	81	9.625e	A	2)	Johannesburg	12 Feb

(Donaldson timed in 9 3/8)

100 metres

Emil Ketterer	Ger	83	10.8	1)	München	26 Jun
Hanns Braun	Ger	86	10.8	1)	Zoppot	24 Jul
Richard Rau	Ger	89	10.8	1)	Duisburg	08 Aug
Hans Mäulen	Ger	88	10.8	1)	Frankfurt/M	13 Aug
Max Herrmann	Ger	85	10.8	1)	Hamburg	21 Aug
Robert Cloughen	USA	89	10.8°	1)	New York	05 Sep
Geo Malfait	Fra		10.8	)		
Rodolfo Hammersley	Chl		10.8	1)	Buenos Aires	30 Sep

° = 110 y. (100.58 m.) time

Doubtful:

V. Galcheran	Arg		10.8	)		

Downhill:

Karl Halt	Ger	91	10.8	1)	Taubenberg	30 May

200 metres (half-to-full turn)

Billy Woodger	NZ		21.7*w		1)	Auckland	26 Feb
John Nelson	USA	85	21.7*		1)	Champaign, IL	04 Jun
Frank Lukeman	Can		21.7*		1)	Montreal	24 Sep
Robert Cloughen	USA	89	22.1*		1)	Hamilton	24 May
George Patching	SA	86	22.1*	A	1)	Pretoria	01 Jun

"Pro":

Charles Holway	USA		21.9		1)	Wigan	11 May

220 yards (straight course)

Ralph Craig	USA	89	21.2	1)	Philadelphia	28 May
Forrest Stanton	USA		21.4	1)		
Fred Ramsdell	USA		21.4e	2)	Philadelphia	28 May
Lee Carey	USA		21.4	1)		
Waldo Throop	USA		21.6	1)	Claremont	19 Mar
F. Burns	USA		21.6	1)	New Haven	14 May
Charles Minds	USA		21.6	1)h1	Philadelphia	27 May
William Martin	USA		21.6	1)	Notre Dame	28 May
Robert Kerr	Can	82	21.6	1)	Winnipeg	12 Sep

4x100 metre relay

Allmänna Idrotts Klubben Stockholm	Swe		44.4	1)	Stockholm	10 Sep
(Stenborg, Åberg, Möller, Lindberg)						
Berlin Team	Ger		45.2	1)	Frankfurt/M	28 Aug
(J.Meyerhoff, M.Hermann, F.Rathmann, R.Rau)						

1911

100 yards

Lee Carey	USA		9.8	1)	Annapolis	13 May
Ralph Craig	USA	89	9.8	1)s1	Cambridge, MA	27 May
Guy Reed	USA		9.8	1)	Kansas City	17 Jun
James Rosenberger	USA	87	9.8	1)	New York	23 Jun
Robert Kerr	Can	82	9.8	1)	Auburn, NY	24 Jun
Gwynn Henry	USA	87	9.8	1)	New York	04 Jul
C. B. Larsson	USA/Swe		9.8	1)	Boston	Aug
Victor D'Arcy	UK	87	9.8	1)	Wien	10 Sep
Ronald Opie	NZ		9.8	1)	Wellington	26 Dec
Russell Cook	USA		9.9e	2)s1	Cambridge, MA	27 May
"Pros":						
Jack Donaldson	Aus	86	9.6 A	1)	Johannesburg	26 Jul
Arthur Postle	Aus	81	9.8 A	1)	Johannesburg	04 Feb

100 metres

Emil Ketterer	Ger	83	10.5	1)	Karlsruhe	09 Jul
Richard Rau	Ger	89	10.5	1)h	Braunschweig	13 Aug
Erwin Kern	Ger	88	10.6	2)	Karlsruhe	09 Jul
Fritz Keppel	Ger	88	10.6	3)	Karlsruhe	09 Jul
Fred Ramsdell	USA		10.7	2)	Berlin	09 Jul
William Stewart	Aus	89	10.7	1)	Malmö	08 Aug
Julien Boullery	Fra		10.8w	1)	Colombes	28 May
Drolhier	Fra		10.8w	2)	Colombes	28 May
Karl Thomsen	Ger	89	10.8	1)	Kiel	23 Jul
Hans Mäulen	Ger	88	10.8	1)	Frankfurt/M	13 Aug
Knut Lindberg	Swe	82	10.8	1)	Göteborg	24 Sep
Ivan Möller	Swe	84	10.8e	2)	Göteborg	24 Sep
"Pros":						
Reginald Walker	SA	89	10.4+	1)	Durban	25 Nov
Jack Donaldson	Aus	86	10.8+	1)	Melbourne	14 Nov

+ = 110 yards (100.58m) time

200 metres (half-to-full turn)

John Nelson	USA	85	21.7*	1)	Pittsburgh	01 Jul
Lee Carey	USA		21.7*	1)	Annapolis	13 May
Ronald Opie	NZ		21.9*	1)	Christchurch	18 Mar
Richard Rau	Ger	89	22.0	1)	Berlin	09 Jul
Guy Reed	USA		22.1*	1)	Lincoln	06 May
Frank Halbhaus	Can		22.1*	1)	Newmarket	24 May
Fred Ramsdell	USA		22.1*	1)	London	01 Jul
Alvah Meyer	USA	88	22.1*	1)	New York	16 Sep
James Rosenberger	USA	87	22.1*	1)	Montreal	23 Sep
Reuben Povey	SA	89	22.1*	1)		

220 yards (straight course)

Ralph Craig	USA	89	21.2	1)	Cambridge, MA	27 May
LeRoy Dorland	USA	89	21.4	1)	New Britain, CT	24 Jun
W. H. Ford	USA		21.6	1)	Ithaca,NY	13 May
Russell Cooke	USA	87	21.8	1)	Princeton	06 May
Guy Reed	USA		21.8	1)	Saint Paul	06 May
Frederick Ross	USA		21.8	1)h3	Cambridge, MA	26 May
Charles Minds	USA		21.8	1)s2	Cambridge, MA	27 May
Howard Drew	USA	90	21.8	1)	Brookline, MA	24 Jun

4x100 metre relay

Sweden	(Stenborg, Åberg, Möller, Lindberg)	44.4	1)	Stockholm	10 Sep

1912

100 yards

James Wasson	USA		9.6	1)	Nashville	11 May
Charles Rice	USA		9.8w	1T)	Amherst	11 May
Howard Drew	USA	90	9.8w	1T)	Amherst	11 May
Lee Carey	USA		9.8	1)	Annapolis	16 May
Ralph Craig	USA	89	9.8	1)h hcp	New York	01 Jun
George Patching	SA	86	9.8	1)	London	22 Jun
William Applegarth	UK	90	9.8	1)	Belfast	29 Jun
Tom Hoover	USA		9.8	1)	Fayetteville	16 Apr

"Pros":

Reginald Walker	SA	89	9.4	A	1)	Johannesburg	26 Dec
Jack Donaldson	Aus	86	9.75		1)	Weaste	07 Sep

100 metres

Richard Rau	Ger	89	10.5	1)	München	12 May
Erwin Kern	Ger	88	10.5	1)	München	26 May
Howard Drew	USA	90	10.6	1)	Stockholm	01 Jul
Donald Lippincott	USA	93	10.6	1)h16	Stockholm	06 Jul
Lorenz Petersen	Ger		10.6	1)	München	25 Aug
William Applegarth	UK	90	10.6	1)	Praha	29 Sep
Alvah Meyer	USA	88	10.7	19q3	Stockhol	07 Jul
Ralph Craig	USA	89	10.7	1)q4	Stockholm	07 Jul
Harold Heiland	USA	90	10.7	1)	Malmö	21 Jul

200 metres (half-to-full turn)

Ralph Craig	USA	89	21.7	1)	Stockholm	11 Jul
William Applegarth	UK	90	21.7*	1)hcp	London	21 Sep
Alvah Meyer	USA	88	21.7*	1)	Pittsburgh	21 Sep
Donald Lippincott	USA	93	21.8	1)s4	Stockholm	10 Jul
David Jacobs	UK	88	21.9*	1)h4	London	22 Jun
Donnell Young	USA	88	21.9	1)s3	Stockholm	10 Jul
Richard Rau	Ger	89	21.9	2)	Berlin	21 Jul
Reuben Povey	SA	89	22.0e*	2)h4	London	22 Jun
Clement Wilson	USA	91	22.0e	2)s2	Stockholm	10 Jul

220 yards (straight course)

Charles Reidpath	USA	89	21.4	1)	Philadelphia	01 Jun
Eugene Mercer	USA	88	21.5e	2)	Philadelphia	01 Jun
Charles Rice	USA		21.6w	1)	Amherst	11 May
James Wasson	USA		21.6	1)	Nashville	11 May
T. H. Cornell	USA		21.6	1)	New Haven	18 May
Carl Cooke	USA	89	21.7*	1)	Evanston	08 Jun
Frederick Cortis	USA		21.8	1)	Columbus	20 Apr
Ira Courtney	USA	90	21.9*	1)	Palo Alto	17 May

4x100 metre relay

Germany	(Rohr, Herrmann, Kern, Rau)	42.3	1)s3	Stockholm	08 Jul
UK	(Jacobs, Macintosh, D'Arcy, Applegarth)	42.4	1)	Stockholm	09 Jul
Sweden	(Möller, Luther, Persson, Lindberg)	42.5	1)s2	Stockholm	08 Jul
Hungary	(Szobota, Racz, Szalai, Jankovicz)	42.9	2)s2	Stockholm	08 Jul
Canada	(McConnell, Lukeman, Beasley, Howard)	43.5	2)s3	Stockholm	08 Jul

1913

100 yards

Albert Robinson	USA	93	9.6	1)	Mercersburg	02 May
Howard Drew	USA	90	9.6	1)	Hartford	01 Sep
Donald Lippincott	USA	93	9.6	1)	Toronto	06 Sep
C. B. Wagner	USA		9.8	1)	Annapolis	19 Apr
Oliver Reller	USA	92	9.8	1)	Philadelphia	17 May
J. E. Bond	USA		9.8w	1)	Ann Arbor	17 May
James Patterson	USA	91	9.8	1)	Cambridge, MA	31 May
Charles Hoyt	USA	94	9.8	1)	Chicago	07 Jun
William Applegarth	UK	90	9.8	1)	Cardiff	28 Jun
Leo Cahill	USA		9.8	1)	East Orange, NJ	04 Jul
Henry MacIntosh	UK	92	9.8	1)	Wien	25 Jul
Albert Tormey	USA		9.8	1)	Minneapolis	02 Aug
Hal Beasley	Can		9.8	1)	Victoria	08 Aug
Baker	USA		9.8	1)		

"Pro":

Jack Donaldson	Aus	86	9.6	1)	Glasgow	26 Jul

100 metres

Erwin Kern	Ger	88	10.7e°	2)hcp	München	04 May
Henry MacIntosh	UK	92	10.7	1)	Wien	27 Jul
Fritz Fleischer	Aut	94	10.8	1)	Wien	20 Apr
Rolf Smedmark	Swe	86	10.8	1)	Stockholm	31 May
Richard Rau	Ger	89	10.8	1)	Praha	15 Jun
Richard Burghaus	Ger	90	10.8	1)	Gelsenkirchen	15 Jun
Hans Meulen	Ger	88	10.8	1)	Freiburg	13 Jul
Paul Neumann	Ger		10.8	1)	Braunschweig	27 Jul
Léon Aelter	Bel		10.8	2)	Wien	27 Jul
Hermann Waffenschmidt	Ger	93	10.8	1)	Essen	03 Aug
Ture Persson	Swe	92	10.8	1)	Randers	03 Aug
Karl Lindblom	Swe	92	10.8w	1)	Aspudden	03Aug
Jenö Rakos	Hun		10.8	1)	Wien	31 Aug
Max Herrmann	Ger	85	10.8	1)	Braunschweig	07 Sep
Pál Szalai	Hun		10.8	1)	Budapest	27 Sep

° = After a false start, Kern was penalized 1m. In the correct race he finished 1m behind a 10.6 handicap runner, so he covered 101 m.

200 metres (half-to-full turn)

William Applegarth	UK	90	21.5*		1)	London	05 Jul
Charles Hoyt	USA	94	21.7*		1)	Chicago	07 Jun
Richard Rau	Ger	89	21.8		1)h	Praha	15 Jun
Richard Rice	UK	86	21.8e		2)	High Wycombe	06 Sep
George Patching	SA	86	21.9*	A	1)	Johannesburg	01 May
Max Herrmann	Ger	85	22.0e		2)h	Praha	15 Jun
Clive Taylor	UK		22.0		1)	London	13 Sep
E. P. Campbell	USA		22.1*		1)	Los Angeles	15 Mar
C. O. Parker	USA		22.1*		1)	Chicago	24 May
Henry MacIntosh	UK	92	22.1		1)	Wien	26 Jul
R. S. Burley	UK		22.1e		3)	High Wycombe	06 Sep

"Pro":

Jack Donaldson	Aus	86	21.15°	1)hcp	Glasgow	26 Jul

° = actually 21.1/4 over 220y.

220 yards (streight course)

Albert Robinson	USA	93	20.8	1)	State College, PA	02 May
H. H. Seward	USA		21.2w	1)	Ann Arbor	17 May
Donald Lippincott	USA	93	21.2	1)	Cambridge, MA	31 May
James Patterson	USA		21.4	1)s2	Cambridge, MA	31 May
J. E. Bond	USA		21.4e	3)	Cambridge, MA	31 May
H. M. Wagner	USA		21.5e	)	Cambridge, MA	31 May
William Applegarth	UK	90	21.5*	1)	Kettering	30 Jun
Maxson	USA		21.6	1)	Baltimore	31 May
Oliver Reller	USA		21.7e	5)	Cambridge, MA	03 May

4x100 metre relay

UK		(Applegarth, Macintosh, Jacobs, D'Arcy)	43.0*	1)	London	07 Jul
Berliner SC	Ger	(Petersen, Matzdorf, Calleja, Kielmann)	43.9	1)	Berlin	29 Jun
Canada		( )	43.9*	1)	Vancouver	06 Oct
Sweden		(Olsson, Persson, Wallenberg, Jacobsson)	44.0	1)	Malmö	27 Jul
MTK	Hun	(Szenes, Radi, Rakos, Szalai)	44.4	1)	Wien	27 Jul

1914

100 yards

Howard Drew	USA	90	9.6	1)	Berkeley	28 Mar
Bill Carter	USA		9.8	1)	Ann Arbor	23 May
H. H. Seward	USA		9.8	1)	Ann Arbor	23 May
J. E. Bond	USA		9.8e	2)	Ann Arbor	23 May
Brooke Brewer	USA	95	9.8	1)		
William Applegarth	UK	90	9.8	1)	Manchester	13 Jun
C. W. Taylor	UK		9.9e	2)	Manchester	13 Jun
Hal Beasley	Can		9.9	1)	Shawnigan Lake	08 Aug

100 metres

Arthur Reinhardt	Ger	93	10.6w	1)	Hamburg	26 Apr
Richard Rau	Ger	89	10.8	1)	Hannover	17 May
Rolf Smedmark	Swe	86	10.8	1)	Stockholm	31 May
István Jankovich	Hun		10.8	1)	Budapest	28 Jun
Erwin Kern	Ger	88	10.8	1)h	Malmö	03 Jul
Fritz Lehmann	Ger	92	10.8w	1)	Malmö	05 Jul
Vasiliy Arkhipov	Rus		10.8	1)s	Riga	06 Jul
Olav Rustad	Nor	94	10.8	1)	Kristiania	12 Jul
Léon Aelter	Bel		10.8	1)	Bruxelles	26 Jul

Rolling start:

Fritz Fleischer	Aut	94	10.7	1)	Wien	19 Jul

200 metres (half-to-full turn)

William Applegarth	UK	90	21.1*	1)	London	04 Jul
Victor D'Arcy	UK	87	21.6e	2)	London	04 Jul
Harry Edward	UK	95	21.7e	2)	Berlin	28 Jun
John Rooney	UK		21.8e	3)	London	04 Jul
Maurice Barancik	USA		21.9*	1)	Chicago	06 Jun
Francis Shaw	Ire		21.9	4)	London	04 Jul

220 yards (straight course)

Howard Drew	USA	90	21.2	1)	Claremont	28 Feb
George Parker	USA		21.2	1)	Fresno	02 Oct
William Barron	USA	92	21.4	1)	Ithaca	09 May
Edward Teschner	USA		21.4	1)	New Haven	16 May
Bill Carter	USA		21.4	1)	Ann Arbor	23 May
Larry Gillette	USA		21.6	2)	Claremont	28 Feb
J. E. Bond	USA		21.6	1)	Ann Arbor	02 May
Edmund Jones	USA	94	21.6	1)	Annapolis?	

4x100 metre relay

TV München	Ger	(Leber, Aicher, Lehmann, Kern)	42.6	1)	Berlin	28 Jun
Sweden		(Jacobsson, Sundell, Persson, Smedmark)	43.6	2)	Malmö	08 Jul
HIFK	Fin	(Engberg, Wickholm, Malinoffsky, Jefimoff)	44.3	1)	Helsinki	06 Sep
Racing CF	Fra	(Gustin, Tissier, Person, André)	44.4	1)	Colombes	21 Jun
Sparta	Cze	(Vorisek, Labik, Novak, Vygoda)	44.8	1)	København	21 Jun

1915

100 yards

Dueson Knight	USA		9.8		1)	Chicago	15 May
Brooke Brewer	USA	95	9.8		1)s	Philadelphia	15 May
Andrew Ward	USA		9.8		1)	Urbana, IL	05 Jun
Willis Teale	USA		9.8		1)	West Point	09 Jun
Jo Loomis	USA		9.8		1)	Chicago	03 Jul
Robert Morse	USA		9.8w		1)	San Francisco	06 Aug
Frank Solomon	SA		9.8	A	1)	Johannesburg	16 Dec

100 metres

Jan Grijseels	Hol	90	10.7	1)	Rotterdam	15 Aug
Agne Holmström	Swe	93	10.8w	1)	Malmö	16 May
Boris Kotov	Rus		10.8	)	Moskva	28 Jun
Vasiliy Arkhipov	Rus		10.8	)	Moskva	28 Jun
Alex Pedersen	Nor	91	10.9	1)	Fredrikstad	29 Aug
John Nelson	Swe	87	10.9	)		

Downhill:

Philip Baldwin	USA	87	10.8	1)hcp	Firenze	25 Jul

200 metres (half-to-full turn)

Andrew Ward	USA		21.5*	1)h3	Urbana, IL	05 Jun
Harold Smith	USA		21.7*	1)	Chicago	03 Jul
Alfred Booth	USA	93	21.9*	1)h2	Urbana, IL	05 Jun
Duerson Knight	USA		22.1*	1)	Chicago	22 May
F. W. Stormer	USA		22.2	1)	Cincinnati	17 Jul
Collins	USA		22.3*	1)	Annapolis	15 May

"Pros":

William Applegarth	UK	90	22.25	1)	Weaste	10 Apr
Jack Donaldson	Aus	86	22.4e	2)	Weaste	10 Apr

220 yards (straight course)

Robert McBride	USA		21.0w	1)	San Francisco	31 Jul
Robert Morse	USA		21.2w	1)	San Francisco	07 Aug
	(also:		21.2	1)	Toronto	11 Sep
Fred Murray	USA	94	21.4	1)		25 Sep
H. Bostock	USA		21.6	1)	Haverford	15 May
Heaton Treadway	USA	95	21.6w	1)	New Haven	15 May
Leo Foley	USA		21.8	1)	Cambridge, MA	08 May
Brooke Brewer	USA	95	21.8	1)	Philadelphia	15 May
James Patterson	USA	91	21.8	1)h1	Philadelphia	28 May

4x100 metre relay

IFK Uppsala	Swe	(Levin, Traung, Lindholm, Ottander)	44.0	1)	Stockholm	26 Sep
Alumni OP	USA	(Kraft, Canwell, Riedel, Bingham)	44.4	1)	Chicago	17 Jun
Berliner SC	Ger	( )	44.7	1)	Berlin	08 Aug
HIFK	Fin	(Engberg, Wickholm, Malinoffsky, Jefimoff)	44.8	1)	Helsinki	20 Jun
IK Tjalve	Nor	(Vinne, Hellum, Amb, Johnsen)	45.5	2)	Kristiania	05 Sep

1916

100 yards

Rusty Frame	USA		9.6	1)	Austin	08 Apr
Edward Teschner	USA		9.8	1)	Cambridge, MA	13 May
Charles Rice	USA		9.8w	1)	Brunswick, ME	13 May
Evan Pearson	USA		9.8	1)	Spokane	20 May
Andrew Kelly	USA		9.8	1)	Springfield, MA	20 May
Henry Williams	USA		9.8	1)	San Diego	19 Aug
Andrew Ward	USA		9.8	1)	Chicago	26 Aug

"Pros":

Jack Donaldson	Aus	86	9.8	1)	London	07 Aug
William Applegarth	UK	90	9.9e	2)	London	07 Aug

100 metres

Olaf Rustad	Nor	94	10.7	1)	Kristiania	17 Sep
Jan Grijseels	Hol	90	10.7	)		
Géza Krepuska	Hun		10.8	1)	Wien	23 Jul
Jo Loomis	USA		10.8	1)	Stockholm	15 Oct

Doubtful:

Otto Thoms	Ger		10.6w	1)	Hamburg	30 Jul
Bernhard Schmidt	Ger		10.8	)		

200 metres (half-to-full turn)

Charles Hoyt	USA		21.3*	1)	Des Moines	22 Apr
Elmo Hohman	USA		21.4e*	2)	Des Moines	22 Apr
Carman Smith	USA		21.5*	1)	Evanston	03 Jun
Henry Williams	USA		21.7*	1)	San Diego	19 Aug
Binga Dismond	USA	91	22.1*	1)	Chicago	20 May
Hans Müller	Ger	99	22.1	1)	Leipzig	30 Jul
Frederick Murray	USA	94	22.2	1)	Stockholm	15 Oct
Vosbury	USA		22.3*	1)	Annapolis	13 May
Olaf Rustad	Nor	94	22.4	1)	Kristiania	17 Sep

"Pro":

William Applegarth	UK	90	21.9e	2)hcp	London	07 Aug

220 yards (straight course)

Andrew Kelly	USA		21.4	1)	Springfield, MA	20 May
Charles Rice	USA		21.4e	2)	Springfield, MA	20 May
Dana Jenkins	USA		21.4	1)	New Orleans	27 May
Frederick Murray	USA	94	21.6	1)	Palo Alto	15 Apr
Edward Teschner	USA		21.6	1)	Cambridge, MA	13 May
Harold Smith	USA		21.6	1)	Ann Arbor	20 May
William Moore	USA		21.6	1)	Cambridge, MA	27 May
Morrison	USA		21.6	1)	Pullman	03 Jun
Andrew Ward	USA		21.6	1)h1	Newark	09 Sep

4x100 metre relay

USA	(Ward, Murray, Simpson, Loomis)	43.0	1)	Kristiania	22 Oct
Swe	(Björck, Luther, Larsson, Holmström)	43.2	1)	Stockholm	09 Jul
Nor	(Frode-Hansen, Frogner, Johnsen, Rustad)	43.9	2)	Stockhlom	09 Jul
SC Charlottenburg	Ger (? , ? , Senftleben, Rau)	43.9	1)	Leipzig	27 Aug
Hol	(Verschoor, Snikkers, Dulker, Grijseels)	44.9	1)	Amsterdam	30 Jul

1917

100 yards

Frank Solomon	SA	9.8A	1)	Johannesburg	06 Apr
Verle Murray	USA	10.0	1)	Whittier, CA	03 Mar
Clyde Gilbert	USA	10.0	1)	Honolulu	17 Mar
Homer Chaney	USA	10.0	1)	Los Angeles	23 Mar

Billy Warren	USA		10.0	1)	Glendora, CA	21 Apr
Jack Melville	USA		10.0	1)	Berkeley	28 Apr
Jackson Scholz	USA	97	10.0	1)		02 Jun
William Hayes	USA		10.0	1)	Saint Louis	31 Aug
Gennaro Saavedra	Phi		10.0	)		
Fortunato Catalon	Phi		10.0	)		
R. Derbyshire	UK		10.0	)		
Collie	UK		10.0	)		

"Pro":

William Applegarth	UK	90	10.0	1)	Salonika	09 Jun

100 metres

Olaf Frogner	Nor	91	10.7	1)	Bergen	17 Jun
Agne Holmström	Swe	93	10.7w	1)	Malmö	10 Sep
Fabian Björk	Swe	93	10.8	1)	Huskvarna	28 May
Sigurd Roll	Nor		10.9	2)	Bergen	17 Jun
G. Kelder	Hol		10.9	)		

200 metres (half-to-full turn)

Charles Hoyt	USA		21.7*	1)	Chicago	09 Jun
Sol Butlter	USA	95	21.9*	1)h1	Chicago	09 Jun
F. Feuerstein	USA		21.9*	1)h3	Chicago	09 Jun
Agne Holmström	Swe	93	22.3	1)	Stockholm	07 Jul
N. Lal	Ind		22.5*	1)		
Olav Frogner	Nor	91	22.6	1)	Kristiania	22 Sep

"Pro":

William Applegarth	UK	90	22.1*	1)	Salonika	09 Jun

220 yards (straight course)

Morris Kirksey	USA	95	21.8	1)	Fresno	28 Sep
Charles Paddock	USA	00	22.0	1)	Long Beach	10 Mar
Constance	USA		22.2	1)		03 Mar
Norwood	USA		22.2	1)		23 Mar
Calden	USA		22.2	1)	Palo Alto	07 Apr
R. Bechtel	USA		22.2	1)	Bethlehem, NY	19 May
Charles Hoyt	USA		22.2	1)		02 Jun
Hans Müller	Ger	99	22.2+	1)	Berlin	03 Jun
Andrew Ward	USA		22.2	1)	Saint Louis	01 Sep
Peter White	USA		22.2e	2)	Saint Louis	01 Sep
Nils Sandström	Swe	93	22.2+	1)	Stockholm	14 Oct

+ = 200 m. time plus 0.1.

4x100 metre relay

SIK Hellas	Swe	(Schorling, Malm, Lindblom, Sandström)	43.1	1)	Stockholm	14 Oct
Chicago AAC	USA	(Landers, Holt, Eby, Ward)	43.8*	1)	Saint Louis	03 Sep
	Nor	(Frogner, Johnsen, Johansen, Roll)	44.2	2)	Kristiania	02 Sep
HIFK	Fin	(Wilén, Wickholm, Stenberg, Bergman)	44.3	1)	Turku	28 Jul
AIK	Den	( )	45.8	2)	København	29 Jul

1918

100 Yards

George Watson	USA		9.8	1)	Honolulu	03 Mar
Jackson Scholz	USA	97	9.8	1)	Columbia, MO	25 May
Woods	USA		10.0	1)	Eagle Rock	08 Feb
Charles Paddock	USA	00	10.0	1)	Los Angeles	16 Feb
Giorgio Croci	Ita	93	10.0	1)	Milano	12 May
Collier	USA		10.0	1)	Bloomington	18 May
Robert Morse	USA		10.0	1)		19 May
Jack Melville	USA		10.0	1)	Palo Alto	25 May
William Ganzemuller	USA		10.0	1)s1	Philadelphia	31 May
Howard Drew	USA	90	10.0	1)	Chicago	05 Jun

Andrew Ward	USA		10.0	1)	Detroit	14 Sep
T. T. Hoskins	USA		10.0	1)h1	Great Lakes, IL	20 Sep
Mahl	USA		10.0	1)h6	Great Lakes, IL	20 Sep
Arthur Henke	USA		10.0	1)	Great Lakes, IL	20 Sep
Jo Loomis	USA		10.0	1)h2	Great Lakes, IL	21 Sep

100 metres

E. Bauer	Ger		10.7w	1)	Hochlarmark	09 Jun
Mario Romero	Cub		10.8	1)	Habana	24 Feb
Giorgio Croci	Ita	93	10.8	1)	Roma	14 Mar
Nils Engdahl	Swe	98	10.8w	1)	Malmö	08 Jun
Curt Reuterwall	Swe		10.8w	)	Stockholm	16 Jun
Olav Frogner	Nor		10.8	1)	Kristiania	30 Jun
John Johnsen	Nor		10.8	2)	København	01 Sep
Hilding Nilsson	Swe	93	10.8	1)	København	29 Sep
Felix Mendizabal	Spa	91	10.8w	1)s1	Madrid	12 Oct
H. Pritchard	UK		10.8	1)		
Umberto Ramirez	Chl		10.8w	1)	Valparaiso	

Doubtful:

Karl Neumann	Ger		10.8	)
Arthur Reinhardt	Ger	93	10.8	)

200 metres (half-to-full turn)

Arthur Reinhardt	Ger	93	21.8w	1)	Hamburg	14 Jul
Mario Romero	Cub		22.0	1)	Habana	24 Feb
Géza Krepuska	Hun		22.2	1)	Budapest	30 Jun
Carl Erler	Ger	92	22.2w	2)	Hamburg	14 Jul
Frank Shea	USA	96	22.3*	1)	Annapolis	11 May
Howard Drew	USA	90	22.3*	1)	Chicago	08 Jun
Olav Frogner	Nor		22.3	1)	Stockholm	08 Jul
Nils Engdahl	Swe	98	22.4	1)	Stockholm	17 Aug
Nils Sandström	Swe	93	22.4	1)	Norrköping	22 Sep
Umberto Ramirez	Chl		22.4w	1)	Valparaiso	

220 yards (straight course)

Collier	USA		21.4	1)	Bloomington	18 May
Creed Haymond	USA		21.6	1)	Philadelphia	21 Jun
Allen Woodring	USA	98	21.6	1)	Princeton	11 May
Charles Carroll	USA		22.0	1)	Urbana, IL	05 May
Jack Melville	USA		22.2	1)	Berkeley	30 Mar
Jo Loomis	USA		22.2	1)h1	Great Lakes, IL	21 Sep
Cornelius Shaughnessy	USA		22.2	1)h2	Great Lakes, IL	21 Sep

4x100 metre relay

Swe		(Holmström, Sandström, Petersson-Björneman, Engdahl)	42.8	1)	København	01 Sep
	Nor	(Frogner, Johnsen, Blegen, Helsing)	43.3	2)	København	01 Sep
Great Lakes NS	USA	(Dover, Erickson, Cass, Murchison)	44.2*	1)	Chicago	23 Sep
	Den	(Andersen, Thorsen, Sörensen, Mathiasen)	44.4	3)	København	01 Sep
HIFK	Fin	(Homberg, Wilén, Bergman, Wickholm)	45.6	1)	Helsinki	14 Sep

1919

100 yards

Charles Paddock	USA	00	9.8	1)	Claremont, CA	12 Apr
Billy Hayes	USA		9.8	1)	Urbana, IL	03 May
Henry Williams	USA		9.8	1)	Tacoma	01 Jul
Homer Chaney	USA		9.9e	2)	Claremont, CA	12 Apr
Harry Edward	UK	95	9.9	1)	London	09 Jun
Roy Burguez	Aus		9.9	1)	Brisbane	26 Jul
William Hill	UK	96	9.9	1)	Cowes	26 Jul
Frederick Mawby	UK	91	9.9	1)	London	21 Aug

"Pro" ?:

Claire Demont	Can		9.9	1)	Glace Bay	19 Sep

100 metres

Géza Krepuska	Hun		10.7w	1)	Budapest	06 Jul
Alfred Steen	Swe		10.7	1)	Malmö	13 Jul
John Johnsen	Nor		10.7	1)	Kalmar	13 Jul
Hilding Nilsson	Swe	93	10.8w	1)	Lund	01 Jun
Arthur Reinhardt	Ger	93	10.8	1)	Nürnberg	01 Jun
Sol Butler	USA	95	10.8	1)h1	Colombes	18 Jun
Charles Paddock	USA	00	10.8	1)	Paris	26 Jun
Richard Rau	Ger	89	10.8	1)	Malmö	29 Jun
Alex Weider	Ger	96	10.8	1)	Frankfurt/M	13 Jul
William Petersson	Swe	95	10.8	2)	Malmö	13 Jul
Karl Preyss	Ger	93	10.8	1)	Stuttgart	20 Jul
Willi Dünker	Ger	93	10.8	1T)	Dortmund	10 Aug
E. Bauer	Ger		10.8	1T)	Dortmund	10 Aug
Kai Mathiassen	Den		10.8	1)	København	10 Aug
Sven Hygum	Den		10.8	1)	Horsens	07 Sep
Paul Brochart	Bel	99	10.8	1)	Bruxelles	07 Sep
Humberto Ramirez	Chl		10.8w	1)	Valparaiso	
August Heyneman	Hol		10.8			

200 metres (half-to-turn)

Henry Williams	USA		21.7*	1)	Philadelphia	13 Sep
William Hill	UK	96	21.9*	1)h	London	05 Jul
Francis Mawby	UK		21.9*	1)	London	04 Sep
Loren Murchison	USA	98	21.9*e	2)	Philadelphia	13 Sep
Morris Kirksey	USA	95	21.9*e	3)	Philadelphia	13 Sep
William Hunt	Aus		22.3*	1)	Sydney	13 Dec
Jock Leadley	Aus		22.3*	1)		
Nils Sandström	Swe	93	22.4	)	København	22 Jun
Humberto Ramirez	Chl		22.4w	1)	Valparaiso	

220 yards (straight course)

Creed Haymond	USA		21.6	1)h2	Cambridge, MA	30 May
Charles Paddock	USA	00	21.7+	1)	Colombes	19 Jun
Billy Hayes	USA		21.8	1)	Cambridge, MA	23 Aug
Homer Chaney	USA		22.0	1)	Claremont, CA	08 Mar
Fred Davis	USA		22.0	1)h1	Cambridge, MA	30 May
Frederick Kunkle	USA		22.0	1)h3	Cambridge, MA	30 May
Henry Williams	USA		22.0	1)	Tacoma, CA	01 Jul
Richard Rau	Ger	89	22.0+	1)h	Berlin	10 Aug

+ = 200 m. time plus 0.1.

4x100 metre relay

Univ.of Pennsylvania	USA	42.6*	1)	Philadelphia	07 Jun
(Landers, Davis, Haymond, C.Smith)					
SoIK Hellas	Swe	43.5	1)	Karlstad	16 Aug
(Andersson-Dennel, Malm, Schorling, Sandström)					
	Den	43.5	1)	Stockholm	31 Aug
(Andersen, Sörensen, Heilmann, Mathiasen)					
IK Tjalve	Nor	44.0	1)	Stockholm	21 Jul
(Johnsen, Roenneberg, Hansen, Hammerstad)					
Berliner SC	Ger	44.0	1)	Berlin	10 Aug
(Skowronnek, Glaser, Krüger, Schoch)					

1920

100 yards

George Davidson	NZ		9.8w		1)	Wellington	17 Jan
Charles Paddock	USA	00	9.8		1)	Berkeley	10 Apr
Jackson Scholz	USA	97	9.8		1)	Des Moines	24 Apr
Morris Kirksey	USA	95	9.8		1)	Palo Alto	09 May
Jack Oosterlaak	SA	96	9.8	A	1)	Johannesburg	16 Dec

100 metres

Joseph Imbach	Swz	94	10.6	1)	Genève	25 Jul
Jackson Scholz	USA	97	10.6	1)	Stockholm	06 Sep

Nils Engdahl	Swe	98	10.7	1)	Stockholm	11 Jul
Agne Holmström	Swe	93	10.7	2)	Stockholm	11 Jul
Richard Rau	Ger	89	10.7	1)	Dresden	15 Aug

Doubful timing:

Otto Kessler	Ger		10.6w	1)	Neunkirchen	20 Jun

200 metres (half-to-full turn)

Jackson Scholz	USA	97	21.5*	1)	Ann Arbor	05 Jun
Harry Edward	UK	95	21.5*	1)	London	03 Jul
George Massengale	USA		21.7*	1)	Chicago	26 Jun
Randolph Brown	USA	98	21.8*e	2)	London	03 Jul
Charles Paddock	USA	00	21.9*	1)	Los Angeles	20 Mar
Roy Haliburton	Can	90	21.9* A	1)	Calgary	23 Jun
Nils Engdahl	Swe	98	21.9	1)	Stockholm	11 Jul
Wilhelm Bukes	SA	96	21.9*	1)		
Sven Malm	Swe	94	22.0	2)	Stockholm	11 Jul
Allen Woodring	USA	98	22.0	1)	Antwerpen	20 Aug

220 yards (straight course)

Charles Paddock	USA	00	21.4	1)	Berkeley	10 Apr
Morris Kirksey	USA	95	21.4w	1)	Berkeley	17 Apr
Smith	USA		21.6	1)		15 May
Billy Hayes	USA		21.6	1)	Notre Dame	22 May
H. King	USA		21.6	1)	Cincinnati	12 Jun
Jackson Scholz	USA	97	21.6	1)	Ames, IA	29 May
Loren Murchison	USA	98	21.6e	3)	Cambridge, MA	17 Jul

4x100 metre relay

USA	(Paddock, Scholz, Murchison, Kirksey)	42.2	1)	Antwerpen	22 Aug
Fra	(Ali Khan, Lorain, Tirard, R.Mourlon)	42.6	2)	Antwerpen	22 Aug
SC Charlottenburg Ger	(Krüger, Dünker, Waffenschmidt, Rau)	42.7	1)	Berlin	04 Jul
Swe	(Holmström, Petersson-Björneman, Malm, Sandström)	42.9e	3)	Antwerpen	22 Aug
UK	(Edward, Hill, D'Arcy, Abrahams)	43.1e	4)	Antwerpen	22 Aug

ALL TIME WORLD LIST OF BEST PERFORMERS AS AT THE END OF 1920

100 yards

James Rector	USA	84	9.4w	1)	Charlettesville	09 May 08
Jack Hempton	NZ	63	9.6w	1)	Dunedin	14 Dec 89
Arthur Duffey	USA	79	9.6	1)	New York	31 May 02
Dan Kelly	USA	83	9.6	1)	Spokane, WA	23 Jun 06
Marion Roberts	USA		9.6w	1)	Amherst	07 May 10
Clement Wilson	USA	91	9.6	1)	Cedar Rapids	11 Jun 10
James Wasson	USA		9.6	1)	Nashville	11 May 12
Albert Robinson	USA	93	9.6	1)	Mercersburg	02 May 13
Howard Drew	USA	90	9.6	1)	Hartford	01 Sep 13
Donald Lippincott	USA	93	9.6	1)	Toronto	06 Sep 13
Rusty Frame	USA		9.6	1)	Austin	08 Apr 16

100 metres

Emil Ketterer	Ger	83	10.5	1)	Karlsruhe	09 Jul 11
Richard Rau	Ger	89	10.5	1)h	Braunschweig	13 Aug 11
Erwin Kern	Ger	88	10.5	1)	München	26 May 12
Knut Lindberg	Swe	82	10.6	1)	Göteborg	26 Aug 06
Fritz Keppel	Ger	88	10.6	3)	Karlsruhe	09 Jul 11

Howard Drew	USA	90	10.6	1)	Stockholm	01 Jul 12
Donald Lippincott	USA	93	10.6	1)h16	Stockholm	06 Jul 2
Lorenz Petersen	Ger		10.6	1)	München	25 Aug 12
William Applegarth	UK	90	10.6	1)	Praha	29 Sep 12
Arthur Reinhardt	Ger	93	10.6w	1)	Hamburg	26 Apr 14
Joseph Imbach	Swz	94	10.6	1)	Genève	25 Jul 20
Jackson Scholz	USA	97	10.6	1)	Stockholm	06 Sep 20

200 metres (half-to-full turn)

William Applegarth	UK	90	21.1*	1)	London	04 Jul 14
James Maybury	USA		21.3*	1)	Chicago	05 Jun 97
Charles Hoyt	USA		21.3*	1)	Des Moines	22 Apr 16
Elmo Hohman	USA		21.4*e	2)	Des Moines	22 Apr 16
Harry Jewett	USA	69	21.5*	1)	Montreal	24 Sep 92
Patrick Walsh	USA		21.5*	1)	Montreal	21 Sep 02
Archie Hahn	USA	80	21.5*	1)	Chicago	30 May 03
Nathaniel Cartmell	USA	83	21.5*	1)	Norfolk, WA	22 Jun 07
Lee Carey	USA		21.5*	1)	Annapolis	08 May 09
Andrew Ward	USA		21.5*	1)h3	Urbana, IL	05 Jun 15
Carman Smith	USA		21.5*	1)	Evanston	03 Jun 16
Jackson Scholz	USA	97	21.5*	1)	Ann Arbor	05 Jun 20
Harry Edward	UK	95	21.5*	1)	London	03 Jul 20

220 yards (straight course)

Albert Robinson	USA	93	20.8	1)	State College, PA	02 May 13
Robert McBride	USA		21.0w	1)	San Francisco	31 Jul 15
Ernard Wefers	USA	73	21.2	1)	New York	30 May 96
A. S. Henderson	USA		21.2	1)	Annapolis	08 May 97
John Tewksbury	USA	76	21.2	1)	Princerton, NJ	22 Apr 99
Dan Kelly	USA	83	21.2	1)	Spokane, WA	23 Jun 06
Ralph Craig	USA	89	21.2	1)	Philadelphia	28 May10
H. H. Seward	USA		21.2w	1)	Ann Arbor	17 May 13
Donald Lippincott	USA	93	21.2	1)	Cambridge, MA	31 May 13
Howard Drew	USA	90	21.2	1)	Claremont	28 Feb 14
George Parker	USA		21.2	1)	Fresno	02 Oct 14
Robert Morse	USA		21.2	1)	Toronto	11 Sep 15

4x100 metre relay

USA	(Paddock, Scholz, Murchison, Kirksey)	42.2	1)	Antwerpen	22 Aug 20
Ger	(Rohr, Herrmann, Kern, Rau)	42.3	1)s3	Stockholm	08 Jul 12
UK	(Jacobs, Macintosh, D'Arcy, Applegarth)	42.4	1)	Stockholm	09 Jul 12
Swe	(Möller, Luther, Persson, Lindborg)	42.5	1)s2	Stockholm	08 Jul 12
Fra	(Ali Khan, Lorain, Tirard, R.Mourlon)	42.6	2)	Antwerpen	22 Aug 20

1921

100 yards

Charles Paddock	USA	00	9.6	1)	Berkeley	26 Mar
Allen Woodring	USA	98	9.6	1)	Syracuse, NY	07 May
Morris Kirksey	USA	95	9.7e	2)	Palo Alto	29 Mar
Edward Gourdin	USA	97	9.8w	1)	State College, PA	19 Apr
Vernon Blenkiron	USA	01	9.8+e	2)	Redlands, CA	23 Apr
Joe Ellis	USA		9.8	1)	Austin	30 Apr
Marion Lindsey	USA		9.8	1)	Waxahachie, TX	06 May
G. Gallagher	USA		9.8w	1)	Columbia, MO	07 May
Edward Smith	USA		9.8w	1)	Lincoln, NE	07 May
Jacobson	USA		9.8	1)		07 May
Alfred LeConey	USA	01	9.8	1)	Baltimore	14 May
Robert Hutchison	USA	96	9.8	1)	Berkeley	14 May
Edward Sudden	USA		9.8e	2)	Berkeley	14 May
Vic Hurley	USA		9.8	1)	Eugene	21 May
Billy Hayes	USA		9.8w	1)	Chicago	04 Jun
Cyril Coaffee	Can	97	9.8	1)hcp	Winnipeg	16 Jul

Downhill:

Henri Nozières	Swz	91	9.6	1)	Histon, Cambridge	28 Jul
Frederick Mawby	UK	91	9.6e	2)	Histon, Cambridge	28 Jul

+ = during 100 m. race.

100 metres

Charles Paddock	USA	00	10.2+	1)	Pasadena	18 Jun
Vernon Blenkiron	USA	01	10.4	1)	Redlads, CA	23 Apr
Martin Reichel	Ger	96	10.5w	1)	Stockholm	10 Jul
Richard Rau	Ger	89	10.6w	1)	Magdeburg	19 Jun
Hubert Houben	Ger	98	10.7	1)	Rotterdam	03 Jul
John Lilja	Swe	93	10.7w	2)	Stockholm	10 Jul
Joseph Imbach	Swz	94	10.7	1)	Oyonnax	31 Jul
Nils Sandström	Swe	93	10.7	1)h2	Stockholm	20 Aug
Lilja			10.7	1)h3	Stockholm	20 Aug
Ulysses Malaguti de Sousa	Bra	96	10.7	1)	Rio de Janeiro	18 Dec

+ = 110 y. (100.58 m.) time

Intrasquad meet:

Nils Sandström	Swe	93	10.7w	1)	Stockholm	16 Aug

No start pistol:

Hubert Houben	Ger	98	10.5w	1)	Düren	07 Aug

200 metres (half-to-full turn)

Jock Oosterlaak	SA	96	21.7*w	1)	Durban	26 Nov
Frederick Mawby	UK	91	21.8	1)hcp	London	14 May
Ernst Krüger	Ger	96	21.8	1)	Berlin	07 Aug
Howard Kinsman	SA	00	21.8*we	2)	Durban	26 Nov
Charles Paddock	USA	00	21.9*	1)	Los Angeles	14 May
Harry Edward	UK	95	21.9*	1)s1	London	01 Jul
John Lilja	Swe	93	21.9	1)h2	Stockholm	20 Aug
Oosterlaak			21.9* A	1)	Johannesburg	24 Sep
Erik Lindvall	Swe	95	21.9w	1)	Malmö	25 Sep
Hans Zirpel	Ger	96	22.0	2)	Berlin	07 Aug
Abelardo Piovano	Arg		22.0	1)	Buenos Aires	12 Oct

Short course (217 y. = 198.4 m.)

Bill Miller	Can		21.6	1)hcp	Winnipeg	16 Jul

220 yards (straight course)

Charles Paddock	USA	00	20.8	1)	Berkeley	26 Mar
Robert Hutchison	USA	96	21.2	2)	Berkeley	26 Mar
Allen Woodring	USA	98	21.2	1)	Syracuse, NY	06 May
Morris Kirksey	USA	95	21.6	1)	Palo Alto	26 Mar
W. Simmons	USA		21.6	1)	Columbus, OH	07 May
Eric Wilson	USA	00	21.6	1)	Iowa City	07 May
Brittingham	USA		21.6	1)	Washington, DC	13 May
Robert Maxam	USA		21.6	1)	Ithaca, NY	14 May
Alfred LeConey	USA	01	21.6	1)	Baltimore	14 May
Vic Hurley	USA		21.6	1)	Pullman, WA	04 Jun

4x100 metre relay

New York AC	USA	(Wefers II, Lovejoy, Ray, Farrell)	42.2*	1)	Pasadena	05 Jul
	Swe	(Lindvall, Lilja, Malm, Sandström)	42.7	1)	Stockholm	28 Aug
SC Charlottenburg	Ger	(Vogel, Krüger, Senftleben, Rau)	42.8	1)	Berlin	03 Jul
IF Örnulf-Oslo	Nor	(Guldager, Iversen, G.Stenersen, R.Stenersen)	43.4	1)	København	03 Jul
	Den	(Thorsen, Sörensen, Böggild, Truelsen)	43.4	2)	Oslo	04 Sep

1922

100 yards

Charles Paddock	USA	00	9.6	1)	Honolulu	01 Apr
Edward Farrell	USA		9.6	1)h	Bridgeport, CT	24 Jun
Cyril Coaffee	Can	97	9.6w A	1)	Calgary	12 Aug
Alfred LeConey	USA	01	9.7	1)	Annapolis	20 May

Billy Hayes	USA		9.7	1)	Iowa City	03 Jun
Loren Murchison	USA	98	9.7	1)	Chicago	24 Jun

Downhill:

Harry Edward	UK	95	9.4	1)hcp	Histon, Cambridge	03Aug

Unconfirmed performance:

Robert McAllister	USA	99	9.7	1)	Danbury	Jun

"Pro":

William Applegarth	UK	90	9.6	1)	Dundee	?17 Jun

100 metres

Hubert Houben	Ger	98	10.5	1)	Frankfurt/M	03 Sep
Paul Brochart	Bel	99	10.6w	1)	Liège	03 Sep
Erik Lindvall	Swe	95	10.6w	1)	København	17 Sep
Marinus Sörensen	Den	98	10.6w	2)	København	17 Sep
Friedrich Reissmann	Ger	99	10.7	1)	Magdeburg	11 Jun
Hans Senftleben	Ger	97	10.7	1)	Stettin	23 Jul
Vittorio Zucca	Ita	96	10.7	1)	Pola	01 Aug
Harry Broos	Hol	98	10.7	)		

Downhill:

Albert Heise	Fra	99	10.6w	1)	Haguenau	25 Jun
Hugo Herr	Ger	98	10.7	1)	Taubenberg	21 May
Louis Téneveau	Frau	01	10.7we	2)	Haguenau	25 Jun

Dobtful timing:

Ludwig Hummerjohann	Ger	02	10.6	1)	Gelsenkirchen	09 Jul
Hermann Reinbold	Ger		10.6	1)	Bad Nauheim	16 Jul

No start pistol:

Erik Lindvall	Swe	95	10.4w	1)	Düren	09 Jul
Heirich Esselen	Ger		10.5w	2)	Düren	09 Jul
Heinrich Mattonet	Ger	01	10.6w	3)	Düren	09 Jul

Short course:

Hubert Houben	Ger	98	10.3	1)	Krefeld	18 Jun
Friedrich Reissmann	Ger	99	10.6	1)s	Krefeld	18 Jun

200 metres (half-to-full turn)

Jock Oosterlaak	SA	96	21.7*	1)	Wellington	25 Feb
Cyril Coaffee	Can	97	21.7*w A	1)	Calgary	12 Aug
Wilhelm Bukes	SA	96	21.8*e	2)	Wellington	25 Feb
Nils Engdahl	Swe	98	21.8	1)	Stockholm	20 Aug
Georg Davidson	NZ		21.9*e	3)	Wellington	25 Feb
Harry Edward	UK	95	21.9*	1)	London	01 Jul
Coaffee			21.9*	1)	Winnipeg	03 Aug
Cecil Hay	Can		21.9*we A	2)	Calgary	12 Aug
Hubert Houben	Ger	98	21.9	1)	Frankfurt/M	03 Sep
Christian Steyn	SA	97	21.9*	1)	London	09 Sep
Alex Wieder	Ger	96	22.0	1)	Frankfurt/M	08 Jul
James Thwaite	UK	99	22.0	1)	London	29 Jul

Short course:

Burkhardt	Ger		21.9	1)	Ludwigshafen	30 Jul
Eric Liddell	UK	02	22.0°	1)hcp	Glasgow	05 Aug

° = 218 y. (199.33 m.) time

220 yards (straight course)

Robert Hutchison	USA	96	21.2w	1)	Berkeley	08 Apr
Louis Clarke	USA	01	21.2	1)	Charlottesville, VA	15 Apr
Alfred LeConey	USA	01	21.3	1)	Cambridge, MA	27 May
Edward Smith	USA		21.3	1)	Lawrenc	27 May
Leonard Paulu	USA		21.4	1)	Grinnell, IA	13 May
Allen Woodring	USA	98	21.4w	1)h3	Cambridge, MA	26 May
Herold Jones	USA		21.4	1)	Detroit	19 Aug
Edwin Carr	Aus	99	21.5	1)	Adelaide	02 Jan

4x100 metre relay

SC Charlottenburg	Ger		42.4	1)	Duisburg	20 Aug
(Cohn, Krüger, Senftleben, Zirpel)						
Univ.of Nebraska	USA		42.6*	1)	Des Moines	29 Apr
(Deering, Lukens, Noble, Ed Smith)						
	Swe		43.3	1)	København	03 Sep
(Lindvall, Engdahl, Malm, Sandström)						
KAOE,Budapest	Hun		43.5	1)	Budapest	10 Sep
(Görög, Juhasz, Koinráth, Kurunczy)						
Stade Français, Paris	Fra		43.6	1)	Colombes	06 Aug
(Durier, Lageix, Pluchet, Jamois)						

Race annulled:

SC Charlottenburg	Ger		42.2	1)	Duisburg	20 Aug

1923

100 yards

Charles Paddock	USA	00	9.6+	1)	Paris	06 May
Fred Tykle	USA	01	9.6w	1)	Lafayette,IN	12 May
Frank Hussey	USA	05	9.6w	1)	Brooklyn, NY	09 Jun
Eugene Goodwillie	USA	04	9.7	1)	Evanston	02 Jun
Eric Liddell	UK	02	9.7	1)	London	07 Jul

+ = during 100 m. race

Downhill:

James Thwaite	UK	99	9.7w	1)	Leeds	12 May

100 metres

Charles Paddock	USA	00	10.4	1)	Paris	06 May
Nils Engdahl	Swe	98	10.5w	1)	Malmö	30 Sep
Edwyn Carr	Aus	99	10.6w	1)	København	22 Jul
Carr			10.6	1)	Pardubice	12 Aug
Gustaf Dahlén	Swe	01	10.6w	2)	Malmö	30 Sep
Harry Broos	Hol	98	10.6	)		
Hubert Houben	Ger	98	10.7	1)	Düsseldorf	20 May
Luis Miquel	Chl		10.7	)	Santiago de Chile	21 May
Paul Brochart	Bel	99	10.7	1)	Liège	08 Jul
André Mourlon	Fra	03	10.7e	2)	Helsinki	23 Sep
Carl Hedberg	Swe	03	10.7w	3)	Malmö	30 Sep

Rolling start:

Lauri Härö	Fin	99	10.5w	1)	Lahti	07 Oct
Reijo Halme	Fin	99	10.7	1)	Helsinki	23 Sep

Downhill:

Josef Düllmann	Ger		10.6w	1)	Solingen	12 Aug

Doubtful timing:

Hubert Houben	Ger	98	10.4	1)hcp	Goch	12 Aug
Max Freund	Ger	01	10.6w	1)h	Leipzig	05 Aug

Short course (97.2 m.):

Harold Lever	USA		10.4	1)	Toronto	08 Sep

200 metres (half-to-full turn)

Charles Paddock	USA	00	21.0		1)	Paris	06 May
Eugene Goodwillie	USA	04	21.3*		1)	Urbana, IL	12 May
Leslie Tracy	NZ		21.5*w		1)	Wellington	24 Mar
Eric Liddell	UK	02	21.5*		1)s3	London	06 Jul
Howard Kinsman	SA	00	21.5*		1)	Ladysmith	18 Aug
Norman Grehan	Aus	02	21.5*		1)	Brisbane	18 Aug
Morris Kirksey	USA	95	21.7*		1)	Wellington	24 Feb
George Dustan	SA	00	21.7*	A	1)	Johannesburg	02 Apr

Unknown irregularity:

Morris Kirksey	USA	95	21.5*	1)	Cambridge, NZ	28 Feb

220 yards (straight course)

Charles Paddock	USA	00	21.2	1)	Berkeley	31 Mar
Eric Wilson	USA	00	21.2	1)h	Ann Arbor	02 Jun
Harry Evans	USA	03	21.3e	2)	Ann Arbor	02 Jun
Ian Campbell	USA		21.4	1)	Berkeley	21 Apr
Fredric Lovejoy	USA	02	21.4	1)	Philadelphia	12 May
Allen Woodring	USA	98	21.4	1)	West Point, NY	19 May
Clarkson Black	USA		21.4	1)	Pawling, NY	02 Jun
Loren Murchison	USA	98	21.4	1)	Yonkers, NY	25 Aug

4x100 metre relay

Univ.of Illinois	USA	(Sweet, Hughes, Evans, Ayres)	42.1*	1)	Des Moines	28 Apr
	Ger	(Houben, Söhngen,Thumm, Reissmann)	42.5	1)h1	Göteborg	02 Jul
	Fin	(Härö, Halme,Wilén, Drisin)	42.6	1)h2	Göteborg	02 Jul
	Fra	(Hirlimann, Lorain, Gavois, A.Mourlon)	42.6	1)	Paris	09 Sep
KAOE Budapest	Hun	(Kurunczy, M.Gerö, Vida, F.Gerö)	42.7	1)	Wien	08 Sep
	Swe	(Engdahl, Österdahl, Branting, Russell)	42.7	2)	Paris	09 Sep

1924

100 yards

Alfred LeConey	USA	01	9.4w	1)	Allentowne, PA	30 Aug
Hubert Houben	Ger	98	9.5w	1)hcp	Köbenhavn	24 Jun
Charles Paddock	USA	00	9.5we	2)	Allentowne, PA	30 Aug
Loren Murchison	USA	98	9.5we	3)	Allentowne, PA	30 Aug
Paddock			9.6	1)	West Orange, NJ	06 Sep
Frank Hussey	USA	05	9.7	1)	Washington, DC	10 May
Murchison			9.7e	2)	Wesr Orange, NJ	06 Sep

Downhill:

Harold Abrahams	UK	99	9.6w	1)	Woolwich	07 Jun
Jackson Scholz	USA	97	9.6	1)hcp	Histon, Cambridge	31 Jul
Cyril Coaffee	Can	97	9.6e	2)hcp	Histon, Cambridge	31 Jul
William Nichol	UK	01	9.7we	2)	Woolwich	07 Jun

100 metres

Francisco Arango	Cub	02	10.4w	1)	Habana	27 Apr
Hubert Houben	Ger	98	10.4w	1)	Recklinghausen	08 Oct
Houben			10.5	1)	Köln	29 May
Jackson Scholz	USA	97	10.5	1)s	New York	07 Jun
Loren Murchison	USA	98	10.5	1)	Stockholm	31 Jul
Heinrich Most	Ger	96	10.5w	2)	Recklinghausen	08 Oct
José E. Barrientos	Cub	04	10.6w	1)h	Habana	13 Apr
Alfred LeConey	USA	01	10.6	1)h	New York	07 Jun
Robert Pepper	USA		10.6	1)	Atlanta	07 Jun
Charles Paddock	USA	00	10.6	1)h3	Cambridge, MA	13 Jun
George Hill	USA	01	10.6e	2)h3	Cambridge, MA	13 Jun
Chester Bowman	USA	01	10.6	1)	Cambridge, MA	14 Jun
Harold Abrahams	UK	99	10.6	1)q4	Colombes	06 Jul
Reijo Halme	Fin	99	10.6	1)	Saint-Gaudens	27 Jul
Gustaf Dalén	Swe	01	10.6w	1)h1	Köbenhavn	21 Sep

Rolling start:

Mogens Truelsen	Den	01	10.5	1)	Köbenhavn	21 Sep

Doubtful:

Robert Suhr	Ger	05	10.5	1)	Karlsruhe	06 Jul
Willi Apfel	Ger	00	10.6	2)	Karlsruhe	06 Jul

200 metres (half-to-full turn)

Harry Evans	USA	03	21.2	1)	Urbana, IL	27 May
Leslie Parker	Aus	03	21.3*w	1)	Brisbane	23 Aug

Charles Paddock	USA	00	21.4	1)	Berlin	06 Aug
Jackson Scholz	USA	97	21.4	1)	Dublin	13 Aug
Norman Grehan	Aus	02	21.4*we	2)	Brisbane	23 Aug
Hubert Houben	Ger	98	21.4 e	1)hcp	Augsburg	21 Sep
Loren Murchison	USA	98	21.5 e	2)	Berlin	06 Aug
Cyril Coaffee	Can	97	21.6	3)hcp	Toronto	07 Jun
Howard Kinsman	SA	00	21.6*	1)	London	21 Jun
André Mourlon	Fra	03	21.6	1)	Colombes	22 Jun

220 yards (straight course)

Charles Paddock	USA	08	20.8	1)	West Orange, NJ	06 Sep
Linsley Dodge	USA		21.0w	1)	Cambridge, MA	24 May
Jackson Scholz	USA		21.0*	1)s1	Cambridge, MA	14 Jun
Louis Clarke	USA	01	21.1*e	2)s1	Cambrdge, MA	14 Jun
Harry Evans	USA	03	21.2	1)	Urbana, IL	16 May
Victor Leschinsky	USA		21.2*w	1)h1	Ann Arbor	30 May
Bernard Otto	USA		21.2*w	1)h2	Ann Arbor	30 May
Eric Wilson	USA	00	21.2*	1)	Iowa City, IA	31 May
Bayes Norton	USA	03	21.2*e	2)	Cambridge, MA	14 Jun
George Hill	USA	01	21.2*e	3)	Cambridge, MA	14 Jun

4x100 metre relay

USA	(Hussey, Clarke, Murchison, LeConey)	41.0	1)s1	Colombes	13 Jul
UK	(Abrahams, Rangeley, Royle, Nichol)	41.2e	2)	Colombes	13 Jul
Hol	(Boot, Broos, de Vries, van den Berge)	41.8e	3)	Colombes	13 Jul
Hun	(Gerö, Kurunczy, Muskát, Rózsahegyi)	42.0e	4)	Colombes	13 Jul
Swz	(Imbach, Moriaud, Hemmi, Borner)	42.2	1)h4	Colmebes	12 Jul
Fra	(Heise, Degrelle, R.Mourlon, A.Mourlon)	42.2e	5)	Colombes	13 Jul

Disqualified:

Swz	(Imbach, Moriaud, Hemmi, Borner)	42.0e	-)	Colombes	13 Jul

1925

100 yards

Jackson Scholz	USA	97	9.5	1)	Greensboro, NC	09 May
Roland Locke	USA	03	9.6	1)h	Lawrence	18 Apr
Jerome Landa	USA		9.7w	1)	Austin	17 Apr
Fred Alderman	USA	05	9.7	1)	East Lansing, MI	23 May
William DeHart Hubbard	USA	03	9.7	1)	Ann Arbor	29 May
Frank Hussey	USA	05	9.7w	1T)h	San Francisco	04 Jul

Doubtful timing (discrepancy in watches):

William DeHart Hubbard	USA	03	9.6	1)	Ann Arbor	09 May

Short course/downhill track:

William Green	UK	04	9.6	1)hcp	Histon, Cambridge	30 Jul

100 metres

Hubert Houben	Ger	98	10.5	1)	Magdeburg	17 Sep
Joachim Büchner	Ger	05	10.5	2)	Magdeburg	17 Sep
Richard Corts	Ger	05	10.5	1)	Ulm	04 Oct
Jakob Schüller	Ger	05	10.6	1)	Neuss	31 May
Helmut Körnig	Ger	05	10.6	2)	Berlin	21 Jun
Charles Paddock	USA	00	10.6	1)	Stockholm	16 Jul
André Théard	Hai	05	10.6	1)	Paris	02 Aug
Werner Wege	Ger	04	10.6w?	1)	Leipzig	30 Aug
André Mourlon	Fra	03	10.6w	1)B	København	02 Sep
István Raggambi-Fluck	Hun	05	10.6	1)	Budapest	06 Sep
Marinus van den Berge	Hol	00	10.6	1)	Colombes	04 Oct

Doubtful timing:

Georg Lammers	Ger	05	10.4	1)	Oldenburg	14 Jun
Paul Artigues	Fra		10.6	1)	Mazères	06 Sep

Unknown irregularity:

Juan Felitto	Uru	10.6	)	Montevideo	15 Mar

200 metres (half-to-full turn)

Harry Evans	USA	03	21.4	1)	Colombes	04 Oct
Loren Murchison	USA	98	21.5*	1)	London	18 Jul
Howard Kinsman	SA	00	21.5*	1)	Durban	16 Dec
Joachim Büchner	Ger	05	21.6	1)	Halle	18 Jul
André Mourlon	Fra	03	21.6	1)	Brighton	25 Jul
Hubert Houben	Ger	98	21.6	1)	Magdeburg	17 Sep
Marinus van den Berge	Hol	00	21.6	2)	Colombes	04 Oct
Jakob Schüller	Ger	05	21.7	2)	Bochum	05 Jul
Walter Rangeley	UK	03	21.7	2)	Brighton	25 Jul
André Cerbonney	Fra	00	21.7	2)	Stockholm	29 Aug

Doubtful timing:

Paul Artigues	Fra		21.6	1)	Mazéres	06 Sep

220 yards (straight course)

Henry Russell	USA	04	20.8w	1)	Ithaca	16 May
Roland Locke	USA	03	20.8w	1)	Norman, OK	30 May
Jackson Scholz	USA	97	20.8w	1)	San Francisco	04 Jul
Oliver MacDonald	USA	04	20.9we	2)	San Francisco	04 Jul
Fred Alderman	USA	05	21.1w+	1)	Columbus	06 Jun
Ball	USA		21.2	1)	Austin	21 Apr
Harry Evans	USA	03	21.2	1)	Urbana, IL	02 May
Russell			21.2	1)	Philadelphia	09 May
Bayes Norton	USA	03	21.2	1)	Princeton	16 May
Alderman			21.2	1)	East Lansing, MI	23 May
Scholz			21.3	1)	Houston	28 Mar
Russell Sweet	USA	04	21.3w	1)	Pullman	02 May
Orthel Roberts	USA		21.3	1)	Grinnell, IA	22 May
Alfred LeConey	USA	01	21.3we	3)	San Francisco	04 Jul

+ = actual time 21.12

4x100 metre relay

New York AC	USA	(Hussey, Todd, MacDonald, Scholz)	41.2*	1)	San Francisco	05 Jul
Deutscher SC, Berlin	Ger	(Hübner, Haltenhoff, Leeske, Wondratschek)	42.2	1)	Berlin	09 Aug
	Fra	(Hirlimann, Rousseaux, Cerbonney, A.Mourlon)	42.4	1)	Stockholm	30 Aug
	Swe	(Ottander, Österdahl, Branting, S.Pettersson)	42.7	2)	Stockholm	30 Aug
KAOE, Budapest	Hun	(Sugár, M.Gerö, Vida, F.Gerö)	42.7	1)	Budapest	04 Oct

1926

100 yards

Roland Locke	USA	03	9.5w	1)	Des Moines	24 Apr
Philip Barber	USA	04	9.5w	1)	San Francisco	08 May
Charles Paddock	USA	00	9.5	1)	Los Angeles	15 May
Charles Borah	USA	06	9.5	2)	Los Angeles	15 May
Jackson Scholz	USA	97	9.6we	2)	San Francisco	08 May
Tom Sharkey	USA	05	9.6	1)	Cincinnati	22 May
(Locke)			9.6	1)	Lincoln	22 May
William DeHart Hubbard	USA	03	9.6	1)	Cincinnati	05 Jun

100 metres

Helmut Körnig	Ger	05	10.3w	1)	Leipzig	08 Aug
Kurt Dreibholz	Ger	04	10.4w	2)	Leipzig	08 Aug
Werner Wege	Ger	04	10.4w	3)	Leipzig	08 Aug
(Körnig)			10.4	1)	Halle	29 Aug
André Théard	Hai	05	10.5	1)	København	01 Aug
Hubert Houben	Ger	98	10.5w	4)	Leipzig	08 Aug
(Wege)			10.5	2)	Halle	29 Aug
George Lammers	Ger	05	10.5w	1)	Oldenburg	12 Sep
José E.Barrientos	Cub	04	10.6w	1)	Habana	29 Apr
Richard Corts	Ger	05	10.6	1)	Ulm	13 Jun
Sándor Hajdu	Hun	05	10.6w	1)	Sátoraljaujhely	11 Jul

Karl Gerke	Ger	04	10.6	1)	Hannover	08 Aug
Willy Thumm	Ger	97	10.6w	5)	Leipzig	08 Aug
Marinus van den Berge	Hol	00	10.6	1)	Stuttgart	15 Aug

Doubtful timing:

Jakob Schüller	Ger	05	10.5	1)	Krefeld	25 Jul
Houben			10.6	3)	Krefeld	25 Jul

200 metres (half-to-full turn)

Roland Locke	USA	03	20.4*	1)	Lincoln	01 May
Jackson Scholz	USA	97	21.3*	1)hcp	Dunedin	20 Feb
Henry Russell	USA	04	21.4*	1)	London	10 Jul
Helmut Körnig	Ger	05	21.5	1)	Leipzig	07 Aug
Norman Grehan	Aus	02	21.5*	1)	Brisbane	21 Aug
Werner Wege	Ger	04	21.6	1)	Düsseldorf	05 Sep
Per Oscar Andersen	Nor	03	21.6	1)	Stockhol	18 Sep
Arthur Porritt	NZ	00	21.7*e	2)	London	10 Jul
Joachim Büchner	Ger	05	21.7	2)	Leipzig	17 Jul
Leslie Parker	Aus	03	21.7*e	2)	Brisbane	21 Aug
Hubert Houben	Ger	98	21.7	2)	Düsseldorf	05 Sep

220 yards (straight course)

Jackson Scholz	USA	97	20.9	1)	San Francisco	08 May
Charles Borah	USA	06	20.9	1)	Los Angeles	15 May
Fred Alderman	USA	05	20.9	1)	Detroit	May
Roland Locke	USA	03	20.9	1)	Chicago	12 Jun
Henry Russell	USA	04	21.0w	1)	Cambridge, MA	29 May
Hale	USA		21.1	1)	Champaign, IL	15 May
Tom Sharkey	USA	05	21.1	1)	Oberlin, OH	29 May
Richard Bartholomew	USA		21.2	1)	State College, PA	08 May
Victor Leschinsky	USA		21.2	1)	Ann Arbor	08 May
Ray Clark	USA		21.2	1)	New Haven, CT	15 May

4x100 metre relay

Newark AC	USA		41.4*	1)	Philadelphia	06 Jul
(Harwood, Cummings, Clarke, Bowman)						
Hol			41.7	1)	Köln	12 Sep
(de Boer, Broos, Lamp, van den Berge)						
Ger			41.8	1)	Basel	22 Aug
(Dreibholz, Wege, Houben, Körnig)						
Budapest Team	Hun		42.1	1)	Budapest	19 Sep
(Rózsahegyi, Hajdu, Vida, Raggambi-Fluck)						
UAI	Fra		42.6	1)	Colombes	11 Jul
(Monteil, R.Mourlon, Jay, A.Mourlon)						
FC Liègeois	Bel		42.6	2)	Haarlem	08 Aug
(Leblanc, Moetbeek, Zinner, Brockart)						

1927

100 yards

Charles Borah	USA	06	9.5	1)	Los Angeles	16 Apr
Kent Farley	USA		9.6	1)	Columbia, MO	09 Apr
James Quinn	USA	06	9.6	1)	Kensington, RI	07 May
John Currie	USA	02	9.6w	1)	Greensboro, NC	07 May
Alfred Miller	USA	04	9.6w	1)	Cambridge, MA	14 May
James Pappas	USA	06	9.6	1)	Ithaca	21 May
Richard Bartholomew	USA		9.6	1)	State College, PA	21 May
Fred Alderman	USA	05	9.6w	1)	East Lansing, MI	21 May
Lowell Grady	USA		9.6w	1)	Lincoln	21 May
Chester Bowman	USA	01	9.6	1)	Lincoln	02 Jul
William deHart Hubbard	USA	03	9.6	1)	Cincinnati	17 Sep

Doubtful timing:

Daniel Joubert	SA	09	9.6w	1)	Dundee	12 Nov

100 metres

José E. Barrientos	Cub	04	10.2w	1)	Habana	08 May

(Barrientos)			10.4	1)	Habana	26 Mar
Helmut Körnig	Ger	05	10.4w	1)	Stettin	22 Jun
George Lammers	Ger	05	10.4w	1)	Bremen	17 Jul
Hubert Houben	Ger	98	10.4	1)	Hannover	04 Sep
Jakob Schüller	Ger	05	10.4	2)	Hannover	04 Sep
Friedrich Wichmann	Ger	01	10.5	1)	Stuttgart	03 Jul
(Lammers)			10.5	1)	Berlin	14 Aug
Per Oscar Andersen	Nor	03	10.5	1)	København	28 Aug
Anselmo Gonzaga	Phi	06	10.5	1)	Manila	15 Dec

Rolling start:

Helmut Körnig	Ger	05	10.4	1)	Berlin	05 Jun

200 metres (half-to-full turn)

Lowell Grady	USA		21.2w	1)	Lincoln	21 May
Jakob Schüller	Ger	05	21.4	1)	Düsseldorf	31 Jul
Georg Lammers	Ger	05	21.5	1)h	Frankfurt/M.	01 May
Charles Borah	USA	06	21,5*	1)	Lincoln	02 Jul
Hubert Houben	Ger	98	21.5	2)	Düsseldorf	31 Jul
José E. Barrientos	Cub	04	21.6	1)	Habana	08 May
Per Oscar Andersen	Nor	03	21.6	1)	Helsinki	03 Sep

220 yards (straight course)

Fred Alderman	USA	05	20.5w	1)	East Lansing, MI	21 May
Ed Haynes	USA		20.8 A	1)		21 May
Charles Borah	USA	06	20.9	1)	Philadelphia	28 May
Frank Wykoff	USA	09	21.0w	1)	Modesto, CA	07 May
(Alderman)			21.0	1)	South Bend, IN	14 May
Joseph Della Maria	USA		21.0	1)	Chicago	18 Jun
John Everingham	USA		21.1	1)	Iowa City	14 May
Les Hables	USA	09	21.2we	2)	Modesto, CA	07 May
Dean Anderson	USA		21.2 e	2)	Los Angeles	04 Jun
Lowell Grady	USA		21.2 e	2)	Chicago	11 Jun
Henry Cummings	USA	05	21.2	1)	Yonkers, NY	18 Jun

4x100 metre relay

Newark AC	USA	(Bowman, Currie, Pappas, Cummings)	40.8*	1)B	Lincoln	04 Jul
	Ger	(Büchner, Wichmann, Houben, Schüller)	41.0	1)	Düsseldorf	31 Jul
Polyt. Harriers	UK	(Hodge, Rice, Simmons, London)	41.4	1)	Hannover	04 Sep
	Fra	(Sylvestre, Crestois, Fischer, Hirliman)	42.2	1)	Colombes	18 Sep
KAOE	Hun	(Sugár, Magyar, Vida, Balázs)	42.6	1)	Budapest	18 Sep
YMCA	Arg	(Butti, Pellosi, Ure Aldao, Pina)	42.6	1)	Buenos Aires	11 Dec

1928

100 yards

Claude Bracey	USA	09	9.5w	1)	Austin	23 Mar
Aubrey Cockrell	USA		9.5w	1)	Austin	12 Apr
Frank Lombardi	USA		9.5+	1)	Selma, CA	05 May
Sam McBain	USA		9.6w	1)	Santa Maria, CA	10 Mar
Gorge Simpson	USA	08	9.6	1)	Colombus	21 Apr
Charles Borah	USA	06	9.6	1)	Fresno	28 Apr
Weldon Draper	USA		9.6	2)	Fresno	28 Apr
Frank Hussey	USA	05	9.6	1)	West Point	05 May
E. A. Weichert	USA		9.6w	1)	Dallas	01 Jun
(Bracey)			9.6	1)	Chicago	09 Jun
Charles Paddock	USA	00	9.6	1)	Santa Barbara	09 Jun
Leigh Miller	Can		9.6	1)	Pictou	29 Aug

+ = actually 9.6 for 101 y. (92.35 m.)

100 metres

José E.Barrientos	Cub	04	10.2w	1)	Habana	31 Mar
(Barrientos)			10.4	1)	Habana	21 Apr
Ernst Geerling	Ger	09	10.4	1)	Frankenthal	01 Jul

Richard Corts	Ger	05	10.4	1)	Dsseldorf	15 Jul
Georg Lammers	Ger	05	10.4	1)h	Oldenburg	26 Aug
Hubert Houben	Ger	98	10.5	2)	Dsseldorf	15 Jul
Edward Hamm	USA	06	10.5	1)	Stockholm	15 Aug
Ferenc Gerö	Hun	00	10.5	1)	Kassel	19 Aug
Arthur Jonath	Ger	09	10.5	2)	Bochum	12 Sep
Helmut Körnig	Ger	05	10.5	1)	Mainz	16 Sep

200 metres (half-to-full turn)

Helmut Körnig	Ger	05	21.0	1)	Bochum	26 Aug
Hubert Houben	Ger	98	21.1	2)	Bochum	26 Aug
Jakob Schüller	Ger	05	21.1	3)	Bochum	26 Aug
Wilfred Legg	SA	06	21.3* A	1)h2	Bloemfontein	18 May
Roland Locke	USA	03	21.4	1)	Colombes	12 Aug
John Rinkel	UK	05	21.5*	1)	Oxford	23 Jun
Hermann Schlöske	Ger	05	21.6	2)	Berlin	30 Jun
Friedrich Wichmann	Ger	01	21.6*	1)	London	07 Jul
Henry Russell	USA	04	21.6	1)	Köln	07 Aug
James Ball	Can	03	21.6+	1)	Dublin	16 Aug

+ = during 220 y. (201.16 m.) race

220 yards (straight course)

Claude Bracey	USA	09	20.9	1)	Chicago	09 Jun
Frank Wykoff	USA	09	20.9°	1)	Los Angeles	16 Jun
Wesley Foster	USA		21.0	1)	Moscow, ID	11 May
Jim Barnes	USA		21.0	1)	Wooster, OH	26 May
George Simpson	USA	08	21.0e	2)	Chicago	09 Jun
Helmut Körnig	GER	05	21.0°	1)	Berlin	19 Aug
Ralph Metcalfe	USA	10	21.1w	1)	Champaign	19 May
Don Bennett	USA	08	21.1	1)	Columbus	26 May

° = 200 m time plus 0.1

4x100 metre relay

German Team	Ger	(Corts, Wichmann, Houben, Körnig)	40.8	1)hcp	Berlin	03 Jun
	USA	(Wykoff, Quinn, Borah, Russell)	41.0	1)	Amsterdam	05 Aug
	Fra	(Cerbonney, Fischer, Dufau, A.Mourlon)	41.6	1)	Colombes	10 Jun
	UK	(Gill, Smouha, Rangeley, London)	41.8e	3)	Amsterdam	05 Aug
Hungarian Team	Hun	(Odri, F.Gerö, Sugár, Raggambi-Fluck)	41.8	2)	Köln	07 Aug

1929

100 yards

Claude Bracey	USA	09	9.4w	1)	Dallas	30 Mar
Russell Sweet	USA	04	9.4w	1)	San Francisco	04 May
George Simpson	USA	08	9.4	1)	Chicago	08 Jun
(Bracey)			9.5	1)	Austin	29 Mar
Cy Leland	USA	10	9.5	1)	Waco	20 Apr
Richard Kent	USA		9.5w	1)	West Point	18 May
Eddie Tolan	USA	08	9.5	1)	Evanston	25 May

100 metres

Eugen Eldracher	Ger	07	10.3w	1)	Seoul	17 Oct
Georg Lammers	Ger	05	10.4	1)	Oldenburg	12 May
Erich Borchmeyer	Ger	05	10.4w	1)h	Ahlen	16 Jun
(Eldracher)			10.4	1)	Mannheim	30 Jun
Marinus van den Berge	Hol	00	10.4w	1)	Rotterdam	Jul
Helmut Körnig	Ger	05	10.4w	1)	Budapest	28 Jul
Eddie Tolan	USA	08	10.4	1)	Köln	31 Jul

200 metres (half-to-full turn)

Eugen Eldracher	Ger	07	21.1	1)	Mannheim	30 Jun
Eddie Tolan	USA	08	21.1	1)	Stockholm	09 Aug
Helmut Körnig	Ger	05	21.2w	1)	Berlin	09 Jun

Friedrich Wichmann	Ger	01	21.2		1)h1	Breslau	20 Jul
Erwyn Gillmeister	Ger	07	21.3		2)	Stockholm	09 Aug
Werner Gerhardt	SA	07	21.3*	A	1)	Pretoria	16 Dec
Erich Borchmeyer	Ger	05	21.4		1)	Duisburg	30 Jun
Frank Wykoff	USA	09	21.4*e		2)	Vancouver	13 Jul
(Körnig)			21.4		1)	Berlin	04 Aug
Reginald Bowen	USA	07	21.4		3)	Stockholm	09 Aug
William Walters	SA	07	21.5*	A	1)	Kimberley	30 Mar
Werner Storz	Ger	04	21.5w		2)	Berlin	09 Jun
James Carlton	Aus	08	21.5*		1)	Sydney	16 Nov

220 yards (straight course)

George Simpson	USA	08	20.6		1)	Columbus	20 Apr
Eddie Tolan	USA	08	20.8e		2)	Evanston	25 May
Hubert Meier	USA	08	20.9		1)	Columbia	04 May
Brutus Beall	USA		21.1w		1)	Shawnee	11 May
Jack Davis	USA		21.1	A	1)	Denver	18 May
John White	USA		21.1	A	2)	Denver	18 May
Crosby Pendleton	USA		21.1		1)	Pullman	25 May
Richard Kent	USA		21.1w		1)	Philadelphia	01 Jun
Claude Bracey	USA	09	21.1		1)h1	Chicago	07 Jun

4x100 metre relay

SC Charlottenburg	Ger	(Körnig, Grosser, Nathan, Schlöske)	40.8	1)	Breslau	22 Jul
Los Angeles AC	USA	(Maurer, Tolan, Bowen, Wykoff)	41.0*	1)	Vancouver	12 Jul
Griquas	SA	(Wigginton, Viljoen, Legg, van Aswegen)	41.8*	1)	Kimberley	30 Nov
	Arg	(Spinassi, Gagliardi, Pages, Ure Aldao)	42.2	1)	Lima	07 May
Polyt. Harriers	UK	(London, Simmons, Ellery, Stagnell)	42.2*	1)	London	06 Jul

Noteworthy performances made in 4x100 y. (365.76 m.) relay:

	Ger	(Körnig, Wichmann, Eldracher, Schlöske)	37.8	1)	London	24 Aug
England	UK	(Crawford, Ellery, Simmons, London)	39.0	2)	London	24 Aug

1930

100 yards

Cy Leland	USA	10	9.4w		1)	Lawrence	19 Apr
Frank Wykoff	USA	09	9.4		1)	Los Angeles	10 May
Hubert Meier	USA	08	9.4		1)	Lincoln	24 May
Claude Bracey	USA	09	9.5w		2)	Lawrence	19 Apr
George Simpson	USA	08	9.5		1)	Columbus	03 May
Les Hables	USA	09	9.5w		1)	San Francisco	03 May
James Carlton	Aus	08	9.6w		1)h	Melbourne	25 Jan
(Leland)			9.6		1)	Fort Worth	15 Mar
Ray Alf	USA		9.6		1)	El Monte, CA	29 Mar
John Hass	USA		9.6		1)		
Hector Dyer	USA	10	9.6		1)	Los Angeles	12 Apr
(Bracey)			9.6		1)h3	Lawrence	19 Apr
DeArmond Hutson	USA		9.6		1)		
Fay Loveridge	USA		9.6w		1)	Sacramento	03 May
Claude Grabert	USA		9.6w	A	1)	Albuquerque	10 May
Ernie Useman	USA		9.6		1)	Champaign	17 May
Percy Williams	Can	08	9.6		1)	Vancouver	26 Jun

Uncertain estimates:

Les Hables	USA	09	9.6	2)	Los Angeles	10 May
Emmett Toppino	USA	09	9.6	3)	Chicago	07 Jun
Eddie Tolan	USA	08	9.6	4)	Chicago	07 Jun

Downhill:

John Hanlon	UK	05	9.6w	1)	Eastleigh	07 Jun

100 metres

Eddie Tolan	USA	08	10.2	1)	Vancouver	01 Jul
George Simpson	USA	08	10.3e	2)	Vancouver	01 Jul

Percy Williams	Can	08	10.3	1)	Toronto	09 Aug
George Lammers	Ger	05	10.4	1)	Flensburg	01 Jun
Helmut Körnig	Ger	05	10.4w	1)	Berlin	13 Jul
(Körnig)			10.4	1)	Stockholm	20 Jul
Arthur Jonath	Ger	09	10.5w	1)	Stockholm	10 Jun
Marinus van den Berge	Hol	00	10.5w	)		
Friedrich-Wilhelm Regener	Ger	06	10.5w	1)h	Königsberg	02 Aug
Christiaan Berger	Hol	11	10.5	1)	Hilversum	17 Aug

200 metres (half-to-full turn)

Christiaan Berger	Hol	11	21.1	1)	Amsterdam	15 Jun
James Charlton	Aus	08	21.2*	1)	Sydney	18 Jan
Helmut Körnig	Ger	05	21.2	1)	Köln	15 Jun
George Simpson	USA	08	21.2*	1)	Pittsburgh	23 Aug
Frank Wykoff	USA	09	21.3*	1)	Los Angeles	05 Apr
Marinus van den Berge	Hol	00	21.3	2)	Amsterdam	15 Jun
Max Mährlein	Ger	06	21.4	1)	Frankfurt/M	15 Jun
Erwin Gillmeister	Ger	07	21.4	1)	Kassel	18 Aug
Werner Gerhardt	SA	07	21.5* A	1)	Johannesburg	21 Apr
John Hanlon	UK	05	21.5*w	1)	Oxford	21 Jun
Erich Borchmeyer	Ger	05	21.5w	1)h	Giessen	20 Jul

220 yards (straight course)

George Simpson	USA	08	20.6	1)	Vancouver	01 Jul
Eddie Tolan	USA	08	20.6	2)	Vancouver	01 Jul
Hector Dyer	USA	10	20.8w	1)	San Francisco	03 May
Cy Leland	USA	10	20.9	1)	College Station	12 May
Hugh Ratliff	USA		21.0	1)		
Ralph Metcalfe	USA	10	21.1w	1)	Champaign	17 May
Crosby Pendleton	USA		21.1	1)	Seattle	24 May
Helmut Körnig	Ger	05	21.1°	1)	Berlin-Grunewald	03 Aug
Claude Bracey	USA	09	21.2	2)	Houston	05 Apr
Charles Farmer	USA		21.2	1)	Chapel Hill	28 Apr
Joe Mendel	USA		21.2	1)	Sioux Falls	24 May

° = 200 m. time plus 0.1

4x100 metre relay

Illinois Univ.	USA	(Useman, Dickenson, Cave, Patterson)	40.8*	1)	Lawrence	19 Apr
DSV 78 Hannover	Ger	(Jonath, Borchmeyer, Renders, Gillmeister)	41.0	1)r2	Kassel	18 Aug
	Fra	(Sureaud, Parrain, Beigbeder, A.Mourlon)	41.6	1)	Colombes	13 Jul
	Ita	(Lucci, Salviati, Maregatti, Toetti)	41.6	2)	Colombes	13 Jul
All India Bengal Team		(M.Sutton, Lesming, W.Sutton, Vernieux)	42.0*	1)	Allahabad	08 Feb
	Can	(Brown, Miller, Adams, Fitzpatrick)	42.0*	1)	Hamilto	23 Aug

Noteworthy performances made in 4x100 yards relay:

USA	(Sweet, Leland, Simpson, Tolan)	37.5	1)	Chicago	27 Aug

1931

100 yards

Daniel Joubert	SA	09	9.3w	1)h	Grahamstown	15 May
(Joubert)			9.4	1)	Grahamstown	16 May
James Carlton	Aus	08	9.4w	1)	Newcastle, NSW	15 Nov
Payton Glass	USA		9.5w	1)h1	Austin	27 Mar
Paul Swift	USA		9.5	1)	Lawrence	18 Apr
Frank Wykoff	USA	09	9.5	1)	Fresno	09 May
Joe Mendel	USA	06	9.5	1)	Huron, SD	23 May
Joe Klaner	USA		9.5w	1)	Lincoln	23 May
Emmett Toppino	USA	09	9.5	1)h	Chicago	05 Jun

100 metres

Helmut Körnig	Ger	05	10.3w	1)	Regensburg	14 May
Eddie Tolan	USA	08	10.3	1)	Vancouver	22 Aug

Georg Lammers	Ger	05	10.4w	1)	Friesoythe	03 May
(Körnig)			10.4	1)	Bremen	17 May
Arthur Jonath	Ger	09	10.4	1)	Köln	27 May
(Lammers)			10.4	1)	Osnabrück	31 May
Gustav Hanssen	Nor	02	10.4	1)	Hamburg	02 Aug
Erhard Pflug	Ger	10	10.4	1)	Flensburg	23 Aug
Juan B. Pina	Arg	07	10.4	1)	Buenos Aires	29 Nov
Christiaan Berger	Hol	11	10.5	1)	Drachten	25 May
Takayoshi Yoshioka	Jap	09	10.5	1)	Koshien	30 May

200 metres (half-to-full turn)

Eddie Tolan	USA	08	20.9*	1)	Lincoln	04 Jul
James Carlton	Aus	09	20.9*	1)hcp	Newcastle, NSW	15 Nov
Ralph Sickel	USA		21.0*w	1)	Lincoln	23 May
Ralph Metcalfe	USA	10	21.0*e	2)	Lincoln	04 Jul
George Simpson	USA	08	21.1*w	1)	Napier	24 Jan
Joe Klaner	USA		21.1*we	2)	Lincoln	23 May
Daniel Joubert	SA	09	21.2*	1)	Grahamstown	16 May
Jack Burnett	USA		21.2*	1)	Lincoln	03 Jul
Joe Mendel	USA		21.2*	2)	Lincoln	03 Jul
Arthur Jonath	Ger	09	21.4	1)	Kassel	12 Jul

Doubtful timing:

Dolf Benz	Hol		21.4w	1)	Zaandam	19 Jul

220 yards (straight course)

Joe Klaner	USA		20.8w	1)	Lawrence	11 Apr
Frank Wykoff	USA	08	20.8	1)	Los Angeles	16 May
Eddie Tolan	USA	08	20.9	1)	Evanston	23 May
Frank Wisner	USA		21.0	1)	Birmingham, AL	16 May
Cy Leland	USA	10	21.0	1)	Los Angeles	19 Jun
George Simpson	USA	08	21.1°	1)	Tokyo	26 Apr
Clifford Mell	USA		21.1	1)		

° = 200 m. time plus 0.1.

Course 2 y. (1.82 m.) short:

Frank Wykoff	USA	08	20.5	1)	Glendale	25 Apr

4x100 metre relay

Univ. of So. California	USA	(Delby, Maurer, Guyer, Wykoff)	40.6*	1)	Fresno	09 May
	Ger	(Körnig, Mölle, Borchmeyer, Jonath)	41.1	1)	Köln	30 Aug
Japan Student Team	Jap	(Inuma, Sasaki, Anno, Yoshioka)	41.6	1)	Tokyo	27 Oct
	UK	(Reid, Saunders, Cohen, London)	41.8	2)	Köln	30 Aug
	Fra	(Imbert, Finat, Beigbeder, Sureaud)	42.0	2)	Colombes	06 Sep

1932

100 yards

Robert Kiesel	USA	11	9.5		1)	Berkeley	09 apr
Dumbar Hunt	USA		9.5w		1)	Los Angeles	16 Apr
Ralph Metcalfe	USA	10	9.5		1)	Des Moines	30 Apr
Don Bennett	USA	08	9.5w		1)	Evanston	21 May
Howard Greenwell	USA		9.5w	A	1)	Salt Lake City	21 May

100 metres (E = electric Kirby Camera time)

Ralph Metcalfe	USA	10	10.2	1)	Chicago	11 Jun
Arthur Jonath	Ger	09	10.3	1)r1	Bochum	05 Jun
Jesse Owens	USA	13	10.3w	1)	Cleveland	11 Jun
Eddie Tolan	USA	08	10.3w	1)	Ann Arbor	25 Jun
Tolan 10.38 E			10.3	1)	Los Angeles	01 Aug
(Metcalfe 10.38 E)			10.3	2)	Los Angeles	01 Aug
Emmett Toppino	USA	09	10.4	1)	New Orleans	03 Apr
Peyton Glass	USA		10.4	1)	Norman, OK	27 May
Robert Kiesel	USA	11	10.4	1)	San Francisco	04 Jun

Ernst Geerling	Ger	09	10.4	2)r1	Bochum	05 Jun
Georg Lammers	Ger	05	10.4	1)	Kassel	14 Jun
Claude Bracey	USA	09	10.4	1)	Houston	18 Jun
Frank Wykoff	USA	09	10.4	1)	Los Angeles	18 Jun
Harold Wright	Can	08	10.4 A	1)	Calgary	25 Jun
Hector Dyer	USA	10	10.4	1)	Long Beach	02 Jul
Burchall Pearson	Can	15	10.4	1)	Hamilton, ONT	15 Jul
Franz Heithoff	Ger	09	10.4w	1)	Rheydt	17 Jul
Franz Buthe-Pieper	Ger	10	10.4w	2)	Rheydt	17 Jul

200 metres (half-to-full turn) (E = Electric Kirby Camera time)

James Carlton	Aus	08	20.5*	1)	Sydney	18 Jan
Arthur Jonath	Ger	09	21.2	1)	Kassel	14 Jun
Eddie Tolan (21.12 E)	USA	08	21.2	1)	Los Angeles	03 Aug
Hector Dyer	USA	19	21.4	1)	Los Angeles	18 Jun
Carlos Bianchi Luti (21.46 E)	Arg	11	21.4	1)q3	Los Angeles	02 Aug
George Simpson	USA	08	21.4	2)	Los Angeles	03 Aug
Edward Hampson	Aus		21.5*w	1)	Sydney	27 Feb
Wolfgang Vent	Ger	11	21.5	2)	Kassel	14 Jun
Roy Delby	USA		21.5	2)	Los Angeles	18 Jun
Ralph Metcalfe (21.49 E)	USA	10	21.5	1)	Palo Alto	16 Jul
William Walters	SA	07	21.5	2)q1	Los Angeles	02 Aug

Uncertain estimate:

Ewan Davidson	Aus		21.4*	2)	Sydney	18 Jan

220 yards (straight course)

Ralph Metcalfe	USA	10	19.8w	1)	Toronto	03 Sep
Don Bennett	USA	08	20.5w	1)	Evanston	21 May
(Metcalfe)			20.5	1)	Chicago	11 Jun
(Bennett)			20.7	1)	Columbus	14 May
Ralph Montague	USA	09	20.7°w	1)	San Francisco	04 Jun
Bill Weems	USA		20.8	)		
James Johnson	USA	12	20.8w	2)	Chicago	28 May
Eddie Tolan	USA	08	20.8°w	1)	Ann Arbor	25 Jun
(Johnson)			20.9e	2)	Chicago	11 Jun
Foy Draper	USA	13	21.0w	1)	Huntington Park	01 Apr
Haskett Derby	USA		21.0	1)	New Haven	14 May
Richard Kent	USA		21.0	1)	Montclair, NJ	11 Jun

° = 200 m. time plus 0.1

4x100 metre relay

USA	(Kiesel, Toppino, Dyer, Wykoff)	40.0	1)	Los Angeles	07 Aug
Ger	(Körnig, Lammers, Borchmeyer, Jonath)	40.6	1)r2	Kassel	14 Jun
Ita	(Salviati, Castelli, Maregatti, Toetti)	41.0	1)	Firenze	26 Jun
Can	(Williams, Brown, Wright, Pearson)	41.3	4)	Los Angeles	07 Aug
Jap	(Yoshioka, Nambu, Anno, Nakajima)	41.3	5)	Los Angeles	07 Aug

Noteworthy performance made in 4x100 y. (365.76 m.) relay:

USA	(Montague, Toppino, Dyer, Metcalfe)	37.8	1)	San Francisco	14 Aug

1933

100 yards

James Johnson	USA	12	9.4w	1)	Bloomington	03 May
Ralph Metcalfe	USA	10	9.4w	1)	Kalamazoo	13 May
Jesse Owens	USA	13	9.4	1)	Chicago (HS ev)	17 Jun
(Metcalfe)			9.4	1)	Chicago (Coll ev)	17 Jun
(Johnson)			9.5	1)	Normal, IL	15 Apr
Frank Wykoff	USA	09	9.5	1)	Santa Barbara	29 Apr
Paul Starr	USA		9.5	2)	Chicago (Coll ev)	17 Jun

Unsanctioned meet:

Carl Nelson	USA		9.5	1)	Clinton, IA	13 Jun

100 metres

Arthur Jonath	Ger	09	10.3	1)	Hamm	23 Jul
Ralph Metcalfe	USA	10	10.3w	1)	Malmö	28 Jul
(Metcalfe)			10.3	1)	Düsseldorf	30 Jul
Erich Borchmeyer	Ger	05	10.3	1)	Köln	12 Aug
Ivo de Pádua Sallowicz	Bra	08	10.3w	1)	São Paulo	01 Oct
Carlos Bianchi Luti	Arg	11	10.4	1)h	Montevideo	06 Apr
James Johnson	USA	12	10.4	1)	Chicago	29 Jun
Christiaan Berger	Hol	11	10.4	1)	Den Haag	02 Jul
George Lammers	Ger	05	10.4	P)	Stuttgart	27 Jul
Friedrich Hendrix	Ger	11	10.4	2)	Köln	12 Aug
Egon Schein	Ger	12	10.4	3)	Köln	12 Aug
Takayoshi Yoshioka	Jap	09	10.4	1)	Tokyo	23 Sep

200 metres (half-to-full turn)

Ralph Metcalfe	USA	10	20.6	1)hcp	Budapest	12 Aug
John Horsfall	Aus		21.2*w	1)	Melbourne	10 May
Ivan Fuqua	USA	09	21.2	2)	Malmö	28 Jul
Arthur Jonath	Ger	09	21.3	1)	Bochum	25 May
Burchall Pearson	Can	15	21.4*	1)	Hamilton,Ont	19 Jul
Erich Borchmeyer	Ger	05	21.4	1)	Köln	13 Aug
Egon Schein	Ger	12	21.4	2)	Köln	13 Aug
James Abbott	USA	14	21.5*	1)	Los Angeles	31 Mar
Robin Murdoch	UK	11	21.5*w	1)	Glasgow	24 Jun
Archie Turner	UK		21.6*we	2)	Glasgow	24 Jun
Erhard Pflug	Ger	10	21.6	3)	Köln	13 Aug
Renos Frangoudis	Gre	09	21.6	1)	Athinai	07 Oct

Timers missed flash, but ratified as a record:

József Kovács	Hun	11	21.0	1)	Budapest	15 Oct

220 yards (straight course)

Ralph Metcalfe	USA	10	20.4	1)	Chicago (Coll ev)	17 Jun
Jesse Owens	USA	13	20.7	1)	Chicago (HS ev)	17 Jun
James Johnson	USA	12	20.7	2)	Chicago (Coll ev)	17 Jun
Elmer Helbing	USA		20.8	1)	Austin	6 May
Paul Starr	USA		20.8	3)	Chicago (Coll ev)	17 Jun
William Fritz	Can	14	20.8	1)hcp	Toronto	02 Sep
Robert Grieve	USA	13	20.9	2)	Chicago (HS ev)	17 Jun
Edwin Toribio	USA		21.0	1)	Batn Rouge	29 Apr
Frank Plumb	USA		21.0w	1)	Pullman	20 May

Doubtful timing:

Burchall Pearson	Can	15	20.4	1)h	Fort William	05 Aug

4x100 metre relay

Oklahoma A&M Coll	USA	(Gallagher, Littlejohn, Harrington, Glass)	41.2*	1)	Lawrence	22 Apr
TuS Bochum	Ger	(Vent, Buthe-Pieper, Borchmeyer, Jonath)	41.5	1)	Bochum	28 May
	Hol	(Benz, Berger, Jansen, van den Berge)	41.9	1)	Amsterdam	13 Aug
	Hun	(Paizs, Forgács, G.Gerö, Nagy)	42.0	1)	Budapest	06 Aug
	UK	(Summers, Yates, Rangeley, Saunders)	42.0	1)	Milano	17 Sep

1934

100 yards

George Anderson	USA	16	9.4	1)	Fresno	12 May
Jesse Owens	USA	13	9.4	1)	Columbus	19 May
Robert Kiesel	USA	11	9.5	1)	Berkeley	07 Apr
Ralph Metcalfe	USA	10	9.5	1)	Escanaba, MI	02 Jun

100 metres

José Xavier de Almeida	Bra	04	10.2w	1)	Rio de Janeiro	23 Sep

Erich Borchmeyer	Ger	05	10.3	1)	Berlin	01 Jul
Eulace Peacock	USA	14	10.3	1)	Oslo	06 Aug
Chriaan Berger	Hol	11	10.3	1)	Amsterdam	26 Aug
Ralph Metcalfe	USA	10	10.3	1)	Osaka	15 Sep
George Anderson	USA	16	10.4	1)	Los Angeles	01 Jun
József Sir	Hun	12	10.4w	1)	Budapest	23 Jun
Jesse Owens	USA	13	10.4e	2)	Milwaukee	30 Jun
(Sir)			10.4	1)s1	Berlin	01 Jul
Gerd Horberger	Ger	10	10.4	2)	Frankfurt/M	22 Jul
Federico Andreini	Arg	13	10.4	1)	Córdoba	12 Oct

200 metres (half-to-full turn)

Edward Hampson	Aus		21.2*w	1)	Blenheim	07 Mar
Ivan Fuqua	USA	09	21.2	1)	Frankfurt/M	22 Jul
Paul Hänni	Swz	14	21.2	1)	Strasbourg	26 Aug
Ralph Metcalfe	USA	10	21.3*	1)	Milwaukee	08 Jun
(Hampson)			21.4*	1)	Melbourne	20 Jan
Howard Yates	Aus		21.4*	1)	Melbourne	24 Feb
Martinus Theunissen	SA	11	21.5*	1)		
József Sir	Hun	12	21.5	1)	Budapest	30 Jun
Christiaan Berger	Hol	11	21.5	1)	Amsterdam	18 Aug
Erich Borchmeyer	Ger	05	21.5	1)	Stuttgart	19 Aug

220 yards (straight course)

Ralph Metcalfe	USA	10	20.3°w	1)	Tokyo	09 Sep
Charles Parsons	USA	11	20.7°w	2)	Tokyo	09 Sep
James LuValle	USA	12	20.8	1)	Los Angeles	03 Mar
Robert Kiesel	USA	11	20.8	1)	Berkeley	17 Mar
Foy Draper	USA	13	20.8	1)	Berkeley	09 Jun
(Metcalfe)			20.9	1)	Los Angeles	23 Jun

° = 200 metre time plus 0.1.

4x100 metre relay

U. of So. California	USA	(Draper, Osburne, Abbott, Parsons)	40.9*	1)	Fresno	12 May
	Ger	(Schein, Gillmeiester, Hornberger, Borchmeyer)	41.0	1)	Torino	09 Sep
Budapest BTE	Hun	(Minai, Paitz, Kovács, Sir)	41.2	1)	Budapest	16 Sep
	Jap	(Sasaki, Suzuki, Taniguchi, Yoshioka)	41.5	2)	Tokyo	08 Sep
	Hol	(Osendarp, Boersma, Janssen, Berger)	41.6	3)	Torino	09 Sep

1935

100 yards

Harvey Wallender	USA	14	9.4w	1)h	Austin	30 Mar
Herman Neugass	USA	15	9.4w	1)	Austin	30 Mar
Jesse Owens	USA	13	9.4	1)	Evanston	18 May
Michael Moran	Aus		9.5w	1)	Sydney	12 Jan
George Anderson	USA	16	9.5w	1)	Berkeley	09 Mar
(Neugass)			9.5	1)	University, AL	06 Apr
Bennie Gastmeyer	USA	11	9.5w	1)	Paris, TX	26 Apr
(Anderson)			9.5	1)	Fresno	11 May
Eulace Peacock	USA	14	9.5	1)	Villanova	18 May
Robert Grieve	USA	13	9.5	2)	Ann Arbor	25 May
Carson Schoemake	USA		9.5	1)	Seattle	01 Jun
Eric Grimbeek	SA	08	9.5w A	1)	Johannesburg	14 Sep
Howard Yates	Aus	13	9.5w	1)	Melbourne	21 Dec

100 metres

Eulace Peacock	USA	14	10.2w	1)h2	Lincoln	04 Jul
Takayoshi Yoshioka	Jap	09	10.3w	1)	Nishinomiya	09 Jun
Ralph Metcalfe	USA	10	10.3we	2)	Lincoln	04 Jul
(Yoshioka)			10.3	1)	Seoul	04 Aug
(Peacock)			10.3	1)	Basel	06 Aug
Herman Neugass	USA	15	10.4	1)	Baton Rouge	03 May
Erich Borchmeyer	Ger	05	10.4w	1)h	Stuttgart	18 May

Mutsuo Taniguchi	Jap	13	10.4w	1)	Nishinomiya	26 May
Bumpei Kondo	Jap		10.4w	2)	Nishinomiya	26 May
Karl Neckermann	Ger	11	10.4w	1)	Baden-Baden	30 Jun
Ralph Sickel	USA		10.4w	1)	Lincoln	03 Jul
Jesse Owens	USA	13	10.4we	3)	Lincoln	04 Jul
Wilhelm Leichum	Ger	11	10.4w	1)	Stettin	06 Jul
Foy Draper	USA	13	10.4	1)	Oslo	02 Aug
Paul Hänni	Swz	14	10.4	2)	Basel	06 Aug
Antonio Fondevila	Arg	16	10.4	1)	Buenos Aires	21 Dec

200 metres (half-to-full turn)

Ralph Metcalfe	USA	10	21.0w		1)	Lincoln	04 Jul
Martinus Theunissen	SA	11	21.0*	A	1)	Johannesburg	14 Sep
Arthur Sweeney	UK	09	21.1*e	A	2)	Johannesburg	14 Sep
Eric Grimbeek	SA	08	21.2*	A	1)	Pretoria	30 Nov
Paul Hänni	Swz	14	21.2		1)	Basel	06 Aug
Mack Robinson	USA	14	21.3*		1)	Santa Barbara	27 Apr
Donald Dunn	USA		21.3w		1)h2	Lincoln	04 Jul
George Anderson	USA	16	21.3we		2T)	Lincoln	04 Jul
Foy Draper	USA	13	21.3we		2T)	Lincoln	04 Jul
Gerd Hornberger	Ger	10	21.3		1)	Darmstadt	14 Jul
Joe Haley	Can		21.3*		1)	Victoria	28 Aug
Martnus Osendarp	Hol	16	21.3		1)	Malmö	14 Sep

220 yards (straight course)

Jesse Owens	USA	13	20.3	1)	Ann Arbor	25 May
Harvey Wallender	USA	14	20.5	1)	Austin	03 May
Bennie Gastmeyer	USA	11	20.6w	1)	Commerce, TX	07 May
Andrew Dooley	USA	14	20.7	2)	Ann Arbor	25 May
Herman Neugass	USA	15	20.8°w	1)	Baton Rouge	04 May
Edward O'Brien	USA	14	20.8	1)	Syracuse	11 May
Carson Shoemake	USA		20.8	1)	Seattle	11 May
Bruce Humber	Can	13	20.8	2)	Seattle	11 May

° = 200 metre time plus 0.1.

4x100 metre relay

Univ. of Iowa	USA	(Dooley, Briggs, Nelson, James Owen)	40.3*	1)	Lavrence	20 Apr
	Ger	(Leichum, Hornberger, Neckermann, Borchmeyer)	41.2	1)	Berlin	31 Aug
	Hol	(Boersma, van Beveren, Osendarp, Berger)	41.4	2)	Düsseldorf	29 Sep
Budapest BTE	Hun	(Minai, Paitz, Kovács, Sir)	41.6	1)	Budapest	28 Jul
	Jap	(Takano, Nakajima, Suzuki, Yoshioka)	41.8	1)	Nishin.	09 Jun
	Ita	(Mariani, Caldana, Ragni, Toetti)	41.8	1)	Torino	22 Sep

1936

100 yards

Jesse Owens	USA	13	9.3w	1)	Madison, WI	16 May
(Owens)			9.4	1)	Columbus	13 Jun
Sam Stoller	USA	15	9.5	1)h	Columbus	22 May
Ralph Metcalfe	USA	10	9.5	1)	Toronto	05 Sep

Doubtful timing:

Jack Brown	Can		9.4	1)hcp	Toronto	05 Sep

100 metres

Jesse Owens	USA	13	10.2	1)	Chicago	20 Jun
Harvey Wallender	USA	14	10.3w	1)h2	Chicago	19 Jun
Foy Draper	USA	13	10.3	2)	Chicago	20 Jun
Sam Stoller	USA	15	10.3	3)	Chicago	20 Jun
Howard McPhee	Can	16	10.3	1)	Vancouver	01 Jul
Ralph Metcalfe	USA	10	10.3	1)	Köln	10 Aug
Lennart Strandberg	Swe	15	10.3	1)	Malmö	26 Sep

Doubtful timing:

Lennart Lindgren	Swe	15	10.3w	1)	Landskrona	24 May

Downhill:

Erich Borchmeyer	Ger	05	10.3	1)r1	Schwenningen	31 May

200 metres (half-to-full turn) (E = "Zielbildkamera" electric time)

Jesse Owens	USA	13	20.7	1)	Berlin	05 Aug
Mack Robinson	USA	14	20.8	1)	Colombes	23 Aug
Robert Rodenkirchen	Ger	16	21.0	1)s3	Cambridge,MA	26 Jun
Martinus Theunissen	SA	11	21.1* A	1)	Pretoria	21 Mar
Harvey Wallender	USA	14	21.1	1)	Houston	06 Jun
Martinus Osendarp	Hol	16	21.1	1)	Amsterdam	28 Jun
Foy Draper	USA	13	21.1	1)	Stockholm	20 Aug
Cyril Holmes	UK	15	21.2*w	1)	Manchester	09 May
Paul Hänni	Swe	14	21.2	1)	Bern	28 Jun
Robert Packard	USA	16	21.2	1)h7	Berlin	04 Aug
Lee Orr (21.37 E)	Can	17	21.2w	1)q1	Berlin	04 Aug
Ralph Metcalfe	USA	10	21.2	1)	Viipuri	24 Aug

220 yards (straight course)

Jesse Owens	USA	13	20.5	1)	Notre Dame	09 May
Harvey Wallender	USA	14	20.5w	1)	Houston	09 May
Ralph Metcalfe	USA	10	20.7	1)	Toronto	05 Sep
Perrin Walker	USA	12	20.8w	1)	New York	16 Aug
Foy Draper	USA	13	20.9	1)	Los Angeles	02 May
(Wallender)			20.9	1)		
Robert Graham	USA		20.9	1)	Walla Walla	30 May
Bryant Allen	USA		20.9	1)	Huntington Park, CA	05 Jun
Rozia Singletary	USA		21.0	1)	Hampton, VA	16 May

Doubtful timing:

Jack Brown	Can		20.9	1)hcp	Toronto	19 Sep

4x100 metre relay (E = "Zielbildkamera" electric timing)

USA	(Owens, Metcalfe, Draper, Wykoff)	39.8	1)	Berlin	09 Aug
Ger	(Leichum, Borchmeyer, Gillmeister, Hornberger)	40.7	1)r1	Köln	21 Jun
Ita	(Mariani, Caldana, Ragni, Gonnelli)	41.1	2)h1	Berlin	08 Aug
Hol	(Boersma, van Beveren, Berger, Osendarp)	41.3	1)h2	Berlin	08 Aug
Jap	(Yoshioka, Sasaki, Taniguchi, Suzuki)	41.4	1)	Helsinki	11 Jul

Disqualified for dropping the baton:

Hol	(Boersma, van Beveren, Berger, Osendarp) (41.28 E)	41.2	-)	Berlin	09 Aug

Noteworthy performance made in 4x100 y. (= 365.76 m.) relay:

USA	(Wykoff, Glickman, Owens, Metcalfe)	37.4	1)	London	15 Aug

1937

100 yards

Adrian Talley	USA	15	9.4w	1)	Fresno	03 Apr
Ben Johnson	USA	14	9.4w	1)	Strasbourg	29 Aug
Robert Packard	USA	16	9.5w	1)h	Birmingham, AL	14 May

100 metres

Ben Johnson	USA	14	10.2w	1)	Colombes	22 Aug
Takayoshi Yoshioka	Jap	09	10.2w	1)	Nishinomiya	11 Sep
Allan Tolmich	USA	17	10.3w	2)	Nishinomiya	11 Sep
Martinus Osendarp	Hol	16	10.4w	1)	Budapest	26 Jun
Gerd Hornberger	Ger	10	10.4	1)	Dillingen	27 Jun
Arthur Sweeney	UK	09	10.4	1)	Wuppertal	02 Jul
Gyula Gyenes	Hun	11	10.4	1)	Budapest	08 Aug
Perrin Walker	USA	12	10.4	1)	Oslo	19 Aug
Alan Pennington	UK	16	10.4w	2)	Colombes	22 Aug
Paul Hänni	Swz	14	10.4	1)	Basel	28 Aug
Karl Neckermann	Ger	11	10.4w	3)	Strasbourg	29 Aug
(Johnson)			10.4	1)	Bern	01 Sep

Cyril Holmes	UK	15	10.4w	2)	Stockholm	07 Sep
Mutsuo Taniguchi	Jap	13	10.4w	3)	Nishinomiya	11 Sep
Orazio Mariani	Ita	15	10.4w	1)	Colombes	12 Sep

200 metres (half-to-full turn)

Ben Johnson	USA	14	20.8	1)	Colombes	22 Aug
Jack Weiershauser	USA	15	20.9	1)	Milwaukee	03 Jul
Dennis Shore	SA	15	21.0* A	1)	Johannesburg	13 Nov
Perrin Walker	USA	12	21.1	1)	København	14 Sep
Harry Coleman	Can		21.3*w	1)	Moose Jaw	18Aug
Paul Hänni	Swz	14	21.3	1)	Karlsruhe	22 Aug
Morris Vandecar	SA	14	21.3* A	1)	Johannesburg	04 Oct
Martinus Osendarp	Hol	16	21.4	1)	Budapest	27 Jun
Karl Neckermann	Ger	11	21.4	1)	Mannheim	03 Oct

Uncertain estimate:

Mack Robinson	USA	14	21.4	2)	Milwaukee	03 Jul

220 yards (straight course)

Clark Crane	USA	14	20.5w	1)	Fresno	03 Apr
Robert Young	USA	16	20.6w	1)	Los Angeles	17 Apr
Randolph Carter	USA	13	20.7	1)	San Diego	08 May
Delmer Brown	USA	14	20.7	1)	Commerce, TX	15 May
Jack Weiershauser	USA	15	20.7	1)	Palo Alto	12 Jun
Clyde Jeffrey	USA	18	20.8w	1)	Riverside, CA	16/17 Apr
Kenneth Chittum	USA	16	20.8	1)	Champaign	17 Apr
Lee Orr	Can	17	20.8	1)	Seattle	22 May
Robert Rodenkirchen	Ger	16	20.8	1)	Yonkers, NY	13 Jun

4x100 metre relay

Pacific Coast Conference	USA	(Boone, Ledford, L.Orr/Can, Weiershauser)	40.5*	1)	Los Angeles	26 Jun
Univ.of So.Cal.	USA	(Boone, Jordan, Crane, Talley)	40.7*	1)	Fresno	15 May
	Ger	(Borchmeyer, Hornberger, Neckermann, Scheuring)	41.1	1)	München	08 Aug
	Ita	(Mariani, Caldana, Ragni, Gonnelli)	41.3	1)	Colombes	12 Sep
	Swe	(Lindgren, Ternström, Stenqvist, Strandberg)	41.6	2)	Berlin	18 Sep
	Hun	(Nagy, Minai, Kovács, Gyenes)	41.7	1T)	Budapest	27 Jun
	Hol	(Boersma, van Beveren, H.Baumgarten, Osendarp)	41.7	1T)	Budapest	27 Jun

1938

100 yards

Arnold Nutting	USA	16	9.4w	1)	Berkeley	26 Mar
Ben Reams	USA	16	9.4w	1)	Reno, NV	30 Apr
Fred Wolcott	USA	17	9.5	1)	Houston	16 Apr
Mozel Ellerbe	USA	13	9.5	1)	Tuskegee, AL	07 May
(Reams)			9.5	1)	Davis, CA	07 May
Robert Lewis	USA	17	9.5w	1)	Bloomington, IN	09 May
Adrian Talley	USA	15	9.5	1)	Fresno	14 May
Lee Orr	Can	17	9.5	1)h1	Seattle	20 May
Martin Glickman	USA	17	9.5	1)	West Point, NY	21 May
Mack Robinson	USA	14	9.5	2)	Seattle	21 May
Dennis Shore	SA	15	9.5 A	1)	Johannesburg	26 Sep

Doubtful timing:

Jimmy Callista	USA		9.1w	1)	Erie, PA	30 Apr

100 metres

José Bento de Assis	Bra	15	10.2w	1)hcp	Rio de Janeiro	22 May
Jennings Blackett	Pan	18	10.3	1)s2	Panama City	06 Feb
Jacinto Ortiz	Cub	13	10.3	1)s3	Panama City	06 Feb
Martinus Osendarp	Hol	16	10.3w	1)	Amsterdam	12 Jun
Ben Johnson	USA	14	10.3	1)	Köln	20 Aug
Conrado Rodríguez	Cub	09	10.4	1)h3	Panama City	06 Feb

Eulalio Villodas	PR		10.4		2)h3	Panama City	06 Feb
Alfred Brown	Jam		10.4		1)h4	Panama City	06 Feb
Mutsuo Taniguchi	Jap	13	10.4		1)	Osaka	14 May
Terunori Kawate	Jap		10.4		1)	Nishinomiya	10 Jul
Mozel Ellerbe	USA	13	10.4		1)r2	Dortmund	07 Aug
Erik Sjövall	Nor	11	10.4		1)	Oslo	21 Aug
Orazio Mariani	Ita	15	10.4		1)s2	Colombes	03 Sep
Wynand van Beveren	Hol	11	10.4		2)s2	Colombes	03 Sep
Lennart Strandberg	Swe	15	10.4w		1)	København	11 Sep
Perrin Walker	USA	12	10.4		1)	Milano	11 Sep
Takayoshi Yoshioka	Jap	09	10.4		1)	Nishinomiya	25 Sep

Race annulled (ran alone):

Wilbur Greer	USA	17	10.4		1)r1	Dortmund	07 Aug

Rolling start:

Manfred Kersch	Ger	13	10.4w		1)	Frankfurt/M	10 Jul

200 metres (half-to-full turn)

Ben Johnson	USA	14	20.9		1)	Stockholm	21 Jul
Perrin Walker	USA	12	20.9		1)	Köln	20 Aug
Cyril Holmes	UK	15	21.1*		1)	Sydney	10 Feb
Clyde Jeffrey	USA	18	21.1		1)	Dortmund	07 Aug
Martinus Osendarp	Hol	16	21.1		1)	Rotterdam	21 Aug
Dennis Shore	SA	15	21.1*	A	1)	Johannesburg	26 Sep
Jacinto Ortiz	Cub	13	21.2		1)s2	Panama City	08 Feb
John Mumford	Aus		21.2*e		2)	Sydney	10 Feb
Mack Robinson	USA	14	21.2*		1)	Minneapolis	18 Jun
Orazio Mariani	Ita	15	21.2		1)	Firenze	26 Jun
Jack Emigh	USA	18	21.2*		1)	Evanston	27 Jun
Morris Vandecar	SA	14	21.2*		1)	Durban	16 Dec

Unconfirmed performance:

Jacinto Ortiz	Cub	13	20.8		1)	Habana	Jan

220 yards (straight course)

Clyde Jeffrey	USA	18	20.5w		1)		
(Jeffrey)			20.6		1)	Claremont, CA	07 May
Wilbur Miller	USA	19	20.6		2)	Claremont, CA	07 May
Jack Emigh	USA	18	20.7		1)	Missoula, MT	30 Apr
Curtis Ledford	USA	16	20.7w		1)	Pullman	30 Apr
E. Y. Steakley	USA		20.8		1)	Austin	05 May
Robert Lewis	USA	17	20.8w		1)	Columbus	04 Jun
Bryant Allen	USA		20.9		1)	Fullerton, CA	05 Apr
Mack Robinson	USA	14	20.9		1)		
Lee Orr	Can	17	20.9		1)	Seattle	21 May

Unconfirmed performance:

Ledford			20.9		(2T)	Seattle	21 May

4x100 metre relay

USA	(Greer, Ellerbe, Jeffrey, B.Johnson)	40.0	1)	Berlin	13 Aug
Ger	(Kersch, Hornberger, Neckermann, Scheuring)	40.3	2)	Berlin	13 Aug
Swe	(Klemming, Stenqvist, Lindgren, Strandberg)	41.1	2)	Colombes	05 Sep
UK	(Scarr, A.G.K.Brown, Sweeney, Page)	41.2	3)	Colombes	05 Sep
Ita	(Daelli, Caldana, Gonnelli, Mariani)	41.2	2)	Milano	11 Sep

1939

100 yards

Wilbur Greer	USA	17	9.5		1)	Austin	01 Apr
Mack Robinson	USA	14	9.5		1)	Whittier, CA	01 Apr
Earl Witcher	USA		9.5	A	1)	El Paso	08 Apr
Mozel Ellerbe	USA	13	9.5		1)	Lawrence	22 Apr
Brian Dunn	Aus	21	9.5w		1)	Sydney	09 May

Fred Wolcott	USA	17	9.5	1)h	College Station, TX	12 May
Clyde Jeffrey	USA	18	9.5w	1)	San Jose	03 Jun

100 metres

Clyde Jeffrey	USA	18	10.2w	1T)h3	Lincoln	04 Jul
Mozel Ellerbe	USA	13	10.2w	1T)h3	Lincoln	04 Jul
Herbert Thompson	USA	15	10.3w	1)h1	Lincoln	04 Jul
Norwood Ewell	USA	18	10.3w	1)h2	Lincoln	04 Jul
Karl Neckermann	Ger	11	10.3	1)	Berlin	08 Jul
Jakob Scheuring	Ger	12	10.3	1)	Lahr	13 Aug
Ted Best	Aus		10.4w	1)	Ballarat	10 Apr
Stanley Nairn	Jam		10.4	1)h2	Montego Bay	13 Apr
Ben Johnson	USA	14	10.4we	5)	Lincoln	04 Jul
Orazio Mariani	Ita	15	10.4	2)	Milano	16 Jul
(Jeffrey)			10.4	1)	Basel	12 Aug
Haakon Tranberg	Nor	17	10.4	1)	Oslo	10 Sep
Luis O.Venini	Arg	18	10.4w	1)	Buenos Aires	18 Nov

200 metres (half-to-full turn)

Jakob Scheuring	Ger	12	21.0		1)	Mannheim	24 Jun
Norwood Ewell	USA	18	21.0		1)	Lincoln	04 Jul
Perrin Walker	USA	12	21.1		1)h2	Lincoln	04 Jul
Clyde Jeffrey	USA	18	21.1e		2)	Lincoln	04 Jul
Karl Neckermann	Ger	11	21.2		2)	Mannheim	24 Jun
Orazio Mariani	Ita	15	21.2		1)	Milano	15 Jul
Lee Orr	Can	17	21.2*		1)	Victoria, BC	15 Jul
Morris Vandecar	SA	14	21.4*	A	1)	Krugersdorp	18 Feb
John Cumberbatch	Tri		21.4*		1)	Siparia	24 Apr
Tullio Gonnelli	Ita	12	21.4		1)	Milano	07 May
José Bento de Assis	Bra	15	21.4		1)	Lima	28 May
Gerd Hornberger	Ger	10	21.4		2)	Frankfurt/M	12 Aug

Doubtful timing:

Heinrich Huth	Ger	20	21.4	1)	Kassel	02 Jul

Unconfirmed performance:

Dennis Shore	SA	15	21.1*	)		

220 yards (straight course)

George Koettel	USA	16	20.5w	1)	Norman	08 Apr
Jack Emigh	USA	18	20.5w	1)	Cheney, WA	21 Apr
Robert Lewis	USA	17	20.8	1)		22 Apr
Clyde Jeffrey	USA	18	20.8	1)	Berkeley	22 Apr
Vernon Akins	USA	15	20.9	1)	Wichita	13 May
Curtis Ledford	USA	16	20.9	1)	Pullman	13 May
Albert Rogers	USA		20.9	1)	Toronto	02 Sep
Wilbur Miller	USA	19	21.0	1)	Los Angeles	11 Mar
Eddie Morris	USA	22	21.0	1)	Huntington B.,CA	18 Mar
Clyde Yakel	USA		21.0	1)	San Diego	01 Apr
Harold Davis	USA	21	21.0	1)	San Jose	03 Jun

Unconfirmed performance:

Bob Christian	USA		20.9	1)		

4x100 metre relay

	Ger	(Borchmeyer, Hornberger, Neckermann, Scheuring)	40.1	1)	Berlin	29 Jul
	Ita	(Daelli, Monacci, Gonnelli, Mariani)	40.8	2)	Berlin	29 Jul
New York AC	USA	(Weast, O'Sullivan, Clapp, P.Walker)	41.0	1)	Lincoln	04 Jul
	Fra	(Valmy, Goldowski, Bucourt, Fusil)	41.3	1)	Amsterdam	13 Aug
	Swe	(Klemming, Stenqvsit, Lindgren, Ivar Nilsson)	41.4	1)	Oslo	23 Sep

1940

100 yards

Clyde Jeffrey	USA	18	9.4	1)	Long Beach	16 Mar

Eddie Morris	USA	22	9.5w	1)	Huntington Beach, CA	01 May
Harold Davis	USA	21	9.5	1)	Fresno	11 May
Leo Tarrant	USA	18	9.5	1)		
Billy Brown	USA	18	9.5	1)h	Birmingham, AL	17 May
Pat Haley	USA	19	9.5	1)	Cheney, WA	18 May

100 metres (E= electric timer)

Harold Davis	USA	21	10.3	1)	Compton	07 Jun
Eddie Morris	USA	22	10.4	1)h3	Fresno	28 Jun
Norwod Ewell (10.34 E)	USA	18	10.4	2)	Fresno	29 Jun
Takayoshi Yoshioka	Jap	09	10.5	1)	Kashihara	01 Jun
Ramón Baltar	Cub	19	10.5	1)	Habana	12 Jun
Leo Tarrant	USA	18	10.5	1)h3	Fresno	28 Jun
Wim Nota	Hol	19	10.5w	1)h	Rotterdam	14 Jul
Martinus Osendarp	Hol	16	10.5w	)		
Carlo Monti	Ita	20	10.5	1)	Milano	21 Jul
Harald Mellerowicz	Ger	19	10.5	1)	København	22 Aug
Orazio Mariani	Ita	15	10.5	3)	Milano	22 Sep
José C. Ferraz	Bra	19	10.5	1)	São Paulo	22 Sep

Doubtful timing:

Ludwig Iffland	Ger	19	10.5w	1)	Essen	09 Jun

200 metres (half-to-full turn)

Norwood Ewell	USA	18	21.0*	1)	Minneapolis	22 Jun
George Koettel	USA	16	21.2*	1)h	Lincoln	17 May
Clyde Jeffrey	USA	18	21.2*	1)	Evanston	17 Jun
Harald Mellerowicz	Ger	19	21.2	1)	Milano	22 Sep
Carlo Monti	Ita	20	21.3	2)	Milano	22 Sep
Nemesio de Guzman	Phi	16	21.4	1)	Manila	18 Feb
Joe Hunte	Tri		21.5*	1)	Arima	09 Jun
Mario Lanzi	Ita	14	21.5	1)r2	Milano	25 Jun
Karl Neckermann	Ger	11	21.6	1)	Frankfurt/O	19 May
Heinz Baumgarten	Hol	16	21.6	)		
Orazio Mariani	Ita	15	21.6	2)	Torino	14 Sep
Tullio Gonnelli	Ita	12	21.6	3)	Torino	14 Sep

Unconfirmed performance:

Dennis Shore	SA	15	21.5*	)		

220 yards (straight course) (E = electric time)

Harold Davis	USA	21	20.5°		1)	Fresno	29 Jun
Eddie Morris	USA	22	20.6w		1)	Huntington Beach, CA	01 May
Robert Owen	USA	18	20.6w		1)	New Haven, CT	11 May
(Morris)			20.7		1)	Huntington Beach, CA	11 May
Frank Ohl	USA	17	20.7		1)	Columbus	14 May
Cyrus Ellsworth	USA	18	20.7	A	1)	Salt Lake City	25 May
Norwood Ewell	USA	18	20.8w		1)	Univ.Park, PA	04 May
Ewell (20.63 E)			20.8°		2)	Fresno	29 Jun

° = 200 m. time plus 0.1.

4x100 metre relay

	Ita	(Tito, Gritti, Daelli, Gonnelli)	40.6	1)	Torino	14 Sep
Pacific Coast Conf.	USA	(Willis, Anderson, Sinclair, Jeffrey)	40.8*	1)	Evanston	17 Jun
	Ger	(Scheuring, Mellerowicz, Neckermann, Kersch)	40.8	2)	Torino	14 Sep
São Paulo	Bra	(Oliveira, Padilha, de Assis, Puschnik)	42.1	1)	Rio de Janeiro	12 Sep
	Hun	(Szigetvári, Korompai, Sándor, Gyenes)	42.1	2)	Budapest	05 Oct

ALL TIME WORLD LIST OF BEST PERFORMERS AS AT THE END OF 1940

100 yards (hand timing)

Daniel Joubert	SA	09	9.3w	1)h	Grahastown	15 May 31
Jesse Owens	USA	13	9.3w	1)	Madison, WI	16 May 36
Alfred LeConey	USA	01	9.4w	1)	Allentown, PA	30 Aug 24
Claude Bracey	USA	09	9.4w	1)	Dallas	30 Mar 29
Russell Sweet	USA	04	9.4w	1)	San Francisco	04 May 29
George Simpson	USA	08	9.4	1)	Chicago	08 Jun 29
Cy Leland	USA	10	9.4w	1)	Lawrence	19 Apr 30
Frank Wykoff	USA	09	9.4	1)	Los Angeles	10 May 30
Hubert Meier	USA	08	9.4	1)	Lincoln	24 May 30
(Joubert)			9.4	1)	Grahamstown	16 May 31
James Carlton	Aus	08	9.4w	1)	Newcastle, NSW	15 Nov 31
James Johnson	USA	12	9.4w	1)	Bloomington	03 May 33
Harvey Wallender	USA	14	9.4w	1)h	Austin	30 Mar 35
Herman Neugass	USA	15	9.4w	1)	Austin	30 Mar 35
(Owens)			9.4	1)	Chicago(HS ev)	17 Jun 33
Ralph Metcalfe	USA	10	9.4	1)	Chicago(Collev)	17 Jun 33
George Anderson	USA	16	9.4	1)	Fresno	12 May 34
Adrian Talley	USA	15	9.4w	1)	Fresno	03 Apr 37
Ben Johnson	USA	14	9.4w	1)	Strasbourg	29 Aug 37
Arnold Nutting	USA	16	9.4w	1)	Berkeley	26 Mar 38
Ben Reams	USA	16	9.4w	1)	Reno, NV	30 Apr 38
Clyde Jeffrey	USA	18	9.4	1)	Long Beach	16 Mar 40

100 metres (hand timing)

Charles Paddock	USA	00	10.2+	1)	Pasadena	18 Jun 21
Jose E.Barrientos	Cu	04	10.2w	1)	Habana	08 May 27
Eddie Tolan	USA	08	10.2	1)	Vancouver	01 Jul 30
Ralph Metcalfe	USA	10	10.2	1)	Chicago	11 Jun 32
José Xavier de Almeida	Bra	04	10.2w	1)	Rio de Janeiro	23 Sep 34
Eulace Peacock	USA	14	10.2w	1)h2	Lincil n	04 Jul 35
Jesse Owens	USA	13	10.2	1)	Chicago	20 Jun 36
Ben Jonhson	USA	14	10.2w	1)	Colombes	22 Aug 37
Takayoshi Yoshioka	Jap	09	10.2w	1)	Nishinomya	11 Sep 37
José Bento de Assis	Bra	15	10.2w	1)hcp	Rio de Janeiro	22May 38
Clyde Jeffrey	USA	18	10.2w	1T)h3	Lincil n	04 Jul 39
Mozel Ellerbe	USA	13	10.2w	1T)h3	Lincoln	04 Jul 39

+ = made in a 110 y. (100.58 m.) race

200 metres (half-to-full turn – hand timing)

Roland Locke	USA	03	20.4*	1)	Lincoln	01 May 26
James Carlton	Aus	08	20.5*	1)	Sydney	18 Jan 32
Ralph Metcalfe	USA	10	20.6	1)hcp	Budapest	12 Aug 33
Jesse Owens	USA	13	20.7	1)	Berlin	05 Aug 36
Mack Robinson	USA	14	20.8	1)	Colombes	23 Aug 36
Ben Johnson	USA	14	20.8	1)	Colombes	22 Aug 37
Eddie Tolan	USA	08	20.9*	1)	Lincoln	04 Jul 31
Jack Weiershauser	USA	15	20.9	1)	Milwaukee	03 Jul 37
Perrin Walker	USA	12	20.9	1)	Köln	20 Aug 38
Ralph Sickel	USA		21.0*w	1)	Lincoln	23 May 31
Martinus Theunissen	SA	11	21.0* A	1)	Johannesburg	14 Sep 35
Robert Rodenkirchen	Ger	16	21.0	1)s3	Cambridge, MA	26 Jun 36
Dennis Shore	SA	15	21.0* A	1)	Johannesburg	13 Nov 37
Jakob Scheuring	Ger	12	21.0	1)	Mannheim	24 Jun 39
Norwood Ewell	USA	18	21.0	1)	Lincoln	04 Jul 39

220 yards (straight course – hand timing)

Ralph Metcalfe	USA	10	19.8w	1)	Toronto	03 Sep 32
Jesse Owens	USA	13	20.3	1)	Ann Arbor	25 May 35

(Metcalfe)			20.4	1)	Chicago	17 Jun 33
Fred Alderman	USA	05	20.5w	1)	East Lansing	21 May 27
Harvey Wallender	USA	14	20.5	1)	Austin	03 May 35
Don Bennett	USA	08	20.5w	1)	Evanston	21 May 32
Clark Crane	USA	14	20.5w	1)	Fresno	03 Apr 37
Clyde Jeffrey	USA	18	20.5w	1)		38
George Koettel	USA	16	20.5w	1)	Norman	08 Apr 39
Jack Emigh	USA	18	20.5w	1)	Cheney, WA	21 Apr 39
Hal Davis	USA	21	20.5°	1)	Fresno	29 Jun 40

° = 200 m. time plus 0.1.

4x100 metre relay (hand timing)

	USA	(Owens, Metcalfe, Draper, Wykoff)	39.8	1)	Berlin	09 Aug 36
	Ger	(Borchmeyer, Hornberger, Neckermann, Scheuring)	40.1	1)	Berlin	29 Jul 39
	Ita	(Tito, Gritti, Daelli, Gonnelli)	40.6	1)	Torino	14 Sep 40
	Swe	(Klemming, Stenqvsit, Lindgren, Strandberg)	41.1	2)	Colombes	05 Sep 38
	UK	(Abrahams, Rangeley, Royle, Nichol)	41.2e	2)	Colombes	13 Jul 24
Budapest BTE	Hun	(Minai, Paitz, Kovács, Sir)	41.2	1)	Budapest	16 Sep 34
	Can	(Williams, Brown, Wright, Pearson)	41.3	4)	Los Angeles	07 Aug 32
	Jap	(Yoshioka, Nambu, Anno, Nakajima)	41.3	5)	Los Angeles	07 Aug 32
	Hol	(Boersma, van Beveren, Berger, Osendarp)	41.3	1)h2	Berlin	08 Aug 36
	Fra	(Valmy, Goldowski, Bucourt, Fusil)	41.3	1)	Amsterdam	13 Aug 39

1941

100 yards

Carlton Terry	USA	20	9.2w	1)	College Station	02 May
Fred Ramsdell	USA	16	9.3w	2)	College Station	02 May
Billy Brown	USA	18	9.4w	1)	Baton Rouge	19 Apr
Harold Davis	USA	21	9.4w	1)	Fresno	17 May
Eddie Morris	USA	22	9.5w	1)	Huntington Beach, CA	05 Apr
(Brown)			9.5	1)	Houston	12 Apr
(Davis)			9.5	1)	Salinas, CA	19 Apr
Payton Jordan	USA	17	9.5	1)	San Diego	26 Apr
Leo Tarrant	USA	18	9.5	)		
Harvey Kelsey	USA	23	9.5	1)	Andover, MA	10 May
McIver Riley	USA		9.5	1)	Raleight, NC	10 May

100 metres

Harold Davis	USA	21	10.2	1)h	Compton	06 Jun
Norwood Ewell	USA	18	10.3	1)	Philadelphia	29 Jun
Payton Jordan	USA	17	10.3	1)	Kingston	26 Jul
Josè Bento de Assis	Bra	15	10.3w	1)	São Paulo	31 Aug
René Valmy	Fra	21	10.4w	1)	Romans	03 Aug
Martinus Osendarp	Hol	16	10.4w	1)	den Haag	10 Aug
Ramón Baltar	Cu	19	10.5	1)	Habana	18 Apr
(Valmy)			10.5	1)	Tunis	04 May
Carlo Monti	Ita	20	10.5	1)	Torino	20 Jul
Orazio Mariani	Ita	15	10.5	2)	Torino	20 Jul
Henri Geul	Hol	16	10.5w	2)	den Haag	10 Aug
Jan Grijseels	Hol	18	10.5w	3)	den Haag	10 Aug
(Bento de Assis)			10.5	1)	São Paulo	30 Aug
Michele Tito	Ita	20	10.5	1)	Prato	07 Sep
(Osendarp)			10.5	1)	Amsterdam	21 Sep
Jakob Scheuring	Ger	12	10.5	1)	Ulm	28 Sep

200 metres (half-to-full turn)

Payton Jordan	USA	17	21.0*		1)	Kingston	23 Jul
Jakob Scheuring	Ger	12	21.0		1)	Stuttgart	30 Aug
José Bento de Assis	Bra	15	21.2		1)	São Paulo	05 Oct
Don Walters	USA		21.4*		1)	Lincoln	24 May
Bob Smith	USA		21.5*		1)	Corvallis	03 May
Harold Davis	USA	21	21.5*		1)	Passaic, NJ	02 Jul
Rafael Cotes	Col		21.5	A	1)	Bucaramanga	Dec
Jannie Joubert	SA		21.6*	A	1)	Johannesburg	24 May

Martinus Osendarp	Hol	16	21.6	1)	Rotterdam	03 Jun
Hern MacKenley	Jam	22	21.6*	1)	Kingston	16 Jul
René Valmy	Fra	21	21.6w	1)	Romans	03 Aug
Orazio Mariani	Ita	15	21.6	1)	Budapest	10 Aug
Gerrit de Pagter	Hol	19	21.6w	1)	Middelburg	17 Aug

Uncertain estimate:

Hubert Kerns	USA	20	21.6*	2)	Passaic, NJ	02 Jul

Unconfirmed performance:

Dennis Shore	SA	15	20.9*w A	1)	Benoni	

220 yards (straight course)

Harold Davis	USA	21	20.2w	1)	Fresno	17 May
Joe Blagg	USA	19	20.4w	1)	College Station	02 May
Billy Brown	USA	18	20.5w	1)	Baton Rouge	19 Apr
(Davis)			20.5	1)	Berkeley	03 May
Eddie Morris	USA	22	20.6w	1)	Huntington Beach, CA	05 Apr
(Brown)			20.6	1)	Birmingham, AL	17 May
Norwood Ewell	USA	18	20.6°	2)	Philadelphia	29 Jun
Howie Campbell	USA	20	20.7	1)	Cambridge, MA	17 May
Doug Pirnie	USA	20	20.7w	1)	New Haven, CT	24 May
Payton Jordan	USA	17	20.7°	3)	Philadelphia	29 Jun

° = 200 m. time plus 0.1.

4x100 metre relay

Univ. of Texas	USA	(Seay, Terry, Ramsdell, Hill)	40.8*	1)h	Des Moines	25 Apr
	Ger	(Fuhrmann, Scheuring, Bönecke, Harbig)	41.0	1)	Bologna	28 Jun
	Ita	(Tito, Gritti, Daelli, Gonnelli)	41.1	2)	Bologna	28 Jun
	Bra	(Oliveira, Padilha, Puschnik, de Assis)	42.1	1)	Buenos Aires	28 Apr
	Hun	(Csányi, Gyenes, Szigetvári, Korompai)	42.1	2)	Budapest	09 Aug

1942

100 yards

Harold Davis	USA	21	9.4	1)	Fresno	16 May
Pete Owens	USA	20	9.5w	1)h	Laredo, TX	05 Mar
Jim Metcalf	USA		9.5w	1)h	Laredo, TX	05 Mar
Bill Smith	USA	23	9.5	1)	San Jose	25 Apr
Enrique Adame	USA		9.5	1)	Arlington, TX	02 May
Ralph Hammond	USA	20	9.5	1)	Columbus	09 May
Owen Joggerst	USA	22	9.5	1)	Lincoln	16 May
Norwood Ewell	USA	18	9.5w	1)	New York	30 May

Doubtful timing:

Edward Greenidge	USA	23	9.3	1)	Tuskegee, AL	09 May
Kjell Qvale	USA		9.4	1)	Corpus Christi	27 Apr

100 metres

Albert Spree	Hol	22	10.3w	1)	Rotterdam	24 May
Jan Grijseels	Hol	18	10.4w	2)	Rotterdam	24 May
Wim Nota	Hol	19	10.4w	3)	Rotterdam	24 May
Harald Mellerowicz	Ger	19	10.4	1)hcp	Kraków	20 Sep
Filiberto Correa	PR		10.5	1)	Ponce	29 Mar
Harold Davis	USA	21	10.5	1)	Kansas City	06 Jun
Martinus Osendarp	Hol	16	10.5	1)	Amsterdam	15 Jun
Bill Smith	USA	23	10.5	1)	New York	19 Jun
Ion Moina	Rom	21	10.5	1)	Predeal	01 Aug
Lennart Strandberg	Swe	15	10.5	1)	Linköping	20 Aug
Sten Ohlsson	Swe	22	10.5	1)	Budapest	26 Sep

Downhill course:

Karl Lehmann	Ger	21	10.5	1)	Chemnitz	05 Jul

200 metres (half-to-full turn)

Norwood Ewell	USA	18	20.8*	1)	Pittsburgh	09 May
Harald Mellerowicz	Ger	19	21.0	1)hcp	Kraków	20 Sep
Harold Davis	USA	21	21.1*	1)	Lincoln	13 Jun
Herb McKenley	Jam	22	21.2	1)	Kingston	01 Jul
Emmanuel McDonald Bailey	Tri	20	21.4	2)	Kingston	01 Jul
Lennart Strandberg	Swe	15	21.4	1)	Malmö	06 Sep
Edward Greenidge	USA	23	21.5*	1)	Halifax	02 Aug
Carlo Monti	Ita	20	21.6	1)	Milano	17 May
Leo Tarrant	USA	18	21.6*	1)h2	Lincoln	12 Jun
Martinus Osendarp	Hol	16	21.6	1)	Oslo	05 Sep

Doubtful timing:

Gerrit de Pagter	Hol	19	21.5w	1)	Rotterdam	24 May

Unconfirmed performance:

Dennis Shore	SA	15	21.1*	)		

220 yards (straight course)

Harold Davis	USA	21	20.4		1)	Evanston	16 Jun
Norwood Ewell	USA	18	20.5w		1)	New York	30 May
Leo Tarrant	USA	18	20.6		1)		
Charles Shaw	USA		20.8w		2)	New York	30 May
Hubert Kerns	USA	20	20.9		1)	Los Angeles	25 Apr
William Carter	USA		20.9w		3)	New York	30 May
Harold Hall	USA		21.0w		1)	Austin	11 Apr
Ralph Hammond	USA	20	21.0		1)	Columbus	21 May
Bob Dey	USA		21.0	A	1)	Salt Lake City	23 May
(Hall)			21.1		1)	Houston	02 May
Enrique Adame	USA		21.1		1)	Arlington,TX	02 May

4x100 metre relay

U. of California	USA	(Rhoades, Shipnuck, Finch, Davis)	40.6*	1)	Fresno	16 May
	Ita	(Tito, Perucconi, Daelli, Noferini)	41.6	1)	Zürich	23 Aug
Trekvogels den Haag	Hol	(Grijseels, Blok, van Osta, Osendarp)	41.7	1)	Berlin	02 Aug
	Swe	(S. Ohlsson, Lidman, Stenqvist, Strandberg)	41.8	1)	Budapest	27 Sep
	Hun	(Solymosi, Szigetvári, Pelsöczy, Gyenes)	42.0	2)	Budapest	27 Sep

1943

100 yards

Jim Metcalf	USA		9.5	1)	Stillwater, OK	17 Apr
Charles Parker	USA	26	9.5w	1)	Austin	08 May
Harold Davis	USA	21	9.5	1)	Fresno	22 May
Lloyd LaBeach	Jam	23	9.5	1)	Kingston	18 Sep
Joe Shy	USA		9.6	1)	Columbia, MO	01 May
Jim Pettit	USA	23	9.6	1)	West Point	29 May
Edward Greenidge	USA	23	9.6	1)	Cambridge, Ma	24 Jul
George Baker	Tri		9.6	1)	Georgetown	04 Oct

Doubtful conditions:

Dennis Shore	SA	15	9.4	A	1)	Pretoria	06 May

Unconfirmed performance:

Dennis Shore	SA	15		9.6	)

100 metres

Lloyd LaBeach	Jam	23	10.2w	1)	Willemstad	09 Aug
Adelio Márquez	Arg	24	10.2w	1)	Buenos Aires	27 Nov
Harold Davis	USA	21	10.3	1)	New York	20 Jun
Leroy Brown	Jam	23	10.3w	2)	Willemstad	09 Aug
Walter Pérez	Uru	24	10.4	1)	Buenos Aires	05 Feb
Lennart Strandberg	Swe	15	10.4	1)	Hudiksvall	04 Jul

Martinus Osendarp	Hol	16	10.4	1)r2	Amsterdam	25 Jul
(LaBeach)			10.4	1)	Willemstad	01 Aug
Albert Brown	Jam	23	10.4w	3)	Willemstad	09 Aug
(Márquez)			10.4	1)r1	Buenos Aires	06 Nov
Gerardo Bönnhoff (Jr. event)	Arg	26	10.4w	1)	Buenos Aires	27 Nov

200 metres (half-to-full turn)

Leroy Brown	Jam	23	21.2	1T)	Kingston	14 Jul
Lloyd LaBeach	Jam	23	21.2	1T)	Kingston	14 Jul
Adelio Márquez	Arg	24	21.3	1)	Buenos Aires	19 Dec
Ion Moina	Rom	21	21.4	1)	Predeal	22 Aug
Ion Zenide	Rom		21.5	2)	Predeal	22 Aug
Martinus Osendarp	Hol	16	21.6	1)	Amsterdam	27 Jun
Lennart Strandberg	Swe	15	21.6	1)	Hälsingborg	31 Aug
Pál Pelsöczi	Hun	19	21.6	1)	Budapest	10 Oct
Cyril Holmes	UK	15	21.7*	1)	Imber Court	14 Aug
Doubtful conditions:						
Douglas Harris	NZ	19	21.7*	1)	Onehunga	13 Feb
Doubtful timing:						
Herbert Sonntag	Ger	20	21.2	1)	Aurich	26 Sep
Track 7 ft. (2.13 m.) short:						
John Stoney	Aus		20.9*w	1)	Melbourne	11 Dec

220 yards (straight course)

Harold Davis	USA	21	20.3°w	1)	New York	20 Jun
Edward Greenidge	USA	23	20.5°w	2)	New York	20 Jun
Charles Parker	USA	26	20.6w	1)	Austin	08 May
George Guida	USA	24	20.8°w	3)	New York	20 Jun
(Davis)			20.9	1)	Los Angeles	08 May
(Guida)			21.0°	1)	New York	19 Jun
Jack Morris	USA	24	21.1	1)	West Point	29 May
James O'Reilly	USA		21.1	)		
Eddie Conwell	USA	24	21.1°w	4)	New York	20 Jun
Melvin Patton	USA	24	21.2	1)	Los Angeles	30 Apr
Joe Shy	USA		21.2	)		
Cliff Bourland	USA	21	21.2	1)	Los Angeles	10 Jul

° = 200 m. time plus 0.1

4x100 metre relay

Univ. of Missouri	USA	(Alexander, Tracy, Joggerst, Shy)	41.2*	1)	Fresno	22 May
	Hol	(Berger, Zwaan, van Osta, Osendarp)	41.9	1)r1 hcp	Amsterdam	22 Aug
	Hun	(Pelsöczi, Csányi, Szigetvári, Csépánfalvi)	41.9	1)	Basel	29 Aug
	Arg	( )	42.1	1)	Buenos Aires	18 Dec
Union Saint-Gilloise	Bel	(Maes, Siroul, Fr.Braekman, Pol.Braekman)	42.3	1)	Bruxelles	24 Aug

1944

100 yards

George Lewis	Tri	16	9.4	1)	Georgetown	09 Aug
Lloyd LaBeach	Jam	23	9.5	1)	Panama City	03 May
Claude Young	USA	23	9.5w	1)	Ann Arbor	13 May
Charles Parker	USA	26	9.6	1)	Austin	01 Apr
(Young)			9.6	1)	Champaign	06 May
Adelio Márquez	Arg	24	9.6	1)	Buenos Aires	11 Jun
M. Lytle	USA		9.6	1)	Delaware, OH	17 Jun
Unconfirmed performance:						
Dennis Shore	SA	15	9.5	)		

100 metres

Walter Pérez	Uru	24	10.4	1)	Montevideo	05 Feb
Adelio Márquez	Arg	24	10.4	1)	Buenos Aires	02 Dec
Gerardo Bönnhoff	Arg	26	10.4	2)	Buenos Aires	02 Dec
Claude Young	USA	23	10.5	1)	New York	18 Jun
António Zapata	Mex		10.5	)	Torreón	25 Jun
Karl Lehmann	Ger	21	10.5	1)h	Lahr	06 Aug
José Bento de Assis	Bra	15	10.5	1)	São Paulo	28 Oct

200 metres (half-to-full turn)

Emmanuel McDonald Bailey	Tri	20	21.1*	1)	Georgetown	09 Aug
Adelio Márquez	Arg	24	21.3	1)	Buenos Aires	22 Oct
Daniel Hugo	SA	24	21.4*w	1)	Stellebosch	27 Mar
Martinus Osendarp	Hol	16	21.4	1)	Rotterdam	13 Aug
Claude Young	USA	23	21.5*	1)	Milwaukee	10 Jun
Walter Pérez	Uru	25	21.5	1)	Montevideo	27 Sep
Ernesto Gómez	Per		21.5	)	Lima	10 Dec
Jos Bento de Assis	Bra	15	21.6	1)	São Paulo	01 Oct
Gerardo Bönnhoff	Arg	26	21.6	1)	Buenos Aires	05 Nov
(Hugo)			21.8*	1)h	Stellenbosch	10 Apr
Georges Foussard	Fra	21	21.8	1)	Paris	25 Jun

Doubtful conditions:

Ion Moina	Rom	21	21.8	1)	Predeal	Aug

220 yards (straight course)

Charles Parker	USA	26	20.7	1)	Austin	06 May
Claude Young	USA	23	20.9	1)	Champaign	06 May
Ralph Ellsworth	USA		21.2	1)	Austin	13 May
James O'Reilly	USA		21.3	1)		Apr
Culbertson	USA		21.4	1)		Apr
Walter Newman	USA		21.4	1)	West Point	06 May

4x100 metre relay

New York Univ.	USA	(Rubin, Parker, Svoboda, Conwell)	42.3*	1)	Philadelphia	28 Apr
	Arg	(Fernández, Ravano, Bönnhoff, Márquez)	42.4	1)	Buenos Aires	02 Jul
Seleção FPA, São Paulo	Bra	(Bento de Assis, Ribeiro, Gherardi, Bastianon)	42.5	1)	São Paulo	28 Oct
	Swz	(H.Nilsson, Ivar Nilsson, Nordin, Håkansson)	42.6	1)	Stockholm	13 Jul
Racing Club de France	Fra	(Foussard, Morisseau, Maignan, Dancette)	42.9	1)	Paris	25 Jun

1945

100 yards

Perry Samuels	USA	26	9.5w		1)	San Antonio	19 May
(Samuels)			9.6		1)h	Austin	05 May
Zane Moon	USA		9.6w		1)h	Rawlins, WY	18 May
George Lewis	Tri	16	9.7		1)	Port-of-Spain	25 Mar
(Moon)			9.7		1)		
Jumal Afzal	USA		9.7		1)		
Grover Klemmer	USA	21	9.7		1)	Great Lakes, IL	26 May
Glenn Willis	USA		9.7		1)	Pasadena, CA	08 Jun
Dennis Shore	SA	15	9.7	A	1)	Johannesburg	29 Sep
John Treloar	Aus	28	9.7		1)	Sydeney	06 Oct

Doubtful timing:

Don Pettie	Can	27	9.6	1)	Winnipeg	11 Aug

Unconfirmed performances:

Harold Davis	USA	21	9.5	1)	Brisbane	
Walter Pérez	Uru	24	9.6	1)		
George Baker	Tri		9.6	1)	Bridgetown	

100 metres

Norwood Ewell	USA	18	10.3		1)	New York	30 Jun
Gerardo Bönnhoff	Arg	26	10.3		1)	Buenos Aires	01 Dec
Dave Day	USA		10.4		1)		
Charles Edwards	USA		10.4		1)	Reims	Jul
Adelio Márquez	Arg	24	10.4		1)	Buenos Aires	24 Nov
José Bento de Assis	Bra	15	10.5		1)h2	Montevideo	15 Apr
Perry Samuels	USA	26	10.5		1)	New York	29 Jun
George Lewis	Tri	16	10.5		1)	Willemstad	04 Nov
Carlos Isaack	Arg	24	10.5		3)	Buenos Aires	01 Dec

Unconfirmed performance:

Ion Moina	Rom	21	10.4		)		

200 metres (half-to-full turn)

Elmore Harris	USA	22	21.2*		1)hcp	New York	09 Jun
José Bento de Assis	Bra	15	21.3		1)	Montevideo	19 Apr
Adelio Márquez	Arg	24	21.4		1)h3	Montevideo	18 Apr
Gerardo Bönnhoff	Arg	26	21.5		1)		02 Feb
Bob Crowson	USA	23	21.5*		1)	Lincoln	19 May
Dennis Shore	SA	15	21.5*	A	1)	Pretoria	17 Oct
John Treloar	Aus	28	21,.6*		1)	Sydney	06 Oct
George Lewis	Tri	16	21.7*		1)h1	Port-of-Spain	29 Mar
Albert McLean	Tri		21.7*		1)	Port-of-Spain	31 May
Lennart Strandberg	Swe	15	21.7		1)	Stockholm	10 Aug

Unconfirmed performances:

Dennis Shore	SA	15	21.1*		)		
Charles Edwards	USA		21.4		)		

220 yards (straight course)

Andy Shurr	USA		21.1	1)		
Elton Correa	USA		21.3	1)		
John Van Velzer	USA	23	21.3	1)	West Point	26 May
Bob Crowson	USA	23	21.3°	1)	New York	29 Jun
Perry Samuels	USA	26	21.5	1)		
Earl Collins	USA		21.5	1)	Dallas	12 May

° = 200 m. time plus 0.1

4x100 metre relay

	Bra	(dos Santos, Bento de Assis, de Luz, Bastianon)	41.9	1)	Montevideo	16 Apr
	Arg	(Ravano, Florio, Márquez, Isaack)	42.0	2)	Montevideo	16 Apr
U. of So.California	USA	(Morris, Moorman, Eagle, Beaman)	42.0*	1)	Modesto	02 Jun
	Swe	(Ohlsson, Strandberg, Laessker, Håkansson)	42.0	1)	København	25 Aug
Combined Team „A"		(Monti/Ita, Lidman/Swe, Pol.Braekman/Bel, Valmy/Fra)	42.5	1)	Bern	22 Jul
Moskva	SU	(Golovkin, Korobkov, S.Kuznyetsov, Karakulov)	42.7	1)	Kiev	Sep

1946

100 yards

Bill Martineson	USA		9.5w		1)h	College Station	10 May
Allen Lawler	USA	22	9.5w		1)h	Collge Station	10 May
Dennis Shore	SA	15	9.5	A	1)	Queenstown	24 May
Billy Mathis	USA	27	9.5		1)	Buffalo	04 Aug

100 metres

Charles Parker	USA	26	10.2	1)	Kyoto	
Carlos Isaack	Arg	24	10.2w	1)	Villa Maria	29 Sep
Gerardo Bönnhoff	Arg	26	10.2w	2)	Villa Maria	29 Sep
George Lewis	Tri	16	10.2	1)	Port-of-Spain	16 Nov
Emmanuel McDonald Bailey	Tri	20	10.3	1)	Göteborg	28 Aug
Jon Moina	Rom	21	10.4	1)	Predeal	24 Aug
Rafael Fortún	Cub	19	10.4	1)h1	Barranquilla	09 Dec

200 metres (half-to-full turn)

Lloyd LaBeach	Jam/Pan	23	20.8*		1)	Kingston	04 Sep
Herb McKenley	Jam	22	20.9*e		2)	Kingston	04 Sep
Norwood Ewell	USA	18	21.0*w		1)	Philadelphia	08 Jun
John Treloar	Aus	28	21.1*		1)	Sydney	21 Dec
George Lewis	Tri	16	21.2		1)	Port-of-Spain	16 Nov
Dennis Shore	SA	15	21.3*	A	1)	Pretoria	07 Oct
Emmanuel McDonald Bailey	Tri	20	21.3		1)r1	Göteborg	29 Aug
(Ewell)			21.3		1)	Praha	24 Jul
Gerardo Bönnhoff	Arg	26	21.4w		1)	Villa Maria	30 Sep
Carlo Monti	Ita	20	21.4		1)	Milano	06 Oct
Bob Crowson	USA	23	21.5*		1)	Lincoln	18 May

Unconfirmed performance:

Dennis Shore	SA	15	21.0*		1)		

220 yards (Straight course)

Herb McKenley	Jam	22	20.0	1)	Champaign	01 Jun
Lloyd LaBeach	Jam/Pan	23	20.8	2)	Champaign	01 Jun
Mel Patton	USA	24	21.1	1)	Westwood, CA	20 Apr
Jack Pierce	USA	26	21.2	1)	Champaign	18 May

4x100 metre relay

Baylor Univ.	USA	(Isaacs, McGillberry, Cotton, Martineson)	40.8*	1)	Lawrence	20 Apr
	Swe	(Danielsson, I.Nilsson, Laessker, Håkansson)	41.5	1)	Oslo	25 Aug
	Ita	(Tito, Perucconi, Monti, Cattoni)	41.8	1)	Zurich	22 Sep
	Arg	(Triulzi, Florio, Márquez, Isaack)	41.9	1)	Santiago de Chile	28 Apr
	Fra	(Lebas, Gonon, Lepève, Valmy)	42.0	2)	Oslo	25 Aug

1947

100 yards

Herb McKenley	Jam	22	9.4w		1)	Champaign	24 May
Mel Patton	USA	24	9.4		1)	Modesto	24 May
Emmanuel McDonald Bailey	Tri	20	9.4w		1)h hcp	Bradford	07 Jun
Bill Martineson	USA		9.5w		1)	College Station	12 Apr
Aubrey Fowler	USA		9.5w		1)	Fayetteville	19 Apr
Webb Jay	USA		9.5w		1)	College Station	19 Apr
Wendell Davis	USA		9.5		1)	St.Louis	10 May
Billy Mathis	USA	27	9.5w		2)	Champaign	24 May
(Martineson)			9.5		2)	Modesto	24 May
(Mathis)			9.5	A	1)	Salt Lake City	20 Jun
Charles Peters	USA	27	9.5	A	2)h3	Salt Lake City	20 Jun
Don Campbell	USA	26	9.5	A	1)h4	Salt Lake City	20 Jun
Morris Curotta	Aus	29	9.5w		1)	Sydney	21 Oct

Rolling start:

Eddie Conwell	USA	24	9.5	A	1)	Provo	26 Apr

Unofficial mark (starter and timers not registered officials):

Daniel Hugo	SA	24	9.5		1)	De Aar	21 Apr

Downhill course:

Hal Fox	USA		9.5		-)	Reno	19 Apr

100 metres

Juan Lopez Testa	Uru	26	10.2w	1)s1	Buenos Aires	14 Oct
Emmanuel McDonald Bailey	Tri	20	10.3	1)	Antwerpen	29 Jun
Allen Lawler	USA	22	10.3	1)	Lincoln	04 Jul
Harrison Dillard	USA	23	10.3	1)	Stockholm	05 Aug
Herb McKenley	Jam	22	10.4	1)	Compton	06 Jun
Richard Houden	USA		10.4	1)h4	Lincoln	04 Jul
Gerardo Bönnhoff	Arg	26	10.4	1)s2	Buenos Aires	14 Oct

Doubtful timing:

Clarrie Hayes	Aus		10.3	1)	Tokyo	03 Oct

200 metres (half-to-full turn)

Herb McKenley	Jam	22	20.3*w		1)	Georgetown	07 Apr
Norwood Ewell	USA	18	21.0		1)	Lincoln	05 Jul
Billy Mathis	USA	27	21.1*		1)	Georgetown	04 Aug
John Treloar	Aus	28	21.1*		1)	Sydney	
Emmanuel McDonald Bailey	Tri	20	21.2		1)	Praha	25 Jun
Richard Houden	USA		21.2		1)	Praha	23 Jul
Harrison Dillard	USA	23	21.2		1)	Oslo	24 Jul
Daniel Hugo	SA	24	21.3*	A	1)	Bulawayo	07 Apr
Joe Cianciabella	USA	25	21.3*		1)	Philadelphia	31 May
Lloyd LaBeach	Pan	23	21.3*		1)	Alhambra, CA	11 Jul
Allen Lawler	USA	22	21.3		2)	Praha	23 Jul
John Wilkinson	UK	29	21.3		1)	Köln	16 Aug
Gerardo Bönnhoff	Arg	26	21.3		1)	Buenos Aires	28 Sep
Dennis Shore	SA	15	21.3*	A	1)	Pretoria	06 Dec
Peter Heath	Aus		21.3*w		1)	Sydney	27 Dec

Doubtful timing:

Clarrie Hayes	Aus		21.2	1)	Tokyo	03 Oct

220 yards (straight course)

Herb McKenley	Jam	22	20.2w		1)	Champaign	24 May
Mel Patton	USA	24	20.4		1)	Riverside, CA	05 Apr
Lloyd LaBeach	Pan	23	20.7+		1)	Los Angeles	13 Jun
(McKenley)			20.7	A	1)	Salt Lake City	21 Jun
Aubrey Fowler	USA		20.9w		1)	StillWater, OK	10 May
Charles Parker	USA	26	20.9		1)	College Station	10 May
Glenn Davis	USA	24	20.9		1)	West Point	24 May
Charles Peters	USA	27	20.9	A	1)h1	Salt Lake City	20 Jun

+ = during 220 y. race.

4x100 metre relay

Univ. of Texas	USA	(Samuels, Lawler, Kidd, Parker)	40.4*	1)	Los Angeles	23 May
	Hun	(Tima, Bartha, Csányi, Goldoványi)	41.1	1)	Milano	04 Oct
	Ita	(Monti, Montanari, Tito, Turrini)	41.6	2)	Milano	04 Oct
	Fra	(Bally, Litaudon, Martel, Valmy)	41.7	1)	Praha	15 Aug
	Cze	(Parácek, Schmid, Horcic, David)	41.8	2)	Praha	15 Aug

1948

100 yards (E= electric time)

Mel Patton	USA	24	9.3	1)	Fresno	15 May
Paul Bienz	USA	26	9.4w	1)	Baton Rouge	01 May
Clyde Scott	USA	24	9.4w	1)	Fayetteville	08 May
Wendell Belfield	USA	28	9.4	1)	Atlanta	15 May
Lloyd LaBeach	Pan	23	9.4	2)	Fresno	15 May

Doubtful timing (one watch):

George Lewis	Pan	16	9.4	1)	California	16 May

100 metres

Lloyd LaBeach	Pan	23	10.2	1)	Fresno	15 May
Norwood Ewell (10.32E)	USA	18	10.2	1)	Evanston	09 Jul
Mel Patton (10.44-E)	USA	24	10.3	2)	Evanston	09 Jul
Harrison Dillard	USA	23	10.3	1)	London	31 Jul

200 metres (half-to-full turn)

Mel Patton	USA	24	20.7w	1)	Minnneapolis	19 Jun
(Patton)			20.7	1)	Evanston	10 Jul
Charles Peters	USA	27	20.8*	1)	Lafayette	01 May
Norwood Ewell	USA	18	20.8	2)	Evanston	10 Jul

Harrison Dillard	USA	23	20.8	1)	Colombes	16 Aug
Charles May	USA	24	20.9*	2)	Lafayette	01 May
Lloyd LaBeach	Pan	23	20.9	1)h	Milwaukee	02 Jul
Cliff Bourland	USA	21	21.0	3)	Evanston	10 Jul
Charles Parker	USA	26	21.1w	2)	Minneapolis	19 Jun
(Parker)			21.1 e	4)	Evanston	10 Jul

Downhill course:

John Treloar	Aus	28	20.8*	1)	Melbourne	26 Jan
John Bartram	Aus	25	21.0*	2)	Melbourne	26 Jan

220 yards (Straight course)

Lloyd LaBeach	Pan	23	20.3	1)	Compton	04 Jun
Bill Napier	USA	19	20.5w	1)	College Station	01 May
Paul Bienz	USA	26	20.6	1)	New Orleans	10 Apr
Eugene Carter	USA	28	20.6w	1)	Abilene	08 May
Mel Patton	USA	24	20.6	1)	Los Angeles	08 May
Charles Parker	USA	26	20.6	1)	Dallas	04 Jun

4x100 metre relay

U. of Texas	USA	(Samuels, Robertson, Lawler, Parker)	40.6	1)	Los Angeles	21 May
	USA	(Ewell, Wright, Dillard, Patton)	40.6	1)	London	07 Aug
	Ita	(Perucconi, Bassetti, Monti, Siddi)	41.0	1)	Firenze	03 Jul
	UK	(McCorquodale, Gregory, Jones, Archer)	41.3	2)	London	07 Aug
	Aus	(Curotta, Bruce, Bartram, Treloar)	41.4*	1)	Sydney	28 Feb
	Fra	(Porthault, Litaudon, Lebas, Valmy)	41.4	1)	Paris	25 Jul
	Hun	(Tima, Bartha, Csányi, Goldoványi)	41.4	2)h2	London	06 Aug

1949

100 yards

Mel Patton	USA	24	9.1w		1)	Westwood	07 May
Telford Neely	USA	25	9.2w		1)	Baton Rouge	30 Apr
Harrison Dillard	USA	23	9.4		1)	Georgetown	16 Apr
Lloyd LaBeach	Pan	23	9.5		1)	Malbourne	29 Jan
Eugene Carter	USA	28	9.5w		1)	Abilene	23 Mar
Dean Smith	USA	32	9.5w		1)	Graham, TX	09 Apr
Paul Bienz	USA	26	9.5w		1)	Atlanta	16 Apr
Don Campbell	USA	26	9.5	A	1)h	Boulder	30 Apr
Bob Tyler	USA	23	9.5		1)	Baltimore	14 May
Perry Samuels	USA	26	9.5		1)	Fayetteville	14 May
Emmanuel McDonald Bailey	Tri	20	9.5		1)	Reykjavik	21 May
(Patton)			9.5		1)h1	Los Angeles	17 Jun

"Whistle" start:

Lloyd LaBeach	Pan	23	9.4	1)	Newcastle, NSW	26 Jan

100 metres

Emmanuel McDonald Bailey	Tri	20	10.2w	1)	Reykjavik	28 May
Mario Fayos	Uru	25	10.3	1)	Montevideo	26 Mar
Andrew Stanfield	USA	27	10.3	1)	Fresno	25 Jun
Herb McKenley	Jam	22	10.3	1)	Kingston	03 Sep
Harrison Dillard	USA	23	10.4	1)	Georgetown	21 Apr
(McDonald Bailey)			10.4	1)h	Reykjavik	15 May
Bob Tyler	USA	23	10.4	1)	Fresno	24 Jun
Charles Peters	USA	27	10.4	1)h3	Fresno	25 Jun
Bob Work	USA		10.4	2)	Fresno	25 Jun
Konrad Wittekindt	Ger	24	10.4	1)	Kassel	17 Jul
Heinz Fischer	Ger	25	10.4	1)	Dortmund	13 Aug
Aroldo Pereira da Silva	Bra	29	10.4	1)	São Paulo	05 Nov

Doubtful timing:

René Valmy	Fra	21	10.4w	1)	Phnom Penh	13 Feb

200 metres (half-to-full turn)

Herb McKenley	Jam	22	20.9*		1)	Sydney	22 Jan
Andrew Stanfield	USA	27	20.9		1)	Oslo	31 Aug
John Bartram	Aus	25	21.0*		2)	Sydney	22 Jan
Telford Neely	USA	25	21.0*		1)	University,MS	07 May
Lloyd LaBeach	Pan	23	21.1*		1)h	Sydney	22 Jan
Irwin Wood	Aus	28	21.1*		4)	Sydney	22 Jan
Charles Peters	USA	27	21.1*		1)	Evanston	21 May
Morris Curotta	Aus	29	21.2*		1)	Napier	26 Feb
Hendrik Lombard	SA	29	21.2*	A	1)	Pretoria	23 Mar
Craig Dixon	USA	26	21.2		1)	Växjö	13 Aug

Short course:

Zdobyslaw Stawczyk	Pol	23	21.2w	1)	Budapest	20 Aug

220 yards (straight course)

Mel Patton	USA	24	20.2	1)	Westwood	07 May
Lloyd LaBeach	Pan	23	20.3 A	1)	Provo	23 Apr
Paul Bienz	USA	26	20.3w	1)	Tuscaloosa	07 May
Eugene Carter	USA	28	20.4w	1)	Abilene	23 Mar
Buddy Fowlkes	USA	28	20.5w	2)	Atlanta	16 Apr
	Bienz		20.5	1)	Atlanta	28 May
Andrew Stanfield	USA	27	20.5	2)	Los Angeles	18 Jun
Bill Napier	USA	19	20.7w	1)	College Station	09 Apr
Ira Kaplan	USA	28	20.7w	1)	New York	11 Jun
Charles Peters	USA	27	20.7	1)	Berkeley	21 Jun
Ted Haggis	Can	26	20.8	1)	Toronto	03 Sep

Short course (199.33 m.):

Bobby Dean	USA		20.5w	1)	Corpus Christi,TX	15 Apr

4x100 metre relay

U. of So. California	USA	(Pasquali, Frazier, Scott, Patton)	40.5*	1)	Fresno	14 May
	Hun	(Szebeni, Bartha, Csányi, Varasdi)	40.7	1)	Budapest	29 Aug
	Ita	(Penna, Leccese, Monti, Siddi)	41.3	2)	Budapest	29 Aug
Victorian AAA	Aus	(Dunne, Watt, Gillon, Bartram)	41.4*	1)	Sydney	22 Jan
	SU	(Golovkin, Koroyev, Sanadze, Karakulov)	41.6	1)	Moskva	23 Jul

1950

100 yards

Charles Parker	USA	26	9.4w	1)	Laredo, TX	11 Mar
Andrew Stanfield	USA	27	9.4w	1)	Georgetown	08 Apr
Ira Kaplan	USA	28	9.4w	1)	New York	10 Jun
John Treloar	Aus	28	9.5w	1)	Sydney	04 Mar
Eugene Carter	USA	28	9.5w	1)	Austin	18 Mar
Perry Samuels	USA	26	9.5w	2)	Austin	18 Mar
Joe Preston	USA	28	9.5w	1)	Beaumont,TX	25 Mar
(Parker)			9.5	1)	Odessa, TX	25 Mar
Lloyd LaBeach	Pan	23	9.5	1)	Los Angeles	28 Mar
(Treloar)			9.5e	2)hcp	Manly, NSW	01 Apr
Don Anderson	USA		9.5	1)	Westwood	15 Apr
Dick Stolpe	USA	25	9.5w	1)	Wichita	18 Apr
Henry Thresher	USA	32	9.5w	1)	Mercersburg	06 May
Charles Peters	USA	27	9.5	1)	Bloomington	06 May
Jim Gehrdes	USA	25	9.5w	1)	State College	13 May
Jim Caffey	USA		9.5	1)	Brookfield, IL	13 May
Bill Fell	USA	30	9.5	1)	Corvallis	13 May
(Stanfield)			9.5	1)	Los Angeles	19 May
Bob Boyd	USA		9.5	1)	Compton	02 Jun
Arthur Bragg	USA	30	9.5	1)	Bailtimore	10 Jun
Bob Tyler	USA	23	9.5w	1)hcp	Berwick-on-Tweed	24 Jul

Professional mark:

Norwood Ewell	USA	18	9.4	1)r1	Wangaratta, Vic	28 Jan

100 metres

Jesus Farres	Cub		10.3w	1)h1	Guatemala City	26 Feb
Lloyd LaBeach	Pan	23	10.3w	1)h3	Guatemale City	26 Feb
Aristipo Lerma	Col		10.3w	1)h4	Guatemala City	26 Feb
Rafael Fortún	Cub	19	10.3w	1)	Guatemala City	27 Feb
(LaBeach)			10.3	1)	Habana	27 May
Emmanuel McDonald Bailey	Tri	20	10.3	1)	Norrköping	04 Sep
George Rhoden	Jam	26	10.3	1)	Kingston	16 Sep
Egbert McNeil	Jam		10.4	1)	Kingston	08 Feb
(Fortún)			10.4	1)s1	Guatemala City	26 Feb
Herb McKenley	Jam	22	10.4w	2)	Guatemala City	27 Feb
Arthur Bragg	USA	30	10.4	1)	College Park, MD	24 Jun
Vladimir Sukharyev	SU	24	10.4w	1)	Moskva	06 Aug
José Zelaya	Par	26	10.4	1)	Asunción	29 Sep
(Sukharyev)			10.4	1)	Bucuresti	21 Oct

Timers missed the flash:

Lloyd LaBeach	Pan	23	10.2w	1)	Nordmaling	27 Jul

Doubtful timing:

Lloyd LaBeach	Pan	23	10.1	1)	Guayaquil	07 Oct
Andres Fernández	Ecu		10.3	2)	Guayaquil	07 Oct

200 metres (half-to-full turn)

Herb McKenley	Jam	22	20.6w	1)	Eskilstuna	08 Sep
Lloyd LaBeach	Pan	23	20.7	1)	Göteborg	11 Aug
Don Campbell	USA	26	20.8*w A	1)	Kimberley	16 Sep
(McKenley)			20.8	1)	Göteborg	24 Sep
Emmanuel McDonald Bailey	Tri	20	20.9	1)	Colombes	10 Sep
Charles Peters	USA	27	21.0*	1)	Madison, WI	20 Jun
Kenneth Wyeth	SA	29	21.0*w A	2)	Kimberley	16 Sep
George Rhoden	Jam	26	21.0	1)	Kingston	16 Sep
Dave Batten	NZ		21.1*	1)	Napier	02 Jan
John Treloar	Aus	28	21.1*	1)	Sydney	25 Feb
Bob Tyler	USA	23	21.1	1)	College Park, MD	24 Jun

Short course:

Óttó Szebeni	Hun	29	20.9w	1)	Budapest	03 Sep
Béla Goldoványi	Hun	25	21.0w	2)	Budapest	03 Sep

220 yards (straight course)

Charles Parker	USA	26	20.0w	1)	Laredo, TX	11 Mar
Dick Stolpe	USA	25	20.2w	2)	Laredo, TX	11 Mar
Andrew Stanfield	USA	27	20.4w	1)hcp	Georgetown	12 Apr
Eugene Carter	USA	28	20.5w	1)	Laredo, TX (coll.ev)	11 Mar
Lloyd LaBeach	Pan	23	20.5w A	1)	Provo	29 Apr
Paul Bienz	USA	26	20.6	1)	New Orleans	06 May
(LaBeach)			20.6	1)	Compton	02 Jun
Henry Thresher	USA	32	20.6w	1)	New York	10 Jun
Emmanuel McDonald Bailey	Tri	20	20.6w	1)hcp	Imber Court	26 Aug
Ira Kaplan	USA	28	20.7w	2)	New York	10 Jun

4x100 metre relay

Stanford Univ.	USA	(Buck, B.Bryan, Taylor, G.Bryan)	40.7*	1)	Los Angeles	19 May
	SU	(Sukharyev, Kalyayev, Sanadze, Karakulov)	40.9	1)	Moskva	30 Jul
	Fra	(Bally, Perlot, Camus, Bonino)	41.0	1)	Colombes	30 Sep
	Hun	(Zarándi, Szebeni, Csányi, Goldoványi)	41.1	2)	Moskva	30 Jul
Southern Germany	FRG	(Zandt, Luther, Sturm, Wittekindt)	41.4	1)	Köln	27 Aug

N.B. Up to 1950, or just about, reliable information on wind assistance was usually hard to find, so we decided to have a consolidated list, simply adding a "w" for marks known to have been wind-assisted.
From 1951 onwards the newly born ATFS deemed it possible and advisable to list wind-assisted marks separately. We will comply with that policy, giving from now on legal marks first and noteworthy wind-assisted marks later.

1951

100 yards

Tom Williams	USA		9.5	1)	San Diego	05 May
Rod Richard	USA	32	9.5	1)	Fresno	12 May
Guy Blackburn	USA		9.5	1)	Berkeley	02 Jun

100 metres

Emmanuel McDonald Bailey	Tri	20	10.2	1)	Beograd	25 Aug
James Golliday	USA	31	10.3	1)	Berkeley	23 Jun
Vladimir Sukharyev	SU	24	10.3	1)	Bucuresti	23 Sep
Dean Smith	USA	32	10.3	1)	New Orleans	30 Dec
Rafael Fortún	Cub	19	10.4	1)	Habana	20 May
Heinz Fütterer	FRG	31	10.4	1)	Oberhausen	10 Jun
Herb McKenley	Jam	22	10.4	1)	Sarpsborg	27 Jul
Angel Kolev	Bul	26	10.4	2)	Bucuresti	23 Sep

200 metres (half-to-full turn)

Andrew Stanfield	USA	27	20.5*	1)	Philadelphia	26 May
Emmanuel McDonald Bailey	Tri	20	20.9	1)	Beograd	26 Aug
Joe Schatzle	USA	31	21.0*	2)	Philadelphia	26 May
Herb McKenley	Jam	22	21.1	1)	Santiago de Chile	17 May
Rafael Fortún	Cub	19	21.1	1)	Habana	21 May
Lindy Remigino	USA	31	21.1*	1)	Philadelphia	25 May
Peter Kraus	FRG	32	21.1	1)	Regensburg	30 Jun
Vladimir Sukharyev	SU	24	21.2	1)	Moskva	15 Jul
Eugene Cole	USA	28	21.3*	1)	Champaign	12 May
George Rhoden	Jam	26	21.3	1)	Oberhausen	18 Jul

Mark made with assisting wind:

John Wilkinson	UK	29	21.2*	1)	Glasgow	09 Jun

220 yards (straight course)

Walt McKibben	USA	29	20.6	1)	Compton	01 Jun
George Rhoden	Jam	26	20.7	1)	Seattle	16 Jun
Mickey Dunn	USA		20.8 A	1)	Denver	11 May
Gary Green	USA		20.8	1)	Hutchinson	19 May
Arthur Bragg	USA	30	20.8	2)	Seattle	16 Jun
Joe Schatzle	USA	31	20.9	1)	West Point	09 May
Charles Thomas	USA	32	20.9°	1)	Berkeley	22 Jun
James Ford	USA	30	20.9°	1)	Berkeley	23 Jun

Marks made with assisting wind:

Carl Otsuki	USA	27	20.5	1)	Commerce, TX	22 Mar
Emmanuel McDonald Bailey	Tri	20	20.5	1)	Imber Court	05 Jul
Charles Thomas	USA	32	20.6	1)	College Station	14 Apr
Richard Smith	USA		20.8	1)	Denton	02 Mar

° = 200 m. time plus 0.1

4x100 metre relay

Univ. of So. California	USA	(Work, R.S.Richard, G.Brown, Wilson)	40.6*	1)	Fresno	12 May
	Cub	(Farres, Garcia, Mazorra, Fortún)	41.2	2)	Buenos Aires	06 Mar
	UK	(McD. Bailey/Tri, Stacey, Gregory, Shenton)	41.2*	1)	London	04 Aug
	SU	(Sukharyev, Sanadze, Kalyayev, Karakulov)	41.4	1)	Moskva	14 Jul
	Cze	(Horcic, Otava, Broz, Pospisil)	41.4	1)	Budapest	25 Aug
	Hun	(Karadi, Varasdi, Csányi,Goldoványi)	41.4	1)	Budapest	25 Sep

1952

100 yards

Charles Johnson	USA		9.5	1)	Lafayette, LA	19 Apr
Alex Burl	USA		9.5 A	1)	Denver	24 May
James Golliday	USA	31	9.5	1)	Ann Arbor	31 May

100 metres

Andrew Stanfield	USA	27	10.3	1)	Zurich	12 Aug
Levan Sanadze	SU	28	10.3	1)	Tbilisi	21 Sep
Emmanuel McDonald Bailey	UK	20	10.4	1)	London	24 May
Dean Smith	USA	32	10.4	1)	San Antonio	31 May
James Golliday	USA	31	10.4	1)	Berkeley	13 Jun
Lindy Remigino	USA	31	10.4	1)h11	Helsinki	20 Jul
Herb McKenley	Jam	22	10.4	1)s2	Helsinki	21 Jul
James Gathers	USA	30	10.4	1)	Tampere	30 Jul
Thane Baker	USA	31	10.4	1)	Wien	06 Aug
Harrison Dillard	USA	23	10.4	2)	Wien	06 Aug
Jerome Biffle	USA	28	10.4	2)	Zurich	12 Aug
Byron LaBeach	Jam		10.4	1)	Eskilstuna	14 Aug

Marks made with assisting wind:

Lindy Remigino	USA	31	10.2	1)	Oslo	31 Jul

200 metres (half-to-full turn)

Andrew Stanfield	USA	27	20.6	1)	Los Angeles	28 Jun
Thane Baker	USA	31	20.8	2)	Helsinki	23 Jul
James Gathers	USA	30	20.8	3)	Helsinki	23 Jul
Herb McKenley	Jam	22	20.8*	1)	Glasgow	02 Aug
Emmanuel McDonald Bailey	UK	20	20.9	1)	London	24 May
James Ford	USA	30	21.0	1)	Berkeley	14 Jun
Jack Davis	USA	30	21.1	2)	Berkeley	14 Jun
Charles Thomas	USA	32	21.2	3)	Los Angeles	28 Jun
Leslie Laing	Jam	25	21.2	5)	Helsinki	23 Jul
Eugene Cole	USA	28	21.2	1)	Gävle	01 Aug
Brian Butterfield	Aus		21.2	1)	Brisbane	29 Nov

220 yards (straight course)

Andrew Stanfield	USA	27	20.4	1)	Compton	04 Jun
George Rhoden	Jam	26	20.5	2)	Compton	04 Jun
Thane Baker	USA	31	20.6	1)	Kansas City	31 May
Horace Goode	USA	31	20.8	1)	Dallas	18 Apr
George Adrian	USA	31	20.8	1)	Kingsville, TX	10 May
James Gathers	USA	30	20.8	3)	Compton	04 Jun

Marks made with assisting wind

Charles Thomas	USA	32	20.4°	1)	Austin	04 Apr
Thomas			20.4	1)	Dallas	10 May
Horace Goode	USA	31	20.5	2)	Dallas	10 May
Paul Wells	USA		20.7°	1)	Norman	24 May
Eugene Cole	USA	28	20.7	1)	Sacramento	31 May

° = 200 m. time plus 0.1

4x100 metre relay

USA	(D.Smith, Dillard, Remigino, Stanfield) (40.26 E)	40.1	1)	Helsinki	27 Jul
SU	(Tokaryev, Sukharyev, Kalyayev, Sanadze) (40.58 E)	40.3	2)	Helsinki	27 Jul
Hun	(Zarandi, Varasdi, Csányi,Goldoványi) (40.83 E)	40.5	3)	Helsinki	27 Jul
UK	(McDonald Bailey, Jack, Gregory, Shenton) (40.85 E)	40.6	4)	Helsinki	27 Jul
Fra	(Porthault, Bally, Camus, Bonino) (40.98 E)	40.8	2)h1	Helsinki	26 Jul

1953

100 yards

Mike Agostini	Tri	35	9.4	1)	Kingston	15 Apr
Thane Baker	USA	31	9.4	1)	Kansas City	30 May
Hector Hogan	Aus	31	9.5	1)	Brisbane	14 Feb
Charles Thomas	USA	32	9.5	1)	College Station	07 Mar
Willie Williams	USA	31	9.5	1)	Berkeley	18 Apr
Arthur Bragg	USA	30	9.5	1)	Baltimore	09 May
Edward Waters	USA	35	9.5	2)	Baltimore	09 May
Kenneth Kave	USA	33	9.5	3)	Baltimore	09 May

Marks made with assisting wind:

Willie Williams	USA	31	9.4	1)	Prairie View, TX	04 Apr

100 metres

Ralph Butler	USA	30	10.3	1)	Nürnberg	19 Jul
Arthur Bragg	USA	30	10.3	1)	Köln	29 Jul
Mike Agostini	Tri	35	10.4	1)	Port-of-Spain	31 Mar
Heinz Fütterer	FRG	31	10.4	1)	Stuttgart	20 Jun
Ewald Schröder	GDR		10.4	1)	Krakow	01 Jul
Abe Butler	USA		10.4	2)	Nürnberg	19 Jul
Thane Baker	USA	31	10.4	1)	Malmö	03 Aug

Marks made with assisting wind:

Thane Baker	USA	31	10.3	1)	Simrishamn	02 Aug

Doubtful timing:

Sumana Navaratnam	Cey		10.4	1)	Madras	Jan

200 metres (half-to-full turn)

Arthur Bragg	USA	30	20.6	1)	Köln	29 Jul
Andrew Stanfield	USA	27	20.8	1)	Port-of-Spain	28 Mar
Mike Agostini	Tri	35	21.0*	1)	Kingston	15 Apr
Václav Janecek	Cze		21.0	1)	Bucuresti	08 Aug
Heinz Fütterer	FRG	31	21.0	1)	Zagreb	06 Sep
Willie Williams	USA	31	21.1*	1)	Lafayette, IN	29 May
Karl-Friedrich Haas	FRG	31	21.1	1)	Nürnberg	04 Jul
Ardalion Ignatyev	SU	30	21.1	1)	Bucuresti	07 Aug
Herb McKenley	Jam	22	21.2*	1)	Kingston	01 Jan
Emmanuel McDonald Bailey	UK	20	21.2*	1)	London	10 Jul

Marks made with assisting wind:

Thane Baker	USA	31	20.4*	1)h2	Lincoln	19 Jun
Leslie Laing	Jam	25	21.0*	1)h3	Lincoln	19 Jun
Fred Hazekamp	USA		21.1*	1)	Trenton, NJ	23 May
Merv Brock	USA		21.1*	2)h3	Lincoln	19 Jun
Joseph Walker	USA		21.1*	2)h2	Lincoln	19 Jun

220 yards (straight course)

Thane Baker	USA	31	20.4	1)	Kansas City	30 May
Leamon King	USA	36	20.5	1)	Tulare	23 May
Charles Thomas	USA	32	20.6	1)	Laredo	14 Mar
Arthur Pollard	USA	34	20.7	1)	State College	16 May
Milton Campbell	USA	33	20.7	1)	Elizabeth, NJ	20 Jun
Andrew Stanfield	USA	27	20.8	1)	Compton	05 Jun

Marks made with assising wind:

Charles Thomas	USA	32	20.5	1)	Waco	09 Apr
J.Frank Daugherty	USA	35	20.5	1)	Austin	08 May
Horace Goode	USA	31	20.6	2)	Waco	09 Apr
Joe Peugh	USA	33	20.6	1)	Waco (Frosh D)	09 Apr

4x100 metre relay

	Ita	(Ghiselli, Vittori, Montanari, Sangermano)	40.8	1)	Milano	28 Jun
	FRG	(Kluck, Kraus, Fütterer, Zandt)	40.8	2)	Milano	28 Jun
Pacific Co. Conf.	USA	(Graffio, Richardson, Blackburn, Richard)	40.9*	1)	Ann Arbor	23 Jun
	Hun	(Zarandi, Varasdi, Csányi, Goldoványi)	40.9	1)	Budapest	12 Sep
Leningrad	SU	(Tokaryev, Kalyayev, Ryabov, Grigoryev)	41.0	1)	Moskva	23 Aug

1954

100 yards

Hector Hogan	Aus	31	9.3	1)	Sydney	13 Mar
James Jackson	USA	35	9.4	1)	Berkeley	22 May

Arthur Bragg	USA	30	9.4		1)	St.Louis	18 Jun
Lindy Remigino	USA	31	9.5		1)	Fairfield, CT	May
Dean Smith	USA	32	9.5		1)	Waco	15 May
Joe Graffio	USA	32	9.5		1)	Seattle	28 May

Marks made with assisting wind:

Dean Smith	USA	32	9.3		1)	Dallas	01 May
Joe Graffio	USA	32	9.4		2)	Dallas	01 May
Willie Williams	USA	31	9.4		1)	Madison, WI	15 May

100 metres

Hector Hogan	Aus	31	10.2		1)	Sydney	13 Mar
Heinz Fütterer	FRG	31	10.2		1)	Yokohama	31 Oct
James Golliday	USA	31	10.3		1)	Oberhausen	02 Jun
Raúl Mazorra Zamora	Cub		10.4	A	1)	México, DF	07 Mar
Levan Sanadze	SU	28	10.4		1)	Moskva	18 Jul
Willie Williams	USA	31	10.4		1)	Saarbrücken	18 Aug
Viktor Ryabov	SU	27	10.4		1)	Kiev	13 Sep
Mikhail Kazantsev	SU	27	10.4		1)	Nalchik	03 Oct
Lev Vasilyev	SU		10.4		2)	Nalchik	03 Oct

Marks made with assisting wind:

Asmundur Bjarnason	Ice	27	10.3		1)	Reykjavik	08 Aug

Doubtful timing:

M. Gabriel	Ind		10.4		1)	Poona	13 Feb

200 metres (half-to-full turn)

Heinz Fütterer	Ger	31	20.8		1)	Osaka	16 Oct
Howard Bugbee	USA	30	20.9*		1)	Tucson	27 Mar
Arthur Bragg	USA	30	21.0*		1)	St.Louis	19 Jun
Charles Thomas	USA	32	21.0*		2)	St.Louis	19 Jun
Andrew Stanfield	USA	27	21.1*		3)	St.Louis	19 Jun
Ardalion Ignatyev	SU	30	21.1		2)	Bern	29 Aug
Leslie Laing	Jam	25	21.2	A	1)	México, D.F.	10 Mar
Hector Hogan	Aus	31	21.2*		1)	Brisbane	20 Mar
Joe Graffio	USA	32	21.2*		2)	Tucson	27 Mar
José Telles da Conceição	Bra	31	21.2		1)	São Paulo	21 Apr
Lindy Remigino	USA	31	21.2*		1)	Glasgow	12 Jun
George Ellis	UK	32	21.2		3)	Bern	29 Aug

Marks made with assisting wind:

Don Jowett	NZ		21.1*		1)	Hamilton	06 Mar
Ralph Aldredge	USA		21.1*		1)	Abilene	05 Jun

Professional mark:

Herb McKenley	Jam	22	20.8° e		1)	Lilydale, Vic.	12 Mar

° Actually 21.1 for 222 y (202.99 m.).

220 yards (straight course)

Art Pollard	USA	34	20.5		1)	New York	28 May
Charles Thomas	USA	32	20.5		1)	Houston	29 May
Larry McBride	USA	32	20.6		1)	Houston	08 May
Gabe Markisohn	USA	32	20.7		1)	Durham	07 Apr
Henry Thresher	USA	32	20.7		1)	New York	29 May
Bill Swisshelm	USA		20.8		1)	Huntington Beach, CA	13 Mar
Jackie Creel	USA		20.8		1)	Birmingham, AL	15 May
J. W. Mashburn	USA	33	20.8		2)	Houston	29 May
James Jackson	USA	35	20.8		1)	Stockton	05 Jun

Marks made with assisting wind:

J. Frank Daugherty	USA	35	20.6		1)	College Station	10 Apr
Clyde Hart	USA	34	20.6		1)	Waco	03 May
Reed Epps	USA		20.7		1)	Prairie View	01 May
Fred Lucas	USA		20.7		1)	San Diego	26 May

4x100 metre relay

U. of Texas	USA	(D.Smith, Prewitt, Frieden, C.A.Thomas)	40.1*	1)	Lawrence	17 Apr
	Hun	(Zárandi, Varasdi, Csányi, Goldoványi)	40.6	1)	Bern	29 Aug
	SU	(Tokaryev, Ryabov, Sanadze, Konovalov)	40.7	1)	Praha	23 Oct
	Bra	(Kadlec, Ferreira, Fonseca, da Conceiçao)	40.8	1)	São Paulo	24 Apr
	FRG	(Fütterer, Kraus, Zandt, Germar)	40.8	1)	Nürnberg	19 Jun
	UK	(Ellis, Box, Jones, Shenton)	40.8	2)	Bern	29 Aug

1955

100 yards

James Golliday	USA	31	9.3		1)	Evanston	14 May
Larry McBryde	USA	32	9.4		1)	Lafayette	16 Apr
Mike Agostini	Tri	35	9.4		1)	Fresno	14 May
Leamon King	USA	36	9.4		2)	Fresno	14 May
Harry Nash	USA	33	9.4		1)	Madison, WI	21 May
Bobby Morrow	USA	35	9.4		1)	Abilene	03 Jun
Robert Green	USA	28	9.4		1)	San Antonio	13 Jun
Marks made with assisting wind:							
Bobby Morrow	USA	35	9.1		1)	Abilene	04 Jun
Dean Smith	USA	32	9.2		1)	College Station	19 Apr
Larry McBryde	USA	32	9.3		1)	Lawrence	23 Apr

100 metres

Willie Williams	USA	31	10.3	A	1)s2	México, D.F.	14 Mar
Mike Agostini	Tri	35	10.3	A	2)s2	México, D.F.	14 Mar
Rod Richard	USA	32	10.3	A	1)s3	México, D.F.	14 Mar
Heinz Fütterer	FRG	31	10.3		1)	Wuppertal	24 Sep
Dean Smith	USA	32	10.4	A	1)s1	México, D.F.	14 Mar
Leonid Bartenyev	SU	33	10.4		1)	Kiev	May
Yuriy Konovalov	SU	29	10.4		1)	Baku	May
Manuel Rivera	PR		10.4		1)	San Juan	25 Jun
Andrew Stanfield	USA	27	10.4		1)	Kingston	06 Jul
Dick Blair	USA	34	10.4		1)	Praha	21 Jul
Boris Tokaryev	SU	27	10.4		2)	Warszaw	03 Aug
Manfred Germar	FRG	35	10.4		2)	Frankfurt/M	07 Aug
Keith Gardener	Jam	29	10.4		1)	Kingston	31 Aug
Vyacheslav Babiyak	SU		10.4		1)	Leningrad	Sep
José Telles da Conceição	Bra	31	10.4		1)	Rio de Janeiro	14 Sep
Ira Murchison	USA	33	10.4		3)	Wuppertal	24 Sep
Ardalion Ignatyev	SU	30	10.4		1)	Odessa	23 Oct
Ector Hogan	Aus	31	10.4		1)	Melbourne	17 Dec
Brian Randall	Aus		10.4		2)	Melbourne	17 Dec
Marks made with assisting wind:							
Hector Hogan	Aus	31	10.3		1)	Bathurst, NSW	13 Mar
Doubtful timing and/or rolling start:							
Heinrich Umlauft	FRG		10.4		1)	Innsbruck	06 Sep

200 metres (half-to-full turn)

Heinz Fütterer	FRG	31	20.6		1)	Köln	04 Sep
Rod Richard	USA	32	20.7	A	1)	México, D.F.	16 Mar
José Telles da Conceição	Bra	31	20.8	A	1)s1	México, D.F.	15 Mar
Andrew Stanfield	USA	27	20.8		1)	Port-of-Spain	07 May
James Golliday	USA	31	20.8*		1)	Los Angeles	17 Jun
J. W. Mashburn	USA	33	20.9*		1)	Tulsa	14 May
Václav Janecek	Cze	29	20.9°		1)	Erfurt	30 May
Boris Tokaryev	SU	27	20.9		1)	Moskva	10 Jul
Dean Smith	USA	32	21.0*	A	1)	Boulder	25 Jun
Dick Blair	USA	34	21.0		1)	Kouvola	18 Jul
Earl Glaze	USA	36	21.0		1)	Athinai	04 Aug
Manfred Germar	FRG	35	21.0		2)	Köln	04 Sep
Ardalion Ignatyev	SU	30	21.0		1)	Tbilisi	16 Nov

Mark made with assisting wind:

Bobby Morrow	USA	35	20.5°	1)	Abilene	03 Jun

Doubtful timing:

Bobby Morrow	USA	35	20.9°	1)	Napier	26 Dec

° = Made during a 220 y. race

220 yards (straight course)

Robert Kyasky	USA	35	20.6	1)	West Point	28 May
Dick Dorsey	USA	36	20.7	1)	Los Angeles	29 Apr
Eddie Southern	USA	38	20.7	1)	Austin	07 May
Bobby Morrow	USA	35	20.7	1)	Abilene	13 May
Deam Smith	USA	32	20.7	1)	Houston	14 May
Larry McBryde	USA	32	20.7	1)	New Orleans	28 May
Dick Blair	USA	34	20.8	1)	Stillwater	16 Apr
Harry Nelson	Can		20.8	2)	Los Angeles	29 Apr
Art Pollard	USA	34	20.8	1)	University Park	07 May
Horace Goode	USA	31	20.8	2)	Houston	14 May

Marks made with assisting wind:

Bobby Whilden	USA	35	20.4	1)	Laredo	12 Mar
Dean Smith	USA	32	20.4	1)	College Station	19 Apr
Bobby Morrow	USA	35	20.5	1)	Laredo	12 Mar
Horace Goode	USA	31	20.5	1)	Houston	16 Apr
Dick Dorsey	USA	36	20.6	1)	Wilmington	15 Apr
Doyle Jones	USA		20.7	2)	Laredo	12 Mar
J. W. Mashburn	USA	33	20.7	3)	Laredo	12 Mar
Ralph Butler	USA	30	20.7	1)	Compton	02 Apr
Harry Nelson	Can		20.7	1)	Long Beach	15 Apr

4x100 metre relay

Univ. of Texas	USA	(D.Smith, Frieden, Prewitt, Whilden)	40.0*	1)	Modesto	21 May
	SU	(Kalyayev, Tokaryev, Konovalov, Bartenyev)	40.5	1)	Bucuresti	02 Oct
	Hun	(Zárandi, Varasdi, Csányi, Goldoványi)	40.7	1)	Warszawa	06 Aug
	FRG	(Knörzer, Kaufmann, Fütterer, Germar)	40.7	1)	Helsinki	23 Aug
	Swe	(Lorentzon, Malmros, Westlund, Carlsson)	40.8	1)	Stockholm	10 Sep

1956

100 yards

Leamon King	USA	36	9.3	1)	Fresno	12 May
Dave Sime	USA	36	9.3	1)	Raleigh, NC	19 May
Bobby Morrow	USA	35	9.4	1)	Melbourne	04 Jan
Mike Agostini	Tri	35	9.4	1)	Stockton	10 Mar
Ed Waters	USA	35	9.4	1)	Baltimore	12 May
Ken Kave	USA	33	9.4	2)	Baltimore	12 May

Marks made with assisting wind:

Bobby Whillden	USA	35	9.2	1)	Fayeteville	12 May
Ken Kave	USA	33	9.3	1)	Lincoln Univ., PA	14 Apr
Thane Baker	USA	31	9.3	1)	Columbus	21 Apr

Rolling start:

Mike Agostini	Tri	35	9.3	1)	Long Beach	05 May

100 metres

Willie Williams	USA	31	10.1	1)h2	Berlin	03 Aug
Ira Murchison	USA	33	10.1	1)s2	Berlin	04 Aug
Leamon King	USA	36	10.1	1)	Ontario, CA	20 Oct
Bobby Morrow	USA	35	10.2	1)	Houston	19 May
Thane Baker	USA	31	10.2	2)h1	Los Angeles	29 Jun
Dave Sime	USA	36	10.2	1)	New Orleans	30 Dec
Leonid Bartenyev	SU	33	10.3	1)	Kiev	27 May
Boris Tokaryev	SU	27	10.3	1)	Kiev	04 Jun
Lester Carney	USA	34	10.3	1)	Bad Hersfeld	12 Aug

Roy Sandstrom	UK	31	10.3	1)	Budapest	19 Aug
Manfred Germar	FRG	35	10.3	1)	Karlsruhe	25 Aug
Yuriy Bashlikov	SU	36	10.3	1)	Odessa	07 Oct

Downhill course:

Abdul Khaliq	Pak	33	10.2	1)	Abbottabad	07 Oct

Doubtful timing:

Jack Parrington	Can	33	10.2	1)	Toronto	21 Jul
Joe Foreman	Can	35	10.3	2)	Toronto	21 Jul
Stan Levenson	Can	38	10.3	3)	Toronto	21 Jul
Muhammad Sharif Butt	Pak	26	10.3w	1)	Quetta	26 Jul
Abdul Khaliq	Pak	33	10.3	1)	Rawalpindi	08 Sep

200 metres (half-to-full turn)

Thane Baker	USA	31	20.6*	1)	Riverside	09 Jun
Bobby Morrow	USA	35	20.6	1)	Berkeley	16 Jun
Andrew Stanfield	USA	27	20.6	2)	Bakersfield	23 Jun
Ardalion Ignatyev	SU	30	20.7	1)	Kiev	14 Jul
Karl-Friedrich Haas	FRG	31	20.7	1)	Köln	14 Oct
Theodius Bush	USA	33	20.9	3)	Bakersfield	23 Jun
Manfred Germar	FRG	35	20.9	1)	Berlin	18 Aug
Yuriy Konovalov	SU	29	21.0	1)	Nalchik	22 Apr
Boris Tokaryev	SU	27	21.0	1)	Kiev	02 Jun
Dick Blair	USA	34	21.0	1)	Berkeley	15 Jun
Rod Richard	USA	32	21.0	1)	Los Angeles	16 Jun
Leonid Bartenyev	SU	33	21.0	1)	Tashkent	14 Oct

Mark made with assisting wind:

Vilém Mandlik	Cze	36	20.9	1)	Ostrava	25 Aug

Downhill course:

Abdul Khaliq	Pak	33	20.8	1)	Abbottabad	07 Oct

220 yards (straight course)

Dave Sime	USA	36	20.0	1)	Sanger, CA	09 Jun
Mike Agostini	Tri	35	20.1	1)	Barkersfield	17 Mar
Art Pollard	USA	34	20.4	1)	University Park, PA	19 May
James Lea	USA	32	20.6	2)	Bakersfield	17 Mar
John Haines	USA	32	20.7	1)	Ithaca	05 May
Jonas Spiegel	USA	39	20.7	1)	Hopewell, VA	12 May
Theodius Bush	USA	33	20.7	1)	Fort Belvoir, MD	17 May

Marks made with assisting wind:

Bobby Whilden	USA	35	20.4	1)	Dallas	27 Apr
Eddie Southern	USA	38	20.5	1)	Faytteville	12 May
John Haines	USA	32	20.5	1)	New York	26 May
Bruce Lenoir	USA	34	20.6	1)	Ruston	24 Mar
Leamon King	USA	36	20.6	1)	Los Angeles	28 Apr
Len Moore	USA	34	20.6	1)	West Point	19 May

4x100 metre relay

USA	(Murchison, King, Baker, Morrow) (39.60 E)	39.5	1)	Melbourne	01 Dec
SU	(Tokaryev, Sukharyev, Konovalov, Bartenyev) (39.93 E)	39.8	2)	Melbourne	01 Dec
FRG	(Knörzer, Steinbach, Pohl, Germar)	40.0	1)	Köln	14 Oct
Ita	(Gnocchi, Lombardo, Ghiselli, Galbiati)	40.1	1)	Firenze	13 Oct
Pol	(Baranowski, Foik, Jarzembowski, Schmidt)	40.5	1)	Warszawa	08 Sep
Hun	(Kiss, Varasdi, Csányi, Goldoványi)	40.5	1)	Budapest	20 Oct

1957

100 yards

Dave Sime	USA	36	9.3	1)	Raleigh, NC	18 May
Bobby Morrow	USA	35	9.3	1)	Austin	14 Jun
Ira Murchison	USA	33	9.3	2)	Austin	14 Jun

Ollan Kassell	USA	36	9.4		1)	Clarksville	11 May
Hayes Jones	USA	38	9.4		1)	Charleston	24 May
Willie White	USA	38	9.4		1)	Modesto	25 May
Paul Williams	USA	35	9.4		1)	Sheppard AFB, TX	13 Jun

Marks made with assisting wind:

Ken Christensen	USA	33	9.3		1)	Missoula	18 May
Ken Kave	USA	33	9.3		1)	Fort Hood, TX	14 Jun
Willie Williams	USA	31	9.3		1)	Fort Hood, TX	14 Jun

Doubtful timing:

Abdul Khaliq	Pak	33	9.4		1)	Rawalpindi	Mar

100 metres

Leamon King	USA	36	10.2		1)	Oslo	16 Jul
Manfred Germar	FRG	35	10.2		1)	Köln	31 Jul
José Telles da Conceição	Bra	31	10.2		1)	São Paulo	24 Nov
Abdul Khaliq	Pak	33	10.3		1)	Sialkot	18 Feb
Björn Nilsen	Nor	37	10.3		1)	Stavanger	23 May
Dave Sime	USA	36	10.3		1)	Bordeaux	30 Jun
Ira Murchison	USA	33	10.3		1)	Milano	06 Jul
Rafer Johnson	USA	35	10.3		1)	Ljubljana	20 Jul
Ed Collymore	USA	38	10.3		2)	Köln	31 Jul
Hilmar Thorbjörnsson	Ice	34	10.3		1)	Reykjavik	18 Aug
Yuriy Konovalov	SU	29	10.3		1)	Kharkov	07 Sep

200 metres (half-to-full turn)

Manfred Germar	FRG	35	20.4		1)	Köln	31 Jul
Ed Collymore	USA	38	20.6		2	Köln	31 Jul
Bobby Morrow	USA	35	20.9*		1)	Austin	15 Jun
Leonid Bartenyev	SU	33	20.9		1)	Kiev	23 Jun
Mike Agostini	Tri	35	21.0*		1)	Newcastle, NSW	06 Jan
Jerry Beck	USA	35	21.0*		1)	Tulsa	10 May
Ollan Cassell	USA	36	21.0*		1)	Clarksville	11 May
Dave Sime	USA	36	21.0		1)	Bordeaux	29 Jun
Leamon King	USA	36	21.0		1)	Oslo	15 Jul
Carl Kaufmann	FRG	36	21.0		3)	Köln	31 Jul
Trevor Finlay	SA	33	21.0	A	1)	Bloemfontein	16 Nov

Marks made with assisting wind:

Maurice Rae	NZ	35	20.8*		1)	Napier	09 Mar
Björn Nilsen	Nor	37	20.9		1)	Haugesund	07 Sep
Gary Bromhead	Aus	37	20.9*		1)	Sydney	15 Dec

Downhill course:

Gordon Day	SA	36	20.6*w		1)	East London	17 Dec
Trevor Finlay	SA	33	20.7*w		2)	East London	17 Dec

220 yards (straight course)

Mike Agostini	Tri	35	20.4		1)	Fresno	25 Apr
Dave Sime	USA	36	20.4		1)	Raleigh	18 May
Ray Norton	USA	37	20.6		1)	San Jose	04 May
Ken Christensen	USA	33	20.6	A	1)	Salt Lake City	04 May
Leonard Lyles	USA	36	20.6		1)	Charleston	07 May
Bobby Morrow	USA	35	20.6		1)	Compton	31 May

Marks made with assisting wind:

Bobby Morrow	USA	35	20.0		1)	Abilene	26 Mar
Bill Woodhouse	USA	36	20.1		2)	Abilene	26 Mar
Bobby Whilden	USA	35	20.3		2)	Laredo	09 Mar
Ray Norton	USA	37	20.3		1)	San Jose	30 Mar
Preston Griffin	USA	39	20.3		1)	Manhattan Beach, CA	03 May
Willie Williams	USA	31	20.3		1)	Fort Hood, TX	15 Jun
Orlando Hazley	USA	33	20.4		1)	Big Springs, TX	16 Mar
Bobby Poynter	USA	37	20.5		1)	Ventura	29 Mar
Bert Coan	USA	40	20.5		1)	Pasadena	26 Apr
Bobby Staten	USA	38	20.5		2)	Ontario	25 May

4x100 metre relay

Univ. of Texas	USA	(Wilson, Southern, Gainey, Whilden)	39.7*	1)	Lawrence	20 Apr
	SU	(Tokaryev, Plaskeyev, Konovalov, Bartenyev)	40.2	1)	Moskva	01 Aug
	FRG	(Pohl, Hary, Fütterer, Germar)	40.4	1)	Berlin	21 Sep
	Pol	(Baranowski, Foik, Jarzembowski, Staniszewski)	40.7	1)	Budapest	06 Jul
	Fra	(Caprice, Larrieu, Lissenko, Davide)	40.7	2)	Bruxelles	27 Jul

1958

100 yards

Ray Norton	USA	37	9.3	1)	San Jose	12 Apr
Eugene White	USA	37	9.4	1)	Tallahassee	29 Mar
John Moon	USA	38	9.4	1)	Montgomery	19 Apr
Dave Sime	USA	36	9.4	1)	Durham	29 Apr
Dee Givens	USA	37	9.4	1)	Stillwater	03 May
Ira Murchison	USA	33	9.4	1)	Kalamazoo	10 May
Hayes Jones	USA	38	9.4	1)	Normal, IL	24 May
Bobby Morrow	USA	35	9.4	1)	Modesto	31 May
Keith Gardner	Jam	29	9.4	1)	Cardiff	19 Jul

Marks made with assisting wind:

Orlando Hazley	USA	33	9.3	1)	Fayetteville	05 Apr
Bill Woodhouse	USA	36	9.3	1)	Abilene	19 Apr
Bobby Morrow	USA	35	9.3	2)	Abilene	19 Apr
Bruce Land	USA	36	9.3	1)	Abilene	23 Apr

No flash or smoke:

Eddy Southern	USA	38	9.4w	1)	Dallas	03 Apr

Rolling start:

James Bates	USA	40	9.4	1)	Los Angeles	11 Apr

100 metres

Heinz Fütterer	FRG	31	10.2	1)s	Hannover	20 Jul
Armin Hary	FRG	37	10.2	2)s	Hannover	20 Jul
Manfred Germar	FRG	35	10.2	1)	Hannover	20 Jul
Ira Murchison	USA	33	10.2	1)	Moskva	27 Jul
Ed Collymore	USA	38	10.2	2)	Moskva	27 Jul
Mike Agostini	Tri	35	10.2	1)	Köln	29 Aug
Marian Foik	Pol	33	10.3	1)	Warszawa	24 May
Zenon Baranowski	Pol	30	10.3	1)	Szczecin	07 Jun
Jocelyn Delecour	Fra	35	10.3	1)	Warszawa	14 Jun
Keith Gardner	Jam	29	10.3	1)	Tranås	26 Jun
Willie White	USA	38	10.3	1)	Ludwigshafen	01 Jul
Edmund Burg	FRG	35	10.3	2)	Ludwigshafen	01 Jul
Glenn Davis	USA	34	10.3	1)	Oslo	18 Jul
Livio Berruti	Ita	39	10.3	1)	Cuneo	31 Aug
Eduard Feneberg	FRG	30	10.3	1)	München	07 Sep
Peter Radford	UK	39	10.3	1)	Colombes	13 Sep
Björn Nilsen	Nor	37	10.3	1)h	Oslo	20 Sep
Edvin Ozolin	SU	39	10.3	1)s	Tbilisi	29 Oct

Doubtful timing:

Luis Carter	Pan		10.3	1)	Balboa	Jul

200 metres (half-to-full turn)

Ed Collymore	USA	38	20.6*	1)	Berkeley	14 Jun
Mike Agostini	Tri	35	20.6	1)	Köln	29 Aug
Manfred Germar	FRG	35	20.6	1)	Wuppertal	01 Oct
Orlando Hazley	USA	33	20.7*	1)	Stillwater	08 May
Lester Carney	USA	34	20.7*	1)	Berkeley	13 Jun
Maurice Rae	NZ	35	20.8*	1)	Lower Hutt	08 Mar
José Telles da Conceição	Bra	31	20.8	1)	Buenos Aires	04 May
Bobby Morrow	USA	35	20.8*	1)	Los Angeles	13 Jun
Ray Norton	USA	37	20.8*	2)	Berkeley	14 Jun
Willie White	USA	38	20.8	2)	Köln	09 Jul
Vilém Mandlik	Cze	36	20.8	1)	Budapest	07 Sep

Peter Radford	UK	39	20.8	1)	Colombes	14 Sep

Marks made with assising wind:

John Luxon	SA	38	20.6* A	1)	Bloemfontein	03 May
Edward Jefferys	SA	36	20.7* A	2)	Bloemfontein	03 May

220 yards (straight course)

Ed Collymore	USA	38	20.3	1)	Compton	06 Jun
Ira Murchison	USA	33	20.4	1)	Kalamazoo	10 May
Keith Gardner	Jam	29	20.4	1)	Columbia, MO	17 May
Dee Givens	USA	37	20.4	2)	Columbia, MO	17 May
Bobby Morrow	USA	35	20.4	1)	Houston	07 Jun
Ray Norton	USA	37	20.5	1)	San Jose	19 Apr
Eddie Southern	USA	38	20.5	1)	Dallas	10 May
Willie White	USA	38	20.5	2)	Compton	06 Jun

Marks made with assisting wind:

Bill Woodhouse	USA	36	20.0	1)	Abilene	19 Apr
Ira Davis	USA	36	20.0	1)	West Chester, PA	09 May
Ray Norton	USA	37	20.0	1)	Sanger, CA	07 Jun

4x100 metre relay

Abilene Christian College (Griggs, Woodhouse, Segrest, Morrow)	USA	39.5*	1)	Modesto	31 May
FRG (Steinbach, Lauer, Fütterer, Germar)		39.5	1)	Köln	29 Aug
British Empire (Agostini/Tri, Omagbemi/Nig, Robinson/Bah, Gardner/Jam)		40.2*	1)	London	04 Aug
UK (Radford, Sandstrom, Segal, Breacker)		40.2	2)	Stockholm	24 Aug
SU (Bartenyev, Konovalov, Tokaryev, Ozolin)		40.3	2)	Moskva	27 Jul

1959

100 yards

Bill Woodhouse	USA	36	9.3	1)	Abilene	05 May
Ray Norton	USA	37	9.3	1)h	Fresno	09 May
Roscoe Cook	USA	39	9.3	1)	Modesto	30 May
Dave Styron	USA	40	9.4	1)	Ruston	17 Mar
Bobby Morrow	USA	35	9.4	1)	Odessa, TX	21 Mar
Dave Sime	USA	36	9.4	2)	Odessa, TX	21 Mar
Sid Garton	USA	39	9.4	1)	Odessa, TX (Coll.ev)	21 Mar
Mike Agostini	Tri	35	9.4	1)	Wangaratta, Vic	18 Apr
Charley Tidwell	USA	37	9.4	1)	Norman	16 May
Orlando Hazley	USA	33	9.4	2)	Norman	16 May
Peter Radford	UK	39	9.4	1)	Wolverhampton	30 May
Jimmy Omagbemi	Nig	30	9.4	1)	Leverkusen	30 May
Armin Hary	FRG	37	9.4	2)	Leverkusen	30 May
Bob Poynter	USA	37	9.4	4)	Modesto	30 May
Paul Drayton	USA	39	9.4	1)	Philadelphia	13 Jun

Marks made with assisting wind:

Bill Woodhouse	USA	36	9.1	1)	Abilene	18 Apr
Charlie Campbell	USA	36	9.2	1)	Pocatello	22 May
Mike Agostini	Tri	35	9.3	1)	Hamilton, Vic	11 Apr
Sid Garton	USA	39	9.3	1)	Commerce	02 May
Charlie Tidwell	USA	37	9.3	1)	Lincoln	13 Jun

100 metres

Ray Norton	USA	37	10.1	1)	San Jose	18 Apr
Bobby Morrow	USA	35	10.2	1)	Austin	03 Apr
Ira Murchison	USA	33	10.2	2)	Austin	03 Apr
Abdoulaye Seye	Fra	34	10.2	1)	Paris	04 Jul
Bill Woodhouse	USA	36	10.3	3)	Austin	03 Apr
Armin Hary	FRG	37	10.3	1T)	Paris	23 May
Jocelyn Delecour	Fra	35	10.3	1T)	Paris	23 May
Peter Radford	UK	39	10.3	3)	Paris	23 May

Mihail Bachvarov	Bul	35	10.3	1)	Budapest	20 Jun
Mike Agostini	Tri	35	10.3	1)	Caroni	30 May
Wilton Jackson	Tri	35	10.3	2)	Caroni	30 May
Leonid Bartenyev	SU	33	10.3	1)	Budapest	20 Jun
Manfred Germar	FRG	35	10.3	2)	Düsseldorf	03 Jul
Bob Poynter	USA	37	10.3	2)	Philadelphia	18 Jul
Marian Foik	Pol	33	10.3	1)	Hamburg	08 Aug
Peter Gamper	FRG	40	10.3	1)	Dortmund	12 Sep

Marks made with assisting wind:

Abdul Khaliq	Pak	33	10.2	1)	Rawalpindi	Feb
Andrzej Zielinski	Pol	36	10.2	1)	Warszawa	16 May
Martin Lauer	FRG	37	10.2	1)D	Düsseldorf	29 Aug

D = made during a decathlon

Rolling start:

László Kiss	Hun	32	10.3	1)s	Budapest	21 Aug

200 metres (Half-to-full turn)

Ray Norton	USA	37	20.6+	1)	San Jose	02 May
Bill Woodhouse	USA	36	20.6*	1)	Abilene	05 May
Wilton Jackson	Tri	35	20.7*	1)	Penal	22 Mar
Orlando Hazeley	USA	33	20.7*	1)	Norman	19 May
Livio Berruti	Ita	39	20.7	1)	Milano	07 Jun
Milkha Singh	Ind	35	20.8	1)	Poona	31 Jan
Sid Garton	USA	39	20.8*	2)	Abilene	05 May
Vilém Mandlik	Cze	36	20.8	1)	Praha	20 Jun
Abdoulaye Seye	Fra	34	20.8	1)	Beograd	23 Aug
Manfred Germar	FRG	35	20.8	1)	Tobata	18 Oct

Mark made with assisting wind:

Edward Jefferys	SA	36	20.6*	1)	Boksburg	14 Oct

220 yards (straight course)

Ray Norton	USA	37	20.2	1)	San Jose	07 Mar
Bobby Poynter	USA	37	20.5	2)	San Jose	07 Mar
Ralph Fabian	USA	38	20.5	1)	Baton Rouge	14 Mar
Bobby Morrow	USA	35	20.5	1)	Modesto	30 May
Billy Cannon	USA	37	20.6	2)	Baton Rouge	14 Mar
Paul Collins	USA	37	20.6	1)		
Ed Collymore	USA	38	20.6	1)	Villanova	09 May

Marks made with assisting wind:

Bill Woodhouse	USA	36	19.9		1)	Abilene	18 Apr
Bobby Poynter	USA	37	20.3		1)	San Jose	18 Apr
Taylor Jones	USA	39	20.4		1)	Houston	02 May
Basil Ince	Tri	33	20.4		1)	Durham	09 May
Paul Collins	USA	37	20.4	A	1)	Denver	16 May
Eddie Southern	USA	38	20.5		1)	Laredo	07 Mar
Wendell Remple	USA	38	20.5		1)	Wichita	15 Apr
George Peterson	USA	37	20.5		2)	Abilene	18 Apr
Pat Mitchell	USA	42	20.5		1)	Dallas	25 Apr
Bill Kemp	USA	41	20.5		1)	Dallas	25 Apr
Ralph Alspaugh	USA	39	20.5		1)	College Station	09 May
Arnold Tripp	USA	41	20.5		1)	Long Beach	23 May

No flash:

Sid Garton	USA	39	19.6w	1)	Commerce	02 May
Fred Schaefer	USA	39	20.1w	2)	Commerce	02 May
Dave Styron	USA	40	20.2w	3)	Commerce	02 May

4x100 metre relay

U. of Texas	USA	(Wilson, Southern, Gainey, Alspaugh)	39.4*	1)	Modesto	30 May
	FRG	(Gamper, Lauer, Mahlendorf, Germar)	39.8	1)	Köln	19 Sep
	SU	(Ozolin, Bartenyev, Konovalov, Arkhipchuk)	40.0	2)	Philadelphia	18 Jul
	Pol	(Zielinski, Foik, Jarzembowski, E.Schmidt)	40.0	2)	Köln	19 Sep
	Cze	(Janecek, Kynos, Mandlik, Mikluscák)	40.2	1)	Praha	10 Oct

1960

100 yards

Ray Norton	USA	37	9.3		1)	San Jose	02 Apr
Bob Poynter	USA	37	9.4		1)	San Jose	12 Mar
Stone Johnson	USA	40	9.4		1)	Baton Rouge	19 Mar
Charley Tidwell	USA	37	9.4		1)	Abilene	16 Apr
Gene White	USA	37	9.4		1)		30 Apr
Larry Dunn	USA	40	9.4		1)	Tempe	7 May
Ralph Alspaugh	USA	39	9.4		1)	Fort Worth	14 May
Doug Smith	USA	39	9.4		1)	Fresno	14 May
Peter Radford	UK	39	9.4		1)h	Wolverhampton	28 May
Fred McCoy	USA	37	9.4	A	1)	Fort Collins, CO	28 May
Harry Jerome	Can	40	9.4		1)	Modesto	28 May

Marks made with assisting wind:

Bruce Land	USA	36	9.2		1)	Abilene	13 Apr
John Lewis	USA	40	9.3		2)	Abilene	13 Apr
R.L.Lasater	USA	41	9.3		1)	Graham, TX	14 May
Peter Radford	UK	39	9.3		1)	Wolverhampton	28 May
Don Bursill	Aus	40	9.3		1)	Sydney	13 Nov

100 metres

Armin Hary (10.25 E)	FRG	37	10.0		1)	Zurich	21 Jun
Harry Jerome	Can	40	10.0		1)	Saskatoon	15 Jul
Charley Tidwell	USA	37	10.1		1)	Houston	10 Jun
Dave Sime	USA	36	10.1		1)	Walnut	12 Aug
Edward Jefferys	SA	36	10.2	A	1)	Benoni	20 Feb
Bobby Morrow	USA	35	10.2		1)	Lafayette, LA	09 Apr
Dave Styron	USA	40	10.2		2)	Lafayette, LA	09 Apr
Bill Woodhouse	USA	36	10.2		1)	Abilene	16 Apr
JimmyWeaver	USA	36	10.2		2)	Abilene	16 Apr
Dave James	USA	35	10.2		1)	Ankara	22 Apr
Livio Berruti	Ita	39	10.2		1)	Verona	26 May
Manfred Germar	FRG	35	10.2		1)	Malmö	07 Jun
Paul Winder	USA	37	10.2		1)s	Berkeley	18 Jun
Leonid Bartenyev	SU	33	10.2		1)	Kiev	25 Jun
Abdoulaye Seye	Fra	34	10.2		1)	Paris	02 Jul
Enrique Figuerola	Cub	38	10.2		1)	Habana	02 Aug
Stone Johnson	USA	40	10.2		2)	Walnut	12 Aug

Mark made with assisting wind:

Dave Styron	USA	40	10.1		1)	Baton Rouge	07 May

Doubtful timing:

Nikolay Politiko	SU	37	10.2		1)	Cairo	30 Jun
Anatoliy Ryedko	SU	40	10.2		1)h	Uzhgorod	30 Oct

200 metres (half-to-full turn)

Peter Radford	UK	39	20.4*		1)	Wolverhampton	28 May
Abdoulaye Seye	Fra	34	20.4		1)	Köln	16 Sep
Ray Norton	USA	37	20.5*		1)	Berkeley	19 Mar
Armin Hary	FRG	37	20.5		1)	Mannheim	01 Jun
Stone Johnson	USA	40	20.5		1)h1	Palo Alto	02 Jul
Livio Berruti	Ita	39	20.5		1)s2	Roma	03 Sep
Santiago Plaza	Mex	38	20.6	A	1)	México, D.F.	05 Jun
Seraphino Antao	Ken	37	20.6*	A	1)h	Nairobi	01 Jul
Marian Foik	Pol	33	20.6		1)	Lódz	31 Jul
Lester Carney	USA	34	20.6		2)	Roma	03 Sep

Doubtful timing:

John Luxon	SA	38	20.6*	A	1)	Windhoek	23 Apr

Made on a 199.60 m. course:

Charley Tidwell	USA	37	20.2		1)	Abilene	16 Apr
Adolph Plummer	USA	38	20.5		2)	Abilene	16 Apr

220 yards (straight course)

Ray Norton	USA	37	20.1°	1)	San Jose	02 Apr
Edward Jefferys	SA	36	20.2°	1)	Valhalla	30 Mar
Ron Harrison	USA	37	20.3	1)	Tallahassee	07 May
Bob Poynter	USA	37	20.4	2)	San Jose	02 Apr
Bobby Sher	USA	40	20.4	2)	Tallahassee	07 May
Dave Styron	USA	40	20.4	1)	Natchitoches, LA	12 May

Mark made with assisting wind:

Dave Styron	USA	40	20.3°	1)	Baton Rouge	07 May

° = 200 m. time plus 0.1.

"Whistle" start:

David Segal	UK	37	20.3	1)	Coral Gables	30 Mar

4x100 metre relay

FRG	(Cullmann, Hary, Mahlendorf, Lauer) (39.61 E)	39.5	1)h3	Roma	07 Sep
USA	(Budd, Norton, S.Johnson, Sime) (39.87 E)	39.7	1)h4	Roma	07 Sep
British Empire & Commonwealth (Radford/UK, D.Jones/UK, S.Antao/Ken, T.Robinson/Bah)		39.9*	2)	London	14 Sep
Ita	(Sardi, Cazzola, Giannone, Berruti) (40.16 E)	40.0	1)h2	Roma	07 Sep
UK	(Radford, D.Jones, Segal, Whitehead)	40.1	1)	London	01 Aug
Nigeria	(Omagbemi, Amu, Smart, Adebayo) (40.25 E)	40.1	2)h2	Roma	07 Sep
SU	(Kosanov, Bartenyev, Konovalov, Ozolin) (40.24 E)	40.1	2)	Roma	08 Sep

Disqualified for passing baton out of zone:

USA	(Budd, Norton, S.Johnson, Sime) (39.60 E)	39.4	1)	Roma	08 Sep

ALL TIME WORLD LIST OF BEST PERFORMERS AS AT THE END OF 1960

100 yards

Mel Patton	USA	24	9.3	1)	Fresno	15 May 48
Hector Hogan	Aus	31	9.3	1)	Sydney	13 Mar 54
James Golliday	USA	31	9.3	1)	Evanston	14 Mar 55
Leamon King	USA	36	9.3	1)	Fresno	12 May 56
Dave Sime	USA	36	9.3	1)	Raleigh	19 May 56
Bobby Morrow	USA	35	9.3	1)	Austin	14 Jun 57
Ira Murchison	USA	33	9.3	2)	Austin	14 Jun 57
Ray Norton	USA	37	9.3	1)	San Jose	12 Apr 58
Bill Woodhouse	USA	36	9.3	1)	Abilene	05 May 59
Roscoe Cook	USA	39	9.3	1)	Modesto	30 May 59

100 metres

Armin Hary	Ger	37	10.0	1)	Zurich	21 Jun 60
Harry Jerome	Can	40	10.0	1)	Saskatoon	15 Jul 60
Willie Williams	USA	31	10.1	1)h2	Berlin	03 Aug 56
Ira Murchison	USA	33	10.1	1)s2	Berlin	04 Aug 56
Leamon King	USA	36	10.1	1)	Ontario, CA	20 Oct 56
Ray Norton	USA	37	10.1	1)	San Jose	18 Apr 59
Charley Tidwell	USA	37	10.1	1)	Houston	10 Jun 60
Dave Sime	USA	36	10.1	1)	Walnut	12 Aug 60

200 metres (half-to-full turn)

Manfred Germar	FRG	35	20.4	1)	Köln	31 Jul 57
Peter Radford	UK	39	20.4*	1)	Wolverhampton	28 May 60
Abdoulaye Seye	Fra	34	20.4	1)	Köln	16 Sep 60
James Charlton	Aus	09	20.5*	1)	Sydney	16 Jan 32
Andrew Stanfield	USA	27	20.5*	1)	Philadelphia	26 May 51

Ray Norton	USA	37	20.5*	1)	Berkeley	19 Mar 60
Harmin Hary	FRG	37	20.5	1)	Mannheim	01 Jun 60
Stone Johnson	USA	40	20.5	1)	Palo Alto	02 Jul 60
Livio Berruti	Ita	39	20.5	1)s2	Roma	03 Sep 60

220 yards (Straight course)

Dave Sime	USA	36	20.0	1)	Sanger	09 Jun 56
Mike Agostini	Tri	35	20.1	1)	Bakersfield	17 Mar 56
Ray Norton	USA	37	20.1	1)	San Jose	02 Apr 60
Mel Patton	USA	24	20.2	1)	Los Angeles	07 May 49
Edward Jefferys	SA	36	20.2	1)	Valhalla	30 Mar 60
Jesse Owens	USA	13	20.3	1)	Ann Arbor	25 May 35
Lloyd La Beach	Pan	23	20.3	1)	Compton	04 Jun 48
Ed Collymore	USA	38	20.3	1)	Compton	06 Jun 58
Ron Harrison	USA	37	20.3	1)	Tallahassee	07 May 60

4x100 metre relay (E=electric time)

Univ. of Texas	USA	(Wilson, Southern, Gainey, Alspaugh)	39.4*	1)	Modesto	30 May 59
	USA	(Murchison, King, Baker, Morrow) (39.60 E)	39.5	1)	Melbourne	01 Dec 56
	FRG	(Cullmann, Hary, Mahlendorf, Lauer) (39.61 E)	39.5	1)h3	Roma	07 Sep 60
	SU	(Tokaryev, Sukharyev, Konovalov, Bartenyev) (39.93 E)	39.8	2)	Melbourne	01 Dec 56
	Pol	(Zielinski, Foik, Jarzembowski, E.Schmidt)	40.0	2)	Köln	19 Sep 59
	Ita	(Sardi, Cazzola, Giannone, Berruti) (40.16 E)	40.0	1)h2	Roma	07 Sep 60
	UK	(Radford, D.Jones, Segal, Whitehead)	40.1	1)	London	01 Aug 60
	Nig	(Omagbemi, Amu, Smart, Adebayo) (40.25 E)	40.1	2)h2	Roma	07 Sep 60
	Cze	(Janecek, Kynos, Mandlík,Mikluscák)	40.2	1)	Praha	10 Oct 59
	Fra	(Delecour, David, Genevay, Seye)	40.3	1)	Colombes	26 Sep 59
	Ven	(Bonas, Murad, N.Romero, R.Romero) (40.49 E)	40.3	2)s1	Roma	08 Sep 50

1961

100 yards

Frank Budd	USA	39	9.2	1)	New York	24 Jun
Dennis Johnson	Jam	39	9.3	1)	San Jose	11 Mar
Harry Jerome	Can	40	9.3	1)	Corvallis	20 May
Bob Hayes	USA	42	9.3	1)h	Sioux Falls, SD	02 Jun
Paul Drayton	USA	39	9.3	2)	New York	24 Jun
David James	USA	35	9.3	3)	New York	24 Jun

Marks made with assisting wind:

Stone Johnson	USA	40	9.2	1)h	Houston	25 Mar
Ralph Alspaugh	USA	39	9.2	1)	Houston	13 May

Rolling start:

John Lewis	USA	40	9.2w	1)	Denton	15 Apr
Dennis Johnson	Jam	39	9.2w	1)	Walnut	29 Apr

100 metres

Rafael Romero	Ven	38	10.2	1)	Caracas	23 Mar
Vilem Mandlík	Cze	36	10.2	1)	Praha	23 Jun
Marian Foik	Pol	33	10.2	1)	Szczecin	15 Jul
Frank Budd	USA	39	10.2	1)	Göteborg	03 Aug
Arquimedes Herrera	Ven		10.3	2)	Caracas	23 Mar
Livio Berruti	Ita	39	10.3	1)	Padova	20 Apr
Jocelyn Delecour	Fra	35	10.3	1)	Hannover	30 Apr
David Jones	UK	40	10.3	2)	Hannover	30 Apr
Seraphino Antao	Ken	37	10.3	1)	Tel-Aviv	02 May
Nikolay Politiko	SU	37	10.3	1)	Leselidze	10 May
Peter Gamper	FRG	40	10.3	1)	Kornwestheim	30 May
Viktor Usatiy	SU	37	10.3	1)	Dnyepropetrovsk	05 Jul
Anatoliy Ryedko	SU	40	10.3	2)	Dnyepropetrovsk	05 Jul
Harry Jerome	Can	40	10.3	1)	Köln	12 Jul

Vyacheslav Voityenko	SU	41	10.3		1)s	Kiev	15 Jul
Enrique Figuerola	Cub	38	10.3		1)	Potsdam	19 Jul
Claude Piquemal	Fra	39	10.3		2)	Colombes	22 Jul
Eduard Lomtazde	SU	36	10.3		1)h	Tbilisi	20 Sep
Yuriy Konovalov	SU	29	10.3		1)	Nalchik	24 Sep
Amin Tuyakov	SU	37	10.3		1)h	Warszawa	14 Oct
Chen Chia-Chuan	Chi	38	10.3		1)s	Peking	15 Oct

Marks made with assisting wind:

Marian Foik	Pol	33	10.1		1)	Palermo	07 Oct
Bouchaib Embark	Mor	43	10.2		1)	Casablanca	26 Aug

200 metres (half-to-full turn)

Livio Berruti	Ita	39	20.5		1)	Milano	18 Jun
Edward Jefferys	SA	36	20.7*	A	1)	Benoni	04 Feb
Abdul Amu	Nig	33	20.7		1)	Yaba	15 Apr
Frank Budd	USA	39	20.7*		1)	Philadelphia	17 Jun
Marian Foik	Pol	33	20.7		1)	Warszawa	18 Jun
Manfred Germar	FRG	35	20.7		1)	Stuttgart	19 Jul
Seraphino Antao	Ken	37	20.7*	A	1)	Nakuru	09 Sep
Gary Holdsworth	Aus	41	20.8*		1)	Brisbane	05 Mar
Peter Vassella	Aus	41	20.8*		2)	Brisbane	05 Mar
Dennis Johnson	Jam	39	20.8*		1)	Palo Alto	01 Apr
Rafael Romero	Ven	38	20.8		1)	Caracas	04 May
Horacio Esteves	Ven	41	20.8		2)	Caracas	04 May
Otis Davis	USA	32	20.8*		1)	Eugene	18 May
Paul Drayton	USA	39	20.8*		1)s	Philadelphia	16 Jun
Armando Sardi	Ita	40	20.8		1)	Saarbrücken	10 Jul
Jocelyn Delecour	Fra	35	20.8		1)	Colombes	23 Jul
Peter Laeng	Swz	42	20.8		1)	Basel	03 Sep
Ove Jonsson	Swe	40	20.8		1)	Budapest	01 Oct

Mark made with assisting wind:

David Jones	UK	40	20.7*	1)	London	20 May

No flash:

Frank Budd	USA	39	20.4*w	1)	Dartmouth, NH	20 May

220 yards (straight course)

Bob Hayes	USA	42	20.1	1)	Atlanta	13 May
Frank Budd	USA	39	20.2	1)	Villanova	06 May
Dave Styron	USA	40	20.2	1)	Logan	13 May
Forrest Beaty	USA	44	20.2	1)	Ontario, CA	27 May
Ed Collymore	USA	38	20.3	1)	University Park, PA	20 May
Overton Williams	USA	40	20.4	1)	Sacramento	20 May
Paul Drayton	USA	39	20.4	2)	Villanova	11 Jun
Wally Johnson	USA	42	20.5	1)	Dickinson, ND	06 May
Ralph Turner	USA	42	20.5	2)	Ontario, CA	27 May

Marks made with assisting wind:

Ralph Alspaugh	USA	39	20.0	1)	Houston	13 May
Herny Carr	USA	42	20.0	1)	Detroit	18 May
Bill Kemp	USA	41	20.2	2)	Houston	13 May
Earl Young	USA	41	20.3	1)	Laredo	11 Mar
Roy Smalley	USA	40	20.3	3)	Houston	13 May
Alvin Washington	USA	43	20.3	1)	New Hartford, NY	10 Jun

4x100 metre relay

USA	(H.Jones, Budd, Frazier, Drayton)	39.1	1)	Moskva	15 Jul
SU	(Ozolin, Politiko, Konovalov, Bartenyev)	39.4	2)	Moskva	15 Jul
Fra	(Genevay, Lagorce, Piquemal, Delecour)	39.9	1)	Thonon-les-Bains	15 Aug
FRG	(Hebauf, Ulonska, Breker, Germar)	40.1	1)	Dortmund	02 Sep
UK	(Carter, Hildrey, D.Jones, Meakin)	40.1	2)	Dortmund	02 Sep

1962

100 yards

Bob Hayes	USA	42	9.2		1)	Coral Gables	17 Feb
Hrry Jerome	Can	40	9.2		1)	Vancouver	25 Aug
Stone Johnson	USA	40	9.3		1)h	Houston	11 May
Frank Budd	USA	39	9.3		1)	Villanova	12 May
Joe Thornton	USA	39	9.3		1)	Petersburg, VA	19 May
Seraphino Antao	Ken	37	9.3	A	1)	Nairobi	22 Sep

Marks made with assisting wind:

R.L.Lasater	USA	41	9.2		1)	Commerce	31 Mar
Seraphino Antao	Ken	37	9.2		1)	Dublin	18 Jun

100 metres

Bob Hayes	USA	42	10.1	1)	Hässleholm	17 Aug
Andrzej Zielinski	Pol	36	10.2	1)	Praha	02 Jun
Dave James	USA	35	10.2	1)	Zurich	10 Jul
Rogern Sayers	USA	42	10.2	2)	Palo Alto	21 Jul
Marian Foik	Pol	33	10.2	1)	Olsztyn	11 Aug
Peter Gamper	FRG	40	10.2	1)	Praha	11 Aug
Paul Drayton	USA	39	10.2	2)	Hässleholm	17 Aug
Anatoliy Ryedko	SU	40	10.2	1)s	Alma-Ata	22 Sep
Gusman Kosanov	SU	35	10.2	2)s	Alma-Ata	22 Sep
Edvin Ozolin	SU	39	10.2	1)	Tashkent	14 Oct

Marks made with assisting wind:

Heinz Schumann	FRG	36	10.1	1)s	Bremen	26 Aug
Marian Foik	Pol	33	10.1	1)	Lodz	01 Sep

Downhill course:

Heinz Erbstösser	FRG	40	10.2	1)	Unterschönau	14 Oct

200 metres (full turn)

Paul Drayton	USA	39	20.4*	1)	Walnut	23 Jun
Steve Haas	USA	41	20.6*	1)	Los Angeles	14 Apr
Homer Jones	USA	41	20.6*	1)	Houston	12 May
Harry Jerome	Can	40	20.6*	1)h	Eugene	15 Jun
Stone Johnson	USA	40	20.7*	2)	Houston	12 May
Andrzej Zierlinski	Pol	36	20.7	1)	Warszawa	10 Jun
Nate Adams	USA	41	20.7*	2)s	Eugene	15 Jun
Bob Hayes	USA	42	20.7*	2)h	Walnut	23 Jun
Roger Sayers	USA	42	20.7*	2)	Walnut	23 Jun
Ove Jonsson	Swe	40	20.7	1)	Zurich	10 Jul
Sergio Ottolina	Ita	42	20.7	2)	Zurich	10 Jul
Dave James	USA	35	20.7	1)	Lausanne	21 Jul
Marian Foik	Pol	33	20.7	1)	Torun	29 Jul
Peter Laing	Swz	42	20.7	2)	Zurich	04 Aug

Marks made with assisting wind:

Seraphino Antao	Ken	37	20.0*	A	1)	Nairobi	22 Sep
Ray Knaub	USA	40	20.4*		1)	Lincoln	12 May
John Lewis	USA	40	20.6*		1)	Abilene	28 Apr

220 yards (straight course)

Frank Budd	USA	39	20.0	1)	Villanova	12 May
Henry Carr	USA	42	20.1	1)	Tempe	05 May
Paul Drayton	USA	39	20.1	2)	Villanova	12 May
Adolph Plummer	USA	38	20.3	1)	Tempe	18 Apr
John Moon	USA	38	20.3	1)	Ft.Campbell, KY	05 May
John Lewis	USA	40	20.3	1)	Stephenville, TX	11 May
Dave Morris	USA	42	20.3	1)	Modesto	26 May
Ira Murchison	USA	33	20.3	1)	Chicago	24 Jun

Marks made with assisting wind:

Adolph Plummer	USA	38	20.0		1)	Abilene	14 Apr
Anthony Watson	USA	41	20.0		1)h	Lawrence	18 May
Odell Barry	USA	41	20.0		1)h	Findlay, OH	19 May
Dennis Richardson	USA	40	20.2		2)	Abilene	14 Apr

4x100 metre relay

FRG	(Ulonska, Gamper, Bender, Germar)	39.5	1)	Beograd	16 Sep
Pol	(Syka, Juskowiak, Foik, Zielinski)	39.5	2)	Beograd	16 Sep
USA	(Hayes Jones, Hayes, Homer Jones, Daryton)	39,6	1)	Palo Alto	21 Jul
UK	(David Jones, Berwyn Jones, Ronald Jones, Meakin)	39.8	1)h2	Beograd	14 Sep
France	(Lambrot, Genevay, Piquemal, Delecour)	39.9	1)	Colombes	29 Sep

1963

100 yards

Bob Hayes	USA	42	9.1		1)s1	St.Louis	21 Jun
Dennis Richardson	USA	40	9.3		1)	Abilene	27 Mar
Gary Ray	USA		9.3		1)	Birmingham, AL	18 May
Henry Carr	USA	42	9.3		1)	Tempe	25 May
Paul Drayton	USA	39	9.3		1)s2	St.Louis	21 Jun

Marks made with assisting wind:

Odell Barry	USA	41	9.2		1)	Hillsdale, MI	02 May
John House	USA	44	9.2		1)	Van Nuys, CA	11 May
John Gilbert	USA	42	9.2		2)	St.Louis	21 Jun

Professional:

Ken Irvine	Aus		9.3		1)	Dubbo, NSW	09 Mar

100 metres

Arquimedes Herrera	Ven	35	10.2		1)h	São Paulo	27 Apr
Andrzej Zielinski	Pol	36	10.2		1)	Warszawa	01 Jun
Bob Hayes	USA	42	10.2		1)	Moskva	20 Jul

Marks made with assisting wind:

Bob Hayes	USA	42	9.9		1)	Walnut	27 Apr
Henry Carr	USA	42	10.0		2)	Walnut	27 Apr
John Gilbert	USA	42	10.0		3)	Walnut	27 Apr
Arquimedes Herrera	Ven	35	10.0	A	1)s2	Cali	29 Jun
Peter Wagner	GDR	40	10.1		1)	Leipzig	16 May
Joe Satow	Bra	39	10.1	A	1)h4	Cali	29 Jun
Enrique Figuerola	Cub	38	10.1		1)h	Praha	26 Jul

Doubtful timing:

John Moon	USA	38	10.0		1)	San Antonio	15 Jun

200 metres (full turn)

Henry Carr	USA	42	20.2*		1)	Tempe	23 Mar
Bob Hayes	USA	42	20.4*		1)	Coral Gables	24 May
Adolph Plummer	USA	38	20.5*		1)	Compton	07 Jun
Larry Questad	USA	43	20.5*	A	2)	Albuquerque	15 Jun
Dick Cortese	USA	42	20.7*		2)	Tempe	23 Mar
Tom Hester	USA	44	20.7*		3)	Tempe	23 Mar
Bouchaib El Maach	Mor	43	20.7*	A	1)	Denver	24 Apr
Dick Burns	USA	42	20.7*	A	1)	Boulder	04 May
Bill Harvey	USA	42	20.7*		1)	Pocatello	04 May
Nate Adams	USA	41	20.7*		1)	Minneapolis	18 May
Jim Wood	USA		20.7*		1)		
Paul Drayton	USA	39	20.7*		1)h4	St.Louis	22 Jun
Don Webster	USA	44	20.7*		2)s2	St.Louis	22 Jun
Dwight Middleton	USA	43	20.7*		3)s2	St.Louis	22 Jun
Seraphino Antao	Ken	37	20.7*	A	1)	Nairobi	23 Jun
Jocelyn Delecour	Fra	35	20.7		1)	Zurich	02 Jul
Alfred Hebauf	FRG	40	20.7		1)	Augsburg	11 Aug

Marks made with assisting wind:

Paul Drayton	USA	39	20.3*		1T)	St. Louis	22 Jun
John Moon	USA	38	20.5*		3)	St. Louis	22 Jun
Don Webster	USA	44	20.5*		4)	St. Louis	22 Jun
Bob Moreland	USA		20.6*		1)h	Minneapolis	17 May
Andrzej Zielinski	Pol	36	20.6		1)	Bydgoszcs	16 Jun
Earl Young	USA	41	20.6*		6)	St. Louis	22 Jun

220 yards (straight course)

Bill Harvey	USA	42	20.2	A	1)	Logan	18 May
Jerry Williams	USA	45	20.5		1)	Richmond, CA	03 May
Edwin Roberts	Tri	42	20.5		1)	Raleigh	18 May
Buren Simmons	USA	38	20.5		1)h	Long Beach	18 May
Bill Thornton	USA	44	20.6		1)	Grand Junction	13 Apr
Aggrey Awori	Uga	39	20.6		1)	Providence	04 May
Gary Ray	USA	41	20.6		1)	Auburn	04 May
John Moon	USA	38	20.6		1)	Williams, MA	25 May

Marks made with assisting wind:

Tim Russell	USA	43	19.9		1)	Long Beach	15 Mar
Gerald Arline	USA		20.1		1)	Fort Lauderdale	27 Apr
John Moon	USA	38	20.1°		1)	San Antonio	15 Jun
Billy Foster	USA	43	20.2		1)	Fayetteville	11 May
Bernie Rivers	USA	44	20.2		1)	Gary	18 May
Bob Poynter	USA	37	20.3°		2)	San Antonio	15 Jun
Dick Cortese	USA	42	20.4		1)	Long Beach	16 Mar
Jim Love	USA		20.4		1)	Commerce	28 Mar
Bill Cowings	USA	42	20.4		)		
Jerry Williams	USA	45	20.4		1)	Richmond	03 May
Jim Childs	USA		20.4	A	1)	Albuquerque	11 May
John House	USA		20.4		1)	Van Nuys, CA	11 May

° = 200 m. time plus 0.1

Doubtful timing:

Bill Del Vecchio	USA		20.2		1)		13 Jul

4x100 metre relay

USA	(Gilbert, Moon, Drayton, Hayes)	39.6	1)	Warszawa	26 Jul
Fra	(Lambrot, Genevay, Piquemal, Delecour)	39.6	1)	Chambery	15 Sep
FRG	(Khnickenberg, Hebauf, Enderlein, Schumann)	39.6	1)	Kornwestheim	21 Sep
UK	(Radford, Meakin, D.Jones, B.Jones)	39.7	1)	London	23 Aug
Pol	(Juskowiak, Foik, Syka, Dudziak)	39.9	1)	Moskva	14 Sep
Hun	(Csutorás, Gyulai, Mihályfi, Rabai)	39.9	2)	Budapest	02 Oct

1964

100 yards

Bob Hayes	USA	42	9. 1		1)	Coral Gables	01 Jan
Edwin Roberts	Tri	41	9.2		2)	Orangeburg, SC	18 Apr
Darel Newman	USA	43	9.2		1)h	Fresno	09 May
Anthony Watson	USA	41	9.3		1)	Norman	11 Apr
Harry Jerome	Can	40	9.3		1)	Eugene	11 Apr
Richard Stebbins	USA	45	9.3		1)	Houston	09 May
John Roderick	USA	44	9.3		1)	Lubbock	09 May
Travis Williams	USA	46	9.3		1)h	Fresno	09 May
Dave Morris	USA	42	9.3		2)h	Fresno	09 May
Mel Pender	USA	37	9.3		1)	Ft. Campbell	19 May
Henry Carr	USA	42	9.3	A	1)	Salt Lake City	23 May

Mark made with assisting wind:

Bernie Rivers	USA	44	9.2	A	1)	Albuquerque	21 Mar

Doubtful timing:

C. F. Crocker	NZ		9.2w		1)	Waipu	01 Jan

Downhill course:

Bernie Rivers	USA 44		9.3		1)	San Diego	13 Jun

100 metres (E = electric time)

Horacio Esteves	Ven	41	10.0		1)	Caracas	15 Aug
Bob Hayes (10.06 E)	USA	42	10.0		1)	Tokyo	15 Oct
Hideo Iijima	Jap	44	10.1		1)	Berlin	14 Jun
Trenton Jackson	USA	42	10.1		1)s1	Eugene	19 Jun
Harry Jerome	Can	40	10.1		1)s2	Eugene	19 Jun
Enrique Figuerola	Cub	38	10.1		1)	Tartu	21 Jun
Arquimedes Herrera	Ven	35	10.1		1)	Caracas	02 Aug

Marks made with assisting wind:

R. L. Lasater	USA	41	9.9		1)	Commerce	17 Apr
Bob Hayes (9.91 E)	USA	42	9.9		1)s1	Tokyo	15 Oct

Rolling start:

Edwin Roberts	Tri	41	10.1		2)	Eugene	20 Jun

200 metres (full turn)

Henry Carr	USA	42	20.1*		1)	Tempe	04 Apr
Edwin Roberts	Tri	41	20.3*		1)	Toronto	07 Sep
Paul Drayton	USA	39	20.4		1)	Quantico	06 Jun
Bob Hayes	USA	42	20.4*		1)	Fresno	13 Jun
Sergio Ottolina	Ita	42	20.4		1)	Saarbrücken	21 Jun
Seraphino Antao	Ken	37	20.4*	A	1)	Kisumu	05 Sep
Richard Stebbins	USA	45	20.5*		1)	Grambling	18 Apr
Bernie Rivers	USA	44	20.5*		1)	Sunnyvale	18 Apr
Arquimedes Herrera	Ven	35	20.5		1)	Caracas	02 Aug
T. J. Bell	USA	42	20.6	A	1)	México, D.F.	02 May

Marks made with assisting wind:

Bob Hayes	USA	42	20.3		1)s1	Eugene	19 Jun
Harry Jerome	Can	40	20.4		2)s2	Eugene	19 Jun

220 yards (straight course)

Edwin Roberts	Tri	41	20.1		1)	Raleigh	16 May

Mark made with assisting wind:

Bob Hayes	USA	42	20.1		1)	Coral Gables	01 Jan

4x100 metre relay

USA	(Drayton, Ashworth,Stebbins, Hayes) (39.06 E)	39.0	1)	Tokyo	21 Oct
Fra	(Genevay, Laidebeur, Brugier, Delecour)	39.2	1)	Annecy	18 Jul
Ita	(Berruti, Preatoni; Ottolina, Giannattasio)	39.3	2)	Annecy	18 Jul
Pol	(Zielinski, Maniak, Foik, Dudziak) (39.36 E)	39.3	2)	Tokyo	21 Oct
GDR	(Erbstösser, Berger, Wallach, Löffler)	39.4	1)	Berlin	23 Aug
Jam	(McNeil, P.Robinson, Headley, D.Johnson) (39.49 E)	39.4	4)	Tokyo	21 Oct
SU	(Ozolin, Zubov, Kosanov, Savchuk) (39.50 E)	39.4	5)	Tokyo	21 Oct

1965

100 yards

Bob Lay	Aus	44	9.2		1)	Sydney	10 Mat
Richard Stebbins	USA	45	9.2		1)	Baton Rouge	10 Apr
George Anderson	USA	42	9.3		1)	PrairieView	03 Apr
George Eriquezzo	USA		9.3		1)	Little Rock	15 Apr
Craig Wallace	USA	46	9.3		1)	Lexington	01 May
Darel Newman	USA	43	9.3		1)	Fresno	01 May
Fred Kuller	USA	45	9.3		1)	Fresno	08 May
Larry Questad	USA	43	9.3		1)	Fresno	08 May
Harry Jerome	Can	40	9.3		1)	Toronto	10 Jun
Mel Pender	USA	37	9.3		2)	Toronto	10 Jun
Jim Freeman	USA	44	9.3		1)	Elizabeth, NJ	20 Aug

Mark made with assisting wind:

Terry Williams	USA	44	9.2		1)	Hobbs, NM	01 May

100 metres

Chen Cia-Chuan	Chi	38	10.0	1)	Chungking	24 Oct
Jean-Louis Ravelomanantsoa	Mad	43	10.1	!9	Tananarive	03 Apr
Darel Newman	USA	43	10.1	1)	Kiev	31 Jul
Wieslaw Maniak	Pol	38	10.1	1)	Szczecin	13 Aug
Thomas Randolph	USA	42	10.1	1)	Caracas	13 Nov
Enrique Figuerola	Cub	38	10.1	1)	Habana	11 Dec

200 metres (full turn)

Edwin Roberts	Tri	41	20.4*	1)	Sioux Falls	05 Jun
Tommie Smith	USA	44	20.5*	1)	San Jose	27 Feb
Clyde Duncan	USA	45	20.5 A	1)	México, D.F.	17 Apr
Clyde Glosson	USA		20.5*	1)	Prairie View	01 May
Richard Stebbins	USA	45	20.5*	1)	Houston	08 May
Claude Piquemal	Fra	39	20.5	1)	Paris	11 Jun
Adolph Plummer	USA	38	20.5*	1)	San Diego	27 Jun
Paul Drayton	USA	39	20.5	1)	Caracas	13 Nov
Thomas Randolph	USA	42	20.5	2)	Caracas	13 Nov
Enrique Figuerola	Cub	38	20.5	1)	Habana	12 Dec

Mark made with assisting wind:

Clyde Glosson	USA		20.3*	1)		

Doubtful timing:

Norman Tate	USA		20.3*	1)	Orangeburg	17 Apr
Charles Copeland	USA		20.5*	2)	Orangeburg	17 Apr

220 yards (straight course)

Tommie Smith	USA	44	20.1*	1)	San Jose	13 Mar
Tony Jones	USA		20.4	1)	Bemidji, MN	07 May
Burgette	USA		20.4	1)	Kansas City	15 Aug

Mark made with assisting wind:

Eli Myers	USA		20.0	1)	Gary	01 May

4x100 metre relay

	Pol	(Zielinski, Maniak, Romanowski, Dudziak)	39.2	1)	Warszawa	07 Aug
	SU	(Ozolin, Tuyakov, Savchuk, Politiko)	39.2	1)	Colombes	02 Oct
	Fra	(Lambrot, Bambuck, Piquemal, Delacour)	39.3	2)	Colombes	02 Oct
Stanford Univ.	USA	(Frische, Rubin, McIntyre, Questad)	39.5*	1)	Fresno	08 May
	USA	(Owens, Hines, Plummer, Anderson)	39.5	2)	Warszawa	07 Aug
	FRG	(Wilke, Metz, Enderlei, Obersiebrasse)	39.5	3)	Stuttgart	11 Sep

Disqualified for running out of lane:

	Ita	(Giani, Berruti, Ottolina, Giannattasio)	39.5	-)	Zurich	29 Jun

1966

100 yards

Harry Jerome	Can	40	9.1	1)	Edmonton	15 Jul
George Anderson	USA	42	9.3	1)	Coral Gables	08 Jan
Gary Holdsworth	Aus	41	9.3	1)	Melbourne	06 Mar
Lennox Miller	Jam	46	9.3	1)	Los Angeles	19 Mar
Edwin Roberts	Tri	41	9.3	1)	Quantico	07 May
Charlie Greene	USA	44	9.3	1)	Columbia	14 May
Tommie Smith	USA	44	9.3+	1)	San Jose	21 May
Paul Nash	SA	47	9.3+	1)	Mainz	27 Jul
Jim Hines	USA	46	9.3	1)	Houston	16 Dec

Marks made with assisting wind:

Reginald Robinson	USA	49	9.1	1)	Prairie View	30 Apr
Clyde Glosson	USA	47	9.2	1)	Fort Worth	5 Mar
Tommie Smith	USA	44	9.2	1)	Berkeley	6 Apr

\+ = made during 100 m. race

Rolling start:

Rene Matison	USA	46	9.1 A	1)	Albuquerque	04 Jun

No flash:

George Anderson	USA	42	9.2	1)	Beaumont, TX	21 May

100 metres

Tommie Smith	USA	44	10.1	1)	San Jose	21 May
Hideo Iijima	Jap	44	10.1	1)	Berlin	26 Jun
Bill Gaines	USA	48	10.2	1)	Caroni	12 Mar
Edwin Roberts	Tri	41	10.2	2)	Caroni	12 Mar
Hermes Ramirez	Cub	48	10.2	1)	Habana	16 Apr
Enrique Figuerola	Cub	38	10.2	2)	Habana	16 Apr
Harald Eggers	GDR	42	10.2	1)	Leipzig	15 May
Detlef Lewandowski	GDR	44	10.2	2)	Leipzig	15 May
Manuel Planchart	Ven		10.2	1)	Caracas	19 May
Roger Bambuck	Fra	45	10.2	1)	Paris	08 Jun
Aleksandr Lebedyev	SU	46	10.2	2)	Odessa	02 Jul
Hans-Jürgen Felsen	FRG	40	10.2	1)	Metzingen	08 Jul
Gaoussou Kone	IC	43	10.2	1)	Manresa	14 Jul
Paul Nash	SA	47	10.2	1)	Kassel	21 Jul
Charlie Greene	USA	44	10.2	1)	Köln	07 Sep
Bernd Darams	FRG	40	10.2	1)	Innsbruck	13 Sep
Wieslaw Maniak	Pol	38	10.2	1)	Warszawa	17 Sep
Manfred Knickenberg	FRG	37	10.2	1)	Lübeck	24 Sep

Marks made with assisting wind:

Roger Bambuck	Fra	45	10.0	1)	Berlin	09 Jul
Edwin Roberts	Tri	41	10.1	1)	Port-of-Spain	09 Apr
Enrique Figuerola	Cub	38	10.1	1)s	San Juan	16 Jun
Claude Piquemal	Fra	39	10.1	1)	Kiev	17 Sep

Doubtful timing:

Wayne Hermen	USA		10.2	2)	San Jose	21 May

200 metres (full turn)

Tommie Smith	USA	44	19.9*	1)	Sacramento	11 Jun
Harry Jerome	Can	40	20.3*	1)	Edmonton	16 Jul
Richard Stebbins	USA	45	20.4*	1)	Coral Gables	08 Jan
Bernie Rivers	USA	44	20.4*	1)	San Diego	19 Mar
Jim Hines	USA	46	20.4*	1)	Houston	08 May
Norm Jackson	USA		20.5*	1)	Los Angeles	02 Apr
Lennox Miller	Jam	46	20.5*	1)	Los Angeles	07 May
Edwin Roberts	Tri	41	20.5*	1)h	Sioux Falls	04 Jun
Harold Busby	USA	47	20.5*	1)	San Diego	11 Jun
Stanley Allotey	Gha	42	20.5*	1)s	Kingston	08 Aug

Mark made with assisting wind:

Adolph Plummer	USA	38	20.4*	2)	New York	26 Jun

220 yards (straight course)

Tommie Smith	USA	44	19.5	1)	San Jose	07 May

4x100 metre relay

USA	(Anderson, Busby, T.Jones, Hines)	39.1	1)	Berkeley	16 Jul
Fra	(Berger, Delecour, Piquemal, Bambuck)	39.2	1)	Kiev	17 Sep
Poland	(Anielak, Werner, Romanowski, Maniak)	39.6	1)	Minsk	25 Jul
Ghana	(E.Addy, Mends, J.Addy, Allotey)	39.6*	1)	Kingston	13 Aug
SU	(Ozolin, Tuyakov, Savchuk, Politiko)	39.7	1)	London	17 Jun
FRG	(Roderfeld, Metz, Enderlein, Knickenberg)	39.7	1)	Wiesbaden	13 Aug
GDR	(Erbstösser, Berger, Burde, Eggers)	39.7	1)	Dresden	24 Sep

1967

100 yards

Name	Nat	Born	Time		Place	Venue	Date
Jim Hines	USA	46	9.1		1)	Houston	13 May
Charlie Greene	USA	44	9.1	A	1)h4	Provo	15 Jun
Paul Nash	SA	47	9.2		1)	Cape Town	25 Mar
Lennox Miller	Jam	46	9.2	A	1)h3	Provo	15 Jun
Arnaldo Bristol	PR		9.3		1)	Grambling	15 Apr
Clarence Ray	USA	45	9.3		1)	Athens, OH	15 Apr
Jacob Henry	USA		9.3		1)	Alpine, TX	04 May
Tommie Smith	USA	44	9.3	A	1)	Provo	06 May
William Miller	USA		9.3		2)	Houston	13 May
Kirk Clayton	USA	47	9.3		3)	Houston	13 May
Bill Gaines	USA	48	9.3		1)	Almonesson, NJ	20 May
Julius Sang	Ken	44	9.3	A	1)	Nairobi	23 Sep

Marks made with assisting wind:

Name	Nat	Born	Time		Place	Venue	Date
Gary Holdsworth	Aus	41	9.1+		1)	Geelong	19 Mar
John Carlos	USA	45	9.2		1)	Commerce	11 Mar
Larry Highbaugh	USA	49	9.2		1)	Mansfield, OH	15 Apr
Bob Rovere	USA	45	9.2	A	1)	Ogden	10 Jun

+ = made during 100 m. race

100 metres

Name	Nat	Born	Time		Place	Venue	Date
Jim Hines	USA	46	10.0		1)	Modesto	27 May
Willie Turner	USA	48	10.0		2)	Modesto	27 May
Enrique Figuerola	Cub	30	10.0		1)	Budapest	17 Jun
Gary Holdsworth	Aus	41	10.1		1)	Geelong	09 Apr
Paul Nash	SA	47	10.1	A	1)	Potchefstroom	22 Apr
Charlie Greene	USA	44	10.1		3)	Modesto	27 May
Harry Jerome	Can	40	10.1		4)	Modesto	27 May
Jerry Bright	USA	47	10.1		5)	Modesto	27 May
Lennox Miller	Jam	46	10.1		1)	Los Angeles	08 Jul
Jean-Louis Ravelomanantsoa	Mad	43	10.1	A	1)	Addis Ababa	17 Dec

Marks made with assisting wind:

Name	Nat	Born	Time		Place	Venue	Date
Gary Holdsworth	Aus	41	10.0		1)	Geelong	19 Mar
Wieslaw Maniak	Pol	38	10.0		1)	Poznan	24 Jun
Ivan Moreno	Chl	42	10.0		1)	Santiago de Chile	02 Sep

200 metres (full turn)

Name	Nat	Born	Time		Place	Venue	Date
Tommie Smith	USA	44	20.0*		1)	Sacramento	10 Jun
Willie Turner	USA	48	20.1*		2)	Sacramento	10 Jun
John Carlos	USA	45	20.2*		1)	Commerce	11 May
Jim Hines	USA	46	20.2*		1)	Sioux Falls	10 Jun
Lennox Miller	Jam	46	20.3*	A	1)s2	Provo	17 Jun
Paul Nash	SA	47	20.4*	A	1)	Potchefstroom	22 Feb
Oliver Ford	USA	47	20.4*		2)	Houston	13 May
Jan Werner	Pol	46	20.4		1)	Warszawa	03 Jun
Roger Bambuck	Fra	45	20.4		1)	Paris	30 Jul
Jerry Bright	USA	47	20.5*	A	3)	Provo	17 Jun
Ed Roberts	Tri	42	20.5		4)	Los Angeles	09 Jun
Tom Randolph	USA	42	20.5*		1)	Baltimore	23 Jul

Marks made with assisting wind:

Name	Nat	Born	Time		Place	Venue	Date
Orin Richburg	USA	45	20.2*		1)	Bowling Green	20 May
Emmett Taylor	USA	47	20.4*		2)	Bowling Green	20 May

220 yards (straight course)

Name	Nat	Born	Time		Place	Venue	Date
Larry Highbaugh	USA	49	20.5		1)	Indianapolis	27 May
Don Schneider	USA		20.5		1)	Sayreville, NJ	17 Jun

Marks made with assisting wind:

Name	Nat	Born	Time		Place	Venue	Date
Jim Green	USA	47	20.0		1)h	Mansfield	15 Apr
Larry Highbaugh	USA	49	20.4		1)	Mansfield	15 Apr

4x100 metre relay

Univ. of So. California	USA/Jam	38.4*	A	1)	Provo	17 Jun
(McCullouch, Kuller, Simpson, L.Miller/Jam)						
Fra	(Berger, Delecour, Piquemal, Bambuck)	38.9		1)	Ostrava	22 Jul
USA	(McCullouch, Bright, Copeland, Hines)	39.0		1)	Los Angeles	08 Jul
British Commonwealth		39.1		2)	Los Angeles	08 Jul
(Eddy/Aus, Holdsworth,/Aus, M.Campbell/UK, L.Miller/Jam)						
Cub	(Eugelles, Morales, Ramirez, Montes)	39.2		2)	Winnipeg	05 Aug
FRG	(Hirscht, Metz, Wilke, Assion)	39.3		2)	Kiev	16 Sep
GDR	(Erbstösser, Klann, Burde, Eggers)	39.4		1)	Chemnitz	10 Jun
Ita	(Laverda, Preatoni, Giani, Giannattasio)	39.4		2)	Ostrava	22 Jul

1968

100 yards

Jim Hines	USA	46	9.2		1)	Corpus Christi	30 Mar
Craig Wallace	USA	46	9.2		1)	Knoxville	18 May
Clyde Glosson	USA	47	9.3		1)	Laredo	09 Mar
Mel Gray	USA	48	9.3		1)	Pittsburg, KS	09 Apr
Fred Kuller	USA	45	9.3		1)	Eugene	13 Apr
Willie Turner	USA	48	9.3		1)	Corvallis	20 Apr
Lennox Miller	Jam	46	9.3		1)	Los Angeles	04 May
William Miller	USA		9.3		1)	Baton Rouge	11 May
Oliver Ford	USA	47	9.3		1)	Beaumont	18 May
Charlie Greene	USA	44	9.3		1)	San Diego	01 Jun
Jim Green	USA	47	9.3		1)	Houston	08 Jun
Bob Rovere	USA	45	9.3		2)	Houston	08 Jun
Jim Freeman	USA	45	9.3		3)	Houston	08 Jun

Marks made with assisting wind:

Tom Griffith	USA		9.2		1)	Oklahoma City	13 Apr
Jim Hunter	USA		9.2		1)	Houston	19 Apr
Ronnie Ray Smith	USA	49	9.2		1)	San Jose	20 Apr

100 metres (fully automatic timing)

Jim Hines	USA	46	9.95	A	1)	México, D.F.	14 Oct
Charlie Greene	USA	45	10.02	A	1)q4	México, D.F.	13 Oct
Lennox Miller	Jam	46	10.04	A	2)	México, D.F.	14 Oct
Hermes Ramirez	Cub	48	10.10	A	1)q2	México, D.F.	13 Oct
Roger Bambuck	Fra	45	10.11	A	2)s1	México, D.F.	14 Oct
Ronnie Ray Smith	USA	49	10.14		2)s1	Sacramento	20 Jun
Pablo Montes	Cub	45	10.14	A	1)h4	México, D.F.	13 Oct
Mel Pender	USA	37	10.15		3)s1	Sacramento	20 Jun

100 metres (hand timing)

Paul Nash	SA	47	10.0	A	1)	Krugersdorp	02 Apr
Oliver Ford	USA	47	10.0	A	1)s	Albuquerque	31 May
Vladislav Sapeya	SU	43	10.0		1)s	Leningrad	20 Jul
John Carlos	USA	45	10.0	A	2)	Echo Summit	31 Aug

Marks made with assisting wind:

Jim Hines	USA	46	9.8		1)h1	Sacramento	20 Jun
Lennox Miller	Jam	46	9.9		1)h3	Sacramento	20 Jun
Bill Gaines	USA	48	9.9		2)h3	Sacramento	20 Jun

200 metres (fully automatic timing)

Tommie Smith	USA	44	19.83	A	1)	México, D.F.	16 Oct
John Carlos	USA	45	19.92	A	1)	Echo Summit	12 Sep
Peter Norman	Aus	42	20.06	A	2)	México, D.F.	16 Oct
Larry Questad	USA	43	20.28	A	3)	Echo Summit	12 Sep
Jerry Bright	USA	47	20.29	A	4)	Echo Summit	12 Sep
Tom Randolph	USA	42	20.29	A	5)	Echo Summit	12 Sep
Edwin Roberts	Tri	41	20.34	A	4)	México, D.F.	16 Oct
Mike Fray	Jam	47	20.39	A	1)q4	México, D.F.	15 Oct

200 metres (hand timing)

Mike Fray	Jam	47	20.1*		1)	Mesa	23 Mar
Paul Nash	SA	47	20.1		1)	Zurich	02 Jul
Clyde Glosson	USA	47	20.1	A	1)	Echo Summit	31 Aug
Jim Haines	USA	46	20.2*		1)	San Diego	01 Jun
Wayne Collett	USA	49	20.2	A	2)	Echo Summit	31 Aug

4x100 metre relay (fully automatic timing)

USA	(Greene, Pender, R.R.Smith, Hines)	38.24	A	1)	México, D.F.	20 Oct
Jam	(Stewart, Fray, Forbes, L.Miller)	38.39	A	1)s1	México, D.F.	19 Oct
Cub	(Ramirez, Morales, Montes, Figuerola)	38.40	A	2)	México, D.F.	20 Oct
Fra	(Fenouil, Delecour, Piquemal, Bambuck)	38.43	A	3)	México, D.F.	20 Oct
GDR	(Erbstösser, Schelter, P.Haase, Eggers)	38.66	A	5)	México, D.F.	20 Oct

1969

100 yards (hand timing)

John Carlos	USA	45	9.1		1)	Fresno	10 May
Earl Harris	USA	48	9.2		1)	Stillwater	22 Apr
Mike Goodrich	USA	48	9.2		1)h	Des Moines	25 Apr
Andy Hopkins	USA	49	9.2		1)	Houston	30 May
Robert Taylor	USA	49	9.2		2)	Houston	30 May
Lennix Miller	Jam	46	9.2		2)	Knoxville	20 Jun
Doug Hawken	USA	49	9.2		1)	Sacramento	21 Jun
Eddie Hart	USA	49	9.2		2)	Sacramento	21 Jun

Marks made with assisting wind:

John Carlos	USA	45	9.0		1)	San Jose	03 May
Mel Gray	USA	48	9.1		1)s2	Knoxville	20 Jun

100 metres (hand timing)

Hermes Ramirez	Cus	48	10.0		1)	Zurich	04 Jun
Valeriy Borzov	SU	49	10.0		1)	Kiev	18 Aug
Charlie Greene	USA	44	10.1		1)	Villanova	18 May
John Carlos	USA	45	10.1		2)	Villanova	18 May
Pablo Montes	Cub	45	10.1		1)	Habana	23 May
Edwin Roberts	Tri	41	10.1		1)	Milano	02 Jul
Mel Pender	USA	37	10.1		1)s	Poitiers	12 Jul
Detlef Lewandowski	GDR	44	10.1		1)h	Berlin	20 Jul
Hermann Burde	GDR	43	10.1		1)	Berlin	23 Jul
William Dralu	Uga	47	10.1		1)h	Kampala	08 Aug
Aleksandr Kornelyuk	SU	50	10.1		1)	Uzhgorod	27 Oct

Marks made with assisting wind:

John Carlos	USA	45	9.9	A	1)	Echo Summit	12 Sep
Ivory Crockett	USA	49	10.0	A	2)	Echo Summit	12 Sep

Rolling start:

Artwell Mandaza	Rho	47	10.0w		1)	Salisbury	20 Dec

200 metres (full turn - hand timing)

John Carlos	USA	45	20.0	A	1)	Echo Summit	12 Sep
Lennox Miller	Jam	46	20.2*		1)	Pullman	26 Apr
Tom Randolph	USA	42	20.3*		2)h	Miami	29 Jun
Philippe Clerc	Swz	46	20.3		1)	Zurich	04 Jun
Julius Sang	Ken	44	20.3*	A	1)	Nairobi	27 Sep
Oliver Ford	USA	47	20.4*		1)	Billings	07 Jun
Ed Roberts	Tri	41	20.4		2)	Zurich	04 Jul
Lee Evans	USA	47	20.4	A	2)	Echo Summit	12 Sep
Paul Nash	SA	47	20.4	A	1)	Potchefstroom	06 Dec
Tommie Smith	USA	44	20.5		3)	Villania	18 May
Ben Vaughan	USA	48	20.5*		1)	Houston	30 May
Gerald Tinker	USA	51	20.5*		4)h	Miami	29 Jun

Mark made with assisting wind:

Edesel Garrison	USA	50	20.4*	1)	Los Angeles	03 May

Professional race (against a horse):

Jim Hines	USA	46	20.1*	-)		04 Jun

4x100 metre relay

San Jose State	USA	(Davis, Clayton, R.R.Smith, Carlos)	38.6*	1)h	Knoxville	20 Jun
Americas	USA	(Greene, Vaughan, Hurd, Carlos)	38.8	1)	Stuttgart	30 Jul
	Fra	(Sarteur, Bourbeillon, Fenouil, Saint-Gilles)	38.8	1)	Athinai	20 Sep
	Cub	(Bandomo, Morales, Ramirez, Montes)	39.2	1)	Zurich	04 Jul
	FRG	(Schmidtke, Wucherer, Krüger, Eigenherr)	39.2	2)	Zurich	04 Jul
	GDR	(Gollos, P.Haase, Burde, Bombach)	39.3	1)	Berlin	11 Sep
	SU	(Lebedyev, Sapeya, N.Ivanov, Borzov)	39.3	2)	Athinai	20 Sep

1970

100 yards (hand timing)

Willie McGee	USA	50	9.1	1)s2	Houston	08 May
Harrington Jackson	USA	47	9.2	1)	El Paso	28 Mar
Mel Gray	USA	48	9.2	1)	Des Moines	24 Apr
John Carlos	USA	45	9.2	1)	Philadelphia	25 Apr
Robert Taylor	USA	49	9.2	1)h	Houston	08 May
Earl Harris	USA	48	9.2	1)	Baton Rouge	09 May
Jim Green	USA	47	9.2	1)s	Wichita	13 Jun
Ivory Crockett	USA	49	9.2	)	Wichita	13 Jun
Doug Hawken	USA	49	9.2	)	Wichita	13 Jun

Marks made with assisting wind:

Robert Taylor	USA	49	9.1	)	Houston	09 May
Mel Gray	USA	48	9.1	)	Lawrence	15 May
Jim Green	USA	47	9.1	)	Wichita	13 Jun

Timed on one watch:

Willie Harrison	USA		9.1	1)	Levelland, TX	21 Nov

100 metres (hand timing)

Gert Metz	FRG	42	10.0	1)	Burg Gretesch	06 Sep
Hermes Ramirez	Cub	48	10.1	1)	Habana	16 Jan
Norman Chihota	Tan	47	10.1	1)	Arusha	24 May
Ben Vaughan	USA	48	10.1	1)	Viareggio	13 Jun
Charlie Greene	USA	44	10.1	2)	Viareggio	13 Jun
Siegfried Schenke	GDR	43	10.1	1)	Erfurt	03 Jul
Franz-Peter Hofmeister	FRG	51	10.1	2)	Burg Gretesch	06 Sep
Manfred Knickenberg	FRG	37	10.1	3)	Burg Gretesch	06 Sep
Klaus-Joh. Ehl	FRG	49	10.1	4)	Burg Gretesch	06 Sep
Pablo Montes	Cub	45	10.1	1)	Bucuresti	12 Sep

Marks made with assisting wind:

Pablo Montes	Cub	45	9.9	1)s1	Panama City	01 Mar
Artwell Mandaza	Rho	47	9.9	1)s	Welkom	02 May
John Carlos	USA	45	10.0	1)	Modesto	23 May
Ben Vaughan	USA	48	10.0	1)	Stuttgart	15 Jul
Hugo Fernandes	Sur	51	10.0	1)	Willemstad	04 Aug

200 metres (full turn - hand timing)

John Carlos	USA	45	20.2*	1)	Melbourne	17 Mar
Mel Gray	USA	48	20.3*	1)h2	Lawrence	15 May
Willie Turner	USA	48	20.3*	1)	West Los Angeles	16 May
All Coffee	USA	50	20.4*	1)	Baton Rouge	28 Mar
Stan Allotey	Gha	42	20.4*	1)	Los Angeles	28 Mar
Reggie Robinson	USA	49	20.4*	1)	Los Angeles	25 Apr
Fred Newhouse	USA	48	20.4*	1)	Dallas	02 May
Eddie Hart	USA	49	20.4*	2)	Los Angeles	16 May
Larry Black	USA	51	20.4*	1)h2	Des Moines	18 Jun

Ben Vaughan	USA	48	20.4		2)	Stuttgart	16 Jul
Curtis Mills	USA	48	20.4		1)	Moskva	26 Jul

Timed on one watch:

Willie Harrison	USA		19.9*		1)	Levelland, TX	21 Nov
Danny Johnson	USA		20.3*		2)	Levelland, TX	21 Nov

4x100 metre relay

Fra	(Sarteur, Bourme, Fenouil, Metz)	39.0	1)	Colombes	08 Jul
USA	(Crockett, Vaughan, Hart, Taylor)	39.1	1)	Leningrad	23 Jul
SU	(Kornelyuk, Sapeya, Maslakov, Borzov)	39.2	2)	Leningrad	23 Jul
Pol	(Gramse, Werner, Wagner, Nowosz)	39.2	1)	Torino	06 Sep
Cub	(Bandomo, Murales, montes, Triana M.)	39.2	2)	Torino	06 Sep

1971

100 Yards

George Daniels	Gha	50	9.2		1)	Accra	24 Apr
Jack Phillips	USA	48	9.2		1)	Houston	08 May
Willie Deckard	USA	51	9.2		1)	Westwood	08 May
Jim Green	USA	47	9.2		1)	Lexington	15 May
Willy McGee	USA	50	9.2		1)h	Itta Bena, MS	15 May
Francis Baldwin	USA	50	9.2		1)h	Pasadena, TX	28 May
Cliff Branch	USA	49	9.2		2)	Wichita	12 Jun

Marks made with assisting wind:

Delano Meriwether	USA	43	9.0		1)	Eugene	25 Jun
Jim Green	USA	47	9.0		2)	Eugene	25 Jun
Willie McGee	USA	50	9.1		1)	Grambling	13 Mar
Cliff Branch	USA	49	9.1		1)s2	Wichita	12 Jun
Don Quarrie	Jam	51	9.1		1)h4	Eugene	25 Jun
Ivory Crockett	USA	49	9.1		2)h4	Eugene	25 Jun
Charlie Greene	USA	44	9.1		4)	Eugene	25 jun

Doubtful timing:

Roland Martin	USA		9.2		1)		

100 metres (hand timing)

Manfred Kokot	GDR	48	10.0		1)	Erfurt	15 May
Hermes Ramirez	Cub	48	10.0		1)h	Praha	11 Jun
Valeriy Borzov	SU	49	10.0		1)	Kiev	21 Jun
Jean-Louis Ravelomanantsoa	Mad	43	10.0		1)	Helsinki	01 Jul
Pablo Montes	Cub	45	10.1		1)	Leipzig	16 Jun
Charles Francis	Can	48	10.1		1)	Richmond	25 Jun
Marshall Dill	USA	52	10.1		1)	Windsor, Ont.	01 Jul
Vassilios Papageorgopoulos	Gre	47	10.1		1)	Athinai	10 Jul
Karl-Heinz Klotz	FRG	50	10.1		1)	Stuttgart	10 Jul
Jim Green	USA	47	10.1		1)	Durham	16 Jul
Ivory Crockett	USA	49	10.1		2)	Durham	16 Jul
Hans-Joachim Zenk	GDR	52	10.1		1)	Berlin	31 Jul
Don Quarrie	Jam	51	10.1	A	1)h3	Cali	31 Jul
Lennox Miller	Jam	46	10.1	A	1)s	Cali	01 Aug
Franz-Peter Hofmeister	FRG	51	10.1		1)	Bonn	11 Sep

Mark made with assisting wind:

Alain Sarteur	Fra	46	10.0		1)	St. Denise	01 May

Doubtful timing:

Gebre Gebre Egzi	Eth		10.1	A	1)	Addis Ababa	06 Jun

Professional:

Robbie Hutchison	UK		10.1		1)	Melbourne	Feb

200 metres (full turn)

Don Quarrie (19.86 E)	Jam	51	19.8	A	1)	Cali	03 Aug
Willie Deckard	USA	51	20.1*		1)	Westwood	08 May

Marshall Dill	USA	52	20.1		1)	Windsor	01 Jul
Valeriy Borzov	SU	49	20.2		1)	Moskva	18 Jul
Ed Roberts	Tri	41	20.3	A	3)	Cali	03 Aug
Larry Black	USA	51	20.4*		1)	Durham	05 May
Edesel Garrison	USA	50	20.4*		2)	Westwood	08 May
Chuck Smith	USA	48	20.4*		2)s1	Eugene	26 Jun
Jörg Pfeifer	GDR	52	20.4		1)	Leipzig	22 Aug

Marks made with assisting wind:

George Daniels	Gha		20.3*	1)	Stillwater	22 May
Larry Black	USA	51	20.3*	1)	Billings	05 Jun

Wind assisted and straight course:

Marshall Dill	USA	52	20.0*	1)	Mansfield	17 Apr

4x100 metre relay

U. of So. California	USA	(Babb, Garrison, Brown, Deckard)	39.0*	1)h	Seattle	18 Jun
All Stars	Jam	(Daley, Lawson, Quarrie, Miller)	39.1	1)	Berkeley	02 Jul
	Fra	(Bourbeillon, Metz, Fenouil, Arame)	39.2	1)	Paris	09 Jun
	Cub	(Morales, Bandomo, Montes, Ramirez)	39.2	1)	Warszawa	20 Jun
Ukr	SU	(Pankratov, Kuzhukin, Sorkin, Borzov)	39.2	1)	Moskva	16 Jul

1972

100 yards

Harold Porter	USA	52	9.2	1)	Lafayette	15 Apr
Herb Washington	USA	50	9.2	1)	Lawrence	22 Apr
Ivory Crockett	USA	48	9.2	2)	Lawrence	22 Apr
Joe Sincere	USA		9.2	1)	Itta Bena, MS	06 May

Marks made with assisting wind:

Willie McGee	USA	50	9.0	1)h2	Baton Rouge	21 Apr
Robert Taylor	USA	48	9.0	1)h3	Baton Rouge	21 Apr
Adrian Capital	USA	48	9.1	2)h3	Baton Rouge	21 Apr

Rolling start and wind assisted:

William Miller	USA		9.1	1)h1	Baton Rouge	21 Apr

100 metres (fully automatic timing)

Valeriy Borzov	SU	49	10.07	1)q3	München	31 Aug
Robert Taylor	USA	49	10.16	2)q3	München	31 Aug
Hasely Crawford	Tri	50	10.18	3)q3	München	31 Aug
Vassilios Papageorgopoulos	Gre	47	10.22	1)	Izmir	04 Aug
Lennox Miller	Jam	46	10.24	2)	München	15 Aug
Jobst Hirscht	FRG	48	10.25	1)q1	München	31 Aug
Jean-Louis Ravelomanantsoa	Mad	43	10.29	2)h10	München	31 Aug

Marks made with assisting wind:

Vassilios Papageorgopoulos	Gre	47	10.16	1)	London	14 Jul
Aleksandr Kornelyuk	SU	50	10.23	1)q4	München	31 Aug

100 metres (hand timing)

Eddie Hart	USA	49	9.9	1)	Eugene	01 Jul
Rey Robinson	USA	52	9.9	2)	Eugene	01 Jul
Warren Edmonson	USA	50	10.0	2)h2	Fresno	13 May
Steve Riddick	USA	51	10.0	1)s2	Ashland	26 May
Cliff Branch	USA	49	10.0	1)s1	Eugene	02 Jun
Harrington Jackson	USA	47	10.0	2)s2	Eugene	02 Jun
Vassilios Papageorgopoulos	Gre	47	10.0	1)	Bratislava	03 Jun
Valeriy Borzov	SU	49	10.0	1)	Milano	16 Jun
Pietro Mennea	Ita	52	10.0	2)	Milano	16 Jun
Hermes Ramirez	Cub	48	10.0	1)	Praha	21 Jun
Robert Taylor	USA	49	10.0	3)	Eugene	01 Jul
Raimo Vilen	Fin	45	10.0	1)	Vuosaari	27 Jul

Marks made with assisting wind:

Ivory Crockett	USA	49	9.9	1)h3	Eugene	01 Jun
Don Quarrie	Jam	51	9.9	2)h3	Eugene	01 Jun
Robert Taylor	USA	49	9.9	1)q4	Eugene	30 Jun
Rey Robinson	USA	52	9.9	1)s1	Eugene	01 Jul
Norbert Payton	USA	49	9.9	2)s1	Eugene	01 Jul
Warren Edmonson	USA	50	9.9	3)s1	Eugene	01 Jul
Eddie Hart	USA	49	9.9	4)s1	Eugene	01 Jul
Willie Deckard	USA	51	9.9	5)s1	Eugene	01 Jul

200 metres (fully automatic timing)

Valeriy Borzov	SU	49	20.00	1)	München	04 Sep
Larry Black	USA	51	20.19	2)	München	04 Sep
Pietro Mennea	Ita	52	20.30	3)	München	04 Sep
Larry Burton	USA	51	20.37	4)	München	04 Sep
Don Quarrie	Jam	51	20.43	2)q4	München	03 Sep
Manfred Ommer	FRG	50	20.49	1)	München	23 Jul
Chuck Smith	USA	49	20.55	5)	München	04 Sep
Siegfried Schenke	GDR	43	20.56	6)	München	04 Sep

200 metres (hand timing)

Larry Black	USA	51	20.0		1)s1	Billings	02 Jun
Steve Williams	USA	53	20.2*	A	1)	El Paso	15 Apr
Larry Burton	USA	51	20.2*		1)	Lafayette	02 May
Ivory Crockett	USA	48	20.2*		1)	Normal	13 May
Pietro Mennea	Ita	52	20.2		1)	Milano	17 Jun
Don Quarrie	Jam	51	20.3*	A	2)	El Paso	15 Apr
Dennis Schultz	USA	51	20.3*	A	1)h2	Boulder	19 May
Siegfried Schenke	GDR	43	20.3		1)	Potsdam	15 Jun
Dave Jenkins	UK	52	20.3		1)	Edinburgh	19 Aug

Mark made with assisting wind:

Willie Deckard	USA	51	20.2	1)h1	Eugene	01 Jun

4x100 metre relay (fully automatic timing)

USA	(Black, Taylor, Tinker, Hart)	38.19	1)	München	10 Sep
SU	(Kornelyuk, Lovyetskiy, Silovs, Borzov)	38.50	2)	München	10 Sep
FRG	(J.Hirscht, Klotz, Wucherer, Ehl)	38.79	3)	München	10 Sep
Czeq	(Matousek, Demec, Kynos, Bohman)	38.82	4)	München	10 Sep
Pol	(S.Wagner, Cuch, Czerbniak, Nowosz)	38.90	3)s1	München	09 Sep
GDR	(Kokot, Borth, Bombach, Schenke)	38.90	5)	München	10 Sep

Manual timing:

Pol	(S.Wagner, Cuch, Czerbniak, Nowosz)	38.8	1)	Warszawa	09 Aug

1973

100 yards (hand timing)

Steve Williams	USA	53	9.1	1)	Fresno	12 May
Herb Washington	USA	50	9.2	1)r2	Lawrence	21 Apr
Ivory Crockett	USA	48	9.2	2)r2	Lawrence	21 Apr

Marks made with assisting wind:

Dennis Schultz	USA	51	9.1	1)	Stillwater	31 Mar
Kent Merritt	USA		9.1	1)h1	Raleigh	27 Apr
Gerald Tinker	USA	51	9.1	1)	Kent, OH	05 May
Larry Burton	USA	51	9.1	1)	Muncie	08 May
Steve Williams	USA	53	9.1	1)h3	Fresno	11 May
Don Quarrie	Jam	51	9.1	1)h1	Eugene	18 May
Earl Harris	USA	48	9.1	1)s	Fort Lewis	27 Jul

100 metres (fully automatic timing)

Steve Williams	USA	53	10.15	1)	Dakar	04 Aug
Silvio Leonard	Cub	55	10.24	1)	Praha	04 Sep

Siegfried Schenke	GDR	43	10.26	1)	Edinburgh	08 Sep
Klaus-Dieter Kurrat	GDR	55	10.32	1)s1	Duisburg	24 Aug
Juris Silovs	SU	50	10.33	1)s2	Moskva	17 Aug
Alekesandr Kornelyuk	SU	50	10.34	2)	Edinburgh	08 Sep

Mark made with assisting wind:

Félix Mata	Ven	51	10.15	1)	Panama City	24 Feb

100 metres (hand timing)

Aleksandr Kornelyuk	SU	50	10.0	1)	Moskva	10 Jul
Michael Drosse	GDR	52	10.0	1)	Dresden	11 Jul
Hans-Jürgen Bombach	GDR	45	10.0	1)s2	Dresden	20 Jul
Siegfried Schenke	GDR	43	10.0	1)	Berlin	29 Aug

Mark made with assisting wind:

Félix Mata	Ven	51	9.9	1)	Maracaibo	28 Jan

200 metres (fully automatic timing)

Steve Williams	USA	53	20.33*	1)	Bakersfield	16 Jun
Mark Lutz	USA	51	20.38*	2)	Bakersfield	16 Jun
Marshall Dill	USA	52	20.44*	3)	Bakersfield	16 Jun
Ivory Crockett	USA	48	20.50*	4)	Bakersfield	16 Jun
Pietro Mennea	Ita	52	20.56	1)	Moskva	20 Aug

* = 220 y. time less 0.12

200 metres (hand timing)

Carl Lawson	Jam	47	20.1*	1)h1	Moscow, ID	18 May
Don Quarrie	Jam	51	20.1*	1)h1	Eugene	18 May
Hans-Jürgen Bombach	GDR	45	20.2	1)	Dresden	21 Jul
Siegfried Schenke	GDR	43	20.2	2)	Dresden	21 Jul
Steve Williams	USA	53	20.3*	1)r2	Bakersfield	19 May
Fred Newhouse	USA	48	20.4	1)	Pointe-à-Pierre	08 Apr
Ivory Crockett	USA	48	20.4*	1)	Durham	12 May
Willie Deckard	USA	51	20.4*	1)r1	Bekersfield	19 May
Chuck Smith	USA	49	20.4*	2)r2	Bekersfield	19 May
Michael Droese	GDR	52	20.4	1)	Dresden	11 Jul
Ossi Karttunen	Fin	48	20.4	1)	Paimio	28 Jul

Marks made with assisting wind:

Carl Lawson	Jam	47	19.8*	1)	Moscow, ID	19 May
Gerald Tinker	USA	51	19.9*	1)	Kent, OH	05 May
Dennis Schultz	USA	51	20.3*	1)	Stillwater	05 May
Mark Lutz	USA	51	20.3*	1)	Manhattan, KS	19 May
Silvio Leonard	Cub	55	20.3	2)	Maracaibo	28 Jul

Straight course and not confirmed:

Earl Harris	USA	48	20.3*	1)	Fort Lewis	27 Jul

4x100 metre relay (fully automatic timing)

USA	(Washington, S.Williams, Dill, Hammonds)	38.91	1)	München	11 Jul
Fra	(Sainte-Rose, Rechal, Ducasse, Echevin)	39.32	2)	Nice	04 Aug
FRG	(Haupt, Ehl, Ommer, Strempel)	39.35	2)	München	11 Jul
SU	(Zhidkikh, Lovyetskiy, Silovs, Atamas)	39.46	2)	Moskva	20 Aug

Hand timing:

Phila. Pioneer Club		38.7*	1)	Durham	12 May
USA	(Crockett, Joseph, Newhouse, Crawford)				
GDR	(Weise, Droese, Bombach, Schenke)	38.8	1)r2	Berlin	29 Aug
Ita	(Guerini, Maccacaro, Benedetti, Mennea)	39.0	1)	Oslo	04 Aug
SU	(Kornelyuk, Izmyestyev, Silovs, Zhidkikh)	39.3	1)	Leningrad	16 Jun

1974

100 yards (fully automatic timing)

Reggie Jones	USA	53	9.34	1)s3	Austin	07 Jun

Steve Williams	USA	53	9.45	1)	Fresno	18 May
James Gilkes	Guy	52	9.45	2)s3	Austin	07 Jun

Marks made with assisting wind:

Reggie Jones	USA	53	9.18	1)	Austin	07 Jun
Steve Williams	USA	53	9.19	1)h4	Austin	06 Jun
Steve Williams II	USA	53	9.26	2)h4	Austin	06 Jun
Clifford Outlin	USA	53	9.29	3)h4	Austin	06 Jun

Hand timing:

Iviry Crockett	USA	48	9.0	1)	Knoxville	11 May
Steve Williams	USA	53	9.1+	1)	Helsinki	01 Aug

Rolling start and wind assisted:

Mike Walker	USA	53	9.0	1)	Baltimore	15 Jun

+ = made during a 100 m. race

100 metres (fully automatic timing)

Steve Riddick	USA	51	10.20	1)	Zurich	16 Aug
Reggie Jones	USA	53	10.23	1)	Durham	05 Jul
Valeriy Borzov	SU	49	10.27	1)	Roma	03 Sep
Manfred Ommer	FRG	50	10.28	1)s1	Hannover	27 Jul
Dominique Chauvelot	Fra	52	10.28	1)s2	Roma	03 Sep
Pietro Mennea	Ita	52	10.29	2)s2	Roma	03 Sep
Steve Williams	USA	53	10.30	2)	Durham	05 Jul
Silvio Leonard	Cub	55	10.32	1)	Praha	28 Jun
Petar Petrov	Bul	55	10.33	1)	Sofia	19 Jul
Klaus Bieler	FRG	49	10.35	3)	Roma	03 Sep
Juris Silovs	SU	50	10.35	4)	Roma	03 Sep

Marks made with assisting wind:

Steve Williams	USA	53	10.16	1)	London	13 Jul
Manfred Ommer	FRG	50	10.20	1)	Hannover	27 Jul
Franz-Peter Hofmeister	FRG	51	10.28	2)	Hannover	27 Jul

Hand timing:

Steve Williams	USA	53	9.9	1)	Westwood	21 Jun
Pablo Montes	Cub	45	10.0	1)s1	Panama City	09 Feb
Don Quarrie	Jam	51	10.0	2)	Westwood	21 Jun
Silvio Leonard	Cub	55	10.0	1)	Milano	02 Jul
Manfred Ommer	RFG	50	10.0	1)r3	Leverkusen	22 Jul

Mark made with assisting wind:

Silvio Leonard	Cub	55	9.9	1)	Panama City	09 Feb

Rolling start and wind assisted:

Adama Fall	Sen	51	9.9	1)	Dakar	05 Apr

200 metres (fully automatic timing)

Don Quarrie	Jam	51	20.06	1)	Zurich	16 Aug
Hans-Joachim Zenk	GDR	52	20.42	1)	Potsdam	13 Jun
Silvio Leonard	Cub	55	20.42	2)	Potsdam	13 Jun
Pietro Mennea	Ita	52	20.53	1)	Roma	31 Jul
Manfred Ommer	FRG	50	20.57	1)	Hannover	28 Jul
Bruno Cherrier	Fra	53	20.58	2)	Zurich	16 Aug
Jörg Pfeifer	GDR	52	20.60	3)	Potsdam	13 Jun

Marks made with assisting wind:

Reggie Jones	USA	53	20.23*	1)s2	Austin	08 Jun
James Gilkes	Guy	52	20.40*	2)s2	Austin	08 Jun
Larry Black	USA	51	20.45*	1)s1	Austin	08 Jun
Joe Pouncy	USA	50	20.47*	1)	Addison, TX	30 Mar

Hand timing:

Don Quarrie	Jam	51	20.1+		1)	Bakersfielf	18 May
Silvio Leonard	Cub	55	20.2		2)	Potsdam	13 Jun
Steve Williams	USA	53	20.2		1)	Viareggio	07 Aug
John Carlos	USA	45	20.3*	A	1)	El Paso	27 Apr

Marks made with assisting wind:

James Gilkes	Guy	52	19.8*		1)	Austin	08 Jun
Reggie Jones	USA	53	19.9*		2)	Austin	08 Jun
Wardell Gilbreath	USA	54	20.0*		3)	Austin	08 Jun
Don Quarrie	Jam	51	20.0*		1)	Eugene	08 Jun
Charles Joseph	Tri	52	20.1		1)	Arima	15 Jun

+ = made during a 220 y. race

Straight course:

Stanley Harris	USA	56	19.9*		1)	Daytona Beach	03 Apr
James Brown	USA	57	20.1*		2)	Daytona Beach	03 Apr

4x100 metre relay (fully automatic timing)

Fra	(Sainte-Rose, Arame, Cherrier, Chauvelot)	38.69	1)	Roma	08 Sep
Ita	(Guerini, Oliosi, Benedetti, Mennea)	38.88	2)	Roma	08 Sep
GDR	(Kokot, Droese, Bombach, Schenke)	38.99	3)	Roma	08 Sep
USA	(Foster, Riddick, Lutz, R.Jones)	39.03*	1)	Durham	05 Jul
FRG	(Ehl, Bieler, Haupt, Hofmeister)	39.03	1)	Zurich	16 Aug
SU	(Borzov, Kornelyuk, Silovs, Aksinin)	39.03	4)	Roma	08 Sep

1975

100 yards (fully automatic timing)

Clifford Outlin	USA	53	9.33	A	1)s3	Provo	06 Jun
Hasley Crawford	Tri	50	9.35	A	1)	Provo	06 Jun
Don Quarrie	Jam	51	9.37		1)	Fresno	10 May
Houston McTear	USA	57	9.39		1)	Atlanta	07 Jun
Ralf Smith	USA	53	9.42		1)h	Arkadelphia	22 May
Reggie Jones	USA	53	9.43	A	1)s2	Provo	06 Jun
Ed Preston	USA	55	9.44	A	1)h1	Provo	05 Jun
Clancy Edwards	USA	55	9.50		2)	Fresno	10 May

Mark made with assisting wind:

Charles Hopkins	USA	55	9.36		1)	Pasedena, TX	23 May

Hand timing:

Houston McTear	USA	57	9.0		1)h	Winter Park, FL	09 May
Steve Williams	USA	53	9.1		1)	Eugene	07 Jun
Mike Roberson	USA	56	9.2		1)h	Winter Park, FL	02 May
James Brown	USA	57	9.2		1)	Winter Park, FL	10 May
Don Quarrie	Jam	51	9.2		1)	Fresno	10 May

Mark made with assisting wind:

Paul Njoroge	Ken		9.1	A	1)	El Paso	22 Mar
Warren Edmonson	USA	50	9.1	A	1)	El Paso	10 May
Jean-Louis Ravelomanatsoa	Mad	43	9.1	A	2)	El Paso	10 May
J.J. Jackson	USA	47	9.1	A	3)	El Paso	10 May

Doubtful timing:

Bill Collins	USA	51	9.2		1)	Houston	08 Aug

100 metres (fully automatic timing)

Steve Riddick	USA	51	10.05		1)	Zurich	20 Aug
Steve Williams	USA	53	10.08		2)	Zurich	20 Aug
Silvio Leonard	Cub	55	10.15	A	1)s1	México, D.F.	13 Oct
Don Quarrie	Jam	51	10.16		1)	Eugene	20 Jun
Valeriy Borzov	SU	49	10.16		3)	Zurich	20 Aug
Pietro Mennea	Ita	52	10.20		1)	Torino	12 Jul
Hasley Crawford	Tri	50	10.21	A	2)	México, D.F.	14 Oct
James Gilkes	Guy	52	10.22	A	1)s2	México, D.F.	13 Oct

Hand timing:

Silvio Leonard	Cub	55	9.9		1)	Ostrava	05 Jun
Steve Williams	USA	53	9.9		1)	Siena	16 Jul
Houston McTear	USA	57	10.0		1)h1	Knoxville	13 Jun
Steve Riddick	USA	51	10.0		2)h1	Milano	02 Jul

Don Quarrie	Jam	51	10.0	1)	Milano	02 Jul
Valeriy Borzov	SU	49	10.0	1)	Kiev	04 Jul
Pablo Montes	Cub	45	10.0	1)	Habana	05 Sep
Pietro Mennea	Ita	52	10.0	1)	Palermo	10 Sep

Marks made with assisting wind:

Hasley Crawford	Tri	50	9.8	2)	Arima	29 May
Charles Joseph	Tri	52	9.9	2)	Arima	14 Jun
Felix Mata	Ven	51	9.9	1)	Maracaibo	19 Jul

Doubtful distance:

Reggie Jones	USA	53	9.9	1)	Boston	26 Jul

200 metres (fully automatic timing)

Don Quarrie	Jam	51	20.12	1)	Eugene	21 Jun
Steve Williams	USA	53	20.16	1)	Stuttgart	26 Aug
Pietro Mennea	Ita	52	20.23	1)	Torino	13 Jul
Steve Riddick	USA	51	20.31	2)	Zurich	20 Aug
James Gilkes	Guy	52	20.39	2)	Eugene	21 Jun
Reggie Jones	USA	53	20.48* A	1)	Provo	07 Jun
Clancy Edwards	USA	55	20.61* A	3)	Provo	07 Jun
Valeriy Borzov	SU	49	20.61	2)	Nice	17 Aug
Larry Brown	USA	51	20.62 A	1)h2	México, D.F.	15 Oct
Fons Brydenbach	Bel	54	20.68	1)	Bruxelles	10 Aug

Hand timing:

Don Quarrie	Jam	51	19.8+	1)	Eugene	07 Jun
Steve Williams	USA	53	19.8*	2)	Eugene	07 Jun
Silvio Leonard	Cub	55	20.1	1)	Ostrava	05 Jun
Pietro Mennea	Ita	52	20.1	1)	Roma	26 Jun
James Gilkes	Guy	52	20.2	1)	Karlskrona	15 Jul
Reggie Jones	USA	53	20.3*	2)	Modesto	24 May
Charles Joseph	Tri	52	20.4	1)	Bridgetown	27 Mar
Ron Whitaker	USA	55	20.4*	1)	San Jose	19 Apr
Ken Randle	USA	54	20.4*	1)h1	Pullman	16 May
Clancy Edwards	USA	55	20.4	1)h2	Eugene	21 Jun
Steve Riddick	USA	51	20.4	3)	Viareggio	06 Aug

Marks made with assisting wind:

Reggie Jones	USA	53	20.2*	1)	Westwood	29 Mar
Clancy Edwards	USA	55	20.2*	2)	San Jose	03 May
Hasley Crawford	Tri	50	20.2	2)	Arima	31 May
Charles Joseph	Tri	52	20.2	1)	Arima	15 Jun
Ron Whitaker	USA	55	20.3*	3)	San Jose	03 May
Rudy Reid	Tri	52	20.3	2)	Arima	15 Jun

+ = made during a 220 y. race

4x100 metre relay (fully automatic timing)

USA	(Edwards, L.Brown, Merrick, Collins)	38.31	A	1)	México, D.F.	20 Oct
Cub	(Ramirez, Casanas, Montes, Triana M.)	38.46	A	2)	México, D.F.	20 Oct
Can	(Fraser, Nash, Dukowski, Martin)	38.86	A	3)	México, D.F.	20 Oct
GDR	(Zenk, Munkelt, Bombach, Thieme)	38.98		1)	Nice	16 Aug
SU	(Kornelyuk, Kolyesnikov, Silovs, Borzov)	39.00		2)	Nice	16 Aug

Hand timing:

SU	(Kornelyuk, Kolyesnikov, Aksinin, Borzov)	38.7		1)	Kiev	04 Jul

1976

100 yards (fully automatic timing)

Dwayne Evans	USA	58	9.44	1)	Tucson	22 May
Raymond Clayborn	USA		9.52	1T)	Austin	13 May
Jerry Thomas	USA		9.52	1T)	Austin	13 May
Reggie Jones	USA	53	9.53	1)	Tempe	24 Mar
Carlton Derrett	USA		9.54	3)	Austin	13 May
Ray Brooks	USA		9.58	4)	Austin	13 May
Lamar Preyor	USA	57	9.63	2)	Tempe	24 Mar

Marks made with assisting wind:

Oberton Spence	Jam	52	9.35	1)	Austin	28 Feb
Keith Davidson	USA		9.35	2)	Austin	28 Feb
Marvin Baker	USA		9.36	3)	Austin	28 Feb
Ray Clayborn	USA		9.46	4)	Austin	28 Feb

Hand timing:

Harvey Glance	USA	57	9.2	1)	Athens, GA	14 May

Marks made with assisting wind:

Harvey Glance	USA	57	9.0	1)	Auburn	17 Apr
Johnnie Jones	USA	58	9.1	1)	Round Rock	23 Apr

100 metres (fully automatic timing)

Hasely Crawford	Tri	50	10.06	1)	Montreal	24 Jul
Don Quarrie	Jam	51	10.07	2)	Montreal	24 Jul
Harvey Glance	USA	57	10.11	1)	Eugene	20 Jun
Valeriy Borzov	SU	49	10.14	3)	Montreal	24 Jul
Steve Riddick	USA	51	10.15	1)	College Park	06 Aug
Houston McTear	USA	57	10.16	2)	Eugene	20 Jun
Zenon Licznerski	Pol	54	10.22	1)	Bydgoszcz	25 Jun
Klaus-Dieter Kurrat	GDR	55	10.22	1)	Karl Marx Stadt	06 Aug
Johnnie Jones	USA	58	10.23	4)	Eugene	20 Jun
Christer Garpenborg	Swe	52	10.25	1)h2	Westwood	11 Jun
Guy Abrahams	Pan	53	10.25	5)	Montreal	24 Jul

Doubtful timing:

Ed Preston	USA	55	10.07	1)	Austin	03 Apr
Robert Woods	USA		10.14	2)	Austin	03 Apr
Albert Lomotey	Gha	55	10.20	3)	Austin	03 Apr

Hand timing:

Steve Williams	USA	53	9.9	1)	Gainesville	27 Mar
Harvey Glance	USA	57	9.9	1)	Columbia	03 Apr
Don Quarrie	Jam	51	9.9	1)	Modesto	22 May

Mark made with assisting wind:

Steve Williams	USA	53	9.8	1)h1	Knoxville	08 May

Doubtful timing:

Claudiu Suselescu	Rom	52	9.9	1)	Bucuresti	14 Aug

200 metres (fully automatic timing)

Millard Hampton	USA	56	20.10	1)	Eugene	22 Jun
Dwayne Evans	USA	58	20.22	2)	Eugene	22 Jun
Don Quarrie	Jam	51	20.22	1)	Montreal	26 Jul
Pietro Mennea	Ita	52	20.23	1)	Viareggio	14 Aug
Wardell Gilbreath	USA	54	20.27	1)	Tucson	01 May
Larry Jackson	USA	53	20.33	1)	Lincoln	15 May
Mark Lutz	USA	51	20.42	3)	Eugene	22 Jun
Dwayne Strozier	USA	57	20.43	2)	Tucson	01 May
Laverne Smith	USA		20.44	2)	Lincoln	15 May
Steve Riddick	USA	51	20.45	4)	Eugene	22 Jun

Hand timing:

Steve Williams	USA	53	19.9	1)	Gainesville	17 Apr
Harvey Glance	USA	57	20.1+	1)	Auburn	17 Apr
Stanley Harris	USA	56	20.2	2)	Gainesville	17 Apr
Bill Collins	USA	51	20.2*	1)	Houston	08 May
Hasely Crawford	Tri	50	20.2	1)	Lappeenranta	29 Jun
Reggie Jones	UDS	53	20.3	2)	Knoxville	08 May
Ainsley Armstrong	Tri	52	20.3	2)	Lappeenranta	29 Jun

Marks made with assisting wind:

Steve Riddick	USA	51	20.1	1)	Fort-de-France	02 May
Ed Preston	USA	55	20.2	1)	Wichita	28 May

+ = made during a 220 y. race.

4x100 metre relay (fully automatic timing)

Team	Members	Time	Place	Venue	Date
USA	(Glance, J.Jones, Hampton, Riddick)	38.33	1)	Montreal	31 Jul
GDR	(M.Kokot, Pfeifer, Kurrat, Thieme)	38.66	2)	Montreal	31 Jul
SU	(Aksinin, Kolyesnikov, Silovs, Borzov)	38.78	3)	Montreal	31 Jul
Pol	(Szierczynski, Woronin, Grzejszczak, Licznerski)	38.83	4)	Montreal	31 Jul
TV Wattenscheid FRG	(Bastians, Bieler, Steinmann, Borchert)	38.90	1)	München	29 May

1977

100 metres (fully automati timing)

Name	Nat	Born	Time		Place	Venue	Date
Silvio Leonard	Cub	55	9.98	A	1)	Guadalajara	11 Aug
Don Quarrie	Jam	51	10.12		1)	Westwood	11 Jun
Eugen Ray	GDR	57	10.12		1)	Helsinki	13 Aug
Houston McTear	USA	57	10.13		1)	Köln	22 Jun
Steve Williams	USA	53	10.13		1)	Düsseldorf	02 Sep
Harvey Glance	USA	57	10.16		1)h2	Tuscaloosa	13 May
Clancy Edwards	USA	55	10.18		1)	Westwood	30 Apr
Petar Petrov	Bul	55	10.19		2)	Sofia	20 Aug
Hasely Crawford	Tri	50	10.20	A	1)h1	Guadalajara	10 Aug
Osvaldo Lara	Cub	55	10.20	A	2)	Guadalajara	11 Aug

Marks made with assisting wind:

Name	Nat	Born	Time	Place	Venue	Date
Johnnie Jones	USA	58	10.08	1)	Austin	20 May
Eugen Ray	GDR	57	10.09	1)s1	Dresden	01 Jul
Bill Collins	USA	51	10.11	2)	Austin	20 May

Hand timing:

Name	Nat	Born	Time	Place	Venue	Date
Harvey Glance	USA	57	9.8	1)	Auburn	09 Apr
Johnnie Jones	USA	58	9.9	1)	Austin	02 Apr

200 metres (fully automatic timing)

Name	Nat	Born	Time		Place	Venue	Date
Silvio Leonard	Cub	55	20.08	A	1)	Guadalajara	12 Aug
Pietro Mennea	Ita	52	20.11		1)	Milano	02 Jul
Don Quarrie	Jam	51	20.11	A	2)	Guadalajara	12 Aug
Clancy Edwards	USA	55	20.13		1)	Westwood	14 May
Steve Williams	USA	53	20.31		2)	Kingston	13 May
Eugen Ray	GDR	57	20.37		1)	Dresden	07 Aug
Steve Riddick	USA	51	20.38		1)	Nice	21 Aug
Cliff Wiley	USA	55	20.41		1)	Lüdenscheid	30 Aug
Millard Hampton	USA	56	20.43		1)	Westwood	13 Mar
Harvey Glance	USA	57	20.47		1)	Tuscaloosa	14 May

Marks made with assisting wind:

Name	Nat	Born	Time	Place	Venue	Date
Derald Harris	USA	58	20.01	1)	San Jose	09 Apr
William Snoddy	USA	57	20.37	1)	Lawrence	21 May

Hand timing:

Name	Nat	Born	Time	Place	Venue	Date
Harvey Glance	USA	57	20.2	1)	Auburn	21 Mar

Mark made with assisting wind:

Name	Nat	Born	Time	Place	Venue	Date
Silvio Leonard	Cub	55	19.9	1)	Habana	22 May

4x100 metre relay (fully automatic timing)

Team	Members	Time	Place	Venue	Date
USA	(Collins, Riddick, Wiley, S.Williams)	38.03	1)	Düsseldorf	03 Sep
GDR	(Kokot, Ray, Kubeck, Thieme) (Europe I)	38.57	2)	Düsseldorf	03 Sep
Americas II	(R.da Silva/Bra, Leonard/Cub, Quarrie/Jam, Lara/Cub)	38.66	3)	Düsseldorf	03 Sep
SU	(Kolyesnikov, Aksinin, Silovs, Ignatyenko)	38.75	1)	Sofia	23 Aug
Pol	(Swierczynski, Licznerski, Nowosz, Tyszka)	38.78	1)	Warszawa	13 Jul
Ita	(Curini, Caravani, Farina, Rasori)	39.15	2)	Sofia	23 Aug

1978

100 metres (fully automatic timing)

Calcy Edwards	USA	55	10.07		1)	Eugene	02 Jun
Eddie Hart	USA	49	10.07	A	1)	Colorado Springs	30 Jul
Steve Williams	USA	53	10.07		1)	Zurich	16 Aug
Silvio Leonard	Cub	55	10.08		1)	Warszawa	19 Jun
Mel Lattany	USA	59	10.09	A	2)	Colorado Springs	30 Jul
Curtis Dickey	USA	56	10.11		2)	Eugene	02 Jun
Osvaldo Lara	Cub	55	10.11		2)	Medellín	16 Jul
Don Coleman	USA	51	10.11	A	3)	Colorado Springs	30 Jul
Mike Roberson	USA	56	10.11	A	4)	Colorado Springs	30 Jul
Harvey Glance	USA	57	10.15		1)h2	Knoxville	12 May
Allan Wells	UK	52	10.15		1)	Edinburgh	15 Jul

Marks made with assisting wind:

William Snoddy	USA	57	9.87		1)	Dallas	01 Apr
Cole Doty	Can	55	9.98		2)	Dallas	11 Apr
Pietro Mennea	Ita	52	9.99		1)	Bari	13 Sep
Don Quarrie	Jam	51	10.03		1)	Edmonton	07 Aug
Ray Brooks	USA	56	10.04		3)	Dallas	01 Apr
Jerome Deal	USA	58	10.06	A	1)	El Paso	06 May

Hand timing:

Harvey Glance	USA	57	9.9		1)	Auburn	22 Apr
Mike Roberson	USA	56	9.9		2)	Auburn	22 Apr
Ronald Desruelles	Bel	55	9.9		1)r1	Merksem	23 Ju

200 metres (fully automatic timing)

Clancy Edwards	USA	55	20.03		1)	Westwood	29 Apr
Silvio Leonard	Cub	55	20.06		1)r1	Warszawa	19 Jun
James Gilkes	Guy	52	20.14		1)	Ingelheim	12 Sep
Pietro Mennea	Ita	52	20.16		1)	Praha	01 Sep
James Sanford	USA	57	20.24		2)	Corvallis	20 May
Steve Williams	USA	53	20.26		1)r2	Zurich	16 Aug
William Snoddy	USA	57	20.27	A	1)	Colorado Springs	30 Jul
Don Quarrie	Jam	51	20.35		1)	Düsseldorf	06 Jul
Greg Foster	USA	58	20.40		3)	Corvallis	20 May
Larry Myricks	USA	56	20.44		1)	Macomb	27 May

Mark made with assisting wind:

Allan Wells	UK	52	20.12		1)	Edmonton	10 Aug

Hand timing:

Clancy Edwards	USA	55	20.0		1)	Tucson	04 Mar
Ray Brooks	USA	56	20.3		1)	Austin	13 May
Larry Myricks	USA	56	20.3	A	1)	México, D.F.	17 Jun

Mark made with assisting wind:

Don Quarrie	Jam	51	20.2		1)	Luxemburg	10 Sep

4x100 metre relay (fully automatic timing)

Tobias Striders			38.55	1	Tempe	27 May
(Abrahams/Pan, Simmons/USA, Quarrie/Jam, Gilkes/Guy)						
Pol	(Nowosz, Licznerski, Dunecki, Woronin)		38.58	1)	Praha	03 Sep
GDR	(Kokot, Ray, Prenzler, Thieme)		38.78	2)	Praha	03 Sep
SU	(Vladimirtsev, Kolyesnikov, Aksinin, Ignatyenko)		38.82	3)	Praha	03 Sep
Univ. of So. California		USA	38.85	1)	Westwood	29 Apr
(K.Williams, Mullins, Edwards, Sanford)						
Fra	(Pat. Barré, Pas. Barré, Sainte-Rose, Panzo)		38.90	4)	Praha	03 Sep

1979

100 metres (fully automatic timing)

Pietro Mennea	Ita	52	10.01	A	1)r1	México, D.F.	04 Sep
James Sanford	USA	57	10.07		1)	Walnut	16 Jun

Mike Roberson	USA	56	10.07	A	1)s1	México, D.F.	08 Sep
Silvio Leonard	Cub	55	10.11		1)	Kingston	11 May
Harvey Glance	USA	57	10.13		1)s1	San Juan	07 Jul
Clancy Edwards	USA	55	10.15		1)	Walnut	21 Apr
Don Coleman	USA	51	10.15		1)	Merksem	21 Jun
Mel Lattany	USA	59	10.16		1)	Tuscaloosa	20 Apr
Emmit King	USA	59	10.16		3)	Walnut	16 Jun
Marian Woronin	Pol	56	10.16		2)	Torino	04 Aug

Mark made with assisting wind:

Jerome Deal	USA	58	10.08	A	1)	El Paso	21 Apr

200 metres (fully automatic timing)

Pietro Mennea	Ita	52	19.72	A	1)	México, D.F.	12 Sep
James Mallard	USA	57	20.07		1)	Tuscaloosa	20 Apr
James Sanford	USA	57	20.19		1)	Westwood	28 Apr
Greg Foster	USA	58	20.20		2)	Westwood	28 Apr
Leszek Dunecki	Pol	56	20.24	A	2)	México, D.F.	12 Sep
Mel Lattany	USA	59	20.28		2)	Tuscaloosa	20 Apr
Dwayne Evans	USA	58	20.28		1)	Walnut	17 Jun
Clancy Edwards	USA	55	20.33		1T)	Walnut	21 Apr
James Gilkes	Guy	52	20.33		1)r2	Zurich	15 Aug
Silvio Leonard	Cub	55	20.34		1)	Montreal	26 Aug

Mark made with assisting wind:

Allan Wells	UK	52	20.19	1)	London	14 Sep

Questionable distance / wind assisted:

Willie Jackson	USA	59	20.16	1)r1	Stockton	11 May

Hand timing:

James Mallard	USA	57	19.8	1)	Tuscaloosa	13 May
Mel Lattany	USA	59	19.9	2)	Tuscaloosa	13 May
LaMonte King	USA	59	20.0	1)	San Jose	12 May

4x100 metre relay (fully automatic timing)

USOC South	USA	(Roberson, Glance, Collins, Lattany)	38.30 A	1)	Colorado Springs	30 Jul
	Ita	(Lazzer, Caravani, Grazioli, Mennea)	38.42 A	1)	México, D.F.	13 Sep
	Pol	(Zwolinski, Licznerski, Dunecki, Woronin)	38.47	1)	Torino	04 Aug
	GDR	(Kurrat, Ray, Prenzler, Thieme)	38.70	2)	Torino	04 Aug
America (Lara/Cub, Rocha dos Santos/Bra, Leonard/Cub, de Araújo/Bra)			38.70	1)	Montreal	25 Aug
	Fra	(Pat.Barr, Pas.Barr, Sainte-Rose, Panzo)	38.71	3)	Torino	04 Aug

1980

100 metres (fully automatic timing)

James Sanford	USA	57	10.02	1)	Westwood	11 May
Stanley Floyd	USA	61	10.07	1)	Austin	24 May
Allan Wells	UK	52	10.11	1)q1	Moskva	24 Jul
Mike Roberson	USA	56	10.12	2)	Austin	06 Jun
Petar Petrov	Bul	55	10.13	2)q1	Moskva	24 Jul
Harvey Glance	USA	57	10.14	1)s2	Eugene	22 Jun
Mel Lattany	USA	59	10.14	1)	Rieti	31 Aug
Silvio Leonard	Cub	55	10.15	1)	Bratislava	06 Jun
Calvin Smith	USA	61	10.17	2)	Austin	24 May
Eugen Ray	GDR	57	10.18	1)h1	Potsdam	10 May
Jerome Deal	USA	58	10.18	3)	Austin	24 May

Marks made with assisting wind:

James Sanford	USA	57	9.88	1)	Westwood	03 May
Allan Wells	UK	52	10.05	1)	Edinburgh	21 Jun
Harvey Glance	USA	57	10.07	1)	Walnut	19 Apr
Mike Roberson	USA	56	10.08	1)s2	Austin	06 Jun
Ellison Portis	USA		10.09	1)s1	Abilene	23 May

Unconfirmed automatic mark:

Andrey Prokofyev	SU	59	10.13		1)	Leningrad	03 Jun

Hand timing:

Aleksandr Aksinin	SU	54	9.9		1)h5	Leningrad	03 Jun

200 metres (fully automatic timing)

Pietro Mennea	Ita	52	19.96	1)	Barletta	17 Aug
LaMonte King	USA	59	20.08	1)	Walnut	15 Jun
Allan Wells	UK	52	20.21	2)	Moskva	28 Jul
James Sanford	USA	57	20.26	1)	Westwood	03 May
Steve Williams	USA	53	20.26	2)	Bruxelles	22 Aug
Don Quarrie	Jam	51	20.29	3)	Moskva	28 Jul
Silvio Leonard	Cub	55	20.30	4)	Moskva	28 Jul
James Mallard	USA	57	20.34	1)	Tuscaloosa	05 Apr
Efrem Coley	USA	59	20.35	1)	Austin	24 May
James Butler	USA	60	20.36	1)s2	Eugene	25 Jun

Marks made with assisting wind:

James Sanford	USA	57	19.94	1)s1	Austin	07 Jun
Mike Roberson	USA	56	19.95	1)h3	Austin	05 Jun
Allan Wells	UK	52	20.11	1)	Edinburgh	20 Jun
James Mallard	USA	57	20.18	1)h2	Austin	05 Jun
James Butler	USA	60	20.22	2)	Austin	07 Jun

Hand timing:

James Sanford	USA	57	19.7	A	1)	El Paso	19 Apr

4x100 metre relay (fully automatic timing)

SU	(Muravyov, Sidorov, Aksinin, Prokofyev)	38.26	1)	Moskva	01 Aug
Pol	(Zwolinski, Licznerski, Dunecki, Woronin)	38.33	2)	Moskva	01 Aug
USA	(W.Smith, Glance, F.Taylor, Floyd)	38.52	1)	Tokyo	20 Sep
Fra	(Richard, Pas.Barré, Pat.Barré, Panzo)	38.53	3)	Moskva	01 Aug
GDR	(Schlegel, Ray, Kurrat, Munkelt)	38.56	1)	Berlin	09 Jul

ALL TIME WORLD LIST OF BEST PERFORMERS AS AT THE END OF 1980

100 metres (fully automatic timing)

Jim Hines	USA	46	9.95	A	1)	México, D.F.	14 Oct 68
Silvio Leonard	Cub	55	9.98	A	1)	Guadalajara	11 Aug 77
Pietro Mennea	Ita	52	10.01	A	1)r1	México, D.F.	04 Sep 79
Charlie Greene	USA	44	10.02	A	1)q4	México, D.F.	13 Oct 68
James Sanford	USA	57	10.02		1)	Westwood	11 May 80
Lennox Miller	Jam	46	10.04	A	2)	México, D.F.	14 Oct 68
Steve Riddick	USA	51	10.05		1)	Zurich	20 Aug 75
Bob Hayes	USA	42	10.06		1)	Tokyo	15 Oct 64
Hasely Crawford	Tri	50	10.06		1)	Montreal	24 Jul 76

100 metres (fully automatic timing)

Pietro Mennea	Ita	52	19.72	A	1)	México, D.F.	12 Sep 79
Tommie Smith	USA	44	19.83	A	1)	México, D.F.	16 Oct 68
Don Quarrie	Jam	51	19.86	A	1)	Cali	03 Aug 71
John Carlos	USA	45	19.92	A	1)	Echo Summit	12 Sep 68
Valeriy Borzov	SU	49	20.00		1)	München	04 Sep 72
Clancy Edwards	USA	55	20.03		1)	Westwood	29 Apr 78
Peter Norman	Aus	42	20.06	A	2)	México, D.F.	16 Oct 68
Silvio Leonard	Cub	55	20.06		1)r1	Warszawa	19 Jun 78

James Mallard	USA	57	20.07	1)	Tuscaloosa	20 Apr 79
LaMonte King	USA	59	20.08	1)	Walnut	15 Jun 80

4x100 metres relay (fully automatic timing)

USA	(Collins, Riddick, Wiley, S.Williams)	38.03		1)	Düsseldorf	03 Sep 77
SU	(Muravyov, Sidorov, Aksinin, Prokofyev)	38.26		1)	Moskva	01 Aug 80
Pol	(Zwolinski, Licznerski, Dunecki, Woronin)	38.33		2)	Moskva	01 Aug 80
Jam	(Stewart, Fray, Forbes, L.Miller)	38.39	A	2)s1	México, D.F.	19 Oct 68
Cub	(Ramirez, Morales, Montes, Figuerola)	38.40	A	2)	México, D.F.	20 Oct 68

1981

100 metres (fully automatic timing)

Carl Lewis	USA	61	10.00	1)	Dallas	16 May
Mel Lattany	USA	59	10.04	1)	Athens, GA	11 Apr
James Sanford	USA	57	10.05	1)	Westwood	10 May
Stanley Floyd	USA	61	10.10	2)	Westwood	10 May
Jeff Phillips	USA	57	10.11	1)s3	Baton Rouge	05 Jun
Ron Brown	USA	61	10.15	2)s1	Baton Rouge	05 Jun
Colin Bradford	Jam	55	10.15	1)	Ciudad Bolivar	14 Aug
Allan Wells	UK	52	10.17	1)	Zagreb	15 Aug
Rudy Levarity	Bah	58	10.18	1)	College Station	25 Apr
Emmit King	USA	59	10.18	3)	Knoxville	23 May

Marks made with assisting wind:

Carl Lewis	USA	61	9.99	1)	Baton Rouge	05 Jun
Jeff Phillips	USA	57	10.00	2)	Baton Rouge	05 Jun
James Sanford	USA	57	10.03	1)	Syracuse	25 Jul
Dwayne Evans	USA	58	10.07	1)r1	Modesto	16 May
Ron Brown	USA	61	10.08	2)r1	Modesto	16 May

Hand timing:

Harvey Glance	USA	57	9.8	1)	Gainesville	28 Mar

200 metres (fully automatic timing)

James Sanford	USA	57	20.20	1)	Westwood	10 May
Mel Lattany	USA	59	20.21	1)	Roma	06 Sep
Allan Wells	UK	52	20.26	1)	Bruxelles	28 Aug
Frank Emmelmann	GDR	61	20.33	1)	Zagreb	16 Aug
Dwayne Evans	USA	58	20.34	2)	Westwood	10 May
LaMonte King	USA	59	20.36	1)	Stanford	23 May
Jeff Phillips	USA	57	20.36	1)	Sacramento	21 Jun
Eric Brown	USA	60	20.38	2)	Stanford	23 May
Stanley Floyd	USA	61	20.41	1)	Budapest	29 Jul
Lanoris Marshall	USA	60	20.46	3)	Westwood	10 May

Marks made with assisting wind:

Allan Wells	UK	52	20.15	1)	Berlin	21 Aug
Dwayne Evans	USA	58	20.20	1)	Baton Rouge	06 Jun
Frank Emmelmann	GDR	61	20.23	1)	Dresden	14 Jun
Erwyn Skamrahl	FRG	58	20.25	1)	Gelsenkirchen	19 Jul

Hand timing:

Paulo Correa	Bra	60	20.2	A	1)	La Paz	08 Nov
Peter Gandy	Aus	61	20.3		1)	Hobart	11 Jan

Mark made with assisting wind:

James Butler	USA	60	20.2	1)	Stillwater	28 Mar

4x100 metre relay (fully automitic timing)

	Pol	(Zwolinski, Licznerski, Dunecki, Woronin)	38.66	1)	Zagreb	15 Aug
Athletic Attic	USA	(Roberson, Myricks, W.Smith, Glance)	38.70	1)	Tempe	04 Apr
	USA	(Lattany, Ketchum, Grimes, C.Smith)	38.70	1)	Bucuresti	26 Jul
Europe/Poland		(Zwolinski, Licznerski, Dunecki, Woronin)	38.73	1)	Roma	05 Sep
	SU	(Shlyapnikov, Sidorov, Aksinin, Muravyov)	38.76	1)	Tbilisi	26 Jun
	GDR	(Hollender, Kübeck, Hoff, Emmelmann)	38.79	2)	Roma	05 Sep
	Fra	(Le Joncour, Petitbois, Richard, Panzo)	38.83	3)	Zagreb	15 Aug

1982

100 metres (fully automatic timing)

Carl Lewis	USA	61	10.00		1)r1	Modesto	15 May
Stanley Floyd	USA	61	10.03	A	1)	Provo	05 Jun
Calvin Smith	USA	61	10.05		1)	Indianapolis	25 Jul
Willie Gault	USA	60	10.10	A	2)	Provo	05 Jun
Mike Miller	USA	59	10.11	A	3)	Provo	05 Jun
Emmit King	USA	59	10.13		1)	Athens, GA	15 May
James Butler	USA	60	10.14	A	1)r2	Provo	05 Jun
Mel Lattany	USA	59	10.14		1)	Roma	14 Sep
Valentin Atanasov	Bul	61	10.15		1)	Sofia	14 Aug
Leandro Peñalver	Cub	61	10.16		1)	Habana	09 Aug

Marks made with assisting wind:

Calvin Smith	USA	61	9.91		1)	Karl-Marx-Stadt	09 Jul
Allan Wells	UK	52	10.02		1)	Brisbane	04 Oct
Ben Johnson	Can	61	10.05		2)	Brisbane	04 Oct
Cameron Sharp	UK	58	10.07		3)	Brisbane	04 Oct
Mike Miller	USA	59	10.08		1)	Lexington	17 Apr

Hand timing:

Jeff Phillips	USA	57	9.8		1)	Knoxville	22 May
Carl Lewis	USA	61	9.9		1)	Port-of-Spain	10 Jul
Mel Lattany	USA	59	9.9		1)	Rhede	01 Sep

Marks made with assisting wind:

Osvaldo Lara	Cub	55	9.7		1)	Santiago de Cuba	24 Feb
Silvio Leonard	Cub	55	9.8		2)	Santiago de Cuba	24 Feb

200 metres (fully automatic timing)

Mike Miller	USA	59	20.15	A	1)h2	Provo	02 Jun
Phillip Epps	USA	58	20.19		1)	College Station	20 Mar
Tony Sharpe	Can	61	20.22	A	1)	Colorado Springs	20 Jul
James Butler	USA	60	20.23	A	2)h2	Provo	02 Jun
Carl Lewis	USA	61	20.27		1T)	San Jose	17 Apr
Jeff Phillips	USA	57	20.27		1T)	San Jose	17 Apr
Calvin Smith	USA	61	20.31	A	1)h1	Provo	02 Jun
Eric Brown	USA	60	20.39	A	1)h3	Provo	02 Jun
Ronnie Taylor	USA	59	20.39	A	1)h4	Provo	02 Jun
Elliott Quow	USA	62	20.39	A	1)r2	Provo	04 Jun
Terron Wright	USA	58	20.39		2)	Karl-Marx-Stadt	10 Jul
Don Quarrie	Jam	51	20.39		1)	Lausanne	14 Jul
Clinton Davis	USA	65	20.39		1)	Barquisimeto	01 Aug

Marks made wth assisting wind:

James Butler	USA	60	20.07	A	1)	Provo	04 Jun
Calvin Smith	USA	61	20.20	A	2)	Provo	04 Jun
Eric Brown	USA	60	20.22	A	4)	Provo	04 Jun

Hand timing and wind assistance:

Perry Williams	USA		20.0		1)	Raleigh	09 Apr

4x100 metre relay (fully automatic timing)

USA	(Lattany, Floyd, C.Smith, Lewis)	38.13		1)	Zurich	18 Aug
GDR	(Schröder, Kübeck, Prenzler, Emmelmann)	38.29		2)	Karl-Marx-Stadt	09 Jul
Canada	(B.Johnson, Sharpe, D.Williams, S.Hinds)	38.43	A	1)	Colorado Springs	19 Jul
SU	(Yevgenyev, Sokolov, Aksinin, Sidorov)	38.56		2)	Indianapolis	02 Jul
FRG	(Zirkelbach, Haas, Klein, Skamrahl)	38.71		3)	Athinai	11 Sep

1983

100 metres (fully automatic timing)

Calvin Smith	USA	61	9.93	A	1)	Colorado Springs	03 Jul
Carl Lewis	USA	61	9.97		1)r1	Modesto	14 May

Mel Lattany	USA	59	10.03		2)	Zurich	24 Aug
Ron Brown	USA	61	10.06		3)	Zurich	24 Aug
Emmit King	USA	59	10.06		4)	Zurich	24 Aug
Leandro Peñalver	Cub	61	10.06		1)	Caracas	24 Aug
Darrell Green	USA	60	10.08		1)	San Angelo	13 Apr
Stanley Floyd	USA	61	10.13		1)	Houston	16 Apr
Allan Wells	UK	52	10.15		5)	Zurich	24 Aug
Christian Haas	FRG	58	10.16		1)s1	Bremen	24 Jun
Juan Nuñez	Dom	59	10.16		1)	Habana	22 Jul

Disqualified for doping offence:

Juan Nuñez	Dom	59	10.14		2)	Caracas	24 Aug

Marks made with assisting wind:

Carl Lewis	USA	61	9.93		1)	Walnut	24 Apr
Willie Gault	USA	60	9.95		1)	Knoxville	02 Apr
Mel Lattany	USA	59	9.95		1)	Athinai	07 May
Ron Brown	USA	61	10.01		2)	Walnut	24 Apr
Emmit King	USA	59	10.05		1)h1	Houston	02 Jun
Stefano Tilli	Ita	62	10.06		1)	Cagliari	09 Oct

Hand timing and assisting wind:

Willie Gault	USA	60	9.8	A	1)	El Paso	26 Mar
Mike Taylor	USA	65	9.8		1)	Shreveport	11 Apr
Mel Lattany	USA	59	9.8		1)r1	Paris	24 Jun

200 metres (fully automatic timing)

Carl Lewis	USA	61	19.75		1)	Indianapolis	19 Jun
Calvin Smith	USA	61	19.99		1)	Zurich	24 Aug
Larry Myricks	USA	56	20.03		2)	Indianapolis	19 Jun
Elliott Quow	USA	62	20.16		4)	Indianapolis	19 Jun
Mel Lattany	USA	59	20.22		1)	Berlin	17 Aug
Pietro Mennea	Ita	52	20.22		1)	Rieti	04 Sep
Bernie Jackson	USA	61	20.26		5)	Indianapolis	19 Jun
Desai Williams	Can	59	20.29	A	1)	Provo	21 May
Clinton Davis	USA	65	20.29		1)	University Park	26 Jun
James Butler	USA	60	20.32		6)	Indianapolis	19 Jun

Hand timing:

Wessel Oosthuizen	SA	61	20.1	A	1)	Germiston	29 Mar

Doubtful mark:

William Snoddy	USA	57	19.6*		1)	San Diego	07 Apr

4x100 metre relay (fully automatic timing)

USA	(King, Gault, C.Smith, Lewis)	37.86	1)	Helsinki	10 Aug
GDR	(Schröder, Bringmann, Prenzler, Emmelmann)	38.30	1)	Berlin	08 Jun
Ita	(Tilli, Simionato, Pavoni, Mennea)	38.37	2)	Helsinki	10 Aug
SU	(Prokofyev, Sidorov, Muravyov, Brizgin)	38.41	3)	Helsinki	10 Aug
Cub	(Peñalver, Leonard, Lara, Isalgué)	38.55	2)	Caracas	28 Aug

1984

100 metres (fully automatic timing)

Mel Lattany	USA	59	9.96		1)r1	Athens, GA	05 May
Carl Lewis	USA	61	9.99		1)r1	Houston	06 May
Marian Woronin	Pol	56	10.00		1)	Warszawa	09 Jun
Sam Draddy	USA	64	10.09		1)h2	Baton Rouge	12 May
Harvey Glance	USA	57	10.09		2)	Zurich	22 Aug
Calvin Smith	USA	61	10.11		1)r5	Walnut	25 Jul
Ron Brown	USA	61	10.12		2)	Walnut	29 Apr
Ben Johnson	Can	61	10.12		3)	Zurich	22 Aug
Osvaldo Lara	Cub	55	10.14		1)r1	Fürth	09 Jun
Leandro Peñalver	Cub	61	10.14		2)r1	Fürth	09 Jun

Marks made with assisting wind:

Calvin Smith	USA	61	9.94	1)	Sacramento	21 Jul
Ben Johnson	Can	61	10.01	1)	Winnipeg	30 Jun
Ron Brown	USA	61	10.05	2)r1	Modesto	12 May
Harvey Glance	USA	57	10.07	2)	Knoxville	14 Apr

Hand timing:

Paul Narracott	Aus	59	9.9	1)	Brisbane	04 Jan

200 metres (fully automatic timing)

Carl Lewis	USA	61	19.80	1)	Los Angeles	08 Aug
Kirk Baptiste	USA	63	19.96	2)	Los Angeles	08 Aug
Albert Robinson	USA	64	20.07	1)	Indianapolis	05 May
Pietro Mennea	Ita	52	20.07	1)	Brindisi	03 Oct
Thomas Jefferson	USA	62	20.26	3)	Los Angeles	08 Aug
Roy Martin	USA	66	20.28	1)q2	Los Angeles	19 Jun
João B. da Silva	Bra	63	20.30	4)	Los Angeles	08 Aug
James Butler	USA	60	20.31	1)	Roma	31 Aug
Calvin Smith	USA	61	20.33	1)q4	Los Angeles	19 Jun
Vladimir Muravyov	SU	59	20.34	1)	Moskva	18 Aug

Marks made with assisting wind:

Brady Crain	USA	56	20.09	1)	San Jose	09 Jun
Dwayne Evans	USA	58	20.21	1)r1	Walnut	29 Apr
Thomas Jefferson	USA	62	20.21	1)s2	San Jose	09 Jun
Dave Smith	Jam		20.22	1)	Bozeman	19 May

Hand timing:

Mike Conley	USA	62	20.0	1)h3	Austin	11 May

4x100 metres relay (fully automatic timing)

USA	(Graddy, R.Brown, C.Smith, Lewis)	37.83	1)	Los Angeles	11 Aug
SU	(Yevgenyev, Sokolov, Muravyov, Sidorov)	38.32	1)	Moskva	17 Aug
GDR	(Huber, Schröder, Prenzler, Emmelmann)	38.46	2)	Berlin	20 Jul
Jam	(A.Lawrence, Meghoo, Quarrie, R. Stewart)	38.62	2)	Los Angeles	11 Aug
Can	(B.Johnson, Sharpe, D.Williams, Mahorn)	38.62	2)	Köln	26 Aug

1985

100 metres (fully automatic timing)

Carl Lewis	USA	61	9.98	1)r1	Modesto	11 May
Ben Johnson	Can	61	10.00	1)	Canberra	04 Oct
Harvey Glance	USA	57	10.05	1)r1	Tampa	30 Mar
Frank Emmelmann	GDR	61	10.06	1)	Berlin	22 Sep
Terry Scott	USA	64	10.08	1)h3	Austin	30 May
Andrés Simon	Cub	61	10.10	1)	Habana	30 Mar
Darwin Cook	USA	62	10.10	2)r1	Modesto	11 May
Calvin Smith	USA	61	10.10	1)h1	Zurich	21 Aug
Kirk Baptiste	USA	63	10.11	1)	Indianapolis	15 Jun
Chidi Imo	Nig	65	10.11	2)	Canberra	04 Oct

Doubtful wind reading:

Ronald Desruelles	Bel	55	10.02	1)	Naimette-X.	11 May

Marks made with assisting wind:

Carl Lewis	USA	61	9.90	1)	Walnut	28 Apr
Andrés Simon	Cub	61	9.97	1)s1	Kobe	30 Aug

Hand timing:

Darwin Cook	USA	62	9.9	1)	Nice	16 Jul
Vladimir Krylov	SU	64	9.9	1)	Odessa	04 Sep

Mark made with assisting wind:

Elliott Hanna	USA	64	9.8	1)	Ames	04 May

200 metres (fully automatic timing)

Lorenzo Daniel	USA	66	20.07	1)	Starkville	18 May
Kirk Baptiste	USA	63	20.11	1)	Indianapolis	16 Jun
Roy Martin	USA	66	20.13	1)r1	Austin	11 May
Calvin Smith	USA	61	20.14	1)h3	Idianapolis	16 Jun
Mike Conley	USA	62	20.21	2)	Fayetteville	18 May
Frank Emmelmann	GDR	61	20.23	1)	Moskva	18 Aug
Joe DeLoach	USA	67	20.24	3)	Los Angeles	08 Jun
Daron Council	USA	64	20.29	2)	Starkville	18 May
Sam Graddy	USA	64	20.30	1)h1	Knoxville	10 May
Brady Crain	USA	56	20.32	4)	Indianapolis	16 Jun

Marks made with assisting wind:

Kirk Baptiste	USA	63	20.03	1)	Austin	31 May
Mike Conley	USA	62	20.12	1)h3	Austin	29 May
Brady Crain	USA	56	20.16	2)r1	Walnut	28 Apr

Hand time and wind assistance:

Desmond Ross	USA	61	19.8	1)	Manhattan, KS	11 May
Chidi Imo	Nig	65	19.9	2)	Manhattan, KS	11 May
Leroy Dixson	USA	63	20.0	3)	Manhattan, KS	11 May
Anthony Small	Can	64	20.0	4)	Manhattan, KS	11 May

4x100 metre relay (fully automatic timing)

USA	(Glance, Baptiste, C.Smith, Evans)	38.10	1)	Canberra	05 Oct
SU	(Shlyapnikov, Semyonov,Yevgenyev, Muravyov)	38.28	1)	Moskva	17 Aug
America	(D.Williams/Can, Simon/Cub, R.da Silva/Bra, B.Johnson/Can)	38.31	2)	Canberra	05 Oct
GDR	(Truppel, Bringmann, Heimrath, Emmelmann)	38.39	4)	Canberra	05 Oct
Cub	(Chacon, Peñalver, Querol, Simon)	38.76	1)	Kobe	04 Sep
Europe/Ita	(Ullo, Tilli, Pavoni, Simionato)	38.76	5)	Canberra	05 Oct

1986

100 metres (fully automatic timing)

Ben Johnson	Can	61	9.95	1)r1	Moskva	09 Jul
Chidi Imo	Nig	63	10.00	1)r1	Berlin	15 Aug
Robson C. da Silva	Bra	64	10.02	1)	Habana	27 Sep
Linford Christie	UK	60	10.04	1)	Madrid	04 Jun
Carl Lewis	USA	61	10.06	3)r1	Moskva	09 Jul
Emmit King	USA	59	10.07	1)	Sevilla	24 May
Lorenzo Daniel	USA	66	10.08	1)h2	Knoxville	17 May
Harvey Glance	USA	57	10.09	1)	Dresden	03 Jul
Anthoine Richard	Fra	60	10.09	1)	Aix-les-Bains	09 Aug
Thomas Schröder	GDR	62	10.10	1)	Jena	27 Jun
Stanley Kerr	USA	67	10.10	1)	Towson, MD	28 jun

Marks made with assisting wind:

Carl Lewis	USA	61	9.91	1)	Eugene	20 Jun
Roy Martin	USA	66	9.97	1)r1	Houston	18 May
Lorenzo Daniel	USA	66	10.00	1)	Knoxville	18 May

Doubtful wind reading:

Victor Brizgin	SU	62	10.03	1)h1	Leningrad	07 Jun

Hand timing and with assistance:

Alrick Munroe	Jam	60	9.9	1)	Plainview, TX	22 Mar

200 metres (fully automatic timing)

Floyd Heard	USA	66	20.12	1)r1	Moskva	07 Jul
Roy Martin	USA	66	20.16	1)	Dallas	12 Apr
Lorenzo Daniel	USA	66	20.17	1)	Atlanta	20 Apr
John Dinam	Aus	59	20.19	1)	Canberra	06 Mar
Mike Timpson	USA	67	20.23	1)	University Park	16 May
Kirk Baptiste	USA	63	20.25	1)	Budapest	11 Aug

Robson C. da Silva	Bra	64	20.28		1)	Madrid	04 Jun
Calvin Smith	USA	61	20.29		1)	Paris	22 Jul
Harvey McSwain	USA	63	20.30		1)	Knoxville	24 May
Wallace Spearmon	USA	62	20.33		2)	Knoxville	24May

Marks made with assisting wind:

Roy Martin	USA	66	19.86		1)r2	Houston	18 May
Floyd Heard	USA	66	20.03		1)	Eugene	21 Jun
Dwayne Evans	USA	58	20.09		1)	Walnut	01 Jun
Stanley Kerr	USA	67	20.10		2)r2	Houston	18 May
Lorenzo Daniel	USA	66	20.11		1)	Knoxville	18 May
Kirk Baptiste	USA	63	20.14		3)	Eugene	21 Jun

Hand timing:

Carl Lewis	USA	61	20.1		1)	San Jose	31 May

4x100 metre relay (fully automatic timing)

USA	(McRae, Heard, Glance, Lewis)	37.98	1)	Moskva	09 Jul
SU	(Yevgenyev, Yushmanov, Muravyov, Brizgin)	38.19	2)	Moskva	09 Jul
GDR	(Schlegel, Bringmann, Prenzler, Schröder)	38.60	1)	Dresden	03 Jul
Hun	(Karaffa, Nagy, Tatár, Kovács)	38.67	1)	Budapest	11 Aug
UK	(Bunney, Thompson, McFarlane, Christie)	38.71	3)	Stuttgart	31 Aug

1987

100 metres (Fully automatic timing)

Carl Lewis	USA	61	9.93		1)	Roma	30 Aug
Linford Christie	UK	60	10.03		1)r1	Budapest	06 Jul
Mark Witherspoon	USA	63	10.04		1)	San Jose	27 Jun
Andrés Simón	Cub	61	10.06		1)	Habana	01 Aug
Lee McRae	USA	66	10.07		1)	Zagreb	14 Jul
Calvin Smith	USA	61	10.07		2)	Zurich	19 Aug
Ray Stewart	Jam	65	10.08		2)	Roma	30 Aug
Max Morinière	Fra	64	10.09		1)	Lyon	03 Jul
Attila Kovács	Hun	60	10.09		1)	Miskolc	20 Aug
Leandro Peñalver	Cub	61	10.10		2)	Habana	01 Aug

Won race but was posthumously disqualified for doping offence:

Ben Johnson	Can	61	9.83		-)	Roma	30 Aug

Marks made with assisting wind:

Ray Stewart	Jam	65	9.89		1)s1	Indianapolis	09 Aug
Mark Witherspoon	USA	63	9.91		2)s1	Indianapolis	09 Aug
Chidi Imo	Nig	63	9.92	A	1)s1	Nairobi	08 Aug
Leandro Peñalver	Cub	61	10.00		1)s2	Indianapolis	09 Aug

Hand timing and wind assistance:

Ben Johnson	Can	61	9.7		1)	Perth	24 Jan
Ray Stewart	Jam	65	9.8		1)	Austin	04 Apr

200 metres (fully automatic timing)

Carl Lewis	USA	61	19.92		1)	Madrid	04 Jun
Floyd Heard	USA	66	19.95		1)	Lubbock	17 May
Dwayne Evans	USA	58	20.08	A	1)	Albuquerque	13 Jun
Calvin Smith	USA	61	20.10		1)	Zurich	19 Aug
Attila Kovács	Hun	60	20.11		1)	Miskolc	21 Aug
Gilles Quenéhervé	Fra	66	20.16		2)	Roma	03 Sep
John Regis	UK	66	20.18		3)	Roma	03 Sep
Robson C. da Silva	Bra	64	20.20		1)	Moskva	07 Jun
Harvey McSwain	USA	63	20.21	A	2)	Albuquerque	13 Jun
Vladimir Krylov	SU	64	20.23		5)	Roma	03 Sep

Mark made with assisting wind:

Lorenzo Daniel	USA	6	19.88		1)	Tuscaloosa	17 May

Hand timing and wind assistance:

Daron Council	USA	64	20.0	1)	Dallas	11 Apr
Roy Martin	USA	66	20.0	2)	Dallas	11 Apr

4x100 metre relay (fully automatic timing)

USA	(McRae, L. McNeill, Glance, Lewis)	37.90	1)	Roma	06 Sep
SU	(Yevgenyev, Brizgin, Muravyov, Krylov)	38.02	2)	Roma	06 Sep
Jam	(Mair, A. Smith, Wright, Stewart)	38.41	3)	Roma	06 Sep
Can	(B.Johnson, Mahorn, D.Williams, Sharpe)	38.49	2)	Zurich	19 Aug
Cub	(Chacon, Peñalver, Querol, Simón)	38.55	1)	Praha	23 Jun
FRG	(Haas, Westhagemann, Klein, Dobeleit)	38.55	2)	Berlin	21 Aug

Finished 4th but lead-off man Ben Johnson was posthumously disqualified for doping offence:

Can	(Johnson, Mahorn, D.Williams, Dwyer)	38.47	-)	Roma	06 Sep

1988

100 metres (fully automatic timing)

Carl Lewis	USA	61	9.92		1)	Seoul	24 Sep
Calvin Smith	USA	61	9.97		2)r1	Zurich	17 Aug
Linford Christie	UK	60	9.97		2)	Seoul	24 Sep
Ben Johnson	Can	61	9.98	A	1)r1	Sestriere	11 Aug
Robson C. da Silva	Bra	64	10.00	A	1)h3	México, D.F.	22 Jul
Joe DeLoach	USA	67	10.03		1)	Eugene	04 Jun
Dennis Mitchell	USA	66	10.03		1)r1	Lausanne	24 Jun
Emmit King	USA	59	10.04		1)	Tampa	17 Jun
Chidi Imo	Nig	63	10.04		4)r1	Zurich	17 Aug
Johan Rossouw	SA	65	10.06	A	1)	Johannesburg	23 Apr

Disqualified for doping offence:

Ben Johnson	Can	61	9.79	-)	Seoul	24 Sep

Marks made with assisting wind:

Carl Lewis	USA	61	9.78	1)	Indianapolis	16 Jul
Dennis Mitchell	USA	66	9.86	2)	Indianapolis	16 Jul
Calvin Smith	USA	61	9.87	1)s2	Indianapolis	16 Jul
Albert Robinson	USA	64	9.88	4)	Indianapolis	16 Jul
Joe DeLoach	USA	67	9.90	5)	Indianapolis	16 Jul
Ben Johnson	Can	61	9.90	1)	Ottawa	06 Aug
Mike Marsh	USA	67	9.94	6)	Indianapolis	16 Jul

Hand timing:

Iziaq Adeyanju	Nig	59	9.9	1)	Bauchi	02 Jul
Olapade Adenike	Nig	69	9.9	2)	Bauchi	02 Jul
Vitaliy Savin	SU	66	9.9	1)	Vladivostok	13 Sep

Mark made with assisting wind:

Ricardo Chacon	Cub	63	9.8	1)	Caracas	24 Jun

200 metres (fully automatic timing)

Joe DeLoach	USA	67	19.75	1)	Seoul	28 Sep
Carl Lewis	USA	61	19.79	2)	Seoul	28 Sep
Lorenzo Daniel	USA	66	19.87	1)	Eugene	03 Jun
Robson C. da Silva	Bra	64	20.04	3)	Seoul	28 Sep
Roy Martin	USA	66	20.05	3)	Indianapolis	20 Jul
Albert Robinson	USA	64	20.05	4)	Indianapolis	20 Jul
Michael Johnson	USA	67	20.07	2)	Austin	15 May
Calvin Smith	USA	61	20.08	2)	Zurich	17 Aug
Linford Christie	UK	60	20.09	4)	Seoul	28 Sep
Henry Thomas	USA	67	20.18	1)	Eagle Rock	14 May

Mark made with assisting wind:

Cyprean Enweani	Can	64	20.05	A	1)	Calgary	03 Jul

4x100 metre relay (fully automatic timing)

SU	(Brizgin, Krylov, Muravyov, Savin)	38.19	1)	Seoul	01 Oct
UK	(Bunney, Regis, McFarlane, Christie)	38.28	2)	Seoul	01 Oct
Fra	(Marie-Rose, Sangouma, Quenéhervé, Morinière)	38.40	3)	Seoul	01 Oct
Jam	(Faulknor, Meghoo, Bright, Mair)	38.47	4)	Seoul	01 Oct
Cub	(Simón, Peñalver, Querol, Jefferson)	38.48	1)	Habana	30 Jul

1989

100 metres (fully automatic timing)

Leroy Burrell	USA	67	9.94		1)	Houston	16 Jun
Ray Stewart	Jam	65	9.97		1)	Waco	20 May
Frank Fredericks	Nam	67	10.02	A	1)	Provo	27 May
Dennis Mitchell	USA	66	10.03		2)	Houston	16 Jun
Andre Cason	USA	69	10.04		3)	Houston	16 Jun
Carl Lewis	USA	61	10.05		1)	Villeneuve d'Ascq	25 Jun
Calvin Smith	USA	61	10.05		1)	Oslo	01 Jul
Mike Marsh	USA	67	10.07		2)	Gainesville	08 Apr
Linford Christie	UK	60	10.10		1)	Barcelona	08 Sep
Sven Matthes	GDR	69	10.11		1)	Rostock	22 Jun
Marks made with assisting wind:							
Ray Stewart	Jam	65	9.90		1)	Vigo	30 Jun
Joe DeLoach	USA	67	9.97		2)	Walnut	22 Apr
Daron Council	USA	64	9.98		1)h4	Houston	15 Jun
Dennis Mitchell	USA	66	10.00		1)h2	Houston	15 Jun
Tim Jackson	Aus	69	10.00		1)	Sydney	02 Dec
Hand timing:							
Vitaliy Savin	SU	66	9.9		1)	Alma-Ata	29 May

200 metres (fully automatic timing)

Robson C. da Silva	Bra	64	19.96		1)	Bruxelles	25 Aug
Dennis Mitchell	USA	66	20.09	A	1)	Provo	02 Jun
Floyd Heard	USA	66	20.09		1)	Houston	17 Jun
Mark Witherspoon	USA	63	20.12		2)	Houston	17 Jun
Joe DeLoach	USA	67	20.13		1)	Abymes	07 May
Danny Everett	USA	66	20.17		1)	Bern	29 Aug
Daniel Sangouma	Fra	65	20.20		1)	Casablanca	18 Jul
Gilles Quenéhervé	Fra	66	20.21		1)	Genève	15 Jul
Félix Stevens	Cub	64	20.24		1)	Sofia	07 Jul
James Butler	USA	60	20.25		2)	Bern	29 Aug
Marks made with assisting wind:							
Michael Johnson	USA	67	20.06		1)	Austin	25 Mar
Frank Fredericks	Nam	67	20.09	A	1)	Albuquerque	20 May
Hand timing:							
Davidson Ezinwa	Nig	71	19.9		1)	Bauchi	18 Mar
Mark made with assisting wind:							
Robson C. da Silva	Bra	64	19.7	A	1)	Bogota	13 Aug

4x100 metre relay (fully automatic timing)

Texas Christian Univ.		38.23 A	1)	Provo	02 Jun
USA/Jam	(Porter/USA, A.Smith/Jam, Sholars/USA, Stewart/Jam)				
USA	(Cason, Dees, Council, Watkins)	38.29	1)	Barcelona	09 Sep
UK	(Callender, Regis, Adam, Christie)	38.34	2)	Barcelona	09 Sep
Fra	(Morinière, Sangouma, Quenéhervé, Marie-Rose)	38.46	2)	Gateshead	05 Aug
Africa	(M'Baye/Sen, Adeniken/Nig, Imo/Nig, Ezinwa/Nig)	38.81	4)	Barcelona	09 Sep
GDR	(Lassler, Matthes, Heimrath, Görmer)	38.84	1)	Bryansk	14 Jul
FRG	(Schütz, Maul, Klein, Zügel)	38.92	1)r2	Ingolstadt	26 Jul

1990

100 metres (fully automatic timing)

Leroy Burrell	USA	67	9.96		1)	Villeneuve d'Ascq	29 Jun
Linford Christie	UK	60	10.02		1)s2	Auckland	28 Jan
Daniel Sangouma	Fra	65	10.02		2)	Villeneuve d'Ascq	29 Jun
Calvin Smith	USA	61	10.04	A	2)r1	Sestriere	08 Aug
Davidson Ezinwa	Nig	71	10.05		1)	Bauchi	03 Jan
Mark Witherspoon	USA	63	10.05		1)	Sevilla	30 May
Carl Lewis	USA	61	10.05		1)	Norwalk	15 Jun
Patrick Williams	Jam	65	10.06		1)	Modesto	05 May
Mike Marsh	USA	67	10.08	A	3)r2	Sestriere	08 Aug
John Drummond	USA	68	10.10		1)	Arlington	14 Apr
Olapade Adeniken	Nig	69	10.10		1)	Malmö	07 Aug

Marks made with assisting wind:

Linford Christie	UK	60	9.93		1)	Auckland	28 Jan
Leroy Burrell	USA	67	9.94		1)	College Station	19 May

Hand timing (doubtful):

Osmond Ezinwa	Nig	71	9.8		2)h1	Bauchi	02 Jan

200 metres (fully automatic timing)

Michael Johnson	USA	67	19.85		1)	Edinburgh	06 Jul
Danny Everett	USA	66	20.08		2)	Norwalk	16 Jun
John Regis	UK	66	20.11		1)	Split	30 Aug
Leroy Burrell	USA	67	20.14		2)	Barcelona	16 Jul
Robson C. da Silva	Bra	64	20.23		3)	Barcelona	16 Jul
Floyd Heard	USA	66	20.27		2)	Athinai	07 Sep
Davidson Ezinwa	Nig	71	20.30		1)h1	Bauchi	03 Jan
Jean-Charles Trouabal	Fra	65	20.31		2)	Split	30 Aug
Frank Fredericks	Nam	67	20.32		2)	Durham	02 Jun
Dennis Mitchell	USA	66	20.33		3)	Zurich	15 Aug
Linford Christie	UK	60	20.33		3)	Split	30 Aug
Tshakile Nzimande	SA	61	20.33	A	1)	Bloemfontein	30 Oct

Marks made with assisting wind:

Leroy Burrell	USA	67	19.61		1)	College Station	19 May
Marcus Adam	UK	68	20.10		1)	Auckland	01 Feb
Andre Cason	USA	69	20.11		3)	College Station	19 May
Olapade Adeniken	Nig	69	20.18	A	1)	Fort Collins	19 May
Frank Fredericks	Nam	67	20.20	A	2)	Fort Collins	19 May

Hand timing:

Kevin Braunskill	USA	69	19.9		1)	Tucson	05 May
John Regis	UK	66	20.1		1)	Nicosia	30 May

Mark made with assisting wind:

Davidson Ezinwa	Nig	71	20.0		1)	Walnut	28 Apr

4x100 metre relay (fully automatic timing)

	Fra	(Morinière, Sangouma, Trouabal, Marie-Rose)	37.79	1)	Split	01 Sep
Santa Monica TC	USA	(Witherspoon, Burrell, Heard, Lewis)	37.93	1)	Barcelona	16 Jul
	UK	(Braithwaite, Regis, Adam, Christie)	37.98	2)	Split	01 Sep
	Ita	(Longo, Madonia, Floris, Tilli)	38.39	3)	Split	01 Sep
	USA	(Marsh, Council, Cason, Mitchell)	38.45	1)	Seattle	26 Jul
	SU	(Zharov, Krylov, Fatun, Goremykin)	38.46	4)	Split	01 Sep

1991

100 metres (fully automatic timing)

Carl Lewis	USA	61	9.86		1)	Tokyo	25 Aug
Leroy Burrell	USA	67	9.88		2)	Tokyo	25 Aug
Dennis Mitchell	USA	66	9.91		3)	Tokyo	25 Aug

Linford Christie	UK	60	9.92		4)	Tokyo	25 Aug
Frank Fredericks	Nam	67	9.95		5)	Tokyo	25 Aug
Ray Stewart	Jam	65	9.96		6)	Tokyo	25 Aug
Andre Cason	USA	69	9.99		1)r3	Koblenz	11 Sep
Chidi Imo	Nig	63	10.03		1)s2	Lagos	02 Aug
Davidson Ezinwa	Nig	71	10.04		2)s2	Lagos	02 Aug
Bruny Surin	Can	67	10.07		3)s1	Tokyo	25 Aug

Marks made with assisting wind:

Carl Lewis	USA	61	9.80	1)q2	Tokyo	24 Aug
Frank Fredericks	Nam	67	9.89	1)q4	Tokyo	24 Aug
Linford Christie	UK	60	9.90	2)q2	Tokyo	24 Aug

Hand timing:

Salaam Gariba	Gha	69	9.9		1)	Atlanta	06 Apr
Kennedy Ondiek	Ken	66	9.9	A	1)	Nairobi	27 Jul

200 metres (fully automatic timing)

Michael Johnson	USA	67	19.88	1)	Barcelona	20 Sep
Frank Fredericks	Nam	67	20.08	1)	Roma	17 Jul
John Regis	UK	66	20.12	1)	Lausanne	10 Jul
Danny Everett	USA	66	20.13	1)	New York	20 Jul
Robson C. da Silva	Bra	64	20.15	1)	Habana	08 Aug
Atlee Mahorn	Can	65	20.17	1)q1	Tokyo	26 Aug
Jimmy French	USA	70	20.20	1)h2	Fayetteville	11 May
Nikolay Antonov	SU	68	20.20	2)q3	Tokyo	26 Aug
Thomas Jefferson	USA	62	20.21	2)	New York	20 Jul
Jean-Charles Trouabal	Fra	65	20.30	1)	Dijon	28 Jul
Olapade Adeniken	Nig	69	20.30	3)q4	Tokyo	26 Aug

Marks made with assisting wind:

Frank Fredericks	Nam	67	19.90	1)	Eugene	01 Jun
Leroy Burrell	USA	67	20.02	1)	San Jose	25 May
Olapade Adeniken	Nig	69	20.09	2)	Eugene	01 Jun
Jimmy French	USA	70	20.15	3)	Eugene	01 Jun

Hand timing:

Frank Fredericks	Nam	67	20.0	A	1)	Windhoek	27 Jul
Joseph Gikonyo	Ken	65	20.0	A	1)	Nairobi	27 Jul

4x100 metre relay (fully automatic timing)

USA	(Cason, Burrell, Mitchell, Lewis)	37.50	1)	Tokyo	01 Sep
Fra	(Morinière, Sangouma, Trouabal, Marie-Rose)	37.87	2)	Tokyo	01 Sep
UK	(Jarrett, Regis, Braithwaite, Christie)	38.09	3)	Tokyo	01 Sep
Nig	(Ogbeide, Adeniken, Omagbemi, D.Ezinwa)	38.43	4)	Tokyo	01 Sep
Jam	(Green, Stewart, Watson, Mair)	38.45	3)h1	Tokyo	31 Aug

1992

100 metres (fully automatic timing)

Mike Marsh	USA	67	9.93	1)r1	Walnut	18 Apr
Davidson Ezinwa	Nig	71	9.96	2)r1	Walnut	18 Apr
Linford Christie	UK	60	9.96	1)	Barcelona	01 Aug
Olapade Adeniken	Nig	69	9.97	1)	Austin	04 Apr
Leroy Burrell	USA	67	9.97	1)s1	Barcelona	01 Aug
Frank Fredericks	Nam	67	10.02	2)	Barcelona	01 Aug
Dennis Mitchell	USA	66	10.04	3)	Barcelona	01 Aug
Bruny Surin	Can	67	10.05	1)	Salamanca	13 Jul
Ray Stewart	Jam	65	10.06	1)s	Kingston	03 Jul
Carl Lewis	USA	61	10.07	1)r1	Zurich	19 Aug

Doubtful wind reading:

Davidson Ezinwa	Nig	71	9.91	1)	Azusa	11 Apr

Marks made with assisting wind:

Andre Cason	USA	69	9.88	1)r1	Modesto	16 May

Frank Kredericks	Nam	67	9.91	1)	Villeneuve d'Ascq	06 Jul
Vitaliy Savin	Kaz	66	9.94	1)	Moskva	22 Jun
Dennis Mitchell	USA	66	9.94	2)	Villeneuve d'Ascq	06 Jul
Carl Lewis	USA	61	9.95	2)	København	25 Aug
Leroy Burrell	USA	67	9.96	2)r1	Modesto	16 May

Rolling start and wind assisted:

Dennis Mitchell	USA	66	9.92	1)	København	25 Aug

Hand timing:

Bruny Surin	Can	67	9.9	1)	Caorle	11 Jul

200 metres (fully automatic timing)

Mike Marsh	USA	67	19.73	1)s1	Barcelona	05 Aug
Michael Johnson	USA	67	19.79	1)	New Orleans	28 Jun
Frank Fredericks	Nam	67	19.97	2)r1	Zurich	19 Aug
Michael Bates	USA	69	20.01	3)r1	Zurich	19 Aug
John Regis	UK	66	20.09	2)s1	Barcelona	05 Aug
Olapade Adeniken	Nig	69	20.11	1)	Austin	06 Jun
Leroy Burrell	USA	67	20.12	1)s1	New Orleans	27 Jun
Mark Witherspoon	USA	63	20.13	2)r1	Austin	09 May
Bryan Bridgewater	USA	70	20.15	1)	San Angelo	30 May
Carl Lewis	USA	61	20.15	4)	New Orleans	28 Jun
Robson C. da Silva	Bra	64	20.15	3)s1	Barcelona	05 Aug

Marks made with assisting wind:

James Jett	USA	70	19.91	1)	Morgantown	18 Apr
Chris Nelloms	USA	71	19.94	1)	Minneapolis	23 May
Olapade Adeniken	Nig	69	20.00 A	1)	Air Force Academy	23 May

4x100 metre relay (fully automatic timing)

USA	(Marsh, Burrell, Mitchell, Lewis)	37.40	1)	Barcelona	08 Aug
Nig	(Kayode, Imo, Adeniken, D.Ezinwa)	37.98	2)	Barcelona	08 Aug
Cub	(Simón, Lamela, Isasi, Aguilera)	38.00	3)	Barcelona	08 Aug
UK	(Adam, Jarrett, Regis, Christie)	38.08	4)	Barcelona	08 Aug
CIS (formerly SU)	(Galkin, Ivanov, Fedoriv, Savin)	38.17	5)	Barcelona	08 Aug
Can	(B.Johnson, Gilbert, Ogilvie, Surin)	38.62	1)	Nice	15 Jul

1993

100 metres (fully automatic timing)

Linford Christie	UK	60	9.87	1)	Stuttgart	15 Aug
Andre Cason	USA	69	9.92	2)	Stuttgart	15 Aug
Daniel Effiong	Nig	72	9.98	2)s1	Stuttgart	15 Aug
Dennis Mitchell	USA	66	9.99	3)	Stuttgart	15 Aug
Leroy Burrell	USA	67	10.02	1)r1	Zurich	04 Aug
Carl Lewis	USA	61	10.02	3)s1	Stuttgart	15 Aug
Bruny Surin	Can	67	10.02	5)	Stuttgart	15 Aug
Frank Fredericks	Nam	67	10.03	6)	Stuttgart	15 Aug
Jon Drummond	USA	68	10.03	1)r1	Rieti	05 Sep
Calvin Smith	USA	61	10.06	2)	Edinburgh	02 Jul

Marks made with assisting wind:

Andre Cason	USA	69	9.79	1)h4	Eugene	16 Jun
Leroy Burrell	USA	67	9.85	2)h4	Eugene	16 Jun
Dennis Mitchell	USA	66	9.85	2)	Eugene	17 Jun
Carl Lewis	USA	61	9.90	3)	Eugene	17 Jun
Jon Drummond	USA	68	9.92	3)h4	Eugene	16 Jun
Mike Marsh	USA	67	9.97	1T)	Austin	08 May
Daniel Effiong	Nig	72	9.97	1T)	Austin	08 May

Hand timing:

Kestytis Klimas	Lit	69	9.9	1)	Kaunas	22 May
Kennedy Ondieki	Ken	66	9.9 A	1)	Nairobi	28 Jul

Doubtful timing:

Orlando Parker	USA	72	9.7	1)	Auburn	01 May

200 metres (fully automatic timing)

Frank Fredericks	Nam	67	19.85	1)	Stuttgart	20 Aug
John Regis	UK	66	19.94	2)	Stuttgart	20 Aug
Carl Lewis	USA	61	19.99	1)r1	Lausanne	07 Jul
Mike Marsh	USA	67	20.04	1)s1	Eugene	18 Jun
Michael Johnson	USA	67	20.06	2)r1	Lausanne	07 Jun
Bryan Bridgwater	USA	70	20.11	1)	Abilene	29 May
Olapade Adeniken	Nig	69	20.12	1)	Bratislava	01 Jun
Joe DeLoach	USA	67	20.15	1)h4	Eugene	17 Jun
Daniel Effiong	Nig	72	20.15	1)r1	Zurich	04 Aug
Robson C. da Silva	Bra	64	20.16	3)r1	Lausanne	07 Jul

Mark made with assisting wind:

Mike Marsh	USA	67	19.97	1)	Eugene	19 Jun

4x100 metre relay (fully automatic timing)

USA	(Drummond, Cason, D.Mitchell, Burrell)	37.40	1)s1	Stuttgart	21 Aug
UK	(C.Jackson, Jarrett, Regis, Christie)	37.77	2)	Stuttgart	22 Aug
Can	(Esmie, Gilbert, Surin, Mahorn)	37.83	3)	Stuttgart	22 Aug
Commonwealth	(M.Adam/UK, Jarrett/UK, Regis/UK R.Stewart/Jam)	38.37	2)	Walnut	17 Apr
Cub	(A.Simón, I. Garcia, Isasi, Aguilera)	38.39	4)	Stuttgart	22 Aug
Aus	(Henderson, D.Marsh, Capobianco, T.Jackson)	38.46	4)s1	Stuttgart	21 Aug

1994

100 metres (fully automatic timing)

Leroy Burrell	USA	67	9.85		1)	Lausanne	06 Jul
Linford Christie	UK	60	9.91		1)	Victoria	23 Aug
Davidson Ezinwa	Nig	71	9.94		1)	Linz	04 Jul
Dennis Mitchell	USA	66	9.94		1)	Oslo	22 Jul
Olapade Adeniken	Nig	69	9.95	A	1)r1	El Paso	16 Apr
Andre Cason	USA	69	9.98		1)h4	Knoxville	15 Jun
Jon Drummond	USA	68	9.99		2)	Oslo	22 Jul
Mike Marsh	USA	67	10.00		1)	Walnut	17 Apr
Bode Osagiobare	Nig	70	10.01	A	2)r1	El Paso	16 Apr
Donovan Bailey	Can	67	10.03		1)	Duisburg	12 Jun

Wind gauge illegally placed (on outside of track):

Tim Montgomary	USA	75	9.96	1)	Odessa, TX	21 May
Daniel Effiong	Nig	72	9.98	2)	Odessa, TX	21 May

Mark made with assisting wind:

Daniel Effiong	Nig	72	9.94	2)	Austin	09 Apr

Disqualified for doping offence:

Horace Dove-Edwin	SLE	67	10.02	2)	Victoria	23 Aug

Hand timing:

Anvar Kuchmuradov	Uzb	70	9.9	1)	Tashkent	05 May
Vladislav Dologodin	Ukr	72	9.9	1)	Kharkov	13 May

200 metters (fully automatic wind)

John Regis	UK	66	19.87	A	1)	Sestriere	31 Jul
Michael Johnson	USA	67	19.94		1)	Monaco	02 Aug
Frank Fredericks	Nam	67	19.97	A	2)	Sestriere	31 Jul
Daniel Effiong	Nig	72	20.10		1)	San Jose	28 May
Jeff Williams	USA	64	20.19		2)r1	Walnut	17 Apr
Kevin Braunskill	USA	69	20.22	A	3)	Sestriere	31 Jul
Andrew Tynes	Bah	72	20.25		1)	Nassau	16 Jun
Olapade Adeniken	Nig	69	20.28		3)	Monaco	02 Aug
Geir Moen	Nor	69	20.30		1)	Helsinki	11 Aug

Aleksandr Porkhomovskiy	Rus	72	20.35		1)	Rieti	28 Aug

Marks made with assisting wind:

Leroy Burrell	USA	67	20.05		1)	Houston	07 May
Renward Wells	Bah	70	20.06		1)	Stillwater	02 Apr
Andrew Tynes	Bah	72	20.20		1)	Boise	04 Jun
Steve Brimacombe	Aus	71	20.22		1)	Melbourne	19 Feb
Olapade Adeniken	Nig	69	20.23		1)r1	Austin	07 May
David Oaks	USA	72	20.24		1)	Lawrence	21 May

Hand timing:

Sebastián Keitel	Chl	73	20.1		1)	Valencia	23 Nov

4x100 metre relay (fully automatic timing)

Santa Monica TC	USA	(Marsh, Burrell, Heard, Lewis)	37.79	1)	Walnut	17 Apr
World All-Stars			37.82	2)	Walnut	17 Apr
(Drummond/USA, Jarrett/UK, Regis/UK, D.Mitchell/USA)						
	Can	(Bailey, Chambers, Gilbert, Surin)	38.39	1)	Victoria	28 Aug
	UK	(Braithwaite, Jarrett, Regis, Christie)	38.46	1)	London	10 Sep
	Fra	(Lomba, Sangouma, Trouabal, Perrot)	38.57	1)	Helsinki	13 Aug
Africa/Nigeria		(Nwankpa, Effiong, Kayode, Adeniken)	38.72	1)	Durham	12 Aug

1995

100 metres (fully automatic timing)

Donovan Bailey	Can	67	9.91		1)	Montreal	15 Jul
Bruny Surin	Can	67	9.97		2)	Montreal	15 Jul
Linford Christie	UK	60	9.97	A	1)	Johannesburg	23 Sep
Deji Aliu	Nig	75	10.02		1)	Bauchi	18 Mar
Ato Boldon	Tri	73	10.03		3)	Göteborg	06 Aug
Frank Fredericks	Nam	67	10.03	A	2)	Johannesburg	23 Sep
Tim Harden	USA	74	10.05		1)	Knoxville	03 Jun
Olapade Adeniken	Nig	69	10.05		2)h2	Zurich	16 Aug
Terry Bowen	USA	71	10.06		1)h3	Fresno	01 Apr
Donovan Powell	Jam	71	10.07		2)	Knoxville	03 Jun

Marks made with assisting wind:

Maurice Greene	USA	74	9.88		1)r1	Austin	08 Apr
Raymond Stewart	Jam	65	9.89		2)r1	Austin	08 Apr
Mike Marsh	USA	67	9.89		1)	Walnut	15 Apr
Bru.ny Surin	Can	67	9.92		1)	New York	21 May
Olapade Adeniken	Nig	69	9.92	A	1)	Sestriere	29 Jul
Carl Lewis	USA	61	9.94		3)r1	Austin	08 Apr
Tim Montgomery	USA	75	9.95		4)r1	Austin	08 Apr
Anthony Barnes	USA	65	9.96		1)	Fresno	01 Apr
Terry Bowen	USA	71	9.97		2)	Fresno	01 Apr

Hand timing:

Donovan Powell	Jam	71	9.7		1)r1	Houston	19 May
Carl Lewis	USA	61	9.7		2)r1	Houston	19 May
Olapaden Adeniken	Nig	69	9.7		3)r1	Houston	19 May
Ron Clark	USA	69	9.8		4)r1	Houston	19 May

200 metres (fully automatic timing)

Michael Johnson	USA	67	19.79		1)	Göteborg	11 Aug
Frank Frederick	Nam	67	19.93	A	1)	Johannesburg	24 Sep
Ato Boldon	Tri	73	20.08		1)	Tucson	20 May
Linford Christie	UK	60	20.11		1)	Villeneuve d'Ascq	25 Jun
Mike Marsh	USA	67	20.14		2)	Bruxelles	25 Aug
Emmanuel Tuffour	Gha	66	20.15	A	2)	Johannesburg	24 Sep
Riaan Dempers	SA	67	20.16	A	1)	Germiston	07 Apr
Iván Garcia	Cub	72	20.17		1)s1	Mar del Plata	21 Mar
Jeff Williams	USA	65	20.18		3)	Göteborg	11 Aug
Robson C. da Silva	Bra	64	20.20		2)s1	Göteborg	11 Aug

Marks made with assisting wind:

Kevin Little	USA	68	19.94		1)s3	Sacramento	17 Jun
Jeff Williams	USA	65	20.08	A	1)	Sestriere	29 Jul
Jon Drummond	USA	68	20.10		2)s3	Sacramento	17 Jun

4x100 metre relay (fully automatic timing)

Can	(Esmie, Gilbert, Surin, Bailey)	38.16	1)s1	Göteborg	12 Aug
Aus	(P.Henderson, T.Jackson, Brimacombe, D.Marsh)	38.17	1)s2	Göteborg	12 Aug
USA	(Greene, Drummond, Marsh, D.Mitchell)	38.25	1)	Monaco	25 Jul
Ita	(Puggioni, Madonia, Cipollini, Floris)	38.41	2)s2	Göteborg	12 Aug
Bra	(A.da Silva, S.T.de Souza, Ribeiro, R.da Silva)	38.48	3)s2	Göteborg	12 Aug

1996

100 metres (fully automatic timing)

Donovan Bailey	Can	67	9.84		1)	Atlanta	27 Jul
Frank Fredericks	Nam	67	9.86		1)r1	Lausanne	03 Jul
Ato Boldon	Tri	73	9.90		3)	Atlanta	27 Jul
Dennis Mitchell	USA	66	9.91		1)	Milano	07 Sep
Mike Marsh	USA	67	9.95		2)	Walnut	21 Apr
Jon Drummond	USA	68	9.98		1)s2	Atlanta	15 Jun
Vincent Henderson	USA	72	10.00		1)	Fayetteville	13 Apr
Jeff Laynes	USA	70	10.01		1)	Tempe	06 Apr
Leroy Burrell	USA	67	10.01		2)q1	Atlanta	14 Jun
Davidson Ezinwa	Nig	71	10.01		1)	Linz	21 Aug

Marks made with assisting wind:

Obadele Thompson	Bar	76	9.69	A	1)	El Paso	13 Apr
Tim Harden	USA	74	9.94		1)	Knoxville	05 May
Carl Lewis	USA	61	9.94		2)	Atlanta	18 May
Ousmane Diarra	MLI	66	9.94		1)	La Laguna	13 Jul
Osmond Ezinwa	Nig	71	9.94		1)	Pula	04 Sep

Hand timing:

Olapade Adeniken	Nig	69	9.8	1)	Lagos	20 Jun

Mark made with assisting wind:

Rod Mapstone	Aus	69	9.7	1)r1	Perth	21 Dec

200 metres (fully automatic timing)

Michael Johnson	USA	67	19.32	1)	Atlanta	01 Aug
Frank Fredericks	Nam	67	19.68	2)	Atlanta	01 Aug
Ato Boldon	Tri	73	19.80	3)	Atlanta	01 Aug
Jeff Williams	USA	65	19.87	1)	Fresno	13 Apr
Mike Marsh	USA	67	19.88	2)	Atlanta	18 May
Jon Drummond	USA	68	20.05	3)	Stockholm	08 Jul
Ramon Clay	USA	75	20.08	4)	Atlanta	23 Jun
Obadele Thompson	Bar	76	20.14	4)	Atlanta	01 Aug
Vincent Henderson	USA	72	20.17	1)r2	Walnut	21 Apr
Geir Moen	Nor	69	20.17	1)	Rieti	01 Sep

Marks made with assisting wind:

Ramon Clay	USA	75	19.99	2)s1	Atlanta	22 Jun
Alvis Whitted	USA	74	20.03	1)	College Park	20 Apr
Tony Wheeler	USA	75	20.07	2)	College Park	20 Apr

Hand timing:

Tod Long	USA	70	20.1	1)h1	Durham	29 Mar

Mark made with assisting wind:

Claudinei da Silva	Bra	70	20.0	1)h1	Americana	27 Apr

4x100 metre relay (fully automatic timing)

Can	(Esmie, Gilbert, Surin, Bailey)	37.69	1)	Atlanta	03 Aug
USA	(Drummond, Harden, Montgomery. Mitchell)	37.96	1)s2	Atlanta	02 Aug
Bra	(Arnaldo Silva, R.da Silva, Ribeiro, André Silva)	38.41	3)	Atlanta	03 Aug
Ukr	(Rurak, Osovich, Kramarenko, Dologodin)	38.53	1)	Madrid	01 Jun
Cub	(Isasi, Lamela, I. Garcia, Pérez)	38.55	2)s2	Atlanta	02 Aug

1997

100 metres (fully automatic timing)

Maurice Greene	USA	74	9.86	1)	Athinai	03 Aug
Ato Boldon	Tri	73	9.87	1)q1	Athinai	02 Aug
Frank Fredericks	Nam	67	9.90	1)	Bruxelles	22 Aug
Donovan Bailey	Can	67	9.91	2)s2	Athinai	03 Aug
Jon Drummond	USA	68	9.92	1)h3	Indianapolis	12 Jun
Tim Montgomery	USA	75	9.92	2)	Indianapolis	13 Jun
Kareem Streete-Thompson	USA	73	9.96	2)h3	Indianapolis	12 Jun
Mike Marsh	USA	67	9.97	1)h4	Indianapolis	12 Jun
Seun Ogunkoya	Nig	77	9.97	1)	Formia	13 Jul
Percy Spencer	Jam	75	9.98	1)	Kingston	20 Jun

Mark made with assisting wind:

Mike Marsh	USA	67	9.87	1)r1	Walnut	20 Apr

200 metres (fully automatic timing)

Ato Boldon	Tri	73	19.77	1)r1	Stuttgart	13 Jul
Frank Fredericks	Nam	67	19.81	1)	Fukuoka	13 Sep
Maurice Greene	USA	74	19.86	2)r1	Stockholm	07 Jul
Obadele Thompson	Bar	76	20.03	1)	Bloomington	07 Jun
Jon Drummond	USA	68	20.03	1)	Bruxelles	22 Aug
Michael Johnson	USA	67	20.05	1)	Des Moines	26 Apr
Tyree Washington	USA	76	20.10	1)	Villeneuve d'Ascq	29 Jun
Rohsaan Griffin	USA	74	20.18	1)	Linz	09 Jul
Patrick Stevens	Bel	68	20.20	4)r1	Stuttgart	13 Jul
Percy Spencer	Jam	75	20.21	1)	San Diego	23 May

Mark made with assisting wind:

Donovan Bailey	Can	67	20.14	1)	Oslo	04 Jul

4x100 metre relay (fully automatic timing)

Can	(Esmie, Gilbert, Surin, Bailey)	37.86	1)	Athinai	10 Aug
Nig	(O.Ezinwa, Adeniken, Obikwelu, D.Ezinwa)	37.94	1)s2	Athinai	09 Aug
USA	(Saddler, Henderson, Griffin, Mitchell)	37.96	1)	Linz	09 Jul
Cub	(A.Garcia, Ortiz, I.Garcia, Pérez Rionda)	38.06	2)s2	Athinai	09 Aug
Gha	(Duah, Nkansah, Zakari, Tuffour)	38.12	1)s1	Athinai	09 Aug

1998

100 metres (fully automatic timing)

Ato Boldon	Tri	73	9.86		1)r1	Walnut	19 Apr
Obadele Thompson	Bar	76	9.87	A	1)	Johannesburg	11 Sep
Bruny Surin	Can	67	9.89		1)	Montreal	01 Aug
Maurice Greene	USA	74	9.90		1)	Stockholm	05 Aug
Seun Ogunkoya	Nig	77	9.92	A	2)	Johannesburg	11 Sep
Frank Fredericks	Nam	67	9.93		2)	Athinai	17 Jun
Donovan Bailey	Can	67	9.93		2)	Montreal	01 Aug
Jon Drummond	USA	68	9.94		1)h1	New Orleans	19 Jun
Vincent Henderson	USA	72	9.95		1)	Leverkusen	09 Aug
Tim Montgomery	USA	75	10.00		1)h3	New Orleans	19 Jun
Koji Ito	Jap	70	10.00		1)s2	Bangkok	13 Dec

Marks made with assisting wind:

Maurice Greene	USA	74	9.79	1)	Eugene	31 May
Tim Harden	USA	74	9.88	1)	New Orleans	20 Jun

Hand timing:

Seun Ogunkoya	Nig	77	9.8		1)	Lagos	17 Jul

Mark made with assisting wind:

Sayon Cooper	Lbr	74	9.7		1)	Abilene	28 Mar

200 metres (fully automatic timing)

Ato Boldon	Tri	73	19.88		1)	Athinai	17 Jun
Frank Fredericks	Nam	67	19.97	A	1)	Johannesburg	13 Sep
Maurice Greene	USA	74	20.03		1)r1	Walnut	19 Apr
Ramon Clay	USA	75	20.06		1)	Doha	07 May
Sebastián Keitel	Chl	73	20.15		1)	Santiago de Chile	17 May
Jon Drummond	USA	68	20.15		1)	Bruxelles	28 Aug
Koji Ito	Jap	70	20.16		1)h2	Kumamoto	02 Oct
Francis Obikwelu	Nig	78	20.17		2)	Bruxelles	28 Aug
Julian Golding	UK	75	20.18		1)	Kuala Lumpur	19 Sep
Tony McCall	USA	74	20.27		1)	Villach	09 Jul

Marks made with assisting wind:

Maurice Greene	USA	74	19.88		1)	Eugene	31 May
Sebastián Keitel	Chl	73	19.93		1)	São Leopoldo	26 Apr
Shawn Crawford	USA	78	20.12		1)r1	College Station	09 May
Joe Criner	USA	74	20.14		1)r2	Walnut	19 Apr
Obadele Thompson	Bar	76	20.17		2)	Eugene	31 May

Hand timing:

Ramon Clay	USA	75	20.0	A	1)	Pietersburg	11 Mar

4x100 metre relay (fully automatic timing)

USA	(Drummond, Harden, Mitchell, Greene)	37.90		1)	Uniondale, NY	22 Jul
UK	(Condon, Devonish, Golding, Chambers)	38.09	A	1)	Johannesburg	12 Sep
Can	(McCuaig, Gilbert, Surin, Bailey)	38.23		2)	Uniondale, NY	22 Jul
Africa		38.29	A	3)	Johannesburg	12 Sep
	(Ogunkoya/Nig, Myles-Mills/Gha, Fredericks/Nam, Nkansah/Gha)					
America	(McCuaig/Can, Ribeiro/Bra, Keitel/Chl, C.da Silva/Bra)	38.33	A	4)	Johannesburg	12 Sep
Aus	(Hunter, Wohlsen, Brimacombe, Shirvington)	38.69		3)	Kuala Lumpur	21 Sep
IC	(N'Dri Pacôme, Zirignon, Douhou, Meité)	38.76		1)	Dakar	20 Aug

1999

100 metres (fully automatic timing)

Maurice Greene	USA	74	9.79		1)r1	Athinai	16 Jun
Bruni Surin	Can	67	9.84		2)	Sevilla	22 Aug
Ato Boldon	Tri	73	9.86		2)r1	Athinai	16 Jun
Tin Harden	USA	74	9.92		1)	Luzern	05 Jul
Frank Fredericks	Nam	67	9.94		1)	Sydney	20 Feb
Obadele Thompson	Bar	76	9.96		2)	Stockholm	30 Jul
Dwain Chambers	UK	78	9.97		3)	Sevilla	22 Aug
Leonard Myles-Mills	Gha	73	9.98		1)	Boise	05 Jun
Jason Gardener	UK	75	9.98		3)r1	Lausanne	02 Jul
Eric Nkansah	Gha	74	10.00		3)	Nürnberg	13 Jun

Marks made with assisting wind:

Leonard Scott	USA	80	9.83		1)r1	Knoxville	09 Apr
Kenny Brokenburr	USA	68	9.90		2)r1	Knoxville	09 Apr

Hand timing:

Randall Evans	USA	70	9.9		1)	Houston	05 Jun
Koji Ito	Jap	70	9.9		1)	Hiratsuka	16 Jun

Mark made with assisting wind:

Aaron Armstrong	USA	77	9.8		1)	Garden City	01 May

200 metres (fully automatic timing)

Francis Obikwelu	Nig	78	19.84	1)s2	Sevilla	25 Aug
Ato Boldon	Tri	73	19.86	1)r1	Athinai	16 Jun
Franck Fredericks	Nam	67	19.87	1)	Osaka	08 May
John Capel	USA	78	19.87	1)	Boise	05 Jun
Claudinei da Silva	Bra	70	19.89	1)	München	11 Sep
Maurice Greene	USA	74	19.90	1)	Sevilla	27 Aug
Michael Johnson	USA	67	19.93	1)	Roma	07 Jul
Marcin Urbas	Pol	76	19.98	2)s2	Sevilla	25 Aug
Coby Miller	USA	76	20.04	2)	Boise	05 Jun
Aaron Armstrong	USA	77	20.08	1)	Norman	10 Apr

Marks made with assisting wind:

Bobby Cruse	USA	78	19.83	1)r1	Knoxville	09 Apr
Rohsaan Griffin	USA	74	19.96	1)s1	Eugene	26 Jun

4x100 metre relay (fully automatic timing)

USA	(Drummond, Montgomery, Lewis, Greene)	37.59	1)	Sevilla	29 Aug
UK	(Gardener, Campbell, Devonish, Chambers)	37.73	2)	Sevilla	29 Aug
Nig	(Asonze, Obikwelu, Effiong, Aliu)	37.91	3)	Sevilla	29 Aug
AIS		38.02	1)	London	07 Aug
	(Drummon/USA, Boldon/Tri, C.Johnson/USA, M.Greene/USA)				
Bra	(de Oliveira, C. da Silva, Ribeiro, A. da Silva)	38.05	4)	Sevilla	29 Aug
Austin All-Stars		38.23	1)	Austin	03 Apr
	(O.Thompson/Bar, Henderson/USA, Streete-Thompson/Cay, Griffin/USA)				
Can	(Bailey, Gilbert, McCuaig, Betty)	38.49	2)	Winnipeg	30 Jul

2000

100 metres (fully automatic timing)

Maurice Greene	USA	74	9.86	1)	Berlin	01 Sep
Ato Boldon	Tri	73	9.95	1)	Lausanne	05 Jul
Jon Drummond	USA	68	9.96	2)	Berlin	01 Sep
Francis Obikwelu	Nig	78	9.97	2)	Lausanne	05 Jul
Obadele Thompson	Bab	76	9.97	2)	Zurich	11 Aug
Coby Miller	USA	76	9.98	1)s1	Durham	02 Jun
Bernerd Williams	USA	78	9.99	2)s1	Durham	02 Jun
Mike Marsh	USA	67	10.01	1)	Raleigh	17 Jun
Tim Montgomery	USA	75	10.01	3)	Berlin	01 Sep
Brian Lewis	USA	74	10.02	4)	Roma	30 Jun

Marks made with assisting wind:

Coby Miller	USA	76	9.88	1)	Auburn	01 Apr
Mike Marsh	USA	67	9.90	1)r7	Walnut	16 Apr
Bryan Howard	USA	76	9.94	2)r7	Walnut	16 Apr

Rolling strart:

Donovan Bailey	Can	67	9.98	1)	Luzern	27 Jun

200 metres (fully automatic timing)

Michael Johnson	USA	67	19.71	A	1)r1	Pietersburg	18 Mar
John Capel	USA	78	19.85		1)	Sacramento	23 Jul
Floyd Heard	USA	66	19.88		2)	Sacramento	23 Jul
Coby Miller	USA	76	19.96		3)	Sacramento	23 Jul
Ato Boldon	Tri	73	19.97		1)	Lausanne	05 Jul
Obadele Thompson	Bar	76	19.97		1)	Yokohama	09 Sep
Francis Obikwelu	Nig	78	20.01		2)	Lausanne	05 Jul
Chris Williams	Jam	72	20.02		1)r5	Walnut	16 Apr
Maurice Greene	USA	74	20.02		1)	Roma	30 Jun
Bernard Williams	USA	78	20.03		4)	Sacramento	23 Jul

Mark made with assisting wind:

Maurice Greene	USA	74	19.93	1)	Eugene	24 Jun

4x100 metre relay (fully automatic timing)

USA	(Drummond, B.Williams, B. Lewis, Greene)	37.61	1)	Sydney	30 Sep
Bra	(Vi. de Lima, Ribeiro, A. da Silva, C. da Silva)	37.90	2)	Sydney	30 Sep
Cub	(Cesar, Pérez-Rionda, I.Garcia, Mayola)	38.04	3)	Sydney	30 Sep
HSI		38.15	1)	Walnut	16 Apr
	(Drummond/USA, Boldon/Tri, B.Howard/USA, C.Johnson/USA)				
Jam	(L.Frater, D.Thomas, C.Williams, Bredwood)	38.20	4)	Sydney	30 Sep
Jap	(Kawabata, K.Ito, Suetsugu, Asahara)	38.31	3)s2	Sydney	29 Sep

ALL TIME WORLD LIST OF BEST PERFORMERS AS AT THE END OF 2000

100 metres (fully automatic timing)

Maurice Greene	USA	74	9.79		1)r1	Athinai	16 Jun 99
Donovan Bailey	Can	67	9.84		1)	Atlanta	27 Jul 96
Bruny Surin	Can	67	9.84		2)	Sevilla	22 Aug 99
Leroy Burrell	USA	67	9.85		1)r1	Lausanne	06 Jul 94
Carl Lewis	USA	61	9.86		1)	Tokyo	25 Aug 91
Frank Fredericks	Nam	67	9.86		1)r1	Lausanne	03 Jul 96
Ato Boldon	Tri	73	9.86		1)r1	Walnut	17 Apr 98
Linford Christie	UK	60	9.87		1)	Stuttgart	15 Aug 93
Obadele Thompson	Bar	76	9.87	A	1)	Johannesburg	11 Sep 98
Dennis Mitchell	USA	66	9.91		3)	Tokyo	25 Aug 91

Disqualified for drug abuse:

Ben Johnson	Can	61	9.79		-)	Seoul	24 Sep 88

200 metres (fully automatic timing):

Michael Johnson	USA	67	19.32		1)	Atlanta	01 Aug 96
Frank Fredericks	Nam	67	19.68		2)	Atlanta	01 Aug 96
Pietro Mennea	Ita	52	19.72	A	1)	México, D.F.	12 Sep 79
Mike Marsh	USA	67	19.73		1)s1	Barcelona	05 Aug 92
Carl Lewis	USA	61	19.75		1)	Indianapolis	19 Jun 83
Joe DeLoach	USA	67	19.75		1)	Seoul	28 Sep 88
Ato Boldon	Tri	73	19.77		1)r1	Stuttgart	13 Jul 97
Tommie Smith	USA	44	19.83	A	1)	México, D.F.	16 Oct 68
Francis Obikwelu	Nig	78	19.84		1)s2	Sevilla	25 Aug 99
John Capel	USA	78	19.85		1)	Sacramento	23 Jul 00

4x100 metre relay (fully automatic timing)

USA	(Marsh, Burrell, Mitchell, C.Lewis)	37.40	1)	Barcelona	08 Aug 92
Can	(Esmie, Gilbert, Surin, Bailey)	37.69	1)	Atlanta	03 Aug 96
UK	(Gardener, Campbell, Devonish, Chambers)	37.73	2)	Sevilla	29 Aug 99
Fra	(Morinière, Sangouma, Trouabal, Marie-Rose)	37.79	1)	Split	01 Sep 90
World All-Stars	(Drummond/USA, Jarrett, Regis/UK, Mitchell/USA)	37.82	2)	Walnut	17 Apr 94
Bra	(de Lima, Ribeiro, A.da Silva, Cl.da Silva)	37.90	2)	Sydney	30 Sep 00

2001

100 metres (fully automatic timing)

Maurice Greene	USA	74	9.82	1)	Edmonton	05 Aug
Tim Mongomery	USA	75	9.84	1)	Oslo	13 Jul
Ato Boldon	Tri	73	9.88	2)	Oslo	13 Jul
Bernard Williams	USA	78	9.94	3)	Edmonton	05 Aug
Francis Obikwelu	Nig	78	9.98	1)	Berlin	31 Aug

Dwain Chambers	UK	78	9.99		5)	Edmonton	05 Aug
Nobuharu Asahara	Jap	72	10.02		4)	Oslo	13 Jul
Kim Collins	SKN	76	10.04	A	1)	C.de Guatemala	20 Jul
Abdul Aziz Zakari	Gha	76	10.04		1)	Linz	20 Aug
Leonard Scott	USA	80	10.05		1)h3	Eugene	31 May

Faulty wind gauge – possibly wind assisted:

Mark Lewis-Francis	UK	82	9.97	1)q3	Edmonton	04 Aug
Dwain Chambers	UK	78	9.97	1)q4	Edmonton	04 Aug
Kim Collins	SKN	76	10.00	2)q1	Edmonton	04 Aug
Obadele Thompson	Bar	76	10.03	2)q3	Edmonton	04 Aug

Marks made with assisting wind:

Kim Collins	SKN	76	9.99	1)r1	Austin	07 Apr
Christie van Wyk	Nam	77	9.99	1)	Abilene	10 May

Rolling start – wind assisted:

Patrick Jarrett	Jam	77	9.89	1)	Eugene	27 May

200 metres (fully automatic timing)

Joshua J. Johnson	USA	76	19.88	1)	Bruxelles	24 Aug
Bernard Williams	USA	78	20.01	2)	Bruxelles	24 Aug
Konstadinos Kedéris	Gre	73	20.03	1)s2	Edmonton	08 Aug
Ramon Clay	USA	75	20.05	1)	Lausanne	04 Jul
Christian Malcolm	UK	79	20.08	1)s1	Edmonton	08 Aug
Chris Williams	Jam	72	20.11	2)s2	Edmonton	08 Aug
Kevin Little	USA	68	20.13	2)s1	Edmonton	08 Aug
Stéphane Buckland	MRI	77	20.15	3)s1	Edmonton	08 Aug
Shawn Crawford	USA	78	20.17	1)	Brisbane	06 Sep
Troy Douglas	Hol	62	20.19	1)	Rieti	02 Sep

Marks made with assisting wind:

Justin Gatlin	USA	82	19.86	1)h2	Eugene	30 May
Kim Collins	SKN	76	20.08	1)h3	Eugene	30 May

4x100 metre relay (fully automatic timing)

USA	(Drummond, B.Williams, C.Johnson, Greene)	37.88	1)	Austin	07 Apr
Bra	(Sousa, Ribeiro, A.da Silva, C.da Silva)	38.23	1)s1	Edmonton	12 Aug
SA	(Nagel, du Plessis, Newton, Quinn)	38.47	2)	Edmonton	12 Aug
UK	(Chambers, Devonish, Malcolm, Barbour)	38.52	3)	London	22 Jul
Jap	(Matsuda, Suetsugu, Fujimoto, Asahara)	38.54	2)s1	Edmonton	12 Aug

2002

100 metres (fully automatic timing)

Dwain Chambers	UK	78	9.87		1)	Paris	14 Sep
Maurice Greene	USA	74	9.89		1)r1	Roma	12 Jul
Frank Fredericks	Nam	67	9.94	A	1)	Windhoek	13 Apr
Shawn Crawford	USA	78	9.94		1)	Suita	11 May
Joshua J. Johnson	USA	76	9.95		1)r6	Walnut	21 Apr
Jon Drummond	USA	68	9.97		2)	Paris	14 Sep
Coby Miller	USA	76	9.98		1)	Gresham	18 May
Kim Collins	SKN	76	9.98		1)	Manchester	27 Jul
Brian Lewis	USA	74	9.99		1)	Cayenne	04 May
Bernard Williams	USA	78	9.99		2)	Monaco	19 Jul

Marks made with assisting wind:

Frank Fredericks	Nam	67	9.85	A	1)	Nairobi	18 May
Maurice Greene	USA	74	9.88		1)	Stanford	22 Jun

Subsequently disqualified for doping offence:

Tim Montgomery	USA	75	9.78	-)	Paris	14 Sep

200 metres (fully automatic timing)

Shawn Crawford	USA	78	19.85	A	1)	Pretoria	12 Apr
Konstadinos Kedéris	Gre	73	19.85		1)	München	09 Aug

Franck Fredericks	Nam	67	19.99		1)	Roma	12 Jul
Coby Miller	USA	76	20.07		1)	Bruxelles	30 Aug
Morné Nagel	SA	78	20.11	A	1)	Germiston	05 Apr
Darvis Patton	USA	77	20.12		2)	Bruxelles	30 Aug
Francis Obikwelu	Por	78	20.18		1)	Madrid	21 Sep
Bernard Williams	USA	78	20.19		1)r1	Athinai	10 Jun
Marlon Devonish	UK	76	20.19		2)	Manchester	29 Jul
Dominic Demeritte	Bah	78	20.21		1)	Nassau	22 Jun
Darren Campbell	UK	73	20.21		3)	Manchester	29 Jul

Mark made with assisting wind:

Darvis Patton	USA	77	20.06	1)r5	Fort Worth	20 Apr

Suspended under IAAF rules:

Justin Gatlin	USA	82	19.86	1)	Starkville	12 May

4x100 metre relay (fully automatic timing)

USA	(Drummond, Smoots, Conwright, Miller)	37.95		1)	Madrid	20 Sep
UK	(Malcolm, Campbell, Devonish, Chambers)	38.19		1)	München	11 Aug
America	(Mayola/Cub, Collins/SKN, C.Williams/Jam, Demeritte/Bah)	38.32		2)	Madrid	20 Sep
Ukr	(Vasyukov, Rurak, Dovgal, Kaydash)	38.53		2)	München	11 Aug
Bra	(V. de Lima, Ribeiro, A. da Silva, F. Silva)	38.58	A	1)	C. de Guatemala	11 May
Jam	(M. Frater, D. Thomas, C. Williams, A. Powell)	30.62		2)	Manchester	31 Jul

2003

100 metres (fully automatic timing)

Patrick Johnson	Aus	72	9.93	1)	Mito	05 May
Maurice Greene	USA	74	9.94	1)	Carson, L.A.	01 Jun
Deji Aliu	Nig	75	9.95	1)	Abuja	12 Oct
John Capel	USA	78	9.97	1T)r1	Zurich	15 Aug
Justin Gatlin	USA	82	9.97	1T)r1	Zurich	15 Aug
Uchenna Emedolu	Nig	76	9.97	2)	Abuja	12 Oct
Mickey Grimes	USA	76	9.99	1)r2	Zurich	15 Aug
Kim Collins	SKN	76	9.99	3)r1	Zurich	15 Aug
Frank Frederics	Nam	67	10.00	1)	Durban	11 Apr
Darvis Patton	USA	79	10.00	2)r2	Zurich	15 Aug

Marks made with assisting wind:

Patrick Johnson	Aus	72	9.88	1)	Perth	08 Feb
Kim Collins	SKN	76	9.92	1)r1	Austin	05 Apr
Erick Wilson	USA	82	9.93	1)	Levelland	10 May

200 metres (fully automac timing)

Bernard Williams	USA	78	20.01		1)	Roma	11 Jul
Shawn Crawford	USA	78	20.02		2)	Roma	11 Jul
Shingo Suetsugu	Jap	80	20.03		1)	Yokohama	07 Jun
Darvis Patton	USA	79	20.03		1)s1	Saint-Denis	29 Aug
Coby Miller	USA	76	20.04		1)	Lausanne	01 Jul
Justin Gatlin	USA	82	20.04		1)	Bruxelles	05 Sep
Joshua J.Johnson	USA	76	20.05		1)	Abuja	17 May
Stéphane Buckland	MRI	77	20.06		1)q3	Saint-Denis	27 Aug
Usain Bolt	Jam	86	20.13		1)	Bridgetown	20 Jul
André D. da Silva	Bra	72	20.15	A	1)	Cochabamba	11 May

4x100 metre relay (fully automatic timing)

USA	(Drummond, B.Williams, Patton, Greene)	37.77	1)	Berlin	10 Aug
Bra	(V.de Lima, Ribeiro, A.da Silva, Sousa)	38.26	2)	Saint-Denis	31 Aug
Ita	(Scuderi, Collio, Donati, Cavallaro)	38.42	1)	Firenze	21 Jun
Pol	(Krzywanski, Chyla, Jedrusinski, Urbas)	38.45	2)	Firenze	21 Jun
Jam	(R. Williams, Thomas, M.Frater, A.Powell)	38.45	2)s1	Saint-Denis	30 Aug
Finished 2nd but disqualified (*athlete subsequently drugs dq)					
UK	(Malcolm, Campbell, Devonish,Chambers*)	38.08	-)	Saint-Denis	31 Aug

2004

100 metres (fully automatic timing)

Justin Gatlin	USA	82	9.85	1)	Athinai	22 Aug
Francis Obikwelu	Por	78	9.86	2)	Athinai	22 Aug
Maurice Greene	USA	74	9.87	3)	Athinai	22 Aug
Asafa Powell	Jam	82	9.87	1)	Bruxelles	03 Sep
Shawn Crawford	USA	78	9.88	1)	Eugene	19 Jun
John Capel	USA	78	9.95	3)	Eugene	19 Jun
Coby Miller	USA	76	9.99	4)	Sacramento	11 Jul
Abdul Aziz Zakari	Gha	76	10.00	1)r1	Stockholm	27 Jul
Kim Collins	SKN	76	10.00	6)	Athinai	22 Aug
Leonard Scott	USA	80	10.01	3)s1	Sacramento	11 Jul

Marks made with assisting wind:

Maurice Greene	USA	74	9.78	1)	Stanford	31 May
Shawn Crawford	USA	78	9.86	1)	Doha	14 May
Darvis Patton	USA	77	9.89	1)	Arlington	27 mar

Hand timing and rolling start:

Souhalia Alamou	Ben	79	9.7	1)	Cotonou	14 May

200 metres (fully automatic timing)

Shawn Crawford	USA	78	19.79	1)	Athinai	26 Aug
Usain Bolt	Jam	86	19.93	1)	Hamilton, BER	11 Apr
Justin Gatlin	USA	82	20.01	2)	Sacramento	18 Jul
Bernard Williams	USA	78	20.01	2)	Athinai	26 Aug
Asafa Powell	Jam	82	20.06	1)	Monaco	19 Sep
Tyson Gay	USA	82	20.07	1)h2	Sacramento	16 Jul
Brian Dzingai	Zim	81	20.12	2)h1	Austin	10 Jun
Francis Obikwelu	Pot	78	20.12	1)	Sait-Denis	23 Jul
Frank Fredericks	Nam	67	20.14	4)	Athinai	26 Aug
Darvis Patton	USA	77	20.17	2)s2	Sacramento	17 Jul

Marks made with assisting wind:

Steve Mullings	Jam	82	19.90	1)	Fort Worth	17 Apr
Stanford Routt	USA	83	20.03	1)	College Station	29 May
Darvis Patton	USA	77	20.07	2)	Fort Worth	17 Apr

4x100 metre relay (fully automatic timing)

USA	(Crawford, Gatlin, Miller, Greene)	37.92	1)	München	08 Aug
UK	(Gardener, Campbell, Devonish, Lewis-Francis)	38.07	1)	Athinai	28 Aug
Nig	(Fasuba, Emedolu, Egbele, Aliu)	38.23	3)	Athinai	28 Aug
HSI	(Grimes, Scott, Greene/USA, Boldon/Tri)	38.30	2)	Austin	02 Apr
Ger	(Bröning, Unger, Kosenkow, Helmke)	38.30	1)	Madrid	17 Jul
Jap	(Asahara, Suetsugu, Yoshino, Omae)	38.35	1)	Osaka	08 May

2005

100 metres (fully automatic timing)

Asafa Powell	Jam	82	9.77	1)	Athinai	14 Jun
Justin Gatlin	USA	82	9.88	1)	Helsinki	07 Aug
Leonard Scott	USA	80	9.94	2)	London	22 Jul
Marc Burns	Tri	83	9.96	1)	Port-of-Spain	25 Jun
Abdul Aziz Zakari	Gha	76	9.99	2)	Athinai	14 Jun
Darrel Brown	Tri	84	9.99	2)	Port-of-Spain	25 Jun
Shawn Crawford	USA	78	9.99	1)s1	Carson	25 Jun
Ronald Pognon	Fra	82	9.99	1)	Lausanne	05 Jul
Kim Collins	SKN	76	10.00	3)	London	22 Jul
Dwight Thomas	Jam	80	10.00	1)	Linz	23 Aug

Marks with assisting wind:

Justin Gatlin	USA	82	9.84	1)	Eugene	04 Jun
Churandy Martina	AHO	84	9.93 A	1)	El Paso	16 Apr

Hand timing:

Olusoji Fasuba	Nig	84	9.8 A	1)s2	Nairobi	07 May

200 metres (fully automatic timing)

Wallace Spearmon	USA	84	19.89	1)	London	22 Jul
Tyson Gay	USA	82	19.93	1)s1	Sacramento	09 Jun
Usain Bolt	Jam	86	19.99	2)	London	22 Jul
Justin Gatlin	USA	82	20.00	1)	Monterrey	11 Jun
Xavier Carter	USA	85	20.02	1)	Bloomington	18 May
Shawn Crawford	USA	78	20.12	3)	Carson	26 Jun
Christian Malcolm	UK	79	20.15	1)	Firenze	19 Jun
Walter Dix	USA	86	20.18	1)s2	Sacramento	09 Jun
Chris Williams	Jam	72	20.19	2)	Monaco	09 Sep
Tobias Unger	Ger	79	20.20	1)	Bochum-Wattenscheid	03 Jul

Mark made with assisting wind:

Aaron Armstrong	Tri	77	19.98	1)	Port-of-Spain	26 Jun

4x100 metre relay (fully automatic timing)

Fra	(Doucouré, Pognon, De Lépine, Dovy)	38.08	1)	Helsinki	13 Aug
Tri	(Pierre, Burns, Harper, D.Brown)	38.10	2)	Helsinki	13 Aug
UK	(Gardener, Devonish, Malcolm, Lewis-Francis)	38.27	3)	Helsinki	13 Aug
Jam	(Carke, Thomas, Waugh, Frater)	38.28	4)	Helsinki	13 Jun
Aus	(Batman, Ross, Neofytou, Johnson)	38.32	5)	Helsinki	13 Jun

ALL TIME LIST
additional performers
(2001 - 2005)

100 metres (qual. mark: 9.91)

Asafa Powell	Jam	82	9.77	1)	Athinai	14 Jun 05
Justin Gatlin	USA	82	9.85	1)	Athinai	22 Aug 04
Francis Obikwelu	Por	78	9.86	2)	Athinai	22 Aug 04
Dwain Chambers	UK	78	9.87	1)	Paris	14 Sep 02
Shawn Crawford	USA	78	9.88	1)	Eugene	19 Jun 04

Subsequently disqualified for doping offence:

Tim Montgomery	USA	75	9.78	-)	Paris	14 Sep 02

200 metres (qual. mark: 19.85)

Shawn Crawford	USA	78	19.79	1)	Athinai	26 Aug 04
Konstadinos Kedéris	Gre	73	19.85	1)	München	09 Aug 02

4x100 metre relay (qual. mark: 37.90)

None

STATISTICS
WOMEN

ALL TIME WORLD LIST OF BEST PERFORMERS AS AT THE END OF 1940

100 yards

Stanislawa Walasiewicz(°)	Pol	11	10.8	1)	Philadelphia	30 May 30
Helen Stephens	USA	18	10.8	1)	Columbia	04 May 35

100 metres

Helen Stephens	USA	18	11.5	1)hcp	Memphis	15 May 36
Stanislawa Walasiewicz(°)	Pol	11	11.6	1)	Cleveland	10 Jun 36
Käthe Krauss	Ger	06	11.8	1)	Berlin	04 Aug 35
Marie Dollinger	Ger	10	11.8	2)	Berlin	04 Aug 35

200 metres (half-to-full turn)

Stanislawa Walasiewicz(°)	Pol	11	23.6	1)	Warszawa	04 Aug 35
Helen Stephens	USA	18	24.1	1)	Wuppertal	19 Aug 36
Decima Norman	Aus	15	24.4*	1)s1	Sydney	10 Feb 38
Käthe Krauss	Ger	06	24.4	2)	Wien	18 Sep 38

Straight course:

Helen Stephens	USA	18	23.1*	1)hcp	Toronto	02 Sep 35

4x100 metre relay

Ger	(Albus, Krauss, Dollinger, Dörffeldt)	46.4	1)h2	Berlin	08 Aug 36
USA	(E.Robinson, Stephens, Bland, Rogers)	46.7	2)	Wuppertal	19 Aug 36
Can	(Mildred Frizzell, Palmer,Mary Frizzell, Strike)	47.0	2)	Los Angeles	07 Aug 32

(°) doubtful gender status.

ALL TIME WORLD LIST OF BEST PERFORMERS AS AT THE END OF 1950

100 yards

Marjorie Jackson	Aus	31	10.7	1)	Newcastle(Aus)	31 Mar 50
Stanislawa Walasiewicz(°)	Pol	11	10.8	1)	Philadelphia	30 May 30
Helen Stephens	USA	18	10.8	1)	Columbia	04 May 35
Fanny Blankers-Koen	Hol	18	10.8	1)	Amsterdam	18 May 44
Cynthia Thompson	Jam	26	10.8	1)	Georgetown	04 Aug 47
Monica Allen	Br.G.		10.8	1)	Georgetown	Apr 50
Shirley Strickland	Aus	25	10.8	1)	Sydney	13 Jan 51

100 metres

Helen Stephens	USA	18	11.5	1)hcp	Memphis	15 May36
Fanny Blankers-Koen	Hol	18	11.5	1)	Amsterdam	13 Jun 48
Stanislawa Walasiewicz(°)	Pol	11	11.6	1)	Cleveland	10 Jun 36
Alice Coach	USA		11.7	2)e	Lakewood, OH	15 Aug 43

Käthe Krauss	Ger	06	11.8	1)	Berlin	04 Aug 35
Marie Dollinger	Ger	10	11.8	2)	Berlin	04 Aug 35
Marjorie Jackson	Aus	31	11.8	)	Sydney	05 Feb 49
Marga Petersen	Ger	19	11.8	)	Hörde	14 Aug 49

200 metres (half-to-full turn)

Stanislawa Walasiewicz(°)	Pol	11	23.6	1)	Warszawa	04 Aug 35
Fanny Blankers-Koen	Hol	18	24.0	1)	Bruxelles	27 Aug 50
Helen Stephens	USA	18	24.1	1)	Wuppertal	19 Aug 36
Marjorie Jackson	Aus	31	24.2*	1)	Auckland	09 Feb 50
Daphne Hasenjager	SA		24.3*	)	Kimberley	10 Apr 50
Käthe Krauss	Ger	06	24.4	2)	Wien	18 Sep 38
Decima Norman	Aus	15	24.4*	1)	Sydney	10 Feb 38
Sylvia Cheeseman	UK		24.4*	)	Southampton	10 Sep 49
Shirley Strickland	Aus	25	24.4*	2)	Auckland	09 Feb 50

4x100 metre relay

Ger	(Albus, Krauss, Dollinger, Dörffeldt)	46.4	1)h2	Berlin	08 Aug 36
USA	(Carew, Furtsch, Rogers, Von Bremen)	46.7	2)	Wuppertal	19 Aug 36
Can	(Mildred Frizzell, Palmer, Mary Frizzell, Strike)	47.0	2)	Los Angeles	07 Aug 32

(°) doubtful gender status.

ALL TIME WORLD LIST OF BEST PERFORMERS AS AT THE END OF 1960

100 yards

Marlene Mathews-Willard	Aus	34	10.3	1)	Sydney	20 Mar 58
Marjorie Jackson	Aus	31	10.4	1)	Sydney	08 Mar 52
Betty Cuthbert	Aus	38	10.4	1)	Sydney	01 Mar 58
Wendy Hayes	Aus		10.4	3)	Sydney	20 Mar 58
Joyce Crotty	NZ		10.5	1)	Te Puke	24 Mar 56
Ernestine Pollards	USA		10.5	1)	Cleveland	11 Jun 60

100 metres

Shirley Strickland	Aus	25	11.3	1)	Warszawa	04 Aug 55
Vyera Krepkina	SU	33	11.3	1)	Kiev	13 Sep 58
Wilma Rudolph	USA	40	11.3	1)s1	Roma	02 Sep 60
Marjorie Jackson	Aus	31	11.4	1)	Gifu	04 Oct 52
Giuseppina Leone	Ita	34	11.4	1)	Bologna	21 Oct 56
Betty Cuthbert	Aus	38	11.4	1)	Melbourne	24 Nov 56
Galina Popova	SU	32	11.4	1)	Warszawa	27 Jun 59
Maria Itkina	SU	32	11.4	1)	Moskva	02 Jul 60
Catherine Capdevielle	Fra	38	11.4	1)	Koblenz	21 Aug 60
Irina Press	SU	39	11.4	1)	Leselidze	23 Sep 60

200 metres (full turn)

Wilma Rudolph	USA	40	22.9	1)	Corpus Christi	09 Jul 60
Betty Cuthbert	Aus	38	23.1*	1)	Hobart	07 Mar 60
Marlene Mathews-Willard	Aus	34	23.3*	1)	Sydney	22 Mar 58
Patricia Duggan	Aus		23.3*	2)	Hobart	07 Mar 60
Marjorie Jackson	Aus	31	23.4	1)	Helsinki	25 Jul 52
Maria Itkina	SU	32	23.4	1)	Tashkent	13 Oct 56
Lucinda Williams	USA	37	23.4	1)	Philadelphia	19 Jul 59
Christa Stubnick	GDR	33	23.5	1)	Riesa	09 Sep 56
Norma Croker	Aus	34	23.5	1)	Brisbane	06 Oct 56

4x100 metre relay

USA	(Hudson, L.Williams, B.Jones, Rudolph)	44.4	1)h2	Roma	07 Sep 60
Aus	(Strickland, Croker, Mellor, Cuthbert)	44.5	1)	Melbourne	01 Dec 56
UK	(Pashley, Scrivens, Paul, Armitage)	44.7	2)	Melbourne	01 Dec 56
FRG/GDR	(Sander/FRG, Stubnic, Köhler, Mayer/GDR)	44.9	2)	Melbourne	01 Dec 56
SU	(Krepkina, Maslovskaya, Itkina, I. Press)	45.0	2)h2	Roma	07 Sep 60

ALL TIME WORLD LIST OF BEST PERFORMERS AS AT THE END OF 1970

100 yards (hand timing)

Chi Cheng	TPE	44	10.0		1)	Portland	13 Jun 70
Marlene Mathews	Aus	34	10.3		1)	Sydney	20 Mar 58
Wyomia Tyus	USA	45	10.3		1)	Kingston	17 Jul 65

100 metres (hand timing)

Wyomia Tyus	USA	45	11.0	A	1)	México, D.F.	15 Oct 68
Chi Cheng	TPE	44	11.0		1)	Wien	19 Jul 70
Renate Stecher-Meissner	GDR	50	11.0		1)	Berlin	02 Aug 70
Irena Kirszenstein	Pol	46	11.1		2)	Praha	09 Jul 65
Barbara Ferrell	USA	47	11.1		1)	Santa Barbara	02 Jul 67
Lyudmila Samotyesova	SU	39	11.1		1)	Leninakan	15 Aug 68
Margaret Bailes	USA	51	11.1		1)	Aurora	18 Aug 68
Raelene Boyle	Aus	51	11.1	A	4)	México, D.F.	15 Oct 68

200 metres (turn - hand timing)

Chi Cheng (E 22.62)	TPE	44	22.4		1)	München	12 Jul 70
Irena Kirszenstein-Szewinska (E 22.58)	Pol	46	22.5	A	1)	México, D.F.	18 Oct 68
Raelene Boyle (E 22.74)	Aus	51	22.7	A	2)	México, D.F.	18 Oct 68
Renate Meissner-Stecher	GDR	50	22.7		1)	Erfurt	04 Jul 70
Margaret Burvill	Aus	41	22.8*		1)	Perth	22 Feb 64
Barbara Ferrell (E 22.87)	USA	47	22.8	A	1)s2	México, D.F.	17 Oct 68
Jennifer Lamy (E 22.89)	Aus	49	22.8	A	2)s2	México, D.F.	17 Oct 68
Wilma Rudolph	USA	40	22.9		1)	Corpus Christi	09 Jul 60
Margaret Bailes (E 22.95)	USA	51	22.9	A	3)s2	México, D.F.	17 Oct 68

4x100 metre relay (hand timing)

USA	(Ferrell, Bailes, Netter, Tyus)	42.8	A	1)	México, D.F.	20 Oct 68
Cub	(Elejarde, Romay, Quesada, Cobian)	43.3	A	2)	México, D.F.	20 Oct 68
Hol	(van den Berg, Sterk, Hennipman, Bakker)	43.4	A	1)h2	México, D.F.	19 Oct 68
SU	(Zharkova, Bukharina, Popkova, Samotyesova)	43.4	A	3)	México, D.F.	20 Oct 68
Aus	(Lamy, Bennett, Boyle, Burge)	43.4	A	5)	México, D.F.	20 Oct 68

ALL TIME WORLD LIST OF BEST PERFORMERS AS AT THE END OF 1980

100 metres (fully automatic timing)

Marlies Göhr	GDR	58	10.88		1)	Dresden	01 Jul 77
Evelyn Ashford	USA	57	10.97		1)s1	Walnut	16 Jun 79
Marita Koch	GDR	57	10.99		2)	Dresden	24 May 80
Annegret Richter	FRG	50	11.01		1)s1	Montreal	25 Jul 76
Romy Müller	GDR	58	11.02		3)	Dresden	24 May 80
Monika Hamann	GDR	54	11.03		2)	Dresden	01 Jul 77
Inge Helten	FRG	50	11.04		1)h1	Fürth	13 Jun 76
Lyudmila Kondratyeva	SU	58	11.06		1)q1	Moskva	25 Jul 80
Renate Stecher	GDR	50	11.07		1)	München	02 Sep 72
Wyomia Tyus	USA	45	11.08	A	1)	México, D.F.	15 Oct 68
Brenda Morehead	USA	57	11.08		1)	Eugene	21 Jun 76
Ingrid Auerswald	GDR	57	11.08		4)	Dresden	24 May 80

Marks made with assisting wind:

Marlies Göhr	GDR	58	10.79		1)	Cottbus	16 Jul 80
Bärbel Wöckel	GDR	55	10.92		2)	Cottbus	16 Jul 80

Sonia Lannaman	UK	56	10.93	1)	Dublin	17 Jul 77
Ingrid Auerswald	GDR	57	10.93	3)	Cottbus	16 Jul 80
Brenda Morehead	USA	57	10.96	1)s2	Walnut	16 Jun79
Gesine Walther	GDR	62	10.97	4)	Cottbus	16 Jul 80

200 metres (turn - fully automatic timing)

Marita Koch	GDR	57	21.71	1)	Karl-Marx-Stadt	10 Jun 79
Evelyn Ashford	USA	57	21.83	1)	Montreal	24 Aug 79
Bärbel Wöckel	GDR	55	22.01	1)	Cottbus	18 Jul 80
Natalya Bochina	SU	62	22.19	2)	Moskva	30 Jul 80
Merlene Ottey	Jam	60	22.20	3)	Moskva	30 Jul 80
Irena Szewinska	Pol	46	22.21	1)	Potsdam	13 Jun 74
Lyudmila Kondratyeva	SU	58	22.31	1)	Moskva	12 Jun 80
Kathy Smallwood	UK	60	22.31	1)	London	08 Aug 80
Denise Boyd	Aus	52	22.35	1)	Sydney	23 Mar 80
Marlies Göhr	GDR	58	22.36	1)	Halle	14 Jun 79

4x100 metre relay (fully automatic timing)

GDR	(Müller, Wöckel, Auerswald, Göhr)	41.60	1)	Moskva	01 Aug 80
SU	(Komisova, Maslakova, V.Anisimova, Bochina)	42.10	2)	Moskva	01 Aug 80
Eur	(Haglund/Swe, Réga/Fra, Richter/FRG, Hunte/UK)	42.19	1)	Montreal	26 Aug 79
UK	(Hunte, Smallwood, Goddard, Lannamann)	42.43	3)	Moskva	01 Aug 80

WORLD YEAR LISTS 1981 - 2000

1981

100 metres (fully automatic timing)

Evelyn Ashford	USA	57	10.90	A	1)r1	Colorado Springs	22 Jul
Merlene Ottey	Jam	60	11.07		1)s1	Austin	29 May
Jarmila Kratochvílová	CSR	51	11.09		1)	Bratislava	06 Jun
Marlies Göhr	GDR	58	11.09		1)	Erfurt	01 Aug
Kathy Smallwood	UK	60	11.10		2)	Roma	05 Sep
Angella Taylor	Can	58	11.12		1)	Fürth	30 May
Bärbel Wöckel	GDR	55	11.13		2)	Erfurt	01 Aug
Marita Koch	GDR	57	11.16		1)r1	Cottbus	30 May
Jeanette Bolden	USA	60	11.18		2)	Westwood	10 May
Lileith Hodges	Jam	53	11.21		2)s1	Austin	29 May
Angela Bailey	Can	62	11.21		2)	Ciudad Bolívar	14 Aug

Marks made with assisting wind:

Evelyn Ashford	USA	57	10.85	1)	Norwalk	14 Jun
Merlene Ottey	Jam	60	10.97	1)h2	Austin	28 May
Linda Haglund	Swe	56	11.06	1)	Berlin	21 Aug

200 metres (turn - fully automatic timing)

Evelyn Ashford	USA	57	21.84	1)	Bruxelles	28 Aug
Jarmila Kratochvílová	CSR	51	21.97	1)	Bratislava	06 Jun
Bärbel Wöckel	GDR	55	22.07	1)	Jena	09 Aug
Merlene Ottey	Jam	60	22.35	1)	Des Moines	11 Apr
Gesine Walther	GDR	62	22.42	1)	Potsdam	29 Aug
Kirsten Siemon	GDR	61	22.50	2)	Jena	09 Aug
Angella Taylor	Can	58	22.55	1)	Les Abymes	15 May
Kathy Smallwood	UK	60	22.58	1)	Koblenz	26 Aug
Chandra Cheeseborough	USA	59	22.65	2)	Les Abymes	15 May
Chantal Réga	Fra	55	22.72	3)	Les Abymes	15 May

Marks made with assisting wind:

Angella Taylor	Can	58	22.46	1)	Regina	02 Aug
Kathy Smallwood	UK	60	22.57	1)	Edinburgh	05 Jul

Hand timing:

Bärbel Wöckel	GDR	5	21.9	1)	Tbilisi	27 Jun

4x100 metre relay (fully automatic timing)

GDR	(Siemon, Wöckel, G.Walther, Göhr)	42.22	1)	Roma	06 Sep
USA	(A.Brown, Bolden, Griffith, Ashford)	42.82	2)	Roma	06 Sep
SU	(Zolotaryova, Nasonova, Kondratyeva, Bochina)	43.01	3)	Roma	06 Sep
UK	(Hoyte, Smallwood, Goddard, Thomas)	43.03	2)	Zagreb	15 Aug
Ame	(Hodges/Jam, Pusey/Jam, Bailey/Can, Taylor/Can)	43.06	4)	Roma	06 Sep
FRG	(Hirsch, Sommer, Gaugel, Steger)	43.48	1)	Rhede	07 Aug

1982

100 metres (fully automatic timing)

Marlies Göhr	GDR	58	10.88		1)	Karl-Marx-Stadt	09 Jul
Evelyn Ashford	USA	57	10.93		1)	Westwood	07 Aug
Bärbel Wöckel	GDR	55	10.95		2)	Dresden	01 Jul
Angella Taylor	Can	58	11.00		1)	Brisbane	04 Oct
Marita Koch	GDR	57	11.01		3)	Dresden	01 Jul
Merlene Ottey	Jam	60	11.03		2)	Brisbane	04 Oct
Jarmila Kratochvílová	CSR	51	11.10		1)	Praha	16 Aug
Florence Griffith	USA	59	11.12		3)	Karl-Marx-Stadt	09 Jul
Gesine Walther	GDR	62	11.13		1)h2	Cottbus	21 Aug
Diane Williams	USA	61	11.14		4)	Karl-Marx-Stadt	09 Jul
Anelia Nuneva	Bul	62	11.14		1)	Sofia	14 Aug

Marks made with assisting wind:

Bärbel Wöckel	GDR	55	10.92		1)	Cottbus	21 Aug
Angella Taylor	Can	58	10.92		1)s2	Brisbane	04 Oct
Merlene Ottey	Jam	60	10.97	A	1)	Provo	04 Jun

200 metres (turn – fully automatic timing)

Marita Koch	GDR	57	21.76		1)	Dresden	03 Jul
Bärbel Wöckel	GDR	55	22.04		1)	Athinai	09 Sep
Evelyn Ashford	USA	57	22.10		1)	Nice	14 Aug
Kathy Smallwood	UK	60	22.13		2)	Athinai	09 Sep
Merlene Ottey	Jam	60	22.17		1)	Knoxville	20 Jun
Gesine Walther	GDR	62	22.24		2)	Dresden	03 Jul
Angella Taylor	Can	58	22.25	A	1)	Colorado Springs	20 Jul
Jarmila Kratochvílová	CSR	51	22.36		1)	Praha	13 Jun
Sabine Rieger	GDR	63	22.37		2)	Cottbus	26 Jun
Florence Griffith	USA	59	22.39	A	1)	Provo	05 Jun

Mark made with assisting wind:

Bärbel Wöckel	GDR	55	21.85		1)	Karl-Marx-Stadt	10 Jul

4x100 metre relay (fully automatic timing)

GDR	(G.Walther, Wöckel, Schölzel, Göhr)	41.97	1)	Potsdam	28 Aug
USA	(Brown, Griffith, Givens, Williams)	42.29	2)	Karl-Marx-Stadt	09 Jul
UK	(Hoyte, Smallwood, Callender, Thomas)	42.66	2)	Athinai	11 Sep
Fra	(Bily, Cazier, Bacoul, Gaschet)	42.68	3)	Athinai	11 Sep
CSR	(Sokolová, Soborová, Kocembová, Kratochvílová)	42.98	1)	Zurich	18 Aug

1983

100 metres (fully automatic timing)

Evelyn Ashford	USA	57	10.79	A	1)	Colorado Springs	03 Jul
Marlies Göhr	GDR	58	10.81		1)	Berlin	08 Jun
Marita Koch	GDR	57	10.83		2)	Berlin	08 Jun
Diane Williams	USA	61	10.94	A	2)	Colorado Springs	03 Jul
Silke Gladisch	GDR	64	11.03		3)	Berlin	08 Jun
Florence Griffith	USA	59	11.06		2)	Bruxelles	26 Aug
Merlene Ottey	Jam	60	11.07		1)	Lincoln	06 May
Anelia Nuneva	Bul	62	11.07		4)	Berlin	08 Jun
Alice Brown	USA	60	11.08		1)	Los Angeles	25 Jun
Nadezhda Georgieva	Bul	61	11.09		1)	Sofia	04 Jun

Marks made with assisting wind:

Florence Griffith	USA	59	10.96	1)	Zurich	24 Aug
Merlene Ottey	Jam	60	10.98	2)	Zurich	24 Aug

200 metres (turn – fully automatic timing)

Marita Koch	GDR	57	21.82	1)	Karl-Marx-Stadt	18 Jun
Evelyn Ashford	USA	57	21.88	1)	Indianapolis	19 Jun
Chandra Cheeseborough	USA	59	21.99	2)	Indianapolis	19 Jun
Merlene Ottey	Jam	60	22.19	2)	Helsinki	14 Aug
Florence Griffith	USA	59	22.23	3)	Indianapolis	19 Jun
Kathy Cook	UK	60	22.26	2)	Zurich	24 Aug
Randy Givens	USA	62	22.31	4)	Indianapolis	19 Jun
Jarmila Kratochvílová	CSR	51	22.40	1)	London	21 Aug
Alice Brown	USA	60	22.41	5)	Indianapolis	19 Jun
Nadezhda Georgieva	Bul	61	22.42	1)	Sofia	22 May
Bärbel Wöckel	GDR	55	22.42	2)	Karl-Marx-Stadt	18 Jun

Mark made with assisting wind:

Merlene Ottey	Jam	60	22.11	1)	Lawrence	23 Apr

100 metre relay (fully automatic timing)

GDR	(Gladisch, Koch, Auerswald, Göhr)	41.53		1)	Berlin	31 Jul
USA	(Brown, Williams, Cheeseborough, Ashford)	41.61	A	1)	Colorado Springs	03 Jul
Bul	(Zagorcheva, Nuneva, Georgieva, Pavlova)	42.38		1)	Sofia	23 Jul
UK	(Baptiste, Cook, Callender, Thomas)	42.71		2)	Helsinki	10 Aug
Jam	(Hodges, Pusey, Cuthbert, Ottey)	42.73		3)	Helsinki	10 Aug

1984

100 metres (fully automatic timing)

Evelyn Ashford	USA	57	10.76	1)	Zurich	22 Aug
Marlies Göhr	GDR	58	10.84	2)	Zurich	22 Aug
Florence Griffith	USA	59	10.99	2)	Berlin	17 Aug
Merlene Ottey	Jam	60	11.01	1)r2	Walnut	25 Jul
Lyudmila Kondratyeva	SU	58	11.02	2)	Praha	16 Aug
Bärbel Wöckel	GDR	55	11.04	2)	Dresden	26 Jul
Diane Williams	USA	61	11.04	3)	Zurich	22 Aug
Ingrid Auerswald	GDR	57	11.04	4)	Zurich	22 Aug
Valerie Brisco	USA	60	11.08	1)	Koblenz	29 Aug
Anelia Nuneva	Bul	62	11.10	3)	Praha	16 Aug
Silke Gladisch	GDR	64	11.10	4)	Praha	16 Aug

200 metres (turn – fully automatic timing)

Marita Koch	GDR	57	21.71	1)	Potsdam	21 Jul
Marlies Göhr	GDR	58	21.74	1)	Erfurt	03 Jun
Valerie Brisco	USA	60	21.81	1)	Los Angeles	09 Aug
Bärbel Wöckel	GDR	55	21.85	2)	Potsdam	21 Jul
Florence Griffith	USA	59	22.04	2)	Los Angeles	09 Aug
Merlene Ottey	Jam	60	22.09	3)	Los Angeles	09 Aug
Kathy Cook	UK	60	22.10	4)	Los Angeles	09 Aug
Grace Jackson	Jam	61	22.20	5)	Los Angeles	09 Aug
Gesine Walther	GDR	62	22.32	1)r2	Potsdam	21 Jul
Randy Givens	USA	62	22.36	6)	Los Angeles	09 Aug

4x100 metre relay (fully automatic timing)

USA	(Brown, Bolden, Cheeseborough, Ashford)	41.65	1)	Los Angeles	11 Aug
GDR	(Gladisch, Koch, Auerswald, Göhr)	41.69	1)	Potsdam	21 Jul
Bul	(Pavlova, Nuneva, Georgieva, Ivanova)	42.44	1)	Berlin	20 Jul
SU	(Kondratyeva, Azarashvili, Zhizdrikova, Antonova)	42.71	2)	Praha	18 Aug
Can	(Bailey, Payne, Taylor, Gareau)	42.77	2)	Los Angeles	11 Aug

1985

100 metres (fully automatic timing)

Marlies Göhr	GDR	58	10.86	1)	Berlin	22 Sep

Merlene Ottey	Jam	60	10.92	1)	Walnut	28 Apr
Marita Koch	GDR	57	10.97	2)	Leipzig	09 Aug
Marina Zhirova	SU	63	10.98	2)	Moskva	17 Aug
Silke Gladisch	GDR	64	10.99	3)	Leipzig	09 Aug
Florence Griffith	USA	59	11.00	1)	Roma	07 Sep
Valerie Brisco-Hooks	USA	60	11.01	1)	Zurich	21 Aug
Alice Brown	USA	60	11.02	1)	Koblenz	28 Aug
Jeanette Bolden	USA	60	11.09	2)h1	Zurich	21 Aug
Irina Slyusar	SU	63	11.11	1)s2	Kobe	29 Aug

Hand timing:

Irina Slyusar	SU	63	10.8	1)	Ordzhonikidze	13 Jul

200 metres (turn - fully automatic timing)

Marita Koch	GDR	57	21.78	1)	Leipzig	11 Aug
Merlene Ottey	Jam	60	21.93	1)	Indianapolis	16 Jun
Valerie Brisco-Hooks	USA	60	21.98	1)r2	Zurich	21 Aug
Silke Gladisch	GDR	64	22.12	2)	Leipzig	11 Aug
Pam Marshall	USA	60	22.39	2)	Indianapolis	16 Jun
Olga Vladykina	SU	63	22.44	1)	Donyetsk	29 Aug
Florence Griffith	USA	59	22.46	1)	Köln	25 Aug
Marina Zhirova	SU	63	22.46	1)	Tokyo	22 Sep
Elvira Barbashina	SU	63	22.50	1)	Leningrad	03 Aug
Kirsten Emmelmann	GDR	61	22.55	1)r1	Jena	12 Jun

Mark made with assisting wind:

Juliet Cuthbert	Jam	64	22.39	1)h3	Austin	29 May

Hand timing - doubtful conditions:

Pam Marshall	USA	60	21.7	1)	Walnut	02 Jun

4x100 metre relay (fully automatic timing)

GDR	(Gladisch, Rieger, Auerswald, Göhr)	41.37	1)	Canberra	06 Oct
SU	(Nastoburko, Pomoshchnikova, Zhirova, Barbashina)	42.00	2)	Moskva	17 Aug
Pol	(Papula, Kasprzyk, Pisiewicz, Tomczak)	42.71	3)	Moskva	17 Aug
Bul	(Pencheva, Nuneva, Pavlova, Zagorcheva)	43.11	1)	Stara Zagora	02 Aug
USA	(Fallace, Finn, Cliette, Torrence)	43.28	1)	Kobe	04 Sep

1986

100 metres (fully automatic timing)

Evelyn Ashford	USA	57	10.88	1)	Rieti	07 Sep
Heike Drechsler	GDR	64	10.91	2)	Moskva	06 Jul
Marlies Göhr	GDR	58	10.91	1)	Stuttgart	27 Aug
Ewa Kasprzyk	Pol	57	10.93	1)	Grudziadz	27 Jun
Silke Gladisch	GDR	64	10.96	1)	Jena	27 Jun
Valerie Brisco-Hooks	USA	60	10.99	1)	Westwood	17 May
Anelia Nuneva	Bul	62	11.04	2)	Stuttgart	27 Aug
Alice Brown	USA	60	11.06	2)	Westwood	17 May
Merlene Ottey-Page	Jam	60	11.06	1)	Sevilla	24 May
Jeanette Bolden	USA	60	11.08	2)	Zurich	13 Aug
Nelli Cooman	Hol	64	11.08	3)	Stuttgart	27 Aug

Marks made with assisting wind:

Pam Marshall	USA	60	10.80	1)	Eugene	20 Jun
Heike Drechsler	GDR	64	10.80	1)	Oslo	05 Jul
Alice Brown	USA	60	10.84	2)	Eugene	20 Jun
Evelyn Ashford	USA	57	10.85	3)	Eugene	20 Jun
Diane Williams	USA	60	10.92	4)	Eugene	20 Jun

Hand timing and wind assisted:

Merlene Ottey-Page	Jam	60	10.7	1)h2	Shizuoka	27 Apr

200 metres (fully automatic timing)

Heike Drechsler	GDR	64	21.71	1)	Jena	29 Jun

Evelyn Ashford	USA	57	21.97	1)	Zurich	29 Aug
Silke Gladisch	GDR	64	22.07	2)	Jena	29 Jun
Pam Marshall	USA	60	22.12	1)	Moskva	08 Jul
Ewa Kasprzyk	Pol	57	22.13	2)	Moskva	08 Jul
Marita Koch	GDR	57	22.20	1)r1	Berlin	20 Aug
Valerie Brisco-Hooks	USA	60	22.24	1)	Stockholm	01 Jul
Elvira Barbashina	SU	63	22.27	3)	Moskva	08 Jul
Marie-Christine Cazier	Fra	63	22.32	2)	Stuttgart	29 Aug
Grace Jackson	Jam	61	22.39	2)	San Jose	31 May

4x100 metre relay (fully automatic timing)

GDR	(Gladisch, Günther, Auerswald, Göhr)	41.84	1)	Stuttgart	31 Aug
USA	(Finn, Williams, Givens, Ashford)	42.12	1)	Moskva	09 Jul
SU	(Zolotaryova, Azarashvili, Slyusar, Barbashina)	42.27	2)	Moskva	09 Jul
Bul	(Zagorcheva, Nuneva, Georgieva, Donkova)	42.68	2)	Stuttgart	31 Aug
FRG	(März, Köninger, Gaugel, Thimm)	42.84	2)	Berlin	15 Aug

1987

100 metres (fully automatic timing)

Anelia Nuneva	Bul	62	10.86	1)	Beograd	17 Jun
Silke Gladisch	GDR	64	10.86	1)	Potsdam	20 Aug
Merlene Ottey	Jam	60	10.87	1)	Walnut	31 May
Marlies Göhr	GDR	58	10.93	1)	Neubrandenburg	10 Jun
Heike Drechsler	GDR	64	10.95	1)s2	Roma	30 Aug
Florence Griffith	USA	59	10.96	2)	Köln	16 Aug
Angella Taylor-Issajenko	Can	58	10.97	3)	Köln	16 Aug
Angela Bailey	Can	62	10.98	2)	Budapest	06 Jul
Gail Devers	USA	66	10.98	1)	Berlin	21 Aug
Alice Brown	USA	60	11.01	1)h4	San Jose	25 Jun
Pam Marshall	USA	60	11.01	2)	Lausanne	15 Sep

Marks made with assisting wind:

Silke Gladisch	GDR	64	10.82	1)s1	Roma	30 Aug
Gail Devers	USA	66	10.85	1)s1	Indianapolis	09 Aug
Diane Williams	USA	61	10.90	1)	San Jose	27 Jun

200 metres (fully automatic timing)

Silke Gladisch	GDR	64	21.74	1)	Roma	03 Sep
Florence Griffith	USA	59	21.96	2)	Roma	03 Sep
Anelia Nuneva	Bul	62	22.01	1)	Sofia	16 Aug
Pam Marshall	USA	60	22.06	1)	Zurich	19 Aug
Merlene Ottey	Jam	60	22.06	3)	Roma	03 Sep
Heike Drechsler	GDR	64	22.18	2)	Karl-Marx-Stadt	21 Jun
Valerie Brisco	USA	60	22.28	1)	Durham	24 Jul
Grace Jackson	Jam	61	22.34	2)s1	San Jose	26 Jun
Lillie Leatherwood	USA	64	22.38	1)	Tuscaloosa	17 May
Gwen Torrence	USA	65	22.40	5)	Roma	03 Sep

Hand timing:

Marina Molokova	SU	62	22.0	1)	Praha	23 Jun

Hand timing and wind assisted:

Pam Marshall	USA	60	21.6	1)	San Jose	26 Jun
Florence Griffith	USA	59	21.7	2)	San Jose	26 Jun

4x100 metre relay (fully automatic timing)

USA	(Brown, Williams, Griffith, Marshall)	41.55	1)	Berlin	21 Aug
GDR	(Gladisch, Drechsler, Auerswald, Göhr)	41.79	1)	Karl-Marx-Stadt	20 Jun
Bul	(Zagorcheva, Nuneva, Georgieva, Donkova)	42.31	2)	Praha	27 Jun
SU	(Slyusar, Pomoshchnikova, German, Antonova)	42.33	3)	Roma	06 Sep
FRG	(März, Sarvari, Gaugel, Thimm)	43.10	1)r2	Feuerbach	06 Jun

1988

100 metres (fully automatic timing)

Florence Griffith-Joyner	USA	59	10.49	1)q1	Indianapolis	16 Jul
Evelyn Ashford	USA	57	10.81	2)	Indianapolis	17 Jul
Sheila Echols	USA	64	10.83	1)q2	Indianapolis	16 Jul
Anelia Nuneva	Bul	62	10.85	1)s1	Sofia	02 Sep
Diane Williams	USA	60	10.86	2)q1	Indianapolis	16 Jul
Marlies Göhr	GDR	58	10.89	1)	Neubrandenburg	09 Jul
Katrin Krabbe	GDR	69	10.89	1)	Berlin	20 Jul
Heike Drechsler	GDR	64	10.91	1)	Oslo	02 Jul
Gwen Torrence	USA	65	10.91	3)	Indianapolis	17 Jul
Alice Brown	USA	60	10.92	2)q2	Indianapolis	16 Jul

Mark made with assisting wind:

Gwen Torrence	USA	65	10.78	1)q3	Indianapolis	16 Jul

200 metres (fully automatic timing)

Florence Griffith-Joyner	USA	59	21.34	1)	Seoul	29 Sep
Grace Jackson	Jam	61	21.72	2)	Seoul	29 Sep
Heike Drechsler	GDR	64	21.84	1)	Rostock	26 Jun
Pam Marshall	USA	60	21.93	2)	Indianapolis	23 Jul
Merlene Ottey	Jam	60	21.99	4)	Seoul	29 Sep
Gwen Torrence	USA	65	22.02	3)	Indianapolis	23 Jul
Silke Gladisch-Möller	GDR	64	22.09	5)	Seoul	29 Sep
Valerie Brisco	USA	60	22.11	4)	Indianapolis	23 Jul
Dannette Young	USA	64	22.23	1)	Monaco	02 Aug
Maya Azarashvili	SU	64	22.24	1)	Kiev	16 Aug

4x100 metre relay (fully automatic timing)

GDR	(Möller, Behrendt, Lange, Göhr)	41.73	1)	Berlin	13 Sep
USA	(Brown, Echols, Griffith-Joyner, Ashford)	41.98	1)	Seoul	01 Oct
SU	(Kondratyeva, Malchugina, Zhirova, Pomoshchnikova)	42.01	1)s1	Seoul	01 Oct
Bul	(Pencheva, Nuneva, Georgieva, Donkova)	42.29	1)	Sofia	26 Jun
FRG	(Richter, Sarvari, Thomas, Thimm)	42.69	2)s2	Seoul	01 Oct

1989

100 metres (fully automatic timing)

Dawn Sowell	USA	66	10.78	A	1)	Provo	03 Jun
Melene Ottey	Jam	60	10.95		1)	Villeneuve d'Ascq	25 Jun
Laurence Bily	Fra	63	11.04		1)	Tours	13 Aug
Evelyn Ashford	USA	57	11.05		1)	Sapporo	26 Aug
Sheila Echols	USA	64	11.07		2)	London	14 Jul
Evette de Klerk	SA	65	11.09	A	1)	Pretoria	29 Apr
Kerstin Behrendt	GDR	67	11.11		1)	Dresden	30 Jun
Silke Gladisch-Möller	GDR	64	11.11		1)	Macerata	05 Sep
Gwen Torrence	USA	65	11.12		1)	Port-of-Spain	21 Mar
Esther Jones	USA	69	11.12	A	2)	Provo	03 Jun

Marks made with assisting wind:

Olga Naumkina	SU	64	10.96		1)r1	Volgograd	11 Jun
Evette de Klerk	SA	65	10.99	A	1)	Pietersburg	08 Apr
Galina Malchugina	SU	62	10.99		1)h3	Volgograd	11 Jun

200 metres (fully automatic timing)

Dawn Sowell	USA	66	22.04	A	1)	Provo	02 Jun
Evette de Klerk	SA	65	22.06	A	1)	Pietersburg	08 Apr
Merlene Ottey	Jam	60	22.21		1)	Bruxelles	25 Aug
Silke Gladisch-Möller	GDR	64	22.23		1)	Neubrandenburg	23 Jul
Dannette Young	USA	64	22.29		1)	Houston	17 Jun
Grace Jackson	Jam	61	22.36		1)	San Juan	29 Jul
Marie José Pérec	Fra	68	22.36		1)	Chaux-de-Fonds	19 Aug
Mary Onyali	Nig	68	22.45	A	2)	Provo	02 Jun
Pauline Davis	Bah	66	22.50		1)	Bern	29 Aug
Esther Jones	USA	69	22.53		2)	Houston	17 Jun

Mark made with assisting wind:

Esther Jones	USA	69	22.37	1)	New York	22 Jul

4x100 metre relay (fully automatic timing)

GDR	(Möller, Krabbe, Behrendt, Günther)	41.87	1)	Gateshead	05 Aug
USA	(Finn, Howard, Miller, Jones)	42.40	1)	Duisburg	30 Aug
SU	(Papalina, Kovtun, Malchugina, Voronova)	42.76	2)	Barcelona	10 Sep
Fra	(Leroux, Sidibe, Bily, Girard)	43.24	1)	Strasbourg	05 Aug
FRG	(Richter, Sarvari, Thomas, Knoll)	42.45	1)	Ingolstadt	26 Jul

1990

100 metres (fully automatic timing)

Merlene Ottey	Jam	60	10.78		1)	Sevilla	30 May
Katrin Krabbe	GDR	69	10.89		1)	Split	28 Aug
Carlette Guidry	USA	68	11.03		1)	Seattle	24 Jul
Sheila Echols	USA	64	11.05		2)	Seattle	24 Jul
Michelle Finn	USA	65	11.05		3)	Seattle	24 Jul
Evette de Klerk	SA	65	11.06	A	1)	Germiston	20 Apr
Evelyn Asford	USA	57	11.07		2)	Rieti	09 Sep
Mary Onyali	Nig	68	11.09		1)	Villeneuve d'Ascq	29 Jun
Laurence Bily	Fra	63	11.09		2)	Monaco	12 Aug
Galina Malchugina	SU	62	11.10		1)h2	Moskva	09 Jun
Silke Gladisch-Möller	GDR	64	11.10		2)	Split	28 Aug

Marks made with assisting wind:

Evette de Klerk	SA	65	10.94	A	1)h2	Germiston	20 Apr
Michelle Finn	USA	65	10.96	A	1)	Sestriere	08 Aug

200 metres (fully automatic timing)

Merlene Ottey	Jam	60	21.66		1)	Zurich	15 Aug
Katrin Krabbe	GDR	69	21.95		1)	Split	30 Aug
Heike Drechsler	GDR	64	22.19		2)	Split	30 Aug
Galina Malchugina	SU	62	22.23		3)	Split	30 Aug
Mary Onyali	Nig	68	22.31		2)	Villeneuve d'Ascq	29 Jun
Evette de Klerk	SA	65	22.36	A	1)	Germiston	21 Apr
Sandra Myers	Spa	61	22.38		4)	Split	30 Aug
Dannette Young	USA	64	22.40		2)	Nice	10 Jul
Silke-Beate Knoll	FRG	67	22.40		5)	Split	30 Aug
Grace Jackson	Jam	61	22.42		3)	Nice	10 Jul

Mark made with assisting wind:

Dannette Young	USA	64	22.19	1)	Minneapolis	15 Jul

4x100 metre relay

GDR	(Gladisch-Möller, Krabbe, Behrendt, Günther)	41.68	1)	Split	01 Sep
USA	(Guidry, Echols, Finn, Young)	42.34	1)	Minneapolis	14 Jul
SU	(Bykova, Malchugina, Kovtun, Sergeyeva)	42.67	2)	Seattle	26 Jul
FRG	(Lippe, Sarvari, Thomas, Knoll)	43.02	2)	Split	01 Sep
UK	(Douglas, Kinch, Jacobs, P.Thomas)	43.32	3)	Split	01 Sep

1991

100 metres (fully automatic timing)

Merlene Ottey	Jam	60	10.79	1)	Vigo	23 Jul
Katrin Krabbe	Ger	69	10.91	1)	Hannover	27 Jul
Carlette Guidry	USA	68	10.94	1)	New York	14 Jun
Gwen Torrence	USA	65	10.96	2)	Lausanne	10 Jul
Marie-José Pérec	Fra	68	10.96	1)	Dijon	27 Jul
Irina Privalova	CIS (ex SU)	68	10.98	2)	Oslo	06 Jul
Mary Onyali	Nig	68	11.04	1)	Villeneuve d'Ascq	01 Jun
Sandra Myers	Spa	61	11.06	2)	Vigo	23 Jul
Beatrice Utondu	Nig	69	11.08	1)s1	Lagos	02 Aug
Evelyn Ashford	USA	57	11.08	2)s1	Tokyo	27 Aug

Marks made with assisting wind:

Merlene Ottey	Jam	60	10.78	1)s2	Tokyo	27 Aug
Gwen Torrence	USA	65	10.85	2)s2	Tokyo	27 Aug

200 metres (fully automatic timing)

Merlene Ottey	Jam	60	21.64	1)	Bruxelles	13 Sep
Katrin Krabbe	Ger	69	21.96	1)	Berlin	10 Sep
Gwen Torrence	USA	65	22.07	2)	Bruxelles	13 Sep
Irina Privalova	CIS (ex SU)	68	22.21	1)	Zurich	07 Aug
Dannette Young	USA	64	22.24	2)	Monaco	03 Aug
Marie-José Pérec	Fra	68	22.26	1)	Dijon	15 Jun
Grit Breuer	Ger	72	22.45	2)	Köln	08 Sep
Galina Malchugina	CIS (ex SU)	62	22.49	3)q1	Tokyo	29 Aug
Kim Walzer	USA	67	22.57	1)	Lincoln	20 May
Heike Drechsler	Ger	64	22.58	3)	Monaco	03 Aug

4x100 metre relay (fully automatic timing)

	Ger	(Breuer, Krabbe, Richter, Drechsler)	41.91	1)h2	Tokyo	31 Aug
	Jam	(Duhaney, Cuthbert, McDonald, Ottey)	41.94	1)	Tokyo	01 Sep
	CIS (ex SU)	(Kovtun, Malchugina, Vinigradova, Privalova)	42.20	2)	Tokyo	01 Sep
	Nig	(Utondu, Ubah, Opara-Thompson, Onyali)	42.72	2)h1	Tokyo	31 Aug
Texas Univ.	USA	(Clack/USA, Saldana/USA, Williams/Jam, Guidry/USA)	42.88	1)	Eugene	31 May
	Fra	(Bily, Nestoret, Jean-Charles, Pérec)	43.05	4)h1	Tokyo	31 Aug

1992

100 metres (fully automatic timing)

Merlene Ottey	Jam	60	10.80		1)r1	Salamanca	13 Jul
Irina Privalova	Rus	68	10.82		1)	Moskva	22 Jun
Gail Devers	USA	66	10.82		1)	Barcelona	01 Aug
Juliet Cuthbert	Jam	64	10.83		2)	Barcelona	01 Aug
Chioma Ajunwa	Nig	70	10.84		1)	Lagos	11 Apr
Gwen Torrence	USA	65	10.86		4)	Barcelona	01 Aug
Galina Malchugina	Rus	62	10.96		2)	Moskva	22 Jun
Lyudmila Narozhilenko	Rus	64	11.04		1)	Khania	31 May
Irina Slyusar	Ukr	63	11.05		1)	Kiev	15 Jul
Evelyn Ashford	USA	57	11.07		1)h2	Jena	28 May
Olga Bogoslovskaya	Rus	64	11.07		3)	Moskva	22 Jun

Marks made with assisting wind:

Irina Privalova	Rus	68	10.81		1)	Rieti	06 Sep
Gwen Torrente	USA	65	10.82	A	1)	Sestriere	21 Jul
Chryste Gaines	USA	70	10.90		2)r1	Austin	09 May
Evelyn Ashford	USA	57	10.94	A	2)	Sestriere	21 Jul
Michelle Finn	USA	65	10.97	A	3)	Sestriere	21 Jul

200 metres (fully automatic timing)

Gwen Torrence	USA	65	21.72	1)s2	Barcelona	05 Aug
Juliet Cuthbert	Jam	64	21.75	2)s2	Barcelona	05 Aug
Irina Privalova	Rus	68	21.93	1)	Köbenhavn	25 Aug
Merlene Ottey	Jam	60	21.94	1)q4	Barcelona	03 Aug
Marie-José Pérec	Fra	68	22.20	4)r1	Zurich	19 Aug
Galina Malchugina	Rus	62	22.22	1)q3	Barcelona	03 Aug
Carlette Guidry	USA	68	22.24	2)	New Orleans	28 Jun
Silke-Beate Knoll	Ger	67	22.29	1)r1	Ingolstadt	19 Jul
Michelle Finn	USA	65	22.39	4)s2	Barcelona	05 Aug
Pauline Davis	Bah	66	22.44	3)q1	Barcelona	03 Aug

Mark made with assisting wind:

Melinda Gainsford	Aus	71	22.26	1)	Sydney	22 Feb

4x100 metre relay (fully automatic timing)

USA	(Ashford, E.Jones, Guidry, Torrence)	42.11	1)	Barcelona	08 Aug
Rus	(Bogoslovskaya, Malchugina, Trandenkova, Privalova)	42.16	2)	Barcelona	08 Aug

Jam	(Freeman, Cuthbert, Duhaney, Ottey)	42.28	1)h2	Barcelona	07 Aug
Nig	(Utondu, Idehen, Opara-Thompson, Onfali)	42.39	2)h2	Barcelona	07 Aug
Ger	(Philipp, Knoll, Thomas, Günther)	42.57	1)	Lindau	18 Jul

1993

100 metres (fully automatic timing)

Gail Devers	USA	66	10.82		1)	Lausanne	07 Jul
Merlene Ottey	Jam	60	10.82		2)	Stuttgart	16 Aug
Gwen Torrence	USA	65	10.86		1)	Bruxelles	03 Sep
Irina Privalova	Rus	68	10.94		2)	Bruxelles	03 Sep
Mary Onyali	Nig	68	10.97		1)q2	Stuttgart	15 Aug
Liu Xiaomei	Chi	72	11.02		1)	Beijing	08 Sep
Zhanna Tarnopolskaya	Ukr	72	11.08		1)	Odessa	21 May
Inger Miller	USA	72	11.11		1)	Walnut	17 Apr
Holli Hyche	USA	71	11.12		1)	Indianapolis	26 May
Marie-José Pérec	Fra	68	11.12		1)	Nice	21 Jul
Marks made with assisting wind:							
Irina Privalova	Rus	68	10.81		1)	Rieti	05 Sep
Holli Hyche	USA	71	10.93		2)h2	Eugene	16 Jun

200 metres (fully automatic timing)

Merlene Ottey	Jam	60	21.77	1)	Monaco	07 Aug
Irina Privalova	Rus	68	21.88	1)	Rieti	05 Sep
Gwen Torrence	USA	65	21.92	1)	Bruxelles	03 Sep
Marie-José Pérec	Fra	68	21.99	1)	Villeneuve d'Ascq	02 Jul
Galina Malchugina	Rus	62	22.22	2)s2	Stuttgart	19 Aug
Mary Onyali	Nig	68	22.32	3)	Monaco	07 Aug
Inger Miller	USA	72	22.33	1)	Walnut	17 Apr
Hooli Hyche	USA	71	22.34	1)	New Orleans	05 Jun
Natalya Voronova	Rus	65	22.35	3)s1	Stuttgart	19 Aug
Cathy Freeman	Aus	73	22.37	3)	Rieti	05 Sep

4x100 metre relay (fully automatic timing)

Rus	(Bogoslovskaya, Malchugina, Voronova, Privalova)	41.49	1)	Stuttgart	22 Aug
USA	(Finn, Torrente, Vereen, Devers)	41.49	2)	Stuttgart	22 Aug
Jam	(Freeman, Campbell, Mitchell, Ottey)	41.94	3)	Stuttgart	22 Aug
Fra	(Girard, Sidibé, Jean-Charles, Pérec)	42.67	4)	Stuttgart	22 Aug
Ger	(Philipp, Zipp, Knoll, Paschke)	42.79	5)	Stuttgart	22 Aug

1994

100 metres (fully automatic timing)

Irina Privalova	Rus	68	10.77		1)r1	Lausanne	06 Jul
Merlene Ottey	Jam	60	10.78		1)	Paris	03 Sep
Gwen Torrence	USA	65	10.82		2)	Paris	03 Sep
Zanna Tarnopolskaya	Ukr	72	10.99		2)r1	Linz	04 Jul
Juliet Cuthbert	Jam	64	11.01		4)r1	Lausanne	06 Jul
Holli Hyche	USA	71	11.03		1)s1	Boise	03 Jun
Mary Onyali	Nig	68	11.03		1)s2	Victoria	23 Aug
Cheryl Taplin	USA	72	11.07		1)	Baton Rouge	25 May
Patricia Girard	Fra	68	11.11		1)s1	Bondoufle	11 Jul
D'Andre Hill	USA	73	11.12		2)s1	Boise	03 Jun
Gail Devers	USA	66	11.12		1)	Knoxville	16 Jun
Melanie Paschke	Ger	70	11.12		1)s1	Erfurt	01 Jul
Melinda Gainsford	Aus	71	11.12	A	1)	Sestriere	31 Jul
Carlette Guidry	USA	68	11.12		4)	Paris	03 Sep
Marks made with assisting wind:							
Gail Devers	USA	66	10.77		1)	San Jose	28 May
Carlette Guidry	USA	68	10.97		2)	San Jose	28 May
Cheryl Taplin	USA	72	10.99		1)	Austin	08 Apr
Inger Miller	USA	72	10.99		1)	Las Vegas	09 Apr
Chryste Gaines	USA	70	10.99		1)	Abilene	12 May

200 metres (fully automatic timing)

Gwen Torrence	USA	65	21.85	1)	Durham	12 Aug
Irina Privalova	Rus	68	22.02	1)	Stockholm	12 Jul
Merlene Ottey	Jam	60	22.07	1)r1	Berlin	30 Aug
Cathy Freeman	Aus	73	22.25	1)	Victoria	26 Aug
Galina Malchugina	Rus	62	22.29	1)	St.Peterburg	16 Jul
Dannette Young	USA	64	22.29	2)	Durham	12 Aug
Melinda Gainsford	Aus	71	22.32	1)	Hobart	26 Feb
Mary Onyali	Nig	68	22.35	2)	Victoria	26 Aug
Carlette Guidry	USA	68	22.38	3)	Durham	12 Aug
Holli Hyche	USA	71	22.41	1)h1	Boise	01 Jun

Marks made with assisting wind:

Irina Privalova	Rus	68	21.82	1)	Lausanne	06 Jul
Dannette Young	USA	64	22.16	2)	Lausanne	06 Jul

4x100 metre relay (fully automatic timing)

USA	(Gaines, Guidry, Taplin, Young)	42.45	1)	Durham	13 Aug
Ger	(Paschke, Zipp, Knoll, Lichtenhagen)	42.90	1)	Helsinki	13 Aug
Nig/Afr	(Idehen, Tombiri, Opara-Thompson, Onyali)	42.92	1)	London	11 Sep
Rus	(Anisimova, Malchugina, Trandenkova, Privalova)	42.96	2)	Helsinki	13 Aug
Bul	(D.Dimitrova, Nuneva, S.Dimitrova, Pendareva)	43.00	3)	Helsinki	13 Aug

1995

100 metres (fully automatic Timing)

Gwen Torrence	USA	65	10.84		1)s1	Göteborg	07 Aug
Merlene Ottey	Jam	60	10.85		2)s1	Göteborg	07 Aug
Irina Privalova	Rus	68	10.90		3)s1	Göteborg	07 Aug
Zanna Pintusevich	Ukr	72	11.01		1)	Luzern	27 Jun
Chryste Gaines	USA	70	11.02		1)s1	Sacramento	15 Jun
Carlette Guidry	USA	68	11.03		1)q4	Göteborg	06 Aug
Melanie Paschke	Ger	70	11.04		1)	Bremen	30 Jun
Gail Devers	USA	66	11.04		1)	Long Beach	15 Jul
Juliet Cuthbert	Jam	64	11.06		2)	Lausanne	05 Jul
Sheila Echols	USA	64	11.09		1)	Baton Rouge	13 May
Ekaterini Thanou	Gre	75	11.09		5)s1	Göteborg	07 Aug

Mark made with assisting wind:

Gwen Torrence	USA	65	10.83	A	1)	Sestriere	29 Jul

Hand timing and wind assisted:

Sevatheda Fynes	Bah	74	10.7	1)	Nassau	22 Jun

200 metres (fully automatic timing)

Gwen Torrence	USA	65	21.77	1)	Köln	18 Aug
Irina Privalova	Rus	68	21.87	2)	Monaco	25 Jul
Merlene Ottey	Jam	60	21.93	2)	Bruxelles	25 Aug
Melinda Gainsford	Aus	71	22.33	1)	Sydney	05 Mar
Galina Malchugina	Rus	62	22.36	3)	Bruxelles	25 Aug
Mary Onyali	Nig	68	22.38	4)	Bruxelles	25 Aug
Silke-Beate Knoll	Ger	67	22.45	1)	Villeneuve d'Ascq	25 Jun
Carlette Guidry	USA	68	22.45	5)	Monaco	25 Jul
Juliet Cuthbert	Jam	64	22.48	3)r1	Lausanne	05 Jul
Cathy Freeman	Aus	73	22.50	1)	San Jose	27 May

4x100 metre relay (fully automatic timing)

USA	(Mondie-Milner, Guidry, Gaines, Torrence)	42.12	1)	Göteborg	13 Aug
Jam	(Duhaney, Cuthbert, McDonald, Ottey)	42.25	2)	Göteborg	13 Aug
Rus	(N.Voronova, Malchugina, Trandenkova, Leshchova)	42.49	2)h2	Göteborg	12 Aug
Fra	(Singa, Bangué, Girard, Combe)	42.56	2)h1	Göteborg	12 Aug
Bah	(Clarke, Ferguson, Fynes, Devis)	42.74	3)h1	Göteborg	12 Aug

1996

100 metres (fully automatic timing)

Merlene Ottey	Jam	60	10.74	1)	Milano	07 Sep
Gwen Torrence	USA	65	10.82	1)	Atlanta	15 Jun
Gail Devers	USA	66	10.83	2)	Milano	07 Sep
D'Andre Hill	USA	73	10.92	3)	Atlanta	15 Jun
Chryste Gaines	USA	70	10.96	2)h1	Atlanta	14 Jun
Inger Miller	USA	72	10.96	4)	Atlanta	15 Jun
Chandra Sturrup	Bah	71	11.00	4)	Atlanta	27 Jul
Mary Onyali	Nig	68	11.00	3)	Milano	07 Sep
Galina Malchugina	Rus	62	11.02	1)	St.Peterburg	02 Jul
Irina Privalova	Rus	68	11.03	3)	Monaco	10 Aug

Hand timing:

Mary Onyali	Nig	68	10.7	1)	Lagos	22 Jun

200 metres (fully automatic timing)

Marie-José Pérec	Fra	68	22.07	1)s1	Atlanta	01 Aug
Mary Onyali	Nig	68	22.07	1)	Zurich	14 Aug
Merlene Ottey	Jam	60	22.08	1)s2	Atlanta	01 Aug
Carlette Guidry	USA	68	22.14	1)	Atlanta	23 Jun
Dannette Young-Stone	USA	64	22.18	2)	Atlanta	23 Jun
Galina Malchugina	Rus	62	22.18	1)s2	St.Peterburg	04 Jul
Juliet Cuthbert	Jam	64	22.24	3)s1	Atlanta	01 Aug
Inger Miller	USA	72	22.25	3)	Atlanta	23 Jun
Gwen Torrence	USA	65	22.25	4)	Atlanta	23 Jun
Irina Privalova	Rus	68	22.27	3)	Zurich	14 Aug

4x100 metres (fully automatic timing)

USA	(Gaines, Devers, Miller, Torrence)	41.95	1)	Atlanta	03 Aug
Bah	(E.Clarke, Sturrup, Fynes, Davis)	42.14	2)	Atlanta	03 Aug
Jam	(Freeman, Cuthbert, Mitchell, Ottey)	42.24	3)	Atlanta	03 Aug
Rus	(Leshchova, Malchugina, Voronova, Privalova)	42.27	4)	Atlanta	03 Aug
Nig	(Ajunwa, Tombini-Shirey, C.Opara, Onfali)	42.56	5)	Atlanta	03 Aug

1997

100 metres (fully automatic timing)

Marion Jones	USA	75	10.76	1)	Bruxelles	22 Aug
Li Xuemei	Chi	77	10.79	1)	Shanghai	18 Oct
Merlene Ottey	Jam	60	10.83	2)	Bruxelles	22 Aug
Zhanna Pintusevich	Ukr	72	10.85	2)	Athinai	03 Aug
Gail Devers	USA	66	10.88	3)	Berlin	26 Aug
Liu Xiaomei	Chi	72	10.89	2)	Shanghai	18 Oct
Christine Arron	Fra	73	11.03	1)	Montauban	22 Jul
Sevatheda Fynes	Bah	74	11.03	3)	Athinai	03 Aug
Inger Miller	USA	72	11.04	1)h2	Indianapolis	12 Jun
Andrea Philipp	Ger	71	11.05	1)r1	Dortmund	08 Jun

Hand timing:

Zhanna Pintusevich	Ukr	72	10.6	1)	Kiev	12 Jun

200 metres (fully automatic timing)

Marion Jones	USA	75	21.76		1)	Zurich	13 Aug
Li Xuemei	Chi	77	22.01		1)	Shanghai	22 Oct
Merlene Ottey	Jam	60	22.06		2)	Monaco	16 Aug
Zhanna Pintusevich	Ukr	72	22.17	A	1)	Monachil	09 Jul
Melinda Gainsford-Taylor	Aus	71	22.23		1)	Stuttgart	13 Jul
Susanthika Jayasinghe	Sri	75	22.33		2)s2	Athinai	07 Aug
Liu Xiaomei	Chi	72	22.36		2)	Shanghai	22 Oct
Inger Miller	USA	72	22.37		2)	Zurich	13 Aug
Marina Trandenkova	Rus	67	22.44	A	2)	Monachil	09 Jul
Yekaterina Leshchova	Rus	74	22.47		2)h4	Athinai	06 Aug

Mark made with assisting wind:

Merlene Ottey	Jam	60	21.92	2)	Fukuoka	13 Sep

Hand timing:

Viktoria Fomento	Ukr	70	22.1	1)	Lisboa	20 Jun

4x100 metres (fully automatic timing)

	USA	(Gaines, Jones, Miller, Devers)	41.47	1)	Athinai	09 Aug
	Jam	(McDonald, Frazer, Cuthbert, Grant)	42.10	2)	Athinai	09 Aug
	Bah	(E.Clarke, Fynes, Ferguson, Davis)	42.19	1)h2	Athinai	08 Aug
	Fra	(Girard, Arron, Combe, Félix)	42.21	3)	Athinai	09 Aug
Sichuan	Chi	(Xiao Lin, Li Yali, Liu Xiaomei, Li Xuemei)	42.23	1)	Shanghai	23 Oct

1998

100 metres (fully automatic timing)

Marion Jones	USA	75	10.65	A	1)	Johannesburg	12 Sep
Christine Arron	Fra	73	10.73		1)	Budapest	19 Aug
Irina Privalova	Rus	68	10.83		2)	Budapest	19 Aug
Ekaterini Thanou	Gre	75	10.87		3)	Budapest	19 Aug
Chryste Gaines	USA	70	10.89		2)	New Orleans	20 Jun
Zhanna Pintusevich	Ukr	72	10.92		4)	Budapest	19 Aug
Li Xuemei	Chi	77	10.95		1)	Beijing	06 Jun
Chandra Sturrup	Bah	71	10.95		1)	Nassau	20 Jun
Debbie Ferguson	Bah	76	10.97		2)	Stockholm	05 Aug
Beverly McDonald	Jam	70	10.99		1)	Doha	07 May

Mark made with assisting wind:

Inger Miller	USA	72	10.84	1)	Walnut	19 Apr

Hand timing:

Svetlana Goncharenko	Rus	71	10.7	1)	Rostov	30 May

200 metres (fully automatic timing)

Marion Jones	USA	75	21.62	A	1)	Johannesburg	11 Sep
Inger Miller	USA	72	22.20		1)	Bruxelles	28 Aug
Falilat Ogunkoya	Nig	69	22.22		1)	Dakar	22 Aug
Berly McDonald	Jam	70	22.24		1)	Villeneuve d'Ascq	11 Jul
Zhanna Pintusevich	Ukr	72	22.35	A	3)	Johannesburg	11 Sep
Svetlana Goncharenko	Rus	71	22.46		1)	Thessaloniki	27 Jul
Damayanthi Darsha	Sri	75	22.48		1)	Bangkok	18 Dec
Melinda Gainsford-Taylor	Aus	71	22.49		2)	Sydney	28 Feb
Debbie Ferguson	Bah	76	22.53		1)	Gainesville	24 May
Marlene Ottey	Jam	60	22.53		1)	Istanbul	30 May
Li Xuemei	Chi	77	22.53		2)	Bangkok	18 Dec

Hand timing:

Svetlana Goncharenko	Rus	71	21.9	1)	Rostov	31 May

4x100 metre relay (fully automatic timing)

USA	(Taplin, Gaines, Miller, Guidry)	42.00	A	1)	Johannesburg	13 Sep
Bah	(Fynes, Sturrup, Ferguson, Davis)	42.19		2)	Uniondale, NY	22 Jul
Fra	(Benth, Bangué, Félix, Arron)	42.43		1)	Villeneuve d'Ascq	11 Jul
Rus	(Leshchova, Malchugina, Voronova, Privalova)	42.49		1)	St.Peterburg	27 Jun
Ger	(Paschke, G.Rockmeier, B.Rockmeier, Philipp)	42.59		2)	St.Petersburg	27 Jun

1999

100 metres (fully automatic timing)

Marion Jones	USA	75	10.70	1)	Sevilla	22 Aug
Inger Miller	USA	72	10.79	2)	Sevilla	22 Aug
Ekaterini Thanou	Gre	75	10.83	2)s1	Sevilla	22 Aug
Glory Alozie	Nig	77	10.90	1)	La Laguna	05 Jun
Sevatheda Fynes	Bah	74	10.91	2)	Lausanne	02 Jul

Zhanna Pintusevich-Block	Ukr	72	10.94	2)q2	Sevilla	21 Aug
Gail Devers	USA	66	10.94	2)s2	Sevilla	22 Aug
Chandra Sturrup	Bah	71	10.96	1)h	Nassau	18 Jun
Christine Arron	Fra	73	10.97	1)	Paris	19 Jun
Debbie Ferguson	Bah	76	10.98	1)s1	Boise	04 Jun

200 metres (fully automatic timing)

Inger Miller	USA	72	21.77	1)	Sevilla	27 Aug
Marion Jones	USA	75	21.81	1)	Eugene	30 May
Merlene Frazer	Jam	73	22.18	1)s2	Sevilla	25 Aug
Debbie Ferguson	Bah	76	22.19	1)	Saint-Denis	03 Jul
Beverly McDonald	Jam	70	22.22	2)	Sevilla	27 Aug
Andrea Philipp	Ger	71	22.25	2)s1	Sevilla	25 Aug
Christine Arron	Fra	73	22.26	2)	Saint-Denis	03 Jul
Fatima Yusuf	Nig	71	22.28	2)q2	Sevilla	24 Aug
LaTasha Jenkins	USA	77	22.29	1)	Boise	05 Jun
Muriel Hurtis	Fra	79	22.31	3)q2	Sevilla	24 Aug

4x100 metre relay (fully automatic timing)

Bah	(Fynes, Sturrup, Davis, Ferguson)	41.92	1)	Sevilla	29 Aug
Fra	(Girard, Hurtis, Benth, Arron)	42.06	2)	Sevilla	29 Aug
Jam	(A.Bailey, Frazer, McDonald, Dowdie)	42.15	3)	Sevilla	29 Aug
USA	(Taplin, Perry, Miller, Devers)	42.28	1)h1	Sevilla	28 Aug
Ger	(Philipp, G.Rockmeier, Möller, Wagner)	42.63	5)	Sevilla	29 Aug

2000

100 metres (fully automatic timing)

Marion Jones	USA	75	10.75	1)	Sydney	23 Sep
Chandra Sturrup	Bah	71	10.86	1)	Nassau	21 Jul
Ekaterini Thanou	Gre	75	10.91	1)	Lausanne	05 Jul
Inger Miller	USA	72	10.91	1)	Monaco	18 Aug
Zanna Pintusevich-Block	Ukr	72	10.93	1)	Oslo	28 Jul
Eldece Clarke-Lewis	Bah	65	10.96	1)	Fort-de-France	29 Apr
Debbie Ferguson	Bah	76	10.96	2)	Nassau	21 Jul
Chryste Gaines	USA	70	10.97	1)r1	Athinai	28 Jun
Pauline Davis-Thompson	Bah	66	10.97	3)	Nassau	21 Jul
Christine Arron	Fra	73	10.99	2)	Roma	30 Jun
Gail Devers	USA	66	10.99	1)h3	Sacramento	14 Jul
Mary Onyali	Nig	68	10.99	1)	Chaux-de-Fonds	13 Aug
Merlene Ottey	Jam	60	10.99	1)	Thessaloniki	30 Aug

200 metres (fully automatic timing)

Marion Jones	USA	75	21.84		1)	Sydney	28 Sep
Inger Miller	USA	72	22.09		2)	Sacramento	23 Jul
Pauline Davis-Thompson	Bah	66	22.27		2)	Sydney	28 Sep
Susanthika Jayasinghe	Sri	75	22.28		3)	Sydney	28 Sep
Beverly McDonald	Jam	70	22.35		4)	Sydney	28 Sep
Debbie Ferguson	Bah	76	22.37		5)	Sydney	28 Sep
Nanceen Perry	USA	77	22.38		3)	Sacramento	23 Jul
Léonie Myriam Mani	CAM	77	22.41		1)	Kourou	21 May
Melinda Gainsford-Taylor	Aus	71	22.42		6)	Sydney	28 Sep
LaTasha Colander-Richardson	USA	76	22.49		1)	Nassau	09 Jun
Mary Onyali	Nig	68	22.49		1)	Chaux-de-Fonds	13 Aug
Marks made with assisting wind:							
Nancheen Perry	USA	77	22.16		1)	Austin	06 May
Melinda Gainsford-Taylor	Aus	71	22.18	A	1)	Pietersburg	18 Mar

4x100 metre relay (fully automatic timing)

Bah	(Fynes, Sturrup, Davis-Thompson, Ferguson)	41.95	1)	Sydney	30 Sep
USA	(Gaines, Devers, Miller, Edwards)	42.13	1)	Monaco	18 Aug
Jam	(Lawrence, V.Campbell, McDonald, Ottey)	42.13	2)	Sydney	30 Sep
Fra	(Citté, Hurtis, Dia, Arron)	42.38	3)	Monaco	18 Aug
Ger	(Schielke, Möller, Philipp, Wagner)	42.73	1)	Chemnitz	22 Jul

ALL TIME WORLD LIST OF BEST PERFORMERS AS AT THE END OF 2000

100 metres (fully automatic timing)

Florence Griffith-Joyner	USA	59	10.49		1)q1	Indianapolis	16 Jul 88
Marion Jones	USA	75	10.65	A	1)	Johannesburg	12 Sep 98
Christine Arron	Fra	73	10.73		1)	Budapest	19 Aug 98
Merlene Ottey	Jam	60	10.74		1)	Milano	07 Sep 96
Evelyn Ashford	USA	57	10.76		1)	Zurich	22 Aug 84
Irina Privalova	Rus	68	10.77		1)r1	Lausanne	06 Jul 94
Dawn Sowell	USA	66	10.78	A	1)	Provo	03 Jun 89
Li Xuemei	Chi	77	10.79		1)	Shanghai	18 Oct 97
Inger Miller	USA	72	10.79		2)	Sevilla	22 Aug 99
Marlies Göhr	GDR	58	10.81		1)	Berlin	08 Jun 83

200 metres (fully automatic timing)

Florence Griffith-Joyner	USA	59	21.34		1)	Seoul	29 Sep 88
Marion Jones	USA	75	21.62	A	1)	Johannesburg	11 Sep 98
Marlene Ottey	Jam	60	21.64		1)	Bruxelles	13 Sep 91
Marita Koch	GDR	57	21.71		1)	Karl-Marx-Stadt	10 Jun 79
Heike Drechsler	GDR	64	21.71		1)	Jena	29 Jun 86
Grace Jackson	Jam	61	21.72		2)	Seoul	29 Sep 88
Gwen Torrence	USA	65	21.72		1)s2	Barcelona	05 Aug 92
Marlies Göhr	GDR	58	21.74		1)	Erfurt	03 Jun 84
Silke Gladisch	GDR	64	21.74		1)	Roma	03 Sep 87
Juliet Cuthbert	Jam	64	21.75		2)s2	Barcelona	05 Aug 92

4x100 metre relay (fully automatic timing)

GDR	(Gladisch, Rieger, Auerswald, Göhr)	41.37	1)	Camberra	06 Oct 85
USA	(Gaines, Jones, Miller, Devers)	41.47	1)	Athinai	09 Aug 97
Rus	(Bogoslovskaya, Malchugina, Voronova, Privalova)	41.49	1)	Stuttgart	22 Aug 93
Bah	(Fynes, Sturrup, Davis-Thompson, Ferguson)	41.92	1)	Sevilla	29 Aug 99
Jam	(Duhaney, Cuthbert, McDonald, Ottey)	41.94	1)	Tokyo	01 Sep 91

2001

100 metres (fully automatic timing)

Zhanna Pintusevich-Block	Ukr	72	10.82		1)	Edmonton	06 Aug
Marion Jones	USA	75	10.84		1)	Saint-Denis	06 Jul
Ekaterini Thanou	Gre	75	10.91		3)	Edmonton	06 Aug
Chandra Sturrup	Bah	71	10.95		2)	Bruxelles	24 Aug
Léonie Myriam Mani	CMR	77	10.98		2)r1	Athinai	11 Jun
Chryste Gaines	USA	70	10.98		1)	Monaco	20 Jul
Kelli White	USA	77	10.99		3)r1	Athinai	11 Jun
LaTasha Jenkins	USA	77	11.02		1)	Athens, GA	05 May
Debbie Ferguson	Bah	76	11.04		5)r1	Athinai	11 Jun
Mercy Nku	Nig	76	11.06		1)r2	Lausanne	04 Jul
Endurance Ojokolo	Nig	75	11.06		1)r2	Zurich	17 Aug

200 metres (fully automatic timing)

Marion Jones	USA	75	22.23		1)h1	Eugene	23 Jun
Kelli White	USA	77	22.38		1)	Bruxelles	24 Aug
LaTasha Jenkins	USA	77	22.39		1)h2	Eugene	23 Jun
Debbie Ferguson	Bah	76	22.39		1)s3	Edmonton	09 Aug
Cydonie Mothersill	Cay	78	22.54	A	1)	C. de Guatemala	21 Jul
Léonie Myriam Mani	CMR	77	22.54		1)	Rieti	02 Sep
Beverly McDonald	Jam	70	22.57		2)	Bruxelles	24 Aug
Aleen Bailey	Jam	80	22.59		1)	Lawrence	21 Apr

Heide Seyerling	SA	76	22.63	1)	Durban	03 Mar
LaTasha Richardson	USA	76	22.63	2)	Lawrence	21 Apr
Susanthika Jayasinghe	Sri	75	22.63	1)	Osaka	12 May
Lorraine Fenton	Jam	73	22.63	1)r2	Kassel	13 Jun

Hand timing:

Natalya Mikhaylovskaya	Rus	75	22.0	1)	Irkutsk	28 Jul

4x100 metre relay (fully automatic timing)

USA	(White, Gaines, Miller, Jones)	41.71	1)	Edmonton	11 Aug
Ger	(Paschke, G.Rockmeier, B.Rockmeier, Wagner)	42.32	2)	Edmonton	11 Aug
Fra	(Félix, Bangué, Hurtis, Sidibé)	42.39	3)	Edmonton	11 Aug
Jam	(J.Campbell, Frazer, McDonald, A.Walker)	42.40	4)	Edmonton	11 Aug
Nig	(Ajunwa, Ojokolo, Nku, Onyali-Omagbemi)	42.52	5)	Edmonton	11 Aug

2002

100 metres (fully automatic timing)

Zhanna Pintusevich-Block	Ukr	72	10.83	1)r1	Heusden	20 Jul
Marion Jones	USA	75	10.84	1)	Monaco	19 Jul
Debbie Ferguson	Bah	76	10.91	1)	Manchester	27 Jul
Tayna Lawrence	Jam	75	10.93	3)	Bruxelles	30 Aug
Chryste Gaines	USA	70	10.94	4)	Bruxelles	30 Aug
Muriel Hurtis	Fra	79	10.96	1)	Annecy	22 Jun
Veronica Campbell	Jam	82	11.00	2)	Manchester	27 Jul
Chandra Sturrup	Bah	71	11.01	1)	Doha	15 May
LaTasha Jenkins	USA	77	11.05	1)	Nashville	20 Apr
Ekaterini Thanou	Gre	75	11.05	1)s2	München	07 Aug

200 metres (fully automatic timing)

Marion Jones	USA	75	22.11	1)	Bruxelles	30 Aug
Debbie Ferguson	Bah	76	22.20	1)	Manchester	29 Jul
Zhanna Pintusevich-Block	Ukr	72	22.24	2)	Bruxelles	20 Aug
Veronica Campbell	Jam	82	22.39	1)	Odessa	18 May
Muriel Hurtis	Fra	79	22.43	1)	München	09 Aug
Stephanie Durst	USA	82	22.48	1)	Starkville	12 May
Kelli White	USA	77	22.50	2)	Stanford	23 Jun
Kim Gevaert	Bel	78	22.53	2)	München	09 Aug
Aleen Bailey	Jam	80	22.54	2)	Starkville	12 May
Juliet Campbell	Jam	70	22.54	2)	Manchester	29 Jul

Marks made with assisting wind:

Muna Lee	USA	81	22.33	1)	San Antonio	10 Aug

Hand timing:

Virgen Benavides	Cub	74	22.3	1)	Habana	30 Nov

4x100 metre relay (fully automatic timing)

Americas	(Lawrence/Jam, Campbell/Jam, McDonald/Jam, Ferguson/Bah)	41.91	1)	Madrid	20 Sep
USA	(Gaines, Jones, Miller, Devers)	42.05	2)	Madrid	20 Sep
Fra	(Girard, Hurtis, Félix, Sidibé)	42.41	1)	Annecy	22 Jun
Bah	(Clarke, Fynes, Sturrup, Ferguson)	42.44	1)	Manchester	31 Jul
Ger	(Paschke, G.Rockmeier, Schielke, Wagner)	42.49	2)	Annecy	22 Jun
Jam	(Gouldbourne, J.Campell, A.Walker, V.Campbell)	42.73	2)	Manchester	31 Jul

2003

100 metres (fully automatic timing)

Kelli White	USA	77	10.85	1)	Saint-Denis	24 Aug
Chryste Gaines	USA	70	10.86	1)	Monaco	14 Sep
Chandra Sturrup	Bah	71	10.89	1)	Roma	11 Jul
Torri Edwards	USA	77	10.93	2)	Saint Denis	24 Aug
Debbie Ferguson	Bah	76	10.97	1)	Durban	11 Apr

Zhanna Block	Ukr	72	10.99	3)	Saint Denis	24 Aug
Christine Arron	Fra	73	11.01	2)s1	Saint Denis	24 Aug
Ekaterini Thanou	Gre	75	11.03	5)	Saint Denis	24 Aug
Muna Lee	USA	81	11.04	2)r1	Walnut	19 Apr
Natalya Safronnikova	Bel	73	11.05	1)	Minsk	28 Jun

Marks made with assisting wind:

Kelli White	USA	77	10.79	1)	Carson	01 Jun
Chandra Sturrup	Bah	71	10.88	3)	Berlin	10 Aug

200 metres (fully automatic timing)

Kelli White	USA	77	22.05		1)	Saint Denis	28 Aug
Allyson Felix	USA	85	22.11	A	1)	México, D.F.	03 May
Torri Edwards	USA	77	22.28		1)	Roma	11 Jul
LaTasha Jenkins	USA	77	22.31	A	2)	México	03 May
Anastasiya Kapachinskaya	Rus	79	22.38		2)	Saint Denis	28 Aug
Muriel Hurtis	Fra	79	22.41		1)s2	Saint Denis	27 Aug
Cydonie Mothersill	Cay	78	22.45		1)	St. George's	06 Jul
Debbie Ferguson	Bah	76	22.50	A	1)	Pretoria	04 Apr
Aleen Bailey	Jam	80	22.59		1)	Kingston	21 Jun
Mary Onyali	Nig	68	22.60		1)	Abuja	17 May

4x100 metre relay (fully automatic timing)

Fra	(Girard, Hurtis, Félix, Arron)	41.78	1)	Saint Denis	30 Aug
USA	(A.Williams, Gaines, Miller, Edwards)	41.83	2)	Saint Denis	30 Aug
Rus	(Fyodorova, Tabakova, Kislova, Kruglova)	42.62	2)h1	Saint Denis	29 Aug
Ukr	(Tkalich, Kravchenko, Pastushenko, Maydanova)	42.96	1)	Kiev	06 Jul
Nig	(Edem, Ojokolo, Odozor, Onyali)	43.04	1)	Abuja	13 Oct

2004

100 metres (fully automatic timing)

Ivet Lalova	Bul	84	10.77	1)	Plovdiv	19 Jun
Veronica Campbell	Jam	82	10.91	1)	Monaco	18 Sep
Yulia Nesterenko	Bel	79	10.92	1)s1	Athinai	21 Aug
Christine Arron	Fra	73	10.95	1)	Sotteville	16 Jul
Lauryn Williams	USA	83	10.96	2)	Athinai	21 Aug
LaTasha Colander	USA	76	10.97	1)	Sacramento	10 Jul
Sherone Simpson	Jam	84	11.01	1)	St. George's	29 May
Marion Jones	USA	75	11.04	1)	Kingston	07 May
Aleen Bailey	Jam	80	11.04	1)	Birmingham	25 Jul
Debbie Ferguson	Bah	76	11.04	4)s1	Athinai	21 Aug

Drugs disqualification:

Torri Edwards	USA	77	11.00	-)	Sacramento	10 Jul

200 metres (fully automatic timing)

Veronica Campbell	Jam	82	22.05	1)	Athinai	25 Aug
Allyson Felix	USA	85	22.18	2)	Athinai	25 Aug
Debbie Ferguson	Bah	76	22.30	3)	Athinai	25 Aug
Aleen Bailey	Jam	80	22.33	2)s2	Athinai	24 Aug
Tonette Dyer	USA	83	22.34	1)	Irvine	02 May
Irina Khabarova	Rus	66	22.34	1)	Tula	31 Jul
Muna Lee	USA	81	22.36	2)	Sacramento	18 Jul
LaTasha Colander	USA	76	22.37	1)	Stanford	31 May
Cydonie Mothersill	Cay	78	22.40	1)h3	Athinai	23 Aug
Lauryn Williams	USA	83	22.46	1)	Coral Gables	10 Apr

Drugs disqualification:

Torri Edwards	USA	77	22.38	-)	Sacramento	17 Jul

4x100 metre relay

USA	(A.Williams, Jones, L.Williams, Colander)	41.67	1)	München	08 Aug
Jam	(Lawrence, Simpson, Bailey, Campbell)	41.73	1)	Athinai	27 Aug

Rus	(Fyodorova, Tabakova, Khabarova, Kruglova)	42.12	1)h2	Athinai	26 Aug
Fra	(Mang, Hurtis, Félix, Arron)	42.41	1)	Bydgoszcz	19 Jun
Bah	(Clarke, Sturrup, Brown, Ferguson)	42.69	4)	Athinai	27 Aug

2005

100 metres (fully automatic timing)

Chandra Sturrup	Bah	71	10.84	1)	Lausanne	05 Jul
Veronica Campbell	Jam	82	10.85	1)	Zurich	19 Aug
Lauryn Williams	USA	83	10.88	2)	Zurich	19 Aug
Christine Arron	Fra	73	10.93	2)	Monaco	09 Sep
Sherone Simpson	Jam	84	10.97	2)	Kingston	25 Jun
Ivet Lalova	Bul	84	11.03	1)	Ostrava	09 Jun
Maria Karastamáti	Gre	84	11.03	1)	Erfurt	16 Jul
Me'Lisa Barber	USA	80	11.04	1)h3	Carson	24 Jun
Allyson Felix	USA	85	11.05	1)	Yokohama	19 Sep
LaTasha Colander	USA	76	11.06	1)	Santo Domingo	14 May

Marks made with assisting wind:

Christine Arron	Fra	73	10.82	1)	Castres	26 Jul
Me'Lisa Barber	USA	80	10.87	1)	Carson	25 Jun

200 metres (fully automatic timing)

Allyson Felix	USA	85	22.13	1)	Carson	26 Jun
Rachelle Boone-Smith	USA	81	22.22	2)	Carson	26 Jun
Lauryn Williams	USA	83	22.27	2)	Carson	22 May
Christine Arron	Fra	73	22.31	3)	Helsinki	12 Aug
LaTasha Colander	USA	76	22.34	3)	Carson	26 Jun
Veronica Campbell	Jam	82	22.35	1)	Torino	03 Jun
Me'Lisa Barber	USA	80	22.37	4)	Carson	26 Jun
Cydonie Mothersill	Cay	78	22.39	1)h	Nassau	10 Jul
Svetlana Pospelova	Rus	79	22.39	1)	Tula	24 Jul
Muna Lee	USA	81	22.46	5)	Carson	26 Jun

4x100 metre relay (fully automatic timing)

USA	(Daigle, Lee, Barber, L.Williams)	41.78	1)	Helsinki	13 Aug
Jam	(Browning, Simpson, Bailey, Campbell)	41.99	2)	Helsinki	13 Aug
Bel	(Nesterenko, Sologub, Nevmerzhitskaya, Dragun)	42.56	3)	Helsinki	13 Aug
Rus	(Fyodorova, Gushchina, Khabarova, Kondratyeva)	42.73	1)	Firenze	18 Jun
Fra	(Buval, Jacques-Sébastien, Dia, Arron)	42.85	4)	Helsinki	13 Aug

ALL TIME LIST
Additional performers
(2001 / 2005)

100 metres (qual. mark 10.81)

Ivet Lalova	Bul	84	10.77	1)	Plovdiv	19 Jun 04

200 metres (qual. mark 21.75)

None

4x100 metre relay (qual. mark 41.94)

Jam	(Lawrence, Simpson, Bailey, Campbell)	41.73	1)	Athinai	27 Aug 04
Fra	(Girard, Hurtis, Félix, Arron)	41.78	1)	Saint Denis	30 Aug 03
Americas	(Lawrence/Jam, Campbell/Jam, McDonald/Jam, Ferguson/Bah)	41.91	1)	Madrid	20 Sep 02

INDEX MEN

(names mentioned in the written text)

D

E

K

L

M

Q

R

S

INDEX WOMEN

(names mentioned in the written text)

BIBLIOGRAPHY

Berendonk, B. "Doping, von der Forschung zum Betrug" (Rowohlt Sport, 1992).

Cowe, E.L. "International Womens Athletics 1890 to 1940, a Statistical History" (1985).

Hamacher, H. "Leichtathletik im 19. Jahrhundert (Band I, 1891-1900).

Hahn, A. "How to Sprint" (American Sports Publishing Company, New York, 1925).

Hendershott, J. "Track's Greatest Women" (Tafnews Press, Los Altos, CA.1987).

Hymans, R. "Progression of World Best Performances and Official IAAF World Records" (IAAF, Monaco, 2003).

Keddie, J.W. "Scottish Athletics 1883-1983" (Scottish Amateur Athletic Association, 1982).

Kök. N., Magnusson R., Potts. D.H., Quercetani, R.L. "Track & Field Performances Through the Years", Volumes 1, 2, 3 and 4 (ATFS/Firenze, Köbenhavn, 1986, '89, '92 and '97).

Lagerström, U. "The Sprinters" (1876/1914).

Lovesey, P. "The Official Centenary History of the AAA" (Guinness Superlatives Limited, 1979).

Mengoni, L., Magnusson R., Sykora, M., Terry, D. "World and National Leaders in Track & Field Athletiocs, 1860-1972 (ATFS, 1973).

Misángyi, O. "Az Ujkori Atletika Története" (Budapest, Országos Testne-velési Tanács, 1932).

Pallicca, G. "I figli del vento" (Storia dei 100 metri ai Giochi Olimpici e ai Campionati Mondiali di Atletica Leggera, Vol.1, Atene 1896 – Los Angeles 1932).

Pietkiewicz, S. "World Yearly Best Men Relays 4x100 m. and 4x400 m." (PZLA, Warszawa, 1997).

Pozzoli, P., "Women's Track & Field World, Yearbook 1967".

Quercetani, R.L., "Athletics" (A History of Modern Track and Field Athletics, 1860-2000, Men and Women) SEP Editrice, Cernusco s.N., Milan, 2000).

Shearman, M. "Athletics and Football" (Longmans, Green, and Co., London, 1888).

Watman, M. "Olympic Track & Field History" (presented by American Track & Field, published by Athletics International Ltd. in association with Shooting Star Media, Inc., 2004).

And almanacs, year-books, periodicals and newspapers from many parts of the world.

Printed in August 2006
Finito di stampare
nel mese di Agosto 2006